THE LAW OF COPYRIGHT
UNDER
THE UNIVERSAL CONVENTION

THE LAW OF
COPYRIGHT

UNDER

THE UNIVERSAL
CONVENTION

by

ARPAD BOGSCH

Third revised edition

A. W. SIJTHOFF   R. R. BOWKER CO.
LEYDEN   NEW YORK

1968

Library of Congress Catalog Card Number: 64-21098

© A.W. Sijthoff's Uitgeversmaatschappij, N.V. 1958, 1964, 1968

Printed in the Netherlands

CONTENTS

PART I

ANALYSIS AND COMMENTARY OF THE UNIVERSAL COPYRIGHT CONVENTION

APPENDIX I
DOCUMENTS OF THE GENEVA CONFERENCE

APPENDIX II
DOCUMENTS OF THE INTERGOVERNMENTAL COPYRIGHT COMMITTEE

PART II

THE COPYRIGHT LAWS OF THE COUNTRIES PARTY TO THE UNIVERSAL COPYRIGHT CONVENTION

INDEXES

PART I

ANALYSIS AND COMMENTARY OF
THE UNIVERSAL COPYRIGHT CONVENTION

INTRODUCTORY OBSERVATIONS
TO PART I

The Universal Copyright Convention was adopted by an intergovernmental conference, fifty countries participating, on September 6, 1952, in Geneva, Switzerland.

The Convention went into effect on September 16, 1955.

Being a multilateral treaty, the list of the countries bound by the Convention is subject to variations as countries adhere to or withdraw from the Convention.[1]

As to the history of the preparation and adoption of the Convention, UNESCO's publications are not only authoritative but also almost entirely complete sources.[2]

This Part is a commentary on the text of the Universal Convention. Each article of the Convention is treated separately in the order in which it stands in the Convention. The Resolution concerning Article XI is discussed together with Article XI, and the Appendix Declaration relating to Article XVII is discussed together with Article XVII.

At the end of this Part short chapters are devoted to the three Protocols which were adopted, together with the Convention, by the Intergovernmental Copyright Conference on September 6, 1952.

---

[1] The status of adherences can be followed through the "Copyright Bulletin" of UNESCO, "Le Droit d'Auteur" of the Berne Copyright Union, and the circulars of the U.S. Copyright Office. Current information can be obtained from the secretariat of UNESCO, Paris, France.

[2] The "Records of the Intergovernmental Conference," published by UNESCO (hereafter referred to as "Records"), contain the text of the Convention in the three authoritative languages, the Report of the Rapporteur General, the list of the delegations and other participants of the Conference, the minutes of the discussions, and the text of all the working documents.

The Geneva Conference was preceded by extensive research and studies carried out by UNESCO's secretariat. The principles and eventually the draft of the Convention are the result of the consultations of several "committees of experts" sponsored by UNESCO between 1947 and 1951. The results of both the studies and the meetings appear in the first six volumes of UNESCO's "Copyright Bulletin."

The Geneva Conference was followed, in 1954 and 1955, by two sessions of the "Interim Copyright Committee" and, starting in 1956, by the sessions of the "Intergovernmental Copyright Committee" established by the Universal Convention. The work of these committees is reported on in detail in the later volumes of UNESCO's "Copyright Bulletin," starting with Volume VII.

PREAMBLE OF THE CONVENTION

"*The Contracting States,*

> *Moved by the desire to assure in all countries copyright protection of literary, scientific, and artistic works,*
>
> *Convinced that a system of copyright protection appropriate to all nations of the world and expressed in a universal convention, additional to, and without impairing international systems already in force, will ensure respect for the rights of the individual and encourage the development of literature, the sciences and the arts,*
>
> *Persuaded that such a universal copyright system will facilitate a wider dissemination of works of the human mind and increase international understanding,*

Have agreed as follows:" (Preamble)

The Preamble of the Convention does not contain legal rules. Approaching its text from a legal angle would, therefore, be out of place. Nevertheless, the Preamble, perhaps more than the rules contained in the various articles of the Convention, reflects the ideology of the epoch in which it was adopted and the general thinking of the men who drafted this treaty.

The Convention was drafted in 1952, in the first decade of the United Nations, which is the latest expression of humanity's desire to live in a world in which harmony reigns among all countries. Hence, the ambitious title "Universal Convention," "the desire to assure in all countries copyright protection" (first paragraph), and the striving for increased "international understanding" (third paragraph).

The more specific objectives pursued are threefold: "respect for the rights of the individual" (second paragraph), "encourage[ment of] the development of literature, the science and the arts" (ibidem), and "wider dissemination of works of the human mind" (third paragraph).

It has become traditional to differentiate between the European and the American philosophy of copyright by alleging that Europeans think that copyright is an inherent or natural right of the individual author, and that Americans think that copyright is a monopoly granted in order to stimulate artistic creation. The first would find its expression in the doctrine of the French Revolution, the second in the Constitution of the United States. This difference in approach, if it exists, does not seem to have significant practical consequences, since the laws of Europe and the United States yield protections which, in their results, are rather similar to each other.

We think that the two doctrines are not mutually exclusive. On the contrary, we think that each is included in the other. How could one encourage creation without protecting the individual who creates? And since all authors create for the public, their protection necessarily is beneficial to the development of the arts.

But, whether one is of the opinion that the two philosophies are reconcilable or not, the fact remains that the Convention reconciles them by alluding to both in the same breath.

There remains the goal of facilitating a wider dissemination of works of the human mind. The underlying philosophy points again to the age of the United Nations. It is one of their articles of faith that if people know each other they will understand each other, and that there is no better means of knowing than through reading the books of other peoples, listening to their music, viewing their motion pictures, and, in general, becoming acquainted with what their minds have created and with that in which their minds rejoice.

In addition to these philosophical considerations, there are a few lines in the Preamble which point to a more political question. The new system instituted by the Convention, the Preamble states, is "additional to" and does not "impair...international systems already in force" (second paragraph). These general terms refer to what are commonly called the "Berne System" and the "Pan American System," the first consisting of the Berne Copyright Convention and its later revisions; the latter of the inter-American multilateral copyright conventions. The Geneva Conference did not want to destroy these systems which, through long decades, proved that they satisfied the needs of those limited regions of the world to which they apply. The continuance of these systems is not only a pious wish: the idea is implemented by legal rules contained in Articles XVII and XVIII of the Convention.

ARTICLE I: OBLIGATION OF STATES TO PROTECT COPYRIGHT

"Each Contracting State undertakes to provide for the adequate and effective protection of the rights of authors and other copyright proprietors in literary, scientific, and artistic works, including writings, musical, dramatic, and cinematographic works, and paintings, engravings, and sculpture." (Art. I)

1. Scope of Article I.—Article I establishes the obligation of each contracting country to provide for adequate and effective protection of copyright. The Convention is based on the principle that each contracting country will grant the same protection, subject to certain exceptions, to works to which the Convention applies as it grants to domestic works (cf. Article II concerning "national treatment" of "assimilation"). Thus the value of the Convention protection depends almost entirely on the level which copyright protection attains, according to national law, in the country where protection is sought.

The Convention contains express minima only on two points: duration (Article IV) and the right of translation (Article V). The provisions on formalities (Article III) may result in deviations from assimilation in order to make the acquisition of protection more simple than this would be if it were left to pure national treatment. On all other points, however, the Convention contains no possible exceptions from national treatment and no express minimum requirements. All that it provides for is that the protection must be "adequate and effective."

2. Meaning of "Adequate and Effective Protection."—The protection that each contracting country must provide for is an "adequate and effective" protection. The word "effective" does not seem to add much to "adequate" since an ineffective protection could hardly be considered as adequate.

But whether the protection is called "adequate and effective" or only "adequate," the main question remains: what is an adequate and effective protection?

According to the Rapporteur-General, the Chairman of the Geneva Conference indicated that the rights conferred on authors by the Convention "should include those given to authors by civilized countries" (Records, page 74).

The Chairman's reply seems to be logical though not overly helpful. The Convention was drafted by representatives of civilized countries which, with a few exceptions, grant to authors protection which, although varying considerably in details, is, on the whole, rather similar from one country to the other. The right of reproduction (copying), public performance, adaptation and recording are recognized in all civilized countries. As stated, there are important differences in details. The right of public performance, for example, is recognized in some highly civilized countries only if the performance is for profit. Some of the rights are subject to compulsory licenses, thus, for example, the right of broadcasting and the right of sound recording, in many civilized countries. The Berne Conventions admit compulsory licenses in respect of these two rights. It is believed that the standard of "adequate and effective" protection, as understood today, would be met under the Universal Convention even if a country would not grant an exclusive right of authorization but only adequate compensation to the author for the broadcasting or sound recording of his work. On the other hand, the now prevailing view in civilized countries requires the recognition of an exclusive right of authorization in the case of copying (reproduction, multiplication), adaptation (arrangement of a musical work, dramatization of a novel, novelization of a drama, filming of a novel or a drama, etc.), and public performance of a musical, dramatic or cinematographic work, at least if the public performance is made with a gainful intent ("for profit").

The lack of enumeration of the rights which must be protected in order that the standard of "adequate and efficient" protection could be considered as met, has both its drawbacks and its advantages. The drawback of this very general language is that there is no sure guide in borderline cases or where uniformity or near-uniformity among civilized countries is missing.

The general, not to say vague, language of Article I, has, on the other hand, the very distinct advantage that as the views of the civilized countries change in respect of what is adequate, so will the obligations of the countries under Article I. Without modifying the language of the Convention, its material content will consequently undergo changes, and the Convention will, so to speak, automatically keep itself modern. As soon as a new method of communication, multiplication, expression or realization of a work is invented, and as soon as the civilized countries recognize in their domestic laws some rights of the authors in connection with these new methods, the recognition of the same right to works (to which the Convention applies) will become mandatory under the Convention, because otherwise the standards of "adequate and effective" protection would not be respected.

It must be recognized, however, that any interpretation based on some transcendent standards of civilized countries is full of difficulties because views may differ widely on the question of which are the countries that ought to be regarded as civilized, and on the question of the degree to which uniformity among such countries should be required, i.e., one shall have to draw fine distinctions between the isolated or rare and the generally or almost generally accepted. The Convention recognizes expressly only one right, the right of translation. It does so not because all countries agree on it but much rather because it is a highly controversial right in many, even civilized, countries. Less controversial rights should be protected as a matter of course. But there, again, views will differ in borderline cases and the Convention's lack of enumerating the rights may be a tempting argument for those who, in a concrete situation, desire to justify denial of protection of a certain right.

3. Meaning of "Authors and Other Copyright Proprietors." —Article I provides that the protection must be granted to the rights "of authors and other copyright proprietors." The fact that the Convention does not refer only to authors but also to "other copyright proprietors" seems to have at least two good reasons.

The first reason is that "author" has a different meaning in the various copyright laws of the world. Some countries recognize as authors only physical persons, others recognize also legal entities. In the case of works made by an employee in the course of his employment, some countries recognize the employer, others the employee as author. The question of who is the author or are the authors of a photograph or a motion picture belongs among the most controversial problems of copyright law and the replies may considerably vary from one country to the other. These differences, however, do not matter as far as Article I is concerned. What this Article prescribes is the protection of the rights of the copyright proprietor: he may be the "author" (whatever this means in the different countries), or he may be a person other than the person who, in the terminology of the copyright laws of at least some countries, is, or would be called, the author, if this person is "copyright proprietor."

The other reason for which the Conference appended "and the copyright proprietors" to "authors" is probably that it wanted to make clear that those who acquire the rights of the author are in the same position as the author himself. Thus Convention protection will extend not only to the author but also to his successors, whether inter vivos, such as assignees, or mortis causa, such as heirs or legatees.

4. Works Protected.—The rights of authors and other copyright proprietors must be protected, according to Article I, insofar as they exist "in literary, scientific and artistic works, including writings, musical, dramatic, and cinematographic works, and paintings, engravings and sculpture."

The Convention gives first a general description of works ("literary, scientific and artistic"). This description is followed by a nonlimitative enumeration of some kind of works, seven in number.

The general description follows a traditional, though illogical and in modern times particularly inadequate, terminology.

The use of the word "scientific" is unfortunate. The scientific character of a work has no relevance from the viewpoint of copyright law. A medical book, a statistical chart, a geographical film is protected because it is a book, a drawing, a motion picture, and not because it deals with the science of medicine, statistics, or geography.

"Scientific, literary and artistic" do not refer to mutually exclusive categories. Is a philosophical essay a scientific or a literary work? Is an opera a literary or an artistic work? And what is a cinematographic work: is it literary, artistic, both, or neither? It is a new category perhaps, as "radiophonic" works are a new category, at least in the terminology of some modern copyright laws. And what is a musical work? It is artistic only if one says that music is an art. But is not literature an art, too?

It is submitted that the words "literary, scientific and artistic works," as used in Article I, should not be analyzed one by one and in their nontechnical meaning. They should be considered together, as an expression, meaning works susceptible of copyright protection.

The general description in question is followed by examples. There are seven of them and they are discussed one by one hereafter. That they are only examples follows from the fact that they are introduced by the word "including" ("such as" in the French and Spanish texts). Thus the enumeration is not limitative. "Literary, scientific and artistic works" may be interpreted as including also other categories than the seven mentioned expressly, if such additional categories are recognized as works by the custom of the civilized countries. On the other hand, the seven categories must be protected, irrespective of the status of said custom.

5. Same: Writings.—The word "writing" has a special meaning in U.S. copyright terminology where it means all kinds of works of an author susceptible of statutory copyright protection. Consequently, it includes not only works the form of expression of which is the written word, but also musical works, paintings, sculptures, photographs, and motion pictures. As used in the Convention, "writing" has a more restricted meaning; otherwise it would duplicate the other categories of works equally mentioned in Article I. "Writing," for the purposes of the Convention, should be understood according to its common, nontechnical meaning. Thus, writing is a work of the human intellect expressed in language and fixed by means of conventional signs susceptible of being read.

The physical form of the writing has no relevance: it may be in "plain language," code or shorthand; it may be handwritten, typewritten, printed, etc. The length of the writing is also, at least in theory, irrelevant, although an extremely short writing, consisting, for example, of one or two words only, would in most cases not be susceptible of protection for practical reasons. The contents of a writing does not make any difference. It may treat any subject: belles lettres, science, information and all the variants and combinations thereof. According to the now prevailing view, however, some kinds of writings may be excluded from copyright protection on account of their contents, such as the official documents emanating from the legislative, administrative and judicial public authorities (for example, laws, decrees, court decisions).

The genre to which a work belongs is irrelevant: novel, essay, poem, play, words of a song, libretto of an opera, are writings and must be protected.

The exterior form of the writing is also irrelevant: books, newspapers, periodicals, single sheets, pamphlets, are equally writings.

"Writing," however, does not include purely oral works, even if their literary genre is one which frequently takes the form of a writing. Thus addresses, sermons, lectures and speeches, if not written down before or after their oral delivery, are not writings.

6. Same: Musical Works, and Dramatic Works. — Since it results from Article I that the contracting countries must protect musical and dramatic works, their combinations (operas, operettas and other "dramatic-musical" works) shall have to be protected, too. Dramatic works are usually reduced to writing and in this case they are protected on two accounts: as writings and as dramatic works.

7. Same: Cinematographic Works. — Silent or sound motion pictures shall be protected irrespective of their destination (theatrical exhibition, television broadcasting, exhibition for a restricted group of spectators), the person of their producers (producers of commercial films, amateurs, broadcasting organizations producing kinescopes), their genre (film dramas, documentaries, news-reels, etc.), length, mode of realization (filming of "nature," cartoons) or technical process used (pictures on transparent films, on electronic tapes, etc.).

8. Same: Paintings and Engravings. — These words should be broadly interpreted, as far as the technique is concerned. Thus "painting" probably includes also drawings, and "engravings" also include lithographs. It will not always be easy to draw the line between paintings and works of applied art. Is a hand-painted wall paper, drapery or furniture fabric a painting or a work of applied art, or both?

9. Same: Sculpture. — Sculptures are three dimensional works of art produced by carving, cutting, hewing wood, stone, modeling plaster, etc. The result may be a statue, an ornament, and perhaps also a useful object. The differentiation between "pure" sculptures and three dimensional works of applied art is frequently very difficult and the views on where the line should be drawn, if one should be drawn at all, between the two are rather different in the various countries.

10. Works Not Necessarily Protected.—Article I does not require the protection of photographic works and of works of applied art. If, however, a country protects photographic works, and works of applied art as artistic works, the term of protection cannot be less than ten years, unless denial of protection results from the application of the rule of the shorter term. These problems are discussed in the Chapter on Article IV, under point 19.

ARTICLE II: FIELD OF APPLICATION OF THE CONVENTION AND NATIONAL TREATMENT

"*1. Published works of nationals of any Contracting State and works first published in that State shall enjoy in each other Contracting State the same protection as that other State accords to works of its nationals first published in its own territory.*

2. Unpublished works of nationals of each Contracting State shall enjoy in each other Contracting State the same protection as that other State accords to unpublished works of its own nationals.

3. For the purpose of this Convention any Contracting State may, by domestic legislation, assimilate to its own nationals any person domiciled in that State." (Art. II)

1. Scope of Article II. — In order that a creation of the human intellect be subject to the provisions of the Universal Convention it must correspond to certain criteria: it must be a "work" within the meaning given this word in the Convention (Article I); it must not be in the public domain for lapse of time (Article IV) or for noncompliance with certain formalities (Article III); and it must have a certain "nationality." The work's nationality usually depends upon the nationality (or domicile) of its author (see point 18, infra), or upon the country of first publication.

Article II defines the kinds of works which are, because of their nationality, subject to the provisions of the Convention.

Article II also defines the "treatment" which a work, subject to the provisions of the Convention because of its nationality, will receive by virtue of the Convention. The word "treatment" includes, in addition to rights, the conditions, exceptions, and limitations, in time and otherwise, to which copyright protection is subject.

These then are the two main subjects regulated by Article II of the Convention. They will be analyzed in the following order: first, (A) the problem of whether the work comes within the provisions of the Convention because of its nationality; second, (B) the treatment that such a work is entitled to by virtue of the Convention.

A. Eligibility under the Provisions of the Convention Because of the Work's Nationality

2. Published and Unpublished Works. — Article II deals in two separate paragraphs with works subject to the provisions of the Convention: paragraph 1 deals with published works, paragraph 2 with unpublished works. Whether a work is published or unpublished for purposes of the Convention must be determined according to Article VI of the Convention and not according to any other rule, in particular not according to possible definitions given to the concept of publication by the domestic copyright law of the country in which protection is sought, of which the author is a national, or in which the work was first published. This follows from the introductory words of Article VI which state that "'publication', as used in this Convention [hence also in Article II], means..." For the definition of publication, see the Chapter on Article VI, infra.

3. Two Classes of Published Works. — In respect to published works Article III, paragraph 1, stipulates that "published works of nationals of any Contracting State and works first published in that State shall enjoy in each other Contracting State [national treatment]." It is clear from the construction of this sentence that there are two classes of published works which are subject to the provisions of the Convention: (i) works of nationals of another contracting country, and, (ii) works first published in another contracting country.

4. Parallel with Other Systems. — The first category is in harmony with the systems of countries in which, as in the United States of America, protection depends on the author's nationality and is independent of the place of the work's first publication. The second category follows the tradition of the Berne Conventions, according to which, for published works, the place of first publication is decisive. In this respect, as in several other respects, the drafters of the Convention wanted to satisfy both systems and this desire accounts for bringing both categories of works within the Convention.

5. Works of Nationals of the Contracting Country in Which Protection Is Sought First Published in Another Contracting Country. — It is not entirely clear whether a country is obligated to protect, by virtue of the Convention, a work of its own national if the work was first published in any other contracting country. Such work seems to qualify as a work first published in another contracting country and thus it ought to be protected. The fact that the work is not a work of a national of another contracting country does not seem relevant since works first published in another contracting country must be protected irrespective of the author's nationality. The requirements of Article II, according to which a work (i) must be authored by a national of another contracting country, or (ii) must be first published in another contracting country, are alternative and not cumulative. This follows from the conjunction expressed by the word "and" as well as from the repetition of the word "works" in the first sentence of Article II, paragraph 1, which states that "published works of nationals of any

Contracting State and works first published in that State" shall be protected in other states. Had the Conference wanted to make the conditions cumulative, the sentence in question ought to have stipulated that works of nationals of any contracting country first published in any contracting country shall be protected by other contracting countries.

6. Works First Published in the Contracting Country in Which Protection Is Sought and Authored by a National of Another Contracting Country.—Analogous considerations lead us to believe that a contracting country is obligated to protect a work first published on its own territory if the author of the work is a national of another contracting country. Such a work shall have to be protected not because it was first published in the territory of the country in which protection is sought but because it is the work of a national of another contracting country and all works of nationals of another contracting country have to be protected, whatever be the place of their first publication.

7. Discussion of Works Under 5 and 6 Above.—Doubts as to the correctness of the interpretation given under 5 and 6 *supra* might stem from the fact that such an interpretation is in conflict with the principle expressed in Article III according to which the provision on formalities does not, or does not necessarily, apply to works first published in the territory of the country in which protection is sought or to works of nationals of such a country. It is believed, however, that the fact this provision appears in Article III and not in Article II shows that it applies only to formalities and thus is an exception to the general rule stated in Article II.

8. Same, in Respect to the U.S.A.—As far as the United States is concerned, our interpretation seems to give satisfactory results. Under Article III, paragraph 2, of the Convention, the United States will continue to be able to require the fulfillment of all the formalities prescribed by Title 17 of the U.S. Code (i.e., the Copyright Law), in respect to works first published in the United States (irrespective of the author's nationality) as well as in respect to all published works authored by U.S. citizens (irrespective of the place of first publication); (as to domiciliaries see point 25, *infra*). The fact that in respects other than formalities the United States will have to give Convention protection to a work of a U.S. citizen first published in a contracting country other than the United States or to a work of a national of a contracting country (other than the United States) first published in the United States, does not seem to involve any difficulties since there is no conflict between the minima prescribed by the Convention and the national treatment resulting from Title 17.

9. Same, in Respect to Certain Other Countries.—In respect to countries, however, in which domestic works receive less protection than prescribed for works subject to the Universal Convention, it becomes quite important that our interpretation be followed. Suppose, for example, that country A would provide for no translation rights for domestic works, but would comply with Article V of the Convention in respect to works protected by virtue of the Universal Convention; could such a country deny the protection of the right of translation in respect to works of U.S. citizens first published in A, or in respect to works of nationals of A first published in the United States? According to our interpretation it could do neither, since, with the exception of the provision concerning the substitution of formalities contained in Article III, all the provisions of the Convention must be applied to works of the kind in question.

10. Works of Nationals of a Contracting Country First Published in a Contracting Country, Seeking Protection in Another Contracting Country.—A published work authored by a national of a contracting country and first published in the same or another contracting country is protected on two accounts in a contracting country which is neither that of the author's nationality nor that in which the first publication occurred: *first*, as a work authored by a national of another contracting country, *second*, as a work first published in another contracting country. If the country of first publication and the country of the author's nationality are the same, there is no problem, since whichever of the two criteria (author's nationality, place of first publication) is taken into account, they will both point to the same country. The situation is different when the country of first publication and the country of the author's nationality are not the same. For example, a work of a French national first published in Switzerland and seeking protection in the United States of America either as a French or a Swiss work. Still, this duality of the work's nationality does not seem to cause any practical difficulties since the protection required by the Convention is, generally, independent from the status of the work in the country in which it was first published or of which its author is a national (cf. point 24, *infra*). But there is an important exception to this general rule. The duration of protection might depend on the duration that a given work enjoys in a given country other than the country in which protection is sought: this is the case of the "shorter term rule" of Article IV (see Section C, under the Chapter on Article IV, *infra*). In such cases it is important that the work be attached not to two countries but only to one country—and a choice must be made between the country of which the author is a national and the country in which the work was first published. This choice is made in Article IV relating to duration, and is discussed there.

11. Works of a National of a Noncontracting Country First Published in the Contracting Country Where Protection is Sought.—Unlike the Berne Conventions, the Universal Copyright

Convention does not require a contracting country to protect works first published on its own territory if the author is a national of a country which is not a contracting country, since such a work is neither first published in an other contracting country nor is it authored by a national of another contracting country. For example, France, under the Berne Conventions, is required to protect a work by a Russian author if first published in France. But France is not obligated to protect the same work under the Universal Copyright Convention (presuming that the U.S.S.R. is not a member of the Berne Union and has not adhered to the Universal Copyright Convention).

12. Works of a National of a Contracting Country First Published in a Noncontracting Country.—On the other hand, a work of a national of a contracting country first published in a non-contracting country has to be protected by another contracting country under the Universal Copyright Convention, but not under the Berne Conventions. For example, France does not apply the Berne Conventions to a work of a Swiss national first published in the U.S.S.R., but France will have to apply the Universal Convention to the same work since Article III, paragraph 1, of the Universal Copyright Convention requires the protection of the works of nationals of other contracting countries irrespective of the place of first publication.

13. Other Published Works.—The Berne Conventions and the Universal Copyright Convention are alike in that both prescribe the protection of works of authors of a noncontracting country first published in another contracting country; and that neither requires the protection of works of authors of a noncontracting country first published in a noncontracting country. The two Conventions are also alike in that neither requires a contracting country to protect the works of their own nationals first published on their own territory or on the territory of a noncontracting country.

14. "First" Publication.—A contracting country must apply the Universal Copyright Convention to published works of nationals of noncontracting countries only if such works were first published in another contracting country. In order to determine which of several publications was the first, all publications made in any country must be taken into consideration. If the work of a national of a noncontracting country was first published in a noncontracting country or was first published in the contracting country in which protection is sought, the work will not fall under the protection of the Convention even if, later, it is published in a (another) contracting country. A simultaneous publication in a noncontracting country (or the contracting country in which protection is sought) and in a contracting country other than that in which protection is sought, if happening on the same day, probably would be enough to satisfy the requirement of first publication.

But a "simultaneous" publication which, in actual fact, takes place between the second and thirtieth day from the first publication and which, under the Berne-Brussels Convention, is considered as first publication, is not a first publication under Article II of the Universal Convention. The thirty-day provision in Article IV, paragraph 6, of the Universal Convention applies only for the purposes of the "rule of the shorter term" as provided in Article IV, paragraph 4, and only if the simultaneous publication took place in two or more contracting countries (in the Berne Conventions the rule applies also between contracting and noncontracting countries); it does not apply in connection with Article II now under consideration. Article IV, paragraph 6, is introduced by the words "For the purposes of the application of paragraph 4 of this [IV] Article," from which it follows, *a contrario*, that the provision does not apply to Article II. (For published works of nationals of a contracting country the place of first publication is irrelevant, as stated in points 4, 6, 10 and 12, *supra*.)

15. Territory of State.—Certain works first published in a Contracting State are protected. The word "State" does not necessarily mean the metropolitan territory of the contracting country. If such a country notified UNESCO that the Convention will also apply to "all or any of the countries or territories for the international relations of which it is responsible" (Article XIII), then works of nationals of non-contracting countries first published in said "countries or territories" will also be protected under the Convention.

16. Unpublished Works.—In respect to unpublished works, Article III, paragraph 2, stipulates that "unpublished works of nationals of each Contracting State shall enjoy in each other Contracting State [national treatment]." It follows *a contrario* that no state is obligated to comply with the Universal Convention in respect to unpublished works of its own nationals or in respect to unpublished works of nationals of noncontracting countries even, it seems to us, if such nationals were the domiciliaries of another contracting country. More is said about this latter aspect of the problem in point 25, *infra*.

17. "Nationals."—The term "national" includes a citizen (i.e., a person who is endowed with full political and civil rights in the body politic of the State) as well as a person who, though not a citizen, owes permanent allegiance to the State and is entitled to its protection (e.g., natives of certain of the outlying possessions of the United States of America); it also includes legal entities such as corporations.

18. Who Must be a National?—It could be argued that there is no explicit reply in the Convention to the question who—the author, other owner of the copyright, the licensee of a particular right, or some other person—must be a national of a contracting country in the cases in which nationality is of relevance, i.e., in respect to works first published in a noncontracting country, and in respect to unpublished works. On the other hand, the more persuasive argument would seem to be that the expression "works of nationals" cannot be interpreted as referring to one other than the author. In our opinion, it seems to be beyond doubt that only the author's nationality is relevant, not only because his is the most natural connection with the work but also because the recognition of the nationality of other persons would lead to arbitrary results and to abuses. Thus, for example, it would obviously be repellent to Article II if an author of a noncontracting country could, by transferring his rights to a national of a contracting country, receive protection without being obligated to publish his work for the first time in a contracting country.

19. Successive Nationalities. —If an author loses his nationality, with or without acquiring a new nationality, which of his nationalities (or his stateless status) controls: the one he had at the moment of his birth, of the creation of the work, of its first publication, of his death, or some other moment? There is no explicit answer to these questions in the Convention. It would seem, however, that the relevant nationality is (i) in the case of unpublished works: the nationality the author had when the work was created, (ii) in the case of published works (only works first published in a noncontracting country are affected): the nationality the author had at the moment the first publication took place. The following three reasons support this interpretation: (a) Article II speaks about the protection of works (not persons) which are in certain situations. It is then in relation to the work that one should examine the nationality of its author. For published works the author's nationality becomes relevant at the moment of first publication. This follows from Article II, paragraph 2. For unpublished works the Convention does not stipulate any definite moment but the moment of creation, i.e., the moment when the work or any of its parts come into existence, seems the natural solution. Once we decide that the relevant nationality is connected with the work and not with the author, the author's nationality at his birth or at his death becomes of no import. (b) If one should take the position that a given work's nationality changes every time its author's nationality changes, a work might be protected or not protected according to whether its author is or is not a national of a contracting country. In other words, a work would walk in and out the public domain, possibly several times. Works protected would be deprived of protection solely because of the changes in the author's nationality and property rights would be destroyed without compensation. Works in the public domain would be removed from the public domain making previously lawful acts unlawful. The absurdity of such results is patent. (c) The prevailing opinion in most countries is the one we advocate. Cf. 17 U.S.C. § 9 (1a).

There is, however, a difficulty with this interpretation in the case of works the author of which changes nationality between their creation and first publication in a noncontracting country. If at the creation the author was a national of a contracting country, the unpublished work was protected, but if, at the moment of the first publication of the same work in a noncontracting country, the author is a national of a noncontracting country, the work will fall into the public domain at that moment. On the other hand if, at the creation the author was a national of a noncontracting country, the unpublished work was in the public domain, but, if at the moment of the first publication of the same work in a noncontracting country the author is a national of a contracting country, the work will be removed from the public domain at that moment. This latter phenomenon—no protection for a work as long as unpublished, protection for the same work from first publication—however, is not a unique one and occurs also independently of a change in the author's nationality, for example, (i) when a country becomes a party to the Convention at a moment which follows the work's creation and precedes its first publication, (ii) when an unpublished work of a national of a noncontracting country is first published in a contracting country.

20. Controverted Nationality.—If there is a controversy whether an author is or is not a national of a given country or which of his two or more nationalities is relevant, according to what rules should such a controversy be decided? The matter of nationality is not regulated by international law (cf. Advisory Opinion No. 4 of the Permanent Court of International Justice, Feb. 7, 1923; Ser. B., No. 4) except, of course, if between given countries there are treaties which regulate the matter. Otherwise the determination of an author's nationality would seem to be solely within the domestic jurisdiction of the country in which protection is sought.

21. Plurality of Authors.—If an unpublished work or a work first published in a noncontracting country has two or more authors of different nationalities, some of them being nationals of noncontracting countries but at least one of them being a national of a contracting country, protection should be granted under the doctrine of *in dubiis benigniora praeferenda sunt*. It has to be conceded, however, that there is no authority in the text of the Convention to support this interpretation.

22. Anonymous and Pseudonymous Works.—The question arises how to determine whether a work is protected if it is an unpublished work or a work first published in a noncontracting country and does not bear the author's name or bears a pseudonym and the author's identity is not known. The Convention does not contain an answer to the question. It would seem, however, that the risk of not knowing whether or not the work is protected rests with the user even if he is honestly mistaken.

23. Works of Employees and Legal Entities; Motion Pictures. —Some difficult problems arise in connection with works which, according to the laws of the different contracting countries, have not the same authors. This is the case for instance: (a) for works created by an employee, when one country considers the employer, the other the employee, as author; (b) for works which in one country are regarded as authored by a legal entity, in others by the agents or employees of the legal entity; (c) for motion pictures, when some countries consider the producer, others the "individual intellectual creators" (authors of the pre-existent works and/or of the scenario, film-music; and/or the director, etc.) as author. (The enumeration is not exhaustive. Similar problems might arise in connection with photographs, and at a somewhat different level, in connection with portraits, letters, etc.)

These problems are not solved in the Convention. At least one of them (the problem of legal entities as authors) was touched upon by the Conference, the president of which "suggested that it was a matter for each Contracting State to interpret the word 'nationals' according to its own rule of law; the Convention was not to be regarded as imposing on any Contracting State the obligation of recognizing for copyright purposes legal and juridical persons as well as physical persons, but only as requiring that a State should apply the same interpretation to foreign nationals as to its own nationals; for example, a State protecting the works of its own incorporated bodies should protect also the works of such bodies of other Contracting States" (Rapporteur General's Report, Records p. 76). This statement is not completely in point with our problem since the real question is not whether A, protecting the works of its own legal entities, should protect the works of legal entities of B (the answer cannot be other than affirmative), but what the obligation of A, not recognizing legal entities as authors, should be in respect to works which, by B, are regarded as authored by a legal entity.

There are, however, two principles in the quoted comment which deserve attention, to wit, (i) that it is a matter for each contracting country to interpret the word "nationals" according to its own rule of law, (ii) that a country should apply the same interpretation to foreign nationals as to its own nationals. These principles seem to be the more reasonable since they are in harmony with the basic principle of the Convention, that is, the principle of national treatment, and since it is more natural for any country to apply its own law than the law of a foreign country.

Applying these principles to our problems it would seem that any contracting country may decide according to its own copyright law who the author (or authors) of a given work is (are). Once this decision is made, the rest follows from the explicit rules of the Convention: the nationality of the persons (juridical or natural) thus found to be authors will decide whether the Convention applies to the work (unpublished, or published for the first time in a noncontracting country).

Thus, if a work was created by an employee who is national of a noncontracting country in the employment of an employer who is national of a contracting country and was first published in a noncontracting country, countries which consider the employee as author may deny protection, but countries which consider the employer as author must grant protection.

If a work appears as a work of a legal entity incorporated in a contracting country but actually was created by a national of a noncontracting country, and was first published in a noncontracting country, countries which recognize legal entities as authors will have to protect the work, whereas countries which do not recognize legal entities as authors may deny protection.

If a motion picture's producer is a national of a contracting country but all the "individual intellectual creators" of the motion picture are nationals of a noncontracting country, and the motion picture was first published in a noncontracting country, countries which consider the producer as author must give protection to the motion picture, whereas protection may be denied by countries which consider as authors of a motion picture its "individual intellectual creators."

The above observations analogously apply also to unpublished works.

It should be noted, however, that as soon as a work is first published in a contracting country—this is far the more frequent case in actual practice—the determination of who the author is and of what his nationality is, become irrelevant, and the work must be protected under the Convention irrespective of the theory the different countries may follow in respect to employer-employee, legal entity-natural person, producer-contributors problems.

24. Protection in the Country of Origin.—Whether the Convention is applicable to a work does not generally depend on whether the work is protected in the country of which its author is a national or in which it was first published. (See, however, some qualifications to this statement at the end of the present point.) Although the Universal Convention does not stipulate, as does the Brussels Convention, that the enjoyment and the exercise of the rights granted by the Brussels Convention are independent of the existence of protection in the country of origin of the work (Article 4, paragraph 2), the same rule is implicit in the Universal Convention. The conditions of protection are those and those alone which are enumerated in the Convention. One cannot read into a convention conditions which are not expressed in its text. Some inter-American Conventions furnish arguments *a contrario*. In these Conventions protection in the work's country of origin is a prerequisite of convention protection (cf. Article IX of the Washington Convention of 1946). The fact that the Brussels Convention explicitly states a rule which, in our opinion, goes without saying, does not contradict our interpretation, since the incorporation of the rule in the Brussels Convention (and some of its precedents) has historical reasons. The original text of the Berne Convention (1886) contained the contrary rule, viz., that the enjoyment of the rights granted by the Convention "is subject to the compliance with the conditions and formalities required by the laws of the country of origin of the work." Thus, only the reverse of this rule necessitated the incorporation of an express stipulation in the later texts of the Berne Union. Finally, at the Geneva Conference Japan proposed that no contracting country be obligated to grant protection to published works not protected in the country of their first publication, or to unpublished works not protected in the country of which the author is a national. This proposal was rejected by the Conference.

If the reason for a work's non-protection in the country in which it was first published (or of which its author is a national, if the work is unpublished) is that the work belongs to a class of works which is not, or not any more, protected, such circumstances might exclude protection by virtue of the Universal Convention (Article IV, paragraph 4). This question is more fully discussed in connection with Article IV, *infra*.

25. Domiciliaries.—Whenever we speak about "nationals," the following rule, contained in paragraph 3 of Article II should be borne in mind: "For the purposes of this Convention any Contracting State may, by domestic legislation, assimilate to its own nationals any person domiciled in that State."

As long as the effects of this provision are limited to the country which assimilates its domiciliaries to its own nationals, the rule is unequivocal. Article III, paragraph 2, allows the contracting countries to refuse to apply to works of its own nationals the provisions concerning the substitution of the notice prescribed by the Convention for domestic formalities. Article II, paragraph 3, permits the same exception to be applied to domiciliaries. Thus the United States, for example, may require nationals of other contracting countries to comply with the formalities prescribed by Title 17 of the U.S. Code, if they are domiciled in the United States, irrespective of the work's place of first publication. Such a rule is consistent with the general principles of international law according to which, barring exceptions, a person domiciled in a country which is not his own cannot object to the application of the law concerning property rights of the country in which he is domiciled.

It is believed that the assimilation in question has an effect limited to the country in which the foreign national is domiciled, and that the other contracting countries have to treat the author according to his nationality and not according to his domicile. A citizen of a contracting country may be denied protection in the country in which he is domiciled, but all the other contracting countries must give him protection because of his nationality. Furthermore, a country may assimilate, because they are domiciled in its territory, nationals of noncontracting countries but this does not mean that other contracting countries will have to grant protection to the works of such persons (unless the works are first published in a contracting country). In other words, assimilation based on domicile does not affect the effects of author's nationality except in the country in which he chose to establish his domicile. Otherwise, the Convention should have stipulated that foreign domiciliaries are assimilated to the nationals of the country of their domicile.

The assimilation must result from domestic legislation, as, for example, 17 U.S.C. § 9(a), i.e., it must be based on a statute or general rule of law and cannot be decided *ad hoc* in respect to individual authors.

The applicable definition of domicile will be the definition of the assimilating country as long as it respects the written or unwritten rules of international law.

26. Stateless Persons and Refugees. — As to the protection of stateless persons and refugees having their habitual residence in a State party to Protocol 1, see the Chapter on Protocol 1, *infra*.

27. Certain Intergovernmental Organizations. — As to works published for the first time by the United Nations, by the Specialized Agencies in relation therewith, or by the Organization of American States, as well as to the unpublished works of the same organizations, governed by Protocol 2, see the Chapter on Protocol 2, *infra*.

28. Overlap with Berne Conventions. — As to works to which both the Berne Conventions and the Universal Convention might otherwise apply, see Article XVII and the Appendix Declaration relating to said Article, discussed in the Chapter of the same title, *infra*.

29. Overlap with Other Treaties. — As to works to which both the Universal Convention and some other international convention, treaty or arrangement (except the Berne Conventions) might otherwise apply, see Articles XVIII and XIX, discussed in the Chapters relating thereto, *infra*.

B. National Treatment

30. Notion of Assimilation. — The treatment that each contracting country has to give works subject to the provisions of the Convention is separately defined for published and unpublished works. To published works each contracting country has to accord "the same protection as [it] accords to works of its nationals first published in its own territory" (Article II, paragraph 1); whereas to unpublished works each contracting country has to accord "the same protection as [it] accords to unpublished works of its own nationals" (Article II, paragraph 2). In other words, each contracting country assimilates works subject to the provisions of the Universal Convention to domestic works (hence the expression "assimilation") by granting them what is currently termed "national treatment."

31. Published Works.—In respect to published works, national treatment is defined as the same protection accorded by the country in which protection is sought "to works of its [own] nationals first published in its own territory." The latter qualification is intended to grant a protection which is the most favorable to the author. The domestic laws of some countries—e.g., the United Kingdom and other members of the Commonwealth—do not protect the works of their own nationals if first published in a country to which their copyright laws do not apply. Thus, assimilation to nationals might have led to no protection. But it is generally believed that the protection that a country grants to the works of its own nationals, if first published on its own territory, represents the optimum from the author's viewpoint.

32. Unpublished Works.—In respect to unpublished works, national treatment is defined as the same protection as accorded by the country in which protection is sought "to unpublished works of its own nationals."

Works which are unpublished, within the meaning of Article VI of the Convention, cannot be given the same treatment as published works receive, even if certain kinds of unpublished works (within the meaning of the Convention) are treated as published works, according to the domestic copyright law. Thus, for instance, if, according to the domestic law of a contracting country, the issuing of phonograph records causes the publication of the otherwise unpublished musical work (the performance of which has been recorded on the phonograph record), such musical work, if otherwise eligible for protection under the Convention, must be treated as an unpublished work. Consequently, there must be means for protection without formalities and the copyright notice as described in Article III, paragraph 1, shall not have to be affixed on such records.

33. Source of Domestic Protection.—The Convention does not state by virtue of what kind of rules domestic works —and, as a result of the Convention, foreign works—have to be protected. In most cases the rules are contained in the copyright statutes of the countries. But it is not necessarily so. They might be, wholly or in part, incorporated in a country's constitution (cf. U.S. Constitution, Article I, § 8), Civil Code (cf. Brazil and Switzerland), Patent Law (cf. Haiti), or other enactments. The applicable rules might also result from the common law, as, for example, in the United States in respect to unpublished works in which a claim to copyright has not been registered in the U.S. Copyright Office. In countries where treaties are part of the laws of the country, the provisions of the Universal Convention may be directly applicable. For fuller discussion of these problems, see the Chapter on Article X, *infra*.

ARTICLE III: FORMALITIES

"*1. Any Contracting State which, under its domestic law, requires as a condition of copyright, compliance with formalities such as deposit, registration, notice, notarial certificates, payment of fees or manufacture or publication that Contracting State, shall regard these requirements as satisfied with respect to all works protected in accordance with this Convention and first published outside its territory and the author of which is not one of its nationals, if from the time of the first publication all the copies of the work published with the authority of the author or other copyright proprietor bear the symbol © accompanied by the name of the copyright proprietor and the year of first publication placed in such manner and location as to give reasonable notice of claim of copyright.*

2. The provisions of paragraph 1 of this article shall not preclude any Contracting State from requiring formalities or other conditions for the acquisition and enjoyment of copyright in respect of works first published in its territory or works of its nationals wherever published.

3. The provisions of paragraph 1 of this article shall not preclude any Contracting State from providing that a person seeking judicial relief must, in bringing the action, comply with procedural requirements, such as that the complainant must appear through domestic counsel or that the complainant must deposit with the court or an administrative office, or both, a copy of the work involved in the litigation; provided that failure to comply with such requirements shall not affect the validity of the copyright, nor shall any such requirement be imposed upon a national of another Contracting State if such requirement is not imposed on nationals of the State in which protection is claimed.

4. In each Contracting State there shall be legal means of protecting without formalities the unpublished works of nationals of other Contracting States.

5. If a Contracting State grants protection for more than one term of copyright and the first term is for a period longer than one of the minimum periods prescribed in article IV, such State shall not be required to comply with the provisions of paragraph 1 of this article III in respect of the second or any subsequent term of copyright." (Art. III)

1. Scope of Article III.—Article III deals with copyright "formalities," i.e., the external conditions of copyright protection as distinguished from conditions of protection inherent in the work itself (whether it is a "work," who is its author, whether it is within the period of protection). The Convention uses the term "formalities" without defining it. Certain formalities, however, are expressly mentioned (deposit, registration, notice, notarial certificate, payment of fees, manufacture in a certain State, publication in a certain State) in the first paragraph of Article III, as will be seen below.

Article III contains five paragraphs which can be divided into two groups: paragraphs 1, 2, 3 and 5 deal with formalities in respect to published works; paragraph 4 deals with formalities in respect to unpublished works. We shall consider them in this order. The question of whether a work is published or unpublished must be decided according to Article VI, discussed in Chapter VI, below.

A. Published Works

2. Nature and Purpose of Paragraph 1. — Article III is, in effect, an exception to the rule of national treatment established in Article II. Pure assimilation of foreigners to nationals would mean that foreign works must comply with the same formalities as domestic works in the country in which protection is sought. But whereas it is relatively simple, in the case of a domestic work, to fulfill the formalities because compliance occurs on the spot, familiarity with the law of one's own country is not difficult, and no transfer restrictions have to be overcome in connection with the payment of registration fees, the contrary of all this applies in the case of foreign works. And these difficulties have to be multiplied by the number of countries requiring formalities because, if one would have to follow strictly the principle of "same" treatment, one would have to comply with the domestic formalities of each such country. In order to avoid these difficulties the Convention exempts foreign works from formalities subject to one condition: the placing of the Convention notice on all copies of the published work. This notice does not imply any expense, does not require the transfer of money from one country to another, does not necessitate knowledge of the rules of foreign law, frequently very complicated in matters of copyright formalities, and does not require manufacture or first publication in the country in which protection is sought. In short, the solution offered by the Convention eliminated most of the difficulties which would exist, in matters of formalities, if the principle of national treatment were followed.

3. Domestic Formalities Not Affected. — Article III does not require the countries having a copyright system based on formalities to abandon such system, even in the case of foreign works. Instead, it provides that the use of the Convention notice will obligate the countries to "regard" all domestic formal requirements "as satisfied." In other words: the placing of the Convention notice puts the foreign works into the same juridical situation in respect to the domestic law as domestic works which have complied with the formalities prescribed by their national law. This is the principle which, in the language of the Convention, is expressed by the following passage: "Any Contracting State which, under its domestic law, requires [compliance with constitutive formalities] shall regard these requirements as satisfied" if the work bears the Convention notice.

4. The Convention Notice.—The Convention notice contains three elements: the symbol © (the letter "c" in a circle), the name of the copyright proprietor, and the year of first publication. This notice is identical with one of the forms of the copyright notice provided for by the U.S. Law (17 U.S.C. § 19). Further elements in common with the U.S. rules are that the Convention notice applies only to published works and that a work has to bear it from first publication. The requirements for location of the notice are not necessarily the same in respect to works to which the United States applies the Convention (17 U.S.C. § 9 (1c)), and in respect to other, particularly the domestic, works (17 U.S.C. § 20). This problem will be discussed below.

5. The Symbol ©.—Whereas, according to the U.S. Law, the copies of the work may bear the word "Copyright", its abbreviation "Copr.", or the symbol © (17 U.S.C. § 19), the requirements of the Convention will not be met by "Copyright" or "Copr." Although the letter "C" in the symbol © undoubtedly derives from the English word "Copyright," the sign © has become, in the Convention, a symbol which does not require understanding of the English word "copyright." Through this denaturalization international significance without language barriers is achieved.

6. The Name of the Copyright Proprietor.—The second element of the Convention notice is "the name of the copyright proprietor."

Under the systems in which copyright is indivisible, copyright can be owned only *in toto*, by the author or his assignee or other successor. In these systems a person who acquired from the proprietor of the copyright a part of the total right only, for example the exclusive right to publish a literary work in book form, is a licensee. Thus the licensor, and not the licensee, is the "proprietor" and the licensor's name must be indicated in the notice on the copies of the book, even though, because of the license, he himself has no right to publish the work in book form.

On the other hand, under some systems copyright is divisible. Thus, the person who acquires, for example, the exclusive right to publish a work in book form, will be considered a copyright proprietor, i.e., the owner of that part of copyright which relates to this particular right. Under these systems the person who, under the first system, is a "licensee," is, here, a copyright owner, although not owner of all the rights which compose copyright. Accordingly, the indication, in the notice, of the name of the part-copyright owner will be appropriate.

Which of the two systems serves the purpose which prompted the Geneva Conference to require that the name of the copyright proprietor be one of the three elements of the Convention notice? The purpose, obviously, is to give an indication of ownership to any prospective user of the work if he wants to trace the person whose permission he needs if he wants to use the work. It is believed that both systems allow the satisfaction of this intent. If, under the first system, the prospective user addresses the owner of the copyright, but the owner cannot contract with him because the right in which the prospective user is interested has been granted to a licensee, the owner will, generally, be able to inform the prospective user about the identity of the licensee. On the other hand, if, under the second system, the prospective user addresses the assignee of that part of the copyright which does not include the right in which the prospective user is interested, the assignee, generally, will be able to inform the prospective user about the identity of the person from whom all rights (including the assignee's rights, and the rights in which the prospective user is interested) are derived.

It would seem natural that copies of an edition published in a country following the system of indivisible copyright would bear the name of the proprietor of the copyright, whereas those of an edition published in a country following the system of divisible copyright would bear the name of the proprietor of that part of the copyright which includes the right to distribute the copies of the edition in question. It is believed likely that no contracting country will consider a notice insufficient because ownership is interpreted according to one system rather than the other. Otherwise one would require that the publisher determine, according to the laws of each contracting country, who the proprietor is and, if he is not the same according to the various laws, indicate them all. This would be a requirement difficult if not impossible to comply with.

If a later edition follows the work's first publication, and, at the time of this later edition, the copyright proprietor is a person other than the copyright proprietor at the time of first publication, should the Convention notice in the copies of the later edition show the name of the new or of the old proprietor? There seem to be arguments both ways.

On the one hand, one could argue that the indication of the proprietor at the time of first publication is more appropriate because the notice indicates the year date of the first publication, and, reading together the date of first publication with the name of a person who only subsequently became copyright proprietor would convey the wrong impression.

On the other hand, one could argue that the purpose of the notice, i.e., to indicate the owner, can, generally, more easily be realized if the latest owner is indicated, because the more recent the information, the easier it will be to find the present owner. It can be argued that this position is stronger than the first, that the purpose of the Convention notice is not to give information as to the first copyright owner, but rather to indicate the year of first publication and the name of the copyright proprietor at the time of the particular later edition. In other words, year date and name serve different purposes: the name indicates the owner but has nothing to do with duration.

It should be noted that according to the U.S. Copyright Law an assignee may indicate his name in the notice only if the assignment has been recorded (17 U.S.C. § 32). In respect to a work to which the United States does not apply Article III of the Convention (for example, because its author is a U.S. citizen or because it was first published in the U.S.), this rule should always be borne in mind, the more so as it has been held (Group Publishers, Inc. v. Winchell, 83 U.S.P.Q. 461 (DCSNY, 1949), that indication of an assignee whose assignment is not recorded may destroy copyright.

In view of the fact that § 9c does not include among the exemptions § 30 on assignments, it would appear that the same rule might apply to works to which the United States applies Article III of the Convention.

The name in the notice may be that of a natural person or of a legal entity, for example, the trade name of a publishing firm. Can it be a pseudonym? Notwithstanding a contrary practice in the United States, it probably cannot (unless it is a generally known penname), because the use of a pseudonym would frustrate the intent of the Convention of making traceable the copyright proprietor. How complete must the name of a natural person be? Does it have to give the first name(s) as well as the last name(s)? Are at least the initial(s) of the first name indispensable? It is believed that compliance with the local laws and customs which prevail in the country in which the edition is published, or of which the author is a national, or in the language of which the work appears, should be acceptable. The pattern of names varies in the different countries of the world. For example, in some there are no surnames, in others there are several. No universal rules seem to exist. As to the names of legal entities, in particular of corporations, they should be indicated in full or in the abbreviated form permitted by the laws or customs of the place of publication.

Whereas the "c" in the circle must always be a "c" of the Latin alphabet (even if printed in a book in Greek, Gothic, Cyrillic, Chinese, etc., alphabet)—since this "c" is a symbol and not an abbreviation— the name of the copyright proprietor will naturally appear in the language and writing of the work itself or the country in which the edition is published or of which the author is a national.

7. The Year of First Publication.—The third element of the Convention notice is "the year of first publication" of the work. Indication of the day and month is not required. The year may be indicated either according to the Christian era or in terms of any other accepted computation having a logical connection with the work or the nationality of the copyright proprietor at the place of first publication. The year may be given in words in the language of the country of first publication or in the language in which the publication is written, or may be given in numbers used in the country in question. It also may be in Roman numbers.

The year indicated must be the one in which first publication effectively occurred, because that is what the Convention stipulates. If a different year is indicated, the notice probably is of no effect. United States courts have held that where the year in the notice antedates the year of actual publication, copyright is not thereby lost, but the statutory term runs from the last day of the year which appears in the notice rather than from the actual (later) date of first publication (Callaghan v. Myers, 128 U.S. 645). But, also according to U.S. courts, postdated notices are fatal to copyright (American Code Co. v. Bensinger, 282 F 829). The distinction between antedated and postdated notices is justified in U.S. law since the term is computed from first publication, and whereas antedating generally does not harm the public interest, postdating generally will. Under the Convention, however, the same considerations do not always apply. For most kinds of works in most foreign countries term runs from the author's death. Usually in such cases the indication of the year of first publication will furnish no clue as to the work's being in the public domain, and antedating or postdating will not mislead one as to the status of the work in regard to copyright. Thus, generally speaking, the purpose served by the indication of the year of first publication is nothing more than an information on this very point. The information should be correct. If a contracting country refuses to accept a year date which is not the true date of first publication, it could not be accused of violating the Convention. Small deviations, which frequently occur in the Christmas book market (when two weeks' difference means a different year date) should, of course, be treated with leniency. Furthermore, if a country wants to be lenient in the case of inaccurate indications—if, for example, the United States wants to maintain its doctrine under the Callaghan case and accept antedated notices—probably no one may complain. And if, in consequence of said doctrine, a foreign work would actually receive in the United Stated protection for less than 25 years from first publication, the copyright proprietor will have no ground to complain because instead of a possible greater loss (denial of all protection because of inaccurate notice) he will only suffer a smaller loss (shorter protection caused by inaccurate notice).

If later unchanged editions follow the first publication, these later editions will have to bear the year of the first publication. The language used in Article III is unequivocal: "the year of *first* publication" (emphasis supplied).

A later edition frequently does not contain the same text (or matter) as the first (or previous not first) edition. If the later edition contains no new copyrightable matter, only the date of first publication can be repeated. If, however, the later edition contains new matters, the edition will be "later" only as to the old matter, whereas it will be "first publication" in respect to the new matter. Such edition is thus both "first" and "subsequent." It would be logical to require that both years be indicated—or, if the edition is based on several previous ones, the years of all editions containing new matter should be indicated.

According to U.S. court decisions in the case of new editions containing new matter, it may be enough to indicate the year date of the first publication of the new matter, West Publishing Co. v. Thompson, 176 F. 833. This harmonizes with the provisions of the U.S. Copyright Law according to which "works republished with new matter, shall be regarded as new works" (17 U.S.C. § 7), without, however, extending the copyright to the "old" matter. Although there is no parallel provision in the Convention, this principle appears to be acceptable also in the case of the Convention. An edition containing previously published matter and new matter usually does not show, in itself, what is new and what is old. This can be found out only by comparing the text (or matter) of the earlier edition with that of the subsequent one. Such comparison is indispensable whether the subsequent edition shows or does not show also the date of the earlier edition. The only inconvenience resulting from showing only the date of the subsequent edition is that the prospective user's attention is not called to the fact that some parts of the new edition have already been published earlier. This inconvenience, however, does not seem to be serious enough to invalidate the Convention notice if, instead of the dates of all editions, only the date of the last edition containing new material is indicated.

8. Combination of the Three Elements of Notice.—According to the language of the first paragraph of Article III the symbol © must be "accompanied" by the name of the copyright proprietor and the year of first publication. This means that the three elements of notice must be grouped together and cannot be scattered in different places. A book, for example, which on its first page would show the author's name after the title placed on top of the page, the publisher's name and a year date on the bottom of the page, and the symbol © somewhere in between, probably would not satisfy the Convention's requirements since one could not tell whether the author or the publisher is the copyright proprietor and whether the year is that of first publication or subsequent printing.

May a notice contain more than prescribed by the Convention and still be regarded good under the Convention? May one indicate not only the year but also the month and day of first publication? May one put the word "by" between the symbol © and the name of the copyright proprietor? Although probably such additions would not vitiate the notice, it is recommended that the provisions of the Convention be followed closely and that nothing be added which might obscure the intention to follow the provisions of the Convention.

As indicated above, the notice prescribed by the Convention is identical with one of the possible forms of the copyright notice required by the U.S. Copyright Law in respect to works to which the United States does not apply the Convention (17 U.S.C. § 19). It is possible but not certain that it also meets the requirements of the Buenos Aires Copyright Convention. The Buenos Aires Convention stipulates that there must "appear in the work a statement that indicates the reservation of the property right" (Article 3). While it is possible that the notice provided for by the Universal Convention has acquired a meaning, universally understood, according to which its appearance indicates "reservation" of a "property right," and while it certainly already has this connotation in the United States where the "C" will always call the word "copyright" to the reader's mind, it might well be that the expression "Derechos Reservados," "Droits reservés," "All Rights Reserved," or a similar statement is a safer device for expressing "reservation" of a "property right" and should be used whenever protection is desired by virtue of the Buenos Aires Convention.

It may be that, as long as the three elements of the Convention notice are given together, in a cohesive group, it is irrelevant in what order they appear; it seems, however, preferable to follow the order in which the elements are enumerated in the Convention and give *first* the symbol, *second* the name of the copyright proprietor, and *last* the year of first publication.

9. Placing of Notice.—The Convention notice must be "placed in such manner and location as to give reasonable notice of claim of copyright" (Article III, par. 1). The Convention is decidedly less formalistic than Section 20 of the U.S. Law which contains detailed rules as to the location of the notice. According to said Section, for example, the notice must be applied, in the case of a book, on the title page or on the page immediately following. Different rules apply to music, periodicals, and other classes of works; and some difficulties arise when a work is a combination of several, as for instance a dramatico-musical work published in book form (is it music or book?).

The question whether a given notice meets the requirements of the Convention is one which has to be decided on the particular circumstances of each case. If it is apt "to give reasonable notice of claim of copyright" to the reasonable reader or "visual perceiver" (cf. Article VI) of the copy, it is a good notice. What is reasonable is a question of fact. It seems that any notice located according to Section 20 of the U.S. Law is reasonable and also good under the Convention (and under Section 9 (1c) of the U.S. Law). But there are also other reasonable locations

for a notice, for instance the last page of a book, and they could well
be equally acceptable under the Convention.

The following list of possible locations does not purport to be a
statement either of the prescriptions of Section 20 of the U.S. Law (in
which many classes of works are not expressly covered) or of the possibilities under the Convention (and Section 9 (1c) of the U.S. Law),
but is an attempt to give a practical guide, and is believed to represent
one set of "reasonable" possibilities of location under the Convention
(and Section 9 (1c) of the U.S. Law) and would also satisfy the prescriptions of Section 20 of the U.S. Law:

> Books and pamphlets: title page, or the page immediately following;
> Newspapers, magazines, and other periodicals; title page;
> One page text: the face or verso;
> Texts on both sides of a single sheet: either side;
> Printed music: title page or first page of music;
> Publications containing both text and music: title page;
> Maps, prints, two dimensional reproduction of artistic works, photographs:
> their face side (not verso), either inside the map, etc. (but somewhere near
> the title or the margin), or on the margin;
> Independent parts for which (separate) copyright is claimed, of a whole for
> which no (or different) copyright is claimed (for example, an article in a
> newspaper): under the title of the part (article);
> Motion picture reels: on the frames which carry its title.

The Intergovernmental Copyright Committee (see the chapter on
Article XI, below), in an advisory opinion adopted in 1957, expressed
the view that the placing of the notice in the following locations would
appear to satisfy the requirements of the Convention:

> "in the case of *books* or *pamphlets*, on the title page or the page immediately
> following, or at the end of the book or pamphlet, in the case of a *single sheet*,
> on either of the sides,
> in the case of *printed music*, on the title page or first page of music, or at the end
> of the printed music,
> in the case of *newspapers*, *magazines* or other *periodicals*, under the main title or
> the "masthead,"
> in the case of *maps*, *prints*, or *photographs*, on their face side, either on the actual
> map or picture (but somewhere near the title or the margin) or on the margin,
> in the case of *independent parts of a whole* (if a separate copyright is claimed in the
> independent parts), under the title of the independent part,
> in the case of *motion pictures*, on the frames which carry its title (whether appear-
> ing at the beginning or the end) or credits."

The notice must not only be placed in such location but also in such
manner as to give reasonable notice of copyright. Thus the notice must
be legible and perceivable to a person looking for it with reasonable
attention.

The last words of Article III, paragraph 1, viz., "as to give reasonable notice of claim of copyright" are to be construed as an adjective
of the manner and location of the symbol, name and year—and not
as meaning that protection by virtue of the Convention is dependent

on a formal claim of copyright stated in a notice. Here lies a difference between the U.S. Law and the Convention. The former considers the copyright notice as a constituent element of copyright; in the latter, the symbol, name and year are only a possible substitute for compliance with the national formalities of other countries. This is the theory. But as a practical matter the use of the Convention notice is imperative because its omission would entail the necessity of complying with all the formalities of all countries having formalities. Compliance with such a multitude of formalities is so highly impractical and so much more burdensome than compliance with the Convention notice that, as a result of practical consideration, the use of the Convention notice becomes a condition of copyright protection in all countries having a system of constitutive formalities.

10. When Must the Notice Appear?—The Convention stipulates that the notice must appear "from the time of the first publication" of the work. If the notice did not appear on the copies which caused the first publication of the work, the placing of the notice on subsequent editions will serve no purpose in contracting countries requiring formalities. This is particularly true in respect to works which were first published before the Convention came into force. To such works the provisions of the Convention will not extend even if editions published after the Convention's coming into force bear the notice, assuming that these works were permanently in the public domain in such countries. Notices affixed after the Convention's coming into force on copies circulated before said event will naturally also have no effect in such countries under the Convention.

For a work first published with the Convention notice before the Convention comes into force, see Article VII, discussed *infra.*

If the copies bear the notice at the time of the work's first publication, but copies of a later edition do not, the benefits of Article III are lost because the requirement according to which "all the copies of the work" must bear the notice, is not fulfilled.

A translation is ordinarily considered a different and separately copyrightable work from the original. Therefore, if the copies of a work in the original language bear the notice but the copies of the same work's translation do not, it would seem that the benefits will continue to subsist in respect to the original work but not in respect to the translation. By analogy: if the original work does not bear the notice but the translation does, the translation benefits of Article III and the original does not.

11. Unauthorized Publications Excepted.—The Convention specifies that the notice must appear on "all the copies of the work published with the authority of the author or other copyright proprietor." The last ten words qualify the word "copies" (somewhat inartistically because, in theory, only the work is published; the copies are distributed, sold, etc.), and not the word "work" since otherwise an unauthorized edition of a work originally lawfully published could make the work fall into the public domain, which would be a patently inadmissible result. The purpose of the provision is that unauthorized editions, not bearing the notice, should not deprive the work of the benefits of Article III—a manifestly desirable result, otherwise it would be enough to make a clandestine edition to deprive the lawful editions of the benefits of Article III.

12. All Copies Must Bear the Notice.—All copies—and not only some or, for example, only those of the first publication—must bear the notice. This raises some difficulty of proof. Once the copies of a work start to circulate in commerce it is impossible to assemble them all in order to prove that each one bears the notice. But if the infringer-defendant produces one or more copies not bearing the notice—and these copies are lawful reproduction—he will have established that not all copies bear the notice. It is believed that the omission of the notice on one or some (but how many?) copies may not always remove the benefits of Article III. Although, strictly construed, such omission violates Article III, the liberal provision of the U.S. Law (§ 21) in similar situations may be followed also in the case of the Convention. Each case shall have to be decided on its own particular circumstances as it is obvious that the omission of the notice on one copy of an engraving existing only in three copies will be measured differently than the omission of the notice on one copy of a book existing in several thousand or million copies.

13. Requirements Satisfiable by Convention Notice.—The "requirements" which shall be regarded "as satisfied" are formalities required "as a condition of copyright." These are the formalities which, if not fulfilled, prevent the acquisition of copyright or result in the loss of the once acquired copyright before the expiration of the applicable term. Other kinds of formalities such as deposit for the purposes of enriching the national libraries (*dépôt légal*), or for the purposes of censorship, customs, or other "administrative" formalities, are not satisfied by use of the Convention notice as long as they are not sanctioned by the denial or loss of copyright protection. Article III, paragraph 3, expressly permits procedural formalities in connection with judicial actions (see below, point 22).

"Condition of copyright" may refer to the totality of copyright or to certain rights embraced therein. Thus, for example, the requirement of the Argentine Law according to which the protection of the right of translation—and this alone—depends on the fulfillment of certain formalities, is a requirement satisfiable by the Convention notice even though all other rights embraced in copyright would be protected without the Convention notice.

The Convention expressly mentions certain formalities, but the enumeration is not exhaustive. It is introduced by the words "such as." As the Rapporteur General noted: "It was the intention [of the Conference] that the particular kind of formalities specified in paragraph 1 are listed as examples only and not limitatively" (Records, page 78). Those expressly mentioned are the following:

14. Same: Deposit and Registration.—Deposit and registration exist, to varying degrees and with various effects, for example, in a number of Latin American countries, Spain, the Philippines, China, Liberia, and, in respect to certain photographic works in Italy. In respect to the United States, the Convention notice will satisfy deposit and registration but not registration of the claim for the renewal term (see point 24, below).

15. Same: Notice.—Notice requirements, varying from cases where they exist only in respect to photographs to çases where they are generally required, exist, for example, in a number of Latin American countries, China, Denmark, Italy, Norway, the Philippines, the United States and the Soviet Union. These requirements will be satisfied by the Convention notice within the limits established in the Convention.

16. Same: Notarial Certificates.—Examples for "notarial certificates" are the affidavits provided for in the U.S. Law setting forth that the requirements of domestic manufacture were met (17 U.S.C. § 17); the "affidavits" provided for by the Philippine Law for attesting the place of printing, the date of publication; and the "super-legalizations" of power of attorney prescribed by the Cuban Law.

17. Same: Payment of Fees.—This is a requirement which frequently accompanies registration; cf. 17 U.S.C. § 215.

18. Same: Manufacture in the Contracting State in Which Protection Is Sought.—The only known example is the "manufacturing clause" of the U.S. Law (17 U.S.C. § 16) applicable to books and periodicals in the English language. If the copies of such works bear the Convention notice they will not have to be manufactured within the limits of the United States. It is obvious that this provision interests the United Kingdom, Canada and other countries of the Commonwealth. It is for this reason that the Rapporteur General noted that "when the [Conference] proceeded to discuss Article III on formalities, the United Kingdom intimated that the adoption of this Article was vital if their country were to accept the Convention" (Records, page 77).

19. Same: Publication in the Contracting State in Which Protection Is Sought.—A great number of States protect a published work—whether by a domestic or foreign author—only if it is first published in their own territory (Australia, Canada, Ceylon, Holy See, India, Ireland, Israel, New Zealand, Pakistan, Thailand, Union of South Africa). Other countries protect a work of a foreign author only if it is first published in their own territory (Austria, Bulgaria, Denmark, Finland, Greece, Hungary, Iceland, Japan, Liechtenstein, Norway, Poland, Sweden, Switzerland, Turkey, Yugoslavia). Because of paragraph 1 of Article III of the Convention these countries cannot require first publication on their territory if the copies of the work bear the Convention notice. In view of the great number of the countries in this category, the use of the Convention notice is doubtless highly useful and advisable.

20. Same: Other Formalities.—In view of the fact that the enumeration is not limitative, other formalities may be also avoided by the use of the Convention notice. Thus, for example, Chile may not require a consular certificate of reciprocity; Honduras, the granting of a patent; Nicaragua, the application addressed to the Ministry of *Fomento* for the recognition of copyright; Peru, a ministerial certificate; Uruguay, the consular certificate showing that the work is protected in its country of origin.

21. Same: General.—In view of the fact that the overwhelming majority of the national laws require one or more formalities, the placing of the Convention notice on all copies of the published work is highly advisable. It is, in fact, a practical necessity. The introductory words of Article III: "Any Contracting State which, under its domestic law, requires as a condition of copyright, compliance with formalities…" applies, in reality, to almost all countries. The only countries which, according to our understanding, would have to apply the Convention to any works the copies of which do not bear the Convention notice, are Belgium, France, Luxemburg and Portugal.

The following passage in paragraph 1: "with respect to all works protected in accordance with this Convention and first published outside its territory and the author of which is not one of its nationals" will be discussed hereafter in connection with paragraph 2 of Article III.

22. Paragraph 2.—Paragraph 2 of Article III states that any contracting country may require constitutive formalities ("formalities or other conditions for the acquisition and enjoyment of copyright") in respect to works first published in its territory or works of its nationals wherever published. The paragraph is superfluous. The same result follows from paragraph 1. When paragraph 1 states that it applies to works first published outside the territory of the country in which protection is sought, it is implicit that it cannot apply to works first published in the same country's territory; and when paragraph 1 states that it applies to works the author of which is not one of the nationals of the country in which protection is sought, it is implicit that it cannot apply to works of a person who is the same country's own national. Thus the two statements lead to exactly the same results. The United Kingdom realized the repetition and formally proposed that the words "first published outside its territory and the author of which is not its national" be omitted in paragraph 1 (Records, page 339). The proposal was not adopted and thus there are now two provisions in Article III (the first in paragraph 1, the second in paragraph 2) from which it follows that works of U.S. authors, wherever published, must comply with all the domestic U.S. formalities—including manufacture in the United States—even if they bear the Convention notice; and that the same applies in respect to works first published in the United States whatever be the nationality of their authors. As to the relations between Article II and the now analyzed provisions of Article III, see points 7 and 8 under the chapter dealing with Article II.

23. Paragraph 3.—Paragraph 3 deals with what we shall call judicial-procedural requirements. They must be distinguished from the constitutive copyright formalities dealt with by paragraph 1. Unlike constitutive copyright formalities, the compliance with judicial-procedural requirements can be required by the country in which protection is sought even if the copies of the work bear the Convention notice: "The provisions of paragraph 1 of this Article shall not preclude any Contracting State from providing that a person seeking judicial relief must, in bringing the action, comply with procedural requirements..." (Article III, paragraph 3).

Compliance with them can be required only:

—from "a person seeking judicial relief";
—for the purposes of the lawsuit ("in bringing the action" and "litigation");
—if they are "procedural";
—if the same are also "imposed on nationals of the State in which protection is claimed."

Thus, compliance with requirements cannot be demanded from a person who does not seek judicial relief. It cannot be required for proceedings before an administrative agency not performing quasi judicial functions; or by a court in a procedure which is not a lawsuit.

The fact that a rule is laid down in the copyright statute—rather than in a judicial code, code of civil or penal procedure or the like—does not deprive it of its intrinsic procedural character. Thus, the last sentence of 17 U.S.C. § 13, "No action or proceeding shall be maintained for infringement of copyright in any work until the provisions of [the U.S. Copyright Law] with respect to the deposit of copies and registration of such work shall have been complied with" is clearly a judicial-procedural requirement within the meaning of Article III, paragraph 3, of the Convention, notwithstanding the fact that it appears in the Copyright Statute of the United States.

The rule according to which no judicial-procedural requirement can be imposed upon a national of another contracting country if such requirement is not imposed on nationals of the country in which protection is claimed, is clearly aimed at the exclusion of discrimination against foreigners. This rule also harmonizes with the general principle of assimilation.

The fact that these judicial-procedural requirements are not to be confused with constitutive copyright formalities also results from the provision according to which failure to comply with the former requirements shall not affect the validity of copyright. Consequently, even if the action is defeated because of failure to comply with a procedural requirement, copyright is not forfeited, and if the rules of procedure do not exclude a new action, new action can be brought against the same defendant after complying with the procedural requirements. And, of course, against a different defendant, infringing the same copyright, action can always be brought after compliance with the procedural formalities.

There is no definition in the Convention of the notion of "procedural requirements." But two examples are given: (a) obligation for the complainant to appear through domestic counsel; (b) obligation for the complainant to deposit with the court or an administrative office, or both, a copy of the work involved in the litigation.

The first example, to say the least, is farfetched. It is rather unlikely that any person, reading the first paragraph, would have or could have arrived at the idea that a counsel is a copyright formality or that a counsel is something that could be replaced by a "c" in a circle.

On the other hand, the key to paragraph 3 is the possibility reserved for each country to ask for the deposit "with the court or an administrative office, or both [of] a copy of the work involved in the litigation." This leaves applicable the above quoted last sentence of 17 U.S.C. § 13 even in respect to works which bear the Convention notice and to which the United States has to extend Convention protection. Thus, if the rights in a work protected by the United States by virtue of the Convention are infringed and action is brought before a U.S. court, the action will be maintainable only if a copy of the work is deposited with the U.S. Copyright Office in Washington, D.C., and if the claim of copyright therein is registered.

24. Paragraph 5.—Paragraph 5 stipulates that "If a Contracting State grants protection for more than one term of copyright and the first term is for a period longer than one of the minimum periods prescribed in Article IV [on duration], such State shall not be required to comply with the provisions of paragraph 1 of this Article III in respect of the second and subsequent term of copyright." At the present time—and until their laws are changed—this provision is of interest only to the United States and the Philippines, both having two terms of protection: twenty-eight plus twenty-eight years, computed from first publication, in the United States, and thirty plus thirty years, computed from registration, in the Philippines. No country provides for more than two terms of copyright.

This paragraph permits the United States to make copyright protection for the second term of 28 years dependent on the fulfillment of the renewal formalities: during the last (i.e., 28th) year of the first term an application for renewal has to be addressed to the U.S. Copyright Office and the renewal claim must be registered in the said Office; in default of the registration of such application the copyright shall expire at the end of the first term (17 U.S.C. § 24).

The effect of this Article is that foreign works to which the provisions of the Convention apply and which bear the Convention notice can avoid the domestic formalities of the United States only in respect to the first term of copyright; whereas if one wants to assure copyright also for the second term, it shall be necessary to comply with the renewal formalities (i.e., application for registration of a claim to renewal), and with the renewal formalities only. The United States could not require, as a prerequisite of renewal, that formalities prescribed for the first term by the U.S. Law (notice according to 17 U.S.C. § 20 rather than according to the Convention, if they are different; deposit and registration in view of the first term; manufacture on U.S. territory, etc.) be complied with, if the Convention notice replaced the domestic formalities for the first term. A contrary view would frustrate the intention of the Convention which obviously is to dispense with formalities for the first term. This interpretation can be justified also on the basis of the provisions of the U.S. Law alone. It follows from 17 U.S.C. § 24 that renewal is possible for all works for which originally (i.e., for the first term) copyright was secured. The securing of copyright for published works happens through publication with notice (§ 10), but the notice, of course, may be the Convention notice (§ 9 (1 c)). It is true that it would be contrary to the Convention to require, at the time of renewal, that the applicant for renewal submit evidence that the work was protected during the first period. For example, one might submit a copy of the first edition, through which the work was first published, and point to the Convention notice in such copy. Whether the U.S. Copyright Office will or will not require such evidence (the question will become of current interest only 28 years after the Convention's entry into force, i.e., in 1983) is a matter of conjecture. It is quite possible that it will not require such evidence. But, if it does, it would not violate the Convention. The thing that it could never require is that the applicant for renewal comply with the first term formalities, that is, the very formalities which, through the Convention notice, the proprietor was entitled to avoid.

In respect to the Philippines, paragraph 5 is more difficult to apply. According to the Philippine Law the first term of protection runs from the date of registration. But this registration, if the copies of the work bear the Convention notice, is unnecessary. From what date will protection be computed and which is going to be the critical 30th year during which the renewal has to be registered? There seems to be no answer to these questions in the present Philippine Law.

B. Unpublished Works

25. Paragraph 4.—This paragraph deals with unpublished works and formalities. It stipulates that "In each Contracting State there shall be legal means of protecting without formalities the unpublished works of nationals of other Contracting States." The word "means" signifies "possibility." In other words, in each contracting country there must exist a possibility ("ways and means") for protection without formalities. If "means" were to signify any positive action on the part of the person seeking protection, this would amount to formalities. Protection must be available "automatically" upon the work's creation.

This provision does not prevent any contracting country from maintaining or establishing protection without formalities in addition to a system which allows—but does not prescribe—fulfillment of formalities in the case of unpublished works. If the protection varies, within the same country, according to whether or not formalities have been complied with in respect to an unpublished work, an unpublished work of a national of another contracting country not fulfilling the national formalities will enjoy the same protection as the country accords to unpublished works of its own nationals which do not comply with formalities; whereas an unpublished work of a national of another contracting country fulfilling the national formalities will enjoy the same protection as the country accords to unpublished works of its own nationals which fulfill formalities.

It is a curiosity of the Convention that there seems to be no minimum term prescribed in respect to unpublished works in which no claim to copyright has been registered, i.e., the very unpublished works in respect to which protection is free of formalities. This problem will be discussed in connection with Article IV concerning duration.

The United States seems to be the only country in which the scope of protection of an unpublished work varies according to whether or not a copy (or photograph, etc.) of such a work has been deposited and the claim to copyright in it registered in the U.S. Copyright Office. If such formalities are complied with, the work will be protected for 28 years, renewable for an additional 28 years, counted from registration; if such formalities are not complied with, the work will enjoy protection under the common law, rather than under the Copyright Statute, and duration is not limited in time. Not all kinds of unpublished works (or, more exactly, works copies of which are not reproduced for sale) are eligible for registration: lectures and similar productions; dramatic, dramatico-musical, and musical compositions; works of art, plastic works or drawings; photographs and motion pictures are eligible for registration—but books, periodicals, maps, reproductions of works of art, prints and pictorial illustrations are not.

As will be discussed in connection with Article VI on publication, the making and general distribution to the public of phonograph records or other exclusively sound devices for the reproduction of performances of musical or literary works do not constitute publication of such works. Consequently, in respect to unpublished works the performances of which are recorded on records or other sound devices reproduced for sale, no formalities have to be complied with. Even if said records and devices do not bear the Convention notice, the unpublished works (the performance of which were recorded thereon), will have to be protected as unpublished works. Thus, if the optional domestic formalities for unpublished works are not complied with in the United States, such works should be protected in the United States for an unlimited time under the common law.

ARTICLE IV: DURATION OF PROTECTION

"*1. The duration of protection of a work shall be governed, in accordance with the provisions of article II and this article, by the law of the Contracting State in which protection is claimed.*

2. The term of protection for works protected under this Convention shall not be less than the life of the author and 25 years after. his death.

However, any Contracting State which, on the effective date of this Convention in that State, has limited this term for certain classes of works to a period computed from the first publication of the work, shall be entitled to maintain these exceptions and to extend them to other classes of works. For all these classes the term of protection shall not be les than 25 years from the date of first publication.

Any Contracting State which, upon the effective date of this Convention in that State, does not compute the term of protection upon the basis of the life of the author, shall be entitled to compute the term of protection from the date of the first publication of the work or from its registration prior to publication, as the case may be, provided the term of protection shall not be less than 25 years from the date of first publication or from its registration prior to publication, as the case may be.

If the legislation of a Contracting State grants two or more successive terms of protection, the duration of the first term shall not be less than one of the minimum periods specified above.

3. The provisions of paragraph 2 of this article shall not apply to photographic works or to works of applied art; provided, however, that the term of protection in those Contracting States which protect photographic works, or works of applied art in so far as they are protected as artistic works, shall not be less than ten years for each of said classes of works.

4. No Contracting State shall be obliged to grant protection to a work for a period longer than that fixed for the class of works to which the work in question belongs, in the case of unpublished works by the law of the Contracting State of which the author is a national, and in the case of published works by the law of the Contracting State in which the work has been first published.

For the purposes of the application of the preceding provision, if the law of any Contracting State grants two or more successive terms of protection, the period of protection of that State shall be considered to be the aggregate of those terms. However, if a specified work is not protected by such State during the second or any subsequent term for any reason, the other Contracting States shall not be obliged to protect it during the second or any subsequent term.

5. For the purposes of the application of paragraph 4 of this article, the work of a national of a Contracting State, first published in a non-Contracting State, shall be treated as though first published in the Contracting State of which the author is a national.

6. For the purposes of the application of paragraph 4 of this article, in case of simultaneous publication in two or more Contracting States, the work shall be treated as though first published in the State which affords the shortest term; any work published in two or more Contracting States within thirty days of its first publication shall be considered as having been published simultaneously in said Contracting States." (Art. IV)

1. Scope of Article IV.—The basic principle which governs the duration of protection is the same which governs the entire Convention. It is the principle of national treatment: a work to which the provisions of the Convention apply must be protected during the same term as a domestic work.

Article IV, however, subjects this basic rule to two qualifications:

First, no contracting country may protect works coming under the provisions of the Convention for less than certain terms specified in the Convention ("minimum terms").

Second, no contracting country is obligated to protect a work coming under the provisions of the Convention for a period longer than that fixed by the work's country of origin for the class of works to which the work in question belongs ("rule of the shorter term").

For brevity's sake we shall use, in this Chapter, the expression "country of origin," meaning: (i) in the case of unpublished works, the country of which the author is a national; (ii) in the case of published works, the country in which they were first published.

For a more complete definition of "country of origin," see point 21, *infra.*

A. Basic Rule (Paragraph 1)

2. National Treatment.—The Convention stipulates that the duration of protection of a work is governed, "in accordance with the provisions of Article II and this Article" (Article IV, paragraph 1) by the law of the contracting country in which protection is claimed. In other words, the principle of national treatment applies also in respect to duration.

Said principle applies "in accordance with the provisions of Article II" (Article IV, paragraph 1), i.e., (i) published works of nationals of country A are protected in country B for the term accorded by B to works of nationals of B first published in B; (ii) works first published in A are protected in B for the term accorded by B to works of nationals of B first published in B; (iii) unpublished works of nationals of A are protected in B for the term accorded by B to unpublished works of nationals of B; (iv) the rules under (i), (ii), and (iii) do not necessarily apply if the work's author is domiciled in B. See, however, the next point.

3. Qualifications. — Article IV, paragraph 1, contains a warning that the rule of national treatment is subject to the qualifications contained in the other paragraphs — i.e., paragraphs 2 to 6 — of the same Article. The qualifications were mentioned briefly in point 1, above, and will be discussed in detail in points 4 to 28, hereafter. In addition to these qualifications, the Convention contains other provisions affecting the term of protection, i.e., Article V which regulates the right to translate, including the minimum term of this right. They are discussed in connection with Article V of the Convention.

B. Minimum Terms (Paragraphs 2 and 3)

4. The Different Kinds of Minimum Terms Set by the Convention. — The Convention contains four kinds of minimum terms: the last in respect to photographic works and works of applied art; the first three in respect to all other works, including writings, musical, dramatic and cinematographic works, and paintings, engravings and sculpture. The four minima are the following:

(i) The term of protection cannot be less than the life of the author and 25 years after his death, except in the cases mentioned hereafter under (ii), (iii), and (iv).

(ii) Any contracting country which upon the effective date of the Convention in that country has limited the term of protection for certain classes of works to a period computed from the first publication of the work, may compute the term from the date of publication but must grant protection for a minimum term of 25 years from the date of first publication; this option is available to the country not only in respect to those classes of works for which protection is computed — on the effective date of the Convention in that country — from the date of first publication, but also in respect to any class of work to which the country may later extend the principle of computation from first publication.

(iii) Any contracting country which, upon the effective date of the Convention in that country, does not compute the term of protection upon the basis of the life of the author, may compute the term from the date of publication in the case of published works, and from the date of registration in the case of unpublished registered works, with a minimum, however, of 25 years from the date of publication or registration.

(iv) Contracting countries which protect photographic works, may, for such works, provide, as a minimum term, 10 years, rather than the minima specified under (i), (ii) and (iii) above. The same option applies in respect to works of applied art in so far as they are protected as artistic works. The starting point of the 10-year term is not fixed by the Convention.

As a rule, therefore, the life plus 25 years is the minimum under the Convention; the other minima are exceptions available only to countries which correspond to certain criteria described in the Convention.

5. Life Plus 25 Years.—Countries in which duration is generally calculated on the basis of the life of the author—and this is the method followed by the overwhelming majority of countries—usually grant protection for a term longer than life plus 25 years. There are, however, a few exceptions. Haiti, Liberia and Poland grant only life plus 20 years (life plus 10 years in Haiti in default of descendants of the author); and the U.S.S.R. grants only life plus 15 years. These countries, if they choose to adhere to the Convention, will have to extend the duration to life plus 25 years for works protected by virtue of the provisions of the Convention.

If the national law of a contracting country provides for a protection longer than life plus 25 years, such country must grant this longer protection to Convention works. This results from the rule of assimilation expressed in paragraph 1 of the Article under consideration. Thus, countries which grant life plus 50 years to the unpublished works of their own nationals, or to works of their own nationals first published in their own territory, must grant protection for life plus 50 years to "works protected under this Convention." As to the question of which are "works protected under this Convention," see Article II.

For possible exceptions, see the "rule of the shorter term" contained in paragraphs 4, 5 and 6 of Article IV, and the provisions applicable to the right to translate, in Article V.

6. Life Plus 25 Years or 25 Years From First Publication; Countries to Which It Applies.—The second subparagraph of paragraph 2 applies only to contracting countries which have a mixed system of computing the term, i.e., if at least to one class they apply the method of computing the term from first publication. If a country computes the term for no class of work on the basis of the author's life (the only known cases are the United States and the Philippines), it is subparagraph 3, and not 2, which will apply. And if a country does not compute duration for any class of work on the basis of first publication, and is a country which computes duration for at least one class of work on the basis of the author's life, subparagraph 1 (and neither subparagraph 2 nor 3) will apply (as stated above, only Haiti, Liberia and Poland seem to belong in this category).

The overwhelming majority of the world's countries which grant copyright protection compute duration for most works on the basis of the author's life plus a term of years, but in respect to at least one class of works, from first publication. To such countries the combined rules of subparagraphs 1 and 2 apply.

7. Same: "Upon the Effective Date of This Convention."— The method of computing the term from first publication at least in respect to one class of works must exist "upon the effective date of this Convention in that State," i.e., September 16, 1955, for the first 12 countries parties to the Convention, and, for subsequent parties, three months after the State has deposited its instrument of ratification, acceptance or accession (Article IX).

8. Same: Extensibility of Computation From First Publication.—If, at the said date, a country follows the method of computation from first publication for certain classes of works, such country is entitled not only to maintain this method in respect to such classes but may also "extend" the same method "to other classes of works." There is no limit to this extension, and it would probably not be contrary to the Convention to extend the method in question to all classes of works.

Subparagraph 2 of paragraph 2 does not apply to the United States, since in the United States computation from first publication is not *an exception* to the rule of computation on the basis of the author's life. In the United States computation from first publication is *the rule* for all classes of works, and for no classes is the life of the author the basis of computation. Consequently, subparagraph 3, discussed under point 14, infra, and not subparagraph 2, applies to the United States.

9. Same: Where Neither Life Nor Publication Is the Basis of Computation.—There are countries in which duration is calculated generally on the basis of the author's life, but for certain classes of works duration is calculated from an event other than the author's death or the work's first publication. Thus, for example, duration is calculated:
—from making, in the case of cinematographic works, in Austria, Poland, and Thailand; and, in the case of certain kinds of cinematographic works, in Italy;
—from the death of the publisher (editor), in the case of anonymous and pseudonymous works, in Cuba, France and Spain, and, in the case of posthumous works, in Argentina and France;
—from the date of first performance, in certain specified cases, in some countries of the British Commonwealth, when posthumous works are involved;
—from the data of registration in the copyright register, in the case of anonymous and pseudonymous works, in Venezuela, and in the case of works of legal entities, in Chile.
—from the death of the employer, in the case of works created by his employees, in the Netherlands;

—from the dissolution of the legal entity, in the case of works "of" legal entities, in France.

The Convention does not prohibit the maintaining of the above starting points. But in no case except for photographs and applied arts and works protected on the basis of the date of publication, can protection end before 25 years from the author's death. This rule, however, is not always simple to apply. Take, for example, a cinematographic work protected, according to the domestic law, for X years from its making or first performance. According to the Convention, protection cannot end before the author's death, plus 25 years. Who is the author of a cinematographic work? If, as author, the national law recognizes one or more natural persons, protection under the Convention could not end earlier than 25 years after he (or they) die. The death of such persons is, however, wholly unrelated to the date of the film's making or first performance and the result may frequently be a shorter term than the Convention minimum. In such cases, protection of works protected by virtue of the Convention would have to be extended to the end of 25 years from the author's death.

In cases in which the work, according to the national law, has a legal entity as author and the term is not computed from first publication, the application of the second subparagraph becomes impossible. The minimum calculated from the death of the author is inapplicable because there is no natural person involved. And the minimum calculated from the work's first publication is inapplicable because the subparagraph in question admits such computation only for classes of works for which, according to the national law, terms are calculated from first publication. The reality is that the Convention neglects to take into account that there are many countries in the world which—although computing the term for certain works on the basis of the author's life—for others do not compute the term from first publication. It could not have been the Conference's intention not to establish minima for such works. Although the only possible solution would be to modify the law by adopting one of the two, it would be unrealistic to hope that all countries which have such other starting points in their laws will abandon them for the sake of adopting either life or first publication as the starting point. The more realistic solution would be to modify the Convention and establish a 25 years minimum also from starting points other than the author's life or first publication.

10. Same: Definition of "Classes" of Works.—Subparagraph 2 uses the expression "classes" of works. What is the definition of a "class" of works? Copyright laws frequently distinguish between works according to their artistic nature. Thus, literary, musical, artistic, etc., works would belong to separate classes. The author's identity may be a cause of classification: thus, there are works bearing the author's real name and pseudonymous works; works authored by natural persons and legal entities; by foreigners or nationals; by employees in the course of their employment and by self-employed authors; works published during the author's life and posthumous works. Published and unpublished works are frequently held to be distinct classes; or unpublished works unregistered as distinguished from registered unpublished works. The U.S. Copyright Law distinguishes between thirteen different classes of works for purposes of registration (17 U.S.C. § 5).

It is believed that any group of works—whether they are grouped according to the above or other bases—is a class if they receive a different treatment than other works. For the purpose of Article IV only those bases of differentiation will be relevant which have a bearing on the length or computation of the term.

11. Same: Where Computation Is From First Publication But Term Is Less Than 25 Years.—There are certain countries in which certain classes of works, for which duration is calculated from first publication, are protected for less than 25 years. Thus, for example, Bolivia protects anonymous and pseudonymous works for 20 years, Italy protects the works of certain legal entities for 2 years, of others for 10 years, Brazil and Norway protect certain works of legal entities for 20 years, China and the U.S.S.R. protect cinematographic works for 10 years, and the Dominican Republic for 20 years. Such terms are in conflict with the Convention and ought to be extended at least to 25 years from publication (or the author's death) in the case of works to which the provisions of the Convention apply.

12. Same: If More.—If a country protects certain classes of works for a period longer than 25 years after publication, it will have to apply the same, longer term to works belonging to the same classes and to which the Convention applies.

13. Same: Unpublished Works.—Countries to which the second subparagraph applies must grant, to unpublished works, protection for not less than 25 years from the author's death.

14. Twenty-Five Years From First Publication or Registration Prior to Publication. Countries to Which It Applies.—The third subparagraph contains rules applicable to "any Contracting State which, upon the effective date of this Convention in that State, does not compute the term of protection upon the basis of the life of the author." Among the countries which have a copyright law, there are only two countries to which the said definition applies: the United States and the Philippines. In the United States, duration is computed from first publication for published works; from registration for unpublished works in which claims to copyright are registered prior to publication; whereas unpublished works in which a claim to copyright has not been registered are perpetually protected by common law. In the Philippines, duration is computed from registration. For these two countries the minima are those specified in the third subparagraph. The first and second paragraphs do not apply to them.

15. Same: Meaning of the Words "Upon the Effective Date of This Convention."—In order that the third subparagraph may apply to a country, the absence of computing the term upon the author's life must exist "upon the effective date of this Convention in that State." This date, for the United States, was September 16, 1955; for the Philippines, October 15, 1955.

16. Same: Minimum for Published Works.—Countries to which the third subparagraph applies are "entitled to compute the term of protection from the date of the first publication of the work... provided the term of protection shall not be less than 25 years from the date of first publication." This minimum is met by the United States where the first term of copyright is 28 years from first publication. The United States, of course, will have to apply not the minimum 25 but the 28 years (or 56 years, see point 23, infra), by virtue of the principle of national treatment stipulated in paragraph 1.

The rule is less easy to apply to the Philippines. According to the Convention, the Philippines "would be entitled to compute the term of protection from the date of the first publication of the work." However, the Philippines does not compute the term from first publication but from registration. The Convention does not admit such method of computation in the case of published works and, unless the Philippines considers publication with Convention notice as the equivalent of registration (which it probably should by virtue of Article III), it would not satisfy one of the requirements for ratification. Supposing that the Philippines follow the suggested interpretation, the 30 years would run from first publication and thus would exceed the required minimum.

17. Same: Minimum for Unpublished Works.—In the United States, claims to copyright in unpublished works may be registered; and it would seem that in the Philippines an unpublished work is protected only if the claim is registered. The Convention prescribes that countries like the United States and the Philippines are "entitled to compute the term of protection from... (the work's) registration prior to publication, provided the term of protection shall not be less than 25 years... from its registration prior to publication." There is no explicit provision in the U.S. Law as to the starting date and duration of protection for unpublished works in which the copyright claim is registered in the U.S. Copyright Office. It has been held however, that such works are protected for the statutory period, i.e., 28 (or 56) years, computed from the date of deposit, Marx v. United States, 37 U.S.P.Q. 380 (C.C.A. 9, 1938), which, for all practical purposes, coincides with the date of registration. In the Philippines, the law itself provides that the term is calculated from registration, and lasts 30 (or

60) years. Thus, term in both countries clearly exceeds the minimum prescribed by the Convention.

So much about unpublished but registered works. As to unpublished works which are not registered prior to their publication the Convention does not contain a minimum. This is an anomaly, since there is no reason to prescribe minima for unpublished works in the case of all countries where duration is based (for one or more or all classes of works) on the life of the author, and not to prescribe minima for unregistered unpublished works in the case of countries like the United States and the Philippines. According to the law prevailing today in the United States, this anomaly has, of course, no practical ill effects, because the protection of unpublished works in which a claim to copyright has not been registered is governed by the common law and is limitless in time. Consequently, it is longer than any conceivable limited term. Technically, however, there is a gap in the Convention which should be filled in a future revision.

18. Minima Apply Only to First Term.—The fourth subparagraph of paragraph 2 stipulates that "if the legislation of a Contracting State grants two or more successive terms of protection, the duration of the first term shall not be less than one of the minimum periods specified above." There are only two countries, the United States and the Philippines, that grant two successive terms of protection; there are none which grant more than two. In both countries the first term is longer than the minimum required by the Convention.

19. Minimum for Photographic Works and Works of Applied Art.—The Convention does not obligate the contracting countries to protect photographic works. If, however, a contracting country does protect photographic works by virtue of its domestic law, such country must protect the photographic works of nationals of other contracting countries or photographic works first published in another contracting country (see, however, the rule of the shorter term, point 21, infra). The term of such protection will be the same as that which domestic photographic works enjoy. This follows, from the rule of national treatment expressed in Article IV, paragraph 1. Such term, however, cannot be less than 10 years (cf. Article IV, paragraph 3). The minimum terms stipulated in Article IV, paragraph 2, do not apply to photographic works. Curiously, Article IV, paragraph 3, does not stipulate from what date the 10 years minimum term must be computed. Thus, the starting date might be any date as long as it is not prior to the date on which the photographic work comes into existence. It may be the date of the making of the photograph, the development of the negative, publication, registration, the death of the author, or some other date.

The above also apply to works of applied art "insofar as they are protected as artistic works" by the domestic law of the contracting country in which protection is sought. "Protected as artistic works" means works of applied art protected by the rules of copyright as distinguished from the rules of industrial property or some other theory, because if industrial or other non-copyright laws apply, it would be illogical to demand that the rules of a treaty on copyright be extended to them.

We are not aware of any law which, if it protects works of applied art as artistic works, protects them for less than 10 years; and all but three countries which protect photographs protect all kinds of photographic works for at least 10 years. The three exceptions are: Bulgaria, the U.S.S.R., and Yugoslavia, which protect certain kinds of photographic works for 5 years only.

20. Nature of Protection During Term of Protection. —The Convention does not contain answers to such questions as what kind of protection must be granted during the term of protection? What kinds of rights must be protected? Are the rights exclusive rights to prohibit unauthorized uses, or only a right to remuneration, or some other kinds of rights? The answers to these questions must be sought in connection with Article I and were discussed there. All that results from Article IV is that the rights—whatever they may be—must be protected during the terms specified in Article IV. The only right in respect to which duration is not regulated by Article IV is the right to translate, governed by Article V and discussed in connection with the same.

C. Rule of the Shorter Term (Paragraph 4 to 6)

21. "Country of Origin" of a Work. —The Convention does not use the expression "country of origin" of a work. In order to simplify the explanation of the somewhat complicated rules of paragraphs 4, 5 and 6 of Article IV, we shall use this shorthand expression. It should be clearly understood, however, that we use this expression only in connection with Article IV, i.e., in connection with duration—and not in connection with other articles of the Convention. It does not apply, in particular, to Article II.

For the purposes of the rules relating to duration, the "country of origin" of a work is:

(A) for unpublished works: the contracting state of which the author is a national (cf. paragraph 4);

(B) for published works:

(1) first published in a contracting state: the contracting state in which the work has been first published (cf. paragraph 4);

(2) first published in a noncontracting state, if the author is a national of a contracting state: the contracting state of which the author is a national (cf. paragraph 5);

(3) first published simultaneously in two or more contracting states: the contracting state which affords the shortest term (cf. paragraph 5).

It is implicit in the above rules that:

a) for a work of a national of a contracting country simultaneously published for the first time in a contracting country and in a non-contracting country, the contracting country will be the country of origin;

b) for a work of a national of a noncontracting country simultaneously published for the first time in a contracting country and in a noncontracting country, the contracting country will be the country of origin;

c) there is no need to define the country of origin:
—of an unpublished work of a national of a noncontracting country,
—of a work of a national of a noncontracting country first published in a noncontracting country,
since to such works the Convention does not apply (cf. Article II).

As noted above, if a work of a national of contracting country A is first published in contracting country B, it is the contracting country in which first publication occurred, i.e., B, which is the country of origin—for the purposes of Article IV. In other words, in matters of duration, the territoriality principle prevails over the nationality principle. This contrasts with Article II which does not differentiate between the two principles. Thus, for example, for the work of a U.S. author first published in Italy the country of origin will be Italy—for the purposes of the rule of the shorter term—when the work seeks protection in France, assuming all three countries to be contracting countries.

It follows from the last sentence of paragraph 6 that simultaneous publication does not have to be effected necessarily on the same day but that, if first publication in a contracting country is followed by other publications in one or more other contracting country or countries within 30 days of the first publication, all such publications will be considered simultaneous.

22. Rule of the Shorter Term.—Works to which the provisions of the Convention apply need not necessarily be protected for the same duration as national works. The term of protection for the former may be shorter than for the latter, by virtue of the fourth paragraph of Article IV which provides that "no Contracting State shall be obligated to grant protection to a work for a period longer than that fixed for the class of works to which the work in question belongs [in its country of origin]."

Contrary to the language used in most other international copyright treaties, the above rule is in a permissive form, i.e., contracting countries have the right but not the duty to "cut back" national duration to the duration prevailing in the work's country of origin.

If a country desires to make use of the permission to "cut back," the question arises whether, as far as the Convention is concerned, it must enact any general rule to this effect. The need for an enacted rule (be it a law emanating from the legislature, an administrative order, or any other rule of a recognized rule-making organ of the country) may, of course, stem from constitutional considerations of the country: for example, in countries where no international treaty is recognized as self-executing, an enactment will be necessary. This, however, is not the problem which is of interest here. The problem here is whether the Convention requires an enactment, irrespective of the countries' views on self-executing effects, i.e., whether the Convention requires an enactment even in countries where the Convention is generally self-executing.

The Convention does not seem to contain a clear answer to this question. One could argue that since the Convention does not provide that a country may "cut back" by its law or other enacted rule, a country may "cut back" in any manner it pleases, i.e., even by remaining silent. On the other hand, and this seems to be a more logical solution, one could argue that the permission given by the Convention to "cut back," is a permission given to the countries (and not to those private persons who may want to use foreign works) and that the will of countries in matters of copyright law is usually manifested by laws, orders, or other general rules. One could also argue that, from a practical viewpoint, unless the will of the country is expressed in the form of a general rule, the owners of copyright and the prospective users are left in such an uncertainty as to their rights and obligations which would be repugnant to common sense. Consequently, this argument would conclude, countries wishing to make use of the permissive rule of Article IV, paragraph 4, must enact general rules to this effect.

If the intention of the Geneva Conference was to achieve this last mentioned result, it would have been clearer to provide, instead of "No Contracting State shall be obliged...," some words like the following: "Any Contracting State may, by its domestic legislation, provide..." (cf. the language used in the beginning of Article V, paragraph 2).

The quoted rule of shorter term of the Universal Convention differs from the corresponding provisions of other conventions not only in the above but also in another respect. Whereas other conventions require the protection of a given work for a term not more than the term of protection this same work is given in its country of origin, under the Universal Convention a contracting country may limit the protection of a given work (during the first term) to the term which prevails in the country of origin in respect to the class of works to which the given work belongs.

The provision of the Universal Convention can probably best be explained if one applies it step by step, for example, in the following manner:

(i) first one has to determine the duration which the national law of the country where protection is sought would grant to the work if this work were a domestic work;

(ii) then one has to determine to what class of works the particular work belongs, according to the laws of its country of origin;

(iii) finally, one has to determine the duration which the laws of the country of origin of the work grant — not necessarily to the particular work in question — but to the class of works to which the particular work belongs.

If the duration under (iii) is shorter than that under (i), the duration under (iii) may be applied.

Naturally, if the duration under (iii) is zero — i.e., when the class is not protected by copyright in the work's country of origin — the country in which protection is sought is free to deny protection to the work even if, under this latter country's law, works of the class to which the particular work belongs enjoy protection.

On the other hand, if the particular work is not protected in its country of origin (due, for example, to failure to comply with initial domestic formalities), this circumstance, in itself, will not excuse the country in which protection is sought from the duty to protect the work if the class to which it belongs according to the law of its country of origin is protected in its country of origin.

The solution adopted by the Conference is a compromise between two principles. According to the first, duration should be regulated only by the law of the country in which protection is sought ("pure" national treatment). According to the other, no work should be entitled to longer protection abroad than in its country of origin (principle of the Berne Conventions). The compromise is characterized by the following: (a) the principle of pure national treatment applies only if the class of works is protected in the country of origin for at least the same duration as in the country in which protection is sought; (b) the principle of pure national treatment applies only as to the first, but not as to the second term of protection (see point 23, infra.); (c) even where deviation from the principle of pure national treatment is contemplated, its application is permissive, and not obligatory.

It has been said that the reason for adopting the "class" as the measure rather than the individual work, lies in the Conference's desire to avoid the possible necessity on the part of the country in which protection is sought to apply a foreign country's law to a particular work. This, it has been argued, is difficult enough for those who, being nationals of the country of origin, are naturally more familiar with the law of the country of origin. Should one demand the application of a foreign law, the difficulties and possibility of erroneous results would probably multiply. The application of the foreign law is, of course, not entirely avoided, since the rules affecting the "class" — and not the individual work—must still be known and applied; and the determination to which class the individual work belongs also implies the application of the law of the country of origin and the country in which protection is sought.

23. Same: Several Terms of Protection.—The second subparagraph of paragraph 4 deals with countries granting "two or more successive terms of protection." As pointed out above, the only countries granting two successive terms are the United States and the Philippines. There are no countries granting more than two terms.

The second subparagraph stipulates that "for the purposes of the application of the preceding provision [i.e., the first subparagraph containing the rule of the shorter term], if the law of any Contracting State grants two or more successive terms of protection, the period of protection of that State shall be considered to be the aggregate of those terms. However, if a specified work is not protected by such State during the second or any subsequent term for any reason, the other Contracting State shall not be obliged to protect it during the second or any subsequent term."

Applied to published works of which the country of origin is the United States, the above rule means that such works will be protected for the term prescribed by the national law of the country in which protection is sought, but if this term is longer than 56 years from first publication the term may be reduced to 56 years from first publication. If, however, copyright has not been renewed for the second term of 28 years, a further reduction of 28 years is permitted, and, if applied, will result in a protection of 28 years from first publication. In this case the comparison of terms between the term according to the law of the country in which protection is sought and the term according to the U.S. Law is not made in relation to the class to which the work belongs, but in relation to the "specified" individual work. If the specified work has fallen into the public domain in the United States for failure of renewal or any other reason after the 28th year from publication, other contracting countries may deny protection from the same moment the work has fallen into the public domain in the United States.

The same considerations apply, analogously, to unpublished works of U.S. nationals in which claims to copyright have been registered in the United States, and to works originating in the Philippines.

24. Same: Different Terms for Different Rights.—There are countries in which certain rights—in the same work—are protected for a shorter period than other rights. In several countries, for example, a literary work is protected for a longer period against unauthorized reproduction or public performance than against unauthorized translation. If a work has such a country as country of origin, may the other contracting countries differentiate between the different rights when they apply the rule of the shorter term? It is submitted that they may do so. They may protect the right of translation for not more than it is protected in the work's country of origin. The underlying thought in the first subparagraph of paragraph 4 is that any country may refuse to give a longer protection than that which prevails for the class of works to which the particular work belongs in the country of origin. "Cutting back" for certain rights (and not for a particular work) is an application of the same principle since all works (and not only the individual work) receive a shorter protection for certain rights than for others.

ARTICLE V: THE RIGHT TO TRANSLATE

"*1. Copyright shall include the exclusive right of the author to make, publish, and authorize the making and publication of translations of works protected under this Convention.*

2. However, any Contracting State may, by its domestic legislation, restrict the right of translation of writings, but only subject to the following provisions:

If, after the expiration of a period of seven years from the date of the first publication of a writing a translation of such writing has not been published in the national language or languages, as the case may be, of the Contracting State, by the owner of the right of translation or with his authorization, any national of such Contracting State may obtain a non-exclusive license from the competent authority thereof to translate the work and publish the work so translated in any of the national languages in which it has not been published; provided that such national, in accordance with the procedure of the State concerned, establishes either that he has requested, and been denied, authorization by the proprietor of the right to make and publish the translation, or that, after due diligence on his part, he was unable to find the owner of the right. A license may also be granted on the same conditions if all previous editions of a translation in such language are out of print.

If the owner of the right of translation cannot be found, then the applicant for a license shall send copies of his application to the publisher whose name appears on the work and, if the nationality of the owner of the right of translation is known, to the diplomatic or consular representative of the State of which such owner is a national, or to the organization which may have been designated by the government of that State. The license shall not be granted before the expiration of a period of two months from the date of the dispatch of the copies of the application.

Due provision shall be made by domestic legislation to assure to the owner of the right of translation a compensation which is just and conforms to international standards, to assure payment and transmittal of such compensation, and to assure a correct translation of the work.

The original title and the name of the author of the work shall be printed on all copies of the published translation. The license shall be valid only for publication of the translation in the territory of the Contracting State where it has been applied for. Copies so published may be imported and sold in another Contracting State if one of the national languages of such other State is the same language as that into which

*the work has been so translated, and if the domestic law in such other
State makes provision for such licenses and does not prohibit such importation and sale. Where the foregoing conditions do not exist, the importation and sale of such copies in a Contracting State shall be governed
by its domestic law and its agreements. The license shall not be transferred by the licensee.*

*The license shall not be granted when the author has withdrawn
from circulation all copies of the work.*" (Art. V)

1. Scope of Article V.—The fifth Article of the Universal Copyright
Convention deals with the right of translation. It is the only provision
in the Convention which mentions expressly a prerogative, a "right,"
of the author.

The Article consists of two paragraphs: the first establishes the rule
(exclusive right of translation), the second, consisting of six unnumbered
subparagraphs, the possible exception (compulsory license).

A. The Rule: Exclusive Right of Translation

2. The First Paragraph.—Article V, paragraph 1, provides that:

"Copyright shall include the exclusive right of the author to make, publish, and
authorize the making and publication of translations of works protected under
this Convention."

The right in question belongs, according to the text, to the author.
Although "other copyright proprietors" are not mentioned, if Article V
is read together with Article I—as it should be, since the Convention
is a whole—it is clear that both the author and other copyright proprietors, or more exactly, the "owner of the right of translation" (cf.
Article V, paragraph 2) are meant.

The right is an exclusive right: without the authorization of the
owner of the right of translation any translation is unlawful, except,
of course, in the particular cases regulated in paragraph 2.

The author has the exclusive right to the following acts:
—to make a translation,
—to publish a translation,
—to authorize the making of a translation,
—to authorize the publication of a translation.

Only the last of these four acts seems to have practical importance
in the ordinary case. The first two point to the author himself. Rarely
does an author himself make or publish a translation of his own work.
And if he does, probably no one would question his right to do so
(unless, of course, he previously assigned his rights).

The third act is the making of a translation by a person other than
the author—without any further act, particularly without publication.

It is open to question whether a translation made for personal use is susceptible of effectively enforceable prohibition. In several countries copying, performance, translation or other use, for purely personal purposes, is free. The language of the Convention would seem to mean that translation for purely personal purposes is unlawful. It is questionable whether the Conference wanted to go this far.

The fourth kind of act prohibited—without the author's authorization—is the publication of a translation. The meaning of "publication" has to be construed according to Article VI which defines publication "as used in this Convention." It results from this definition that the recording of a translation (or more exactly, of the recitation of a translation) or the public performance of a translation are not "publication." Neither are they the "making" of a translation. Consequently, recordings, performances or other uses of a translation, as long as they are not "publication," are outside the scope of Article V. In these respects the general rules contained in, and discussed in connection with, Article I, and not the special rules of Article V, apply. Consequently, the rules in respect to the compulsory license (Article V, paragraph 2) are also inapplicable to recordings and performances.

The objects of the first paragraph are works, as distinguished from "writings" to which the second paragraph applies. The meaning of this difference is discussed in connection with paragraph 2.

The duration of the right of translation is regulated by Articles II (national treatment), IV (duration), and by the present Article (V).

In general, the duration of the right of translation shall be governed by the law of the contracting country in which protection is claimed (subject to the rule of the shorter term).

There are, however, certain minima, in respect to both the exclusive and the non-exclusive right of translation.

The right of translation must be protected as an exclusive right during the general term of protection prescribed by the law of the country in which protection is sought in countries which do not introduce a compulsory license system within the limits of paragraph 2, and in cases in which paragraph 2 of Article V is inapplicable (although the country introduced a compulsory license system within limits of paragraph 2).

The provisions of paragraph 2 do not apply if the object of the translation is a work which is not a writing (cf. paragraph 2); if the translation is into a language other than a national language of said country (cf. paragraph 2); or if the translation is into a national language, but translation into the same language has been published within 7 years of the first publication of the original writing and the editions of the translations are not out of print (cf. paragraph 2).

Even where a country has introduced a compulsory license system, the right of translation must be protected as an exclusive right during at least the first seven years which follow the date of first publication of the work to be translated.

If a country has adopted a compulsory license system, the term of the non-exclusive right of translation will start not earlier than the end of the above mentioned seven years and will end according to the general rules of duration (Article IV). If, for example, in a given country the general term of protection comprises the author's life and 50 years thereafter; and the same country adopts a compulsory license system, the right of translation will be protected as an exclusive right for 7 years from the first publication of the original writing, and as a non-exclusive right from the end of the 7th year to the end of the 50th year after the author's death (unless the rule of the shorter term reduces this to some extent; see Article IV).

B. The Exception: Compulsory License

3. In General.—The rule of exclusive right of translation is subject to the exception provided for in paragraph 2. This paragraph contains an unusual wealth of detail and is introduced by the first subparagraph reading as follows:

> "However, any Contracting State may, by its domestic legislation, restrict the right of translation of writings, but only subject to the following provisions: "...

It is to be noted that the restrictions must be stipulated by legislation. It is, consequently, not possible to restrict the right of translation in an *ad hoc* manner, in respect to a given work (unless a special law is passed), for example by administrative decision, even if the restriction would respect the limits established by paragraph 2.

The restriction, resulting from statute, can relate only to writings. The expression "writing" is nowhere defined in the Convention. In the U.S. Law it has been given a very broad interpretation. The natural meaning of the word would be, in the context of Article V of the Convention, any work the form of expression of which is language, susceptible of translation into another language, if it exists in a written form. Thus, works not reduced to writing, purely oral sermons, addresses, etc., would not come under the provisions of Article V, paragraph 2. It is somewhat confusing that the word "writing" is used, in Article I, as distinct from dramatic and cinematographic works. Dramatic works are usually written, and thus Article V, paragraph 2, should apply to them. The dialogues in a motion picture also exist, usually, in "writing." Although Article I causes some doubt, the better opinion seems to be to regard dramatic works, cinematographic works, and also the words of songs, and the libretti of dramatico-musical works, as writings, as long as they do exist in a written form, and apply to them paragraph 2 of Article V. Such application, however, as will be seen below, must be preceded by the publication of said writings.

It must be understood that the compulsory license may extend only to the making and publication of the translation—i.e., to the reproduction in tangible form and the general distribution to the public of copies of the translation from which it can be read—and not to the recitation of a non-dramatic literary writing, to the performance of a dramatic writing or words of a song or libretto, nor to the public exhibition of the dialogue (written and published) of a talking motion picture.

4. Cases in Which Compulsory License May Be Granted.— A compulsory license of translation may be granted in two cases, viz.:

> "If, after the expiration of a period of seven years from the date of the first publication of a writing, a translation of such writing has not yet been published in the national language or languages, as the case may be, of the Contracting State, by the owner of the right of translation or with his authorization, any national of such Contracting State may obtain a non-exclusive license from the competent authority thereof to translate the work and publish the work so translated in any of the national languages in which it has not been published..." (Article V, paragraph 1, subparagraph 2, first sentence); or, "...if all previous editions of a translation in such language are out of print" (Article V, paragraph 1, subparagraph 2, second sentence).

In other words, there are two cases in which a translation may be published without the authorization of the owner of the right of translation, or notwithstanding his opposition:

(i) if no translation in the national language has been published within 7 years of the original's first publication;

(ii) if a translation into the national language has been published within 7 years of the original's first publication, but all editions of the translation are out of print after the expiration of said term of 7 years.

As will be seen below, even in these two cases the license can be granted only after certain steps have been made (point 5, *infra*) and if the author has not withdrawn from circulation all copies of the work.

In both cases license for translating may be granted only "after the expiration of seven years from the date of first publication of a writing." Consequently, a license cannot be granted in the case of unpublished works. The seven years must be calculated from the date on which the writing has been first published. This will usually have happened in the language in which the writing was originally written. But it is not necessarily so. If it has been first published in translation, the date of the first publication of such translation will start the running of the seven years. As to the meaning of "writing," see point 3, above. "Publication" must be construed according to the definition of Article VI (see there); and, consequently, a public performance or recording of a translation will not make the seven years start to run.

In order to make a license possible, not only must the seven years have expired but there must be a lack of available translation, either because the writing has never been published in translation into the language in question or because, so published, the editions of said translation are out of print.

The license may be granted only for the publication of translations into the national language or languages of the contracting country granting the license. The Convention does not define the concept of "national" language. A national language is not necessarily an official language: Switzerland, for example, has four national languages (German, French, Italian, Romansh) but only three of them (the first three) are official. All languages which are the mother tongue of a minority in a region seem to be "national" for the purposes of the Convention. There might be cases when a language, without being the mother tongue of a linguistic minority, has the status of an official language, as, for example, the English in India, or the Dutch in Indonesia. It is doubtful whether these could be regarded as "national." According to the report of the Rapporteur-General "it was also understood [by the Geneva Conference]... that a State could determine which were the national languages... Thus, India could provide for translation into the official regional languages which are used in parts of that country and which are not national languages of other countries [e.g., English], as well as providing for translation into the national languages used more generally in India." (Records, page 81).

The Convention also specifies that license may be granted if, during the seven years, the translation has not been published "by the owner of the right of translation or with his authorization." In other words, if, within the seven years, a translation has been published without the authorization of the owner of the right of translation, such translation, being illicit, cannot prevent the granting of a compulsory license after the expiration of the seven years.

Even if a translation authorized by the owner of the right of translation has been published during the seven-year period, a license may be granted "if all previous editions... are out of print," at any moment, after the seventh year and before the expiration of the general term of protection. An edition is out of print if the publisher has no copies, or sufficient copies, in his stock to satisfy demands. The fact that a few copies are still available in retail bookshops or on the secondhand book market does not mean that an edition is still in print.

In these cases, and after the steps to be discussed below have been made, a license can be obtained. "License" means a permission, an authorization which, in this case, will be granted by a "competent authority" of the country and will be in lieu of the consent of the person who owns the right of translation.

The license is granted by "the competent authority thereof," i.e., of the country in the national language of which the writing will be translated and published. The Convention does not specify whether this authority is an administrative authority. The State is free to designate the authority, but the designation must be made by a legislative measure.

The beneficiary of the license must be a national of the contracting country granting the license. Such national, of course, may be a legal entity, as long as it is, according to the laws of the country, a domestic corporation or other domestic legal entity. Probably foreigners domiciled in the country may be also beneficiaries of the license because, according to Article II, paragraph 3, any contracting country may, by domestic legislation, assimilate to its own nationals any person domiciled in that country.

The license is "non-exclusive." Consequently, the author or other owner of the right of translation preserves the right of granting an authorization even if all the conditions of a State-license are present. The author, or the owner of the right of translation, has the right to grant the right of translation, and to do this, he does not need the consent of the State authority. The right of the State authority and of the author exist side by side, and none can prevent the other of granting a license. Non-exclusivity also means that the State may issue several licenses to different licensees in respect to the same writing.

The license is granted "to translate the work [or more correctly: the writing] and publish the work so translated." License for performance, recording, cinematographic adaptation, broadcasting, etc., cannot be granted on the basis of Article V. Possibility for some of such licenses may exist on the basis of the strict application of national treatment. But this is an altogether different question discussed under Article I, supra.

5. Prerequisites of Securing a License to Publish a Translation.—The State license of translation can be accorded only if certain steps, specified in the proviso of the second subparagraph, have been taken. In certain cases, these steps have to be supplemented by others specified in the third subparagraph.

According to the proviso of the second subparagraph the license may be granted

> "provided that such national [i.e., the applicant], in accordance with the procedure of the State concerned, establishes either that he has requested, and been denied, authorization by the proprietor of the right to make and publish the translation, or that, after due diligence on his part, he was unable to find the owner of the right."

The third subparagraph specifies the meaning of "due diligence" in the following terms:

> "If the owner of the right of translation cannot be found, then the applicant for the license shall send copies of his application to the publisher whose name appears on the work, and, if the nationality of the owner of the right of translation is known, to the diplomatic or consular representative of that State of which such owner is a national, or to the organization which may have been designated

> by the government of that State. The license shall not be granted before the expiration of a period of two months from the date of the dispatch of the copies of the application."

In other words, there are two situations under which a license can be granted—other conditions present:

The first is when the owner denies authorization. The cause of denial is irrelevant. There cannot be denial unless there was a previous request by the applicant. And the denial must be referable to the applicant's request. A general denial ("I will not authorize anyone") not addressed to the applicant, or a denial vis-á-vis another person than the applicant is probably not a denial. A denial, however, may be implicit. If it is proved that the owner received the request and did not reply within a reasonable period of time, the denial can be assumed. It is, of course, sometimes quite difficult to establish who the owner of the right of translation is, and it would seem that the applicant will have to bear the risk of any error in respect to the owner's identity.

The second case is that in which there could be no denial, explicit or implicit, because the applicant was "unable to find the owner of the right" notwithstanding "due diligence on his part." Whether inability to find the owner means only inability to verify who the owner is, is not clear from the Convention. Although the word "find" would rather point to the ability of locating and contacting, it probably should be understood as also referring to the inability to reply to the question who the owner is. The publisher is a rather likely person to know who the owner is, and communication with him may have been provided for in the Convention for the very reason of preventing the granting of a license on the pretext that the applicant did not know who the owner was. Under these circumstances the applicant must send a copy of his application to the publisher whose name appears on the work. He does not have to request the publisher to authorize the translation, but merely to send him a copy of his application to the State authority. Of course, if the publisher happens to be the owner or if he knows who the owner is and informs the applicant accordingly, then the applicant will have to request the authorization—and the case becomes one of the first kind, i.e., where the admissibility of a license will depend on request and denial.

By "the publisher whose name appears on the work" one probably should understand (a) in the case of an application for translation into a language in which no translation has been published: the publisher of the work in the language in which it was first published; (b) in the case of an application for the re-publication of a translation out of print: the publishers of all previous editions of the translation and/or the publisher of the work in the language in which it was first published, particularly if the translation for which the license is applied for is a new translation and not a mere reprint of the translation out of print.

If the applicant is unable to find the owner but the nationality of the owner is known, the copy of his application will have to be sent not only to the publisher but also to (i) the diplomatic or consular representative of the State of which the owner is a national, or (ii) to the organization, which may have been designated by the government of the same State. This provision is cumulative with, and not alternative to, the provision of communication to the publisher. It implies two frequently difficult questions. Who is the owner? What is his nationality? If the applicant does not know, and after due diligence is unable to find out, who the owner is, or what his nationality is, he probably is exempt from the requirement of sending copies to diplomatic or consular representatives or the "organization" mentioned above.

The last sentence of the third subparagraph means that there must be a waiting period of two months (after the dispatch of the copies of the application) before the license may be granted. This usually will be ample time for the owner to contact the applicant. If they cannot agree on the conditions under which the applicant may publish the translated work, there is denial, and the license may be issued.

6. Pecuniary Rights of the Author.—According to the fourth subparagraph of the second paragraph:

> "Due provision shall be made by domestic legislation to assure to the owner of the right of translation a compensation which is just and conforms to international standards, to assure payment and transmittal of such compensation..."

In other words, the domestic legislation establishing a system of compulsory license must provide for (a) compensation, and (b) the effective payment and transfer of the compensation.

The compensation must be just and conform to international standards. What is meant, probably, is that it must be just judged by prevailing rates in international contracts involving translations, and not by domestic standards. Thus, it is avoided that a State may be its own judge as to what is just.

The methods by which a State will assure "payment and transmittal" are left to the domestic legislation. A safe procedure would be to accord the license only after the compensation was paid or security given. "Transmittal" probably refers to the restrictions of transfer (convertibility) of currency from one country to another. Consequently, if the sums were held at the disposal of the owner of the right of translation in the country in which the translation was published, but this country would not grant authorization for their transfer into the country where the owner of the translation right lives, the requirements of the Convention would not be met.

7. Non-Pecuniary Rights of the Author.—In addition to the remuneration, the Convention requires that certain non-pecuniary rights of the author be respected. They are not called "moral" rights, so as to avoid this controversial designation, but the assurances in question refer to prerogatives which, in the European copyright terminology, are nothing else but moral rights. They are (i) the respect of authorship, (ii) the respect of the integrity of the text, and (iii) the right to withdraw from circulation. They are worded as follows:

> (i) "The original title and the name of the author of the work shall be printed on all copies of the published translation" (paragraph 2, subparagraph 5).
> (ii) "Due provision shall be made by domestic legislation… to assure a correct translation of the work" (paragraph 2, subparagraph 4).
> (iii) "The license shall not be granted when the author has withdrawn from the circulation all copies of the work" (paragraph 2, subparagraph 6).

(i) The "original title" means probably the title of the work in the language in which the writing was first published. The "name of the author" probably can be indicated only if it appears on the original writing; if the original is anonymous, the translation cannot bear the author's name; if it was published under a pseudonym, the translation must bear the same pseudonym. That the title and the name must be "printed" probably does not have to be taken literally; if the process of multiplication of the copies of the published translation was other than printing, that other method will be sufficient for indicating author and title.

(ii) It is not always easy to decide what constitutes a "correct" translation. A literal translation is not necessarily correct, and a correct translation is not necessarily literal. Probably "correct" is a translation which conveys with the greatest possible fidelity the thoughts expressed in the original. It is more difficult to see how a State can "assure" that a translation is correct. Possibly the license should be granted only after the correctness of the translation has been checked and certified by a State-appointed authority. Or it could be made clear in the license that if the translation is not correct, the license will be withdrawn, the copies of the translation destroyed or the inexactitudes in it corrected.

8. Territorial Validity of License.—The second, third and fourth sentences of subparagraph 5 of paragraph 2 read as follows:

> "The license shall be valid only for publication of the translation in the territory of the Contracting State where it has been applied for. Copies so published may be imported and sold in another Contracting State if one of the national languages of such other State is the same language as that into which the work has been so translated, and if the domestic law in such other State makes provision for such licenses and does not prohibit such importation and sale. Where the foregoing conditions do not exist, the importation and sale of such copies in a Contracting State shall be governed by its domestic law and agreements."

The license is valid only for "publication" in the territory of the country where it has been applied for. Publication, according to Article VI, means general distribution to the public. Consequently, such general distribution must be effectuated in the country granting the license. Quaere whether there may be distribution also in another country? On the face of the second sentence, distribution would seem to be limited to the country where the license was granted, since the license for publication is only valid for publication in the territory of the country granting the license. This, however, is contradicted by the following sentences provided for the "conditions" of importation of copies. Importation into another country presupposes exportation from the country in which the license was granted. Consequently, exportation, i.e., distribution outside the country granting the license, is also admitted.

This is not the only contradiction in this paragraph. Its third sentence gives the impression that importation of copies into a country other than the one granting the license is possible only (a) if one of the national languages of the importing country is the same language as that into which the work has been translated under the license, and (b) if the importing country itself introduced the compulsory licensing system for translations, and, finally (c) if the importing country does not prohibit the importation. However, the fourth sentence destroys all these seeming conditions, by stipulating that "where the foregoing (i.e., (a), (b), and (c)) conditions do not exist, the importation will... be governed by... domestic law and... agreements." As we understand these long and complicated provisions, they do not amount to more than the following: copies of translations reproduced under license in a Contracting State may be exported into another State which does not prohibit the importation. Prohibition of importation may, of course, be illegal from an international viewpoint if, by treaty, a country obliged itself not to prohibit importation. However, there is nothing in the Convention which would limit the powers of any country in respect to the permission of prohibition of importation of writings translated and published under a compulsory license.

9. Non-Transferability of License.—The fifth sentence of paragraph 5 stipulates that "the license shall not be transferred by the licensee." This provision is a necessary supplement to the rule according to which a State may grant licenses only to its own nationals (paragraph 2). Otherwise, by a simple transfer, licenses would end up in the hands of persons who are not nationals of the State granting the licenses.

ARTICLE VI: DEFINITION OF "PUBLICATION"

"'Publication', as used in this Convention, means the reproduction in tangible form and the general distribution to the public of copies of a work from which it can be read or otherwise visually perceived." (Art. VI)

1. Scope of Article VI.—"Publication" is the only concept defined in the Universal Copyright Convention. It is one of the key words in the Convention. It occurs several times in the basic articles II, III, IV and V. If it were interpreted differently by the various contracting countries, this would lead to confusion in respect to almost the whole Convention.

Definition of this concept is all the more necessary because the word "publication" has widely varying meanings in the national laws, and its meaning in the Berne Conventions is notoriously vague.

As to national laws it would be outside the scope of this book to attempt to survey them all. A few typical examples will be enough to illustrate the great diversity.

According to the British Law, the following acts do not constitute publication: "the performance, or the issue of records, of a literary, dramatic or musical work, the construction of a work of architecture or of a sculpture." (Copyright Act, 1956, s. 49).

Several laws in Continental Europe employ two different expressions both of which are usually translated by the English word "publication": one is what the Germans call *veröffentlichen*, the other what they call *erscheinen*. The Austrian law, for example, defined these two as follows: "A work is published (*veröffentlicht*) when it is made available to the public with the authorization of the person entitled thereto" (Law 111/1936, Section 8). "A work is published (*erschienen*) when, with the authorization of the person entitled thereto, copies in sufficient numbers are made available for sale or circulation to the public" (Law 111/1936, Section 9, paragraph 1).

Some of the differences between the national laws can be accounted for by the fact that the term "publication" is used for different purposes in the different laws. In the U.S. Law "publication" marks the necessity of fulfilling formalities and serves as starting point in computing duration for published works. The Law does not define "publication" in general, but it does define the concept of the "date of publication"

(17 U.S.C. § 26). Before the Universal Copyright Convention was adopted, the place of first publication, with one minor exception, did not have relevance in the U.S. Law, according to which the work's eligibility for protection depended on the nationality of the author rather than on the place of first publication. This may be the reason why the place of first publication is not defined in the U.S. Law.

On the other hand, subject to important but relatively rare exceptions, the reverse of the U.S. situation is true in most European countries. These have no constitutive formalities and duration is computed from the author's death. Consequently, publication has generally no bearing either on formal requirements or duration. But a published work, particularly if authored by a foreigner, is generally eligible for protection only if it is first published in the country in which protection is sought. This, generally, is not a relevant factor under the U.S. Law.

As to the Berne Conventions, the difficulties of interpretation of the concept of "publication" are illustrated by the debates of the Brussels Conference. The "official program" (i.e., the suggestion of the Belgian Government and the Berne Bureau) proposed that the sentence "published works shall be understood to be works copies of which have been issued" be completed by the words "whatever may be the means of manufacture of the copies (printings, discs, films, etc.)." This proposal, strongly supported by the French delegation, was, with equal strength, opposed by the British delegation which "was of the opinion that the right of performance and the right of reproduction are two clearly distinct rights and the performance of a work is not a copy, according to Anglo-Saxon law. A film or disc is the fixation of a performance of the work but is not a copy of the work. This is the reason why the British Delegation resolutely opposed the French proposal which was the same as the proposal contained in the program" (translated from *Actes de la Conférence de Bruxelles*, page 177). In the end, the Conference adopted the words "whatever may be the means of manufacture of the copies" but omitted the parentheses, containing, among others, the words "discs" and "films." Thus, the Conference did not resolve the problem. Whether the issuance of discs amounts to publication depends on the question whether a disc is a copy or not, and, at least according to the records of the Brussels Conference, France believes it is, and Great Britain believes that it is not; and what is worse, both interpretations seem to be compatible with the text of the Brussels Convention.

It is against this background that the Geneva Conference had to adopt a definition for the word "publication." The controversy centered around the question whether the issuance of phonograph records amounts to publication of the work, a performance of which was fixed on the records. It was the intention of the Conference to answer this question in the negative, not so much for theoretical reasons but mainly because it was considered a prerequisite for United States acceptance of the Convention. It was, in effect, believed that according to the U.S. Law the issuance of phonograph records does not amount to publication, and that an unpublished work remains unpublished, i.e., requires no fulfillment of formalities and is "perpetually" protected at common law, notwithstanding the issuance of phonograph records. It was believed that a contrary provision in the Convention would require an amendment of the U.S. Copyright Statute unlikely to be accepted by Congress. To avoid these difficulties was the principal reason for adopting the definition which now is Article VI of the Convention.

Whether it is a logical solution from other points of view is a wholly different question which is beyond the scope of this book.

A. The Definition

2. The Two Key Words in the Definition.—The sole sentence of Article VI defines publication. It reads as follows:

> "'Publication', as used in this Convention, means the reproduction in tangible form and the general distribution to the public of copies of a work from which it can be read or otherwise visually perceived."

The interpretation of this provision turns on the meaning of the words "copies" and "distribution."

3. Meaning of "Copies."—The word "copy" in the English language has at least two meanings. It means, on the one hand, what the French word *exemplaire* means, and it also means what the French word *copie* means.

Copy-*exemplaire* is the object which results whenever the work of an author is multiplied. The objects resulting from the multiplications are equivalent, in artistic value, with the object created by the author. Since they are equivalent, they are all like the original.

Books, newspapers, periodicals, and sheet music clearly illustrate the meaning of copy-*exemplaire*. They all originate in a manuscript which is then multiplied and the objects resulting from this multiplication, for example, the thousands of "copies" of the printed book, are all equivalent with the original manuscript because they include the very words or notes wich make the intellectual contents of the manuscript. There are, of course, as will be discussed below, other kinds of works which are susceptible of multiplication and, thus, of existing in several copies-*exemplaires*.

The other meaning of the English word "copy" is what the French *copie* means. This copy-*copie* is the object which results whenever the work of an author is imitated. The objects resulting from the imitation are not equivalent with the object created by the author. Of course, the copy-*copie* may itself be a work, a secondary work or adaptation, which is susceptible of multiplication. But the results of such multiplication will be exemplaires of the secondary work and not of the primary, original work.

Photographs made of paintings illustrate the meaning of copy-*copie*. A photograph made from a painting even if in color and so similar to the original that only the expert's eye can distinguish it, is not equivalent with the painting and is not a multiplication thereof. A hundred photographic prints of the same painting do not result in a hundred paintings, but in a hundred photographs of the painting. They are copies-*exemplaires* of the secondary work (i.e., the photograph) but not of the work (i.e., the painting).

It seems clear from the French, Spanish, German, Italian and Portuguese texts of the Convention—which all use the word *exemplaire*—that the English word "copy" in the Convention has to be understood as meaning copies of the work, as distinguished from copies of adaptations of the work. Hereinafter, unless expressly stated otherwise, the word copy will be used as meaning *exemplaire* and not *copie*.

4. Same: Works Existing in One or More Copies.—Some works can exist only in one copy. Paintings and drawings are the typical examples. A painter may paint several times the same subject, but in such a case each painting will be a self-contained original work and not a copy of the first painting.

A painting may be imitated, either by color-photography or by a "copyist" who, using the same implements and techniques as the original painter, tries to achieve something which visually will have the same, or nearly the same, effects as the original. Both will be secondary works in relation to the original. Neither is a copy (*exemplaire*) of the painting.

Probably most other works may exist either in one or in several copies. Books, newspapers, magazines, periodicals, sheet music, photographs, engravings, cinematographic works, may exist in one copy (manuscript; negative film; stone, wood or copper plate, etc.) or several copies (issues, copies, prints, impressions, positive films). Sculptural works, if susceptible of multiplication by casting from moulds, may exist in several copies; otherwise they may belong to the category of works for which only one copy is conceivable.

5. Same: Oral Works.—An oral literary or musical work, i.e. a work expressed by the language or musical sounds but not fixed in writing or musical notation, cannot have copies in the Convention sense because a copy is a tangible thing and ideas only expressed by voice or sound are not tangible.

6. Same: Sound Recordings.—By sound recordings we mean phonograph records or discs, tapes, wires, and similar contrivances fixing the recitations, deliveries or performances of literary, dramatic or musical works.

It is submitted that sound recordings are not copies of the works the performances of which are fixed on them. They are not copies because a sound recording is not equivalent with the creation of the author. A recording is only a more or less accurate interpretation of the author's creative ideas. Even if it were assumed that the recording fixes the work, it also fixes something additional, i.e., the performance of the work; and work plus performance cannot be equivalent with the work only.

There are some countries the copyright laws of which consider recordings as works. In this case, naturally, records, discs, etc., are copies: but copies of the recording and not copies of the musical (or other) work of which the performance is fixed.

7. Cinematographic Works.—Cinematographic works are sui generis works, equivalent from a legal viewpoint with any other class of works, such as dramatic or musical works. They enjoy the status of work generally; a status which in most countries is denied to phonograph records.

A cinematographic work is the sum total of different arts: literary, dramatic, musical, photographic, interpretative and performing arts, and of other arts, like that of direction, peculiar to cinematography. These are amalgamated in a unified whole and incorporated by the cinematographic film. This film is capable of having one or more copies.

Cinematographic films usually contain two bands or tracks: a visual or picture band and a sound track. If the sound track is separated from the visual band, it has striking resemblances to what we called sound recordings which we declared are not copies of the works the performances of which are fixed thereon.

It is believed that the same is true in respect to the sound track: it is not a copy of the musical, etc., work, the performance of which is fixed on the sound track. On the other hand, a sound track is part of a copy of the cinematographic work.

In other words: neither phonograph records nor the sound tracks of films are copies of the musical work; films (the sound track and the picture band together) are copies of the cinematographic work, just as records are copies of phonographic works if one accords the status of work to sound recordings.

8. Copies Distinguished From Secondary Works.—To draw the line between copies of a work and adaptations of a work is not always easy.

We are of the opinion that translations are not copies of the published original work. "Romeo and Juliet" may exist in millions of copies in Japanese translation, but these copies—although fully based on Shakespeare's work—are copies of the translation, work of the translator, and not of Shakespeare's work.

Analogous considerations apply to musical arrangements. Copies of the arrangement are not copies of the work on which the arrangement is based; and copies of the original composition are not copies of the arrangement.

The same is true in respect to the cinematographic adaptation of a drama, novel or other literary work; or the dramatization of a novel or another literary work.

In general, a secondary work is never a copy of the original work: the former is the adaptation of the latter, and the copies of the secondary work are copies of the secondary work only and not only of the primary work.

This principle applies, of course, also to artistic works and their adaptations. The non-juridical usage of the words "copy" and "reproduction" must be distinguished from the meaning of the same words in Article VI of the Convention. We have mentioned above that the hand-painted "copy" as used in the non-technical sense is not a copy (according to the Convention) but a new, although secondary, work of art, like the translation is a secondary literary work. A photograph, "art reproduction," "color reproduction," "color print," diapositive slide, film, etching, etc., of a painting or drawing is also not a copy of the original painting or drawing which can exist only in one copy, but a secondary work which may exist in several copies. It is an adaptation.

The difference between adaptations and primary works is more patent when one is two dimensional and the other three dimensional. Photographs, etchings, drawings, etc., of sculptures, architectural works of art, works of applied art, are not copies (although they are sometimes called, in non-technical language "reproductions"); and the same is true when a photograph, painting, etc., is adapted to a sculptural work, such as a bas-relief.

9. Meaning of "Reproduction in Tangible Form."—If grammatically analyzed, Article VI would seem to indicate that two acts are necessary for publication: "reproduction in tangible form" and "general distribution to the public of copies of a work..." Some support for this view has been expressed by some persons in the United States.

It is believed that, in reality, the use of the words "reproduction in tangible form" expresses an idea which is inherent in the word "copies" and that, strictly speaking, the use of the words "reproduction in tangible form" is redundant, being implicit in the word "copies." Copies (not one copy but *copies*) cannot exist without reproduction, they are necessarily the result of reproduction; as reproduction necessarily results in copies. Copies are equivalent objects with the original; and after the original was produced by the author, a repeated producing of the same, i.e., a reproduction, will result in equivalent objects; if they were not equivalent they would not be reproductions but transformations, modifications, imitations, etc. Incidentally, "reproduction" is perhaps not the happiest term. In locutions like "color-reproduction" it means adaptation, and it might have been better to use the word "multiplication" as does the German text of the Convention (*vervielfältigen*). What it means is simply copying, or making many copies (*exemplaires*). This, in itself, shows that the use of the word "reproduction" is a redundancy.

The use of the words "in tangible form" is a further redundancy. A copy is a thing, a physical object, a movable, a chattel, something corporeal. Thus, it is tangible by definition.

The probable reason for employing the words "reproduction in tangible form" is that the Geneva Conference wanted to emphasize that public performances, recitations, exhibitions or showings do not amount to publication. Performances, etc., are not tangible. They are not reproductions. Thus, it has been made clear that a performance is not a publication. Since, however, a performance is not a distribution of copies, the words "distribution of copies" in themselves make it clear that a performance is not a publication within the meaning of the Universal Convention which, in this respect, is in harmony with the Berne Conventions. Whether this is a logical solution, in other words, whether distribution of copies should be regarded as the only means of publication, and diffusion by performance (e.g., to millions of radio listeners or television viewers) should not be so regarded, is a different question and will not be discussed here.

10. Meaning of "Copies . . . From Which [the Work] Can Be Read or Otherwise Visually Perceived."—As it has been stated above (point 1), the Geneva Conference was particularly anxious to make it clear that phonograph records and other like sound recordings are not copies of the musical or other work, the performance of which is fixed on them. It is for this purpose that the Convention expressly states that only the issue of copies from which the work can be read, or otherwise visually perceived, can result in publication. A sound recording cannot be read, nor can the work, the performance of which is fixed on the recording, be visually perceived, from a sound recording. Thus, the purpose of the Conference has been achieved. From a practical viewpoint the qualification in question is adequate.

From the angle of economy and art in drafting, however, the choice of words may be unfortunate. It is believed that they are superfluous. As demonstrated above, phonograph records are not copies of the work, the performance of which is fixed on them (point 6). Since there is publication only if copies are distributed, if there are no copies—and phonograph records are *not* copies—there is no publication.

On the other hand, there is a possibility that the words "read or otherwise visually perceived" may lead to misunderstanding if applied to cinematographic works. A cinematographic work is perceived both visually and by the ear, at least if it is a sound film, as the overwhelming majority of modern cinematographic works are. There is no doubt that the negative and positive films (comprising both picture band and sound track) are copies of the cinematographic work; and that if these copies are generally distributed to the public, for example, by selling thousands of copies, the cinematographic work will be published. However, it may be argued that not any copy can cause publication but only copies serving visual perception; that sound films serve not only visual perception but also perception by the ear. There may be some merit in this argument. However, sound films are intended also for visual perception. Once this element is present, it satisfies the words "read or otherwise visually perceived" of Article VI. The first meeting of the Interim Copyright Committee established by the Geneva Conference expressed the view that the "sole purpose" of Article VI was to exclude phonograph records. Consequently, it could not intend to exclude also films. The views of the Committee have not the force of a judicial interpretation, but they carry enough weight to be seriously considered.

There is one more unfortunate implication in the words "read and otherwise visually perceived." They may be understood as implying that there are two kinds of copies of works: copies perceivable by the eye, and copies perceivable by the ear. But, within the meaning of the word "copies" in Article VI, copies perceivable by the ear do not exist, and consequently the qualification is superfluous and confusing.

The above considerations, of course, are based on the assumption that records are not works. If a record is a work, i.e., if the producer of the record is an author, then the definition of the Convention is inadequate, because the thousands of "pressings" made of an original recording are obviously copies of the original recording, and these pressings are perceivable by the ear.

11. Meaning of "General Distribution to the Public."—It is probably not possible to define with accuracy the meaning of the word "distribution," as used in Article VI. The common, non-technical, meaning of "distribute" is to "deal out." Consequently, whenever copies of the work are dealt out or handed out, there is distribution, i.e., publication.

As stated above, the U.S. Copyright Law does not define publication, but it does define the date of publication and it is implicit in this rule that placing on sale, sale and public distribution are acts resulting in publication (17 U.S.C. § 62). In this enumeration sale and distribution are different concepts, and the Congressional hearings show that distribution is meant to be gratuitous distribution as contrasted with sale (Arguments before the Committees on Patents of the Senate and House of Representatives on S. 6330 and H.R. 19853, 59th Congress, 1st Session 160 (June 1906), 101 (December 1906)). Since the Convention does not use the word "sale," it is believed that "distribution" is meant to cover both gratuitous and non-gratuitous distribution, i.e., sale. Otherwise, the most common and, from the author's viewpoint, the most lucrative kind of distribution, that for a sale's price, would be excluded, which would lead to a manifestly impossible result. On the other hand, it is questionable whether, according to the Convention, "placing on sale" (exposure on stalls or counters, or keeping in stock, with the intent to sell) is distribution, because distribution would seem to imply not only an intent to distribute but also the accomplished distribution, i.e., a transfer of the copies.

The vagueness of the term "distribution" is illustrated by the great variety of terms used in the other texts of the Convention.

The French text uses the words *mise à disposition*, i.e., putting at the disposition of the public. In one sense disposition means exactly distribution. Understood in this sense it is an *idem per idem* and thus of no help in understanding the word distribution. In another sense putting at the disposition implies that it is enough to offer the copies and that acceptance is not necessary. If this meaning is accepted, placing on sale would be also a form of distribution. In a third sense, however, disposition may be understood as implying the necessity of owning, by members of the public, of copies, because only a person who acquired the property in the copy can dispose of the copy. If this meaning is accepted, distribution would mean transfer of property (either for a valuable consideration or gratuitously) and mere lending, leasing, loaning of the copy or permission to use it, would not amount to distribution. In a fourth sense, however, "putting at the disposition" may be understood as lending, leasing, loaning, or permitting to use, without transfer of the property rights. When I put my car at your disposition for the afternoon, I do just this; and I have no idea of parting with the property.

The Spanish text is an exact translation of the French (*poner a disposición*).

The non-authoritative but official German text translates "distribution" by "making accessible" (*zugänglich machen*). This expression is just as vague as the French, if not even broader. When is a work accessible to me, a member of the public, through a copy? If I buy it or otherwise obtain the property in it, it obviously becomes accessible. But it would seem that even if I am given a chance to read or visually perceive a copy, without acquiring its property, I have access to the work. It is not an unlimited or exclusive access, but it is nevertheless a kind of access.

The official Portuguese text uses the expression which probably is the broadest of all. It speaks about the "communication" of the copies to the public (*communicaçao ao público*).

To summarize: the various versions of the Convention consider distribution, putting at the disposition, making accessible, and communication, as acts resulting in publication.

In view of the variety and vagueness of these terms, any definite interpretation seems to be impossible. It seems to be clear that the sale of the copies or their free handing out come within the meaning of "distribution." It may be argued that offering for sale is not a distribution. Whether lending, leasing, and other licenses to use the copies under reservation of the property in them amounts to distribution, seems to be a widely open question.

12. Same: Meaning of "To the Public."—The words "to the public" seem to mean that anyone who wishes to obtain one of the copies available for distribution should be able to do so, by paying the required price of fulfilling the other conditions which the distributor of the copies is free to set as long as a reasonable number of copies have been made available. The setting of certain conditions, other than price, involves some difficult cases of interpretation. If, for example, copies of a book are distributed only to certain individuals, e.g., to the members of a club, is such a distribution a distribution to the public? It seems to be impossible to establish abstract rules. One shall have to look to the facts and circumstances in each particular case. Thus, for example, if books are distributed only to the members of a club, there may be a great difference between cases which involve clubs of ten members and clubs of ten thousand members.

13. Same: Meaning of "General."—According to the Convention distribution must not only be "to the public" but it also must be "general." In one sense the two qualifications are redundant. A distribution, the potential beneficiary of which is any member of the public and not a particular member of it, is necessarily a general distribution; and vice-versa: the target of a general distribution is necessarily the public. It may be, however, that the Geneva Conference inserted the adjective "general" in order to emphasize that the copies should be available to any prospective purchaser as long as the copies last.

14. Meaning of the Plural in the Word "Copies."—According to the Convention in order to achieve publication it is necessary to distribute copies. One copy is not enough. Consequently, works which cannot exist but in one copy, such as paintings (cf. point 4, supra), or works which are capable of existing in several copies but actually exist in one copy only (e.g., a manuscript of a book, existing in one copy only and not yet multiplied) are not susceptible of publication.

15. Meaning of Words "As Used in This Convention."—These words seem to be superfluous. On the one hand, it is evident that the Convention can give definitions only for the purposes of the Convention. On the other hand, if the national law of a potential contracting country contains a definition different from the definition of the Convention, such contracting country will have to take, with regard to Convention works, the necessary measures to give effect to the definition contained in the Convention (cf. Article X).

16. Date and Place of Publication.—As will be seen, in respect to the application of other provisions of the Convention (particularly Articles II, III, IV and V), not only the question whether a given work is a published or an unpublished work is relevant, but also the questions of the date and place of first publication of a work.

The date of first publication is the date on which copies of the work were first distributed to the public. The objects of the distribution are copies; these copies are the result of reproduction. Reproduction, by definition, is not publication. But reproduction, in itself, i.e., without distribution, is not publication. Thus, the date of reproduction cannot be the date of publication. The act of publication is completed only when distribution starts. For this reason we believe that the date of distribution, and not the date of reproduction, must be controlling in determining the date of publication.

For analogous reasons we submit that the place of first publication is the country in which copies of the work were first distributed. It is to be noted that this interpretation implies that the place of reproduction is irrelevant. Thus, for example, a work, copies of which were first reproduced in a noncontracting country, but were first distributed in a contracting country, is a work which must be regarded as a work first published in a contracting country. Or, if the copies were reproduced in contracting country A, and distributed in contracting country B, the country of first publication is B. Or, if the copies were reproduced in a contracting country but first distributed in a noncontracting country, such work must be regarded as a work first published in a noncontracting country.

Our interpretation may be regarded as contrary to the literal meaning of Article VI, because Article VI would, on its face, seem to consider reproduction and distribution as two acts each of which is a requirement of publication. However, as discussed above (point 9), the use of "reproduction" is redundant and the word "reproduction" probably serves only the purpose of emphasizing that reproduced, tangible, etc., copies, and not performances, etc., must be distributed in order to achieve publication.

17. General Observations.—As already intimated at the end of point 9, supra, whether the solution adopted by the Geneva Conference is a logical solution is questionable. The definition was adopted for practical considerations, on the insistence chiefly of the U.S. Delegation, and for the purpose of assuring that the distribution of phonograph records of an unpublished musical or literary work should not amount to publication. While we believe that it is logically correct to consider that phonograph records are not copies of the musical or literary work, we are rather inclined to think that the distribution of records should have similar effect as publication. Such a theory would help to eliminate the artificial differentiation between the publication of talking motion pictures and phonograph records. And for those countries that consider records as sui generis works, the question of when records are published would find a natural answer. All this, however, is speculation for the possible improvement, by revision, of the Convention. As it is worded today, there is no doubt that the distribution of phonograph records does not cause the musical or literary work to be published.

B. THE APPLICATION OF THE DEFINITION TO THE OTHER PROVISIONS OF THE CONVENTION

18. Provisions Using the Concept of Publication.—The concept of "publication" is used several times in Articles II, III, IV and V of the Convention.

The concept of publication is of relevance also in connection with the Appendix Declaration relating to Article XVII, but there it is used within the meaning of the Berne Conventions, and not within the meaning of Article VI of the Universal Copyright Convention. It will be discussed in the analysis of the Appendix Declaration.

19. "Publication" and Article II.—In respect to the eligibility of a work for protection under the Convention, "publication" plays a role only if the work's author is not a national of a contracting country. If he is a national, the work is protected whether published or not, and if so, irrespective of the place of first publication. But, if the author is not a national of a contracting country, the Convention applies only if the work is a published work and has been first published in a contracting country.

"Publication" plays an important role in determining the treatment contracting countries must accord to works to which the Convention applies: published works must be accorded the same protection as the domestic law accords to works of domestic authors first published in the country in which protection is sought; and unpublished works must be accorded the same protection as the domestic law accords to unpublished works of nationals of the country in which protection is sought. This differentiation is particularly important in connection with formalities and duration to be examined in the following points.

20. "Publication" and Article III (Formalities).—In respect to formalities (Article III), the concept of "publication" has relevance in the following instances:

(a) The possibility of substituting the Convention notice for domestic formalities exists only in respect to works first published outside the territory of the country in which protection under the Convention is sought (and if the author is not a national of the same country) (cf. Article III, paragraphs 1 and 2).

(b) Among the domestic formalities that may be replaced by the Convention notice, is publication in the contracting country in which protection is sought (Article III, paragraph 1).

(c) The Convention notice, to be effective, must appear in "all the copies of the work published with the authority of the author or other copyright proprietor" (Article III, paragraph 1).

(d) Said notice must appear "from the time of the first publication" of the work (Article III, paragraph 1).

(e) One of the elements of the Convention notice is "the year of first publication" (Article III, paragraph 1).

(f) In each contracting country there must be "legal means of protecting without formalities the unpublished works" of nationals of other contracting countries (Article III, paragraph 4).

All these problems have been examined in detail in the chapter dealing with Article III.

21. "Publication" and Article IV (Duration).—In respect to the term of protection (Article IV) the concept of publication has relevance in the following instances:

(a) Only countries which compute term for certain classes of works from first publication are allowed to apply the minimum stipulated in Article IV, paragraph 2, subparagraph 2, i.e., "25 years from the date of first publication," to the said classes and also to other classes (see, however, the following point).

(b) Only countries which do not compute term on the basis of the life of the author are allowed to compute the term of protection "from the date of the first publication of the work or from its registration prior to publication"; and the minimum will be "25 years from the date of first publication or from registration prior to publication" (Article IV, paragraph 2, subparagraph 2).

(c) According to the rule of the shorter term, no contracting country is obliged "to grant protection to a work for a period longer than that fixed for the class of works to which the work in question belongs, in the case of unpublished works by the law of the Contracting State of which the author is a national, and in the case of published works by the law of the Contracting State in which the work has been first published" (Article IV, paragraph 4, subparagraph 1).

(d) For the purposes of the foregoing rule "the work of a national of a Contracting State, first published in a non-Contracting State, shall be treated as though first published in the Contracting State of which the author is a national" (Article IV, paragraph 5).

(e) For the purposes of the rule mentioned under point (c) above "in the case of simultaneous publication in two or more Contracting States within thirty days of its first publication shall be considered as having been published simultaneously in said Contracting States" (Article IV, paragraph 6).

These provisions have been examined in some detail in the chapter dealing with Article IV.

22. "Publication" and Article V (Right of Translation).—In respect to the right of translation (Article V) the concept of publication has relevance in the following instances:

(a) The possibility of subjecting the right of translation to a compulsory license system exists, among others, in respect to writings of which a translation "has not been published" within "seven years from the date of the first *publication* of the writing" (Article V, paragraph 2, subparagraph 2).

(b) The compulsory license entitles the licensee to translate and publish (Article V, paragraph 2, subparagraph 2) but, subject to exceptions, only to publish in the contracting country where the license has been applied for (Article V, paragraph 2, subparagraph 5).

These provisions have been examined in some detail in the chapter dealing with Article V.

ARTICLE VII: WORKS PERMANENTLY IN THE PUBLIC DOMAIN

" This Convention shall not apply to works or rights in works which, at the effective date of the Convention in a Contracting State where protection is claimed, are permanently in the public domain in the said Contracting State." (Art. VII)

1. Scope of Article VII.—Article VII denies Convention protection to a class of works (and rights in works), viz., to works (or rights in works) which "at the effective date of the Convention in a Contracting State where protection is claimed, are permanently in the public domain in the said Contracting State."

The use of the indefinite article ("in a Contracting State") seems unfortunate, because the work "said" refers to a given State, viz., to the very State in which protection is claimed. It would have been better, from a grammatical viewpoint, to use the definite article, like the French and Spanish texts of the Convention do, and stipulate that the Convention shall not apply to works or rights in works which, at the effective date of the Convention in the Contracting State where protection is claimed, are permanently in the public domain in the said Contracting State.

The effective date of the Convention in a given contracting country, according to Article IX (see below), is the day which follows by three months the day on which the said country has deposited its instrument of ratification, acceptance or accession, and, in the case of the first twelve countries that have deposited their instruments of ratification or accession (among them the United States), it was September 16, 1955.

In the following analysis, for the sake of brevity, "critical date" will be used to designate the date on which the Convention becomes effective in the contracting country in which protection is claimed.

2. Transitional Character of Article VII.—In dealing with works (and rights in works) in relation to a certain date—the critical date—Article VII is limited in its scope: it deals only with works (and rights in works) which, at the said date, were in existence. To any work created after the said date, Article VII is inapplicable.

For the sake of brevity, in the following analysis "existing work" will be used to designate works the creation of which terminated on or before the critical date.

3. Status of Work Outside the Country in Which Protection Is Claimed.—Article VII specifies that the Convention shall not apply to works (or rights in works) which, on the critical date, are permanently in the public domain in the country in which protection is claimed. The implication is that the question whether the work (or right) is permanently in the public domain in any country other than the country in which Convention protection is actually claimed (e.g., is permanently in the public domain in the country of which the author is a national, or in which the work was first published, as long as it is other than the country in which protection is claimed) is, as far as Article VII is concerned, irrelevant. In other words, no country can deny protection, on the basis of Article VII, to a work (or a right) only on the ground that it has fallen permanently in the public domain in another country. Denial of protection may, of course, follow from the application of Article IV, or other provisions.

4. Meaning of "In the Public Domain."—Works (or rights in works) "in the public domain" are works (or rights) which are not protected. The cause of non-protection is irrelevant: it may result from the fact that the work is of a kind not eligible for protection, that formalities constitutive of copyright were not complied with, that the term of protection expired, or any other cause. The same is true in respect to rights in a work, i.e., the cause of non-protection is irrelevant. The right of translation, for example, may be in the public domain because, before the critical date, it was not recognized by the law, or because the special formalities necessary for the preservation of this right were not complied with, or because the special, shorter term of protection granted to this right expired before the critical date, or for other reasons.

As illustrated by the above examples, a work, as such, may not be in the public domain at the critical date, and application of the Convention to certain rights in the same work may still be denied if such rights were, at the critical date, in the public domain. This is the significance of the words "or rights in works" in Article VII. If, for example, country A grants 10 years from first publication for translation rights, but grants 50 years from the author's death for all other rights (e.g., for the right of reproduction), and this country becomes bound, under the Convention, with country B, in which the work was first published eleven years before the critical date, A may refuse to protect the right of translation (notwithstanding Article V), although it may not, because of Article VII, refuse to protect the other rights (e.g., the right of reproduction).

Whether the state of non-protection at the critical date was or was not preceded by a state of protection, is irrelevant. This is particularly clear in the Spanish and French texts of the Convention which, instead of speaking of works (or rights) "in the public domain," speak of works (or rights) "which have definitely ceased to be protected or which have never been protected."

5. Works (and Rights) Not Permanently in the Public Domain on the Critical Date.—Article VII provides that a country shall not apply the Convention to works (or rights in works) which in the same country—or, more exactly, according to the laws or international agreements (other than the Universal Convention) of that country—are permanently in the public domain.

The question arises whether this rule was intended to contain a negative implication that all existing works (or rights) provisionally in the public domain on the critical date, and all existing works (or rights) neither provisionally nor permanently in the public domain on the critical date, are works (or rights) to which the Convention shall apply.

While recognizing the possibility of arguing that the Convention does not apply to any work created prior to the critical date, because there is no express language to this effect in the Convention, it is submitted that the better view is that the Convention does apply to works (or rights) which are not permanently in the public domain on the critical date, provided, naturally, that they satisfy the other requirements which make a work (or right) eligible for Convention protection.

Had the Convention wanted to exclude from Convention protection works (or rights) provisionally in the public domain, it would have been dangerous and illogical to use the word "permanently." And had the Conference wanted to exclude from Convention protection any work (works permanently, provisionally or not in the public domain) existing on the critical date, it could have done so by stipulating that the Convention only applies to works created after the critical date, or by stipulating that the Convention shall not apply to any existing work. The Conference adopted neither of these two all-embracing formulas. Instead, it used restrictive language ("permanently in the public domain") and it would seem difficult to argue that the Conference, speaking about works (or rights) permanently in the public domain, also meant works (or rights) not permanently in the public domain.

6. Same: Works Provisionally in the Public Domain.—As stated above, it is submitted that, according to the better interpretation, Article VII implicitly provides that the Convention shall apply to works provisionally in the public domain.

Examples of the institution of a provisional public domain exist in the copyright laws of several Latin American countries, according to which the failure to register the copyright claim within a stated period may cause the work's falling into the public domain for a definite time, for example two years, whereafter the claim becomes registrable within a new stated period (e.g., 6 months). Only if this second possibility of complying with the formalities is missed, is the work considered as having "permanently" fallen into the public domain.

In some countries, unpublished works of aliens are not protected (except on the basis of special provisions such as treaties) but works first published in them are protected irrespective of the author's nationality. In such a country the work of an alien is always first in the public domain (since a state of non-publication necessarily precedes publication) but will come under copyright protection if it is first published in the country. The United Kingdom, for example, grants no protection to the unpublished work of a Cuban citizen but if the same work is first published in London, it will be protected by the U.K. Copyright Law. It is submitted that in countries having such systems unpublished works should be regarded as works which, necessarily, cannot be permanently in the public domain (unless the term of protection, computed from the author's death, expired).

ARTICLE VIII: SIGNATURE OF AND ADHESION TO THE CONVENTION

"*1. This Convention, which shall bear the date of September 6, 1952, shall be deposited with the Director-General of the United Nations Educational, Scientific and Cultural Organization and shall remain open for signature by all States for a period of 120 days after that date. It shall be subject to ratification or acceptance by the signatory States.*

2. Any State which has not signed this Convention may accede thereto.

3. Ratification, acceptance or accession shall be effected by the deposit of an instrument to that effect with the Director-General of the United Nations Educational, Scientific and Cultural Organization." (Art. VIII)

1. Scope of Article VIII.—Article VIII provides for the methods by which States may become parties to the Convention. The Article also provides implicitly that any State may become party thereto.

2. Methods Whereby States May Become Parties to the Convention.—Article VIII distinguishes between States which have and which have not signed the Convention. Signature was possible only for a period of 120 days starting on September 6, 1952. Paragraph 1 stipulates:

"This Convention, which shall bear the date of September 6, 1952, shall be deposited with the Director-General of the United Nations Educational, Scientific and Cultural Organization [UNESCO] and shall reamin open for signature by all States for a period of 120 days after that date..."

Forty States signed the Convention during the stated period:

Andorra	Belgium
Argentine Republic	Brazil
Australia	Canada
Austria	Chile
Cuba	Luxemburg
Denmark	Mexico
El Salvador	Monaco
Finland	Netherlands
France	Nicaragua
German Federal Republic	Norway
Guatemala	Peru
Haiti	Portugal
Holy See	San Marino

Honduras	Spain
India	Sweden
Ireland	Switzerland
Israel	United Kingdom
Italy	United States of America
Japan	Uruguay
Liberia	Yugoslavia

Those States which signed the Convention become bound by it if they "ratify" or "accept" the same. The second sentence of paragraph 1 provides:

"It [the Convention] shall be subject to ratification or acceptance by the Signatory States."

Those States which did not sign the Convention become bound by it if they "accede" to the same. Paragraph 2 provides:

"Any State which has not signed this Convention may accede thereto."

Signing of the Convention has no legal consequences. It does not carry with it any rights or obligations.

Ratification, acceptance and accession (the three will be designated hereafter by the word "adherence") have exactly the same legal effects. The difference is only one in denomination: the first two denominations (ratification, acceptance) being reserved for signatories, the latter (accession) being reserved for non-signatories.

A signatory State which adheres to the Convention has a free choice to call its adherence "ratification" or "acceptance." Their legal effects, as already stated, are the same: it is stated in the Rapporteur-General's report that "whether [a signatory State] ratified or accepted, the effect in binding the State was the same. In some countries the term or word used made no difference, but in others, such as the United States, acceptance was by a different procedure from ratification and might be easier in practice" (Records, page 84). Still, the United States ratified rather than accepted.

Following the contemporary trend of depositing the original text of multilateral conventions (cf. paragraph 1) and the instruments of adherence with the secretariat of intergovernmental organizations rather than with the government of a (usually the host) country, Article VIII, paragraph 3, provides that:

"Ratification, acceptance or accession shall be effected by the deposit of an instrument to that effect with the Director-General of the United Nations Educational, Scientific and Cultural Organization [UNESCO]."

UNESCO's headquarters are in Paris.

3. Convention Open to all States.—Signatory States may become parties to the Convention (if they wish to adhere, they "ratify" or "accept" the Convention); "any State which has not signed" the Convention may become party to it too (if it wishes to adhere, it "accedes"). In other words, the Convention is open to all States ("Universal" Convention).

Although Article X provides that "at the time an instrument of ratification, acceptance or accession is deposited on behalf of any State, such State must be in a position under its domestic law to give effect to the term Convention," no individual or body is designated in the Convention who or which would have the task of determining whether a prospective Contracting State is or is not in the said position.

Article XXI provides that the Director-General of UNESCO has the task of informing the interested countries about the date on which the Convention comes into force. It might be argued perhaps that this task necessarily involves a weighing by the Director-General whether the deposits of the instruments of adherence are acceptable with reference to Article X which, as already stated, provides that at the time of the deposit the depositing country "must be in a position under its domestic law to give effect to the terms of this Convention." The better view, however, seems to be that, because of the Convention's silence on this matter, such important function cannot be imputed to the Director-General and that his duty is merely a mechanical one, i.e., counting the deposited instruments, and if they attain the number of twelve, as prescribed in Article IX, notify the countries of the Convention's coming into force. That, in fact, the Director-General regarded his role to be just this, can be deducted from his passive attitude in the case of the first twelve instruments, since there is no evidence of his attempting to determine whether such instruments emanated from countries which complied with the requirements of Article X.

Neither is the Intergovernmental Committee established under Article XI entitled to refuse an instrument of adherence, because its rights and obligations limitatively enumerated in the Convention (Articles XI and XII) do not include the task of deciding whether a country is eligible to become a party to the Convention.

Consequently, even if a country is not in the position to give effect to the terms of the Convention, nobody will prevent it from depositing its instrument of adherence. As to the available remedies, see the analysis of Article X below.

4. Effect of Deposit.—The question has arisen whether an instrument of adherence can be withdrawn during the period (three months in the case of the twelfth or any subsequent adherer) which elapses between the date of deposit and the entry into force of the Convention (within the meaning of Article IX).

It is believed that such withdrawal of the instrument of adherence is not possible. If the act of depositing the instrument were in the nature of an offer, it could be withdrawn. But it is not an offer. It could be regarded as an offer only if it required acceptance. But it does not require acceptance by the countries already bound by the Convention.

They have no power to refuse to enter into contractual relations with any country wishing to adhere.

It is believed that the act of deposit is an acceptance. The Convention is an offer kept open by all countries already parties of the Convention to any new country to enter into contractual relationship with them. Once the new country deposits its instrument of adherence, it accepts the offer and the contract is concluded.

ARTICLE IX: COMING INTO FORCE OF THE CONVENTION

"1. This Convention shall come into force three months after the deposit of twelve instruments of ratification, acceptance or accession, among which there shall be those of four States which are not members of the International Union for the Protection of Literary and Artistic Works.

2. Subsequently, this Convention shall come into force in respect of each State three months after that State has deposited its instrument of ratification, acceptance or accession." (Art. IX)

1. Scope of Article IX.—Article IX establishes the dates on which the Convention comes into force. The rules are not the same for all contracting countries. Differentiation must be made between two groups of countries, i.e., the first twelve which deposit their instruments of adherence, and any subsequent country.

2. Entry Into Force of Convention Between the First Twelve Countries.—In respect to the first twelve countries, the Convention establishes the following rule, in Article IX, paragraph 1:

"1. This Convention shall come into force after the deposit of twelve instruments of ratification, acceptance or accession, among which there shall be those of four States which are not members of the International Union for the Protection of Literary and Artistic Works."

The words "among which there shall be those of four States which are not members of the [Berne] Union..." should be understood as a minimum of four, rather than a fixed number, since the intent behind this qualification was to make the Universal Convention effective only if it is adhered to by countries other than countries members of the Berne Copyright Union (the Berne countries being bound, in their mutual relations, by the Berne Conventions). The condition, if so interpreted, was met since seven of the first twelve adherents were non-Berne countries (i.e., Andorra, Cambodia, Chile, Costa Rica, Haiti, Laos, United States of America).

The first twelve instruments of adherence were deposited by the said seven countries and the Federal Republic of Germany, Israel, Monaco, Pakistan and Spain.

The twelfth, that of Monaco, having been deposited on June 16, 1955, the Convention came into force, within the meaning of Article IX, paragraph 1, on September 16, 1955 (3 years and 10 days after its adoption in Geneva). See, however, point 8 of the Chapter dealing with Article X.

3. Entry Into Force of Convention Between Other Countries.
—Between a country that is not among the first twelve and all other
countries that deposited their instruments earlier than said country,
the Convention goes into effect on the day which follows by three
months the day on which said country deposited its instrument of
adherence. The rule is contained in Article IX, paragraph 2, reading
as follows:

> "2. Subsequently, this Convention shall come into force in respect of each
> State three months after the State has deposited its instrument of ratification,
> acceptance or accession."

The word "subsequently" relates to the previous paragraph and
should be understood as meaning, "except the date fixed in paragraph
1."

The words "in respect of each State... that... has deposited its instrument" of adherence subsequently to the twelfth State, does not mean,
of course, that the Convention goes into force on the provided date only
in respect of that State, but that it goes into force between that State
and all the other States which effectuated deposit earlier than the State
in question.

ARTICLE X: GIVING EFFECT TO THE CONVENTION

"1. Each State party to this Convention undertakes to adopt, in accordance with its Constitution, such measures as are necessary to ensure the application of this Convention.

2. It is understood, however, that at the time an instrument of ratification, acceptance or accession is deposited on behalf of any State, such State must be in a position under its domestic law to give effect to the terms of this Convention." (Art. X)

1. Scope of Article X.—Basically, Article X provides that the contracting countries must apply the Universal Convention: paragraph 1 providing that the measures necessary to this end must be adopted by each country, paragraph 2 fixing the date on which such measures must exist.

2. Paragraph 1: Adoption of "Measures."—Paragraph 1 provides that each contracting country undertakes to "adopt" such "measures" as are necessary to ensure the application of the Convention.

Statutes, emanating from the legislative branch of the government, are "measures." So, also, are rules, regulations, orders, decrees or similar enactments emanating from the executive or administrative branches of government. All these are "express" laws.

The question arises whether "tacit" laws, such as the common law, court decisions, custom, and other similar "sources of law" not emanating from the legislative, executive or administrative branches of government, existing under different names in countries of different legal systems, are "measures."

As to the common law, different theories exist. According to one theory it is a body of law which always existed, independently of enactment, and is found and enunciated by the courts. Consequently, common law is not a "measure" that is "adopted," since both imply some action by man, of which a pre-existing body of laws is naturally independent. Under another theory, common law exists only as far as it is expressed by court diciseons.

This leads us to court decisions, whether relating to common law or not. If judges are regarded as the "makers" of law, perhaps it could be said that when they hand down opinions, they "adopt" legal "measures." It could be argued, however, that opinions are not measures and that the activity of a judge consists in applying rather than adopting the law.

In any case, it could be argued that it is not necessary to resolve the problem, since the obligation of countries to adopt measures is not unconditional but is required only where the domestic law is insufficient. Such a contention would derive its force from paragraph 2 of Article X. This paragraph provides that a contracting country must be in a position, "under its domestic law" to give effect to the Convention. If "domestic law" is interpreted as comprising also the "tacit" law, then, to the extent this tacit law (or existing express law) is in harmony with the Convention, there is no need for adopting measures, i.e., new "express" law. Both the word "necessary" in paragraph 1, and the word "however" in paragraph 2, would support this interpretation.

As stated, this interpretation is based on the premises that "law," as used in paragraph 2, means not only "express" law but also "tacit" law. Comparison with the French and Spanish texts of the Convention, which use the word "legislation," would indicate that "law" has the narrow meaning of positive enactments, i.e., of "express" law. On the other hand, it could be argued that the word "legislation" itself has a broader meaning and that, in any case, the English word "law" may be interpreted as referring also to "tacit" law.

The argument is of great practical significance. Several countries which adhered to the Convention have not, or not on all points provided for by the Convention, statutory or other "express" rules. France's copyright legislation was, at the time she adhered to the Convention, notoriously fragmentary; in the United States of America protection of unpublished works, in which claims to copyright have not been registered, is based on common law, and in both countries court decisions are an important source of copyright law. Other countries (e.g., Andorra, Cambodia) have no copyright statutes, unless the fragmentary French statutes apply to them. Whether these countries satisfy the requirements of Article X, depends, at least in part, on whether other than "express" sources of law are also recognized as "law." It is believed that the better view is to recognize these sources. Whether, in the concrete case, they exist and meet the Convention's requirements is a different question which, from an international viewpoint, could be tested only in the adjudication of a concrete dispute between two or more contracting countries by the International Court of Justice. Pending a negative finding to this effect by the Court, we suggest that the requirements should be presumed to having been met.

The matter is the more serious as noncompliance with Article X may void a country's adherence of its legal validity and would render the deposit of its instrument of adherence an unsuccessful attempt to adhere rather than an adherence (see point 8, below). It seems to conform with the traditional view that nullity of contracts is not presumed and to hold that violation of Article X must be proved before, and found by, the International Court before such grave consequences can be attached to the absence of "express" law.

3. Same: "In Accordance With Its Constitution."—Paragraph
1 provides that each contracting country undertakes to adopt "in
accordance with its constitution" such measures as are required. The
quoted passage is superfluous because it is self-evident. To suppose the
contrary would mean that countries consider themselves entitled to
conclude unconstitutional conventions, or adopt unconstitutional
domestic measures.

4. Same: "As Are Necessary."—Paragraph 1 provides that the
contracting countries undertake to adopt such measures "as are
necessary" to ensure the application of the convention.

Article I provides that "each Contracting State undertakes to provide
for the adequate and effective protection" of the rights of copyright
proprietors. Other articles of the Convention spell out in further details
the obligations of the contracting countries. Article X is a corollary of
these undertakings or obligations: if they can be fulfilled only if the
country adopts certain measures, then, naturally, the country will have
to adopt said measures. Otherwise, it would violate the Convention.

It has been argued that Article X, paragraph 1, intends to provide
that the Convention is not a so-called self-executive treaty, i.e., that
its rules are not directly enforceable in the domestic courts of a contracting country. Under this theory, contracting countries assume the
obligation of providing, usually by legislation, the rules which "implement" the treaty, i.e., which make the application of the Convention
both possible and unavoidable.

It is believed that some of the substantive provisions of the Convention
are, by their nature, not directly enforceable, but require implementation. Thus, for example, the general undertaking in Article I to
protect the rights of copyright proprietors evidently requires the
definition of these rights by domestic law, since the Convention itself
does not mention any rights except the right of translation in Article V.
Another example of the need of domestic measures is furnished by
Article IV on duration: the Article establishes alternate minima, but
it will depend on the domestic law which of these minima is followed
(or exceeded). Still another example for the possible need of domestic
measures is constituted by Article V, paragraph 2, on the compulsory
license in the case of translation rights. In this last respect it is also clear
that the implementation must be by legislation ("…Contracting State
may, by its domestic legislation, restrict the right of translation…").

On the other hand, there are provisions in the Convention, which,
by their legal nature, would be directly enforceable before the domestic
courts in countries where the direct application of treaty provisions is
legally possible. Thus, for example, the rules on the field of application
of the Convention (Article II), the substitution of the Convention notice
for domestic formalities (Article III), the definition of publication
(Article VI) and some other provisions are drafted as self-sufficient

rules, i.e., they do not refer to the domestic law of each country and, consequently, by their intrinsic nature, they do not require implementation by domestic measures. Whether, for a given country, corresponding domestic measures will be necessary, will depend on whether the Convention has become the law of the land and whether, as such, it supersedes inconsistent domestic measures.

It could be argued that not even in respect to these, by their legal nature directly enforceable, provisions can the Convention be regarded as self-executing, in countries which generally admit the self-executing effects of treaties, because Article X is directed to all countries, because it calls for the adoption of certain measures, and because measures "to ensure the application" of a treaty are necessarily other than the treaty itself.

Such argument, however, seems to have the weakness that it disregards the word "necessary" in Article X, paragraph 1. If a country admits the self-executing effects of those provisions of the Convention which are cast in an otherwise directly applicable form, then, it is submitted, for such a country no implementing measures are necessary.

5. Same: "Ensure the Application of the Convention."—The measures to be adopted are such as are necessary "to ensure the application of the Convention." Such measures are not only measures of copyright law but also measures of procedural character which will admit, as plaintiff, before the domestic courts the alien copyright proprietor, or which will criminally punish the infringer of his rights, as well as measures which will enforce the court's judgment if the losing defendant does not comply with it voluntarily.

6. Same: "State Party to This Convention."—Paragraph 1 is the only place in the Convention which uses the expression "State party to this Convention" rather than "Contracting State." This inconsistency in drafting has no legal significance. The expression means the same as "Contracting State."

7. Paragraph 2.—Paragraph 2 provides that at the time an instrument of ratification, acceptance or accession is deposited on behalf of a contracting country, such country must be in a position under its domestic law to give effect to the terms of this Convention. If, prior to such time, the country had a law which would have not allowed giving effect to the Convention, then, as seen above, such country had "to adopt... such measures as are necessary to ensure the application of this Convention" (paragraph 1).

That a State must be in the said position "under its domestic law" appears to be true only if one construes, as one probably should, "domestic law" as including the treaty itself in respect to all countries where treaties have self-executing effect.

As to the meaning of "law," see point 2, above.

8. Same: the Date of Deposit.—The date on which a country must be in a position to give effect to the Convention is, curiously, not the date on which the Convention comes into force in respect to such country (Article IX) but the date on which the country deposits its "instrument of ratification, acceptance or accession" (Article X). (There is a difference of three months between the two dates in the case of the twelfth or any subsequent country adhering to the Convention, and there was a difference of more than 3 months in the case of the first eleven adherences.)

Reference to the date of deposit rather than the date of entry into force, would be justified, had the Convention provided machinery for establishing and certifying whether a country, desirous of becoming a party to the Convention, is in a position to give effect to the Convention. In the negative, then, the country would not be admitted to the Convention.

No such machinery is, however, provided for in the Convention (see point 3 in the chapter on Article VIII).

Under such circumstances, what can a contracting country (or group of contracting countries) do which finds that another contracting country was not, at the time it deposited its instrument of adherence, "in a position under its domestic law to give effect to the terms of this Convention?"

Can it consider the Convention a nullity, i.e., a void contract, in its relations with the country not living up to the requirements of Article X?

Perhaps it could, but it would probably be more advisable not to trust only its own judgment but ask, under Article XV, the International Court of Justice to determine whether the defendant country was in the position required under Article X at the time it deposited its instrument of adherence. Should the Court find the defendant's act of deposit an unsuccessful attempt at adherence, it would declare the Convention void between the defendant and all other countries which have deposited their instruments. Should this situation arise in respect to one or more of the first twelve adherences, the date of entry into effect of the Convention as provided for under Article IX, paragraph 1, (i.e., September 16, 1955), would itself become questionable. In integrum restitutio or damages, depending on the case, could be claimed, too. Since any such judgment would involve the interpretation ("construction") of a multilateral treaty (the Universal Convention), if the claim was not presented by all contracting countries, any of them could intervene (Statute of the International Court of Justice, Article 63).

The foregoing considerations apply to the case in which the validity of the adherence of a contracting country is challenged by one or more other contracting countries before the International Court of Justice. It is conceivable, theoretically, that the domestic court of a country could find that the adherence of the same country was not valid because of non-compliance with the requirements of Article X. Such self-condemnation is, if for no other than for political reasons, most unlikely, but it is, as said above, a theoretical possibility. Such finding of the domestic court, however, would have no international effects, since no country can, vis-à-vis the other contracting countries, be the judge of its own actions.

If the domestic court of a country finds that another country did not meet the requirements of Article X, the private litigants will have to conform with the court's decision. But the latter country could, if it wished, enter a complaint against the country of the domestic court before the International Court of Justice and ask for the determination of the issue.

9. Same: Continuing Obligation.—Paragraph 2, if interpreted literally, could be understood as establishing the obligation of being in a position to give effect to the terms of the Convention as an obligation existing only on the date of deposit of the instrument of ratification, acceptance or accession. This is, of course, not true. The same position must exist throughout the entire period during which the country is bound by the Convention. It would have been more appropriate to state the rule as relating from the date of deposit to the effective date of denunciation.

ARTICLE XI AND RESOLUTION RELATING THERETO

INTERGOVERNMENTAL COPYRIGHT COMMITTEE

"*1. An Intergovernmental Committee is hereby established with the following duties:*

a) to study the problems concerning the application and operation of this Convention;

b) to make preparation for periodic revisions of this Convention;

c) to study any other problems concerning the international protection of copyright, in co-operation with the various interested international organizations, such as the United Nations Educational, Scientific and Cultural Organization, the International Union for the Protection of Literary and Artistic Works and the Organization of American States;

d) to inform the Contracting States as to its activities.

2. The Committee shall consist of the representatives of twelve Contracting States to be selected with due consideration to fair geographical representation and in conformity with the Resolution relating to this article, annexed to this Convention.

The Director-General of the United Nations Educational, Scientific and Cultural Organization, the Director of the Bureau of the International Union for the Protection of Literary and Artistic Works and the Secretary-General of the Organization of American States, or their representatives, may attend meetings of the Committee in an advisory capacity." (Art. XI)

Resolution Concerning Article XI

"*The Intergovernmental Copyright Conference*

Having considered the problems relating to the Intergovernmental Committee provided for in Article XI of the Universal Copyright Convention

resolves

1. The first members of the Committee shall be representatives of the following twelve States, each of those States designating one representative and an alternate: Argentina, Brazil, France, Germany, India, Italy, Japan, Mexico, Spain, Switzerland, United Kingdom, and United States of America.

2. The Committee shall be constituted as soon as the Convention comes into force in accordance with Article XI of this Convention;

3. The Committee shall elect its Chairman and one Vice-Chairman. It shall establish its rules of procedure having regard to the following principles:

a) the normal duration of the term of office of the representative shall be six years; with one-third retiring every two years;

b) before the expiration of the term of office of any members, the Committee shall decide which State shall cease to be represented on it and which States shall be called upon to designate representatives; the representatives of those States which have not ratified, accepted or acceded shall be the first to retire;

c) the different parts of the world shall be fairly represented;

and expresses the wish

that the United Nations Educational, Scientific, and Cultural Organization provide its Secretariat."

1. Scope of Article XI and the Resolution Relating Thereto. —Article XI creates an "Intergovernmental Committee." Its duties are outlined in paragraph 1 of Article XI. Its composition is regulated by paragraph 2 of Article XI, and by a "Resolution concerning Article XI" adopted by the Intergovernmental Copyright Conference on the same day as the Convention, viz., September 6, 1952. This Resolution, from a legal viewpoint, has the same value as if it were part of the text itself of the Convention: it precedes the signatures; and countries which ratify, accept or accede to the Convention, necessarily ratify, accept or accede also to the Resolution.

2. Duties of the Committee.—The duties of the Committee are enumerated in Article XI, paragraph 1, reading as follows:

"1. An Intergovernment Committee is hereby established with the following duties:

a) to study the problems concerning the application and operation of this Convention;

b) to make preparation for periodic revisions of this Convention;

c) to study any other problems concerning the international protection of copyright, in co-operation with the various interested international organizations, such as the United Nations Educational, Scientific and Cultural Organization, the International Union for the Protection of Literary and Artistic Works and the Organizations of American States."

It follows from the above that the Committee has no judicial authority: it cannot decide disputes and it cannot give authoritative interpretations of the Convention, which would have a binding force vis-à-vis the Contracting States. The Committee has no legislative authority either: it cannot amend the Convention. It has no administrative functions either, unless one considers the preparation (Article XI, paragraph 1b), and convocation (Article XII), of conferences of revision as administrative functions.

The Committee's main duty is to study two kinds of problems, viz., "problems concerning the application and operation of this [Universal] Convention" (Article XI, paragraph 1a), and "any other problems concerning the international protection of copyright" (Article XI, paragraph 1c). One of the differences between the two sets of problems is that the first set is limited to problems concerning the Universal Convention, whereas the second set is not limited thereto. Consequently, under paragraph 1c, the Committee may and should study such problems of international copyright which are not dealt with in the Convention. Rapprochement or ultimate merger of the Berne Conventions with the Universal Convention and/or the Pan American Conventions would seem to be a most interesting task and desirable goal which the Committee could usefully study. It is believed that the Committee could, either upon its own initiative, or on request by a State or an intergovernmental organization, give opinions and advice on the meaning of the various provisions of the Convention and on the question whether the copyright law of a given country, or its proposed copyright legislation, meets the requirements of the Convention. Such an opinion, however, would not be binding on anybody, not even the Committee, which may freely reverse itself.

If the studies relate to other problems than those concerning the application and operation of the Universal Convention, i.e., if they are carried out under the authority of paragraph 1c (rather than paragraph 1a), the Committee must co-operate "with the various interested international organizations" (paragraph 1c). UNESCO, the Berne Union and the Organization of American States are named as examples of such organizations. These examples seem to indicate that by "international organizations" the Conference meant intergovernmental, rather than non-governmental ("private"), organizations.

According to paragraph 1b, the Committee has the duty "to make preparation for periodic revisions of this Convention." It follows from Article XII that the revisions are to take place at intergovernmental conferences. Their convocation is also the task of the Committee (see Article XII). "Periodic" is not defined in the Convention. Although "periodic" would seem to imply revisions at stated, regular intervals, there are no guarantees for such periodicity in the Convention since the date of any conference is freely set by the Committee and/or a certain number of contracting countries (cf. Article XII).

According to paragraph 1d, the Committee must "inform the Contracting States as to its activities." This is natural, otherwise the Committee would work in a vacuum. In view of the fact that UNESCO provides the Secretariat of the Committee, the Committee's communications reach the governments of the contracting countries through UNESCO's Director-General (cf. Resolution concerning Article XI).

3. Composition of the Committee.—The members of the Committee are states, notably twelve of the contracting countries (Article XI, paragraph 1). The first members were elected during the Geneva Conference in 1952 (Resolution, par. 1). As any country may be reelected any number of times (Rules 2 and 37), whether there will be any rotation among the contracting countries, and, if so, to what extent, is within the discretion of the twelve original members.

Extraordinary grounds for losing a seat are denunciation of the Convention or unjustified absence at two consecutive regular annual sessions. Whether the absence was justified, is a matter to be decided by the Committee itself (Rule 4).

The designation of new members (or the election of the old members) is decided by a simple majority vote of the members (Rule 36, par. 3, and Rule 28). The outgoing members have the right to participate in the vote. An amendment of the Rules to effect the contrary result would appear to be logical.

Each member state is represented by one representative and one alternate, who may be accompanied to the sessions of the Committee by advisors (Rule 1).

4. Rules of Procedure.—The Committee has adopted its own Rules of Procedure (reprinted on pages 203 to 207, infra). In addition to the questions of membership, discussed above, the Rules regulate the frequency of the sessions, the election and duties of the officers, the establishment of agenda, the methods of working through sub-committees and consultants, the role of the secretariat, the conduct of business, the procedure of voting, the use of languages, the keeping of the records, the methods of amending the rules, and other related matters.

ARTICLE XII: REVISION OF THE CONVENTION

*"The Intergovernmental Committee shall convene a conference for
revision of this Convention whenever it deems necessary, or at the request
of at least ten Contracting States, or of a majority of the Contracting
States if there are less than twenty Contracting States."* (Art. XII)

1. Scope of Article XII.—Article XII provides for the method
whereby conferences for revision are convened. It is nowhere stated in
the Convention that it should or could be revised. This idea is, however,
implicit both in Article XI, paragraph 1b, and Article XII.

The result of a "revision" is a new convention, which, although in
its non-"revised" parts identical with the old, is both in respect to the
revised parts and to its entirety (both revised and non-revised parts)
a new contract. Only those countries will be bound by the new convention which ratify it. Those countries which do not ratify the new
convention continue to be bound by the old convention. For such
countries the new convention is *res inter alios acta*.

The Universal Convention does not provide any rules as to the vote
necessary for adopting the "revised," or more correctly, new convention.
Whether the conference of revision will prescribe unanimity, a qualified
or simple majority of the States parties to the old convention and/or
voting in the conference of revision, are questions which are left to the
discretion of the conference of revision itself. It will regulate these
matters in its rules of procedure.

2. Condition of Convocation of the Conference.—There are
two conditions, each of which is sufficient in itself, and which, if ma-
terialized, prompt the convocation of a "conference of revision": (a) the
will of the Intergovernmental Committee ("whenever [the Committee]
deems necessary"), or, (b) the will of a certain number of contracting
countries. The number of contracting countries which can provoke a
convocation must be at least:

—ten, if the total number of contracting countries is 18 or more,
—nine, if the total number of contracting countries is 16 or 17,
—eight, if the total number of contracting countries is 14 or 15,
—seven, if the total number of contracting countries is 12 or 13,
—six, if the total number of contracting countries is 10 or 11,
—five, if the total number of contracting countries is 8 or 9,
—four, if the total number of contracting countries is 6 or 7,
—three, if the total number of contracting countries is 4 or 5,
—two, if the total number of contracting countries is 2 or 3.

This follows from the words "…at the request of at least ten Contracting States, or of a majority of the Contracting States if there are less than twenty Contracting States." If the stated number of contracting countries request the convocation, the Committee has to convene the conference, whether it deems it necessary or not.

3. Convocation Issues From Committee.—The convocation is an act of the Intergovernmental Committee. No organ of UNESCO has to approve the Committee's action. The invitations should be signed by the Chairman of the Committee or its members.

ARTICLE XIII: APPLICATION OF THE CONVENTION TO NON-SELF-GOVERNING TERRITORIES

"Any Contracting State may, at the time of deposit of its instrument of ratification, acceptance or accession, or at any time thereafter, declare by notification addressed to the Director-General of the United Nations Education, Scientific and Cultural Organization that this Convention shall apply to all or any of the countries or territories for the international relations of which it is responsible and this Convention shall thereupon apply to the countries or territories named in such notification after the expiration of the term of three months provided for in Article IX. In the absence of such notification, this Convention shall not apply to any such country or territory." (Art. XIII)

1. Scope of Article XIII.—Article XIII provides for the methods whereby the Convention may be made applicable to non-self-governing territories. Adherence by a country to the Convention does not automatically have the effect of extending the application of the Convention to the non-self-governing territories "for the international relations of which it [i.e., the country in question] is responsible." Such extension requires an express declaration. Its form is a notification addressed to the Director-General of UNESCO, and emanating from the country which is responsible for the international relations of the territory. Three months after the date of the deposit (but September 16, 1955, in case of the first twelve adherences), the Convention becomes applicable to the territory or territories mentioned in the notification. From that time on the Convention applies, both as to rights and obligations, between the non-self-governing territory and all contracting countries other than the contracting country which made the notification.

For the communication of such notifications, see Article XXI.

ARTICLE XIV: DENUNCIATION OF THE CONVENTION

" 1. Any Contracting State may denounce this Convention in its own name or on behalf of all or any of the countries or territories as to which a notification has been given under Article XIII. The denunciation shall be made by notification addressed to the Director-General of the United Nations Educational, Scientific and Cultural Organization.

2. Such denunciation shall operate only in respect of the State or of the country or territory on whose behalf it was made and shall not take effect until twelve months after the date of receipt of the notification."
(Art. XIV)

1. Scope of Article XIV.—Article XIV provides for the method by which a contracting country may terminate its contractual relations under the Convention: the method is denunciation. The provision is self-explanatory.

Denunciation is the only method whereby a country can terminate its contractual relations. Since the Convention does not establish a "Union" or other legal entity consisting of the contracting countries, there was no need that the Convention should provide for withdrawal by, or expulsion of, a country.

Concerning the question whether a country may withdraw its instrument of adherence in the course of the three months which follow the deposit of such instrument, see point 4 under Article VIII.

Concerning the question whether the International Court of Justice can declare an adherence void in relation to certain countries, see point 8 under Article X.

The Convention is not concluded for any definite time. It will remain in force as long as two or more countries remain bound by it.

Although Article VIII requires, for the Convention's entry into force, adherence by twelve countries (among them four non-Berne countries), there is no provision in the Convention which would make the Convention's continued existence dependent on the same conditions. Consequently, the Convention will remain in force even if the number of the contracting countries would become less than twelve, or even if less than four were non-Berne countries.

ARTICLE XV: JURISDICTION OF THE INTERNATIONAL COURT OF JUSTICE

"A dispute between two or more Contracting States concerning the interpretation or application of this Convention, not settled by negotiation, shall, unless the States concerned agree on some other method of settlement, be brought before the International Court of Justice for determination by it." (Art. XV)

1. Scope of Article XV.—This Article establishes the jurisdiction of the International Court of Justice (hereafter referred to as "the Court").

2. Disputes.—The Court has jurisdiction over "a dispute between two or more Contracting States concerning the interpretation or application of this [Universal] Convention."

This provision finds its complement in the Statute of the Court (hereafter referred to as "Statute") which, in its Article 36, provides that "The jurisdiction of the Court comprises... all matters specially provided for... in the treaties and conventions in force." The Universal Convention is one of such treaties or conventions. The dispute must, as a matter of course, be of legal nature (cf. Statute, Article 36, paragraph 2).

Questions of "interpretation" are questions relating to the exact meaning of the Convention's provisions. They are also called questions of construction.

Typical disputes of "application" of the Convention would be disputes concerning the existence of any fact which, if established, would constitute a breach of an obligation under the Universal Convention (cf. Statute, Article 36, paragraph 1c), or disputes concerning the nature or extent of the reparation to be made for the breach of an obligation resulting from the Universal Convention (cf. Statute, Article 36, paragraph 1d).

3. Parties.—The disputes must exist "between two or more Contracting States." This is in accordance with Article 34, paragraph 1, of the Statute which provides that "Only States may be parties in cases before the Court."

The question arises whether the Court is open to all States parties to the Universal Convention. If such States are parties to the Statute, the Court is open to them. Such States are: (1) ipso facto, the States members of the United Nations, by virtue of Article 93, paragraph 1, of the Charter of the United Nations, and (2) upon acceptance of the conditions determined by the General Assembly of the United Nations, States which apply for becoming parties to the Statute, (cf. Charter of the United Nations, Article 93, paragraph 2). Such States are, today, Japan, Liechtenstein, San Marino, and Switzerland.

If a State party to the Universal Convention is not party to the Statute of the Court, the Court will be open to it if it previously declares to accept the jurisdiction of the Court, and to undertake to comply in good faith with the decision of the Court (cf. Statute, Article 34, paragraph 1; Resolution of the Security Council of the United Nations of October 15, 1946). If the country not party to the Statute is plaintiff, it doubtlessly will be diligent in depositing such declaration. It is less certain whether it would do the same, if it is a defendant. It is not entirely clear whether the Court could proceed in said case, viz., when the defendant country is not a party to the Statute and has not deposited the required declaration. "The conditions under which the Court shall be open to other States" than States parties to the Statute (Statute, Article 35, paragraph 2) have not been complied with, consequently the Court could be deemed as not open to them. On the other hand, "open" may be interpreted as referring to the plaintiff only. It could also be argued that, by accepting the Court's jurisdiction in Article XV of the Universal Convention, any country not party to the Statute, implicitly assumed the obligation to deposit the required declaration; not to deposit would be a breach; and, according to the maxim *nemo ex proprio dolo…,* no one can derive rights from his own breach; consequently, if the Court would refuse to proceed against such countries, it would, in essence, approve the breach of an international obligation, which it obviously cannot do.

It should be noted that others than States cannot be parties in a dispute before the Court. Consequently, natural persons, corporations, etc., can neither sue nor be sued before the Court. If they think that their rights are violated and if they cannot obtain remedy before the national courts of the country which has jurisdiction over the infringer, they may try to persuade the government of their own country to sue the other country before the International Court. Thus, the dispute is elevated to the level of a dispute between States and will become cognizable by the International Court.

4. Bringing of Action.—According to Article XV, disputes may "be brought" before the Court. "Cases are brought before the Court, as the case may be, either by the notification of the special agreement or by a written application addressed to the Registrar [of the Court]" (Statute, Article 40). For the Procedure see Statute, Chapter III; and the Rules of Court adopted on May 6, 1946.

5. Determination.—According to Article XV, the disputes are brought before the Court "for determination by it." Determination is made by judgment, and the judgment states the reasons on which it is based (Statute, Article 55).

6. States Not Parties to the Original Dispute.—The Universal Convention being a multilateral convention, a dispute does not necessarily involve all contracting countries. The determination of the dispute, however, may be of relevance to them. To safeguard their rights, whenever the construction of the Universal Convention is in question, the Registrar of the Court will notify them, and they will have the right to intervene in the proceedings (Statute, Article 63). If they use such right, the construction given by the judgment will be equally binding upon them (Statute, Article 63). This is an exception to the general rule laid down in Article 59 of the Statute, according to which "The decision of the Court has no binding force except between the parties and in respect of that particular case."

7. Meaning of "Not Settled by Negotiation."—Article XV provides that disputes "not settled by negotiation" may be brought before the Court. This seems to be a pleonasm, because a dispute which is settled is no longer a dispute, and if there is no dispute there is nothing to be brought before the Court (as to advisory opinions, which may be requested by certain international organizations and not States, see point 9 below). "By negotiation" is not quite accurate, since a dispute settled in any manner, whether by negotiation or otherwise, ceases to be a dispute and cannot be brought before the Court. A dispute settled, for example, by an arbitration award can also not be brought before the Court.

8. Meaning of "Unless the States Concerned Agree on Some Other Method of Settlement."—According to Article XV disputes between two or more Contracting States will be brought before the Court "unless the States concerned agree on some other method of settlement." This proviso simply means that if all countries concerned in a dispute agree not to go before the Court, nothing in the Universal Convention prevents them from doing so. It goes without saying that if one or more of the countries between which the dispute exists desires, or desire, to go before the Court, it (they) can force the others to face it (them) before the Court. See, however, point 3 supra.

9. Advisory Opinion by the International Court.—In connection with the Universal Convention, the International Court may proceed not only in the case provided for in Article XV of the Universal Convention, viz., in the case of dispute between States. It may also give advisory opinions on the request of authorized bodies.

The Court's competence in such cases does not depend on the Universal Convention but on the Charter of the United Nations and the Statute of the Court.

Advisory opinions may be requested by the General Assembly or the Security Council on "any legal question" (U.N. Charter, Article 96, paragraph 1).

Other organs of the United Nations as well as Specialized Agencies so authorized by the General Assembly of the United Nations may also request advisory opinions of the Court but only on such legal questions which arise "within the scope of their activities." (U.N. Charter, Article 96, paragraph 2). Certain problems which may arise in connection with the role of UNESCO as provided for in Articles VIII, XI, XIII, XIV, XXI, the Resolution concerning Article XI, and the three Protocols annexed to the Universal Convention, would be proper subjects for advisory opinions. And so would questions arising in connection with the protection of works published for the first time by the United Nations or by its Specialized Agencies, as well as of unpublished works of the same organizations—insofar as their protection or non-protection in countries parties to Protocol 2 is concerned.

Among the organs and Specialized Agencies entitled to request such opinions there are the Economic and Social Council of the United Nations (ECOSOC) and UNESCO. A full list of these organizations is given in the Yearbooks of the International Court of Justice.

ARTICLE XVI: LANGUAGES OF THE CONVENTION

"*1. This Convention shall be established in English, French, and Spanish. The three texts shall be signed and shall be equally authoritative.*

2. Official texts of this Convention shall be established in German, Italian, and Portuguese.

Any Contracting State or group of Contracting States shall be entitled to have established by the Director-General of the United Nations Educational, Scientific and Cultural Organization other texts in the language of its choice by arrangement with the Director-General.

All such texts shall be annexed to the signed texts of this Convention."
(Art. XVI)

1. Scope of Article XVI.—Only paragraph 1 of this Article has legal consequences. It establishes the rule that the English, French and Spanish texts are equally authoritative. And only these three texts are authoritative, i.e., if there are differences between these three texts on the one hand, and a text in another language on the other hand, the three named ones govern. If there are differences among the English, French and Spanish texts, such differences must be resolved according to the general rules of legal interpretation, as any other possible ambiguity or obscurity in the text.

The texts in German, Italian and Portugese are "official" texts. No legal consequence is attached to this adjective, which seems to reflect an act of courtesy on the part of the Geneva Conference. The texts in other languages, established on the request of one or more contracting countries, with the co-operation of UNESCO, are not called "official." Their legal significance, however, is the same as that of the official texts, i.e., the authoritative texts will always prevail over them in cases of possible different interpretations.

ARTICLE XVII AND APPENDIX DECLARATION RELATING THERETO

RELATIONS TO THE CONVENTIONS OF THE BERNE UNION

"*1. This Convention shall not in any way affect the provisions of the Berne Convention for the Protection of Literary and Artistic Works or membership in the Union created by that Convention.*

2. In application of the foregoing paragraph, a Declaration has been annexed to the present article. This Declaration is an integral part of this Convention for the States bound by the Berne Convention on January 1, 1951, or which have or may become bound to it at a later date. The signature of this Convention by such States shall also constitute signature of the said Declaration, and ratification, acceptance or accession by such States shall include the Declaration as well as the Convention." (Art. XVII)

Appendix Declaration Relating to Article XVII

"*The States which are members of the International Union for the Protection of Literary and Artistic Works, and which are signatories to the Universal Copyright Convention,*

Desiring to reinforce their mutual relations on the basis of the said Union and to avoid any conflict which might result from the coexistence of the Convention of Berne and the Universal Convention,

Have, by common agreement, accepted the terms of the following declaration:

(a) Works which, according to the Berne Convention, have as their country of origin a country which has withdrawn from the International Union created by the said Convention, after January 1, 1951, shall not be protected by the Universal Copyright Convention in the countries of the Berne Union;

(b) The Universal Copyright Convention shall not be applicable to the relationships among countries of the Berne Union insofar as it relates to the protection of works having as their country of origin, within the meaning of the Berne Convention, a country of the International Union created by the said Convention."

1. Scope of Articles XVII, XVIII, XIX, and Appendix Declaration Relating to Article XVII. — When the Universal Copyright Convention was adopted, a dozen or more multilateral and almost a hundred bilateral treaties were in existence governing copyright relations between countries. The need for establishing norms for the co-existence of the Universal Convention with the other multilateral conventions and the bilateral treaties was clearly recognized by the Geneva Conference. Articles XVII, XVIII and XIX, as well as the Appendix Declaration relating to Article XVII resulted from the recognition of this need.

Article XVII and the Appendix Declaration deal with the Conventions of the International Union for the Protection of Literary and Artistic Works (Berne Union), i.e., the Berne Convention, Additional Article, and Final Protocol (1886); the Paris Additional Act and Interpretative Declaration (1896); the Berlin Convention (1908); the Berne Additional Protocol (1914); the Rome Convention (1928); and the Brussels Convention (1948), (hereafter referred to as "Berne Conventions," or "Conventions (or texts) of the Berne Union"). Between two countries members of the Union those provisions apply which both have ratified and which are latest in date. Consequently, not all the countries members of the Union are bound to each other by the same text, and some are probably not bound to each other at all. The latter situation would seem to exist in cases where the countries have not ratified the same text, for example: if A ratified only the Brussels and B only the Rome text, there appears to be no Convention relations between A and B, although both are members of the Berne Union.

Article XVIII deals with the "multilateral or bilateral copyright conventions or arrangements that are or may be in effect exclusively between two or more American Republics."

Article XIX deals with those "multilateral or bilateral conventions or arrangements" which are covered neither by Article XVII nor by Article XVIII.

2. Scope of Article XVII and the Appendix Declaration Relating Thereto.—These provisions pursue three aims: (A) to emphasize that the Universal Convention does not affect the Berne Conventions, (B) to establish sanctions against countries withdrawing from the Berne Union, (C) to determine the extent of applicability of the Universal Convention by countries members of the Berne Union.

A. BERNE CONVENTIONS NOT AFFECTED

3. Article XVII, Paragraph 1.—That the Universal Convention does not replace or repeal the conventions of the Berne Union, is expressed in Article XVII, paragraph 1, of the Universal Convention which reads as follows:

> "This Convention shall not in any way affect the provisions of the Berne Convention for the Protection of Literary and Artistic Works or membership in the Union created by that Convention."

In other words, the provision states that the Universal Copyright Convention will not do two things: (i) it "shall not in any way affect the provisions of the Berne Convention" ("Berne Convention" meaning all texts or any text of the Berne Union) and, (ii) it "shall not in any way affect... membership in the Union created by [the Berne] Convention" ("Berne Convention" meaning all texts or any text of the Berne Union).

These two points are not provisions of the kind which order or prohibit something. They are statements of facts wholly independent from the Universal Copyright Convention since the Geneva Conference had no power to modify, and the Universal Convention did not purport to modify the Berne Conventions or affect membership in the Berne Union.

The original Berne Convention established, as far back as 1886, the rule according to which "no alteration in the Convention shall be binding on the Union except by the unanimous consent of the countries comprising it" (Art. XVII), this consent being formulated at conferences of revision. These rules have been reaffirmed in the texts adopted in Berlin (Art. 24), Rome (Art. 24), and Brussels (Art. 24). The Geneva Conference, not being a conference of revision of the Berne Union, and the Universal Convention, not being the expression of the unanimous consent of the countries which compose the Berne Union, could not change the Brussels Convention or any of the earlier texts of the Berne Union. For this latter the Universal Convention is *res inter alios acta*.

It follows from the above that the sentence according to which the Universal Copyright Convention in no way affects membership in the Union, is the recording of an existing state of facts and not a rule, since the rules of membership (how to accede to, and withdraw from, the Berne Union) are part of the provisions of the different Berne Conventions which, as demonstrated above, are unaffected by the Universal Convention. The conditions for withdrawal from the Union, in particular, are expressly regulated in the various Berne Conventions; and it follows from the relevant provisions that the only way by which a country may cease to be a member of the Union is by its denunciation of the Convention or Conventions to which such country is a party.

Consequently, Article XVII, paragraph 1, of the Universal Convention is, from a legal viewpoint, not necessary. Its presence in the Universal Convention shows that some countries of the Berne Union present at the Geneva Conference considered it advisable to emphasize the point that the provisions of the Berne Conventions and membership in the Berne Union are an internal affair of the Berne countries.

It could be argued that Article XVII, paragraph 1, was intended to establish that the Berne Conventions continue to be applicable between countries even after they have adhered to the Universal Convention, and that, notwithstanding the Universal Convention being the *lex posterior* and the Berne Conventions the *lex prior*, the rule *lex posterior derogat priori* will not apply. If such was the intent, the words chosen to express it are not the most fortunate, because the thing which the advent of the Universal Convention left unaffected is the relation or mutual protection between countries parties both to the Berne and the Universal Conventions, and not the "provisions" of the Berne Conventions or the "membership" in the Berne Union. Furthermore, the intent in question, and with some qualifications at that, finds expression in proviso b) of the Appendix Declaration, discussed below, and thus Article XVII, paragraph 1, would be redundant with proviso b) of the said Declaration.

4. Article XVII, Paragraph 2.—Article XVII, paragraph 2, establishes a link between the Convention itself and the Appendix Declaration. It reads as follows:

> 2. In application of the foregoing paragraph, a Declaration has been annexed to the present article. This Declaration is an integral part of this Convention for the States bound by the Berne Convention on January 1, 1951, or which have or may become bound to it at a later date. The signature of this Convention by such States shall also constitute signature of the said Declaration, and ratification, acceptance or accession by such States shall include the Declaration as well as the Convention.

Whether the statement according to which the Declaration has been annexed "in application of the foregoing paragraph," i.e., of Article XVII, paragraph 1, is a correct statement, is questionable. As will be seen in connection with its analysis, the Declaration provides for a sanction against countries withdrawing from the Berne Union and determines the extent of applicability of the Universal Convention by countries parties to the Universal and one or more of the Berne Conventions. Neither of these questions follows from or is connected with the provisions of the first paragraph.

The second sentence of paragraph 2 provides that the Declaration is an integral part of the Convention "for the States bound by the Berne Convention on January 1, 1951, or which have or may become bound to it at a later date." The words "Berne Convention" meaning any text of the Berne Union, the provision in question applies to any state which was a member of the Berne Union on January 1, 1951, or which has become a member of it at any later date, whether this date precedes or follows the date of the Universal Convention.

The provision according to which the Declaration is an integral part of the Universal Convention "for the States bound by the Berne Convention" carries the negative implication that countries not bound by the Berne Conventions are not bound by the Declaration. As will be seen below (under C.), such implication may be in contradiction to the provisions contained in proviso (b) of the Declaration.

The third sentence of Article XVII, paragraph 2, provides that signature, ratification, acceptance of, or accession to the Convention also constitutes signature, ratification, acceptance of, or accession to the Declaration. The sentence in question is redundant with the previous one: that the Declaration is an integral part of the Convention, or that acceptance, etc., of the Convention is also acceptance, etc., of the Declaration, mean exactly the same thing. If one could accept, etc., the Convention and exclude from the acceptance, etc., the Declaration, the Declaration would cease to be an integral part of the Convention. Furthermore, Article XX, too, excludes partial acceptance, etc., of the Convention. Thus, the third sentence of paragraph 2 is also redundant with Article XX.

The words "such States" in the third sentence referring to countries members of the Berne Union on or after January 1, 1951, carry the same negative implication as the second sentence, i.e., that countries not members of the Berne Union are not bound by the Declaration. As will be seen below (under C.), such implication may be in contradiction to the provisions contained in proviso (b) of the Declaration.

5. Introduction of Declaration.—Similar negative implications result from the introductory words of the Declaration since they provide that the Declaration is the reflection of a "common agreement" between States parties to both the Universal and one or more of the Berne Union texts, which would seem to mean that countries parties only to the Universal Convention did not agree to the Declaration.

The use of the word "signatories" in the introductory paragraph of the Declaration:

"The States which are members of the International [Berne] Union for the Protection of Literary and Artistic Works, and which are signatories of the Universal Copyright Convention"

is improper, because mere signature of the Universal Convention does not obligate the countries to apply the Declaration; only ratification or acceptance (following signature), or accession (not preceded by signature), will obligate a country to apply the Declaration.

The second paragraph of the introduction of the Declaration:

"Desiring to reinforce their mutual relations on the basis of the said Union and to avoid any conflict which might result from the co-existence of the Convention of Berne [*meaning here all texts or any text of the Berne Union*] and the Universal Copyright Convention"

is not an enforceable rule but only a declaration of intent or preliminary explanation for the reasons of concluding the Declaration.

The third and last paragraph of the introduction to the Declaration reads as follows:

"Have, by common agreement, accepted the terms of the following Declaration."

The use of the word "declaration" is not fortunate. "Declaration" is usually employed for designating pronouncements of principles which are not legally enforceable. The Declaration relating to Article XVII is more than that: it contains rules of the same kind as the various articles of the Convention contain, i.e., rules enforceable before the courts. "Additional Article" or similar terms would have been more appropriate.

B. Sanction for Withdrawal from the Berne Union

6. Proviso (a) of the Declaration.—Certain countries, members of the Berne Union, feared that accession to the Universal Convention might induce Berne countries to abandon the Union, should they believe that "by ratifying the so-called Universal Convention [they have] adequately fulfilled [their] international duties in the domain of copyright protection" (see Switzerland's reply to UNESCO's "Request for Views on a Universal Copyright Convention, Vol. III (1950), No. 2 UNESCO Copyright Bulletin 47). Consequently, a strong movement started, particularly in the circles of the Permanent Committee of the Berne Union, in favor of finding a device by which the risk of withdrawals could be effectively minimized. Since the Berne Conventions expressly allow withdrawal from the Berne Union, and since the Universal Copyright Convention could not, for the reasons stated under A., above, prohibit withdrawal from the Berne Union, indirect means were sought to achieve the desired goal. Such means were recommended by the Lisbon meeting of the Permanent Committee of the Berne Union (1950 Le Droit d'Auteur 131) and were, with only slight changes, eventually adopted by the Geneva Conference. The deterrence of withdrawals is achieved by putting a prohibitive price on withdrawals. Stated in general terms, the price is denial of protection under the Universal Convention in the other Berne countries. This provision, which can properly be termed a sanction, is contained in proviso (a) of the Declaration reading as follows:

> "Works which, according to the Berne Convention, have as their country of origin a country which has withdrawn from the International Union created by the said Convention after January 1, 1951, shall not be protected by the Universal Copyright Convention in the countries of the Berne Union."

7. Category of Works to Which the Sanction Applies.—The sanction, i.e., non-protection under the Universal Convention, applies to "works which, according to the Berne Convention, have as their country of origin a country which has withdrawn from the International Union created by the said Convention after January 1, 1951."

The words "under the Berne Convention" should be understood as meaning that text of the Berne Union which, in the particular case, would be applicable in the ex-Berne country had it not withdrawn from the Berne Union.

The definition of the country of origin is not exactly the same in all texts of the Berne Union. According to the most recent ones (cf. Brussels Convention, Article 4), works having a Berne country as their country of origin are those which:

—if unpublished, were authored by a national of a Berne country;

—if published, were (a) either first published in a Berne country or (b) were simultaneously published for the first time in two or more Berne countries, or in one or more Berne countries and one or more non-Berne countries.

Consequently, works which, according to the above definition, have as their country of origin a Berne country which withdrew from the Berne Union (hereafter designated as "ex-Berne country") after the stated date, are denied protection in the Berne countries under the Universal Convention. The following kinds of works will fall clearly in this category: (i) unpublished works created by a national of an ex-Berne country after the effective date of withdrawal by the same country, and/or (ii) works first published in the ex-Berne country after the same date, whatever be the author's nationality and even if creation took place before said date.

The situation is less clear in respect to works which (i) were authored by a national of a prospective withdrawing country and were unpublished at the date of withdrawal, or, (ii) were first published in a prospective withdrawing country before the date of withdrawal. In one sense these works have as their country of origin an ex-Berne country, namely, if one gives to the term "ex-Berne country" a retrospective meaning. Under this theory, proviso (a) would apply to them and Universal Convention protection would be denied. In another sense, however, such works have originated in a country which is a Berne country, and not an ex-Berne country, because, at the time they originated in it, the country still belonged to the Berne Union. If one accepts this latter interpretation, proviso (a) is inapplicable.

According to this view, application of the Universal Convention to such works could not be denied by invoking proviso (a) of the Declaration. Whether the Universal Convention will apply in the concrete case is, of course, dependent on the other circumstances of the case, namely, whether the work meets the other requirements of the Universal Convention.

8. Countries Which Must Apply the Sanction.—It results from proviso (a) of the Declaration that the sanction—no protection under the Universal Convention—shall be applied by "countries of the Berne Union."

"Countries of the Berne Union" probably means any country member of the Berne Union, including those which maintained no Berne relationship with the ex-Berne country. In other words, the sanction will be applied not only by a Berne country with which the withdrawing country terminated its Berne relationship by withdrawing from the

Berne Union, but also by a Berne country which never had any Berne relationship with the withdrawing country. The reason for the lack of relationship is irrelevant: it may be the result of the fact that the "punishing" and the "punished" country ratified unidentical texts of the Berne Union or because the "punishing" country entered the Berne Union only after the date of withdrawal by the "punished" country. The latter is particularly curious.

> Let us suppose, for example, that Greece, now a Berne Union member, with-draws from the Berne Union in 1965; and that the United States, now not a member of the Berne Union, will adhere to it in 1970. Let us also suppose that since 1955, both countries are parties to the Universal Convention. Works originating in Greece (at least after 1970 but perhaps even prior to 1970) would be denied, after 1970, protection under the Universal Convention because the United States, in our example, and after 1970, is "a country of the Berne Union" and Greece is a "country which has withdrawn from the [Berne Union]... after January 1, 1951." And all this in spite of the fact that, between 1955 and 1970, the United States granted Universal Convention protection to works originating in Greece.

To avoid these curious results it would have been more logical to provide that the sanction will apply only in cases where the withdrawal severed theretofore existing Berne relationships.

The rule according to which the sanction contained in proviso (a) is applied by "countries of the Berne Union" carries with it the negative implication that an ex-Berne country shall not apply the sanction. In other words, a Berne Union country will apply the sanction only as long as it is a member of the Berne Union, but as soon as it leaves the Berne Union, i.e., becomes an ex-Berne country, it will have to start applying the Universal Convention to works originating in other ex-Berne countries if otherwise such works qualify for Universal Convention protection.

9. Relevance of Date of Withdrawal.—The sanction is applicable to works which, according to the Berne Conventions, have as their country of origin a country "which has withdrawn from the International Union created by the said Convention, after January 1, 1951."

It is, therefore, not applicable to Haiti, the only country which has ever withdrawn (in 1943) from the Berne Union.

It is believed that the sanction is equally inapplicable to those new countries which have not themselves adhered to the Berne Union, although one or more texts of the Union formerly applied in territories of which such countries were constituted before they became sovereign and eligible for membership in the Berne Union. For example, the Rome Convention formerly applied to the Island of Ceylon as a British colony. Ceylon is now fully independent and eligible for membership. Should Ceylon, however, decide not to apply the Rome Convention, such decision could not be considered a withdrawal. To be able to withdraw, a country must be a member. Ceylon, as a country, was never a member, and, consequently, it cannot withdraw.

The date of January 1, 1951, is an arbitrary one. It probably was chosen by the preparatory meeting of 1951 which established the draft of the Convention to discourage withdrawal in anticipation of the conclusion of the Universal Convention. The date of the signature of the Universal Convention (Sept. 6, 1952) could have been substituted with equal effect since no withdrawals occurred between Jan. 1, 1951, and Sept. 6, 1952.

The entire proviso (a) of the Appendix Declaration, i.e., the sanction, will naturally find no application until a country, party to both the Universal and one or more of the Berne Conventions, withdraws from the Berne Union. Between January 1, 1951, and the present, no country has left the Berne Union. If this remains the situation in the future, proviso (a) of the Declaration will never be applied.

C. Applicability of the Universal Convention by Countries Members of the Berne Union

10. The Problem of Co-Existence Between the Texts of the Berne Union and the Universal Convention.—The texts of the Berne Union and the Universal Convention regulate the same matters, i.e., international copyright, in a very similar manner in some respects but in other respects in quite different manner. To avoid overlaps and conflicts, the Geneva Conference, theoretically, could have chosen between several solutions. It could have stipulated that in case of conflict the Universal Copyright Convention would prevail over the Berne Convention according to the maxim *lex posterior derogat priori*. The opposite result, i.e., that in case of conflict the Berne Convention would prevail over the Universal Convention, might have been reached under the maxim *lex specialis derogat generali*. A third possibility might have been the principle adopted by the Berne Union that as between two conflicting copyright treaties the one more favorable to the author prevails (cf. Article 20 of the Brussels Convention).

None of these principles were followed by the Geneva Conference which refused to examine the differences existing between the Universal Copyright Convention and the Berne Conventions and to establish rules for regulating the conflicts arising from such differences. It preferred to choose a radical solution by deciding, in proviso (b) of the Declaration, that:

> "The Universal Copyright Convention shall not be applicable to the relationships among countries of the Berne Union insofar as it relates to the protection of works having as their country of origin, within the meaning of the Berne Convention, a country of the International Union created by said Convention."

As to the meaning of the words "country of origin, within the meaning of the Berne Convention," see point 6 above.

11. Relationship Between Two Berne Countries Linked by a Text of the Berne Union.—If a work originates, within the meaning of the Berne Conventions, in a country "of the International Union created by the said Convention" (hereafter referred to as a "Berne country"), the Universal Convention shall not be applicable as far as "relationships among countries of the Berne Union" are concerned. It is not stated in the Declaration, probably because it goes without saying, that in these relationships the relevant text of the Berne Union applies.

> If, for example, Canada and France are both parties to the Universal and the Rome Conventions and an unpublished work is authored by a Canadian citizen or a work is first published in Canada alone, France will not apply the Universal Convention to this work but will protect it under the Rome Convention. And Canada will act in a similar manner in respect to works first published in France, or, if unpublished, authored by a French citizen.

If a work has a non-Berne country as country of origin, within the meaning of the Berne Conventions, the Universal Convention will become applicable even in the relationships between two countries of the Berne Union.

> Supposing, for example, that Canada and France are parties to both the Rome and the Universal Conventions, and the United States is a party to the Universal Convention only, if a work of a French citizen is first published in the United States, Canada will extend Universal Convention protection to such work, since it fulfills the requirements of Article II of the Universal Convention but has a non-Berne country as country of origin, according to the Rome Convention.

12. Relationship Between Two Berne Countries Not Linked by a Text of the Berne Union.—The meaning of proviso (b) of the Declaration is uncertain when one tries to apply it between two countries which, although each a member of the Berne Union, have not ratified the same text of the Berne Union.

A work of a national of one of the two countries if unpublished or first published in the same country, does not seem to be entitled to Berne protection in the other country since there appears to be no Berne text in force between the two countries. The question arises whether the Universal Convention will be applicable or inapplicable to such a work.

According to one view, the Universal Convention is inapplicable because the work has, as country of origin, a country member of the Berne Union, and the country, where protection is sought, is also member of the Berne Union.

The result is repellent to common sense. An example will illustrate it:

> As of today, the Netherlands has ratified all texts still in force of the Berne Union except the Brussels text; and Turkey has ratified only the Brussels text. The two countries give no protection to each other under any Berne text

although they are both members of the Berne Union. Let us suppose that they are both parties to the Universal Convention. A work is first published in Turkey. It will not be protected by any Berne text in the Netherlands. It would be denied protection also under the Universal Convention. And this in the face of a situation in which both countries are linked by the Universal Convention and the Universal Convention only, i.e., in a situation where conflicts, confusion and overlaps with the Berne Conventions are impossible.

According to another view, the Convention would be applicable in such situations. This view is based on the following arguments: first, that proviso (b) refers to "relationships among countries of the Berne Union" and that between two Berne countries not linked by a Berne text there are no relationships, and, second, that if one looks upon a work from the viewpoint of the country in which protection is claimed, and the work originates in a Berne country with which the former country is not linked by any Berne text, then such work has a non-Berne country as country of origin, since, for the country in which protection is claimed "Berne Convention" can mean only those texts by which it is bound—and the country of origin would result from a text by which it is not bound.

13. Relationship Between Berne and Non-Berne Countries. —If a work of a national of a country party to both the Universal and one of the Berne Conventions claims protection in another country party to the same Conventions, the Universal Convention is clearly inapplicable, because of proviso (b) of the Declaration, whenever the work is unpublished or was first published in a country party to both Conventions. Although such a work would qualify for protection under the Universal Convention under Article II, proviso (b) of the Declaration makes it inapplicable because such a work has, "within the meaning of the Berne Convention," a Berne country as country of origin and the relationship involved is "among countries of the Berne Union."

> To illustrate the above, let us suppose that Canada, France and Japan are parties to both Conventions. Protection is claimed in Japan for the unpublished work of a French citizen; or for a work of a French citizen first published in France or Canada. Japan may not apply the Universal Copyright Convention to such works, because the country of origin is France or Canada, and the relationships involved are those between Japan and France, or between Japan and Canada.

A difficult question of interpretation arises, however: (i) if the author is not a national of a country party to both Conventions and the work is first published in a country party to both Conventions, or, (ii) if the work is simultaneously published for the first time in a country party to both Conventions and in a country party to the Universal Convention only (the author's nationality is irrelevant).

> To illustrate the above set of cases, let us suppose that Canada, France and Japan are parties to both Conventions; that the United States is party to the

Universal Convention only; and the U.S.S.R. is party to neither. Protection is claimed in Japan for:

(i) a work of an American or Russian citizen first published in Canada;

(ii) a work simultaneously published for the first time in Canada and the United States (the author may be Canadian or American or Russian).

In all these cases the work undoubtedly has, or has also, a Berne country of origin (Canada). Consequently, one of the requirements of proviso (b) of the Declaration, which makes the Universal Convention inapplicable, is met.

There is, however, a second requirement in proviso (b). Proviso (b) makes the Universal Convention inapplicable "to the relationships among countries of the Berne Union." In all the above cases two kinds of relationships are involved: first, relationship between two Berne countries (Japan-Canada), second, relationship between a Berne and a non-Berne country (Japan-U.S.A., Japan-U.S.S.R.).

When the second relationship is with a non-Berne country (U.S.S.R.), this second relationship may probably be ignored because such country (of which the author is a national) cannot properly claim that a Convention (the Universal Convention) to which it is not a party be applied. In reality, the second relationship is non-existent and properly should not be called a relationship since there is no contract between the two countries (Japan-U.S.S.R.). In these cases the country of first publication (Canada) is the only country having a relationship to the country of forum (Japan), and both being Berne countries proviso (b) seems to be clearly applicable.

If, however, the second relationship is with a non-Berne country party to the Universal Convention (U.S.A.), serious uncertainty arises as to the applicability of proviso (b) of the Declaration.

Turning to the above examples the uncertainty consists of the following:

(i) Work of a U.S. citizen is first published in Canada. Canada cannot require that Japan apply the Universal Convention because the work has, under the terms of the Berne Conventions, Canada as country of origin, and the relationship involved is between two Berne countries (Canada-Japan). On the other hand, the U.S.A. may require that Japan apply the Universal Convention (and not the Berne Conventions) because the work qualifies for Universal Convention protection (because of the author's U.S. nationality; cf. Art. II) and the relationship is between two Universal Convention countries (U.S.A.-Japan).

(ii) Work simultaneously published for the first time in Canada and the U.S.A. Canada cannot require the application of the Universal Convention for the reasons stated above. But the U.S.A. may require that Japan apply the Universal Convention (and not the Berne Conventions) because the work qualifies for Universal Convention protection and the relationship is between two Universal Convention countries (U.S.A.-Japan). (The work qualifies for Universal Convention protection because it was simultaneously, i.e., first published also in the U.S.A.; if its author is a U.S. citizen, it qualifies also for this reason).

14. Same: Ambiguity of Declaration.—As seen above, whenever a work has, within the meaning of the Berne Conventions, a Berne country as country of origin, but the international relationships involved are not purely between two countries parties to both the Universal and Berne Conventions but also between a country party to both Conventions and a country party to the Universal Convention alone, it is uncertain whether or not the Universal Convention may be invoked.

The basic principle is national treatment in both Conventions. Consequently, in many cases application of one Convention will lead to the same result as application of the other. There are, however, cases in which the Conventions are in conflict. Thus, for example, in matters of duration it is relevant whether the rule of the shorter term relates to the term for which the work is protected in a Berne country (minimum 50 years after the author's death in Brussels countries; 50 years after the author's death in most Rome countries) or in a Universal Convention country (28 or 56 years after publication in the U.S.A.; minimum 25 years in general; cf. Article IV of the Universal Convention). It is also relevant whether the minimum of the right to translate is governed by the rules prevailing in the Berne "reservatory" countries (no protection if no translation is made during 10 years from first publication) or by Article II, paragraph 2, of the Universal Convention (a possibility of compulsory license if no translation is made during 7 years from first publication or if all translations are out of print at the end of the 7-year term).

The arguments which would favor the interpretation according to which the Universal Convention is applicable in the cases in question are the following:

(i) Proviso (b) of the Declaration provides that "the Universal Copyright Convention shall not be applicable to the relationships among countries of the Berne Union." The relationships existing here are not only between two countries parties to both Conventions but also between a country party to both Conventions and a country party to the Universal Convention only.

(ii) Countries which are not members of the Berne Union are not bound by the Declaration because the Declaration, according to its introduction, is an agreement between "The States which are members of the International Union for the Protection of Literary and Artistic Works, and which are signatories to the Universal Copyright Convention" and between these States only; because, according to Article XVII, paragraph 2, the Declaration is an integral part of the Universal Convention "for the States bound by the Berne Convention on January 1, 1951, or which have or may become bound to it at a later date" and only for these States; and because, also according to Article XVII, paragraph 2, acceptance of the Universal Convention constitutes acceptance of the Declaration "by such [i.e., Berne member] States," and by such States only.

On the other hand, arguments which would favor the contrary interpretation, i.e., that the Universal Convention is inapplicable in the cases in question may be the following:

(i) The Declaration is appended to Article XVII of the Convention. Article XVII, like any Article of the Convention, binds all States parties to it.

(ii) Article XVII, paragraph 2, is "in application of the foregoing [i.e., first] paragraph [of Article XVII]" and Article XVII is, in no way, limited to countries parties to both Conventions; it also binds countries parties to the Universal Convention only.

(iii) Perhaps one ought to differentiate between the obligation of States actively to apply certain provisions of the Convention and the passive requirement to suffer the effects of certain provisions. Article XVII, paragraph 2, puts active obligations (the active obligation to apply the Berne texts rather than the Universal Convention) only on Berne countries. In this sense the provisions in question apply to them. Countries parties only to the Universal Convention are neither required to apply the Berne Conventions nor to refuse to apply the Universal Convention. All they are asked is to suffer that other States do not apply the Universal Convention in certain cases.

(As a practical matter, nationals of countries parties only to the Universal Convention can avoid non-application of the Universal Convention by not publishing their works for the first time, or simultaneously for the first time, in a Berne country. If they do publish it for the first time, or simultaneously for the first time, abroad—which is an act depending on their free will—they must suffer the consequences.)

It must be recognized that both sets of arguments have some merit and that the Convention contains no clear answer to the problem.

This, of course, leaves the country in which protection is claimed with a very serious practical problem. Which one of the Conventions, the Universal Convention or the relevant Berne text, should it apply? One could resolve the problem by cutting the Gordian knot with a sword and protect works to which both Conventions may apply to the extent and in a manner which satisfy both Conventions.

Under this solution, for example, Japan, a reservatory country under the Berne Convention, would neither apply the Berne Convention nor the Universal Convention in respect of the right of translation in a work which may be considered as qualifying for protection under both Conventions but the sum total of the two regimes, i.e., it would grant exclusive right for 10 (and not 7) years from first publication and if the work is not translated within these 10 (not 7) years, for the rest of the general term of protection there would be obligation of payment to the copyright owner (not free use).

This solution is not equitable for the country in which protection is claimed because it puts on it a double burden. It is not juridical either, because it cannot be supported by any language in the Convention. But it would be a safe course to take.

ARTICLE XVIII: RELATIONS TO INTER-AMERICAN COPYRIGHT CONVENTIONS

"This Convention shall not abrogate multilateral or bilateral copyright conventions or arrangements that are or may be in effect exclusively between two or more American Republics. In the event of any difference either between the provisions of such existing conventions or arrangements and the provisions of this Convention, or between the provisions of this Convention and those of any new convention or arrangement which may be formulated between two or more American Republics after this Convention comes into force, the convention or arrangement most recently formulated shall prevail between the parties thereto. Rights in works acquired in any Contracting State under existing conventions or arrangements before the date this Convention comes into force in such State shall not be affected." (Art. XVIII)

1. Scope of Article XVIII.—Article XVIII regulates possible problems arising from the co-existence of the Universal Convention with multilateral or bilateral copyright conventions or "arrangements" concluded between American Republics. The three sentences of Article XVIII contain three basic ideas, viz., (A) that the Universal Convention does not abrogate inter-American conventions or arrangements, (B) that in case of difference between the Universal Convention and an inter-American convention or arrangement, the one later in date prevails, and, (C) that the Universal Convention does not affect rights acquired under earlier conventions or arrangements.

A. Universal Convention does not Abrogate Inter-American Conventions or Arrangements

2. Principle of Non-Abrogation.—This principle is expressed in the first sentence of Article XVIII, reading as follows:

"This Convention shall not abrogate multilateral or bilateral copyright conventions or arrangements that are or may be in effect exclusively between two or more American Republics."

3. Meaning of "Multilateral Or Bilateral Copyright Conventions Or Arrangements."—"Convention" means contracts between sovereign States. The title, if any, that is given to the instrument ("treaty," "convention," "agreement," "arrangement," etc.), or instruments ("diplomatic notes," "letters," etc.), embodying the contract is irrelevant.

"Arrangement" includes all the above. The question is, does it also include something else? Does it include, for example, an exchange of notes between the governments of two countries which contain no undertaking for the future but which merely record the fact that, on the date of the exchange of notes (or any other date referred to in the exchange of notes), each of the two countries granted copyright protection to the other? (Exchanges of notes of this kind frequently precede proclamations made by the President of the United States extending the benefits of the U.S. Copyright Law to nationals of foreign countries. The proclamation in itself, of course, is not an arrangement, because a proclamation is a unilateral act by the U.S. President, whereas an arrangement must, according to Articles XVIII and XIX, be either multilateral or bilateral). Does it also include, for example, a mere situation in which two or more countries grant each other copyright protection without even recording this state of fact in mutual declarations? (Some proclamations of the President of the United States are issued without a previous exchange of notes, and are based on the President's own finding that the proclaimed foreign country grants adequate protection to U.S. citizens).

Although it must be recognized that "arrangement" is a very broad term and, according to one of its meanings does not imply any undertaking, it is believed that the better view is that in the context of Articles XVIII and XIX, arrangement is an undertaking (or contract) between States. In these two articles, "conventions or arrangements" are contrasted with the Universal Convention. The purpose of the Article is to regulate co-existence between a given copyright treaty (the Universal Convention), and something else. This else must be also copyright treaties, otherwise the basis of comparison is missing.

4. Meaning of "In Effect Exclusively Between Two Or More American Republics."—"American Republics" are the sovereign republics of the Western Hemisphere, i.e., at the present time the following twenty-four: Argentina, Barbados, Bolivia, Brazil, Chile, Colombia, Costa Rica, Cuba, Dominican Republic, El Salvador, Ecuador, Guayana, Guatemala, Haiti, Honduras, Jamaica, Mexico, Nicaragua, Panama, Paraguay, Peru, United States of America, Uruguay, and Venezuela. Canada, not being a republic, is not among the countries in question. Neither are the non self-governing territories (colonies).

Article XVIII applies only to conventions or arrangements in effect "exclusively" between American republics. Consequently, the Montevideo Convention of 1889, although originally signed by American republics only, does not come under Article XVIII, because later several European countries adhered thereto, and thus it ceased to be a convention in effect exclusively between American republics.

5. Meaning of "That Are Or May Be in Effect."—Conventions or arrangements "that are... in effect" are those which were in effect on the date of the signature of the Universal Convention, i.e., September 6, 1952. Conventions or arrangements "that... may be in effect" are those which come into force any time after September 6, 1952.

6. Meaning of "Shall Not Abrogate."—Article XVIII provides that the Universal Convention "shall not abrogate" conventions or arrangements "that are or may be in effect."

As to conventions or arrangements in effect prior to September 6, 1952, the statement is not quite accurate. Doubts as to the continued existence of a convention or arrangement, because of the Universal Convention, can arise not as of September 6, 1952, but only as of the date on which all parties to the other convention or arrangement become bound by the Universal Convention.

The conventions or arrangements, as such, will without any doubt continue, and not be abrogated, between such countries which do not adhere to the Universal Convention. Doubts may only arise as to the continued effects of the convention or arrangement between those countries which adhere to the Universal Convention. As to the scope of the non-abrogation principle in this latter case, see point 13 below.

As to conventions or arrangements which come into effect subsequent to the signing of the Universal Convention, one must differentiate between those formulated before and after September 6, 1952. If they were formulated before this date (for example the Buenos Aires Convention of 1910 in respect of Argentina which ratified it in 1953, and in respect of Chile which ratified it in 1955; or the Washington Convention of 1946 in respect of Cuba which ratified it in 1955), the observations set out in the previous paragraph apply. If they are formulated after September 6, 1952, the Universal Convention cannot "abrogate" them because "abrogate" refers, by definition, to something existent and not future. In respect of such conventions or arrangements the first sentence is logically correct but superfluous.

B. Later Convention or Arrangement Prevails

7. Principle of Later Convention Or Arrangement Prevailing Over Earlier.—The second sentence of Article XVIII deals with the situation in which differences exist between the Universal Convention and an inter-American convention or arrangement. In such a situation the instrument more recent in date prevails. The rule is formulated in the following manner:

> "In the event of any difference either between the provisions of such existing conventions or arrangements and the provisions of this Convention, or between the provisions of this Convention and those of any new convention or arrangement which may be formulated between two or more American Republics after this Convention comes into force, the convention or arrangement most recently formulated shall prevail between the parties thereto."

In other words, the sentence in question envisages two situations, viz., possible differences between:

(i) "existing" conventions or arrangements and the Universal Convention,
(ii) the Universal Convention and conventions or arrangements which may be formulated "...after this [Universal] Convention comes into force,"
and provides that, in either case, "the most recently formulated shall prevail."

According to the Report of the Rapporteur-General "...the most recent agreement shall prevail and... the date of formulation of an agreement rather than the date of ratification [is] its effective date for this purpose" (Records, page 91). In other words, "formulation" means the date on which the treaty was signed, if it is a bilateral treaty, and the date on which the Conference adopted it (and the first signatories signed it), if it is a multilateral convention. In the case of a multilateral convention open for signature not only on but also after the date on which the Conference adopted it, the date of formulation will remain the date of adoption by the Conference, even in respect to countries which sign it at a later date or become party thereto without ever signing it. The date of ratification or the date of entry into force of the convention or arrangement is irrelevant. Only the date of "formulation" counts, for example, in the case of the Buenos Aires Convention August 11, 1910, and in the case of the Washington Convention June 22, 1946.

If this definition of the date of "formulation" is applied to the word "existing," it means September 6, 1952, for the Universal Convention, and any date prior to September 6, 1952, in respect to "existing" conventions or arrangements. Whereas situation (i) deals with the Universal Convention and conventions or arrangements prior to September 6, 1952, situation (ii) deals with the Universal Convention and conventions or arrangements subsequent to the date of coming into force of the Universal Convention, i.e., September 16, 1955. This leaves a period of 3 years and 10 days unprovided for. The reason is probably an oversight in drafting. It has, however, no practical consequences because, as far as we know, no copyright conventions or arrangements were formulated between two or more American republics during the period from September 6, 1952, and September 16, 1955.

Whereas it is both logical and useful to provide for differences between the Universal Convention and earlier conventions and arrangements, it seems to be superfluous to provide for differences between the Universal Convention and later conventions and arrangements. Later conventions or arrangements are concluded because the Universal Convention does not satisfy the parties of the later convention or arrangement. Such later convention or arrangement is concluded in order to institute a regime different from that of the Universal Convention.

The significance of speaking about later conventions or arrangements lies less in the conflict rule than in that that it implies the recognition of the principle that American republics may, even after September 16, 1955, conclude new copyright conventions or arrangements, and may do so even if not all, but only some, parties to the Universal Convention adhere to the new convention or arrangement. If all parties to the Universal Convention adhere to the new convention or arrangement, their right to do so is self-evident. If, however, only two, or more, but not all, parties to the Universal Convention conclude a new convention or arrangement, their right to do so is perhaps less self-evident because it could be maintained that adherence to the Universal Convention by a country is not only in consideration of the protection that this country will receive from the others but also of the protection that the other countries will give each other. In any case, a new convention or arrangement cannot affect the rights of parties to the old convention or arrangement which are not also parties to the new convention or arrangement. This goes without saying but, by superabundance of prudence, Article XVIII expresses it by the use of the words "between the parties thereto" at the end of the second sentence.

8. Meaning of the Word "Difference."—According to Article XVIII, the Universal Convention will prevail over inter-American conventions or arrangements earlier formulated whenever there is a "difference" between one of the latter and the Universal Convention.

Views differ as to the meaning of the word "difference."

According to one view, stricter in its interpretation, there is "difference" ("divergence" in the French and Spanish texts) between the two conventions or arrangements whenever the application of them to a given work does not lead to the same results. Under this interpretation, if, according to the Universal Convention the work is protected, and according to an earlier convention or arrangement it would not, the Universal Convention will prevail and the work shall be protected. Under the same interpretation, if, according to the Universal Convention the work does not qualify for protection, and according to an earlier convention or arrangement it would, the work will not be protected, because the Universal Convention prevails. The same would be true in respect to the conditions, duration, extent, etc., of protection. Illustrations of these problems are given under point 9, below.

According to another view, more liberal, "difference" is only a difference when it works to the benefit of the author and not to his disadvantage. This would mean that the Universal Convention would not prevail over an earlier convention or arrangement if the Universal Convention is less favorable to the author than the earlier convention or arrangement; and that the Universal Convention would prevail over an earlier convention or arrangement only if the Universal Convention is more favorable to the author than the earlier convention or arrangement. This argument would be based on the idea that the intent behind the Universal Convention is to change the existing situation only where the change increases or facilitates protection of copyright proprietors, and this is the principle which guided the drafters of the Convention when, in the Introduction to the same, they stated that the Universal Convention is a system of copyright protection "additional to" and not "impairing international systems already in force."

This latter, more liberal interpretation is a tempting one, but we are slightly more inclined to believe that the first, more strict view is the better. The main reasons are the following:

(a) If there is a contradiction between the Introduction and Article XVIII of the Convention, more weight has to be given to the Article, because it contains a norm or rule, than to a text which reflects "convictions" having no binding legal effect.

(b) The Introduction is satisfied by the first sentence of Article XVIII stating that the Universal Convention "shall not abrogate" the existing conventions or arrangements (cf. point 13, below). If it does not abrogate them, "it is additional to" and does not "impair" the existing international "systems" as such. The undeniable fact, following from the second sentence of Article XVIII, that certain isolated provisions of the existing conventions or arrangements are superseded by the Universal Convention, does not affect the continuance either of the conventions or arrangements as conventions or arrangements, or the systems as systems. A system can continue even if in certain particulars it undergoes modifications.

(c) Copyright laws, conventions or arrangements are not instruments solely intended to serve the interests of authors or other copyright owners. Their scope is to strike a balance, believed to be just or opportune, between the copyright owners on the one hand and the users and the public on the other. When copyright is not protected perpetually, when certain rights are subject to compulsory licenses, or when fulfillment of certain formalities is required, the interests of users and/or the public rather than those of the authors are served. And there is no reason to believe that the Universal Convention is an exception: it, too, may not only recognize the rights of the authors but also limit the same.

(d) There is at least one other instance in which the Geneva Conference was confronted with the possibility of choosing between improving or not the author's protection and preferred not to improve it: proviso (c) of the draft of the appendix Declaration (then called "Protocol") would have established that the author could rely on the Universal Convention conferring "rights greater than those conferred by the Berne Conventions" so far as concerns the protection of works simultaneously published in a country party to both Conventions and a country party only to the Universal Convention; the Geneva Conference, however, omitted this proviso.

(e) The Berne Conventions illustrate that if a Conference desires to differentiate between more favorable and less favorable treaties, it can do and does so (cf. Article 20 of Brussels Convention). Consequently, when the Geneva Conference did not follow the precedent established by the Berne Union, it probably did not follow it because it did not want to arrive at the same results as the Berne Conventions.

(f) The word "difference" is used without any qualification in the Universal Convention. There seems to be no basis in the text of the Convention to consider that differences favorable to the author are the only "real" differences, and to ignore differences which would be favorable to the public and/or the users of works.

9. Application of the Rule to the Buenos Aires and Washington Conventions.—There are six, i.e., Mexico City 1902, Rio de Janeiro 1906, Buenos Aires 1910, Caracas 1911, Havana 1928, and Washington 1946, conventions between American Republics.

We shall deal here only with the Buenos Aires and Washington Conventions. The other four are left aside for the following reasons:

The Mexico City Convention of 1902 is, today, in force only between Salvador and the Dominican Republic, and Salvador and the United States of America. Prerequisite of the application of the Convention is compliance with extremely complicated formalities. As far as we know, they were complied with in less than a dozen cases during the more than 50 years of the Convention's existence.

The main objective of the Rio de Janeiro Convention of 1906, i.e., the creation of international registries in two regional offices in the Western Hemisphere, was never realized. For this reason it is not even sure whether the Convention can be considered as ever having entered into force. Even if it did, it is in force today only in the relations of Salvador with the following countries: Brazil, Chile, Costa Rica, Ecuador, Guatemala, Honduras, Nicaragua, and Panama.

The Caracas Agreement of 1911 seems to remain in force only between Bolivia and Venezuela, Ecuador and Venezuela, Peru and Venezuela.

The Havana Convention of 1928 was ratified by only five countries, but since four of them later adhered to the Washington Convention, the former remains in force only in the relations of Panama with Costa Rica, Ecuador, Guatemala and Nicaragua.

The Buenos Aires Convention of 1910 has been ratified to date by the following seventeen countries: Argentina, Bolivia, Brazil, Chile, Colombia, Costa Rica, Dominican Republic, Ecuador, Guatemala, Haiti, Honduras, Nicaragua, Panama, Paraguay, Peru, United States of America and Uruguay; whereas the Washington Convention of 1946 by the following fourteen countries: Argentina, Bolivia, Brazil, Chile, Costa Rica, Cuba, Dominican Republic, Ecuador, Guatemala, Haiti, Honduras, Mexico, Nicaragua, and Paraguay.

Since the Washington Convention replaced the Buenos Aires Convention, it is the Washington Convention, and not the Buenos Aires Convention, which governs relations between countries which ratified both Conventions.

10. Same: Formalities.—One of the main differences between the Universal Convention and the Buenos Aires and Washington Conventions relates to the rules concerning formalities.

(a) *Buenos Aires Convention: published works.*—The Buenos Aires Convention applies "provided always there shall appear in the work a statement that indicates the reservation of the property right" (Article 3). According to the Universal Convention the country in which

protection is claimed cannot require that the formalities prescribed by
its law be fulfilled if the published work bears the Convention notice
as prescribed by Article III. The provision of the Buenos Aires Convention does not prescribe any definite form. "Derechos reservados,"
"all rights reserved," or similar statements would seem to satisfy the
requirement. Such statements would not satisfy the Universal Convention. Whether the Universal Convention notice ("c" in a circle,
date, name) would amount to a "statement" of the kind referred to in
the Buenos Aires Convention, is uncertain. We are rather inclined to
think it would, particularly if the "c" in the circle becomes a generally
known symbol of copyright protection.

Consequently, and under the strict interpretation (cf. point 8 above)
of the word "difference," if two countries are bound both by the Buenos
Aires and the Universal Conventions, the country which, in its domestic
law, prescribes the fulfillment of formalities, could refuse protection
under either one of the Conventions if the published work, originating
in the other country, does not bear the Universal Convention copyright
notice. Under the liberal interpretation of the word "difference" (cf.
point 8, above), the opposite result would be obtained, i.e., if two
countries are bound by both Conventions, the country which, in its
domestic law, prescribes the fulfillment of formalities, would have to
protect published works originating in the other country even if the
copies of such works do not bear the Universal Convention notice but
only the "statement" prescribed by the Buenos Aires Convention.

(b) *Buenos Aires Convention: unpublished works.* —If the Buenos Aires
Convention is considered applicable to unpublished works, the "statement" would seem to be necessary also in such works. On the other
hand, the Universal Convention expressly exempts unpublished works
from formalities.

Consequently, if two countries are bound both by the Buenos Aires
and the Universal Conventions, a country cannot refuse the protection
of an unpublished work of the national of another country even if the
work does not bear the "statement" mentioned in Article 3 of the Buenos
Aires Convention.

(c) *Washington Convention: published works.*—According to the Washington Convention, works originating and protected in a contracting
country are protected in the others without having to bear any Convention notice. Under the Universal Convention, the use of the Convention notice becomes a practical necessity if a work claims protection
in a country which, on the domestic level, prescribes certain formalities
(cf. Article III).

Consequently, and if the strict interpretation of the word "difference"
is followed (cf. point 8, above), if two countries are bound both by the
Universal and Washington Conventions, the country in which protection is claimed may refuse protection if the published work does not

bear the Universal Convention notice and if this country, by its national law, would otherwise require the fulfillment of formalities.

Under the liberal interpretation of the word "difference" (cf. point 8, above), the opposite result would be obtained, i.e., if two countries are bound by both Conventions, the country which, in its domestic law, prescribes the fulfillment of formalities, would have to protect published works originating in the other country even if the copies of such works do not bear the Universal Convention notice.

(d) *Washington Convention: unpublished works.*—There is no difference between the Universal and Washington Conventions in respect to unpublished works. They will be protected under both, even if the work has complied with no formalities.

11. Same: Duration of Protection.—(a) *Buenos Aires Convention: rule of shorter term.*—The general rule is the same under the Buenos Aires and the Universal Conventions: both prescribe the application of the term which follows from the domestic law of the country in which protection is claimed (Article 6 of the Buenos Aires Convention, Article 5 of the Universal Convention). Under the Buenos Aires Convention, this term must be reduced to the term granted, presumably to the particular work, in its country of origin (Article 6). According to the Universal Convention, a reduction of the term to that prevailing in the country of origin is permissive and is permitted only if the category (and not the particular work) is protected for a lesser period (Article IV)

Consequently, if two countries are bound by both the Buenos Aires and Universal Conventions, one country can terminate protection at the moment the work ceases to be protected in its country of origin only if the reason of the cessation of protection (in the country of origin) relates to the whole category to which the work belongs, and not only to the particular work involved.

(b) *Washington Convention: rule of shorter term.*—Unlike the Universal and Buenos Aires Conventions, the Washington Convention provides that "the duration of the copyright protection shall be governed by the law of the Contracting State in which the protection was originally obtained" (Article VI), and not of the State in which protection is claimed. The law of the latter, however, is relevant too, because, according to the same Article of the Washington Convention, the protection "shall not exceed the duration fixed by the law of the Contracting State in which the protection is claimed."

Consequently, if two countries are bound both by the Washington and the Universal Conventions, the country in which protection is claimed will protect the work according to its national law, and cannot terminate protection earlier, at the moment the work ceases to be protected in its country of origin (which it could do under the Washington Convention), except if the category, rather than the individual work, ceases to be protected at said date.

(c) *Minimum of duration.*—The most important difference, however, concerns the minimum term. Whereas the Universal Convention prescribes a minimum of 25 years for published works, none of the inter-American Conventions provides for any minimum term.

Consequently, a country bound by both the Universal and one of the inter-American Conventions cannot refuse to protect a work for less than 25 years, notwithstanding the fact that protection for 20 years, or, in fact, for any duration less than 25 years, would satisfy its obligations under the inter-American Convention.

12. Same: Right of Translation.—The Buenos Aires (Article 4) and Washington (Article II, point f) Conventions recognize the right of translation as an exclusive right. So does the Universal Convention (Article V, paragraph 1), but it permits, after 7 years (if the work has not been translated or is out of print), and subject to certain precautions, that the exclusive right be replaced by a compulsory license.

In view of the fact that the right of translation is not guaranteed for any minimum term in the inter-American Conventions, a country could give lesser rights than required under the Universal Convention and still not violate the inter-American Conventions.

Consequently, if two countries are bound both by an inter-American and the Universal Conventions, they must grant a protection which is not less than that prescribed by Article V of the Universal Convention.

13. Effect of "Later Convention Or Arrangement Prevails" Rule on "Non-Abrogation" Principle.—If the above analysis (points 7 to 12) is right, i.e., if whenever there is a difference between the effects of the Universal Convention and the earlier inter-American conventions or arrangements, the Universal Convention prevails, and if the strict interpretation of the word "difference" (cf. point 8, above) is followed, then the inter-American conventions or arrangements remain applicable only when their effect is the same as the effect of the Universal Convention. In such cases, however, it becomes irrelevant whether the Universal Convention or the inter-American conventions or arrangements are applied.

What, under these circumstances, is the practical importance of the statement made in the first sentence of Article XVIII, i.e., that the Universal Convention "shall not abrogate" inter-American conventions or arrangements?

As long as two countries are bound by both the Universal and an earlier inter-American convention or arrangement, the fact that they are also bound by the inter-American does not have any practical significance. On points where the two differ from each other, the Universal Convention prevails; this means that the situation would be the same if the inter-American would not exist. On points where the two do not differ from each other, any of them may be applied, and the protection would remain the same even if the inter-American would not exist. "Non-abrogation" under such circumstances and for the said purposes, consequently has no practical effect.

"Non-abrogation" of the inter-American conventions or arrangements will, however, have a practical effect in cases where one or both of the two countries, hitherto bound by both, ceases or cease to be bound by the Universal Convention. In such cases the relationships of the two countries will be governed by the inter-American convention or arrangement without the necessity of adhesion to it anew. In other words, the effects of the inter-American convention or arrangement, dormant during the period when the two countries were also bound by the Universal Convention, will become automatically active.

But if "difference" is interpreted in the more liberal manner, i.e., is understood to exist only where the difference is in favor of the author or other copyright proprietor (cf. point 8, above), then whenever an inter-American convention or arrangement has more favorable effects on the copyright proprietor than the Universal Convention would have, the principle according to which the later convention or arrangement prevails would not be applied.

C. Acquired Rights Unaffected

14. Principle Incorporated in Third Sentence.—The third and last sentence of Article XVIII provides that:

> "Rights in works acquired in any Contracting State under existing conventions or arrangements before the date this Convention comes into force in such State shall not be affected."

The sentence means that the general rule (i.e., the rule according to which in the event of any difference between the provisions of any earlier convention or agreement and the provisions of the Universal Convention, the Universal Convention will prevail), will not apply if its application would affect rights in works acquired under a convention or agreement earlier than the Universal Convention. "Affect" probably should be understood as meaning adversely affect. This follows from the general intent of the clause which is to safeguard acquired rights and not to prevent their possible extension (as long as such extension does not adversely affect another person's acquired rights). The French text of the Convention makes this particularly clear by using the words *porter atteinte* which means to prejudice or violate.

ARTICLE XIX: RELATIONS TO OTHER TREATIES

"This Convention shall not abrogate multilateral or bilateral conventions or arrangements in effect between two or more Contracting States. In the event of any difference between the provisions of such existing conventions or arrangements and the provisions of this Convention, the provisions of this Convention shall prevail. Rights in works acquired in any Contracting State under existing conventions or arrangements before the date on which this Convention comes into force in such State shall not be affected. Nothing in this article shall affect the provisions of article XVII and XVIII of this Convention." (Art. XIX)

1. Scope of Article XIX.—Article XIX regulates possible problems arising from the co-existence of the Universal Convention with multilateral or bilateral conventions or "arrangements" other than the Berne Conventions or the inter-American treaties. The Article consists of four sentences. The first three express the following three basic ideas: (A) that the Universal Convention does not abrogate the conventions or arrangements in question, (B) that in case of difference between the said conventions or arrangements and the Universal Convention, the Universal Convention prevails, (C) that the Universal Convention does not affect rights acquired under said conventions or arrangements.

The fourth sentence, viz.:

"Nothing in this Article shall affect the provisions of Article XVII and XVIII of this Convention"

should be read together with the words "multilateral or bilateral conventions or arrangements in effect between two or more Contracting States [i.e., States bound by the Universal Convention]" of the first sentence. Consequently, Article XIX applies neither to the Berne Conventions treated in Article XVII, nor the inter-American conventions or arrangements treated in Article XVIII. In the following analysis, the words "conventions or arrangements" should be understood as not referring to the Berne Conventions or the inter-American conventions or arrangements.

A. Universal Convention does not Abrogate other Conventions or Arrangements

2. Principle of Non-Abrogation.—This principle is expressed in the first sentence of Article XIX, reading as follows:

"This Convention shall not abrogate multilateral or bilateral conventions or arrangements in effect between two or more Contracting States."

3. Meaning of "Multilateral or Bilateral Conventions or Arrangements."—For the analysis of these words, see point 3 in the chapter dealing with Article XVIII, above.

4. Meaning of "In Effect."—It could be argued that the words "in effect" is not related to any specific date and, consequently, Article XIX deals with any convention or arrangement in force, irrespective of the date of its formulation or entry into force. According to the Rapporteur-General's Report, however, Article XIX would refer only to "existing arrangements" and "avoid reference to future international agreements" (Records, page 92). This would be in contradiction to Article XVIII which also deals with future conventions or arrangements. The argument can be supported by the comparison of the wording of the two Articles: whereas Article XVIII mentions conventions or arrangements "that are or may be in effect," Article XIX speaks only about conventions or arrangements "in effect." Furthermore, the second sentence of Article XIX refers to said conventions or arrangements "in effect" as "existing" treaties. The date of formulation being indicated as criterion in Article XVIII, it is fairly clear that, as far as inter-American conventions or arrangements are concerned, September 6, 1952, is the dividing line between existing (or past) and future conventions or arrangements. In Article XIX, however, there is no mention of the dates of formulation. Consequently, it would seem to be more logical to understand "existing" in its natural meaning, i.e., as meaning any convention or arrangement that went into force prior to, and is in force between two States at, the moment the Universal Convention comes into force between the same two States. The date of formulation of the convention or arrangement other than the Universal Convention naturally precedes the date on which the Universal Convention enters into force between the two States, but would not necessarily be prior to September 6, 1952. If, for example, two States become bound by a bilateral treaty in 1958 and by the Universal Convention in 1960, Article XIX of the Universal Convention does apply to the bilateral treaty.

The above observations apply also to multilateral conventions other than the Berne and inter-American conventions. There is only one of them at the present time: the Montevideo Convention of 1889. The most recent adherence to the Montevideo Convention occurred in 1931 and probably no country will adhere to it in the future. If, however, a country would become bound by the Montevideo Convention at a date which follows the date on which the same country became bound by the Universal Convention, then the relations of such country with other countries parties to both Conventions will be regulated by the Montevideo Convention rather than by the Universal Convention, because in such relations the Montevideo Convention was not an "existing" convention, or a convention "in effect," when the Universal Convention went into force as between the same countries. This is another illustration of the consequences of the fact that Article XIX, in opposition to Article XVIII, does not apply the criterion of "date of formulation."

5. Meaning of "Shall not Abrogate."—Article XIX provides that the Universal Convention "shall not abrogate" conventions or arrangements in effect between parties to the Universal Convention. The practical purport of this rule, with reference to the second sentence, is discussed in point 10, infra.

B. Universal Convention Prevails

6. Prevalence of Universal Convention.—The second sentence of Article XIX deals with the situation in which differences exist between the Universal Convention and another "existing" convention or arrangement (other, of course, than the Berne and inter-American treaties). In such a situation the Universal Convention prevails:

> "In the event of any difference between the provisions of such existing conventions or arrangements and the provisions of this Convention, the provisions of this Convention shall prevail."

In opposition to the parallel provision of Article XVIII, Article XIX does not specify that, under the said circumstances, the Universal Convention shall prevail "between the parties thereto." This, however, goes without saying, since no rule contained in the Universal Convention can be invoked by, or vis-à-vis, a country not bound by the same Convention. Consequently, if, for example, France, Argentina and Uruguay are parties to the Montevideo Convention of 1889, and France and Argentina, but not Uruguay, later become bound by the Universal Convention, then, in the cases of differences between the provisions of the two conventions, the Universal Convention will prevail only between Argentina and France, but not between France and Uruguay, or between Argentina and Uruguay.

7. Meaning of the Word "Difference."—Analogous observations apply here as under Article XVIII (cf. point 8 in the Chapter dealing with Article XVIII).

8. Application of Article XIX to the Montevideo Convention of 1889.—At the present time the Montevideo Convention of 1889 is the only multilateral copyright convention to which Article XIX of the Universal Convention may apply (cf. point 4, in-fine, above). There are basic differences between the two conventions. To mention only one, the Universal Convention prescribes the application of the law of the country in which protection is claimed (cf. Article II), whereas the Montevideo Convention prescribes the application of the law of the country in which the work's first publication or production took place (Article 2). The latter means that a contracting country would not apply its own domestic law to foreign works but the foreign law, i.e., the law of the work's country of origin. Because of Article XIX, however, as between countries bound by both conventions, the Universal Convention will prevail and each country will apply its own domestic law to foreign works; subject only to the qualifications resulting from the Universal Convention.

9. Application of Article XIX to Bilateral Conventions or Arrangements.—Article XIX applies to any "existing" bilateral conventions or arrangements except if both parties are American republics.

The question arises whether Article XIX applies to conventions or arrangements "in effect" between two countries members of the Berne Union. In other words, the problem is that of two countries bound by three instruments, the Universal Convention, Berne Convention, and a bilateral convention or arrangement.

If the work for which protection is claimed is a work, which, according to the terms of one of the Berne Conventions, has, as country of origin, a country party to the same Berne Convention, the Universal Convention does not apply (Universal Convention, Appendix Declaration, proviso b). Possible conflicts between the applicable Berne Convention and the bilateral convention or arrangement will be solved according to Article XX of the applicable convention of the Berne Union.

If, however, the work for which protection is claimed, is a work which does not have a Berne country as country of origin, and there is a difference between the provisions of the bilateral convention or arrangement and the Universal Convention, the provisions of the Universal Convention shall prevail.

10. Effect of "Universal Convention Prevails" Rule on "Non-Abrogation" Principle.—The analysis of the parallel problem in Article XVIII, contained in point 13 of the chapter dealing with Article XVIII, applies, *mutatis mutandis*, also to Article XIX.

C. Acquired Rights Unaffected

11. Principle Incorporated in Third Sentence.—The third sentence of Article XIX is, except for a difference in drafting not affecting its meaning ("before the date this Convention comes into force" in Article XVIII, "before the date on which this Convention comes into force" in Article XIX), identical with the third sentence of Article XVIII. The analysis of the sentence in question, given in point 14 of the Chapter dealing with Article XVIII, applies *mutatis mutandis* also to Article XIX.

ARTICLE XX: RESERVATIONS TO THE CONVENTION

"Reservations to this Convention shall not be permitted." (Art. XX)

1. Scope of Article XX.—The provision means that once a country adheres to the Convention, it is bound by every provision thereof and cannot, at the time it deposits its instrument of adherence, or at any other time, declare that it does not consider itself bound by one or more provisions of the Convention. In other words, the Convention can be adhered to only in its entirety.

ARTICLE XXI: COPIES AND NOTIFICATIONS

"*The Director-General of the United Nations Educational, Scientific and Cultural Organization shall send duly certified copies of this Convention to the States interested, to the Swiss Federal Council and to the Secretary-General of the United Nations for registration by him.*

He shall also inform all interested States of the ratifications, acceptances and accessions which have been deposited, the date on which this Convention comes into force, the notifications under Article XIII of this Convention, and denunciations under Article XIV." (Art. XXI)

1. Scope of Article XXI.—According to the first paragraph, the Director-General must send "duly certified copies" of the Convention to (1) "the States interested," (2) the "Swiss Federal Council," and (3) "the Secretary-General of the United Nations for registration by him."

The certification was effectuated by the following paragraph, stamped, dated and signed by the Legal Adviser of UNESCO: "Certified a true and complete copy of the original Universal Copyright Convention, signed at Geneva on 6 September, 1952, and of a resolution concerning Article XI thereof, annexed thereto."

"States interested" are not only the signatory States and/or States members of UNESCO. Any State may obtain a certified copy from UNESCO.

The Swiss Federal Council is the chief executive authority of the Swiss Confederation. The transmittal of a second copy to Switzerland (it received the first as one of the interested States) has no legal significance. It was an act of courtesy vis-à-vis the country on the territory of which the Conference adopting the Convention was held.

Article 102 of the Charter of the United Nations provides that:

"1. Every treaty and every international agreement entered into by any Member of the United Nations after the present Charter comes into force [October 24, 1945], shall as soon as possible be registered with the Secretariat and published by it.

"2. No party to any such treaty or international agreement which has not been registered in accordance with the provisions of paragraph 1 of this Article may invoke the treaty or agreement before any organ of the United Nations."

The General Assembly of United Nations adopted, by resolutions passed on December 14, 1946, December 1, 1949, and December 12, 1950, regulations to give effect to Article 102 quoted above (U.N. Treaty Series, Vol. 76, page XX). According to Article 4 of the Regulations a treaty of the kind referred to in Article 102 of the Charter may be registered with the Secretariat of United Nations by a Specialized Agency (UNESCO is one) where the Specialized Agency has been authorized by the treaty to effect registration. The date of registration is the date of receipt of the treaty by the Secretariat of United Nations (Regulations, Article 6). The Universal Convention was registered on September 27, 1955. It was published in the United Nations Treaty Series under the serial number 2937.

The second paragraph of Article XXI of the Universal Convention provides that the Director-General shall inform all interested States (1) of the ratifications, acceptances and accessions which have been deposited, (2) of the date on which the Convention comes into force, (3) of the notifications relating to non-self-governing territories (cf. Article XIII), and (4) of the denunciations under Article XIV. These communications are made by circular letters of UNESCO's Director-General to the governments of the various countries. The information also results from the U.N. Treaty Series and from UNESCO's Copyright Bulletin.

As to the question whether the Director-General has the authority to examine whether the country which deposits an instrument of adherence has complied with the requirement provided for in Article X, paragraph 3, see point 3 of the Chapter dealing with Article VIII.

PROTOCOL 1: EXTENSION OF CONVENTION TO WORKS OF STATELESS PERSONS AND REFUGEES

"1. Stateless persons and refugees who have their habitual residence in a State party to this Protocol shall, for the purposes of the Convention, be assimilated to the nationals of that State.

2. (a) This Protocol shall be signed and shall be subject to ratification or acceptance, or may be acceded to, as if the provisions of Article VIII of the Convention applied hereto.

(b) This Protocol shall enter into force in respect of each State, on the date of deposit of the instrument of ratification, acceptance or accession of the State concerned or on the date of entry into force of the Convention with respect to such State, whichever is the later." (Protocol 1)

1. Scope of Protocol 1.—This Protocol provides for the protection of works of stateless persons and refugees. It consists of two paragraphs. Paragraph 1 contains the substantive rule. Paragraph 2 deals with the methods whereby countries may become parties to the Protocol and with the entry into force of the Protocol.

Paragraph 1 provides that "stateless persons and refugees who have their habitual residence in a State party to this Protocol shall, for the purposes of the Convention, be assimilated to the nationals of that State."

2. Stateless Persons.—A "stateless person" is a person who is not a citizen, subject or national of any country for whatever reason.

3. Refugees.—The word "refugee" has no generally accepted meaning. However, the Convention on the Status of Refugees signed in 1951 may be considered as a basis of interpretation. The following elements of the definition given by said Convention may be taken into consideration: a refugee is a person who, having good reason to fear he will be persecuted because of his race, religion, nationality, social group or political opinions, lives outside the country of which he is a national or, if he is stateless, lives outside the country in which he had his habitual residence and who cannot, or, because of said fear, does not desire to, claim the protection of said country. These elements, of course, have the force of indications only, since the definition as such is not a part of the Universal Convention.

A refugee may be stateless or not. If he is stateless, he will be treated as any other stateless person, refugee or not refugee.

If a refugee is not stateless because he acquired the nationality of a country other than the country from which he fled (e.g., he acquired the nationality of the country in which he took refuge), he probably should not be considered a refugee under the Universal Convention.

4. Habitual Residence.—The words "who have their habitual residence" relate both to "stateless persons" and to "refugees." "Habitual residence" is probably a broader concept than "permanent residence" or "domicile." (Article II, paragraph 3, uses the concept of domicile.)

5. Assimilation.—Assimilation means that stateless persons and refugees who have their habitual residence in a country party to both the Convention and the Protocol will be treated, by the country of their habitual residence as well as by the other countries parties to both instruments, as if they were nationals of the country of their habitual residence. In other words, any provision of the Convention in which the concept "national of a contracting State" appears must be read, by countries parties to both instruments, as if the text would refer to (1) nationals of the contracting country, (2) stateless persons having their habitual residence in the contracting country, and (3) refugees having their habitual residence in the contracting country.

6. Paragraph 2: Final Clauses.—According to paragraph 2(a) of the Protocol the methods whereby a country may become party to the Protocol are similar to those whereby a country may become party to the Convention. According to paragraph 2(b) of the Protocol, the Protocol will enter into force in respect to a State adhering thereto on the later of the following two dates: (a) the date on which the Convention enters into force in respect to that State, (b) the date on which the State deposits its instrument of adherence to the Protocol. The second alternative means, for example, that if a State adheres to the Protocol at a time when the Convention has already entered into force in that State, there will be no three months delay between deposit and entry into effect, but the Protocol will enter into force the same day the instrument relating thereto is deposited.

The concluding sentence of the Protocol follows the pattern established in Articles VIII, XVI and XXI of the Convention.

PROTOCOL 2: EXTENSION OF CONVENTION TO WORKS OF CERTAIN INTERGOVERNMENTAL ORGANIZATIONS

"*1. (a) The protection provided for in Article II(1) of the Convention shall apply to works published for the first time by the United Nations, by the Specialized Agencies in relationship therewith, or by the Organization of American States;*

(b) Similarly, Article II(2) of the Convention shall apply to the said organization or agencies.

2. (a) This Protocol shall be signed and shall be subject to ratification or acceptance, or may be acceded to, as if the provisions of Article VIII of the Convention applied hereto.

(b) This Protocol shall enter into force for each State on the date of deposit of the instrument of ratification, acceptance or accession of the State concerned or on the date of entry into force of the Convention with respect to such State, whichever is the later." (Protocol 2)

1. Scope of Protocol 2.—According to its official title, this Protocol concerns the application of the Convention to the works of certain international organizations; and this, undoubtedly, is the general intent. Whether the rules contained in the body of the Protocol fully achieve this objective, is less certain, and will be examined below.

The Protocol consists of two paragraphs. Paragraph 1 contains the substantive rules; paragraph 2 the final clauses. The latter being identical with the final clauses of Protocol 1, contained in paragraph 2 of said Protocol, reference is made to the observations made in respect to Protocol 1, paragraph 2, *supra*.

2. Paragraph 1(a).—This paragraph provides that "The protection provided for in Article II(1) of the Convention shall apply to works first published by the United Nations, by the Specialized Agencies in relationship therewith, or by the Organization of American States."

"Specialized Agencies in relationship with the United Nations" are those intergovernmental organizations which, in their respective field of competence, are recognized by the United Nations as "specialized agency." This recognition and the relationship with the United Nations are established in the Agreements that each specialized agency concludes with the Economic and Social Council of the United Nations. The agreements are approved by the General Assembly of the United Nations. Cf. Articles 57 and 63 of the Charter of the United Nations.

At the time the Protocol went into force there were ten specialized agencies, viz.:

1. ILO   – International Labor Organization
2. FAO   – Food and Agriculture Organization
3. UNESCO   – United Nations Educational, Scientific and Cultural Organization
4. ICAO   – International Civil Aviation Organization
5. BANK   – International Bank for Reconstruction and Development
6. FUND   – International Monetary Fund
7. UPU   – Universal Postal Union
8. ITU   – International Telecommunications Union
9. WHO   – World Health Organization
10. WMO   – World Meteorological Organization

To these ten specialized agencies, as well as to the United Nations and the Organization of American States we shall refer by the word "Organizations" in the remaining part of this chapter.

The Protocol provides not that the Convention but that "the protection provided for in Article II (1) of the Convention" shall apply to works published for the first time by the Organizations. Literally read, this provision would seem to mean that only Article II, paragraph 1, of the Convention would apply to such works and that the other provisions, particularly those relating to formalities (Article III), duration (Article IV), and the right of translation (Article V) would not apply to the same. This interpretation is contrary to the title of the Protocol, which speaks about the application of the Convention to the works of the Organizations. Of course, not all the provisions of the Convention are applicable to the works in question, since, for example, the entry into force of the Protocol, regulated in its paragraph 2(b), is not necessarily the same as that of the Convention, regulated by Article IX of the Convention. There is no reason to believe that the Geneva Conference did not want to extend all the provisions of the Convention which, by their nature, are applicable to the works first published by the Organizations, to such works. There is, for example, no reason to believe that the substitution of domestic formalities by the Convention notice was intended to be denied in the case of published works of the Organizations. The Rapporteur General's report states that "In its first paragraph, it [the Protocol] extended the protection provided by the Convention to..." the works in question (Report, page 75). It is, however, an undeniable fact that the Protocol speaks of Article II, paragraph 1, rather than of the Convention as such and that, consequently, it could be argued that all the Protocol gives is national treatment, not subject to the qualification which would otherwise result from Articles I and III to V of the Convention.

The reason for an express reference to Article II, paragraph 1, lies probably in the desire to emphasize that the published works of the Organizations receive the same treatment as published domestic works.

since Article II, paragraph 1 of the Convention regulates the treatment of published works as distinguished from unpublished works, and paragraph 1(a) of the Protocol also deals only with published works.

The works which are to be protected by virtue of paragraph 1(a) of the Protocol are "works published for the first time by the [Organization]." The author's nationality or the place of the first publication is irrelevant. If the work is first published by one of the Organizations, the Protocol applies to it even if its author is a national of a non-contracting country and the publication takes place in a non-contracting country.

The question arises whether a contracting country can deny the recognition of the Convention notice as a substitute for domestic formalities in the case of works first published by the Organizations in its own territory or authored by its own nationals. Such denial would be based on Article III, paragraph 2 of the Convention.

The question may prove to have practical importance in the United States, for example, since the headquarters of the United Nations are located in New York, and the U.S. Copyright Law requires the fulfillment of formalities which cannot be substituted by the Convention notice in the case of works first published on the territory of the United States or in the case of works authored by U.S. citizens.

As a practical matter, a copyright notice complying with the requirements of both the U.S. Law and the Convention, will, of course, avoid the problems of the notice. But other formalities, particularly manufacture, still remain.

In the case of a work first published by the United Nations on the territory of its headquarters (and the author of which is not a U.S. citizen) one might argue that, for the purposes of the Convention, the headquarters are not the territory of the United States. Whether such an argument would resist the modern trends of international public law consisting in the very narrow interpretation of exterritoriality, is doubtful.

In any case, the rules of the Protocol and the Convention do not entirely fit each other and there is an area of doubt as to the applicability of Article III in general, and of Article III, paragraph 2, in particular.

3. Paragraph 1(b).—This provision is quite cryptic. It provides that "Similarly, Article II(2) of the Convention shall apply to said organizations or agencies." The provision does not speak expressly of unpublished works. The reference to Article II, paragraph 2 of the Convention makes it clear, however, that only unpublished works can be meant because the Convention, in paragraph 2 of its Article II, deals with unpublished works and nothing else. The question arises, however, what should be the link between an unpublished work and a particular Organization to bring it under paragraph 1(b) of the Protocol. The Protocol does not speak about unpublished works of the Organizations, probably because in the view of certain countries a legal entity can never be author, but only natural persons can be authors. As a matter of common sense it is suggested that the works that paragraph 1(b) of the Protocol intends to cover are primarily such unpublished documents and letters which appear or are intended to appear under the heading or with the signature of the Organizations in question. Contractual arrangements between the Organization and the natural person actual drafter of a document, or special factual circumstances prevailing between them, may, of course, exclude or limit the ownership of copyright by the Organization, in which case even said unpublished writings would remain outside the field of application of paragraph 1(b) of the Protocol.

4. Paragraph 2.—This paragraph is similar to paragraph 2 of Protocol 1. The observations made in connection with the latter apply here too.

PROTOCOL 3: CONDITIONAL ADHERENCE TO CONVENTION

"*1. Any State party hereto may, on depositing its instrument of ratification or acceptance of or accession to the Convention, notify the Director-General of the United Nations Educational, Scientific and Cultural Organization (hereinafter referred to as "Director-General") that that instrument shall not take effect for the purposes of Article IX of the Convention until any other State named in such notification shall have deposited its instrument.*

2. The notification referred to in paragraph 1 above shall accompany the instrument to which it relates.

3. The Director-General shall inform all States signatory or which have then acceded to the Convention of any notifications received in accordance with this Protocol.

4. This Protocol shall bear the same date and shall remain open for signature for the same period as the Convention.

5. It shall be subject to ratification or acceptance by the signatory States. Any State which has not signed this Protocol may accede thereto.

6. a) Ratification or acceptance or accession shall be effected by the deposit of an instrument to that effect with the Director-General.

b) This Protocol shall enter into force on the date of deposit of not less than four instruments of ratification or acceptance or accession. The Director-General shall inform all interested States of this date. Instruments deposited after such date shall take effect on the date of their deposit." (Protocol 3)

1. Scope of Protocol 3.—This Protocol enables any country to deposit its instrument of adherence to the Convention without the deposit causing the effects which Article IX attaches to deposits: if a country makes use of the possibility offered by the Protocol, it makes its deposit of no effect pending deposit by another country, named in the instrument of deposit of the first country. Since the Protocol uses the singular ("any other State"), it would seem that the conditional deposit may relate to the deposit of only one other country.

2. Entry Into Force of Protocol.—Paragraph 6 (b) of the Protocol contains the curious provision according to which the Protocol "shall enter into force on the date of deposit of not less than four instruments of ratification or acceptance or accession." This would seem to mean that had only one, two or three countries made a conditional deposit before the number of countries required by Article IX of the Convention deposited their instruments, the deposits of said one, two or three countries would have been unconditional, or perhaps even void, since their conditions were related to an international instrument without force because not adhered to by at least four countries.

As a matter of fact, the fourth instrument of adherence to Protocol 3 was deposited on July 5, 1955, and on the same date Protocol 3 formally entered into force. In reality, however, the Protocol does not, as yet, have any effect since none of the countries which adhered to it named a country upon the deposit of whose instrument it would make the effect of its own deposit depend. It is hard to understand why a country bothers to adhere to Protocol 3, the sole purpose of which is to allow conditional deposit, when such country does not attach any condition to the deposit of the instrument of its ratification or acceptance of, or adherence to, the Convention.

APPENDIX I

DOCUMENTS OF THE GENEVA CONFERENCE

TEXT OF THE CONVENTION IN ENGLISH

The Contracting States,

Moved by the desire to assure in all countries copyright protection of literary, scientific and artistic works,

Convinced that a system of copyright protection appropriate to all nations of the world and expressed in a universal convention, additional to, and without impairing international systems already in force, will ensure respect for the rights of the individual and encourage the development of literature, the sciences and the arts,

Persuaded that such a universal copyright system will facilitate a wider dissemination of works of the human mind and increase international understanding,

Have agreed as follows:

Article I

Each Contracting State undertakes to provide for the adequate and effective protection of the rights of authors and other copyright proprietors in literary, scientific and artistic works, including writings, musical, dramatic and cinematographic works, and paintings, engravings and sculpture.

Article II

1. Published works of nationals of any Contracting State and works first published in that State shall enjoy in each other Contracting State the same protection as that other State accords to works of its nationals first published in its own territory.

2. Unpublished works of nationals of each Contracting State shall enjoy in each other Contracting State the same protection as that other State accords to unpublished works of its own nationals.

3. For the purpose of this Convention any Contracting State may, by domestic legislation, assimilate to its own nationals any person domiciled in that State.

Article III

1. Any Contracting State which, under its domestic law, requires as a condition of copyright, compliance with formalities such as deposit, registration, notice, notarial certificates, payment of fees or manufacture or publication in that Contracting State, shall regard these requirements as satisfied with respect to all works protected in accordance with this Convention and first published outside its territory and the author of which is not one of its nationals, if from the time of the first publication all the copies of the work published with the authority of the author or other copyright proprietor bear the symbol © accompanied by the name of the copyright proprietor and the year of first publication placed in such manner and location as to give reasonable notice of claim of copyright.

2. The provisions of paragraph 1 of this Article shall not preclude any Contracting State from requiring formalities or other conditions for the acquisition and enjoyment of copyright in respect of works first published in its territory or works of its nationals wherever published.

3. The provisions of paragraph 1 of this Article shall not preclude any Contracting State from providing that a person seeking judicial relief must, in bringing the action,

comply with procedural requirements, such as that the complainant must appear through domestic counsel or that the complainant must deposit with the court or an administrative office, or both, a copy of the work involved in the litigation; provided that failure to comply with such requirements shall not affect the validity of the copyright, nor shall any such requirement be imposed upon a national of another Contracting State if such requirement is not imposed on nationals of the State in which protection is claimed.

4. In each Contracting State there shall be legal means of protecting without formalities the unpublished works of nationals of other Contracting States.

5. If a Contracting State grants protection for more than one term of copyright and the first term is for a period longer than one of the minimum periods prescribed in Article IV, such State shall not be required to comply with the provisions of paragraph 1 of this Article III in respect of the second or any subsequent term of copyright.

Article IV

1. The duration of protection of a work shall be governed, in accordance with the provisions of Article II and this Article, by the law of the Contracting State in which protection is claimed.

2. The term of protection for works protected under this Convention shall not be less than the life of the author and 25 years after his death.

However, any Contracting State which, on the effective date of this Convention in that State, has limited this term for certain classes of works to a period computed from the first publication of the work, shall be entitled to maintain these exceptions and to extend them to other classes of works. For all these classes the term of protection shall not be less than 25 years from the date of first publication.

Any Contracting State which, upon the effective date of this Convention in that State, does not compute the term of protection upon the basis of the life of the author, shall be entitled to compute the term of protection from the date of the first publication of the work or from its registration prior to publication, as the case may be, provided the term of protection shall not be less than 25 years from the date of first publication or from its registration prior to publication, as the case may be.

If the legislation of a Contracting State grants two or more successive terms of protection, the duration of the first term shall not be less than one of the minimum periods specified above.

3. The provisions of paragraph 2 of this Article shall not apply to photographic works or to works of applied art; provided, however, that the term of protection in those Contracting States which protect photographic works, or works of applied art in so far as they are protected as artistic works, shall not be less than 10 years for each of said classes of works.

4. No Contracting State shall be obliged to grant protection to a work for a period longer than that fixed for the class of works to which the work in question belongs, in the case of unpublished works by the law of the Contracting State of which the author is a national, and in the case of published works by the law of the Contracting State in which the work has been first published.

For the purposes of the application of the preceding provision, if the law of any Contracting State grants two or more successive terms of protection, the period of protection of that State shall be considered to be the aggregate of those terms. However, if a specified work is not protected by such State during the second or any subsequent term for any reason, the other Contracting States shall not be obliged to protect it during the second or any subsequent term.

5. For the purposes of the application of paragraph 4 of this Article, the work of a national of a Contracting State, first published in a non-Contracting State, shall be treated as though first published in the Contracting State of which the author is a national.

6. For the purposes of the application of paragraph 4 of this Article, in case of simultaneous publication in two or more Contracting States, the work shall be treated as though first published in the State which affords the shortest term; any work published in two or more Contracting States with 30 days of its first publication shall be considered as having been published simultaneously in said Contracting States.

Article V

1. Copyright shall include the exclusive right of the author to make, publish, and authorize the making and publication of translations of works protected under this Convention.

2. However, any Contracting State may, by its domestic legislation, restrict the right of translation of writings, but only subject to the following provisions:

If, after the expiration of a period of seven years from the date of the first publication of a writing, a translation of such writing has not been published in the national language or languages, as the case may be, of the Contracting State, by the owner of the right of translation or with his authorization, any national of such Contracting State may obtain a non-exclusive licence from the competent authority thereof to translate the work and publish the work so translated in any of the national languages in which it has not been published; provided that such national, in accordance with the procedure of the State concerned, establishes either that he has requested, and been denied, authorization by the proprietor of the right to make and publish the translation, or that, after due diligence on his part, he was unable to find the owner of the right. A licence may also be granted on the same conditions if all previous editions of a translation in such language are out of print.

If the owner of the right of translation cannot be found, then the applicant for a licence shall send copies of his application to the publisher whose name appears on the work and, if the nationality of the owner of the right of translation is known, to the diplomatic or consular representative of the State of which such owner is a national, or to the organization which may have been designated by the government of that State. The licence shall not be granted before the expiration of a period of two months from the date of the dispatch of the copies of the application.

Due provision shall be made by domestic legislation to assure to the owner of the right of translation a compensation which is just and conforms to international standards, to assure payment and transmittal of such compensation, and to assure a correct translation of the work.

The original title and the name of the author of the work shall be printed on all copies of the published translation. The licence shall be valid only for publication of the translation in the territory of the Contracting State where it has been applied for. Copies so published may be imported and sold in another Contracting State if one of the national languages of such other State is the same language as that into which the work has been so translated, and if the domestic law in such other State makes provision for such licences and does not prohibit such importation and sale. Where the foregoing conditions do not exist, the importation and sale of such copies in a Contracting State shall be governed by its domestic law and its agreements. The licence shall not be transferred by the licencee.

The licence shall not be granted when the author has withdrawn from circulation all copies of the work.

Article VI

"Publication," as used in this Convention, means the reproduction in tangible form and the general distribution to the public of copies of a work from which it can be read or otherwise visually perceived.

Article VII

This Convention shall not apply to works or rights in works which, at the effective date of the Convention in a Contracting State where protection is claimed, are permanently in the public domain in the said Contracting State.

Article VIII

1. This Convention, which shall bear the date of 6 September 1952, shall be deposited with the Director-General of the United Nations Educational, Scientific and Cultural Organization and shall remain open for signature by all States for a period of 120 days after that date. It shall be subject to ratification or acceptance by the signatory States.

2. Any State which has not signed this Convention may accede thereto.

3. Ratification, acceptance or accession shall be effected by the deposit of an instrument to that effect with the Director-General of the United Nations Educational, Scientific and Cultural Organization.

Article IX

1. This Convention shall come into force three months after the deposit of twelve instruments of ratification, acceptance or accession, among which there shall be those of four States which are not members of the International Union for the Protection of Literary and Artistic Works.

2. Subsequently, this Convention shall come into force in respect of each State three months after that State has deposited its instrument of ratification, acceptance or accession.

Article X

1. Each State party to this Convention undertakes to adopt, in accordance with its Constitution, such measures as are necessary to ensure the application of this Convention.

2. It is understood, however, that at the time an instrument of ratification, acceptance or accession is deposited on behalf of any State, such State must be in a position under its domestic law to give effect to the terms of this Convention.

Article XI

1. An Inter-governmental Committee is hereby established with the following duties:

(a) to study the problems concerning the application and operation of this Convention;

(b) to make preparation for periodic revisions of this Convention;

(c) to study any other problems concerning the international protection of copyright, in co-operation with the various interested international organizations, such as the United Nations Educational, Scientific and Cultural Organization, the International Union for the Protection of Literary and Artistic Works and the Organization of American States;

(d) to inform the Contracting States as to its activities.

2. The Committee shall consist of the representatives of twelve Contracting States to be selected with due consideration to fair geographical representation and in conformity with the Resolution relating to this article, annexed to this Convention.

The Director-General of the United Nations Educational, Scientific and Cultural Organization, the Director of the Bureau of the International Union for the Protection of Literary and Artistic Works and the Secretary-General of the Organization of American States, or their representatives, may attend meetings of the Committee in an advisory capacity.

Article XII

The Inter-governmental Committee shall convene a conference for revision of this Convention whenever it deems necessary, or at the request of at least ten Contracting States, or of a majority of the Contracting States if there are less than twenty Contracting States.

Article XIII

Any Contracting State may, at the time of deposit of its instrument of ratification, acceptance or accession, or at any time thereafter declare by notification addressed to the Director-General of the United Nations Educational, Scientific and Cultural Organization that this Convention shall apply to all or any of the countries or territories for the international relations of which it is responsible and this Convention shall thereupon apply to the countries or territories named in such notification after the expiration of the term of three months provided for in Article IX. In the absence of such notification, this Convention shall not apply to any such country or territory.

Article XIV

1. Any Contracting State may denounce this Convention in its own name or on behalf of all or any of the countries or territories as to which a notification has been given under Article XIII. The denunciation shall be made by notification addressed to the Director-General of the United Nations Educational, Scientific and Cultural Organization.

2. Such denunciation shall operate only in respect of the State or of the country or territory on whose behalf it was made and shall not take effect until twelve months after the date of receipt of the notification.

Article XV

A dispute between two or more Contracting States concerning the interpretation or application of this Convention, not settled by negotiation, shall, unless the States concerned agree on some other method of settlement, be brought before the International Court of Justice for determination by it.

Article XVI

1. This Convention shall be established in English, French and Spanish. The three texts shall be signed and shall be equally authoritative.

2. Official texts of this Convention shall be established in German, Italian and Portuguese.

Any Contracting State or group of Contracting States shall be entitled to have established by the Director-General of the United Nations Educational, Scientific and Cultural Organization other texts in the language of its choice by arrangement with the Director-General.

All such texts shall be annexed to the signed texts of this Convention.

Article XVII

1. This Convention shall not in any way affect the provisions of the Berne Con-

vention for the Protection of Literary and Artistic Works or membership in the Union created by that Convention.

2. In application of the foregoing paragraph, a Declaration has been annexed to the present article. This Declaration is an integral part of this Convention for the States bound by the Berne Convention on January 1, 1951, or which have or may become bound to it at a later date. The signature of this Convention by such States shall also constitute signature of the said Declaration, and ratification, acceptance or accession by such States shall include the Declaration as well as the Convention.

Article XVIII

This Convention shall not abrogate multilateral or bilateral copyright conventions or arrangements that are or may be in effect exclusively between two or more American Republics. In the event of any difference either between the provisions of such existing conventions or arrangements and the provisions of this Convention, or between the provisions of this Convention and those of any new convention or arrangement which may be formulated between two or more American Republics after this Convention comes into force, the convention or arrangement most recently formulated shall prevail between the parties thereto. Rights in works acquired in any Contracting State under existing conventions or arrangements before the date this Convention comes into force in such State shall not be affected.

Article XIX

This Convention shall not abrogate multilateral or bilateral conventions or arrangements in effect between two or more Contracting States. In the event of any difference between the provisions of such existing conventions or arrangements and the provisions of this Convention, the provisions of this Convention shall prevail. Rights in works acquired in any Contracting State under existing conventions or arrangements before the date on which this Convention comes into force in such State shall not be affected. Nothing in this article shall affect the provisions of Articles XVII and XVIII of this Convention.

Article XX

Reservations to this Convention shall not be permitted.

Article XXI

The Director-General of the United Nations Educational, Scientific and Cultural Organization shall send duly certified copies of this Convention to the States interested, to the Swiss Federal Council and to the Secretary-General of the United Nations for registration by him.

He shall also inform all interested States of the ratifications, acceptances and accessions which have been deposited, the date on which this Convention comes into force, the notifications under Article XIII of this Convention, and denunciations under Article XIV.

Appendix Declaration relating to Article XVII

The States which are members of the International Union for the Protection of Literary and Artistic Works, and which are signatories to the Universal Copyright Convention,

Desiring to reinforce their mutual relations on the basis of the said Union and to avoid any conflict which might result from the co-existence of the Convention of Berne and the Universal Convention,

Have, by common agreement, accepted the terms of the following declaration:

(a) Works which, according to the Berne Convention, have as their country of origin a country which has withdrawn from the International Union created by the said Convention, after January 1, 1951, shall not be protected by the Universal Copyright Convention in the countries of the Berne Union;

(b) The Universal Copyright Convention shall not be applicable to the relationships among countries of the Berne Union insofar as it relates to the protection of works having as their country of origin, within the meaning of the Berne Convention, a country of the International Union created by the said Convention.

Resolution concerning Article XI

The Inter-governmental Copyright Conference

Having considered the problems relating to the Inter-governmental Committee provided for in Article XI of the Universal Copyright Convention

resolves

1. The first members of the Committee shall be representatives of the following twelve States, each of those States designating one representative and an alternate: Argentina, Brazil, France, Germany, India, Italy, Japan, Mexico, Spain, Switzerland, United Kingdom, and United States of America.

2. The Committee shall be constituted as soon as the Convention comes into force in accordance with Article XI of this Convention.

3. The Committee shall elect its chairman and one vice-chairman. It shall establish its rules of procedure having regard to the following principles:

(a) the normal duration of the term of office of the representatives shall be six years; with one-third retiring every two years;

(b) before the expiration of the term of office of any members, the Committee shall decide which States shall cease to be represented on it and which States shall be called upon to designate representatives; the representatives of those States which have not ratified, accepted or acceded shall be the first to retire;

(c) the different parts of the world shall be fairly represented;

and expresses the wish

that the United Nations Educational, Scientific and Cultural Organization provide its secretariat.

In faith whereof the undersigned, having deposited their respective full powers, have signed this Convention.

Done at Geneva, this sixth day of September, 1952, in a single copy.

PROTOCOL 1

Annexed to the Universal Copyright Convention concerning the application of that Convention to the works of stateless persons and refugees

The States parties hereto, being also parties to the Universal Copyright Convention (hereinafter referred to as the "Convention"),

Have accepted the following provisions:

1. Stateless persons and refugees who have their habitual residence in a State party to this Protocol shall, for the purposes of the Convention, be assimilated to the nationals of that State.

2. (a) This Protocol shall be signed and shall be subject to ratification or acceptance, or may be acceded to, as if the provisions of Article VIII of the Convention applied hereto.

(b) This Protocol shall enter into force in respect of each State, on the date of deposit of the instrument of ratification, acceptance or accession of the State concerned or on the date of entry into force of the Convention with respect to such State, whichever is the later.

In faith whereof the undersigned, being duly authorized thereto, have signed this Protocol.

Done at Geneva this sixth day of September 1952, in the English, French and Spanish languages, the three texts being equally authoritative, in a single copy which shall be deposited with the Director-General of Unesco. The Director-General shall send certified copies to the signatory States, to the Swiss Federal Council, and to the Secretary-General of the United Nations for registration.

PROTOCOL 2

Annexed to the Universal Copyright Convention, concerning the application of that Convention to the works of certain international organizations

The States parties hereto, being also parties to the Universal Copyright Convention (hereinafter referred to as the "Convention"),

Have accepted the following provisions:

1. (a) The protection provided for in Article II(1) of the Convention shall apply to works published for the first time by the United Nations, by the Specialized Agencies in relationship therewith, or by the Organization of American States;

(b) Similarly, Article II(2) of the Convention shall apply to the said organization or agencies.

2. (a) This Protocol shall be signed and shall be subject to ratification or acceptance, or may be acceded to, as if the provisions of Article VIII of the Convention applied hereto.

(b) This Protocol shall enter into force for each State on the date of deposit of the instrument of ratification, acceptance or accession of the State concerned or on the date of entry into force of the Convention with respect to such State, whichever is the later.

In faith whereof the undersigned, being duly authorized thereto, have signed this Protocol.

Done at Geneva, this sixth day of September 1952, in the English, French and Spanish languages, the three texts being equally authoritative, in a single copy which shall be deposited with the Director-General of Unesco.

The Director-General shall send certified copies to the signatory States, to the Swiss Federal Council, and to the Secretary-General of the United Nations for registration.

PROTOCOL 3

Annexed to the Universal Copyright Convention concerning the effective date of instruments of ratification or acceptance of or accession to that Convention

States parties hereto,

Recognizing that the application of the Universal Copyright Convention (hereinafter referred to as the "Convention") to States participating in all the international copyright systems already in force will contribute greatly to the value of the Convention;

Have agreed as follows:

1. Any State party hereto may, on depositing its instrument of ratification or acceptance of or accession to the Convention, notify the Director-General of the United Nations Educational, Scientific and Cultural Organization (hereinafter referred to as "Director-General") that that instrument shall not take effect for the purposes of Article IX of the Convention until any other State named in such notification shall have deposited its instrument.

2. The notification referred to in paragraph 1 above shall accompany the instrument to which it relates.

3. The Director-General shall inform all States signatory or which have then acceded to the Convention of any notifications received in accordance with this Protocol.

4. This Protocol shall bear the same date and shall remain open for signature for the same period as the Convention.

5. It shall be subject to ratification or acceptance by the signatory States. Any State which has not signed this Protocol may accede thereto.

6. (a) Ratification or acceptance or accession shall be effected by the deposit of an instrument to that effect with the Director-General.

(b) This Protocol shall enter into force on the date of deposit of not less than four instruments of ratification or acceptance or accession. The Director-General shall inform all interested States of this date. Instruments deposited after such date shall take effect on the date of their deposit.

In faith whereof the undersigned, being duly authorized thereto, have signed this Protocol.

Done at Geneva, the sixth day of September 1952, in the English, French and Spanish languages, the three texts being equally authoritative, in a single copy which shall be annexed to the original copy of the Convention. The Director-General shall send certified copies to the signatory States, to the Swiss Federal Council, and to the Secretary-General of the United Nations for registration.

TEXT OF THE CONVENTION IN FRENCH

Les États contractants,

Animés du désir d'assurer dans tous les pays la protection du droit d'auteur sur les œuvres littéraires, scientifiques et artistiques;

Convaincus qu'un régime de protection des droits des auteurs approprié à toutes les nations et exprimé dans une convention universelle, s'ajoutant aux systèmes internationaux déjà en vigueur, sans leur porter atteinte, est de nature à assurer le respect des droits de la personne humaine et à favoriser le développement des lettres, des sciences et des arts;

Persuadés qu'un tel régime universel de protection des droits des auteurs rendra plus facile la diffusion des œuvres de l'esprit et contribuera à une meilleure compréhension internationale,

Sont convenus de ce qui suit:

Article I

Chaque État contractant s'engage à prendre toutes dispositions nécessaires pour assurer une protection suffisante et efficace des droits des auteurs et de tous autres titulaires de ces droits sur les œuvres littéraires, scientifiques et artistiques, telles que les écrits, les œuvres musicales, dramatiques et cinématographiques, les peintures, gravures et sculptures.

Article II

1. Les œuvres publiées des ressortissants de tout État contractant ainsi que les œuvres publiées pour la première fois sur le territoire d'un tel État jouissent, dans tout autre État contractant, de la protection que cet autre État accorde aux œuvres de ses ressortissants publiées pour la première fois sur son propre territoire.

2. Les œuvres non publiées des ressortissants de tout État contractant jouissent, dans tout autre État contractant, de la protection que cet autre État accorde aux œuvres non publiées de ses ressortissants.

3. Pour l'application de la présente Convention, tout État contractant peut, par des dispositions de sa législation interne, assimiler à ses ressortissants toute personne domiciliée sur le territoire de cet État.

Article III

1. Tout État contractant qui, d'après sa législation interne, exige, à titre de condition de la protection des droits des auteurs, l'accomplissement de formalités telles que dépôt, enregistrement, mention, certificats notariés, paiement de taxes, fabrication ou publication sur le territoire national, doit considérer ces exigences comme satisfaites pour toute œuvre protégée aux termes de la présente Convention, publiée pour la première fois hors du territoire de cet État et dont l'auteur n'est pas un de ses ressortissants, si, dès la première publication de cette œuvre, tous les exemplaires de l'œuvre publiée avec l'autorisation de l'auteur ou de tout autre titulaire de ses droits portent le symbole © accompagné du nom du titulaire du droit d'auteur et de l'indication de l'année de première publication; le symbole, le nom et l'année doivent être apposés d'une manière et à une place montrant de façon nette que le droit d'auteur est réservé.

2. Les dispositions de l'alinéa 1 du présent article n'interdisent pas à un État contractant de soumettre à certaines formalités ou à d'autres conditions, en vue d'assurer l'acquisition et la jouissance du droit d'auteur, les œuvres publiées pour la première fois sur son territoire, ou celles de ses ressortissants, quel que soit le lieu de la publication de ces œuvres.

3. Les dispositions de l'alinéa 1 ci-dessus n'interdisent pas à un État contractant d'exiger d'une personne estant en justice qu'elle satisfasse, aux fins du procès, aux règles de procédure telles que l'assistance du demandeur par un avocat exerçant dans cet État ou le dépôt par le demandeur d'un exemplaire de l'œuvre auprès du tribunal ou d'un bureau administratif ou des deux à la fois. Toutefois, le fait de ne pas satisfaire à ces exigences n'affecte pas la validité du droit d'auteur. Aucune de ces exigences ne peut être imposée à un ressortissant d'un autre État contractant si elle ne l'est pas aux ressortissants de l'État dans lequel la protection est demandée.

4. Dans chaque État contractant doivent être assurés des moyens juridiques pour protéger sans formalités les œuvres non publiées des ressortissants des autres États contractants.

5. Si un État contractant accorde plus d'une seule période de protection et si la première est d'une durée supérieure à l'un des minimums de temps prévus à l'article IV de la présente Convention, cet État a la faculté de ne pas appliquer l'alinéa 1 du présent article III en ce qui concerne la deuxième période de protection ainsi que pour les périodes suivantes.

Article IV

1. La durée de la protection de l'œuvre est réglée par la loi de l'État contractant où la protection est demandée conformément aux dispositions de l'article II et aux dispositions ci-dessous.

2. La durée de protection pour les œuvres protégées par la présente Convention ne sera pas inférieure à une période comprenant la vie de l'auteur et vingt-cinq années après sa mort.

Toutefois, l'État contractant qui, à la date de l'entrée en vigueur de la présente Convention sur son territoire, aura restreint ce délai, pour certaines catégories d'œuvres, à une période calculée à partir de la première publication de l'œuvre, aura la faculté de maintenir ces dérogations ou de les étendre à d'autres catégories. Pour toutes ces catégories, la durée de protection ne sera pas inférieure à vingt-cinq années à compter de la date de la première publication.

Tout État contractant qui, à la date de l'entrée en vigueur de la Convention sur son territoire, ne calcule pas la durée de protection sur la base de la vie de l'auteur, aura la faculté de calculer cette durée de protection à compter de la première publication de l'œuvre ou, le cas échéant, de l'enregistrement de cette œuvre préalable à sa publication; la durée de la protection ne sera pas inférieure à vingt-cinq années à compter de la date de la première publication ou, le cas échéant, de l'enregistrement de l'œuvre préalable à la publication.

Si la législation de l'État contractant prévoit deux ou plusieurs périodes consécutives de protection, la durée de la première période ne sera pas inférieure à la durée de l'une des périodes minima déterminée ci-dessus.

3. Les dispositions du numéro 2 du présent article ne s'appliquent pas aux œuvres photographiques, ni aux œuvres des arts appliqués. Toutefois, dans les États contractants qui protègent les œuvres photographiques et, en tant qu'œuvres artistiques, les œuvres des arts appliqués, la durée de la protection ne sera pas, pour ces œuvres, inférieure à dix ans.

4. Aucun État contractant ne sera tenu d'assurer la protection d'une œuvre pendant une durée plus longue que celle fixée, pour la catégorie dont elle relève, s'il s'agit d'une œuvre non publiée, par la loi de l'État contractant dont l'auteur est ressortis-

sant, et, s'il s'agit d'une œuvre publiée, par la loi de l'État contractant où cette œuvre a été publiée pour la première fois.

Aux fins de l'application de la disposition précédente, si la législation d'un État contractant prévoit deux ou plusieurs périodes consécutives de protection, la durée de la protection accordée par cet État est donsidérée comme étant la somme de ces périodes. Toutefois, si pour une raison quelconque une œuvre déterminée n'est pas protégée par ledit État pendant la seconde période ou l'une des périodes suivantes, les autres États contractants ne sont pas tenus de protéger cette œuvre pendant cette seconde période ou les périodes suivantes.

5. Aux fins de l'application du numéro 4 de cet article, l'œuvre d'un ressortissant d'un État contractant publiée pour la première fois dans un État non contractant sera considérée comme ayant été publiée pour la première fois dans l'État contractant dont l'auteur est ressortissant.

6. Aux fins de l'application du numéro 4 susmentionné du présent article, en cas de publication simultanée dans deux ou plusieurs États contractants, l'œuvre sera considérée comme ayant été publiée pour la première fois dans l'État qui accorde la protection la moins longue. Est considérée comme publiée simultanément dans plusieurs pays toute œuvre qui a paru dans deux ou plusieurs pays dans les trente jours de sa première publication.

Article V

1. Le droit d'auteur comprend le droit exclusif de faire, de publier et d'autoriser à faire et à publier la traduction des œuvres protégées aux termes de la présente Convention.

2. Toutefois, chaque État contractant peut, par sa législation nationale, restreindre, pour les écrits, le droit de traduction, mais en se conformant aux dispositions suivantes:

Lorsque, à l'expiration d'un délai de sept années à dater de la première publication d'un écrit, la traduction de cet écrit n'a pas été publiée dans la langue nationale ou, le cas échéant, dans l'une des langues nationales d'un État contractant par le titulaire du droit de traduction ou avec son autorisation, tout ressortissant de cet État contractant pourra obtenir de l'autorité compétente de cet État une licence non exclusive pour traduire l'œuvre et publier l'œuvre ainsi traduite dans la langue nationale en laquelle elle n'a pas été publiée.

Cette licence ne pourra être accordée que si le requérant, conformément aux dispositions en vigueur dans l'État où est introduite la demande, justifie avoir demandé au titulaire du droit de traduction l'autorisation de traduire et de publier la traduction et, après dues diligences de sa part, n'a pu atteindre le titulaire du droit d'auteur ou obtenir son autorisation. Aus mêmes conditions, la licence pourra également être accordée si, pour une traduction déjà publiée dans une langue nationale, les éditions sont épuisées.

Si le titulaire du droit de traduction n'a pu être atteint par le requérant, celui-ci doit adresser des copies de sa demande à l'éditeur dont le nom figure sur l'œuvre et au représentant diplomatique ou consulaire de l'État dont le titulaire du droit de traduction est ressortissant, lorsque la nationalité du titulaire du droit de traduction est connue, ou à l'organisme qui peut avoir été désigné par le gouvernement de cet État. La licence ne pourra être accordée avant l'expiration d'un délai de deux mois à dater de l'envoi des copies de la demande.

La législation nationale adoptera les mesures appropriées pour assurer au titulaire du droit de traduction une rémunération équitable et conforme aux usages internationaux, ainsi que le paiement et le transfert de cette rémunération, et pour garantir une traduction correcte de l'œuvre.

Le titre et le nom de l'auteur de l'œuvre originale doivent être également imprimés sur tous les exemplaires de la traduction publiée. La licence ne sera valable que pour l'édition à l'intérieur du territoire de l'État contractant où cette licence est demandé.

L'importation et la vente des exemplaires dans un autre État contractant sont possibles si cet État a la même langue nationale que celle dans laquelle l'œuvre a été traduite, si sa loi nationale admet la licence et si aucune des dispositions en vigueur dans cet État ne s'oppose à l'importation et à la vente; l'importation et la vente sur le territoire de tout État contractant dans lequel les conditions précédentes ne peuvent jouer sont réservées à la législation de cet État et aux accords conclus par lui. La licence ne pourra être cédée par son bénéficiaire.

La licence ne peut être accordée lorsque l'auteur a retiré de la circulation les exemplaires de l'œuvre.

Article VI

Par «publication» au sens de la présente Convention, il faut entendre la reproduction sous une forme matérielle et la mise à la disposition du public d'exemplaires de l'œuvre permettant de la lire ou d'en prendre connaissance visuellement.

Article VII

La présente Convention ne s'applique pas aux œuvres ou aux droits sur ces œuvres qui, lors de l'entrée en vigueur de la Convention dans l'État contractant où la protection est demandée, auraient cessé définitivement d'être protégées dans cet État ou ne l'auraient jamais été.

Article VIII

1. La présente Convention, qui portera la date du 6 septembre 1952, sera déposée auprès du Directeur général de l'Organisation des Nations Unies pour l'éducation, la science et la culture et restera ouverte à la signature de tous les États pendant une période de cent vingt jours à compter de sa date. Elle sera soumise à la ratification ou à l'acceptation des États signataires.

2. Tout État qui n'aura pas signé la présente Convention pourra y adhérer.

3. La ratification, l'acceptation ou l'adhésion sera opérée par le dépôt d'un instrument à cet effet, auprès du Directeur général de l'Organisation des Nations Unies pour l'éducation, la science et la culture.

Article IX

1. La présente Convention entrera en vigueur trois mois après le dépôt de douze instruments de ratification, d'acceptation ou d'adhésion, y compris les instruments déposés par quatre États ne faisant pas partie de l'Union internationale pour la protection des œuvres littéraires et artistiques.

2. Par la suite, la Convention entrera en vigueur, pour chaque État, trois mois après le dépôt de l'instrument de ratification, d'acceptation ou d'adhésion spécial à cet État.

Article X

1. Tout État partie à la présente Convention s'engage à adopter, conformément aux dispositions de sa constitution, les mesures nécessaires pour assurer l'application de la présente Convention.

2. Il est entendu toutefois qu'au moment du dépôt de son instrument de ratification, d'acceptation ou d'adhésion tout État doit être en mesure, d'après sa législation nationale, d'appliquer les dispositions de la présente Convention.

Article XI

1. Il est créé un Comité intergouvernemental ayant les attributions suivantes:

a) Étudier les problèmes relatifs à l'application et au fonctionnement de la présente Convention;

b) Préparer les revisions périodiques de cette Convention;

c) Étudier tout autre problème relatif à la protection internationale du droit d'auteur, en collaboration avec les divers organismes internationaux intéressés, notamment avec l'Organisation des Nations Unies pour l'éducation, la science et la culture, l'Union internationale pour la protection des œuvres littéraires et artistiques et l'Organisation des États américains;

d) Renseigner les États contractants sur ses travaux.

2. Le Comité est composé des représentants de douze États contractants désignés en tenant compte d'une équitable représentation géographique et conformément aux dispositions de la résolution concernent le présent article, annexée à la présente Convention.

Le Directeur général de l'Organisation des Nations Unies pour l'éducation, la science et la culture, le Directeur du Bureau de l'Union internationale pour la protection des œuvres littéraires et artistiques et le Secrétaire général de l'Organisation des États américains, ou leurs représentants, peuvent assister aux séances du Comité avec voix consultative.

Article XII

Le Comité intergouvernemental convoquera des conférences de revision chaque fois que cela lui semblera nécessaire ou si la convocation est demandée par au moins dix États contractants ou par la majorité des États contractants aussi longtemps que le nombre de ces derniers demeurera inférieur à vingt.

Article XIII

Tout État contractant peut, au moment du dépôt de l'instrument de ratification d'acceptation ou d'adhésion, ou par la suite, déclarer, par une notification adressée au Directeur général de l'Organisation des Nations Unies pour l'éducation, la science et la culture, que la présente Convention est applicable à tout ou partie des pays ou territoires dont il assure les relations extérieures; la Convention s'appliquera alors aux pays ou territoires désignés dans la notification à partir de l'expiration du délai de trois mois prévu à l'article IX. A défaut de cette notification, la présente Convention ne s'appliquera pas à ces pays ou territoires.

Article XIV

1. Tout État contractant aura la faculté de dénoncer la présente Convention en son nom propre ou au nom de tout ou partie des pays ou territoires qui auraient fait l'objet de la notification prévue à l'article XIII. La dénonciation s'effectuera par notification adressée au Directeur général de l'Organisation des Nations Unies pour l'éducation, la science et la culture.

2. Cette dénonciation ne produira effet qu'à l'égard de l'État ou du pays ou territoire au nom duquel elle aura été faite et seulement douze mois après la date à laquelle la notification a été reçue.

Article XV

Tout différend entre deux ou plusieurs États contractants concernant l'interprétation ou l'application de la présente Convention qui ne sera pas réglé par voie de négociation sera porté devant la Cour internationale de justice pour qu'il soit statué par elle, à moins que les États en cause ne conviennent d'un autre mode de règlement.

Article XVI

1. La présente Convention sera établie en français, en anglais et en espagnol. Les trois textes seront signés et feront également foi.
2. Il sera établi des textes officiels de la présente Convention en allemand, en italien et en portugais.

Tout État contractant ou groupe d'États contractants pourra faire établir par le Directeur général de l'Organisation des Nations Unies pour l'éducation, la science et la culture, en accord avec celui-ci, d'autres textes dans la langue de son choix.

Tous ces textes seront annexés au texte signé de la Convention.

Article XVII

1. La présente Convention n'affecte en rien les dispositions de la Convention de Berne pour la protection des œuvres littéraires et artistiques ni l'appartenance à l'Union créée par cette dernière convention.
2. En vue de l'application de l'alinéa précédent, une déclaration est annexée au présent article. Cette déclaration fait partie intégrante de la présente Convention pour les États liés par la Convention de Berne au 1er janvier 1951 ou qui y auront adhéré ultérieurement. La signature de la présente Convention par les États mentionnés ci-dessus vaut également signature de la déclaration; toute ratification ou acceptation de la Convention, toute adhésion à celle-ci par ces États emportera également ratification, acceptation ou adhésion à la déclaration.

Article XVIII

La présente Convention n'infirme pas les conventions ou accords multilatéraux ou bilatéraux sur le droit d'auteur qui sont ou peuvent être mis en vigueur entre deux ou plusieurs républiques américaines, mais exclusivement entre elles. En cas de divergences soit entre les dispositions, d'une part, de l'une de ces conventions ou de l'un de ces accords en vigueur et, d'autre part, les dispositions de la présente Convention, soit entre les dispositions de la présente Convention et celles de toute nouvelle convention ou de tout nouvel accord qui serait établi entre deux ou plusieurs républiques américaines après l'entrée en vigueur de la présente Convention, la convention ou l'accord le plus récemment établi prévaudra entre les parties. Il n'est pas porté atteinte aux droits acquis sur une œuvre, en vertu de conventions ou accords en vigueur dans l'un quelconque des États contractants antérieurement à la date de l'entrée en vigueur de la présente Convention dans cet État.

Article XIX

La présente Convention n'infirme pas les conventions ou accords multilatéraux ou bilatéraux sur le droit d'auteur en vigueur entre deux ou plusieurs États contractants. En cas de divergences entre les dispositions de l'une de ces conventions ou accords et les dispositions de la présente Convention, les dispositions de la présente Convention prévaudront. Ne seront pas affectés les droits acquis sur une œuvre en vertu de conventions ou accords en vigueur dans l'un des États contractants antérieurement à la date de l'entrée en vigueur de la présente Convention dans ledit État. Le présent article ne déroge en rien aux dispositions des articles XVII et XVIII de la présente Convention.

Article XX

Il n'est admis aucune réserve à la présente Convention.

Article XXI

Le Directeur général de l'Organisation des Nations Unies pour l'éducation, la science et la culture enverra des copies dûment certifiées de la présente Convention aux États intéressés et au Conseil fédéral suisse ainsi qu'au Secrétaire général des Nations Unies pour enregistrement par les soins de celui-ci.

En outre, il informera tous les États intéressés du dépôt des instruments de ratification, d'acceptation ou d'adhésion, de la date d'entrée en vigueur de la présente Convention, des notifications prévues à l'article XIII de la présente Convention et des dénonciations prévues à l'article XIV.

Déclaration annexe relative à l'article XVII

Les États membres de l'Union internationale pour la protection des œuvres littéraires et artistiques parties à la Convention universelle du droit d'auteur,

Désirant resserrer leurs relations mutuelles sur la base de ladite Union et éviter tout conflit pouvant résulter de la coexistence de la Convention de Berne et de la Convention universelle,

Ont, d'un commun accord, accepté les termes de la déclaration suivante:

a) Les œuvres qui, aux termes de la Convention de Berne, ont comme pays d'origine un pays ayant quitté, postérieurement au 1er janvier 1951, l'Union internationale créée par cette convention, ne seront pas protégées par la Convention universelle du droit d'auteur dans les pays de l'Union de Berne;

b) La Convention universelle du droit d'auteur ne sera pas applicable, dans les rapports entre les pays liés par la Convention de Berne, en ce qui concerne la protection des œuvres qui, aux termes de cette Convention de Berne, ont comme pays d'origine l'un des pays de l'Union internationale créée par cette convention.

Résolution concernant l'article XI

La Conférence intergouvernementale du droit d'auteur,

Ayant considéré les questions relatives au Comité intergouvernemental prévu à l'article XI de la Convention universelle du droit d'auteur,

Prend les décisions suivantes:

1. Les premiers membres du Comité seront les représentants des douze États suivants, à raison d'un représentant et d'un suppléant désigné par chacun de ces États: Allemagne, Argentine, Brésil, Espagne, États-Unis d'Amérique, France, Inde, Italie, Japon, Mexique, Royaume-Uni et Suisse.

2. Le Comité sera constitué dès que la Convention sera entrée en vigueur conformément à l'article XI de cette Convention.

3. Le Comité élira un président et un vice-président. Il établira son règlement intérieur, qui devra sssurer l'application des règles ci-après:

a) La durée normale du mandat des représentants sera de six ans, avec renouvellement par tiers tous les deux ans;

b) Avant l'expiration de la durée du mandat de chaque membre, le Comité décidera quels sont les États qui cessent d'avoir des représentants dans son sein et les États qui seront appelés à désigner des représentants; cesseront en premier lieu d'avoir des représentants dans le Comité les États qui n'auront pas ratifié, accepté ou adhéré;

c) Il sera tenu compte d'une équitable représentation des différentes parties du monde;

Et émet le vœu que l'Organisation des Nations Unies pour l'éducation, la science et la culture assure le secrétariat du Comité.

En foi de quoi les soussignés, ayant déposé leurs pleins pouvoirs respectifs, ont signé la présente Convention.

Fait à Genève, le six septembre 1952, en un exemplaire unique.

PROTOCOLE No 1

annexe à la Convention universelle pour la protection du droit d'auteur, concernant la protection des œuvres des personnes apatrides et des réfugiés

Les États parties à la Convention universelle pour la protection du droit d'auteur (ci-dessous désignée sous le nom de «Convention») et devanant parties au présent Protocole,

Sont convenus des dispositions suivantes:

1. Les personnes apatrides et les réfugiés ayant leur résidence habituelle dans un État contractant sont, pour l'application de la présente Convention, assimilés aux ressortissants de cet État.

2. *a)* Le présent Protocole sera signé et soumis à la ratification ou à l'acceptation par les États signataires, et il pourra y être adhéré, conformément aux dispositions de l'article VIII de la Convention.

b) Le présent Protocole entrera en vigueur pour chaque État à la date du dépôt de l'instrument de ratification, d'acceptation ou d'adhésion y relatif, à condition que cet État soit déjà partie à la Convention.

En foi de quoi les soussignés, dûment autorisés, ont signé le présent Protocole.

Fait à Genève, le 6 septembre 1952, en français, en anglais et en espagnol, les trois textes faisant foi, en un exemplaire unique qui sera déposé auprès du Directeur général de l'Unesco, qui en adressera une copie certifiée conforme aux États signataires, au Conseil fédéral suisse, ainsi qu'au Secrétaire général des Nations Unies pour enregistrement par les soins de celui-ci.

PROTOCOLE No 2

annexe à la Convention universelle pour la protection du droit d'auteur, concernant l'application de la Convention aux œuvres de certaines organisations internationales

Les États parties à la Convention universelle pour la protection du droit d'auteur (ci-dessous désignée sous le nom de «Convention») et devanant parties au présent Protocole,

Sont convenus des dispositions suivantes:

1. *a)* La protection prévue à l'alinéa 1 de l'article II de la Convention universelle pour la protection du droit d'auteur s'applique aux œuvres publiées pour la première fois par l'Organisation des Nations Unies, par les institutions spécialisées reliées aux Nations Unies ou par l'Organisation des États américains.

b) De même la protection prévue à l'alinéa 2 de l'article II de la Convention s'applique aux susdites organisations ou institutions.

2. *a)* Le présent Protocole sera signé et soumis à la ratification ou à l'acceptation par les États signataires, et il pourra y être adhéré, conformément aux dispositions de l'article VIII de la Convention.

b) Le présent Protocole entrera en vigueur pour chaque État à la date du dépôt de l'instrument de ratification, d'acceptation ou d'adhésion y relatif, à condition que cet État soit déjà partie à la Convention.

En foi de quoi les soussignés, dûment autorisés, ont signé le présent Protocole.

Fait à Genève, le 6 septembre 1952, en français, en anglais et en espagnol, les trois textes faisant foi, en un exemplaire unique qui sera déposé auprès du Directeur général de l'Unesco, qui en adressera une copie certifiée conforme aux États signataires, au Conseil fédéral suisse, ainsi qu'au Secrétaire général des Nations Unies pour enregistrement par les soins de celui-ci.

PROTOCOLE No 3

annexe à la Convention universelle pour la protection du droit d'auteur, relatif à la ratification, acceptation ou adhésion conditionnelle

Les États parties au présent Protocole,

Considérant que l'application de la Convention universelle pour la protection du droit d'auteur (ci-dessous désignée sous le nom de «Convention») à des États parties aux divers systèmes existants de protection internationale du droit d'auteur augmenterait considérablement la valeur de la Convention,

Sont convenus de ce qui suit:

1. Tout État partie au présent Protocole pourra, au moment du dépôt de son instrument de ratification, d'acceptation ou d'adhésion, déclarer, par notification écrite, que le dépôt de cet instrument n'aura d'effet, aux fins de l'article IX de la Convention, qu'à la date où un autre État nommément désigné aura déposé son instrument de ratification, d'acceptation ou d'adhésion.

2. La notification prévue au paragraphe 1 ci-dessus sera jointe à l'instrument auquel elle se rapporte.

3. Le Directeur général de l'Organisation des Nations Unies pour l'éducation, la science et la culture informera tous les États qui auraient signé la Convention ou qui y auraient adhéré de toute notification reçue conformément au présent Protocole.

4. Le présent Protocole portera la même date et restera ouvert à la signature durant la même période que la Convention.

5. Le présent Protocole sera soumis à la ratification ou à l'acceptation des États signataires. Tout État qui n'aura pas signé le présent Protocole pourra y adhérer.

6. *a)* La ratification, l'acceptation ou l'adhésion sera opérée par le dépôt d'un instrument à cet effet auprès du Directeur général de l'Organisation des Nations Unies pour l'éducation, la science et la culture.

b) Le présent Protocole entrera en vigueur au moment du dépôt du quatrième instrument de ratification, d'acceptation ou d'adhésion. Le Directeur général informera tous les États intéressés de la date d'entrée en vigueur du Protocole. Les instruments déposés après cette date produiront leurs effets à dater de leur dépôt.

En foi de quoi les soussignés, dûment autorisés, ont signé le présent Protocole.

Fait à Genève, le 6 septembre 1952, en français, en anglais et en espagnol, les trois textes faisant foi, en un exemplaire unique qui sera annexé à l'exemplaire original de la Convention. Le Directeur général an adressera une copie certifiée conforme aux États signataires, au Conseil fédéral suisse, ainsi qu'au Secrétaire général des Nations Unies pour enregistrement par les soins de celui-ci.

TEXT OF THE CONVENTION IN SPANISH

Los Estados contratantes;

Animados del deseo de asegurar en todos los países la protección del derecho de autor sobre las obras literarias, científicas y artísticas;

Convencidos de que un régimen de protección de los derechos de autor adecuado a todas las naciones y formulado en una convención universal, que se una a los sistemas internacionales vigentes sin afectarlos, contribuirá a asegurar el respeto de los derechos de la personalidad humana y a favorecer el desarrollo de las letras, las ciencias y las artes;

Persuadidos de que un tal régimen universal de protección de los derechos de los autores facilitará la difusión de las obras del espíritu y una mejor comprensión internacional,

Han convenido lo siguiente:

Artículo I

Cada uno de los Estados contratantes se compromete a tomar todas las disposiciones necesarias a fin de asegurar una protección suficiente y efectiva de los derechos de los autores, o de cualesquiera otros titulares de estos derechos, sobre las obras literarias, científicas y artísticas tales como los escritos, las obras musicales, dramáticas y cinematográficas y las de pintura, grabado y escultura.

Artículo II

1. Las obras publicadas de los nacionales de cualquier Estado contratante, así como las obras publicadas por primera vez en el territorio de tal Estado gozarán en cada uno de los otros Estados contratantes de la protección que cada uno de estos Estados conceda a las obras de sus nacionales publicadas por primera vez en su propio territorio.

2. Las obras no publicadas de los nacionales de cada Estado contratante gozarán, en cada uno de los demás Estados contratantes, de toda la protección que cada uno de estos Estados conceda a las obras no publicadas de sus nacionales.

3. Para la aplicación de la presente Convención todo Estado contratante puede, mediante disposiciones de su legislación interna, asimilar a sus propios nacionales toda persona domiciliada en ese Estado.

Artículo III

1. Todo Estado contratante que, según su legislación interna, exija como condición para la protección de los derechos de los autores el cumplimiento de formalidades tales como depósito, registro, mención, certificados notariales, pago de tasas, manufactura o publicación en el territorio nacional, considerará satisfechas tales exigencias, para toda obra protegida de acuerdo con los términos de la presente Convención, publicada por primera vez fuera del territorio de dicho Estado por un autor que no sea nacional del mismo, si, desde la primera publicación de dicha obra, todos sus ejemplares, publicados con autorización del autor o de cualquier otro titular de sus derechos, llevan el símbolo © acompañado del nombre del titular del derecho de autor y de la indicación del año de la primera publicación; el símbolo, el nombre y

el año deben ponerse de manera y en sitio tales que muestren claramente que el derecho de autor está reservado.

2. Las disposiciones del párrafo 1 del presente artículo no impedirán a ningún Estado contratante el someter a ciertas formalidades, u otras condiciones, para asegurar el goce y ejercicio del derecho de autor, a las obras publicadas por primera vez en su territorio o a las obras de sus nacionales dondequiera que sean publicadas.

3. Las disposiciones del párrafo 1 de este artículo no impedirán a ningún Estado contratante el exigir de quien reclame ante los Tribunales, que cumpla, al ejercitar la acción, con reglas de procedimiento tales como el ser asistito por un abogado en ejercicio en ese Estado, o el depósito por el demandante de un ejemplar de la obra en litigio en el tribunal, en una oficina administrativa, o en ambos. Sin embargo, el hecho de no haber cumplido con estas exigencias no afectará a la validez del derecho de autor, ni ninguna de esas exigencias podrá ser impuesta a un nacional de otro Estado contratante, si tal exigencia no se impone a los nacionales del Estado donde la protección se reclama.

4. En cada Estado contratante deben arbitrarse los medios legales para proteger, sin formalidades, las obras no publicadas de los nacionales de los otros Estados contratantes.

5. Si un Estado contratante otorga más de un único período de protección, y si el primero es de una duración superior a alguno de los mínimos de tiempo previstos en el artículo IV de la presente Convención dicho Estado tiene la facultad de no aplicar el párrafo 1 del presente artículo III, en lo que se refiere al segundo período de protección, así como a los períodos sucesivos.

Artículo IV

1. La duración de la protección de la obra se regirá por la ley del Estado contratante donde se reclame la protección, de conformidad con las disposiciones del artículo II y con las contenidas en esta artículo.

2. El plazo de protección para las obras protegidas por la presente Convención no será inferior a la vida del autor y 25 años después de su muerte.

Sin embargo, aquellos Estados contratantes que, en la fecha de entrada en vigor en su territorio de la presente Convención, hayan limitado este plazo, para ciertas categorías de obras, a un período calculado a partir de la primera publicación de la obra, tendrán la facultad de mantener tales excepciones o de extenderlas a otras categorías. Para todas estas categorías, la duración de la protección no será inferior a 25 años a contar de la fecha de la primera publicación.

Todo Estado contratante que en la fecha de entrada en vigor de la Convención en su territorio, no calcule la duración de la protección basándose en la vida del autor, podrá calcular el término de protección a contar desde la primera publicación de la obra, o, dado el caso, desde su registro anterior a la publicación; la duración de la protección no será inferior a 25 años a contar desde la fecha de la primera publicación o, dado el caso, desde el registro anterior a la publicación.

Si la legislación de un Estado contratante otorga dos o más plazos de protección consecutivos, la duración del primer plazo no podrá ser inferior a uno de los períodos mínimos que se han especificado anteriormente.

3. Las disposiciones del párrafo 2 de este artículo no se aplican a las obras fotográficas, ni a las de artes aplicadas. Sin embargo, en los Estados contratantes donde se hallen protegidas las obras fotográficas, y como obras artísticas, las de artes aplicadas, la duración de la protección no podrá ser, para tales obras, inferior a 10 años.

4. Ningún Estado contratante estará obligado a proteger una obra durante un plazo mayor que el fijado para la clase de obras a que pertenezca, por la ley del Estado del cual es nacional el autor cuando se trate de una obra no publicada y, en el caso de una obra publicada, por la ley del Estado contratante donde ha sido publicada por primera vez.

Para la aplicación de la disposición anterior, si la legislación de un Estado contratante otorga dos o más' períodos consecutivos de protección, la duración de la protección concedida por dicho Estado será igual a la suma de todos los períodos. Sin embargo, si por una razón cualquiera, una obra determinada no se halla protegida por tal Estado durante el segundo período, o alguno de los períodos sucesivos, los otros Estados contratantes no están obligados a proteger tal obra durante este segundo período o los períodos sucesivos.

5. Para la aplicación del párrafo 4 de este artículo, la obra de un nacional de un Estado contratante, publicada por primera vez en un Estado no contratante, se considerará como si hubiere sido publicada por primera vez en el Estado contratante del cual es nacional el autor.

6. Para la aplicación del mencionado párrafo 4 de este artículo, en caso de publicación simultánea en dos o más Estados contratantes, se considerará que la obra ha sido publicada por primera vez en el Estado que conceda la protección más corta. Será considerada como publicada simultáneamente en varios países toda obra que haya aparecido en dos o más países dentro de los 30 días a partir de su primera publicación.

Artículo V

1. El derecho de autor comprende el derecho exclusivo de hacer, de publicar y de autorizar que se haga y se publique la traducción de las obras protegidas por la presente Convención.

2. Sin embargo, cada Estado contratante podrá restringir en su legislación nacional el derecho de traducción para los escritos, pero sólo ateniéndose a las disposiciones siguientes:

Si a la expiración de un plazo de siete años a contar de la primera publicación de un escrito, la traducción de este escrito no ha sido publicada en la lengua nacional o en una de las lenguas nacionales de un Estado contratante, por el titular del derecho de traducción o con su autorización, cualquier nacional de ese Estado contratante podrá obtener de la autoridad competente de tal Estado una licencia no exclusiva para traducir y publicarla en la lengua nacional en que no haya sido publicada la obra. Tal licencia sólo podrá concederse si el solicitante, conforme a las disposiciones vigentes en el Estado donde se presente la petición, demuestra que ha pedido al titular del derecho la autorización para hacer y publicar la traducción, y que después de haber hecho las diligencias pertinentes no pudo localizar al titular del derecho u obtener su autorización. En las mismas condiciones se podrá conceder igualmente la licencia si están agotadas las ediciones de una traducción ya publicada en una lengua nacional.

Si el titular del derecho de traducción no hubiere sido localizado por el solicitante, éste deberá transmitir copias de su solicitud al editor cuyo nombre aparezca en los ejemplares de la obra y al representante diplomático o consular del Estado del cual sea nacional el titular del derecho de traducción, cuando la nacionalidad del titular de este derecho es conocida, o al organismo que pueda haber sido designado por el gobierno de este Estado. No podrá concederse la licencia antes de la expiración de un plazo de dos meses desde la fecha del envío de la copia de la solicitud.

La legislación nacional adoptará las medidas adecuadas para asegurar al titular del derecho de traducción una remuneración equitativa y de acuerdo con los usos internacionales, así como el pago y el envío de tal remuneración, y para garantizar una correcta traducción de la obra.

El título y el nombre del autor de la obra original deben imprimirse asimismo en todos los ejemplares de la traducción publicada. La licencia sólo será válida para la publicación en el territorio del Estado contratante donde ha sido solicitada. La importación y la venta de los ejemplares en otro Estado contratante serán posibles si tal Estado tiene como lengua nacional aquélla a la cual ha sido traducida la obra, si su legislación nacional permite la licencia y si ninguna de las disposiciones en vigor en tal Estado se opone a la importación y a la venta; la importación y la venta en todo Estado contratante en el cual las condiciones precedentes no se apliquen reservará a la legislación de tal Estado y a los acuerdos concluídos por el mismo. La licencia no podrá ser cedida por su beneficiario.

La licencia no podrá ser concedida en el caso de que el autor haya retirado de la circulación los ejemplares de la obra.

Artículo VI

Se entiende por «publicación», en los terminos de la presente Convención, la reproducción de la obra en forma tangible a la vez que el poner a disposición del público ejemplares de la obra que permitan leerla o conocerla visualmente.

Artículo VII

La presente Convención no se aplicará a aquellas obras, o a los derechos sobre las mismas, que en la fecha de la entrada en vigor de la Convención en el Estado contratante donde se reclama la protección hayan perdido definitivamente la protección en dicho Estado contratante.

Artículo VIII

1. La presente Convención, que llevará la fecha de 6 de septiembre de 1952, será depositada en poder del Director General de la Organización de las Naciones Unidas para la Educación, la Ciencia y la Cultura y quedará abierta a la firma de todos los Estados durante un período de 120 días a partir de su fecha. Será sometida a la ratificación o a la aceptación de los Estados signatarios.

2. Cualquier Estado que no haya firmado la Convención podrá acceder a ella.

3. La ratificación, la aceptación o la accesión, se efectuarán mediante el depósito de un instrumento a tal efecto dirigido al Director General de la Organización de las Naciones Unidas para la Educación, la Ciencia y la Cultura.

Artículo IX

1. La presente Convención entrará en vigor tres meses después del depósito de doce instrumentos de ratificación, de aceptación o de accesión, entre los que deben figurar los depositados por cuatro Estados que no formen parte de la Unión Internacional para la Protección de las Obras Literarias y Artísticas.

2. La Convención entrará en vigor, para cada Estado, tres meses después del depósito de su respectivo instrumento de ratificación, de aceptación o de accesión.

Artículo X

1. Todo Estado contratante se compromete a tomar, de conformidad con su Constitución, las medidas necesarias para asegurar la aplicación de la presente Convención.

2. Se conviene, sin embargo, que, en el momento del depósito de su instrumento de ratificación, de aceptación o de accesión, todo Estado deberá tener su legislación nacional en condiciones de poder aplicar las disposiciones de la presente Convención.

Artículo XI

1. Se crea un Comité Intergubernamental con las siguientes atribuciones:

a) estudiar los problemas relativos a la aplicación y funcionamiento de la presente Convención;

b) preparar las revisiones periódicas di,esta Convención;

c) estudiar cualquier otro problema relativo a la protección internacional del derecho de autor, en colaboración con los diversos organismos internacionales interesados, especialmente con la Organización de las Naciones Unidas para la Educación, la Ciencia y la Cultura, la Unión Internacional para la Protección de las Obras Literarias y Artísticas, y la Organización de Estados Americanos;

d) informar a los Estados contratantes sobre sus trabajos.

2. De acuerdo con la Resolución relativa a este artículo aneja a esta Convención, el Comité se compondrá de representantes de doce Estados contratantes, teniendo en cuenta al designarlos una representación geográfica equitativa.

El Director General de la Organización de las Naciones Unidas para la Educación, la Ciencia y la Cultura; el Director de la Oficina de la Unión Internacional para la Protección de las Obras Literarias y Artísticas, y el Secretario General de la Organización de los Estados Americanos, o sus representantes, podrán asistir a las reuniones del Comité con carácter consultivo.

Artículo XII

El Comité intergubernamental convocará conferencias de revisión siempre que lo crea necesario o cuando lo soliciten por lo menos diez Estados contratantes, o la mayoría de los Estados contratantes si el número de éstos es inferior a veinte:

Artículo XIII

Todo Estado contratante podrá, en el momento del depósito del instrumento de ratificación, de aceptación o de accesión, o con posterioridad, declarar, mediante notificación dirigida al Director General de la Organización de las Naciones Unidas para la Educación, la Ciencia y la Cultura, que la presente Convención es aplicable a todos o parte de los países o territorios cuyas relaciones exteriores ejerza, y la Convención se aplicará entonces a los países o territorios designados en la notificación, a partir de la expiración del plazo de tres meses previsto en el artículo IX. En defecto de esta notificación, la presente Convención no se aplicará a esos países o territorios.

Artículo XIV

1. Todo Estado contratante tendrá la facultad de denunciar la presente Convención, en su propio nombre, o en nombre de todos o de parte de los países o territorios que hayan sido objeto de la notificación prevista en el artículo XIII. La denuncia se efectuará mediante notificación dirigida al Director General de la Organización de las Naciones Unidas para la Educación, la Ciencia y la Cultura.

2. Tal denuncia no producirá efecto sino con respecto al Estado, país o territorio, en nombre del cual se haya hecho, y solamente doce meses después de la fecha en que la notificación se haya recibido.

Artículo XV

Toda diferencia entre dos o varios Estados contratantes respecto a la interpretación o a la aplicación de la presente Convención, que no sea resuelta por vía de negociación, será llevada ante la Corte Internacional de Justicia para que ésta decida, a menos que los Estados interesados convengan otro modo de solucionarla.

Artículo XVI

1. La presente Convención será redactada en francés, inglés y español. Los tres textos serán firmados y harán igualmente fe.

2. Serán redactados textos oficiales de la presente Convención en alemán, italiano y portugués.

Todo Estado contratante, o grupo de Estados contratantes, podrá hacer redactar por el Director General de la Organización de las Naciones Unidas para la Educación, la Ciencia y la Cultura, y de acuerdo con éste, otros textos en las lenguas que elija. Todos estos textos se añadirán, como anejos, al texto firmado de la Convención.

Artículo XVII

1. La presente Convención no afectará en nada a las disposiciones de la Convención de Berna para la protección de las obras literarias y artísticas, ni al hecho de pertenecer a la Unión creada por esta Convención.

2. En aplicación del párrafo precedente, aparece una declaración como anejo del presente artículo. Esta Declaración forma parte integrante de la presente Convención para los Estados ligados por la Convención de Berna el 1º de enero de 1951, o que se hayan adherido a ella ulteriormente. La firma de la presente Convención por los Estados arriba mencionados implica, al mismo tiempo, la firma de la mencionada Declaración, y su ratificación, aceptación o accesión por esos Estados, significa a la par la de la Declaración y de la Convención.

Artículo XVIII

La presente Convención no deroga las convenciones o acuerdos multilaterales o bilaterales sobre derecho de autor que se hallan o puedan hallarse en vigor exclusivamente entre dos o más repúblicas americanas. En caso de divergencia, ya sea entre las disposiciones de cualquiera de dichas convenciones o acuerdos existentes, de una parte, y las disposiciones de esta Convención de otra, o entre las disposiciones de esta Convención y las de cualquiera otra nueva convención o acuerdo que se concierte entre dos o más repúblicas americanas, después de la entrada en vigor de la presente Convención, prevalecerá entre las partes la Convención o acuerdo redactato más recientemente. Los derechos adquiridos sobre una obra en cualquier Estado contratante en virtud de convenciones y acuerdos existentes con anterioridad a la fecha en que esta Convención entre en vigor en tal Estado, no serán afectados por la misma.

Artículo XIX

La presente Convención no deroga las convenciones o acuerdos multilaterales o bilaterales sobre derecho de autor vigentes entre dos o más Estados contratantes. En caso de divergencia entre las disposiciones de una de dichas convenciones o de esos acuerdos, y las disposiciones de esta Convención, prevalecerán las disposiciones de esta última. No serán afectados los derechos adquiridos sobre una obra en virtud de convenciones o acuerdos en vigor en uno de los Estados contratantes con anterioridad a la fecha de entrada en vigor de la presente Convención en dicho Estado. El presente artículo no afectará en nada las disposiciones de los artículos XVII y XVIII de la presente Convención.

Artículo XX

No se permitirán reservas a la presente Convención.

Artículo XXI

El Director General de la Organización de las Naciones Unidas para la Educación, la Ciencia y la Cultura enviará copias debidamente autorizadas de la presente Convención a los Estados interesados y al Consejo de la Confederación Helvética, así como al Secretario General de las Naciones Unidas, para que las registre.

También informará a todos los Estados interesados del depósito de los instrumentos de ratificación, aceptación o accesión; de la fecha de entrada en vigor de la presente Convención; de las notificaciones previstas en el artículo XIII y de las denuncias previstas en el artículo XIV.

Declaración aneja relativa al artículo XVII

1. Los Estados miembros de la Unión Internacional para la Protección de las Obras Literarias y Artísticas, signatarios de la Convención Universal sobre Derecho de Autor, deseando estrechar sus lazos mutuos sobre la base de la mencionada Unión y evitar todo conflicto que pudiera surgir de la coexistencia de la Convención de Berna y de la Convención Universal, han acaptado, de común acuerdo, los términos de la siguiente declaración:

a) Las obras que, según la Convención de Berna, tengan como país de origen un país que se haya retirado de la Unión Internacional creada por esta Convención, después del 1° de enero de 1951, no serán protegidas por la Convención Universal sobre Derecho de Autor en los países de la Unión de Berna.

b) La Convención Universal sobre Derecho de Autor no será applicable en las relaciones entre los Estados ligados por la Convención de Berna, en lo que se refiera a la protección de las obras que, de acuerdo con esta Convención de Berna, tengan como país de origen uno de los países de la Unión Internacional creada por dicha Convención.

Resolución relativa al artículo XI

La Conferencia Intergubernamental sobre Derecho de Autor,

Habiendo considerado los problemas relativos al Comité Intergubernamental previsto por el artículo XI de la Convención Universal sobre Derecho de Autor, Resuelve:

1. los primeros miembros del Comité şerán los representantes de los doce Estados siguientes, cada uno de los cuales designará un representante y un suplente: Alemania, Argentina, Brasil, España, Estados Unidos de América, Francia, India, Italia, Japón, México, Reino Unido y Suiza.

2. El Comité se constituirá tan pronto entre en vigor la Convención, conforme al artículo XI de la presente Convención.

3. El Comité eligirá su presidente y su vicepresidente. Establecerá su reglamanto interno basándose en los principios siguientes:

a) La duración normal de los mandatos de los representantes será de seis años; cada dos años se retirará una tercera parte de los representantes;

b) Antes de la expiración del mandato de cualquiera de sus miembros, el Comité decidirá cuáles de los Estados dejarán de estar representados y cuáles de los Estados han de disignar representantes; los representantes de aquellos Estados que no hubieren ratificado, aceptado o accedido, se retirarán los primeros;

c) Las diversas partes del mundo estarán equitativamente representadas en su seno;

Y formula el voto de que la Organización de las Naciones Unidas para la Educación, la Ciencia y la Cultura, garantice la Secretaría del Comité.

En fe de lo cual, los infrascritos, que han depositado sus plenos poderes, firman la presente Convención.

En la ciudad de Ginebra, a los seis días de septiembre de 1952, en ejemplar único.

PROTOCOLO 1

anejo a la Convención Universal sobre Derecho de Autor relativo a la aplicación de la Convención a las obras de apatridas y refugiados

Los Estados partes en el presente Protocolo, que también lo son de la Convención Universal sobre Derecho de Autor (en adelante denominada la «Convención») han aceptado las siguientes disposiciones:

1. Los apátridas y los refugiados que tengan su residencia habitual en un Estado contratante serán, para los efectos de la presente Convención, asimilados a los nacionales de ese Estado.

2. *a*) El presente Protocolo se firmará y se someterá a la ratificación, aceptación o accesión come si las disposiciones del Artículo VIII de la Convención se aplicaran al mismo.

b) El presente Protocole entrará en vigor, para cada Estado, en la fecha del depósito del instrumento de ratificación, aceptación o accesión del Estado interesado o en la fecha de entrada en vigor de la Convención con respecto a tal Estado, de acuerdo con la fecha que sea posterior.

En fe de lo cual, los infrascritos, estando debidamente autorizados para ello, firman el presente Protocolo.

En la ciudad de Ginebra, a los seis días del mes de septiembre de 1952, en inglés, francés y español, siendo igualmente auténticos los tres textos, en una sola copia, la cual será depositada con el Director General de la Organización de las Naciones Unidas para la Educación, la Ciencia y la Cultura. El Director General enviará copias certificadas a los Estados signatarios y al Consejo de la Confederación Helvética, así como al Secretario General de las Naciones Unidas para su registro.

PROTOCOLO 2

anejo a la Convención Universal sobre Derecho de Autor relativo a la aplicación de la Convención a las obras de ciertas organizaciones internacionales

Los Estados partes en el presente Protocolo, y que son partes igualmente en la Convención Universal sobre derecho de autor (en adelante denominada la «Convención») han adoptado las disposiciones siguientes:

1. *a*) La protección prevista en el artículo II.1 de la Convención se aplicará a las obras publicadas por primera vez por las Naciones Unidas, por las instituciones especializadas ligadas a ellas, o por la Organización de Estados Americanos.

b) Igualmente el artículo II.2 de la Convención se aplicará a dichas organizaciones e instituciones.

2. *a*) El Protocolo se firmará y se someterá a la ratificación, aceptación o accesión come si las disposiciones del artículo VIII de la Convención se aplicara al mismo.

b) El presente Protocol entrará en vigor para cada Estado en la fecha del depósito del instrumento de ratificación, aceptación o accesión del Estado interesado o en la fecha de entrada en vigor de la Convención con respecto a tal Estado, de acuerdo con la fecha que sea posterior.

En fe de lo cual, los infranscritos, estando debidamente autorizados para ello, firman el presente Protocolo.

Firmado en la ciudad de Ginebra, a los 6 días del mes de septiembre de 1952, en inglés, francés y español, siendo igualmente auténticos los tres textos, en una sola copia la cual será depositada ante el Director General de la Organización de las Naciones Unidas para la Educación, la Ciencia y la Cultura. El Director General enviará copias certificadas a los Estados signatarios y al Secretario General de las Naciones Unidas para su registro.

PROTOCOLO 3

anejo a la Convención Universal sobre Derecho de Autor, relativo a la fecha efectiva de los instrumentos de ratificación, aceptatión o accesión a dicha Convención

Los Estados partes,

Reconociendo que la aplicación de la Convención Universal sobre Derecho de Autor (en adelante denominada «la Convención») en los Estados participantes en los sistemas internacionales de Derecho de Autor, actualmente en vigencia, contribuirá grandemente a la importancia de esta Convención;

Han acordado lo siguiente:

1. Cada Estado parte en el presente Protocolo podrá, al depositar su instrumento de ratificación, aceptación o accesión a la Convención, notificar al Director General de la Organización de las Naciones Unidas para la Educación, la Ciencia y la Cultura (en adelante denominado «el Director General») que tal instrumento no tendrá efecto para los propósitos del artículo IX de la Convención hasta tanto cualquier otro Estado citado por nombre en tal notificación hubiere depositado su instrumento.

2. La notificación a que se refiere el párrafo 1 anterior acompañará el instrumento al cual corresponde.

3. El Director General informará a todos los Estados signatarios o a aquellos que hubieren accedido hasta entonces a la Convención de las notificaciones recibidas conformes al presente Protocolo.

4. El presente Protocolo llevará la misma fecha y quedará abierto a firma durante el mismo período de la Convención.

5. El presente Protocolo se someterá a la ratificación o aceptación de los Estados signatarios. Cualquier Estado que no haya firmado el presente Protocolo podrá acceder al mismo.

6. *a)* Su ratificación, aceptación o accesión se efectuará por medio del depósito del instrumento respectivo ante el Director General.

b) El presente Protocolo entrará en vigor en la fecha del depósito de no menos de cuatro instrumentos de ratificación, aceptación o accesión. El Director General informará a los Estados interesados de tal fecha. Los instrumentos depositados después de tal fecha, entrarán en vigor en la fecha de deposito.

En fe de lo cual, los infrascritos, estando debidamente autorizados para ello, firman al presente Protocolo.

Firmado en la ciudad de Ginebra, a los seis días del mes de septiembre de 1952, en inglés, francés y español, siendo igualmente auténticos los tres textos, en una sola copia, la cual aparecerá como anejo al texto original de la Convención. El Director General enviará copias certificadas a los Estados signatarios, y al Consejo Federal de la Confederación Helvética, así como al Secretario-General de las Naciones Unidas para su registro.

REPORT OF THE RAPPORTEUR-GENERAL

It is now my duty as Rapporteur-Général of the Conference to present my report. I am afraid that it is a long one, but its length is a reflection of the earnest and concentrated endeavours of all delegations over the past three weeks. Even so, this report can be no more than a faint echo of the serious discussions and considerations which have engaged the attention of us all. It has been prepared in great haste and I apologize for its inadequacies.

The Conference sat in public and was attended by delegations from 50 nations and by observers from nine intergovernmental organizations and six non-governmental organizations.

The Conference was the logical development of the desire expressed by many nations for many years and on many different occasions for some international agreement on the rights of authors which would be acceptable to the member States of the Berne Union for the Protection of Literary and Artistic Works, and to the members of the Organization of American States, and if possible, also to those other States which were not members of either. The work of the Copyright Division of Unesco, under the able direction of Mr. François Hepp, and the work of the committees of experts convened by the Division, had crystallized the desire into a definite project, which was given shape at the Sixth Session of the General Conference of Unesco held in Paris in 1951. This was the origin of the Draft Universal Copyright Convention (DA/2) considered at the present Conference, which is referred to in this report as the "programme text". It is thanks to this careful preparatory work, which had fully explored all practical possibilities and exposed the dangers and difficulties underlying the project, that the Conference has made rapid headway and been brought to a successful conclusion.

The work of the Conference has been facilitated by and certainly could not have been achieved in so brief a period as three weeks but for the excellent accommodation and technical services for simultaneous translation provided by the Government of Switzerland and the most able work of the translators and of the secretariat provided by Unesco. The Conference has had a most helpful and excellent secretary in Dr. Arpad Bogsch of the Copyright Division. Moreover, success could never have been achieved at this Conference but for the spirit of co-operation and goodwill shown by all the delegations and their manifest desire to understand and make allowances for the difficulties and points of view of other delegations and for the different concepts of copyright law in other countries. All strove to bring into being not merely a convention acceptable to the largest possible number of States, but also a convention which would be effective in producing a real improvement in the international copyright position and in securing as wide a recognition as possible throughout the world of the fundamental rights of authors.

OPENING PLENARY SESSION

The Conference was opened on 18 August by Mr. Torres Bodet, the Director-General of Unesco, who paid a well-deserved tribute to the preliminary work which had been achieved in bringing the Conference into being, and to the part played by the Berne Union in achieving a high standard of international protection of the works of authors.

The Conference was warmly welcomed to Geneva by Federal Counsellor Mr. Max Petitpierre, and by Mr. Picot, Vice-President of the State Council of Geneva. I take this opportunity of extending to them, and recording, the cordial thanks of the Conference and of expressing our appreciation of the traditional role played by Switzerland in the international protection of the works of authors. The foresight and hospitality of Switzerland were responsible for the foundation of the Brene Union in 1886 and have contributed since then at all times to the continued improvement and widening of that Union. And now Switzerland is instrumental in sponsoring the formation of what we all hope will be an even more comprehensive international convention. It is our earnest desire that the new Convention, whilst being complementary to the other great international conventions in the field of copyright, will be acceptable to all States and will gather strength as time goes on to serve the high purpose for which it is designed.

The first act of the opening plenary session of the Conference was to elect Mr. Plinio Bolla as President, on the proposal of Mr. Marcel Plaisant, the chief delegate of France, seconded by Mr. Luther Evans, chief delegate of the United States of America. Both paid tribute to Mr. Bolla's qualities as an international jurist and as a leader of thought in the field of copyright, and no words of mine are necessary to record the charming and brilliant way in which he has conducted our proceedings and brought them to a satisfactory conclusion, surmounting in friendly and firm manner the many formidable tasks which have faced him as President and steering us successfully past many dangers which, but for his careful control and wise counsel, might well have wrecked our whole endeavour.

CREDENTIALS COMMITTEE, STEERING COMMITTEE AND DRAFTING COMMITTEE

The Conference then selected a Credentials Committee under the chairmanship of Mr. Julio Dantas, chief delegate of Portugal, consisting of distinguished diplomatic members of the Conference, namely, in addition to their chairman, delegates of France, Japan, Sweden, the United States of America and Uruguay. Of the 50 delegations present, 44 presented credentials empowering them to sign a convention.

Following a meeting of the chiefs of delegations, the Conference decided to appoint nine vice-presidents, instead of six as proposed in the draft rules of procedure. The heads of the following delegations were then appointed as vice-presidents: Brazil, Dr. Ildefonso Mascarenhas da Silva; Canada, Dr. Victor L. Doré; France, Mr. Marcel Plaisant; Germany, Dr. Eugen Ulmer; India, Mr. B. N. Lokur; Italy, Dr. Antonio Pennetta; Mexico, Dr. Germán Fernández del Castillo; Spain, Mr. M. Sebastian de Erice O'Shea; United States of America, Dr. Luther H. Evans.

The Conference also appointed me, chief delegate of the United Kingdom, to act as Rapporteur-Général.

It was agreed that the Steering Committee should consist of the President of the Conference, the Chairman of the Credentials Committee, the nine vice-presidents and the Rapporteur-Général.

It was also agreed to appoint a Drafting Committee of nine members to be entrusted with the tentative drawing up of the text of the Convention in three languages. The Drafting Committee was divided into three groups, each designed to accept responsibility for the preparation of the text in one language. Mr. Puget of France was appointed chairman of the Drafting Committee; Mr. Guislain of Belgium and Mr. Bodenhausen of the Netherlands, were appointed to complete the French group. Mr. Fisher of the United States, Mr. Wilmot of Australia and Mr. Girling of the United Kingdom, were appointed to form the English group. Mr. Forns of Spain, Mr. Mendilaharzu of Argentina and Mr. Chediak of Cuba were appointed to form the Spanish group.

RULES OF PROCEDURE

The Conference made rapid progress in considering the draft rules of procedure. A new rule, 10 *bis*, was approved to provide for the Drafting Committee, and the remaining draft rules were quickly dealt with and adopted, modified in view of the appointment of a Drafting Committee and of nine vice-chairmen, *except* Rule 17 dealing with the working languages of the Conference. In that connexion, Mr. Dantas, on behalf of the delegations of Portugal and Brazil, proposed that Portuguese be made a working language of the Conference. He stressed the historic importance of Portugal in the world of culture and asked other delegations to accept Portuguese as a working language. It was, however, pointed out that the adoption of this proposal would create practical difficulties for the secretariat of the Conference.

Ultimately, the President, Mr. Bolla, announced that this difficult question had been satisfactorily settled. He paid tribute to Portugal and the Portuguese language and pointed out that Rule 19 of the Rules of Procedure permitted delegates to speak in any language, and fortunately the official interpreters of the Conference could translate from Portuguese. The Portuguese and Brazilian delegates would accordingly be free to address the Conference in Portuguese if they so desired. In these circumstances the delegations of Portugal and Brazil did not press their proposal but they reserved the right to raise the question of the use of the Portuguese language at future conferences of Unesco, and regarded the present arrangement as being without prejudice to the general question. The Rules of Procedure were then approved (DA/10 rev.).

GENERAL OPENING DISCUSSION

The chief delegate of Italy opened the general discussion by expressing appreciation of the preliminary work done by the Copyright Division of Unesco, and by recalling that it was in Rome in 1928, at the instance of Brazil and France, that the idea of a universal convention had its origin. He was most happy at the prospect of a universal convention, provided that such a convention in no way threatened or impaired the Berne Union, that is to say, provided that Article XV and Protocol of the programme text were, in substance, adopted. Mr. Mentha, the Director of the Bureau of the Berne Union, expressed warm thanks to Mr. Pennetta.

The chief delegate of Cuba (Dr. Remos) expressed the view that an author should possess the fullest possible rights and that the right of translation should not be subject to restriction.

The chief delegate of Japan (Mr. Haguiwara) suggested that the object of the Convention should be to attract the greatest number of participants rather than to aim at a high standard of protection, which might deter certain countries from joining. He therefore entered a plea for a restriction of the right of translation.

The chief delegate of the United Kingdom felt that the Universal Convention should be regarded as the first step to a just world protection of coypright. At this stage a high level of protection should not be sought. He hoped delegates would not judge proposals before the Conference by what would be best suited to their own legislation, but would always consider whether acceptance of proposals would be difficult for other countries.

The chief delegate of the United States thought that fears of damage to the Berne Convention by the Universal Convention had probably been overcome and appealed to the Berne Union countries to have special regard for the position of other countries and not to insist upon too high a standard of protection.

The chief delegate of France made a special appeal to the United States to ratify the Convention. He considered that the Convention could not come into force until ratified by that country.

The delegates of Greece, Liberia, India, Switzerland, Mexico and Spain also spoke.

MAIN COMMISSION

The conference then proceeded to sit as a Main Commission. It was agreed that individual speeches should be limited to 10 minutes and that advisers and experts should be permitted to participate in debates subject to the approval of the chief of their delegation.

WORKING PARTIES

It was agreed also to appoint working parties on special matters to expedite the proceedings and that the discussion in the Main Commission should be limited, when a working party reported back, to two speeches of five minutes each for each delegation. One working party under the chairmanship of Mr. Haguiwara, chief delegate of Japan, was appointed to consider the Preamble and Articles VIII, XI, XII, XIII and XIV of the programme text before these were discussed in detail in the Main Commission. In this Working Party were included representatives of all countries having more than two delegates. A representative of Uruguay was subsequently added to the Party. Another working party was appointed under the chairmanship of Mr. Pennetta, chief delegate of Italy, to consider Articles IX and X on Administration, before discussion of them in the Main Commission. Representatives of Cuba, France, Mexico, the Netherlands, the United Kingdom and the U.S.A. were appointed to this Working Party.

The Main Commission then proceeded to consider the Preamble and Draft Articles of the programme text one by one prior to their reference to the Drafting Committee. The texts prepared by the Drafting Committee were then considered in Plenary Session which finally adopted the text of the Convention and annexed Resolution, Declaration and Protocols as signed.

In what follows in this report, the work of the Main Commission and Plenary Session will be noted Article by Article in numerical order irrespective of the time or order of discussion. The discussions referred to took place in general in the Main Commission unless reference is made specially to the Plenary Session. Also, for convenience in future reference, the Articles will be referred to by their numbers in the signed text unless the contrary is stated.

THE PREAMBLE

As regards the Preamble, the chairman of the working party reported to the Main Commission that they had had the advantage of having before them a draft prepared by Mr. Marcel Plaisant, chief delegate of France, at the request of the Steering Committee, and had based on this as well as on the programme draft their work in preparing the text presented by them to the Main Commission. This text had regard to the desire of some delegations to refer to human rights and also to the desire of others to avoid reference to *"droit moral"*. When the Preamble was discussed in the Main Commission some delegations favoured the introduction into the Preamble of a reference to the Declaration of Human Rights, but the United States Delegation pointed out that, keen supporters as they were of the Declaration, it seemed to them that the covenants implementing the Declaration, and not the present Convention, were the proper place for references to it. The delegate of France said that the Berne Convention was universal and suggested that the reference in the draft Preamble to "a universal system of copyright" should be replaced by a reference to "a system open to all States and contained in a universal convention". This point was left for the Drafting Committee, and the text of the Preamble was adopted.

ARTICLE I

In discussing Article I in the Main Commission, some delegations were of the opinion that the works to be protected should be specified but only by way of example and not by way of limitation. Among works suggested for inclusion in the enumeration were oral works, works of architecture, engraving and national art, works of dramatic art, technical drawings and translations. Other delegations were of the opinion that such enumeration was dangerous, both because it might be read limitatively and because the inclusion of certain works would make it difficult for certain countries to join the Convention. For example, the Constitution of the United States of America would not permit the protection of works of architecture whilst in other countries works of applied art were the subject of independent forms of protection. Canada suggested (DA/31) that the works should not be enumerated but that the Article should refer briefly to literary and artistic works in any form, the word "scientific" being in their view unnecessary. The President explained that the word "scientific" was considered necessary to cover clearly such things as logarithm tables and works on nuclear physics. A proposal by Yugoslavia (DA/27) that works of national art and folklore be specified was defeated.

Again, some delegations were of the opinion that the Article should specify or guarantee the rights to be conferred on authors, such as rights of reproduction and performance. The possibilities and dangers of such an enumeration of rights, either limitatively or by way of example, were discussed. A proposal by Greece (DA/43) including a reference to the "*droit moral*" of the author was defeated. Canada suggested (DA/31) that the Article might refer to reproduction, representation or communication through any medium. Finally the delegations of France, Italy, the United States of America and the United Kingdom made a joint proposal (DA/48) following the general wording of the draft Article but referring also to works of engraving, and this was adopted.

A later proposal by Spain (DA/19) for a new Article defining copyright to include the exclusive right to make or authorize adaptations, arrangements and other transformations of a work was rejected, having regard to the decision taken by the Main Commission in connexion with Article 1 that the rights conferred on authors by the Convention should not be enumerated in it. The President indicated that it was considered that these rights should include those given to authors by civilized countries but that an enumeration was dangerous, because it might read limitatively.

ARTICLE II AND PROTOCOLS 1 AND 2

As Article II stated the general principle of national treatment whereby each Contracting State undertakes to extend to works originating in the other States the protection it gives to works of its own nationals, the general principle being subject to the special provisions or exceptions of Articles III, IV and V on formalities, duration and translation rights (for example, Article III limiting formalities for works originating in other States whilst leaving a State free to impose what formalities it chooses on works of its own nationals), there were few objections to paragraph 2 of the programme text of the Article, but as regards paragraph 1 some delegations suggested in the Main Commission that published works must be protected solely according to their country of first publication, as was done in the Berne Convention. Other delegations pointed out that published works were protected in some parts of the world according to the nationality of the author, and that paragraph 1 was a compromise in the nature of a fusion of both ideas and so providing the widest scope for the protection of published works. A proposal by Japan (DA/16), intended to exclude from protection certain works not protected in their country of origin, was defeated. A proposal by Yugoslavia (DA/49), intended to allow Contracting States to restrict the protection given to published works of nationals of non-Contracting States which do not sufficiently protect the works of authors of any Contracting State, was also defeated.

It was agreed to appoint a working party to consider the Unesco proposal to protect works of the United Nations and like international organizations, and it was pointed out that works first published, or the copyright of which is owned, by these organizations were those to be considered. The chief delegate of Mexico, Mr. Fernández del

Castillo, was appointed chairman of the party, and the other countries appointed to it were Belgium, Cuba, Germany, Italy, the Netherlands, Spain, the United Kingdom and the United States of America. It was agreed that observers from Specialized Agencies, the United Nations and the Organization of American States could also attend the meetings of the working party, if they so desired. The working party's report suggested a protocol (2 as signed) on this subject and this suggestion was adopted. There were difficulties about extra-territoriality, about the status of international organizations as legal persons, and about the vesting of copyright in those organizations, and the protocol was intended to avoid these. In its first paragraph, it extended the protection provided by the Convention to works first published by the United Nations Organization, by Specialized Agencies in relationship with the United Nations, and also, at the request of the Organization of American States, by the last-named organization. Its second paragraph assimilated the specified organizations and agencies to nationals of Contracting States. The Director of the Berne Bureau stated that this approach was not contrary to the rule that only natural persons could produce original works. Japan would have preferred to extend the benefits of the Convention to other international organizations. When the Protocol was considered in Plenary Session, India asked whether the publications of the Intergovernmental Committee to be referred to in the Convention could not be included, but the President pointed out that this committee was not likely to have much time for writing publications and that these would, in any case, probably be published by Unesco.

As regards paragraph 3 of the programme text of Article II, some States including the Holy See, were of the opinion that the works of stateless persons and political refugees should be specifically protected, but others thought that this was unnecessary or might raise difficulties in defining such persons in national legislations. The Convention for the Protection of Stateless Persons, with its industrial property clauses, was referred to as rendering paragraph 3 unnecessary, but attention was drawn to the fact that the Convention had not yet been ratified by many States. Some delegations pointed out, however, that the protection of all works first published in Contracting States as specified in the agreed paragraph 1 of the Article would cover most works of stateless persons, and therefore complication of the Convention in this respect might well be avoided by cancelling paragraph 3. The United States indicated that, for the purpose of their domestic copyright law, domicile must be regarded as the equivalent of nationality, and for this reason they proposed an extension of the paragraph to include not only stateless persons but all persons who had adopted one of the Contracting States as their permanent home. Opinions were divided as to whether nationals of one Contracting State, who published works in that State but resided permanently in another Contracting State, should be assimilated to nationals of the latter for the purposes of the present Convention. France proposed that a provision designed to prevent such assimilation should be included in paragraph 3. The United States intimated, however, that they could not accept the implications of Article III on formalities without being allowed to assimilate persons domiciled in the United States to their own nationals for the purpose of formalities, and that acceptance by the Conference of this French proposal would make it impossible for the United States to ratify the Convention. France thereupon withdrew the proposal. A joint proposal was made by France, the Netherlands, Sweden, the United Kingdom and the United States of America (DA/74 rev.) to replace the draft paragraph 3 by two provisions, one requiring a Contracting State to assimilate to its nationals all stateless persons and refugees habitually risiding there, and a second allowing a Contracting State to assimilate to its own nationals any person who is domiciled therein. It was decided that the first provision should form the subject of a protocol (1 as signed) to the Convention and that the second should be adopted to form a new paragraph 3 to the Article.

The Netherlands proposed (DA/47) that a reference to legal bodies incorporated in a Contracting State should be added to paragraph 3 of Article II. Some delegations were of the opinion that the word "nationals" in the Article included legal and moral persons as well as physical persons, but Liberia pointed out that the works of incorporated bodies were not necessarily and automatically protected in that country. The President suggested that it was a matter for each Contracting State to interpret the word "nationals" according to its own rule of law; the Convention was not to be regarded as imposing on any Contracting State the obligation of recognizing for copyright purposes legal and moral persons as well as physical persons, but only as requiring that a State should apply the same interpretation to foreign nationals as to its own nationals; for example, a State protecting the works of its own incorporated bodies should protect also the works of such bodies of other Contracting States. On this understanding the Netherlands proposal was withdrawn.

The right of the publisher of *anonymous or pseudonymous works* to sue for infringement was raised by Austria. Several countries considered that questions concerning such works required consideration in connexion with more than one article of the Convention and the matter was referred to a working party consisting of delegates of Austria, Belgium, Brazil, France and the United States of America under the chairmanship of Mr. Guislain of Belgium. The working party left to the Main Commission the decision whether any provision dealing particularly with anonymous and pseudonymous works was really necessary in the Convention, but presented a text (DA/128) which reflected the results of their discussions and which stated that the rights of the author in such works ought to be exercised by the copyright proprietor or by the publisher, depending on the law of the State where protection was claimed. The Main Commission decided that it was not necessary to include this in the Convention.

When Article II was considered in the Plenary Session, it was made clear that the French word "ressortissants" was to be considered as equivalent to the English word "nationals".

Article III

When the Main Commission proceeded to discuss Article III on formalities, the United Kingdom intimated that the adoption of this Article was vital if their country were to accept the Convention. The United States made it clear that the provisions of the Article on formalities could be accepted by them only with reference to the first term of protection of 28 years in the United States law, and on the understanding that formalities to secure the second term of 28 years, as provided for in that law, were not excluded. India suggested (DA/53) that a State should not require even the symbol © on works already published in another Contracting State before the effective date of the Convention.

Mexico stated that a requirement for publication in the State where protection is claimed is a condition of copyright and proposed (DA/67) that publication be listed as another example of formality in paragraph 1.

Some delegations proposed that the affixing of the symbol © upon any copies of a work should imply that the symbol had been applied to all copies of the work, the onus of proof to the contrary devolving upon a defendant. The United States explained that the existence of the symbol © upon all copies would be proved in their country by producing one copy bearing the symbol and by testimony that the symbol appeared upon all copies, the onus then being on the other party to prove that all copies did not bear the symbol. A proposal by Austria (DA/37), that a printed copy of a work bearing the symbol should constitute *prima facie* evidence that all published copies bore the symbol was not pressed, and the President suggested that this was a rule of procedure too detailed for inclusion in the Convention, but rather one to be followed by judges.

Germany proposed (DA/46) that the Article should contain a provision to the effect that unpublished works should be protected without formalities. The United States explained that in their country unpublished works were protected by the common law, without formalities, and could also obtain statutory protection by registration. They would therefore support the German proposal provided it was understood that the United States was free to continue formalities for statutory copyright of unpublished works, so long as they gave protection to unpublished works without formality by another means, that is, by the common law.

Some delegates were doubtful whether paragraph 3 of the Article should provide for deposit of copies of the work with an administrative office as well as with the Court, but this appeared to others to be a detailed matter of procedure which must be left to the country where the action was brought.

France and the Netherlands proposed (DA/71) that works which exist in a sole original copy or in a few copies only, such as works of painting or sculpture, should be assimilated to published works if they bear the symbol © from their first communication to the public. The President explained that such works would be regarded as published or unpublished according to the definition of publication to be agreed under Article VI, and that in cases where they were so regarded as published, they could obtain the benefit of Article III if the author ensured that the symbol was placed on all copies of the works published. On this understanding, the proposal was not pressed.

Finally, a proposal by France, Italy, Spain, the United Kingdom and the United States of America (DA/98) provided a revised and enlarged wording of Article III to take account as far as possible of the views of delegates expressed in the discussion, and was adopted by the Main Commission, subject to the possible reconsideration and revision of the last paragraph (dealing with formalities in relation to a second term of protection) when Article IV on the duration of copyright had been settled. Such revision appeared unnecessary when the Article was adopted in Plenary Session. It was the intention that the particular kinds of formalities specified in paragraph 1 are listed as examples only and not limitatively and that paragraphs 1 and 4 together would provide for the protection of published and unpublished works without formalities, except for the requirement for the symbol © if the work were published within the meaning of the definition of Article VI.

ARTICLE IV

Article IV on the duration of copyright proved to be one of the most controversial articles. Some delegations expressed in the Main Commission a strong preference for the principle recognized in Article 7 of the Berne Convention whereby protection is given until the end of a period of years counted from the death of the author. Several delegations were opposed to any possibility of protection ceasing before the death of the author and thought that an overall period of 25 years was too short. These delegations therefore preferred paragraphs 1 and 2 of Proposition C of the programme text. Japan suggested (DA/17) that the period of protection for cinematographic and photographic works and recordings of musical works be left to national legislations. Other delegations pointed out that the principle of a fixed term of protection following first publication was inherent in the law of the United States, and that the possibility of such a form of protection must be retained if the Convention was to attract that country. They therefore preferred paragraphs 1 and 2 of Proposition A or B. The United Kingdom observed that a country might adopt both principles, the Berne principle for most works and the American principle for others, and they understood Propositions A and B as not precluding this: the United Kingdom belonged to the Berne Union but might desire to give or to continue to give a fixed duration of protection to certain special kinds of works, and considered it unwise to complicate the Convention by attempting to make special exceptions for special kinds of works, as would in any case seem necessary if Proposition C were retained.

Many delegations supported the principle of comparison of terms expressed in paragraph 3 of Proposition B or C, arguing that this was similar to a provision of the Berne Convention prior to the Brussels revision; that it was just; and that it might serve to provide an incentive to any country granting a relatively short term of protection to increase this term. Some delegations considered that a work not protected in its own country need not be protected in other States. Some delegations pointed out that the programme text of paragraph 3 was not clear in a number of respects, including its application to cases where copyright was renewable for a second period. The United States preferred Proposition A and were unfavourable to the provisions of paragraph 3 of Proposition B or C: they doubted whether this principle of comparison of terms would be effective as an incentive, and they pointed to the manifold complications which it introduced in practice.

After considerable discussion, a joint proposal was made by Austria, Denmark, Finland, France, Italy, Mexico, Norway, Sweden, the United Kingdom and the United States of America (DA/137), elaborating paragraphs 2 and 3 of Proposition B to meet the criticisms which had been expressed in the discussion. The joint proposal was amended to define "simultaneous publication", a matter which some countries thought might be left to national legislation. The revised and amended joint proposal was finally adopted. It indicated in its second paragraph that the general duration of protection under the Convention should not be less than the life of the author and 25 years after his death, but provided that countries like the United Kingdom, which reckon the term of protection from first publication for special classes of works, such as anonymous works and official publications, could continue to do so for these and other classes of works; and that a country like the United States of America which does not compute the term of protection upon the basis of the life of the author, could continue to compute the term from first publication or from registration prior to publication, this term to be not less than 25 years. A third paragraph of the proposal provided for exceptions to be made to this general rule in the case of photographic works and also of works of applied art when protected as artistic works, a protection of not less than 10 years being specified for these. It was understood that this third paragraph had no reference to the protection of works of applied art under industrial property law, such as that of registered designs, but merely indicated that if such works were protected in any Contracting State as artistic works under the general copyright law, alternatively or additionally to being protected under the industrial property law, the term of protection as artistic works should not be less than 10 years. The date of the commencement of this term was not specified in the paragraph, having regard to the fact that some countries protect photographic works from the date of creation and not from the date of publication. A fourth paragraph in the adopted joint proposal dealt with the principle of comparison of terms. It provided that a Contracting State need not protect a work for a period longer than that fixed in the country of origin for the class of works to which the work belonged, the country of origin being defined in this and succeeding paragraphs. It was understood that the words "class of work" in this fourth paragraph and also in the second paragraph included not only kinds of works, such as photographs and cinematographic works, but also other recognized categories of works, such as anonymous, pseudonymous and posthumous works. It was also understood that if the class to which a work belonged was not protected in the country of origin, so that the period of protection there was zero, other Contracting States need not protect the work, whereas, if the class of work was protected in the country of origin, the fact that the work itself was not so protected, due for example to failure to comply with formalities, would not relieve other countries from protecting it. It was further understood that in a special case where a Contracting State granted the same term of protection for all classes of works, other States need not grant to works originating in the first State more than that term of protection. The latter part of paragraph 4 of the joint proposal dealt with the special case in which the country of origin of the work grants two successive terms of protection, and made it clear that if the work is not protected for the second term, other States were not obliged to protect it for this second term. The joint proposal was criticized by some delegations as unnecessarily complicated, but was supported by the majority as representing a reasonable compromise and was adopted in the Main Commission and Plenary Session.

ARTICLE V

The discussion in the Main Commission on Article V dealing with translation rights revealed wide differences of opinion and it was apparent from the outset that this was one of the most difficult subjects before the Conference.

On the one side were countries which felt that the author should have the exclusive right to authorize translations throughout the entire term during which copyright subsisted in his work. Some suggested that even the first paragraph of the programme text might be dangerous as implying that authors' rights were not generally exclusive. On the other side were countries which considered that the author's exclusive right in this field should be limited to a relatively brief period. Many, whilst anxious to ensure translations into their official or national languages, were fully prepared, if a satisfactory system could be evolved, that the author should receive equitable remuneration during the period in which copyright subsisted in his work. The countries which desired limitation of the author's right of translation regarded it as vital that works of foreign authors should be readily available in their national languages. This was the position strongly defended by the Mexican delegate and supported by others. Certain of these countries were already parties to the Berne Convention and had made the reservation as regards the right of translation under which an author's exclusive right of translation into their language lapsed if he failed to publish such a translation within 10 years of the date of first publication of his work: these countries suggested that they could not be expected to subscribe to a convention which gives authors larger translation rights, and they added that other countries had been unable to join the Berne Convention at all because it was felt that even this reservation would not be sufficient to ensure that translations of foreign works became available to their peoples at a sufficiently early date. Specific suggestions for the duration of exclusive rights having ranged from 3 years to 20 years, many countries were inclined to favour 10 years.

The programme text of the Article was criticezed in several respects. Some countries said that it failed to make clear that, in the case of countries having more than one national language, translations into any of such languages would be covered. Others criticized sub-paragraphs (a), (b) and (c) of paragraph 2 of the text on the grounds of alleged impracticability in operation, and vagueness.

Many countries suggested that works of a scientific character, which often went quickly out of date, should enjoy a shorter period of exclusive protection as regards translation, say three to five years, than works of other kinds. Others pointed to the difficulty of defining scientific works.

There were also differences of opinion as to whether some tribunal should have the power and responsibility of authorizing a translation of an author's work when he himself could not be traced or did not authorize it. In the opinion of many delegations, such a tribunal should be set up by, and should be a competent authority of, the importing country, that is, the country into whose language the translation was to be made. They urged that any tribunal would face a difficult task, and that the courts and tribunals of all Contracting States must in any case be trusted to act fairly, if the whole Convention was to be of value. Other delegations thought that the tribunal should be a competent authority of the exporting country, that is, the country of origin of the work, or at least an international authority.

Some pointed out that private translating could hardly be stopped and that the real problem was to deal with the publication of translations. Others suggested that a minimum remuneration for the author should be specified in the Article.

A working party was set up to seek a compromise. The working party, under the chairmanship of the chief United States delegate, Dr. Luther H. Evans, studied the problem but reached no final agreement. It included representatives of Argentina, Australia, Austria, Belgium, Brazil, Canada, Chile, Cuba, Denmark, El Salvador, France, Germany, India, Italy, Japan, Liberia, Mexico, the Netherlands, Portugal, Spain, Turkey, United Kingdom, Uruguay, United States of America and Yugoslavia. Finally, Italy, Mexico, the United Kingdom and the U.S.A. put forward a compromise proposal (DA/173) which was adopted by the Main Commission. The proposal sought to reconcile the different views and positions of the majority of States and to provide for the interests and effective remuneration of the author, and for notice of any proposal to translate his work. It made no distinction between scientific and other works but gave an exclusive right for seven years for all works. It was understood that the compulsory licence procedure of the second paragraph of the proposal applied only to the translation of writings, and the duplication and issue of copies of the translations. It was also understood that the licenses granted would be personal and non-exclusive, and that a State could determine which were the national languages for this purpose. Thus, India could provide for translation into the official regional languages which are used in parts of that country and which are not the national languages of other countries, as well as providing for translation into the national languages used more generally in India. The delegate of India noted that the draft had no reference to the translation of domestic works within a country such as his. France suggested that the final sentence of the draft should apply to works out of print, as well as those withdrawn. Greece, Japan and Turkey (DA/167; DA/182) made proposals for the addition of a paragraph which would allow any reservation made before 6 September 1952 on the right of translation in one of the international conventions, and particularly the reservation of the Berne Convention, to be maintained as regards the language or languages of the country making the reservation. This was at first accepted on a roll call, after two delegations had changed their vote, by a majority of one with many abstentions, but it was finally agreed to defer the proposal until the whole question of reservations was discussed after all the draft Articles had been dealt with in the Main Commission, and the final conclusions in this respect are recorded later in this report in connexion with Article XX.

When Article V was dealt with in the Plenary Session, some countries raised the question whether copies of translations published under a licence in one Contracting State could be exported to other States. To clarify the position in this respect, a proposal was made by France, Mexico, the United Kingdom and the United States (DA/232), to amend the second paragraph of the Article to specify that copies so published might be imported and sold in another Contracting State, if one of the national languages of the latter State is the same language as that into which the work had been so translated, and if the domestic law of the latter State makes provision for such licences and does not prohibit such importation and sale. When the foregoing conditions do not exist, the importation and sale of such copies in a Contracting State shall be governed by its domestic law and its agreements. Substantially equivalent texts in French and English were agreed upon. The proposal was widely supported, and the Article amended according to the proposal was adopted after a roll call. The assurance that a State such as India can declare a regional language to be a national language was repeated as in the Main Commission.

ARTICLE VI

When Article VI, which defines publication for the purposes of the Convention, was discussed in the Main Commission, some countries favoured the inclusion in the definition of a reference to means whereby works may be aurally perceived, so that the issue of gramophone records of a work would in itself constitute publication of the work. They pointed out that many works were now first made available to the public as gramophone records and not as printed sheets, and that it was illogical to distinguish between records and printed sheets in considering publication. Some even suggested that the Article already effected this result, since records could be seen and their contents presumed, but added that this would be clearer if the Article referred, not to copies of a work from which it can be read or otherwise visually perceived, but merely to copies from which it can be visually perceived. Others indicated that they regarded records as fixations of performances and not as copies of works, and that the suggested extension of the definition, however logical it might appear, would be embarrassing to some countries. Many pointed out that the practical effect of the definition should be considered rather than its logical aspect. The works of nationals of Contracting States were to be protected according to Article II wherever the dividing line between unpublished and published works was drawn, published works being protected provided the requirement of Article III, paragraph 1, was complied with. The proposed extension of the definition of "publication" in Article VI to cover gramophone records would therefore result primarily in the protection of works of nationals of non-Contracting States issued first as records in Contracting States. Germany therefore proposed ((DA/125) that the programme text be retained, but completed by a provision protecting such works specifically. The proposal to make this addition, when put to the vote, resulted in 13 votes both for and against, and was therefore not carried. The Article as in the programme draft was adopted.

ARTICLE VII

Article VII relating to retroactivity was referred to a working party after discussion in the Main Commission had disclosed a considerable divergence of views. The working party included Mr. Boutet, France (Chairman), and delegates of Argentina, Italy, Sweden, the United Kingdom and the United States of America, but, after fully exploring various proposals, it could reach no agreement and reported back accordingly. In the ensuing discussion in the Main Commission, many countries supported not only the Article but also the addition as a second paragraph to the Article of the note or postscript at the foot of the programme text. They argued that this note did not provide for retroactivity but merely protected, as was only just and reasonable, those works which had not in fact yet been published in the State where protection was claimed. Other countries argued that the inclusion of a provision on the lines of the note was dangerous as imposing an obligation to bring into protection some works already in the public domain. Those works, having regard to the definition of "publication" in Article VI, might well have been utilized by the public, and third-party rights would thus be involved. Some countries saw difficulty in passing legislation to implement such an obligation and so in securing ratification of a Convention containing it. The United States considered that this would certainly jeopardize their ratification of the Convention. Some countries therefore urged strongly that the Conference should content itself with protecting works not yet in the public domain, and should not attempt to go further, thus risking the whole Convention.

Similar arguments were expressed in respect of a proposal by Austria (DA/59) and a joint proposal by Denmark, Finland, Norway and Sweden (DA/127), the latter being a limited version of the note or postscript, with provision for protecting third-party rights. The various proposals were put to the vote. Proposals for a second paragraph to the Article on the lines of the note or postscript of the programme text or on the lines proposed by the Nordic countries were rejected. A revised wording of Article VII, generally similar in substance to it and proposed by the United States (DA/163, par. 1), was adopted. A proposal by the United States (DA/163, par. 2) to add a second paragraph calling on Contracting States to take all possible measures to protect existing works but containing no obligation to do so, was withdrawn. A proposal by France (DA/177) to revise Article VII so that the works specified in the

Article as outside the Convention should be works definitely in the public domain on the date of signature of the Convention, was rejected.

When the Article was considered in Plenary Session, the chairman of the Drafting Committee explained that, whereas the term "public domain" appeared in the English text, the term "*domaine public*" was avoided in the French text, since that term had a significance in relating to property of a State.

ARTICLES VIII AND IX AND PROTOCOL 3

The chairman of the working party, Mr. Haguiwara, reported to the Main Commission that the party proposed (DA/136) that Article VIII of the programme text, concerning deposit and ratification, be replaced by two Articles, so as to avoid too long an Article. The first of these dealt with signature and ratification of, or accession to, the Convention and appeared finally as Article VIII; and the second, which dealt with its entry into force, was referred to as Article VIII (b) in the Main Commission but finally appeared as Article IX. The first paragraph of this newly proposed Article VIII had been prepared, said Mr. Haguiwara, after considering three possibilities, the first requiring signature at the end of the Conference by all delegations, the second allowing a limited period for signature as in the text presented, and the third allowing an indefinite or perpetual period for signature. The second possibility would allow delegates to refer, if necessary, to their governments before signing, and was adopted. It was explained that a non-signatory State could accede to the Convention and that a signatory State could later ratify or accept the Convention. Whether it ratified or accepted, the effect in binding the State was the same. In some countries the word or term used made no difference, but in others, such as the United States, acceptance was by a different procedure from ratification and might be easier in practice. Mr. Haguiware further explained that a check had been made with existing international instruments and that it might well be the word "accession" in English should appear as "*adhésion*" in French. The Chairman of the Main Commission explained that in this and other connexions the texts of the Convention in the different languages should not be literal translations but should have regard to real meanings. These matters could be dealt with by the Drafting Committee. As regards the place of deposit of instruments of ratification, Mr. Haguiwara said that the Swiss Government had been considered as appropriate and several delegations had paid tribute to Switzerland, but that on the whole Unesco was better suited in the opinion of the working party. In the ensuing discussion in the Main Commission, Cuba suggested that the Convention should be deposited with the United Nations Organization, since many countries were members of that organization but not of Unesco. Italy stated that her opposition to the choice of Unesco for this purpose need be maintained no longer now that any threat to the Berne Union had disappeared and that precedents for deposit of a Convention with Unesco had been made. Liberia pointed out that some countries, such as Italy and Japan, were not members of the United Nations but were members of Unesco. The text of Article VIII, as presented by the working party, including the provision for deposit with Unesco, was accordingly adopted.

Mr. Haguiwara explained that Article IX included two important additions to the programme draft, the first allowing for ratification by one country, conditional on ratification by another, and the second requiring ratification by a certain number of non-Berne countries before the Convention could come into effect. As regards the first addition, Mr. Haguiwara said that the working party had considered, but rejected, the possibility of naming or referring to two States—the United States of America and the United Kingdom—in this provision, that is to say, the possibility of other countries making their ratifications conditional on ratifications by these two countries. In the ensuing discussion some countries suggested that the first addition proposed by the working party was unnecessary since a State could always attach a condition to its ratification. Others suggested that it might appear in a protocol, and others said that the inclusion of this provision might expedite ratification and avoid hesitation by certain countries to ratify before the United States of America. As regards the second proposed addition, some countries pointed out that four ratifications, not six, by countries not belonging to the Berne Union should be sufficient on a numerical basis of representation at the Conference, and also having regard to the fact that there were several important countries which did not belong to the Berne Union. The working party had proposed a reference to 12 ratifications including either four or six from non-Berne countries, and the Main Commission chose the former alternative by a majority vote. The text of Article IX was then adopted, and the provision for conditional ratification was adopted as a Protocol (3 as signed).

ARTICLE X

A proposal by the United States of America (DA/151) for a new article (originally numbered VIII-*ter* and finally numbered X), as an alternative to an article proposed by the working party (DA/148), relating to national implementation of the obligations imposed by the Convention, was adopted, subject to minor and drafting amendments. It was stated that in some States the Convention, when ratified, would be immediately effective as domestic law without special legislation; that in other States the domestic law would be amended before ratification; and that in still others a period would be required following ratification for revision of the domestic law. Having regard to the last-named class of States, some countries had suggested that it would be better to specify a definite period of say 18 months, in addition to the three months referred to in Article IX, to be allowed for implementation to the initial 12 States ratifying the Convention. Other countries had favoured a mere statement in the Convention that States should implement it in their domestic law as soon as possible, but it was pointed out that this would lead to difficulties and that there might be long delays unfair to those States which implemented the Convention promptly. The difference in this respect between the position of the 12 States ratifying first to bring the Convention into effect, and those States ratifying subsequently, was noted. The Article X as adopted was intended to avoid these difficulties, and the Commission considered but decided against the revision of the period of three months specified in Article IX.

In the Plenary Session, Austria suggested that the first paragraph of the Article repeated the substance of Article I. The paragraph was however retained, since it related to the implementation of the Convention in certain States.

ARTICLE XI AND RESOLUTION CONCERNING INTERGOVERNMENTAL COMMITTEE
VOEU CONCERNING PROVISIONAL ADMINISTRATION

The report of the working party on the Article on Administration (IX of the programme text and finally XI) was presented by the President, Mr. Pennetta. The party had considered the printed Unesco proposal (DA/5) circulated before the Conference and also a proposal by Italy (DA/135), and they recommended (DA/161) that the Article should provide for the establishment of a permanent intergovernmental Committee of 12 States with the Director-General of Unesco, the Director of the Berne Bureau and the Secretary-General of the Organization of American States or their representatives as advisers. The Convention would require development, Mr. Pennetta said, and the working party recommended the establishment of a temporary intergovernmental Committee. As to the secretariat of the Committee, no decisions binding Unesco could in his view be taken at the Conference, but the Executive Board of Unesco, which was due to meet in November, could then consider the matter.

In the ensuing discussion some countries raised questions about the expenses of a secretariat for any intergovernmental Committee. Some doubted the necessity for an intergovernmental Committee, pointing out that the Berne Union had been successful without such a Committee for many years. Others said the Berne Union now had a most useful Permanent Committee and that a similar Committee was desirable if the present Convention was to live and be developed: the Unesco Copyright Division could be the tool to be controlled by this Committee, but the development of the Convention could best be controlled by a special committee and not indirectly from the General Conference of Unesco. Many expressed appreciation of the work done by Unesco and desired that Unesco should undertake the work of the secretariat, so avoiding any need for a new international body.

The questions before the Main Commission were, firstly, whether a permanent intergovernmental committee was required and, if so, its status, and, secondly, whether a temporary intergovernmental Committee was necessary before the permanent Committee came into being and, if so, its relationship to Unesco. On the first question, the Main Commission decided in favour of the Permanent Committee and adopted paragraphs 1 and 2 of the draft Article proposed by the working party, but deleted its paragraph 3 concerning the organization of a secretariat.

On the second question, one suggestion was that the Steering Committee of the Conference should constitute the intergovernmental Committee. However, the Main Commission did not adopt in this respect the proposals of the working party (DA/161) nor a variant of them proposed by Sweden (DA/189), but adopted a resolution proposed by Argentina, Chile, Colombia, El Salvador, Honduras, Nicaragua and Spain (DA/183), to the effect that Unesco should continue its present activities until the permanent intergovernmental Committee was set up, and should be advised in the meantime by a provisional consultative Committee.

When these matters were reviewed in Plenary Session, a *Resolution to be appended to the Convention* was adopted. It referred to the constitution and renewal of the permanent intergovernmental Committee and was based on the report of the working party (DA/161) revised on the proposal of Sweden, in the passage concerning a secretariat for this Committee, to express a *voeu* that Unesco would take care of the secretariat, and on the proposal of France, in the passage concerning the constitution of the Committee, to refer to one representative and one alternate of each of the 12 States represented on the Committee. The President recalled that the Steering Committee had suggested that the following 12 States should be so represented at first: Argentina, Brazil, France, Germany, India, Italy, Japan, Mexico, Spain, Switzerland, the United Kingdom and the United States. The chief delegate of Japan proposed that as he was doubtful whether his country would sign or adhere to the Convention, the name Japan in the list should be replaced by, for example, Thailand, but he agreed to withdraw this proposal when pressed to do so by many delegations. It was made clear that the appearance of the name of any State in this list did not imply an obligation to sign or adhere to the Convention. Colombia, supported by Spain, suggested that the list favoured the Berne countries and that it would give a more equitable geographical distribution if one of the European countries was replaced by a Pan American country. The President drew attention to the fact that one or more of the 12 States whose names had been proposed for the Committee might not have ratified the Convention when it somes into force. The Committee could then consider the suggestion of Colombia when co-opting other States to the Committee.

A *voeu* (DA/227) concerning a provisional administration of the Universal Convention and based on the resolution adopted by the Main Commission on the proposal of Argentina and others (DA/183), was agreed in Plenary Session, although opposed by Italy. It indicated that Unesco should continue its activities to strengthen copyright protection throughout the world, should designate a provisional advisory Committee and, in co-operation with Contracting States, should concern itself with the setting up of the intergovernmental Committee referred to on Article XI.

Article XII

The report of the working party (DA/161) on the draft Article on revision of the Convention (X of the programme text and finally XII) recommended that a decision as to the majority required for revision be left to future conferences. Suggestions had been made that revision should require unanimity (DA/94) or should require at least a two-thirds majority (DA/61), but it was agreed that no provision to this effect should be inserted into the Convention at this stage.

Some countries opposed a suggestion that conferences of revision could be called when the permanent intergovernmental Committee deemed it necessary, as well as on the request of 10 Contracting States or of a majority of the Contracting States if this majority were less than 10. Brazil proposed (DA/176) that Unesco should call future conferences as they had called this one. The Draft Article as agreed provided for the calling of conferences by the Committee, as well as by 10 or a majority of Contracting States.

Article XIII

The Article dealing with the application of the Convention to colonial and other territories (XII of the programme text and finally XIII) was considered in the Main Commission on the basis of a draft which had been prepared by the working party under the chairmanship of Mr. Haguiwara and which corresponded to paragraph 1 of the programme text Article XII, simplified by reference generally to territories for the conduct of whose foreign relations a Contracting State is responsible. In this connexion Germany drew attention to the problem of Berlin and said that the new draft was satisfactory. Viet-Nam suggested that countries, as well as territories, should be referred to. Israel proposed (DA/145) that a provision should be made in the draft for a delay of say three months in the coming into force of the Convention for the territories, following ratification or the equivalent, on the lines already agreed in connexion with the Article IX dealing with its coming into force for Contracting States. This was agreed. Liberia pointed out the importance to that country of the coming into force of the Convention in territories adjacent thereto, for whose foreign relations France and the United Kingdom were responsible. Cuba proposed (DA/84) the deletion of the Article, or its replacement by an article applying the Convention automatically to such territories until a notification to the contrary was given. In the Cuban view, the Article was unnecessary and was contrary to modern ideas of the self-determination of peoples. A Contracting State was a unity with its colonies and should accept the Convention as a unity. France and the United Kingdom stated that their practice was to consult overseas territories and to consider their views before binding them to a convention of this kind, and that the provision was therefore necessary. Cuba withdrew the proposal to delete the Article, and the proposal to replace it was rejected. Spain drew attention to the Tangier problem and desired the early application of the Convention to Tangier, and requested the delegates of countries on the Control Commission of Tangier to urge their countries to take quick action.

Article XIV

The Article on Denunciation (XI in the programme text, XII in the report of the working party and finally XIV) was agreed in the Main Commission in the form suggested by the working party, subject to drafting amendments.

Article XV

Mr. Haguiwara as Chairman of the working party reported to the Main Commission that there had been controversy in the party on the jurisdictional clause (Article XIII of the programme text, finally Article XV) but they had agreed on a text identical with Article 27 *bis* of the Berne Convention. Germany proposed (DA/149) an addition to the Article to specify that each Contracting State cited before the Court by another State must recognize the Court's competence. Germany feared that the statute of the International Court might be read as referring to treaties in force at that date, and that the Resolution of the Security Council of 1946 about the submission of States to the jurisdiction of the Court might be regarded as avoiding any implication that Contracting States of the present Convention accepted the Court's jurisdiction. Others thought that the Article as it stood necessarily implied the substance of the German proposal, and in their view the proposed addition was unnecessary. The amendment was then withdrawn on the understanding that the Conference interpreted this jurisdictional clause in the sense that it implied an obligation on a Contracting State which is not a party to the statute and is taken before the Hague Court by another Contracting State to accept and not to deny the competence of that Court.

Article XVI

The President of the Main Commission explained that the Chairman of the working party had asked him to present their report on the Article dealing with official texts of the Convention (XIV of the draft programme and XVI finally). The questions for the Main Commission were whether one text only, or three texts in different languages, should prevail, and if one, which one; also, which texts should be signed and whether other official texts should be mentioned in the Convention. Some countries suggested that a text in one language should prevail to secure clarity and certainty in cases of doubt and in the event of any dispute, and some suggested that this text should be in French, having regard to the historical and diplomatic importance of the French language and its general acceptance in the field of copyright, as seen in the Berne Convention. Switzerland, a country with three national languages, favoured the suggestion that one language should prevail. Other delegations suggested that texts in three languages, equally authoritative, were desirable. This would allow disputes between countries having a common language to be settled in many cases on the basis of a text in that language, and would also allow a comparison of texts to assist in determining doubts arising from one text. The practice in Canada of having laws in two languages, and comparing the two texts when necessary, was referred to, and so was the practice of the Permanent Court of International Justice at The Hague as regards its working languages, namely, English and French and other languages when the parties so requested. It was agreed that this difficult question was a matter of practical convenience, and that the Convention should be signed in French, English and Spanish. It was further agreed by a majority vote taken by roll call that these three texts should be equally authoritative. Proposals that official texts be established in Portuguese, Italian and German were agreed, but it was understood that these texts would not be signed. The final paragraph of the Article dealing with texts to be prepared at the request of Contracting States was also agreed, but some expressed doubt as to the distinction between these texts and the texts referred to as "official".

In the Plenary Session, a proposal by Israel (DA/210) intended to clarify the Article and refer to "texts established officially" instead of to "official texts" was rejected. It was clear that many delegations attached importance to the adjective "official" in relation to the texts in the German, Italian and Portuguese languages which were not to be signed.

Article XVII and Related Declaration

When the Main Commission discussed the Article relating to the Berne Convention (XV of the programme text and XVII finally) and the associated Protocol, many delegations of leading countries of the Berne Union declared that this provision to the effect that the Berne Convention must prevail for countries of the Union was in their view essential, and several made it clear that they could neither sign nor ratify the Convention if the Protocol were omitted. Cuba, whilst expressing a desire to strengthen the Berne Union, proposed (DA/131) that this Article be abandoned as contrary to principles of international law and derogatory to the sovereignty of States. On the other hand, Portugal suggested (DA/117) that the provisions be strengthened by including the Protocol in the body of the Convention. Canada disliked the Protocol, paragraph 1 (a) in their view savouring of a threat and being contrary to the spirit of the Berne Convention. Japan asked whether a State belonging to the Berne Union could sign the Convention and not the Protocol. The chairman said that the intention was that signature of the Convention would imply acceptance of the Protocol and that no separate signature of the Protocol would be required. The Main Commission rejected the proposal of Cuba to delete the Article and appointed a working party under the chairmanship of Mr. Bodenhausen, delegate of the Netherlands, with delegates of Canada, France, Italy, Japan, Portugal and Switzerland serving on the Party, together with Mr. Hepp of Unesco and Mr. Mentha, Director of the Bureau of the Berne Union. The working party's report suggested that the substance of the Protocol be retained separate from the Convention and be referred to as an Appendix Declaration, signature of the Convention implying acceptance of the Declaration. Having regard to the views of other delegations, Canada and Japan had withdrawn objections, and the Article and Declaration were adopted by the Main Commission.

In the Plenary Session, the Director of the Berne Bureau thanked those delegations who had supported the Article. He had confidence in the future of the Berne Union and at the same time wished the new Universal Convention all success. The Declaration was at first adopted in the form agreed in the Main Commission, but sub-paragraph (c) of paragraph 1 was later deleted as reported under Article XX on Reservations.

Article XVIII

The Article referring principally to the Pan American Conventions (XVI of the programme text and XVIII finally) was discussed in the Main Commission with reference to the text prepared in Washington in January 1952 (DA/2 Add). This text was based on the principle that the most recent agreement shall prevail and, as pointed out by Argentina, that the date of formulation of an agreement rather than the date of ratification was its effective date for this purpose. Austria proposed (DA/64) that the Berne Convention be specifically excepted from the Article and declared they wished to retain the benefit of the Montevideo Convention. Cuba proposed (DA/131) the abandonment of Article XVIII but withdrew the proposal after discussion. Cuba also proposed (DA/134) that Articles XVII and XVIII be combined to form a single Article which should protect all conventions equally. The United States pointed out that the whole problem had been fully explored by the American countries early in the year, when it was agreed that the Universal Convention should not abrogate the existing American conventions but should prevail over them in the event of conflict: the differences between the highly-developed Berne Convention and the old and confused Pan American Conventions justified in their view the different treatment of them in separate Articles, and they pointed out that they had many bilateral and multilateral arrangements with other countries, which must also be considered. Italy agreed that bilateral arrangements and other agreements should not be ignored. Some countries thought that Article XVIII was important in connexion with international agreements other than those between the American Republics. Some suggested that conventions and agreements other than those between the American Republics and the Berne Convention should be dealt with separately and that Article XVIII should refer only to the conventions of the American Republics. A working party under the chairmanship of Mr. Galliano, delegate of Chile, attended by delegates from the American Republics and by Mr. Canyes, the observer of the Pan American Union, was appointed and reported back to the Main Commission with a new draft of Article XVIII (DA/142) limited strictly to the multilateral or bilateral copyright conventions or agreements effective between the American Republics. The Article as so revised was adopted.

ARTICLE XIX

Consequent on the limitation of Article XVIII to agreements exclusively between the American Republics, India proposed to the Main Commission a new Article (XIX) (DA/138) dealing with international conventions and arrangements other than these agreements and other than the Berne Convention and providing that, in the case of conflict, the latter should prevail. The United States supported the proposal and pointed out that they had no intention of abrogating the many bilateral and other arrangements between their country and non-American countries. In their view, the rule should be that the Universal Convention should prevail in cases of conflict and this would be a valuable result for their country. Several countries supported the new Article, but others pointed out that it attempted to govern the operation of future agreements and conventions as well as the interaction of the Universal Convention with existing agreements. In their view, it was wrong to make a provision which, in effect, might open the door to individual groups of Contracting States modifying their obligations under the Universal Convention without denouncing it. They doubted the wisdom of referring to future arrangements and they wondered whether the reference to existing arrangements was not a normal application of a rule of international law and so need not be stated. The United States agreed that the Article need not refer to future arrangements but urged that it should be retained with reference to existing arrangements, in order to avoid any implication which might arise from the wording of the Preamble and Articles XVII and XVIII to the effect that the rule of international law did not apply. The new Article XIX, revised to avoid reference to future international agreements, was then adopted.

ARTICLE XX

The Main Commission then considered two proposals for a new Article relating to the possibility of reservations. A proposal of Cuba (DA/193) was directed to allowing States to make reservations on one or more Articles, whereas a proposal by Argentina, the Netherlands, the United Kingdom and the United States (DA/190) would allow no such reservations beyond any specific provisions of the text of the Convention itself. Some countries urged that an Article allowing reservations would facilitate signature of the Convention by certain States. Others urged that such an Article would destroy the whole basis of the Convention and should not be adopted; the Articles of the Convention had been drafted as compromises to meet as far as possible the different viewpoints and difficulties of individual States. The proposal of Cuba was rejected and the proposal against reservations adopted to form Article XX.

It was understood that this adoption did not rule out from consideration in the Main Commission a proposal by Greece, Japan and Turkey (DA/167; DA/182) to append to Article V a provision intended to allow those States which were members of the Berne Union, with the reservation on translation rights, to maintain their national law, corresponding to the reservation, in respect of all translations into their national language. Japan pointed out that, without such a provision, those States would be required to have a dual system of law on translation rights and would not be clear about the effect of sub-paragraph (c) in paragraph 1 of the Declaration adopted in connexion with Article XVII safeguarding the Berne Convention. The United States opposed the proposal of Japan. Some countries said that if Japan or any other State remained in the Berne Convention with the reservation on translation rights and gave the same 10-years' protection to her own hationals, and also joined the Universal Convention, the granting by her of translation rights subject to Article V on works originating in Contracting States not members of the Berne Union should constitute compliance with the Universal Convention, even though Article II refers to national treatment. Some countries agreed with Japan that sub-paragraph (c) of paragraph 1 of the Declaration presented a difficulty in the sense that authors of Berne countries might, in Berne countries retaining the reservation, claim the benefits of Article V of the Universal Convention, should these be considered in any particular case to confer greater rights on authors than the Berne Convention.

The proposal by Japan having been rejected after a roll call, the chief Japanese delegate intimated that as a result of this decision it would not be possible for Japan to sign the Convention, and his delegation would remain only as observers. Accession to the Convention as it was then drafted would lead in his country to a dual system of translating rights and difficulties under sub-paragraph (c) of paragraph 1 of the Declaration. A proposal was then put forward by the Netherlands to the Main Commission that sub-paragraph (c) of paragraph 1 of the Declaration be deleted. Some delegates considered that this sub-paragraph was of no real value as a safeguard to the Berne Union, since the essential safeguards were contained in sub-paragraphs (a) and (b). Moreover, subparagraph (c) might give rise to ambiguities or difficulties in practice, particularly as regards which of the two systems governing translation rights was the more favourable in any particular case. The United Kingdom suggested that if the paragraph were not deleted it should at least be re-worded to make it clear that it had no application to rights of translation. Other countries, principally France and Germany, favoured retention of sub-paragraph (c) as an integral part of the safeguard of the Berne Convention; this retention might, in their view, make it easier for those Berne countries with a reservation in respect of translation rights to become members of the Universal Convention. The Netherlands' proposal failed to secure a majority in the Main Commission and the President explained that, that being so it would have to be left to the national courts, if authors claimed particular rights, to decide which of the two systems governing translation rights gave the greater rights in the particular case.

When the matter was reconsidered in Plenary Session, sub-paragraph (c) of paragraph 1 of the Declaration relating to the Berne Convention was deleted. This met one of two points of difficulty previously raised by Japan, and to clarify the other point, the President declared that a State which was a member of the Berne Convention with reservation with regard to translating rights, and was also a member of the Universal Convention, and the national legislation of which was based on the requirements of the Berne Convention, would fulfil its obligations under the Universal Convention towards Contracting States not members of the Berne Union if it applied to the works of such States the treatment indicated in Article V: Article II could not be cited against it to allege that it should give to these works the treatment provided for in its national legislation and in the Berne Convention. The United States indicated agreement with this declaration and it was clear that it corresponded to the general understanding. The chief delegate of Japan expressed gratitude at this clarification of his two points of difficulty. He regretted that, having regard to the rejection of his proposal in the Main Commission for an addition to Article V, he still could not sign the Convention at the end of the Conference, but he would now recommend to his government that the question of signature by Japan within 120 days be considered.

Article XXI

This article dealing with notifications to be issued by Unesco [XII (b) in the report of the working party on final clauses and finally XXI] was revised on the proposal of Cuba (DA/140), to make it more specific and to refer to the Swiss Federal Council. This reference was understood to be a tribute to the special part played by Switzerland in connexion with the Convention.

DECLARATION RELATING TO ARTICLE XVII AND RESOLUTION CONCERNING ARTICLE XI

These are dealt with in this report under the corresponding Articles.

PROTOCOLS 1, 2 AND 3

Protocol 1, concerning works of stateless persons and refugees and Protocol 2, concerning works of certain international organizations, are dealt with in this report under Article II. Protocol 3, concerning ratification or acceptance of the Convention, is dealt with under Article IX. It was finally agreed in Plenary Session that the three Protocols should be annexed to the Convention without reference to them in any Article and that each should be separately signed.

VOEUX

The *Voeu* cencerning the activities of Unesco in the field of copyright pending the setting up of the intergovernmental Committee referred to in Article XI is dealt with in this report under that Article.

The Main Commission concluded its proceedings by adopting four other *voeux* which were agreed in Plenary Session. One of these corresponded to a *voeu* adopted at the Brussels Conference of the Berne Union and referred to the possibility of utilizing systems of "*domaine public payant*", involving small royalties on the exploitation for profit of works in the public domain, in order to help benevolent organizations or assistance funds for authors. The other three *voeux* related to foreign exchange restrictions on copyright royalty payments; to the desirability of the United Nations Organization, Unesco and individual States continuing to study double taxation problems; and to the examination as soon as possible by the States represented in the Tangier Control Committee, of the application of the Convention to that territory.

Thus the text of the Convention and Protocols was adopted ready for signature.

May your Rapporteur-Général thank all delegates for the honour conferred on him in appointing him to his task and for the friendly manner in which you have listened to him. May he express the hope that many countries will sign the Convention and Protocols today and that all States will presently ratify, accept or adhere to the new Convention.

6 September 1952   SIR JOHN BLAKE

APPENDIX II

DOCUMENTS OF THE INTERGOVERNMENTAL
COPYRIGHT COMMITTEE

RULES OF PROCEDURE
AS IN FORCE ON JANUARY 1, 1968

SECTION I. MEMBERSHIP AND DUTIES

Rule 1

The Intergovernmental Copyright Committee (hereinafter called "the Committee") established by Article XI of the Universal Copyright Convention (hereinafter called "the Convention") shall consist of 12 States, each State designating one representative and one alternate, who may be accompanied to the sessions of the Committe by advisers.

Rule 2

Except as otherwise provided in the present Rules, the term of office of the Member States of the Committee expires at the end of the regular session held in the fifth calendar year following the session at which their designation took place; or if no regular session is held in the said fifth year then at the end of the next regular session. The term of office of a retiring State may be renewed immediately.

Rule 3

1. (a) In the course of the regular session at the end of which the term of office of a State expires by virtue of Rules 2 or 37, the Committee shall, unless it renews the term of office of such State, designate another Contracting State as a member of the Committee.

   (b) If a State ceases to be a member by virtue of Rule 4, paragraph I, the Committee shall, in the course of the session at the end of which such State will cease to be a member, designate another Contracting State as a member of the Committee for the unexpired term of the retiring State.

   (c) If a State ceases to be a member by virtue of Rule 4, paragraph 2, the Committee shall, in the first session following the date of notification of the denunciation, designate another Contracting State as a member of the Committee for the unexpired term of the retiring State. Such designation shall be effective when it is made or, if the twelve months referred to in Rule 4, paragraph 2, have not yet expired, at the expiration of this period.

2. The Committee shall, when the designations are made, apply the principle of fair representation of the different parts of the world.

Rule 4

1. A State which is not represented at two consecutive regular sessions of the Committee shall, unless the Committee feels that its absence is justified, cease to be a member of the Committee, at the end of the second such session.

2. A State which denounces the Convention shall cease to be a member of the Committee twelve months after the date of receipt of the notification of such denunciation.

Rule 5

Each State represented on the Committee shall notify the Secretariat of the names of its designated representative and alternate.

Rule 6

The Director-General of the United Nations Educational, Scientific and Cultural Organization, the Director of the Bureau of the International Union for the Protection of Literary and Artistic Works, the Secretary-General of the Organization of American States and the Secretary-General of the Council of Europe, or their representatives, may attend meetings of the Committee in an advisory capacity. They shall not be entitled to vote.

Rule 7

The following may be represented at sessions of the Committee by observers: (a) States parties to the Convention not members of the Committee; (b) Member States of the United Nations or of the United Nations Educational, Scientific and Cultural Organization not parties to the Convention; (c) intergovernmental organizations; and (d) nongovernmental organizations, whether national or international, authorized by the Committee or by its Chairman.

Rule 8

The duties of the Committee shall be: (a) to study the problems concerning the application and operation of the Convention; (b) to make preparation for periodic revisions of the Convention; (c) to study any other problems concerning the international protection of copyright or which may affect copyright, in co-operation with the various interested international organizations, such as the United Nations Educational, Scientific and Cultural Organization, the International Union for the Protection of Literary and Artistic Works, the International Labour Organisation, the Organization of American States, the Council of Europe and the Latin Union; (d) to inform the Contracting States as to its activities.

Section II. Sessions

Rule 9

1. The Committee shall meet in regular session at least once every two years.

2. The Chairman shall convene the Committee in special session at the request of four Member States of the Committee.

3. In case of emergency, the Chairman may convene the Committee in special session on his own initiative.

4. A session of the Committee can only be held if at least six States are represented at such session.

Rule 10

The Chairman shall fix the date and place of the meeting, after consulting the Director-General of Unesco, and shall take into consideration the wishes expressed thereon by the Committee.

Section III. Officers

Rule 11

The Committee shall elect, at the opening of each regular session, from among its members, a Chairman and a Vice-Chairman. They shall serve until the election of their successors in Office at the beginning of the next regular session. Such officers shall not be eligible for immediate re-election.

Rule 12

If the Chairman and Vice-Chairman are unable to act at any meeting, an acting Chairman shall be elected who shall act until one of the regular officers is able to resume his duties.

Rule 13

At the end of each session, a report on the work accomplished shall be submitted to the Committee for approval. The preparation of this report shall be entrusted to a Rapporteur-General, appointed from among the members of the Committee, or to the Secretariat.

Section IV. Agenda

Rule 14

1. The Chairman of the Committee shall, in consultation with the Director-General of Unesco, establish a provisional agenda for each regular session after taking into consideration the suggestions, if any, made by the Contracting States.

2. In calling for a special session, the Chairman shall inform the Member States of the Committee of the reasons for the session and shall communicate a provisional agenda.

3. Except in the case of a special session convened by the Chairman of the Committee, the provisional agenda shall be distributed at least three months before the proposed date of the session.

4. Appropriate documentation shall be distributed with the provisional agenda or as soon thereafter as possible.

Rule 15

1. The Committee shall establish the final agenda of the session at its first meeting.

2. The Committee may, during a session, modify the order of items on the agenda or add new items to it.

Section V. Sub-Committees and Consultants

Rule 16

For the study of special questions the Committee, or between two sessions, the Chairman of the Committee, may appoint sub-committees or consultants who shall continue to serve until the next regular session of the Committee; they shall submit their reports to the Committee.

Section VI. Secretariat

Rule 17

The members of the Secretariat of Unesco designated for that purpose by the Director-General shall constitute the Secretariat of the Committee and its sub-committees.

Section VII. Conduct of Business

Rule 18

The meetings of the Committee and of its sub-committees shall not be open to the public. Only persons invited or authorized by the Chairman of the Committee or of the sub-committee concerned may be admitted to the meetings.

Rule 19

Observers, invitees and advisers may be authorized to make oral or written statements before the Committee or its sub-committees.

Rule 20

A simple majority of the States represented at a session shall constitute a quorum at any meeting of a session.

Section VIII. Duties of the Officers

Rule 21

The Chairman of the Committee shall declare the opening and closing of each meeting, direct the discussion, ensure observance of these Rules, accord the right to speak, put questions and announce decisions. He shall rule on points of order and, subject to these Rules, shall have complete control of the proceedings of the body concerned and over the maintenance of order at its meetings.

Rule 22

The Chairman shall call upon speakers in the order in which they have expressed their desire to speak.

Rule 23

The Vice-Chairman, or in his absence, the Acting Chairman, shall preside at the meetings during the temporary absences of the Chairman, and, while so presiding, shall exercise all the powers of the Chairman.

Rule 24

During the discussion on any matter, a representative on the Committee may at any time raise a point of order, and the point of order shall be forthwith decided upon by the Chairman. Any representative on the Committee may appeal against the ruling of the Chairman which can only be overruled by a majority of votes cast. A representative speaking on a point of order may speak only on this point, and may not speak on the substance.

Rule 25

Reopening of a debate already completed by a vote on a given question during the same session shall require a majority of two-thirds of votes cast. Reopening of a debate already completed by a vote on a given question during a previous session shall require a majority of votes cast. Permission to speak on a motion to reopen shall be accorded only to the proposer and to one speaker in opposition, after which it shall be immediately put to the vote.

Section IX. Voting

Rule 26

Each State member of the Committee shall have one vote.

Rule 27

The Chairman, the Vice-Chairman and the Acting Chairman of the Committee shall have the right to vote on behalf of the States they represent.

Rule 28

Except as otherwise provided in these Rules, decisions shall be by a majority of votes cast and an abstention shall not be considered as a vote.

Rule 29

Voting shall normally be by voice, by show of hands, or by standing. In meetings of the Committee there shall be a roll call if requested by two Member States. The votes or abstentions of each State participating in a roll call shall be recorded in the minutes.

Rule 30

On request of any member and unless the Committee decides otherwise, parts of a motion shall be voted on separately. The resulting motion shall then be put to a final vote in its entirety.

Rule 31

Any amendment to a motion shall be voted on before a vote is taken on the motion. When two or more amendments are moved to a motion, the vote should be taken on them in their order of remoteness from the original motion, commencing with the most remote. The Chairman shall determine whether a proposed amendment is so related to the motion as to constitute a proper amendment thereto, or whether it must be considered a substitute motion.

Rule 32

Substitute motions shall, unless the Committee otherwise decides, be put to the vote in the order in which they are presented, and after the disposal of the original motion. The Chairman shall decide whether it is necessary to put the substitute motion to the vote in the light of the vote on the original motion and any amendments thereto. This ruling may be reversed by a majority of votes cast.

Section X. Languages

Rule 33

1. Documents of the Committee and its sub-committees, including the text of draft conventions, recommendations, resolutions, and decisions shall be prepared and circulated in the English, French and Spanish languages, except as dispensed with by unanimous consent.

2. The English, French and Spanish languages shall be used in the deliberations of the Committee and its sub-committees. Speeches made in any of the three languages shall be interpreted into the other two languages, except where such interpretation is dispensed with by unanimous consent of all those concerned.

Section XI. Records of Proceedings

Rule 34

Minutes of the meetings of the Committee shall be prepared by the Secretariat, and approved by the members of the Committee.

Section XII. Amendments to the Rules

Rule 35

1. The Committee may make at the beginning of any session such amendments to these Rules as may be deemed appropriate.

2. Any proposed amendment of the Rules may be adopted by a simple majority of the States represented at the session, when the proposal for the amendment appears in the provisional agenda. Otherwise, a majority of two-thirds of the States represented at the session shall be necessary for the adoption of an amendment to the Rules of Procedure but in no case less than six affirmative votes in this respect shall be effective.

Section XIII. Transitional Provisions

Rule 36
(Repealed.)

Rule 37
(Obsolete.)

Section XIV. General Provision

Rule 38

The Rules can in no case be interpreted in a manner which could be at variance with the provisions of the Universal Copyright Convention.

ADVISORY OPINION ON THE LOCATION OF THE CONVENTION NOTICE

Considering that Article III, paragraph 1, of the Universal Copyright Convention provides that: "any Contracting State which, under its domestic law, requires as a condition of copyright, compliance with formalities such as deposit, registration, notice, notarial certificates, payment of fees or manufacture or publication in that Contracting State, shall regard these requirements as satisfied with respect to all works protected in accordance with this Convention and first published outside its territory and the author of which is not one of its nationals, if from the time of the first publication all the copies of the work published with the authority of the author or other copyright proprietor bear the symbol © accompanied by the name of the copyright proprietor and the year of first publication placed in such manner and location as to give reasonable notice of claim of copyright".

Considering that it is desirable that this rule be applied liberally in order to avoid the danger of loss of protection merely for technicalities of formalities,

Considering that local practices vary from country to country and that a respect for such practices, within the provisions of the Convention, is consistent with the spirit of universality of the Convention,

Considering that guidance, taking into account local practices and the desirability of liberal application of Article III, paragraph 1, may facilitate, for persons seeking protection, compliance with the said provision,

The Intergovernmental Copyright Committee

1. *Expresses the view*

(a) that placing the notice (i.e., the symbol © accompanied by the name of the copyright proprietor and the year of first publication) for example:

in the case of *books* or *pamphlets*, on the title page or the page immediately following, or at the end of the book or pamphlet, in the case of a *single sheet*, on either of the sides,

in the case of *printed music*, on the title page or first page of music, or at the end of the printed music,

in the case of *newspapers*, *magazines* or other *periodicals*, under the main title or the "masthead",

in the case of *maps*, *prints*, or *photographs*, on their face side, either on the actual map or picture (but somewhere near the title or the margin) or on the margin,

in the case of *independent parts of a whole* (if a separate copyright is claimed in the independent parts), under the title of the independent part,

in the case of *motion pictures*, on the frames which carry its title (whether appearing at the beginning or the end) or credits,

would appear to satisfy that provision contained in Article III, paragraph 1, of the Universal Copyright Convention, according to which the notice should be placed "in such... *location* as to give reasonable notice of claim of copyright";

(b) that, if the three elements of the notice (i.e., the symbol ©, the name of the copyright proprietor, the year of first publication) appear in close juxtaposition to each other and in letters and numbers large enough to appear legible to an ordinary reader, then the condition contained in Article III, paragraph 1, of the Universal Copyright Convention, according to which the notice should be placed "in such *manner*... as to give reasonable notice of claim of copyright", appears to be satisfied;

2. *Calls the attention to the following:*

(a) the list appearing in point 1 (a), above, does not exhaust all the kinds of works, copies of which may bear a notice;

(b) the locations indicated in point 1 (a), above, are not necessarily the only locations giving reasonable notice;

(c) the applicability of the Universal Copyright Convention to a given work depends on several circumstances; use of a notice, if at all pertinent, is only one of such circumstances;

3. *Emphasizes,* as in all cases in which its views may be expressed in connexion with the application or operation of the Universal Copyright Convention, that such views are advisory only and do not purport to be binding upon any court or other authority with jurisdiction as to the interpretation of the Convention.

PART II

THE COPYRIGHT LAWS OF THE COUNTRIES PARTY TO THE UNIVERSAL COPYRIGHT CONVENTION

INTRODUCTORY OBSERVATIONS
TO PART II

This Part is divided into as many chapters as there were countries party to the Universal Copyright Convention at the time of going to press (April 1968).

Each chapter consists of an exposition of the law of copyright of one such country, *but only to the extent that it is considered to be of practical interest in determining the copyright status of works which that country is supposed to protect as a country party to the Universal Copyright Convention.*

This limitation of the scope of each chapter means that no attempt has been made to give information on the copyright status of domestic works, works which have a Berne Union country as country of origin, and other works which are not works entitled to protection under the Universal Copyright Convention.[1] It also means that requirements of protection (for example, certain formalities) that need not be met by works entitled to protection under the Universal Copyright Convention, or provisions inapplicable to such works (for example, the "manufacturing clause" of the U.S. statute), are usually not mentioned, or are referred to only briefly.

The attempt to limit information to that deemed to be of practical usefulness to the reader led to the somewhat summary treatment of questions relating to civil litigation and criminal prosecution (since in such cases assistance by local counsel becomes a practical, if not legal, necessity), and a few minor details of infrequent application.

Whenever practical, each chapter follows the same order: 1. Sources (Domestic Law, Universal Copyright Convention); 2. Acquisition of Copyright under the Universal Copyright Convention; 3. Protected Works; 4. Protected Persons; 5. Assignment and Licensing; 6. Protected Rights (Economic Rights, Moral Rights, Limitations); 7. Term of Protection (including the "rule of the shorter term," if any); and, 8. Infringements (Civil Remedies, Penal Sanctions).

---

[1] In fact, however, such information is to a great extent actually furnished since in most countries, and in most respects, the copyright status of such works is the same as that of works entitled to protection under the Universal Copyright Convention.

ANDORRA

Andorra became bound by the Universal Copyright Convention, Protocol 2, and possibly, Protocol 1, on September 16, 1955.[1]

There is no Copyright Law in Andorra.

The Bishop of Urgel informed UNESCO on February 10, 1954, that "with regard to copyright and industrial property, which have very little application in Andorra (where, for example, there is no publishing house), only the case of *Radio-Andorra* has arisen. Its broadcasts are governed by private agreements between the station and authors' societies in Spain, France and other countries whose authors have an interest in such broadcasts."[2]

---

[1] The rights of the sovereign are jointly exercised in Andorra by the Bishop of Urgel and the President of the French Republic as co-Princes of Andorra. The Convention and Protocol 2 were ratified by both co-Princes; Protocol 1 was ratified only by the President of France. *See* CLTW, Andorra: Item 2, and CLTW, Universal Copyright Convention: Item 2.

[2] CLTW, Andorra: Item 1.

ARGENTINA

SOURCES

Internal Law.—The main source of the law of copyright in Argentina is the Law No. 11.723 of September 28, 1933.[1] It was amended by Legislative Decree No. 12.063 of October 2, 1957.[2] Hereinafter it is referred to as "the Law," and references to Articles, without further specification, are references to Articles of this Law.

Universal Copyright Convention.—Argentina became bound by the Universal Copyright Convention and its Protocols 1 and 2 on February 13, 1958.[3] The granting of licenses for the publication of translations provided for in Article V of the Universal Copyright Convention is regulated by Decree No. 1155 of January 31, 1958.[4,5]

English translations of the legislative texts in force in Argentina appear in "Copyright Laws and Treaties of the World."

ACQUISITION OF PROTECTION UNDER THE UNIVERSAL COPYRIGHT CONVENTION

With the exception of certain questions concerning the right of translation,[6] Argentina passed no special legislation for bringing its Law into harmony with certain requirements of the Universal Copyright Convention. In particular, there is nothing in the Law which would

[1] Boletín Oficial, September 30, 1933. Otherwise the general rules of law apply (Art. 12).
[2] Boletín Oficial, October 11, 1957.
[3] *See* CLTW, Argentina: Item 2A.
[4] Boletín Oficial, February 13, 1958.
[5] Argentina is a party to the Brussels Convention (1948) of the Berne Copyright Union, the Montevideo Copyright Convention of 1889, the Buenos Aires Copyright Convention of 1910, and the Washington Copyright Convention of 1946. Decree No. 106, 901 of June 3, 1937, provides protection for Danish authors, but since the adherence of Denmark to the Universal Copyright Convention, this Decree has only a limited importance. *See* CLTW, Argentina: Items 2, 3, 4, and 5.

The best commentaries on the law are the three-volume book of Carlos Mouchet and Sifrido A. Radaelli, entitled "Derechos intelectuales sobre las obras literarias y artísticas," published at Buenos Aires in 1948, and an essay of Carlos Mouchet, entitled "Protección de las obras literarias y artísticas en la Argentina (Relaciones internacionales en la materia)", published in the October 3, 1959, issue of "La Ley" in Buenos Aires.

[6] *See below,* page 220.

provide that formalities the fulfilment of which is required under the Law do not apply or may be avoided in Article III of the Universal Copyright Convention in the case of works which Argentina is supposed to protect under that Convention. It will be assumed in this chapter that in the case of possible conflicts between the Convention and the Law, the provisions of the Convention apply. In the absence of court decisions on the question, the correctness of this assumption cannot be regarded as officially confirmed.

The Law does not contain provisions on the question of what works are protected by Argentina by virtue of the Universal Copyright Convention. On the basis of the provisions contained in the Convention and its Protocols, and subject to the exceptions stated below, it is assumed that such works are: (i) published works of nationals of a Convention Country, irrespective of the place of first publication, (ii) works first published in a Convention Country, irrespective of the nationality of the author, (iii) unpublished works of nationals of a Convention Country other than Argentina, (iv) works of stateless persons and refugees who have their habitual residence in a State party to Protocol 1 (except perhaps Argentina) whether unpublished or published, and, if published, irrespective of the place of first publication, (v) works published for the first time by the United Nations, by any of the Specialized Agencies of the United Nations, or by the Organization of American States, as well as unpublished works of any of these Organizations.[7] It is assumed that, with the possible exception of the rule of the shorter term (discussed below),[8] works belonging to any of these categories are protected in Argentina, without deposit and registration and without the need of registering certain translation contracts,[9] provided always that, in the case of published works, the provisions of Article III of the Universal Copyright Convention concerning notice have been complied with. If a work, falling within any of the above categories is a work which has, as its country of origin, within the meaning of the Conventions of the Berne Union, a country member of that Union, protection in Argentina is available under the applicable Convention of the Berne Union rather than the Universal Copyright Convention.

Argentina has no renewal system, so that there is nothing in this country which would correspond to the renewal formalities existing in the United States.

---

[7] *See* Universal Copyright Convention, Article II, and Protocols 1 and 2.
[8] Article 15. *See* page 224, *below.*
[9] That is, it is assumed that the following provisions of the Law will not apply to these works: articles 13, 14, 30, 34(3), 57 to 70.

PROTECTED WORKS

The Law protects scientific, literary and artistic works. They are defined as including: writings of all kinds and any length; dramatic works; musical and dramatico-musical compositions; cinematographic, choreographic, and pantomimic works; drawings, paintings, works of sculpture and architecture; models and works of art or science applied to commerce or industry; printed matter (*impresos*), plans and maps; plastic works (*plásticos*), photographs, engravings and phonographic records; in general, every scientific, literary, artistic or educational production, whatever its process of reproduction.[10]

PROTECTED PERSONS

Copyright originally vests in the author of the work.[11] Unless assigned, it devolves upon his heirs.[12] Persons who, with the permission of the author, translate, rearrange, adapt, modify or transpose his work, have copyright in the new intellectual work resulting from such acts.[13] Unless and until the creator of an anonymous or pseudonymous work claims the copyright for himself by establishing his identity, copyright in such works belongs to the publisher; authors using a pseudonym may have it registered and thereby they acquire ownership over their pseudonymous works.[14]

In the absence of agreement to the contrary, collaborators in a work enjoy equal rights. Anonymous collaborators in a collective work have no copyright in the contributions which were commissioned from them; the publisher is their legal representative.[15] In the case of musical compositions with words, the composition and the text are considered distinct works.[16] In the absence of an agreement to the contrary, collaborators in a cinematographic work have equal rights; the author of the plot (*argumento*), the composer of the film music, and the film producer are considered as collaborators.[17] Any person who adapts, transposes (*transportar*), modifies, or parodies, a work with the authorization of the author is, unless otherwise agreed by contract, to be considered as co-author of the adaptation, transposition, modification, or parody.[18]

Unsigned articles, anonymous contributions, feature stories (*repor-*

---

[10] Article 1.   [11] Articles 2 and 3.   [12] Article 4.
[13] Article 4. The translator of a work not protected by copyright, while having copyright in his own translation, cannot oppose that other persons translate the same work (art. 24).
[14] Article 3.   [15] Article 16.   [16] Article 17.   [17] Article 20.
[18] Article 25. If these acts are done in relation to a work in the public domain, the adaptor, etc., will alone own the copyright, but he cannot oppose adaptation, etc., of the same work by other persons (art. 26).

tajes), drawings, engravings, or news in general, having an original and peculiar character, published by a daily newspaper, review or other periodical publication, and which have been obtained, as exclusive features (*con carácter de exclusividad*) by it or by a news agency, are considered as the property of such publication or agency.[19] If the contribution to a daily newspaper, review or other periodical publication is signed, the author is considered the owner of the copyright in the contribution. If the contribution is not signed, the author has only the right to publish it in a collection, unless there is a different agreement with the owner of the periodical publication.[20]

The Law also contains provisions concerning the protection of performing artists.[21] However, since their protection is generally considered as being outside the scope of the Universal Copyright Convention, it is believed that protection under these provisions of the Law cannot be claimed *by virtue of that Convention.*

ASSIGNMENT AND LICENSING

The author or his successor in title may, totally or partially, alienate or assign the work (*obra*), or rather the rights in the work. Alienation is only effective for the term fixed by law and confers upon the assignee the right to the economic exploitation of the work. He is not entitled to alter the title, form or contents of the work.[22] Alienation or assignment of pictorial, sculptural, or photographic works or of works of analogous arts, does not, unless otherwise agreed, mean that the right of reproduction has been alienated or assigned; this right remains with the author or his successor in title.[23] The alienation of plans, sketches and similar works give the assignee only the right to execute the work for which they were designed; he may not alienate, reproduce or use them for other purposes.[24]

Publishing Contracts.—When an author licenses the publication of his work, he does not thereby lose his copyright, unless he expressly renounces it in the publication contract. Consequently, he retains his right to translate, transform, recast, etc., the work, and he may defend his copyright against any infringers, including the publisher himself. The only rights the publisher acquires by virtue of the publishing contract are the rights to print, distribute and sell. If the work, prior to its publication, is lost or destroyed while in the possession of the publisher, he is liable to indemnify the author or his successors in title to an extent equal to the royalties or proceeds that would have been payable in the event of publication of the work. If the work is lost or destroyed

[19] Article 28(1).
[20] Article 29.　　[21] Article 56.　　[22] Article 51.　　[23] Article 54.
[24] Article 55. Contrary contractual arrangements are, of course, possible.

while in the possession of the author or his successor in title, he is liable to the publisher for any sum received as advance royalties, as well as for indemnification in respect of damages. If the publication contract is limited to a definite term and if, at the expiration of such term, the publisher possesses unsold copies of the work, the copyright owner may purchase them at cost plus ten per cent. If the copyright owner does not exercise this right, the publisher may continue the sale of the copies on the same conditions as those stipulated in the expired contract. Irrespective of the stipulated term, a publishing contract terminates if the agreed editions are all sold.[25]

Performance Contracts.—If an unpublished theatrical work is accepted for first performance by a theatrical manager (*empresario*), it must be performed within one year from delivery; if it is not performed within this period of time, the author may require as indemnity an amount equal to the author's royalties (*regalia*) for twenty performances of a work of the same kind. Acceptance of a theatrical work for performance does not give the person accepting it the right to reproduce it, or to have it performed by another enterprise, or in a form other than that stipulated, or to reproduce copies other than the indispensable ones, or to hire or sell such copies without the permission of the author. The manager is responsible in the event of the total or partial destruction of the original work, and if, owing to his negligence, the work is lost, or, without the authorization of the author or his successor in title, is reproduced or performed, the manager is required to give an indemnity for the resulting damage. Radiotelephonic transmission, cinematographic exhibition, television transmission, or any other methods of mechanical reproduction of literary or artistic works, are considered public performance.[26]

Registration of Assignments.—The alienation or assignment (*la enajenación o cesión*), whether total or partial, of a literary, scientific or musical work (*sic!*), must be inscribed in the *Registro Nacional de la Propiedad Intelectual* (National Registry of Intellectual Property); otherwise the alienation or assignment is not valid (*no tendrá validez*) in relation to third parties.[27]

PROTECTED RIGHTS

Economic Rights

The author has the right to dispose of, publish, perform, publicly exhibit, translate, and adapt his work; furthermore he has the right to authorize its translation and to reproduce it in any form.[28]

[25] Articles 37 to 44.   [26] Articles 45 to 50.   [27] Article 53.   [28] Article 2.

The right of translation is an exclusive right of authorization for the entire duration (generally the life of the author and 50 years after his death[29]) of copyright in the case of (i) works whose original is in the Spanish language, (ii) unpublished works, (iii) published works which have been published in Spanish translation within seven years of first publication of the work in its original language, provided the Spanish translation is not out of print. In case of published works (i) not published in Spanish translation within the stated period of seven years, or (ii) so published but out of print, the right of translation is an exclusive right of authorization during those seven years or until the Spanish translation is out of print, as the case may be. Thereafter the right is subject to compulsory licensing: the *Ministerio de Educación y Justicia* (Ministry of Education and Justice) grants to any national or foreigner domiciled in Argentina, who so requests, through the intermediary of the *Registro Nacional de la Propiedad Intelectual,* a non-exclusive license to translate and publish within Argentina any such work originally written in a language other than Spanish and protected by the Universal Copyright Convention. In order to obtain such license, the applicant must comply with the following conditions: (a) He must prove that the work corresponds to the definition given above. (b) He must establish that he has requested, and been denied, authorization by the owner of the translation right to make and publish the translation, or that, after due diligence on his part, he was unable to find the owner of the right of translation. (c) He must prove that, having failed to find the owner of the right of translation, he has sent copies of his application to the publisher whose name appears upon the work, and, if the nationality of the owner of the right of translation is known, to the diplomatic or consular representative of the State of which such owner is a national. In such cases, the license is not granted until after the expiration of two months from the date of the despatch of the copies of the application, which fact must be proved by the applicant by producing appropriate evidence of mailing. (d) He must entrust the making of the translation of the work to a person deemed to be competent by a committee consisting of a representative of the *Dirección General de Cultura,* a representative of writers, and a representative of book publishers. (e) He must declare the number of copies which would constitute the edition to be published, and the retail selling price of each copy. (f) He must deposit with the *Banco de la Nación Argentina,* to the order of the said Ministry and for handing over to the owner of the right of translation, an amount equal to one third of 10 per cent of the total value of sales to the public of the declared edition. (g) He must provide sufficient guarantee for the payment of the remaining two thirds of the 10 per cent; the corresponding amount

[29] *A contrario* from the Decree cited in the following footnote.

must be remitted within a period of two years from the date of grant of the license. The license cannot be transferred.[30]

Speeches, etc.—Political or literary speeches, and, in general, lectures on intellectual topics, may not be published without the express consent of their authors. The same holds for parliamentary speeches if publication is for profit.[31]

Music and Text.—The author of a libretto or of any other text set to music has an exclusive right to sell, print or perform his literary work separately from the music; and the composer of the music has the same right in respect of his musical work.[32]

Dramatic and Musical Works Resulting from Collaboration. —If two or more authors have collaborated in a dramatic or musical work, the authorization granted by one of them suffices for its public performance.[33]

Cinematographic Films.—Unless otherwise agreed by contract, (i) the producer of a cinematographic film has the right to exhibit it, even without the consent of the author of the plot or of the composer; (ii) the author of the plot has the exclusive right to publish the plot separately and to transform it into a literary or artistic work of another kind; (iii) the composer has the exclusive right to publish and perform his musical work separately.[34]

MORAL RIGHTS

No work may be published or performed, in whole or in part, other than with the title of and in the form given to it by its author.[35] Even where the author has alienated the copyright in his work, he retains the right to require faithful adherence to its text and to its title when printed, copied or reproduced; he also retains the right to require the mention of his name or pseudonym as author.[36] The producer of a cinematographic film, when publicly exhibiting it, must, in addition to his own name, mention the name of the author of the scenario or plot, or that of the authors of the original works from which the plot of the film is derived, the name of the composer, the artistic director or adapter, and the principal performers.[37]

LIMITATIONS

Any person may include, without the consent of the owner of the copyright, into commentaries, criticisms, notes, collections and an-

[30] Decree No. 1155 of January 31, 1958; Boletín Oficial of February 13, 1958; English translation in CLTW, Argentina: Item 2A.
[31] Article 27.
[32] Article 18.   [33] Article 19.   [34] Article 21.
[35] Article 36.   [36] Article 52.   [37] Article 22.

thologies published for educational purposes, up to 1000 words from literary or scientific works, or up to eight bars from musical works.[38]

News items of general interest may be freely utilized, transmitted or re-transmitted; but, when published in their original form, an indication of the source is required.[39]

The Law contains measures for the protection of privacy in connection with the publication of letters and portraits.[40]

TERM OF PROTECTION

Generally.—Copyright belongs to the author during his lifetime and to his heirs or successors in title for fifty years from the date of his death.[41] If the author dies without heirs, his rights pass to the State, without prejudice to the rights of third parties.[42] The Law provides that the heirs or successors in title may not oppose that a third person republish the work, or publish a translation of the work, if they have allowed more than ten years to elapse from the author's death, without themselves arranging for such republication or publication; and that the compensation to be paid to them by the third person is determined by arbitration if there is no agreement among the parties.[43] It is assumed that where this provision conflicts with the provisions concerning the right of translation, the latter will prevail.[44]

Collaborators.—In the case of a work of collaboration, the fifty-year *post mortem auctoris* term is computed from the death of the collaborator who dies last.[45]

Posthumous Works.—In the case of posthumous works, the fifty-year term is computed from the death of the author.[46]

Anonymous Works.—Copyright in anonymous works belonging to organizations (*instituciones*), corporate bodies (*corporaciones*), or juridical persons (*personas jurídicas*), lasts for fifty years, computed from the publication of the work.[47] When the various parts or volumes of the same work have been published separately in different years, the term runs, for each part or volume, from the year in which it was published; and when a work is published in instalments (*por entregas o folletines*) the date of publication of the last instalment is determinative.[48]

Photographic Works.—For photographic works, the term of

---

[38] Article 10, first and second paragraphs.   [39] Article 28, second paragraph.
[40] Articles 31, 32, 33, 35.
[41] Article 5, first paragraph.   [42] Article 5, fourth paragraph.
[43] Article 6.   [44] *See* page 220, above.   [45] Article 5, second paragraph.
[46] Article 5, third paragraph.   [47] Article 8.   [48] Article 11.

copyright is twenty years from first publication.[49] The Law contains no special provision concerning the duration of protection of unpublished photographic works.

Cinematographic Works.—For cinematographic works, the term of copyright is thirty years from the date of first publication, without prejudice to the protection of the works adapted to or reproduced in the cinematographic work.[50] The Law contains no special provision concerning the term of protection of unpublished cinematographic works.

Rule of the Shorter Term.—Where the work is the work of an author who is not a citizen of Argentina, and where it was first published outside Argentina, the term of protection in Argentina is cut back to the term provided in the law of the country of publication if that term is shorter than the term otherwise provided for by the Law of Argentina.[51] Apparently, this rule of the shorter term does not apply in the case of unpublished works.

INFRINGEMENTS

Preventive Measures.—Courts may order: the suspension of theatrical, cinematographic, philharmonic or other similar performances; the seizure of infringing works or the proceeds already obtained and any other measures which may adequately safeguard the rights protected by the Law.[52]

Penal Sanctions.—Most infringements are sanctioned by penalties (fine or imprisonment).[53]

Works in the Public Domain.—Complaints may be lodged with the *Registro Nacional de la Propiedad Intelectual* (National Registry of Intellectual Property) if a work, whose term of protection has expired, is mutilated, otherwise altered, or incorrectly translated. Corrective measures, or the payment of fines, or both, may be ordered by a panel whose composition is regulated in the Law.[54]

[49] Article 34, first paragraph.   [50] Article 34, second paragraph.
[51] Article 15.
[52] Article 79, first paragraph.
[53] Articles 71 to 78. For civil procedure, *see* Articles 80 to 82.
[54] Article 83.

AUSTRIA

SOURCES

Internal Law.—The main source of the law of copyright in Austria is Law No. 111 of 1936, as revised by Laws No. 206 of 1949, and No. 106 of 1953.[1] Hereinafter, it is referred to as "the Law" and references to Sections, without further specification, are references to Sections of this Law, as amended.

Universal Copyright Convention.—Austria became bound by the Universal Copyright Convention and Protocols 1 and 2 on July 2, 1957.[2]

ACQUISITION OF PROTECTION UNDER THE UNIVERSAL COPYRIGHT CONVENTION

The laws of Austria do not contain any special provision in respect of works to which Austria is supposed to grant protection by virtue of the Universal Copyright Convention.[3] The provisions of that Convention, particularly Articles II and XVII, and Protocols 1 and 2, determine which are the works protected under the Universal Copyright Convention. Briefly stated, such works are—except if excluded by virtue of Article XVII of the Universal Copyright Convention and the Appendix Declaration relating to the same Article (in which case the applicable Convention of the Berne Copyright Union rather than the

[1] The dates of these Laws are: April 9, 1936; July 14, 1949, and July 8, 1953. They were published in the Bundesgesetzblatt 1936, page 131; 1959, page 913; and 1953, page 487. English translation in CLTW, Austria: Item 1.

An excellent and detailed commentary on the Austrian copyright statute is Wilhelm Peter's "Das Österreichische Urheberrecht," published at Vienna in 1956 by Manzsche Verlags- und Universitätsbuchhandlung.

[2] Published under No. 108 of the Bundesgesetzblatt 1957, page 671; CLTW, Austria: Item 2A. Austria has also ratified the Berlin, Rome and Brussels Conventions of the Berne Copyright Union (CLTW, Austria: Item 3). It is a party to the Montevideo Copyright Convention and is bound thereunder with Argentine, Bolivia and Paraguay (CLTW, Austria: Item 4, and Montevideo Copyright Convention: Item 3). An Ordinance of 1907 concerning works of United States citizens (CLTW, Austria: Item 5), and a bilateral treaty concluded in 1930 with Germany (CLTW, Austria: Item 6) are of limited significance so long as the United States and the German Federal Republic, as well as Austria, continue to be parts to the Universal Copyright Convention.

[3] However, see "Rule of the Shorter Term," below.

Universal Copyright Convention governs): (i) published works of nationals of a Convention country, irrespective of the place of first publication, (ii) works first published in a Convention country, irrespective of the nationality of the author, (iii) unpublished works of nationals of a Convention country other than Austria, (iv) works of stateless persons and refugees who have their habitual residence in a State party to Protocol 1 (except perhaps Austria), whether published or unpublished, and if published, irrespective of the place of first publication, (v) works first published by the United Nations, by any of the Specialized Agencies of the United Nations, or by the Organization of American States, as well as unpublished works of any of these Organizations.

There seems to be no need to distinguish, as far as protection in Austria is concerned, between works protected under the Berne Conventions and the Universal Copyright Convention, since, once protection is available under any of these Conventions, the extent of the protection is the same in Austria.

Austria has no copyright formalities. Consequently, registration, deposit, or compliance with other formalities is neither required nor possible in Austria, and the absence, in itself, of a Convention notice on the copies of a published work is no bar to claiming protection in Austria. Furthermore, Austria has no renewal system, so that there is nothing in this country which would correspond to the renewal formalities existing in the United States.

PROTECTED WORKS

Works are original intellectual creations (*eigentümliche geistige Schöpfungen*) in the fields of literature, music (*Tonkunst*), art (*bildende Künste*) and artistic cinematography (*Filmkunst*).[4]

Works of literature are: (i) works in which the form of expression is language (*Sprachwerke*), (ii) choreographic and pantomimic works, (iii) works of scientific or educational nature consisting in two-dimensional or three-dimensional pictorial representations, as long as they do not come under the category of works of art.[5]

Works of art include, among others, works of the art of photography (*Werke der Lichtbildkunst, Lichtbildwerke*), architecture (*Baukunst*), and industrial arts (*Kunstgewerbe*).[6]

Translations and other adaptations (*Bearbeitungen*) are protected as new works, provided they are original intellectual creations of the translator or adaptor.[7] Compilations (*Sammlungen*) which constitute original intellectual creations by reason of the combination of separate

[4] Sections 1(1) and 4.   [5] Section 2.   [6] Section 3.   [7] Section 5(1).

contributions into a homogeneous whole are protected as "collective works" (*Sammelwerke*).[8]

Photographs (*Lichtbilder*), i.e., images produced by a photographic process or by a process similar to photography, must be distinguished from photographic *works*. The same applies to motion pictures (*Laufbilder*), i.e., productions (*Erzeugnisse*, not "works") of cinematography, as distinguished from cinematographic *works*. The difference between the two kinds lies in the presence or absence of original, artistic creativity. If artistic creativity is lacking, the "products," i.e., photographs or motion pictures, do not enjoy full copyright protection but only a protection of a lesser degree called neighboring rights (*verwandte Schutzrechte*).[9] It is not entirely clear whether, where protection depends on the applicability of the Universal Copyright Convention, Austria protects only photographic works and cinematographic works or also photographs and motion pictures. Since the Convention protects "works," it could be argued that Austria might deny protection to photographs and motion pictures since the Austrian Law does not recognize them as works.[10]

PROTECTED PERSONS

Generally.—Copyright originally vests in the author, i.e., the person who created the work.[11] Where several persons have jointly created a work and their creations merge in an inseparable unit, copyright belongs jointly to all co-authors.[12,13]

The author of a translation or other adaptation may exercise his right of exploitation (discussed below) only insofar as the author of the work from which the translation or other adaptation was made has granted the translator or adaptor the exclusive right or the permission to do so.[14]

The rights of exploitation of commercially produced cinematographic works vest in the film producer (*Filmhersteller*, the owner of the enterprise). The rights of the authors of the works used in the cinematographic work are not affected.[15]

In the absence of proof to the contrary, the person who is designated in the usual manner as author on the copies (*Vervielfältigungsstücke*) of

---

[8] Section 6.   [9] Section 73.

[10] Photographs and motion pictures are protected for only twenty years. For details concerning rights, duration, etc., *see* sections 74 and 75. Hereinafter, only photographic works and cinematographic works are taken into account.

[11] *See* section 10(1).

[12] Section 11(1): the combination of works of different kinds, such as music plus words, does not, in itself, constitute authorship of the above kind (section 11(3)).

[13] For presumption of authorship and anonymous works, *see* sections 12 and 13.

[14] Section 14(2).   [15] Section 38(1).

a published work, or on the original (*Urstück*) of a work of art, is presumed to be the author thereof, provided the designation gives his true name or a pseudonym by which he is known, or, in the case of works of art, a known signature.[16] The same applies to the person who is designated in the usual manner as author when the work is publicly delivered or recited, publicly performed or exhibited, or broadcast, unless, under the provision concerning published copies, another person is presumed to be the author.[17]

Anonymous Works.—As long as the author of a published work is not designated, the editor (*Herausgeber*), or, if no editor is designated on the copies, the publisher (*Verleger*), is considered as an agent entrusted by the author with the administration of the copyright.[18]

Letters, Portraits, etc.[19]—Letters, diaries and similar confidential writings may not be read in public or be distributed in any manner which would make them available to the public, if to do so would violate legitimate interests of the author or, if he died without having permitted or ordered their publication (*Veröffentlichung*), of a close relative.[20] Similar principles apply to the addressee of a letter.[21] Close relatives are defined as lineal ascendants and descendants and the surviving spouse. The protection is independent of copyright and lasts, in the case of children, parents and spouse, until their deaths and, in the case of other relatives, until the expiration of the tenth calendar year following the death of the author, or the addressee of a letter, as the case may be.[22]

Portraits of persons may not be exhibited in public or distributed in any manner which would make them available to the public if to do so would violate legitimate interests of the person portrayed or, if he died without having permitted or ordered them to be made public (*Veröffentlichung*), of a close relative.[23] The principles referred to in connection with letters apply analogously.[24]

ASSIGNMENT AND LICENSING

Transmission Mortis Causa.—Copyright is subject to inheritance; it may be bequeathed.[25]

Inalienability.—Copyright is inalienable (*unübertragbar*) *inter vivos*.[26]

Licensing.—The author may authorize other persons to use the

[16] Section 12(1).   [17] Section 12(2).   [18] Section 13.
[19] The provisions discussed onder this heading protect privacy rather than copyright. Consequently, it might be that the Universal Copyright Convention may not be invoked as a basis for applying these provisions to works protectable in Austria under that Convention.
[20] Section 77(1).   [21] Section 77(3).   [22] Section 77(2).   [23] Section 78(1).
[24] Section 78(2).   [25] Section 23(1).   [26] Section 23(3).

work (*Werknutzungsbewilligung*, "simple" license) by certain or all the methods recognized by the Law. He may grant to other persons the exclusive right to do so (*Werknutzungsrecht*, "exclusive" license).[27]

Exclusive Licenses.—The methods, the means, the territorial and time limitations of the use an exclusive licensee may make of the work are governed by the contract concluded with the author.[28] Exclusive licenses are subject to inheritance and alienation.[29] As a rule, exclusive licenses may be transferred to a third person (other than a general successor) only with the consent of the author.[30]

The transferor is a surety for the performance of his obligations *vis-à-vis* the author by the transferee.[31]

Where the exclusive license is not exercised in accordance with the purpose for which it was granted, or is exercised only to an extent so inadequate as to impair important interests of the author, the latter, if he is not at fault, may terminate the contract before the expiration of its contemplated duration.[32]

Dispositions made in advance concerning works to be created in the future are valid.[33] Either party may, however, terminate such contracts after five years from their conclusion if the author undertakes to grant exclusive licenses in respect of all his future works not specifically (*näher*) designated, or in respect of all his future works designated only as to their kinds, to be created during his lifetime or during a term exceeding five years.[34]

Rules of Interpretation.—Where there is no agreement to the contrary, (i) the grant of an exclusive license to use a work does not include a permission to translate or adapt it, (ii) the grant of an exclusive license to "multiply" a literary or musical work does not include a permission to "multiplication" on visual or sound fixations (*Bild- oder Schallträger*), (iii) the grant of an exclusive license to broadcast a work does not include a permission to make visual or sound fixations during the broadcasting or for the purposes of broadcasting.[35]

In case of doubt, transfer of the property of the physical object incorporating or being the work (*Werkstück*) is not deemed to include the grant of a simple or exclusive license to use the work.[36]

Where a work is accepted as a contribution to a periodical publication (newspaper, periodical, yearbook, almanac, and the like), the author retains the right to multiply and distribute his work in any other manner, unless there is an agreement to the contrary or the circumstances reflect a different intention of the parties.[37] Even where the publisher acquired an exclusive right, this expires (i) immediately after the publication of

[27] Section 24. [28] Section 26. [29] Section 27(1).
[30] Section 27(2), (4), (5), and section 28.
[31] Section 27(3). [32] Section 29. [33] Section 31(1). [34] Section 31(2).
[35] Section 33(1). [36] Section 33(2). [37] Section 36(1).

the contribution, if publication was in a newspaper, (ii) at the end of the calendar year following the year in which publication took place, if publication was in a periodical publication other than a newspaper or in a non-periodical compilation (*Sammlung*) and no payment for the author was stipulated.[38]

Collective Editions.—The author who has granted to another person an exclusive license to multiply and distribute a literary or musical work may nevertheless multiply and distribute the same work in a complete collective edition of his works (*Gesamtausgabe*) from the expiration of the calendar year in which the work was first published (*erschienen*); this right cannot be limited or waived by contract.[39]

Rights of Film Producers.—The rights of exploitation belonging to a film producer[40] are subject to inheritance and alienation.[41] Exclusive licenses concerning the exploitation of commercially-produced cinematographic works may be transferred by the exclusive licensee to a third person without the consent of the film producer, except where it has been otherwise agreed between the film producer and the exclusive licensee.[42]

PROTECTED RIGHTS

ECONOMIC RIGHTS

Generally.—The author has the exclusive right to exploit his work (*Verwertungsrecht*), but only by the methods enumerated in the Law.[43]

Right of Multiplication.—The author has the exclusive right to multiply the work.[44] The fixing of a delivery, recitation or performance of work on any device serving to reproduce it repeatedly for the eye or for the ear (visual and sound fixations), such as film strips or phonograph records, are considered a "multiplication."[45] Where the author has permitted another person to "multiply" and distribute a musical work (together with the words, if any, belonging thereto) on sound recordings, any phonograph record manufacturer may require that he be given a permission to so "multiply" and distribute the same work for an equitable compensation. If the author refuses to grant the permission for an equitable compensation, the courts may grant the permission. Permissions granted under such compulsory licenses are valid only for "multiplication" and distribution in Austria and countries where the

[38] Section 36(2).   [39] Section 34.
[40] Discussed on page 231, below.
[41] Section 40(1).   [42] Section 40(3).   [43] Section 14(1).
[44] Section 15(1). The Execution of artistic works on the basis of plans or designs is multiplication (section 15(4)).
[45] Section 15(2).

author is not protected against the "multiplication" and distribution of his works on sound recordings. These compulsory licenses apply only to purely sound recordings and not to audio-visual recordings, such as sound films.[46]

Right of Distribution.—The author has the exclusive right to distribute (*verbreiten*) copies of the work (*Werkstücke*). This includes keeping in stock for the purposes of sale (*feilhalten*) and putting into circulation in a way that makes the work accessible to the public.[47] The right of distribution does not extend to copies of the work (*Werkstücke*) which, with the authorization of the person entitled thereto, have been put into circulation by transfer of the property of such copies; however, where such authorization has been given only for a specified territory, the right to distribute (*verbreiten*), outside such territory, copies (*Werkstücke*) which have been put into circulation (*in Verkehr gebracht*) in such territory is not affected.[48] The right of distribution does not extend to copies (*Werkstücke*) of a work of art which are fixtures on realty.[49]

Right of Broadcasting.—The author has the exclusive right to broadcast (*senden*) the work by radio or any similar method.[50]

Right of Performance.—The author has the exclusive right publicly to deliver (*vortragen*) or perform (*aufführen*) a work of which the form of expression is language (*Sprachwerk*); to perform (*aufführen*) a choreographic or pantomimic work by gestures and other motions of the body; to perform (*aufführen*) a musical work; to exhibit (*aufführen*) a cinematographic work; to exhibit (*vorführen*) a cinematographic work; to exhibit (*vorführen*) a work of art by means of optical contrivances.[51] It is immaterial whether these acts are done directly, or by means of sound or visual fixations,[52] radio or television receiving sets,[53] or loudspeakers operated outside the place (theatre, hall, etc.) where these acts occur.[54]

Right of Exploitation of Cinematographic Works.—The film producer has the exclusive right to exploit commercially (*gewerbsmässig*) produced works;[55] however, the authorization of the authors

---

[46] Section 58.
[47] Section 16(1). As long as the work remains unpublished, the right of distribution includes also the exclusive right to make the work accessible to the public by publicly posting, showing, hanging or exhibiting (*anschlagen, auflegen, aushängen, ausstellen*) copies of the work (*Werkstücke*) (section 16(2)).
[48] Section 16(3).   [49] Section 16(4).   [50] Section 17(1).   [51] Section 18(1).
[52] Section 18(2).
[53] Section 18(3). However, the received radio broadcasts of works of which the form of expression is language, and of musical works, may be publicly performed by means of loudspeakers, provided permission has been obtained from the competent performing rights society (section 59).
[54] Section 18(3).   [55] Section 38(1).

of the cinematographic work, as well as of the producer, is required for the exploitation of adaptations and translations of the cinematographic work.[56]

MORAL RIGHTS

The author has the right to the recognition of his authorship;[57] he cannot waive this right.[58] He has the right to determine whether the work should bear a designation of his authorship, and the character of such designation.[59] Without the authorization of the author, his work may not, as a rule, be abridged, added to, or otherwise altered.[60] Even where the author has agreed to alterations, he retains the right to oppose distortions, mutilations, or other alterations seriously violating his moral interests in the work.[61]

LIMITATIONS

The Law provides for various kinds of free uses of certain kinds of works in the interest of the administration of justice and public administration;[62] for personal use;[63] in connection with certain speeches,[64] newspaper or other periodical articles;[65] for the purposes of instruction, churches, schools;[66] in the case of certain single passages, small portions, etc.;[67] certain non-profit and charitable performances;[68] and some other cases.[69]

TERM OF PROTECTION

Works Other than Cinematographic Works.—Protection of works, other than cinematographic works, generally ends at the expiration of the fiftieth year following the death of the author, (i) if the author has been designated in a manner that creates a presumption of authorship in his favor (see above), (ii) even if the author is not so designated, provided his name is notified to the Ministry of Education.[70] Otherwise, protection generally ends at the expiration of the fiftieth year following the publication (*Veröffentlichung*) of the work.[71]

[56] Section 39(4). The author may refuse their authorization only for sufficient reason (section 39(5)).
[57] Section 19(1).   [58] Section 19(2).   [59] Section 20(1).
[60] Sections 21(1) and 39(3). This rule applies also to the producer of a cinematographic work (section 38(2)).
[61] Section 21(3).   [62] Section 41.   [63] Section 42.   [64] Section 43.
[65] Section 44.   [66] Sections 45, 51, 54.   [67] Sections 46, 47, 48, 49, 52.
[68] Sections 50, 53.   [69] *See* sections 54, 55, 56, 57.
[70] Sections 60, 61, 63, 64, 65; *see* also Order No. 171 of 1936 concerning the register kept for this purpose (Bundesgesetzblatt 1936, page 370; CLTW, Austria: Item 2).
[71] Sections 61, 63, 64, 65.

Cinematographic Works.—One must differentiate between (i) cinematographic works published (*veröffentlicht*) before the expiration of the thirtieth calendar year following filming (*Aufnahme*), and (ii) cinematographic works not so published. In the first case, protection lasts until the expiration of the thirtieth year following publication; in the second case, until the expiration of the thirtieth year following filming.[72]

Extension on Account of the Second World War.—The terms of 50 and 30 years have been prolonged by seven years (to a total of fifty-seven and thirty-seven years, as the case may be) for works which meet the following two conditions: (i) they were created prior to January 1, 1949; (ii) their term of protection had not expired before October 14, 1953.[73] Where the author has granted an exclusive or "simple" (i.e., non-exclusive) license to use a work before October 14, 1953, such grant, in case of doubt, does not extend to the additional period of seven years; however, any person who, for a consideration, has acquired an exclusive or "simple" license to use the work is entitled to continued use during the added period of seven years, upon payment of an equitable compensation.[74] Works by authors who are not Austrian nationals and which were not first published in Austria benefit from the seven-year extension only insofar as the country of which the author is a national grants Austrian works a longer term than Austrian works would have in Austria without this extension.[75] The applicability of the seven-year extension has been expressly stated in respect of (i) works of Norwegian citizens and works of which the country of origin is Norway;[76] (ii) works of Spanish nationals.[77]

Rule of the Shorter Term.—Subject to what has been referred to in connection with the possible extension by seven years, works entitled to protection in Austria under the Universal Copyright Convention enjoy protection in Austria for the terms described above, irrespective of the duration of protection they enjoy in other countries. In other words, Austria does not apply the rule of the shorter term permitted under Article IV (4) of the Universal Copyright Convention.[78]

[72] Section 62.   [73] Act No. 106 of 1953, Section III(1).
[74] Act No. 106 of 1953, Section III (3).   [75] Act No. 106 of 1953, Section III (2).
[76] Note of the Minister of Foreign Affairs of Austria to the Chargé d'Affaires of Norway in Vienna, of December 12, 1957; published in the Bundesgesetzblatt 1957, page 380. *See* CLTW, Austria: Item 7.
[77] *See* file No. Zl. 129.254/59 of the Austrian Bundesministerium für Justiz (Federal Ministry of Justice).
[78] Law No. 109 of 1957 (Bundesgesetzblatt 1957, page 702; CLTW, Austria: Item 8) authorized the Federal Ministry of Justice to reduce, by decree, in accordance with Article IV of the Universal Copyright Convention, the term of protection of works protected in Austria by virtue only of that Convention, if such reduction is necessary in order to protect Austrian interests in a given country. So far, no use has been made of this authorization.

INFRINGEMENTS

Civil Remedies.—Injunctions are available to prevent anticipated infringements or the continuation or repetition of actual infringement.[79] Actions for the elimination of unlawful situations (destruction of the products and instruments of infringement, etc.) may be claimed.[80] The right to damages, surrender of profits, equitable compensation, and the liability of master for infringements committed by his servants, are regulated in some detail.[81]

Penal Sanctions.—Some of the infringements, committed intentionally, are punishable by fine. Prosecution takes place only upon request of the injured party.[82] Infringing articles and contrivances serving infringement may be ordered by the court to be destroyed.[83]

---

[79] Section 81.   [80] Sections 82 to 84.   [81] Sections 86 to 90.   [82] Section 91.
[83] Section 92. For seizure, *see* section 93.

BELGIUM

SOURCES

Internal Law.—The basic instrument is the Law on Copyright of March 22, 1886, amended by the Laws of March 5, 1921, June 25, 1921, and March 11, 1958.[1] Hereinafter, it is referred to as "the Law," and references to Articles, without further specification, are references to the Articles of this Law, as amended.

The Law of July 27, 1953, provides that Belgian nationals may claim, for their benefit, the application of the provisions of the Berne-Brussels Convention in all cases where these provisions are more favorable than those of the Law of 1886, and its amendments.[2]

The Law of June 25, 1921, introduced the *droit de suite*,[3] but since it appears to be applicable only to the artistic works of Belgian and French[4] nationals, it is not further taken into consideration in this book.

Universal Copyright Convention.—Belgium became bound by the Universal Copyright Convention and Protocols 1 and 2 as from August 31, 1960.[5]

---

[1] Published in Moniteur Belge, March 26, 1886; March 27, 1921, August 20, 1921; May 7, 1953. An English translation appears in CLTW as Belgium: Item 1.

The best and most up-to-date commentaries on Belgian copyright law are "Le Droit d'auteur en Belgique; la législation belge mise en concordance avec la Convention de l'Union de Berne et annotée d'après la doctrine et la jurisprudence", by Pierre Recht, published at Brussels by the Maison Ferdinand Larcier, S.A., Editeurs, in 1955, and "Le droit d'auteur sur les exécutions musicales", by the same author, published by the same publisher, in 1960. The first of these books contains the full text of the laws and regulations of Belgium in French.

[2] Published in "Moniteur Belge," July 27, 1953. English translation: CLTW, Belgium: Item 1A.

[3] Published in "Moniteur Belge," August 20, 1921. English translation: CLTW, Belgium: Item 2.

[4] Royal Decree of September 5, 1923, published in "Moniteur Belge," October 13, 1923. English translation: CLTW, Belgium: Item 3.

[5] *See* CLTW, Belgium: Item 4A. Belgium is a member of the Berne Union since its foundation and has ratified all the Conventions of that Union. It became bound by the latest (Brussels) Convention on August 1, 1951 (*see* "Le Droit d'auteur", 1951, page 85).

ACQUISITION OF PROTECTION UNDER
THE UNIVERSAL COPYRIGHT CONVENTION

Applicable Provisions of Belgian Law.—None of the Belgian statutes dealing with copyright law contains any reference to the Universal Copyright Convention. Belgian courts do not seem to have had before them cases involving the Convention. This situation creates some uncertainty as to exactly what provisions of the Belgian law apply to works which, under the terms of the Universal Copyright Convention, Belgium should protect (hereinafter referred to as "Convention works"). The difficulty of interpretation is increased by the fact that it seems to be rather doubtful whether Belgian courts would recognize the supremacy of a treaty over Belgian statutes conflicting with the treaty.[6]

Subject to two exceptions, the Belgian Law of 1886, as amended, does not differentiate between Belgian and non-Belgian works, since it provides that foreigners shall enjoy in Belgium the rights guaranteed by that Law.[7] The two exceptions concern the rule of the shorter term and material reciprocity:

Rule of the Shorter Term.—The Law provides that "Foreigners enjoy in Belgium the rights guaranteed by this law except that their duration cannot, as far as they are concerned, exceed the duration fixed by the Belgian law. However, if they expire earlier in their country, they terminate at the same instant in Belgium."[8] The provision is perhaps not entirely clear. Is it the nationality of the author or the place of first publication which decides, in the case of a published work which foreign law is applicable? Is the comparison to be effected between the durations provided for *in general* by the Belgian and the foreign laws, or between the durations of the protection that a *particular* work (or a particular right(?)) enjoys under the Belgian and the foreign laws? The basic idea of the provision is the same as that of Article IV, paragraph (3), of the Universal Copyright Convention. In view of the vague language of the Belgian provision, it is perhaps not impossible to interpret it in the sense of the Convention. On the other hand, while the Convention provides, the Law does not provide for (i) differentiation between published and unpublished works, (ii) simultaneous publication, (iii) comparison by "classes" of works.[9] It seems therefore equally possible that these qualifications by the Convention of the basic rule of comparison of terms will not apply in Belgium.

[6] *See* Court of Appeals of Brussels, July 5, 1953.

[7] Article 38, first paragraph.

[8] "*Les étrangers jouissent en Belgique des droits guarantis par la présente loi sans que la durée de ceux-ci puisse, en ce qui les concerne, excéder la durée fixée par la loi belge. Toutefois, s'ils viennent à expirer plus tôt dans leurs pays, ils cesseront au même moment en Belgique.*" (Article 38, first paragraph.) The above translation tries to reflect all the obscurities of the original French.

[9] Universal Copyright Convention, Article IV, paragraphs 4, 5, and 6.

Material Reciprocity.—The Law also provides that if it is "established" (*constaté*) that Belgian authors receive less extensive protection in a foreign country, the nationals (*ressortissants*) of such country, as regards their works published abroad, may benefit only to the same extent from the provisions of the Belgian Law.[10] This rule of material reciprocity—if applicable also in the case of works that are supposed to be protected in Belgium by virtue of the Universal Copyright Convention—would be contrary to that Convention since (subject to the sole exception of the rule of the shorter term) the Universal Copyright Convention prescribes national treatment irrespective of the existence or absence of reciprocity.

The Law of 1953.—As already indicated, the Law of July 27, 1953, provides that Belgians may claim, for their benefit, the application of the provisions of the Berne-Brussels Convention in all cases where these provisions are more favorable than those of the Belgian Law on Copyright. There is no doubt that the basic principle of the Universal Copyright Convention is national treatment, by virtue of which Belgium would have to give, in all respects, the same protection to nationals of Convention countries (and to works first published in Convention countries) as it gives to its own nationals. Consequently, it could be argued that the Law of 1953 applies to works protectable under the Convention. On the other hand, the very specific character of the Law, namely that it extends certain provisions of the *Brussels* Convention to *Belgians*, throws some doubt on the possibility of extending benefits of that Law to nationals who are not Belgians and whose country may not be party to the Brussels Convention. If Belgium found it necessary to adopt a special measure extending the benefits of the Brussels Convention to its *own* nationals, would it not be logical to suppose that, in the absence of a special measure, Belgium may refuse to extend the benefits of the Brussels Convention to works protectable only by virtue of the Universal Copyright Convention? In view of these doubts, the following analysis of the protection granted by Belgium *qua* party to the Universal Copyright Convention will, to be on the safe side, disregard any provision which, on the basis of the Law of 1953, might be applicable to works to which the Universal Copyright Convention is applicable in Belgium.

Nature of Protection.—It follows from the above considerations that it would seem that Belgium grants a different protection to works whose country of origin, within the meaning of the Berne Convention, is a Berne Union country,[11] than to works which have no such country as country of origin. Furthermore, it would seem that the protection

[10] Article 38, second paragraph.
[11] As to which works are "Berne works" *see* the chapter on Article XVII of the Universal Copyright Convention, page 110, above.

available to works belonging to the latter category (i.e., "non-Berne works") is the same[12] whether or not the work is eligible for protection under the Universal Copyright Convention.

Subject to one exception concerning a rather special situation,[13] acquisition of copyright is not subject to the fulfillment of any formality in Belgium. Consequently, registration, deposit, or compliance with other formalities is neither required nor possible in Belgium, and the absence, in itself, of the Convention notice on the copies of a published work is no bar to claiming protection in Belgium.[14] Furthermore, Belgium has no copyright renewal system, so there is nothing in Belgium which would correspond to the renewal formalities existing, for example, in the United States.

Formalities.—Belgium has no copyright formalities. Consequently, registration, deposit, or compliance with other formalities is not required, and the absence, in itself, of a Convention notice on the copies of a published work is no bar to claiming protection in Belgium. Furthermore, Belgium has no renewal system, so that there is nothing in this country which would correspond to the renewal formalities existing in the United States.

PROTECTED WORKS

Literary and artistic works are protected.[15] The Law contains no definitions and no examples, but it does expressly mention musical works,[16] and provides that literary works comprise not only writings, but also lessons, sermons, lectures, speeches, and any other oral manifestations of thought.[17] It also provides that the fact that a work of art is reproduced by an industrial process or is applied to an industrial product does not affect the applicability of the Copyright Law.[18] Photographic works[19] and cinematographic works[20] are protected.

[12] Except, perhaps, certain details of comparison of terms; *see above* (preceding page) As to which works are Universal Copyright Convention works, see the chapters on Articles II and XVII of the Universal Copyright Convention, above.

[13] In the case of posthumous works, discussed on page 15, below.

[14] However, protection against copying by a newspaper of a newspaper article previously published in another newspaper depends on the existence of a special notice, accompanying the article, prohibiting reproduction (Article 16).

[15] Article 1.

[16] *See* Articles 16 to 18.

[17] Article 10, first paragraph. However, speeches made in deliberative assemblies, at public court proceedings, or at political gatherings may be freely published; but only the author has the right to have reprints made (*tirer à part*) thereof (Article 10, second paragraph).

[18] Article 21. Floral motifs of table napkins were held to be artistic works (Court of Appeals of Brussels, January 22, 1961).

[19] Tribunal of Ghent, February 23, 1955.

[20] Cour de Cassation, February 13, 1941, and November 11, 1943.

PROTECTED PERSONS

Copyright originally vests in the author. In the case of works created by employees in the course of their employment, implied assignment of the copyright to the employer is presumed.[21]

In the case of published anonymous and pseudonymous works, the publisher is deemed to be author, as far as third parties are concerned.[22]

When copyright is undivided, its exercise is regulated by agreement among the co-owners; in the absence of agreement, no co-owner may exercise the copyright by himself; failing agreement, the courts decide.[23]

In the case of works consisting of music and words (or a libretto), neither the composer nor the author may combine his work with that of a third person. However, the composer may independently authorize the publication or public performance of his work; and the author may independently authorize the publication, public performance, or translation of his work.[24]

In the case of a portrait, neither the author nor the proprietor thereof may reproduce or publicly exhibit it without the consent of the person portrayed or his successors in title during twenty years following the death of such person.[25]

ASSIGNMENT AND LICENSING

Generally.—Copyright is movable property; it is assignable and transmissible, in whole or in part, according to the rules of the Civil Code.[26] The transfer of a work of art does not transfer the right of reproduction on the person acquiring such work.[27]

Safeguard of Moral Rights.—The assignee of copyright or of the physical object incorporating the literary or musical work or work of the figurative arts (*œuvre ... des arts de dessin*), may neither alter the work in order to sell or exploit it, nor publicly exhibit the altered work, without the consent of the author or his successors in title.[28]

---

[21] Corr., Brussels, March 11, 1942; I.C., 1943, page 70.
[22] Article 7, first paragraph; upon revealing his identity, the author resumes the exercise of his rights also vis-à-vis third parties (Art. 7, second para.).
[23] Article 6, first paragraph; the courts have discretion in fixing the conditions of publication; they may deprive the objecting co-owner of any right to royalties and may even authorize the omission of his name on the work (Art. 6, third para.).
[24] Article 18.
[25] Article 20, first paragraph; even authorized reproductions may not bear the author's name (Art. 20, second para.).
[26] Article 3.   [27] Article 19.   [28] Article 9.

PROTECTED RIGHTS

Economic Rights

Reproduction.—The author has the exclusive right to reproduce his work and to authorize its reproduction in any manner or form.[29] Sound and visual fixation constitutes reproduction.[30] The erection of a building according to the plans of the architect constitutes reproduction of the plans.[31] Photographing of works of art, whether two-dimensional or three-dimensional, constitutes reproduction of such a work.[32] Slavish imitation of, or danger of confusion with, the plaintiff's work is not a prerequisite of infringement.[33]

Sale, etc.—Manuscript copies of a printed or manuscript musical score may not be sold, published, or hired without the authorization of the owner of the copyright; if such copies were made for the use of performing artists only, their sale constitutes infringement.[34]

Translation.—Copyright in a literary work includes the exclusive right to make, or authorize the making of, translations.[35]

Performance.—Literary and musical works may be publicly performed only with the consent of their authors.[36] To cause a work to be seen or heard in public by means of a radio or television receiving set constitutes public performance.[37]

Use of Works in Cinematography.—It appears that the consent of the owner of the copyright is required for the fixation or public exhibition of a work by cinematographic means.[38]

Broadcasting.—The consent of the owner of the copyright is required for the sound or television broadcasting of a work.[39] It is one of the peculiar features of the Belgian copyright law that the broadcasting of a commercial disk is held to be both reproduction and performance; consequently, when a work is broadcast by means of a

[29] Article 1.
[30] Court of Cassation, February 13, 1941, Pasicrisie Belge, 1941, I, page 40.
[31] Tribunal of Brussels, June 16, 1954, Journal des Tribunaux, 1955, page 109.
[32] Court of Cassation, December 14, 1953, Pasicrisie Belge, 1953, I, page 215.
[33] Tribunal of Brussels, May 23, 1951, Pasicrisie Belge, 1951, III, page 90.
[34] Tribunal of Verviers, June 24, 1931.
[35] Article 12.
[36] Articles 15 and 16. The composer of the music in a cinematographic work has a separate right of public performance whether the composition existed prior to and independently of the cinematographic work, or whether it was composed for and used only in the cinematographic work (Court of Appeals of Brussels, March 10, 1949).
[37] Court of Cassation, July 12, 1934; December 23, 1937; February 26, 1960.
[38] *A contrario* Article 21bis.
[39] *A contrario* Article 21bis.

commercial disk, consent of the owners or exclusive licensees of both the right of recording ("right of mechanical reproduction or mechanical adaptation") and the right of public performance is required.[40]

Arrangement.—Copyright in musical works includes the exclusive right of making arrangements based upon themes (*motifs*) from the original work.[41]

Moral Rights

The author may require his name to appear on all copies of his work.[42]

The author has a right to protection against any alterations to or omissions from his work which may be prejudicial to his honor or reputation.[43]

Exceptions and Limitations

Quotations.—Copyright in literary works does not prevent quotations from a work for the purposes of criticism, polemics or teaching.[44] The freedom of quotation does not extend to musical and artistic works; consequently, a newspaper may not freely publish a photograph of a painting.[45]

Newspaper Articles.—Newspaper articles not bearing a special notice prohibiting reproduction may be freely reproduced in other newspapers, but the source from which they were taken must be indicated.[46] News of the day is not protected.[47]

Reporting Current Events.—The authorization of the copyright proprietor is not required for the reproduction, recording and public communication of short extracts from literary and artistic works for the purposes of reporting current events by means of (i) photography, (ii) cinematography, (iii) broadcasting (sound or television). The same applies as regards the reproduction and public communication of works of plastic art (*œuvres plastiques*) in their entirety, but only if the use of the entire work is necessary in connection with such reporting.[48]

TERM OF PROTECTION

Generally.—Copyright expires fifty years after the death of the author, or, when the work is the result of collaboration, the last sur-

[40] Court of Cassation, January 19, 1956.
[41] Article 17.
[42] Tribunal of Brussels, February 25, 1954, Journal des Tribunaux, 1954, page 279.
[43] Tribunal of Brussels, June 17, 1931, Pasicrisie Belge, 1931, III, page 161.
[44] Article 13.
[45] Court of Cassation, December 4, 1952, Pasicrisie Belge, 1953, I, page 215.
[46] Commercial Tribunal of Brussels, June 25, 1923, J.C.B., 1923, page 301.
[47] Article 14.   [48] Article 21bis.

viving author.[49] This rule applies also to the composer of the music and the author of the libretto of an opera.[50]

Posthumous Works.—The proprietors of posthumous works enjoy copyright for fifty years from the date on which the work is published, performed, or exhibited, provided the date of publication, performance, or exhibition is registered in a special register of the *Ministère de l'Education nationale et de la Culture* within six months of these acts.[51]

Extension on Account of the First World War.—Works which fulfil the following two conditions, namely, (i) were not in the public domain on June 25, 1921, (ii) were first published before August 4, 1924, are protected, not for fifty, but for sixty, years *p.m.a.*[52]

Rule of the Shorter Term.—As to the application of the rule of the shorter term (comparison of terms), *see* page 236 above.

INFRINGEMENTS

Injunctions and seizure are specially regulated in the Law.[53]

Any wilful (*méchante*) or fraudulent violation of copyright is a delict.[54]

It constitutes a *délit* (offence) to sell, expose for sale, stock for purposes of sale, or import into Belgium for commercial purposes copies that the defendant knows to be infringing objects (*objets contrefaits*).[55]

The wilful (*méchante*) or fraudulent application to a work of art, literature or music of the name or sign of an author (who, in reality, is not the author of the work) is an offence, and so is the sale, exposition for sale, stocking for purposes of sale, or importation into Belgium for commercial purposes of objects that the defendant knows to carry such markings.[56]

Offences are punishable by fines or imprisonment; the instruments of the infringement as well as the infringing objects must or may be confiscated; the proceeds of an infringing performance may be seized.[57]

[49] Articles 2 and 5.
[50] Tribunal of Liège, January 20, 1927, Pasicrisie Belge, 1928, III, page 1949.
[51] Article 4; Royal Decree of March 27, 1886 (Moniteur Belge, May 6, 1886), and Decree of the Minister of Agriculture, Industry, and Public Works of April 3, 1886 (Moniteur Belge, May 6, 1886).
[52] Law of June 25, 1921, published in Moniteur Belge.
[53] Articles 29 to 37.   [54] Article 22, first paragraph.
[55] Article 22, second paragraph.   [56] Article 25.   [57] Articles 23, 24, 25.

BRAZIL

SOURCES

Internal Law.—The main source of the law of copyright in Brazil is the Civil Code: under Book II, Title II ("Property") a separate chapter deals with "Literary, Scientific and Artistic Copyright." The bulk of the provisions dates from 1916.[1] Another important source of the domestic law is Decree No. 4790 of January 2, 1924, particularly dealing with the right of public performance,[2] hereinafter referred to as "the Decree." The Penal Code provides punishments for copyright infringements.[3]

Hereinafter, references to Articles, without further specification, are references to Articles of the Civil Code.

Universal Copyright Convention.—Brazil became bound by the Universal Copyright Convention and Protocols 1 and 2 as from January 13, 1960.[4]

ACQUISITION OF PROTECTION UNDER THE UNIVERSAL COPYRIGHT CONVENTION

The laws of Brazil do not contain any special provisions in respect of works to which Brazil is supposed to grant protection by virtue of

[1] The Civil Code was promulgated by Law No. 3071 of January 1, 1916; amendments affecting provisions dealing with copyright were made by the Laws No. 3725 of January 15, 1919, and No. 3447 of October 23, 1958. See "Diario Oficial" of July 13, 1919, and October 25, 1958, respectively. English translation in CLTW, Brazil: Item 1. Provisions particularly dealing with copyright are contained in Articles 48, 178, 649 through 673, 1346 through 1362. The registration of works is regulated by Decree No. 4857 of November 9, 1939 ("Diario Oficial," of November 23, 1939: English translation in CLTW, Brazil: Item 2).

[2] "Diario Oficial," January 6, 1924. English translation in CLTW, Brazil: Item 3.

[3] The Penal Code was promulgated by Decree No. 2848 of December 7, 1940 ("Diario Oficial," December 31, 1940: English Translation in CLTW, Brazil: Item 4).

[4] CLTW, Brazil: Item 4a. Brazil is a party to the Berne Copyright Union, having ratified the Berlin Convention 1908, the Rome Convention 1928, and the Brussels Convention 1948 (CLTW, Brazil: Item 5). It is also a party to the Rio de Janeiro Copyright Convention of 1906, the Buenos Aires Copyright Convention of 1910, and the Washington Copyright Convention of 1946 (CLTW, Brazil: Items 6, 7, and 8). A bilateral copyright treaty was concluded with Portugal in 1922 ("Diario Oficial," January 23, and April 9, 1924: *see* English translation in CLTW, Brazil: Item 9).

the Universal Copyright Convention. The provisions of that Convention, particularly of Articles II and XVII and Protocols 1 and 2, determine which are the works protected under the Universal Copyright Convention. Briefly stated, such works are, except if excluded by virtue of Article XVII of the Universal Copyright Convention and the Appendix Declaration relating to the same Article (in which case the applicable Berne Convention rather than the Universal Convention governs): (i) published works of nationals of a Convention country, irrespective of the place of first publication, (ii) works first published in a Convention country, irrespective of the nationality of the author, (iii) unpublished works of nationals of a Convention country other than Brazil, (iv) works of stateless persons and refugees who have their habitual residence in a State party to Protocol 1 (except perhaps Brazil), either published or unpublished, and if published, irrespective of the place of first publication, (v) works first published by the United Nations, by any of the Specialized Agencies of the United Nations, or by the Organization of American States, as well as unpublished works of any of these organizations.

The only case in which it might be necessary to distinguish between works protected under the Universal Copyright Convention and works protected under a Convention of the Berne Copyright Union is the case of the rule of the shorter term, discussed below.

Deposit and registration of each work disclosed by means of typography, lithography, engraving, moulding, or any other system of reproduction is required in the *Biblioteca Nacional, Instituto Nacional de Música,* or *Escola Nacional de Belas Artes de Distrito Federal,* according to the nature of the work.[5] Such deposit and registration is required as a condition of protection but may be avoided, in the case of works protected under the Universal Copyright Convention, if the Convention notice is applied as provided for by Article III of the Universal Copyright Convention.[6] Unpublished works are protected without any formalities.[7] Works originating in a country member of the Berne Copyright Union are protected without any formality.[8]

Brazil has no renewal system, so that there is nothing in this country which would correspond to the renewal formalities existing in the United States.

PROTECTED WORKS

Literary, scientific and artistic works are protected.[9] They are not defined. Theatrical works (tragedies, dramas, comedies and other

[5] Article 673; Decree, article 1.
[6] *See* page 3 above.
[7] Universal Copyright Convention, Article III (4).
[8] Cf. Brussels Convention, Article 4(2).
[9] Article 649.

theatrical productions) and musical compositions are specifically referred to.[10]

PROTECTED PERSONS

Copyright vests in the author of the work.[11]

If a work is made up of articles or extracts from the works of different authors, whether gathered in a single volume or distributed in instalments (*series*) such as newspapers, magazines, dictionaries, encyclopaedias and collections of selected works, the rights of economic exploitation rest in the publisher (*editor de publicação*), but the authors of the different works included retain the copyright in their individual productions and may reproduce them separately.[12]

In the case of anonymous or pseudonymous works, the publisher exercises the rights of economic exploitation; however, if the author discloses his identity, he assumes the exercise of such rights (without prejudice to the rights acquired by the publisher).[13]

In the absence of an agreement to the contrary, collaborators who have jointly created a work, hold equal rights therein. None of them may reproduce the work or authorize its reproduction without the permission of the other collaborators, except in the case of a collection of the complete works of any such collaborators.[14] If they disagree, the majority decides; if there is no majority, the Court decides.[15]

The translator of a work in the public domain or the writer of authorized versions or translations of a work protected by copyright has copyright in his translation or revision.[16] Any person who reproduces a work of art by means of a different artistic process or by the same artistic process, if the latter involves originality in the composition, has copyright in his reproduction.[17] Any person who, with the authorization of the composer of a musical work, writes arrangements or variations based upon the themes (*motivos*) of such work, has copyright in his arrangement or variation.[18]

The author of an abridgment or résumé owns the copyright therein if he made it with the consent of the owner of the copyright of the work from which the abridgment or résumé was derived.[19] The same holds where a novel is converted into a play, a play into a novel, a poem into a work written in prose, a work written in prose into a poem, or where the episodes, theme or general plot of a work is developed into a new work.[20]

[10] Decree, articles 1 and 2.
[11] Article 649.   [12] Article 650.
[13] Article 651.   [14] Article 653.   [15] Article 654.
[16] Article 652.
[17] Article 656; the authorization of the owner of the original work, if still under copyright protection, is a prerequisite of protection of the reproduction.
[18] Article 658.   [19] Article 664.   [20] Article 665.

ASSIGNMENT AND LICENSING

Copyright is transmissible by assignment and inheritance.[21] Unless otherwise agreed by contract, the assignment of a newspaper article is only effective for a period of 20 days from its publication: once this period expires, the author recovers his full copyright.[22]

PROTECTED RIGHTS

Economic Rights

Authors have the exclusive right to authorize the reproduction of their works.[23] This right includes the right to authorize translation and the making of new versions;[24] the making of abridgments and resumés;[25] the conversion of a novel into a play, a play into a novel, a work written in prose into a poem, a poem into a work written in prose, and the development into a new work of the episodes, theme or general plot of a pre-existing work.[26]

Musical compositions, tragedies, dramas, comedies and other like works may not be performed in a theatre or at public spectacles if an entrance fee is charged, without the authorization of the author.[27] The author of a musical composition combined with a poetic text may perform and publish the composition or transfer his right therein, independently of the authorization of the author of the words. He must, however, identify the author of the words, who has the right to reproduce his text without the music.[28]

Moral Rights

Assignment and transmission by inheritance of the copyright in the work, or of the actual work, does not transfer the right to modify it. However, the author has the right to modify his work whenever a new edition thereof is being prepared, as long as the modifications he makes do not prejudice the rights of the publisher.[29] The publisher may not take away from, add to, or otherwise modify the work without the author's permission.[30]

Authors have a right to their names' being associated with their works. This right is capable of assignment.[31]

---

[21] *Cf.* Article 659.   [22] Article 659.
[23] Article 649. See also articles 1346 to 1358 for publishing contracts.
[24] Article 652.   [25] Article 664.   [26] Article 665.
[27] Decree, article 2; *see also* articles 1359 to 1362, dramatic performances.
[28] Article 655.   [29] Article 659.   [30] Article 1357.   [31] Article 667.

LIMITATIONS

If the owner of a published work refuses to authorize the publication of new editions thereof, the federal or the state governments may order its expropriation, after indemnification, for reasons of public utility.[32]

The following acts do not require the authorization of the owner of the copyright: (i) reproduction of passages or excerpts from a published work, or of the entire work if it is a short work, into a major scientific work or a compilation having a literary, educational or religious purpose;[33] (ii) the reproduction in newspapers and periodicals of news items and articles not having a literary or scientific character and which have been published in other newspapers or periodicals;[34] (iii) the reproduction in newspapers and periodicals of speeches delivered at public meetings;[35] (iv) the quotation in books, newspapers or magazines of passages from any work for purposes of criticism or discussion;[36] (v) the making of a copy by hand of any work, provided that the copy is not intended for sale;[37] (vi) the reproduction, in the body of a written work, of works of art, provided that the written work is the main feature and that the pictorial reproductions are only used to explain the text;[38] (vii) the utilization of a work of art (*arte figurativa*) for the purposes of obtaining a new work;[39] (viii) the reproduction of a work of art situated in a street or square;[40] (ix) the reproduction by the owner of a privately commissioned portrait or bust, of such portrait or bust.[41]

TERM OF PROTECTION

Generally.—One must distinguish between three situations: (i) the author dies without heirs up to the second degree of consanguinity or without any successors in title; (ii) the author's estate is transmitted to his children, parents or surviving spouse; (iii) neither case (i) nor case (ii) applies. In case (i), copyright expires upon the death of the author; in case (ii), copyright expires upon the death of the child, parent or surviving spouse, as the case may be; in case (iii), copyright expires 60 years from the author's death.[42] It is open to question whether

[32] Article 660.

[33] Article 666 (I); the source from which the reproduction is made and the name of the author of the reproduced work must be indicated.

[34] Article 666 (II); the names of the authors of the items or articles and of the newspapers or periodicals from which they are taken must be indicated.

[35] Article 666 (III). [36] Article 666 (V). [37] Article 666 (VI).

[38] Article 666 (VII); the names of the authors and the sources used must be indicated.

[39] Article 666 (VIII). [40] Article 666 (IX).

[41] Article 666 (X); the person portrayed, or his immediate successors, may oppose reproduction or public exhibition.

[42] Article 649. If the work is made by several persons, the copyright of those dying without heirs or successors accrues to the surviving collaborators (art. 653).

these provisions always lead to a result compatible with the minimum term requirements of the Universal Copyright Convention and the Berne Conventions.

Rule of the Shorter Term.—Since there is no provision in the law of Brazil for the "rule of the shorter term" permitted under Article IV (4) of the Universal Copyright Convention, it would appear that works which are protectable in Brazil under the Universal Copyright Convention alone will be protected there until the expiration of the terms indicated above even if in other countries they fall into the public domain at an earlier date. Works protectable in Brazil under the Universal Copyright Convention alone are the works indicated above under "Acquisition of protection under the Universal Copyright Convention" except if they have a Berne Union member country as country of origin. Works fall into this category (i) if they are unpublished and their authors are nationals (*ressortissants*) of a Berne Union member country, (ii) if they are published and they were first published in a Berne Union member country or they were published, within 30 days of their first publication in a country not member of the Berne Union, in a Berne Union member country. In the case of works falling into this category, the rule of the shorter term, as provided in the Berne Conventions, probably applies.

INFRINGEMENTS

Civil Remedies.—The usurpation of the name of the author or the substitution of another name gives rise to a claim for damages, and the perpetrator of the usurpation or substitution must insert in the work the name of the real author.[43]

Any person who, without the required authorization, publishes an unpublished work or reproduces a published work, forfeits in favor of the owner of the copyright all unauthorized copies, and must pay him the value of the whole edition, less the forfeited copies, at the selling price of the authorized copies or at the price at which the unauthorized copies may be appraised. When the number of the unauthorized copies is not known, the infringer must pay the value of one thousand copies, apart from all forfeited copies.[44] Any person who sells, exposes for sale, or hires to the public fraudulently printed copies is jointly responsible with the publisher; and if the copies were so printed outside Brazil, the seller or the person exposing the copies for sale is responsible as if he were the publisher.[45]

The author, publisher, assignee or duly authorized translator, or the successor to the rights of any of them, may request the competent police

---

[43] Article 667(1) and (2).   [44] Article 669.   [45] Article 670.

authority to prohibit the unauthorized performance of dramatic or musical works;[46] if the performance is carried out without the required authorization, they are entitled to the seizure of the gross receipts collected for the unauthorized performance.[47]

Penal Sanctions.—Violations of copyright are punishable by imprisonment or fine. The sale, exposition for sale, or acquisition or holding for sale, of infringing copies is also punishable by imprisonment or fine.[48]

False attribution of authorship to a person through the use of the name of, or pseudonym or mark adopted by, such person is punishable by imprisonment or fine.[49]

---

[46] Decree, article 3.   [47] Decree, article 6.
[48] Penal Code, article 184.   [49] Penal Code, article 185.

CAMBODIA

Cambodia has no special law on copyright. Its Penal Code makes it punishable to reproduce, for the use of third parties, literary, artistic, musical and scientific works, without the authorization of their authors, even if the appearance of the works is modified with a view to disguising their origin.[1]

According to a communication of September 28, 1955, of the Minister of Education of Cambodia, the said provision is considered as adopting, in Cambodia, with the exception of the actual penalties, the French law, or at least the notions of "reproduction for the use of third parties," "authorization of the authors," and "modification of the appearance of the works."[2]

Cambodia is bound by the Universal Copyright Convention and Protocols 1 and 2 as from September 16, 1955.[3]

---

[1] Penal Code, article 516, promulgated by Royal Order No. 103, of July 23, 1934, published in "Bulletin Administratif du Cambodge," 1934, No. 8, page 991; English translation in CLTW, Cambodia: Item 1.

[2] Letter of September 28, 1955, to UNESCO. *See* CLTW, Cambodia: Item 1.

[3] *See* CLTW, Cambodia: Item 2. A special Kram (Order) of July 20, 1953, provides for the protection of works of authors who are citizens of the United States of America (published "Journal Officiel du Cambodge," July 23, 1953, page 1767; English translation in CLTW, Cambodia: Item 3).

CANADA

SOURCES

Internal Law.—The main source of the law of copyright in Canada is Chapter 55 of the Revised Statutes of Canada which consists of the Copyright Act of 1921 and its subsequent amendments. Hereinafter, it is referred to as "the Act," and references to Sections, without further specification, are references to Sections of this Act.[1]

Universal Copyright Convention.—Canada became bound by the Universal Copyright Convention as from August 22, 1962.[2]

ACQUISITION OF PROTECTION UNDER THE UNIVERSAL COPYRIGHT CONVENTION

The laws of Canada do not contain any provision on the question of whose works are protected in Canada by virtue of the Universal Copyright Convention. The Act provides, in effect, that it protects original literary, dramatic, musical and artistic works:

a) if the author was at the date of the making of the work (i) a British subject or (ii) a citizen or subject of a country which has adhered to the Berlin or Rome Conventions[3] of the Berne Copyright Union, or

---

[1] Published in "Revised Statutes of Canada," Volume II, page 2003; reprinted in CLTW as Canada: Item 1. *See also* the "Copyright Rules" of December 1, 1954 (published in "Statutory Orders and Regulations," 1954, Vol. 1, page 664; (reprinted in CLTW as Canada: Item 1A).

[2] Canada is a member of the Berne Copyright Union, the most recent text which it ratified being the Rome Convention of 1928 (CLTW, Canada: Item 1). Protection to the works of U.S. nationals and works first published in the United States was extended by a Government decree ("certificate") dated December 26, 1923 (published in "The Canada Gazette," 1923, page 2157; text reprinted in CLTW as Canada: Item 3.

[3] The Act refers to countries that have "adhered to the Convention and the Additional Protocol thereto set out in the Second Schedule" (Paragraph 4, (1)). The Second Schedule reproduced the Berlin Convention of 1908 and the Berne Additional Protocol of 1914. Thus, if read literally, countries parties to the Rome Convention of 1928, would seem to be excluded, notwithstanding the fact that Canada ratified the Rome Convention of 1928 and the Third Schedule of the Act reproduced the text of the Rome Convention. Countries members of the Berne Union which have only ratified or adhered to the Brussels Convention of 1948 seem to be excluded, not only because paragraph 4(1) does not refer to the Brussels Convention, but also because Canada has not ratified that Convention.

(iii) a citizen or subject of a country named in a Governmental "certificate," or (iv) a resident within Her Majesty's Dominions,

b) if, in the case of a published work, the work was first published: (i) within Her Majesty's Dominions, or (ii) in a country which had adhered to the Berlin or Berne Conventions of the Berne Copyright Union, or (iii) in a country named in a Governmental "certificate." A work is deemed to be first published in these places even if it has been first published in another place but, within 14 days of its first publication in such other place, it is also published in any of the places referred to under (i), (ii), or (iii).[4]

It seems that eligibility under (a) is limited to unpublished works so that published works are only protected if first publication occurred in one of the countries referred to in (b). Consequently, if first publication occurred outside such countries, the work is not protected even if its author comes within one of the descriptions given under (a). Such a result would be at variance with the requirements of the Universal Copyright Convention, according to which a published work must be protected, even if its first publication occurred in a non-Contracting State, provided the author is a national of a Contracting State.

The countries named in Canadian Governmental certificates are the United States of America;[5] Andorra, Argentina, Cambodia, Chile, Costa Rica, Cuba, Ecuador, Haiti, Laos, Liberia, Mexico, Nicaragua, Nigeria, Paraguay[6] and Panama.[7] These are the countries which are party to the Universal Copyright Convention without being members of the Berne Copyright Union.

Canada has no copyright formalities. Consequently, registration, deposit, or compliance with other formalities is not required, and the absence, in itself, of a Convention notice on the copies of a published work is no bar to claiming protection in Canada. Furthermore, Canada has no renewal system, so that there is nothing in this country which would correspond to the renewal formalities existing in the United States.

PROTECTED WORKS

Original literary, dramatic, musical and artistic works are protected. They include "every original production in the literary, scientific and artistic domain, whatever may be the mode or form of its expression, such as books, pamphlets, and other writings, lectures, dramatic or

[4] Section 3(4).

[5] Certificate of December 26, 1923, published in the "Canada Gazette," 1923, page 2157.

[6] Certificate of August 7, 1962, published in the "Canada Gazette," Part II, page 868.

[7] Certificate of October 17, 1962, published in the "Canada Gazette," Part II, page 1171.

dramatico-musical works, musical works or compositions with or without words, illustrations, sketches, and plastic works relative to geography, topography, architecture or science.[8] Copyright also subsists in records, perforated rolls, and other contrivances by means of which sounds may be mechanically reproduced (hereinafter sometimes referred to as "sound recordings").[9]

"Literary work" includes maps, charts, plans, tables, and compilations.[10] "Dramatic work" includes (i) any piece for recitation, choreographic work or entertainment in dumb show, the scenic arrangement or acting form of which is fixed in writing or otherwise, and (ii) any cinematograph production where the arrangement of acting from or the combination of incidents represented give the work an original character.[11] "Musical work" means any combination of melody and harmony, or either of them, printed, reduced to writing, or otherwise graphically produced or reproduced.[12] "Artistic work" includes works of painting, drawing, sculpture and artistic craftsmanship, and architectural works of art and engravings and photographs.[13]

The Copyright Act is inapplicable to designs capable of being registered under the Industrial Design Act except designs that, though capable of being so registered, are not used or intended to be used as models or patterns to be multiplied by any industrial process.[14]

[8] Sections 4(1) and 2(v). "Work" includes the title thereof when such title is original and distinctive. "Book" includes every volume, part or division of a volume, pamphlet, sheet of letter-press, sheet of music, map, chart or plan separately published (sec. 2(c)). "Lecture" includes address, speech and sermon (sec. 2(l)).

[9] Section 4(3).   [10] Section 2(n).

[11] Section 2(g). "Cinematograph" includes any work produced by any process analogous to cinematography (sec. 2(d)).

[12] Section 2(p).

[13] Section 2(b). "Work of Sculpture" includes casts and models (sec. 2(t)). "Architectural work of art" means any building or structure having an artistic character or design, or any model for such building or structure, but the protection afforded by the Act is confined to the artistic character and design and does not extend to processes or methods of construction (sec. 2(a)). "Engravings" include etchings, lithographs, woodcuts, prints, and other similar works, not being photographs (sec. 2(h)). "Photograph" includes photo-lithograph and any work produced by any process analogous to photography (sec. 2 (s)).

[14] Section 46(1). A design is deemed to be used as a model or pattern to be multiplied by an industrial process: (i) where the design is reproduced or is intended to be reproduced in more than 50 single articles, unless all the articles in which the design is reproduced or is intended to be reproduced together form only a single "set," (ii) where the design is to be applied to printed paper hangings; carpets, floor cloths, or oil cloths manufactured or sold in lengths or pieces; textile piece goods, or textile goods manufactured or sold in lengths or pieces; and, lace, not made by hand. A "set" means a number of articles of the same general character ordinarily on sale together, or intended to be used together, all bearing the same design, with or without modification not sufficient to alter the character or not substantially affect the identity thereof. Where there is a doubt whether given articles do or do not constitute a set, the doubt is determined by the Commissioner of Patents, (Industrial Design Rules, 1954, sec. 11).

PROTECTED PERSONS

Subject to the exceptions stated below, the first owner of the copyright in a work is the author of the work.[15]

Engravings, Photographs and Portraits Made on Order.— Where, in the case of an engraving, photograph, or portrait, the plate or other original was ordered by some other person and was made for valuable consideration in pursuance of that order, then, in the absence of any agreement to the contrary, the person by whom such plate or other original was ordered is the first owner of the copyright.[16] "Plate" includes any stereotype or other plate, stone, block, mould, matrix, transfer, or negative used or intended to be used for printing or reproducing copies of any work.[17]

Work of Employees.—Where the author was in the employment of some other person under a contract of service or apprenticeship and the work was made in the course of his employment by that person, the employer is—in the absence of any agreement to the contrary—the first owner of the copyright; but where the work is an article or other contribution to a newspaper, magazine, or similar periodical, the right of publication otherwise than as part of a newspaper, etc., is presumed to belong to the author-employee.[18]

Sound Recordings.—The first owner of copyright in records, perforated rolls, and other contrivances by means of which sounds may be mechanically reproduced, is the person who, at the time it is made, is the owner of the original plate from which such contrivances are directly or indirectly derived.[19] "Plate" includes any matrix or other appliance by which records, perforated rolls or other contrivances for the acoustic representation of the work are or are intended to be made.[20]

Photographs.—The first owner of copyright in a photograph is the person who, at the time the negative (from which the photograph was directly or indirectly derived) was made, owned such negative.[21]

ASSIGNMENT AND LICENSING

Generally.—The owner of the copyright in any work may assign the right (i) either wholly or partially, (ii) either generally or subject to territorial limitations in Canada, (iii) either for the whole term of the copyright or any part thereof. He may grant any interest in the right by license. Assignments and licenses are valid only if they are in writing signed by the owner of the right in respect to which the assignment or grant is made, or by his duly authorized agent.[22] Where, under any

[15] Section 12(1).   [16] Section 12(2).   [17] Section 2(r).   [18] Section 12(3).
[19] Section 10.   [20] Section 2(r).   [21] Section 9.   [22] Section 12(4).

partial assignment of copyright, the assignee becomes entitled to a given right, the assignee is treated as the owner of the copyright as far as the said given right is concerned.[23]

Cumpulsory License After Twenty-five Years Post Mortem Auctoris.—Twenty-five years after the death of the author, any of his works, if published before the expiration of these twenty-five years, may be reproduced for sale without the authorization of the owner of the copyright if the person so reproducing the work proves (i) that he has given the prescribed notice in writing of his intention to reproduce the work, and (ii) that he has paid a ten per cent royalty on the publication price after each copy sold.[24]

Cumpulsory License After the Death of the Author.—If, at any time after the death of the author of a literary, dramatic, or musical work which has been published or performed in public, a complaint is made to the Governor in Council that the owner of the copyright has refused to republish or to allow the republication of the work or has refused its public performance, and if by reason of such refusal the work is withheld from the public, the owner of the copyright may be ordered to grant a license to reproduce the work or perform the work in public, as the case may be, on such terms and conditions as the Governor in Council may think fit.[25]

Reversion of Copyright to the Author's Estate.—Where the author of a work is the first owner of the copyright therein, no assignment of license by him (otherwise than by will) has effect beyond the expiration of 25 years from his death. The reversionary interest in the copyright on the termination of this 25-year period devolves, on the death of the author—and notwithstanding any agreement made by him during his life—on his legal personal representatives.[26]

Cumpulsory License for Failure to Do Certain Acts in Canada. —If at any time after publication (and while the work is still under copyright protection) the copyright owner (i) fails to print his book in Canada or fails to cause it to be printed in Canada, or (ii) fails to supply by means of copies so printed the reasonable demands of the Canadian market for such book—then, any person may apply to the

[23] Section 12(6).
[24] Section 7(1). In the case of works which are unpublished, not delivered or performed in public, at the date of the author's death, the term of 25 years starts running from the date of first publication, performance or delivery after the author's death (sec. 6).
[25] Section 13.
[26] Proviso to section 5(2). These provisions do not apply to collective works. "Collective work" means: (i) an encyclopaedia, dictionary, year book, or similar work; (ii) a newspaper, review, magazine, or similar periodical; (iii) any work written in distinct parts by different authors, or in which works or parts of works of different authors are incorporated (sec. 2(e)).

Government for a license to print and publish the book in Canada. The licensee must pay a royalty to the owner of the copyright at a rate determined by the Government.[27]

Recording of Assignments and Licenses.—Any grant of an interest in copyright, either assignment or license, may be registered at the Copyright Office. If such a grant is not so registered, it is to be adjudged void against any subsequent assignee or licensee for valuable consideration without actual notice.[28]

PROTECTED RIGHTS

Economic Rights

Generally.—Subject to the exceptions stated below, "copyright" means the sole right: (i) to publish the work if it is an unpublished work; (ii) to produce or reproduce the work in any material form whatsoever; (iii) to perform[29] the work in public; (iv) in the case of lectures,[30] to deliver[31] them in public; (v) to produce, reproduce, perform or publish a translation of a work; (vi) in the case of a novel or other non-dramatic work, or an artistic work, to convert it into a dramatic work, by way of performance in public or otherwise; (vii) in the case of a dramatic work, to convert it into a novel or other non-dramatic work; (viii) in the case of a literary, dramatic, or musical work, to make any record, perforated roll, cinematograph film or other contrivance by means of which the work may be mechanically performed or delivered; (ix) in the case of any literary, dramatic, musical or artistic work, to reproduce, adapt and publicly present such work by cinematography, if the author has given such work an original character (if such original character is absent, the cinematographic production is protected as a photograph); (x) in case of any literary, dramatic, musical or artistic work, to communicate such work by radio communication—and to authorize any of the acts referred to under (i) through (x).[32]

---

[27] Section 14. Similar compulsory license may be available if a book, published in a periodical in a serial from outside Canada, is not also so "serialized" in Canada (sec. 15). These compulsory license provisions are inapplicable to works of authors who are nationals of a country party to the Berlin (and Rome?) Conventions of the Berne Copyright Union, other than Canada (sec. 16(8)).

[28] Section 40.

[29] "Performance" means any acoustic representation of a work and any visual representation of any dramatic action in a work, including a representation made by means of any mechanical instrument or by radio communication (sec. 2(q)).

[30] "Lecture" includes address, speech, and sermon (sec. 2(b)).

[31] "Delivery" in relation to a lecture, includes delivery by means of any mechanical instrument (sec. 2(f)).

[32] Section 3(1).

Legal Licenses for Sound Recordings.—Sound recordings may be made without the consent of the owner of the copyright of musical, literary or dramatic works if such recordings have been previously made by, or with the consent or acquiescence of, such owner. The royalty is two cents (of one Canadian dollar) for each playing surface of a record sold.[33]

MORAL RIGHTS

Independently of the author's copyright, and even after the assignment, either wholly or partially, of the said copyright, the author has the right to claim authorship of the work, as well as the right to restrain any distortion, mutilation or other modification of the said work which would be prejudicial to his honor or reputation.[34]

LIMITATIONS

The Acts provides that certain acts, normally subject to the authorization of the owner of the copyright, may be performed without such authorization. Among such acts are: (i) any fair dealing with the work for purposes of private study, research, criticism, review or newspaper summary; (ii) publishing of pictures of certain three-dimensional works of art when they are permanently situated in a public place; (iii) certain uses in schools; (iv) certain uses in newspapers or lectures publicly delivered; (v) public reading or recitation of reasonable extracts from a published work.[35]

Furthermore, no church, college or school, and no religious, charitable or fraternal organization is liable to pay any compensation to the owner of any musical work (or to any person claiming through him) by reason of the public performance of any musical work in furtherance of a religious, educational or charitable object.[36] Finally, addresses of a political nature, delivered at a public meeting, may be reported in newspapers without the permission of the owner of the copyright in the address.[37]

TERM OF PROTECTION

Generally.—Subject to the exceptions stated below, copyright subsists for the life of the author and fifty years from the first day of January next after his death.[38] In the case of works of joint authorship, the 50 years start running from the date of the death of the co-author

[33] Section 19.
[34] Section 12(7). *See also* section 19(2).
[35] Section 17(2).   [36] Section 17(3).   [37] Section 18.   [38] Section 5.

who dies last.[39] In the case of a literary, dramatic, or musical work, or an engraving, in which copyright subsists at the date of the death of the author, but which has not been published (nor, in the case of a dramatic or musical work, been performed in public; nor, in the case of a lecture, been delivered in public) before the date of the author's death, copyright subsists until publication, performance, or delivery, whichever happens first, and for a term of 50 years thereafter.[40]

Sound Recordings.—Copyright in records, perforated rolls, and other contrivances by means of which sounds may be mechanically reproduced subsists for 50 years from the making of the original plate from which the contrivance was directly or indirectly derived.[41]

Photographs.—Copyright in photographs subsists for 50 years from the making of the original negative from which the photograph was directly or indirectly derived.[42]

Rule of the Shorter Term.—The Act provides—but only in case of works of joint authorship—that authors who are nationals of any country that grants a term of protection shorter than that provided for works of joint authorship by the Act (i.e., 50 years after the death of the last surviving co-author) are not entitled to claim a longer term of protection in Canada.[43] Consequently, it would seem that the "rule of the shorter term" permitted under Article IV, paragraph (4) of the Universal Copyright Convention, does not apply in Canada to any works other than works of joint authorship, and that all works—except works of joint authorship—are protected in Canada until the expiration of the terms indicated above, even if in other countries such works fall into the public domain at an earlier date.

INFRINGEMENTS

Generally.—Subject to the exceptions stated elsewhere,[44] copyright is deemed to be infringed by any person who, without the consent of the owner of the copyright, does anything the sole right to do which is conferred on the owner of the copyright.[45] Furthermore, copyright in a work is deemed to be infringed by any person who does any of the following acts in relation to a work which, to his knowledge, infringes copyright, or would infringe copyright if it had been made in Canada: (i) sells or lets for hire, or by way of trade exposes or offers for sale or hire; (ii) distributes, either for the purposes of trade or to such an

---

[39] Section 8(1). "A work of joint authorship" means a work produced by the collaboration of two or more authors in which the contribution of one author is not distinct from the contribution of the other author or authors (sec. 2(k)).
[40] Section 6.   [41] Section 10.   [42] Section 9.   [43] Section 8(2).
[44] *See above*, page 257.   [45] Section 17(1).

extent as to affect prejudicially the owner of the copyright; (iii) by way of trade exhibits in public; (iv) imports for sale or hire into Canada.[46] Infringement is also committed by any person who permits a theatre, or other place of entertainment, to be used for the public performance for profit of a work, without the consent of the owner of the copyright, unless such person was not aware and had no reasonable grounds for suspecting that the performance would be an infringement of copyright.[47]

Civil Remedies.—The injured party is generally entitled to all remedies by way of injunction, damages, accounts, and otherwise, as are conferred by law for the infringement of a right.[48] Infringing copies and plates may be handed over to the injured party.[49] Injunction is the only available remedy where the defendant proves that at the date of the infringement he was not aware and had no reasonable ground for suspecting that copyright subsisted in the work.[50] The statute of limitations is three years from the date of the infringement.[51]

Penal Sanctions.—Most of the infringing acts, if committed knowingly, constitute offences and are punishable by fine or imprisonment.[52]

Importation of Infringing Copies.—Copies made outside Canada of any work in which copyright subsists which, if made in Canada, would infringe copyright, cannot be imported into Canada.[53]

---

[46] Section 17(4).   [47] Section 17(5).   [48] Section 20(1).
[49] Section 21.   [50] Section 22.   [51] Section 24.
[52] Sections 25 and 26.   [53] Sections 27 and 28.

CHILE

SOURCES

Internal Law.—The main source of the law of copyright in Chile is Decree-Law No. 345 of March 17, 1925, as amended by Law No. 9549 of December 28, 1949.[1] Hereinafter, it is referred to as "the Law," and references to Articles, without further specification, are references to Articles of this Law.

Universal Copyright Convention.—Chile became bound by the Universal Copyright Convention and Protocol 2 as from September 16, 1955.[2]

ACQUISITION OF PROTECTION UNDER THE UNIVERSAL COPYRIGHT CONVENTION

Chile passed no special legislation for bringing its law into harmony with certain requirements of the Universal Copyright Convention. In particular, there is nothing in the Law which would provide that formalities the fulfilment of which is required under the Law for the acquisition of copyright[3] do not apply or may be avoided as provided in Article III of the Universal Copyright Convention in the case of works which Chile is supposed to protect under that Convention. It will be assumed hereinafter that in the case of possible conflicts between the Convention, including in particular its Article III, and the Law, the provisions of the Convention apply. In the absence of court decisions on the question, the correctness of this assumption cannot be regarded as officially confirmed.

The laws of Chile do not contain any provision on the subject of what works are protected in Chile by virtue of the Universal Copyright Convention. On the basis of the provisions of the Convention and the Protocols, it is assumed that they are: (i) published works of nationals of a Convention country, irrespective of the place of first publication, (ii) works first published in a Convention country, irrespective of the

[1] Published in "Diario Oficial," March 17, 1925, page 630, and January 21, 1950, page 129, respectively. English translations in CLTW, Chile: Item 1.

[2] CLTW, Chile: Item 7. Chile is also party to the Rio de Janeiro Copyright Convention of 1906, the Buenos Aires Copyright Convention of 1910, and the Washington Copyright Convention of 1946; see CLTW, Chile: Items 8, 9, and 10.

[3] Articles 1, 5, 14, 15, 18.

nationality of the author, (iii) unpublished works of nationals of a Convention country other than Chile, (iv) works first published by the United Nations, by any of the Specialized Agencies of the United Nations, or by the Organization of American States, as well as unpublished works of any of these Organizations. It is assumed that, with the possible exception of the rule of the shorter term (discussed below), works belonging to any of these categories are protected in Chile without deposit and registration, provided always that, in the case of published works, the provisions of Article III of the Universal Copyright Convention concerning notice have been complied with.

Chile has no renewal system, so that there is nothing in this country which would correspond to the renewal formalities existing in the United States.

PROTECTED WORKS

Any "product of the mind," such as writings, musical compositions, paintings, drawings, sculpture, maps and plans, engineering and architectural plans, theatrical works, cinematographic works, and photographic works, are protected.[4]

PROTECTED PERSONS

Copyright generally vests in the author, "the person to whom the first idea in a scientific, literary or artistic production belongs."[5] Copyright in a translation or compilation belongs to the translator or compiler, as the case may be, provided he has not infringed the rights of the copyright owner in the pre-existing work or works and has clearly indicated the sources. The same applies to transcriptions, adaptations and arrangements having individual character. Mere transposition to another key, or adaptation to different instruments, of musical works are not considered as having such character.[6]

The copyright of a work intended to be sung belongs jointly to the author of the words and the composer of the music; however, the composer of the music is presumed to be the sole owner unless the author of the words has previously acquired copyright in the words or has expressly reserved his rights in such words.[7] Persons who have jointly created a work in such a way that their respective contributions cannot be separated from each other hold joint copyright as collaborators. They may dispose of their rights only jointly.[8]

[4] Articles 1, 2. Pseudonyms are protected (art. 17).
[5] Article 2. For presumptions of authorship, *see* article 16.
[6] Article 4.   [7] Article 3.   [8] Article 12.

Copyright in posthumous works belongs to the heirs of the author. If, however, the author was not, at the time of his death, the owner of the original work, copyright is equally shared between the owner of the original and the heirs of the author (unless otherwise stipulated by contract or provided by will).[9]

ASSIGNMENT AND LICENSING

Copyright may be transferred by act *inter vivos* and may be transferred *mortis causa*.[10] Transfer of one or more of the rights does not imply the transfer of the other rights. Transfers must be made by public deed (*escritura publica*) inscribed in the *Rejistro de la Propiedad Intelectuel* maintained in the *Biblioteca Nacional* (National Library).[11] Licenses must be merely executed in writing.[12]

PROTECTED RIGHTS

ECONOMIC RIGHTS

Subject to the possible exceptions stated below, copyright consists of the exclusive right to distribute, sell or exploit for profit by means of printing, lithography, engraving, copying, moulding, casting, photography, cinematography, phonograph discs, rolls for mechanical instruments, performance, lecture, recitation, translation, adaptation, exhibition, broadcasting, or any other means of reproduction, multiplication or dissemination.[13]

It would appear that public performance rights, whether by broadcasters, in theatres ("grand" rights), or in bars, restaurants, etc. ("small" rights), are subject to compulsory licensing. The royalty rates are fixed by a Government-appointed body, or, in the case of "small rights," in a rate schedule established by the University of Chile.[14]

MORAL RIGHTS

Theatrical companies may not, without the author's consent, change the title of the work; they may not modify, alter or cut the original text;

[9] Article 8.   [10] Article 7.   [11] Article 9.
[12] Article 10.   [13] Article 1.
[14] Law No. 5563 of January 10, 1935 ("Diario Oficial," January 11, 1935, page 117) and Decree No. 1070 of the Vice President of the University of Chile of May 16, 1951 ("Diario Oficial," April 25, 1952, page 835). English translation in CLTW, Chile Items 5 and 6A. *See also* Decree No. 2620 of the President of the University of Chile on the distribution of small performing rights, of September 28, 1953 ("Diario Oficial," January 19, 1954, page 148; English translation in CLTW, Chile: Item 6B).

and may not perform the work under a name other than that of the actual author.[15]

LIMITATIONS

Speeches made at public meetings may be reproduced in accounts made of such meetings, except where express reservation of copyright has been announced in advance. Unless reproduction is expressly prohibited, articles published in periodicals may be freely reproduced in other periodicals.[16]

Subject to a clear indication of source, and solely for the purpose of explaining the text of a work, drawings, engravings, literary, musical, scientific or technical works, or short extracts therefrom, may be reproduced, recited, or performed in scientific, literary or critical works, at public lectures, or in educational texts.[17]

TERM OF PROTECTION

Copyright subsists for the life of the author and, "when it is transmitted *mortis causa*, it shall expire 50 years after death."[18] Presumably, death means the death of the author. Curiously, the Law does not seem to contain a provision concerning the length of the *post mortem auctoris* protection, if any, in cases where copyright is not transmitted *mortis causa* but has been transferred by an act *inter vivos*. "If the State is the heir, the work passes into the public domain,"[19] presumably upon the author's death. Where two or more authors have worked in collaboration, the term of copyright for successors (*sucesores*) is calculated from the death of the last surviving author.[20] If the author is a professional corporate body (*cuerpo colegiado*), copyright lasts 40 years from registration.[21] Under the Universal Copyright Convention protection is, or should be, available without registration; but there is no provision in the law of Chile as regards duration in such cases.

Since there is no provision in Chilean law for the "rule of the shorter term" permitted under Article IV (4) of the Universal Copyright Convention, it would appear that works are protected in Chile until the expiration of the terms indicated above, even if, in other countries, they fall into the public domain at an earlier date.[22]

---

[15] Law No. 5563 (citation given in footnote 14, above), article 17. It is a misdemeanour knowingly to publish or exhibit a work in the public domain under a name other than that of the real author (art. 24).
[16] Article 6.　　[17] Article 11.　　[18] Article 7, first paragraph.
[19] Article 7, second paragraph.　　[20] Article 7, third paragraph.
[21] Article 7, fourth paragraph.　　[22] Article 13.

INFRINGEMENTS

Civil Remedies.—Violation of any of the exclusive rights of the author constitutes infringement.[23] The utilization for profit of copies manufactured or put into circulation in violation of the said rights constitutes infringement, unless good faith is proved in the acquisition and use of the copies.[24] During the course of the proceedings, the court may order the immediate suspension of the sale, circulation, exhibition or performance of the work; at the time of fixing the compensation for damages, the Court may order the delivery to the injured party, the sale, or destruction of the fruits or implements of infringement.[25]

Penal Sanctions.—Infringements of copyright are misdemeanours punishable by fine.[26] Criminal actions prescribe after three years from the date of the infringement; penalty prescribes after five years from the condemnatory sentence.[27]

[23] Article 19, first paragraph.   [24] Article 19, second paragraph.
[25] Article 20.
[26] Article 22. *See also* articles 23 and 25, as well as Law No. 5563 (citation given in footnote 14, above), articles 14, 15, 17.
[27] Article 26.

COSTA RICA

SOURCES

Internal Law.—The main source of the law of copyright in Costa Rica is the Decree-Law on Intellectual Property, No. 40 of June 27, 1896, amended by Decree-Law No. 32 of May 25, 1948.[1] Hereinafter, it is referred to as "the Law," and references to Articles, without further specification, are references to the Articles of this Law.

Universal Copyright Convention.—Costa Rica became bound by the Universal Copyright Convention and Protocols 1 and 2 as from September 16, 1955.[2]

ACQUISITION OF PROTECTION UNDER THE UNIVERSAL COPYRIGHT CONVENTION

Costa Rica passed no special legislation for bringing its law into harmony with certain requirements of the Universal Copyright Convention. In particular, there is nothing in the Law which would provide that formalities, the fulfilment of which is required under the Law for the acquisition of copyright,[3] do not apply, or may be avoided as provided in Article III of the Universal Copyright Convention, in the case of works which Costa Rica is supposed to protect under that Convention. It will be assumed hereinafter that in the case of possible conflicts between the Convention, including, in particular, its Article III, and the Law, the provisions of the Convention apply. In the absence of court decisions on the question, the correctness of this assumption cannot be regarded as officially confirmed.

[1] Published in "Colección de las Leyes y Decretos emitidos en el año 1896," page 201; and "La Gaceta-Diario Oficial," No. 120, of May 29, 1948. English translation in CLTW, Costa Rica: Item 1.

[2] CLTW, Costa Rica: Item 3. Costa Rica is also party to the Copyright Conventions of Rio de Janeiro (1906), Buenos Aires (1910), Havana (1928) and Washington (1946). Costa Rica has concluded bilateral copyright treaties with Spain in 1893 (supplemented by a Protocol in 1896) and with France in 1896. It issued a decree protecting the works of U.S. nationals (Decree No. 6 of August 26, 1899, published in "La Gaceta-Diario Oficial," of September 5, 1899). These bilateral treaties and this decree have only limited significance since the adhesion of Costa Rica, France, Spain, and the United States of America, to the Universal Copyright Convention. *See* CLTW, Costa Rica: Items 4 to 10.

[3] Article 53.

The laws of Costa Rica do not specify what works are protected in Costa Rica by virtue of the Universal Copyright Convention. On the basis of the provisions of the Convention and the Protocols, it is assumed that they are: (i) published works of nationals of a Convention country, irrespective of the place of first publication, (ii) works first published in a Convention country, irrespective of the nationality of the author, (iii) unpublished works of nationals of a Convention country other than Costa Rica, (iv) works of stateless persons and refugees who have their habitual residence in a State party to Protocol 1 (except perhaps Costa Rica), either published or unpublished, irrespective of the place of first publication, (v) works first published by the United Nations, by any of the Specialized Agencies of the United Nations, or by the Organization of American States, as well as unpublished works of any of these Organizations. It is assumed that works belonging to any of these categories are protected in Costa Rica, without deposit and registration, provided always that, in the case of published works, the provisions of Article III of the Universal Copyright Convention concerning notice have been complied with.

Costa Rica has no renewal system, so that there is nothing in this country which would correspond to the renewal formalities existing in the United States.

PROTECTED WORKS

The Law protects all kinds of scientific, literary and artistic works, whatever the manner of their expression (*cualquiera que sea el medio por el cual se den á luz*).[4] Dramatic and musical works,[5] plans, designs, drawings, and maps,[6] are expressly mentioned.

PROTECTED PERSONS

Copyright originally vests in the author.[7]

The translator of a work enjoys the same protection as the author of an original work; but a translator has copyright only in his own translation, and cannot oppose the making of further translations of the same work by other persons.[8]

The authors or translators of works published in newspapers or reviews may collect and publish their works in whole or in part, provided the initial agreement with the publisher of the newspaper or review does not provide otherwise.[9]

If the author of the libretto of a dramatico-musical work prohibits the

[4] Article 2.   [5] Article 26.   [6] Article 39.
[7] Article 3.   [8] Article 18.   [9] Article 17.

performance of his work, the author of the music is entitled to replace the libretto by another libretto. The author of the libretto has similar rights in the converse situation.[10]

The publisher of an anonymous or pseudonymous or posthumous work enjoys the same rights as an author; but when the identity of the author, translator or proprietor of an anonymous or pseudonymous work is legally established, such person immediately enters into the possession of his rights, and the publisher loses his rights, without indemnity.[11]

ASSIGNMENT AND LICENSING

Copyright may be assigned, and if it is assigned, it belongs to the assignee for his lifetime and to his successors in title for 20 years, after which it reverts to the author, or if he is dead, to his heirs or legatees.[12]

PROTECTED RIGHTS

Economic Rights

Copyright includes the exclusive right to authorize publication, translation,[13] reproduction,[14] and, in the case of dramatic and musical works, performance in any theatre or other public place.[15]

Authors or owners of dramatic or musical works may fix the royalties for the performance of their works; if they fail to do so, they are only entitled to claim the fees fixed by Melevant Government regulations.[16] In the absence of agreement to the contrary, the author of the music of a dramatico-musical work is entitled to one half of the royalties, and the author of the libretto to the other half.[17] If a dramatic or musical work has not been published, the author's consent is required to the making, sale or hiring copies thereof.[18] The authors of a dramatico-musical work may publish and sell their respective works separately.[19] Royalties due to the author of, or owner of copyright in, a dramatic or musical work cannot be seized by the creditors of the enterprise organizing the performance of the work.[20]

[10] Article 35.   [11] Articles 21 and 22.   [12] Article 4.

[13] Articles 7, 26, 38, 39, 40. Private letters may not be published without the consent of their authors (art. 8). It is unlawful to publish on the basis of notes (taken by shorthand or otherwise) or phonograph recordings made during the recitation, reading or performance, whether public or private, of a work, including lectures of professors or teachers (arts. 11 and 12); but the publication of extracts is lawful (art. 13).

[14] Articles 9, 26, 38, 39, 40.

[15] Article 29. This applies also to performances given by societies of any kind, if there is a charge for admission (art. 30).

[16] Article 31.   [17] Article 32.   [18] Article 33.   [19] Article 34.   [20] Article 37.

MORAL RIGHTS

The person acquiring a work, or the publisher of a work, may not introduce any alterations therein without the permission of the author or, if the author is dead and there is no different testamentary provision, without the permission of his heirs or legatees.[21] When a dramatic or musical work is publicly performed, it is not lawful to alter its title, or to suppress, modify or make additions to the text of the work.[22]

, LIMITATIONS

For the purposes of commentaries, additions (*adiciones*), notes or criticisms, a scientific or literary work—but not a musical work—may be reproduced to the extent necessary for the said purpose.[23]

Any matter published in a public periodical (*en órganos de publicidad periódica*) may be reproduced by other periodicals of the same nature unless a notice prohibiting reproduction appears at the end of the item as published in the first-mentioned periodical.[24]

TERM OF PROTECTION

Copyright is protected during the life of the author[25] and after his death for a period, the length of which appears to depend on whether the copyright, at the time of the death of the author, belonged to the author or to an assignee. If it belonged to the author, copyright passes to his heirs or legatees and expires 50 years after his death.[26] If, at the time the author died, copyright belonged to an assignee, it remains protected until the expiration of 50 years, computed from the death of the assignee (*adquirente*). During the last 30 years of this 50-year period, copyright belongs to the author, or if he is no longer living, to his heirs or legatees. During the first 20 years of this 50-year period, copyright belongs to the successors (*sucesores a título universal ó particular*) of the assignee.[27] It is not clear what happens if the assignee is a corporation or other legal entity.[28] If copyright would pass to heirs or legatees, and none exist, the work falls into the public domain.[29]

Copyright in posthumous works of an author belongs to his heirs or

---

[21] Article 19.   [22] Article 36.   [23] Articles 10 and 27.   [24] Article 16.
[25] Article 3.   [26] Article 3.   [27] Article 4.
[28] Article 6 provides that the State, municipalities, official and private corporations legally established also enjoy the benefits of the Law; and that insofar as the State, municipalities, and official corporations are concerned, the term of protection is 25 years. It is not stated from what event these 25 years must be computed, and there is no provision as regards private corporations.
[29] Article 5.

legatees for a term of 50 years.[30] The Law does not state whether this term is to be computed from the death of the author or from the date of the posthumous publication.

Scientific, literary and artistic works which, during a period of 25 years have not been reprinted by their author or owner, pass into the public domain.[31] It is assumed that the provisions according to which failure to comply with domestic formalities in Costa Rica may cause works to fall into the public domain[32] do not apply to (i) unpublished works protectable under the Universal Copyright Convention, (ii) such published works protectable under the Universal Copyright Convention which comply with the notice requirements of Article III of the Universal Copyright Convention.

Since there is no provision in the law of Costa Rica for the "rule of the shorter term" permitted under Article IV (4) of the Universal Copyright Convention, it would appear that works to which the Universal Copyright Convention applies are protected in Costa Rica until the expiration of the terms indicated above even if in other countries they fall into the public domain at an earlier date.

INFRINGEMENTS

Infringers of copyright are civilly responsible.[33] Whether they are also responsible criminally in the case of works not registered in Costa Rica seems to be less certain since the Penal Code of 1941 provides punishment only in connection with works registered in Costa Rica.[34]

If the infringement is committed by publication, the author, and if he proves his innocence, the publisher, and if the publisher also proves his innocence, the owner of the typographical establishment, is held liable.[35] If the infringement is committed by public performance or exhibition, the person or enterprise organizing the performance or exhibition, and if they prove their innocence, the performer or exhibitor, is held liable.[36]

[30] Article 23. Posthumous works are: (i) works that have not been published in the lifetime of the author, (ii) works that the author, at his death, left recast, modified, annotated or corrected in such a way that they may be considered as new works (art. 24).

[31] Article 64.

[32] Articles 63, 68, 69, 70. The Law also provides that dramatic or musical works which have been registered and deposited in Costa Rica pass into the public domain if they are not published within a period of 30 years from the date of registration (art. 65). This provision is based on the assumption that registration is a condition of protection. Since it is assumed that Costa Rica does not require registration in the case of unpublished works to which the Universal Copyright Convention applies, the provision appears to be inapplicable to such works, since the starting date of the 30-year period (i.e., registration) is missing.

[33] Article 71.   [34] Penal Code, of August 21, 1941, article 307, para. (2).
[35] Article 72.   [36] Article 73.

CUBA

SOURCES

Internal Law.—The Copyright Law of January 10, 1879, of Spain was extended to Cuba,[1] and does not appear to have been repealed. Nevertheless, a Law of August 11, 1960, has introduced sweeping changes in respect to the exploitation of musical and dramatico-musical works.[2] These supersede the inconsistent provisions of the 1879 Law.

Hereinafter, the Spanish Law of 1879 is referred to as "the Law," and references to Articles, without further specification, are references to Articles of the Law. The Law of August 11, 1960, is referred to as "the 1960 Law."

Universal Copyright Convention.—Cuba became bound by the Universal Copyright Convention and Protocols 1 and 2 as from June 18, 1957.[3]

ACQUISITION OF PROTECTION UNDER THE UNIVERSAL COPYRIGHT CONVENTION

The laws of Cuba do not contain any special provisions in respect of works to which Cuba is supposed to grant protection by virtue of the Universal Copyright Convention. The provisions of that Convention, particularly of Articles II and Protocols 1 and 2, determine which are the works protected under the Universal Copyright Convention. Briefly stated, such works are (i) published works of nationals of a Convention country, irrespective of the place of first publication, (ii) works first published in a Convention country, irrespective of the nationality of the author, (iii) unpublished works of nationals of a Convention country other than Cuba, (iv) works of stateless persons and refugees who have their habitual residence in a State party to Protocol 1 (except perhaps Cuba), either published or unpublished,

[1] Published in "Gaceta de Madrid" of January 12, 1879, No. 12, page 107. Provisions on registration were amended by Decree-Law No. 283 of June 8, 1934 ("Gaceta Oficial de la República de Cuba," June 12, 1934, page 9363). English translation in CLTW, Cuba: Item 1.
[2] No. 860, published in "Gaceta Oficial," August 11, 1960; English translation in CLTW, Cuba: Item 5A.
[3] CLTW, Cuba: Item 6A. Cuba is also party to the Washington Copyright Convention, 1946.

and if published, irrespective of the place of first publication, (v) works first published by the United Nations, by any of the Specialized Agencies of the United Nations, or by the Organization of American States, as well as unpublished works of any of these Organizations.

The Law requires, as a condition of copyright protection, deposit and registration in the Copyright Registry in the case of all works other than works of the fine arts;[4] this requirement, however, is inapplicable in the case of works to be protected by virtue of the Universal Copyright Convention.[5] It would seem that Cuba grants protection to such works even if the Convention notice is missing from the copies of published works, since protection of such works is exempt from any formality.

Cuba has no renewal system, so there is nothing in this country which would correspond to the renewal formalities existing in the United States.

PROTECTED WORKS

Scientific, literary and artistic works are protected, whatever the manner of their expression (*que puedan darse a luz por cualquier medio*).[6] The Law expressly mentions maps, scientific drawings, musical compositions, reproductions of works of art,[7] dramatic works,[8] translations.[9] Indirect reference is made to authorized recasts, extracts and abridgments.[10] The Decree extends copyright protection to authorized phonographic adaptations, transformations and reproductions, and calls them "phonographic works."[11]

According to the Regulations, all works produced or capable of publication by means of writing, drawing, printing, painting, engraving, lithography, stamping, autography, photography, or by any other means of printing or reproduction, are deemed to be works for the purposes of the Law.[12]

PROTECTED PERSONS

Copyright belongs to: (i) the author in his own work, (ii) the translator in his translation, which must be an authorized one if the original work is protected, (iii) to any person who recasts, copies, extracts from, abridges or reproduces original works, insofar as concerns the product of his effort (but permission of the author of the original work, if protected by copyright, is required), (iv) to the publishers (*editores*) of

---

[4] Articles 29, 33 to 39.
[5] *Cf.* Article 51.   [6] Article 1.   [7] Articles 3 and 19.   [8] Article 19.
[9] Article 14.   [10] Article 2.   [11] Decree, article 1.
[12] Regulations, article 1.

hitherto unpublished works whose owner is not known, and to the publishers of hitherto unpublished works of known authorship which have passed into the public domain, (v) the composers of music, (vii) the authors of works of art in respect of any kind of reproductions of such works, (viii) to the successors in title (*derechohabientes*), whether by inheritance or by any other title conveying ownership, of the above-mentioned persons.[13]

ASSIGNMENT AND LICENSING

Copyright devolves upon the author's heirs or legatees. It is also transferable by act *inter vivos*. In the latter case, it belongs to the assignee during the life of the author and for 80 years thereafter, if the author leaves no "compulsory heirs" (*herederos forzosos*), i.e., heirs whose rights cannot be put aside by will unless there is a legitimate cause for disinheriting them. If the author does not leave compulsory heirs, the rights of the assignee end 25 years after the death of the author, and, for the remaining 55 years, they pass to the compulsory heirs.[14]

In the absence of agreement to the contrary, alienation of a work of art does not imply alienation of the right of reproduction, nor the right of public exhibition.[15]

Every contract concluded between authors or composers and other persons for the publication, performance, interpretation or diffusion of their works or the administration of their rights, or which in any manner affects the copyright therein, or the income therefrom, requires the prior approval of the "Cuban Institute of·Musical Rights," and its registration in the "Register of Agreements" of this Body, in order that it shall be valid between the contracting parties and effective against third parties. Any sums which may be receivable in advance by the author or·composer as a consequence of such contracts cannot be claimed if the contract is not approved. A sum to be fixed by the Institute, and which may not exceed ten pesos M.O. ($ 10,00) is payable in respect of each request for the examination of a contract.[16]

A contract is prohibited and therefore is not to be approved by the Governing Council, and is not capable of entry in the Register of Agreements of the Cuban Institute of Musical Rights, if it contains any of the following terms or conditions: (a) the author or composer contracts in respect of his future productions; (b) he contracts for an unspecified term or a term in excess of 10 years in respect of the rights of administration or economic control of one or more musical or

---

[13] Articles 2, 3, 14, 26. The person who conceives and gives form to the scientific or literary work, or who creates and executes the artistic work, is deemed to be the author of the work (Regulations, art. 2).
[14] Article 6.   [15] Article 9.   [16] 1960 Law, article 31.

dramatico-musical works; (c) the contract contains provision for prorogation, and such prorogation, when added to the basic term, exceeds 10 years; (d) in violation of the foregoing provisions, the contract affects or impinges upon rights emanating from copyright in musical or dramatico-musical works; (e) the contract contains provisions contrary to law, morality or public order.[17]

A contract is void if it authorizes successive transmissions of rights without reserving to the author or composer the minimum percentage royalty fixed for the production of the work by the previous publisher, which minimum is determined and revised by the Institute whenever necessary.[18]

The originals of all agreements between parties referred to in Article 34 must be submitted to the Institute, together with as many copies as there are parties, and with their signatures legalized by a notary public. The Institute retains the originals of the said documents, forming with them the "Register of Transactions" and supplies to each of the contracting parties one copy, bearing an indication of having been approved and registered by the Cuban Institute of Musical Rights.[19]

The appropriate portion of monies in respect of works that have been assigned in the manner permitted by law, and in respect of which agreements have been approved by the Institute is payable directly to the publisher. Monies due to an author or composer are likewise payable, as deposits, when due to persons not registered with the Institute or any kindred foreign society with which an agreement has been concluded. In any case, the Institute retains the payments when the publishers, by reason of representing authors or composers in other countries where there are no kindred societies with whom agreements have been concluded, receive the amounts to which they would be entitled and which do not normally reach the Institute.[20]

PROTECTED RIGHTS

Economic Rights

No person has the right to *publish*, without the permission of the author, a scientific, literary or artistic work, including lectures, taken down by means of shorthand, or noted or copied during its reading, performance or public or private exhibition.[21]

No person may, even for the purpose of annotating, adding to or improving the edition of a work, *reproduce* the work of another person without the permission of the owner thereof.[22] In the case of musical

---

[17] 1960 Law, article 32. [18] 1960 Law, article 33.
[19] 1960 Law, article 34. [20] 1960 Law, article 35.
[21] Article 8. [22] Article 7, first paragraph.

works, the prohibition equally extends to the total or partial publication of the melody, with or without accompaniment, transposed or arranged for other instruments, or with different words, or in any other form different from that in which the work was published by the author.[23] Authors of works of art have an exclusive right of *public exhibition* as well as reproduction.[24]

As to the public performance or any other diffusion of musical and dramatico-musical works, authors do not seem to have a right of authorization but merely a right to remuneration through the Cuban Institute of Musical Rights.[25]

MORAL RIGHTS

Authors are protected against changes in the title or text of their works.[26]

Enterprises, societies or private persons who, when proceeding to the public performance of a dramatic or musical work, announce it with a change in title, or suppress, add to or alter certain passages thereof, without the permission of the author, are deemed infringers of copyright.[27]

LIMITATIONS

Any person may publish, as his own property, commentaries, criticisms or notes referring to the work of another person, but including therewith only those parts of the work as are necessary for the purpose.[28]

Writings and telegrams included in periodical publications may be reproduced in any other publication of a like kind, provided that in the original publications no indication is given immediately following the title, or at the end of the article, to the effect that reproduction is prohibited: in all cases, the source from which the reproduction is made must be indicated.[29]

TERM OF PROTECTION

Generally.—Subject to the exceptions referred to below, copyright is protected during the life of the author and 80 years thereafter.[30] As to the reversionary interest of heirs, see "Assignment and Licensing," above.[31]

---

[23] Article 7, second paragraph.   [24] Articles 9 and 10.
[25] *Cf.* Law of 1960, articles 26 to 30.   [26] Articles 47 and 48.
[27] Article 24.   [28] Article 7, first paragraph. *See also* article 23.
[29] Article 31. *See also* article 32.
[30] Article 6. *See also* article 10.
[31] Page 4, above.

Works which are not republished by their owner over a period of 20 years may, in certain circumstances, fall into the public domain.[32] It is uncertain whether this provision is also applicable when its effect would lead to a protection shorter than the minimum terms provided in the Universal Copyright Convention.

Rule of the Shorter Term.—It would appear that a given work does not enjoy copyright protection in Cuba beyond the date on which it falls into the public domain in the country "of its proprietor," and copyright in the translation of a work is not protected in Cuba beyond the date on which the original work falls into the public domain in the country of the proprietor of the copyright in the original work.[33]

INFRINGEMENTS

Civil Remedies.—The law provides that copyright is governed by the general rules of law.[34] These undoubtedly include the general rules concerning compensation for damage caused by infringing acts.

Criminal Sanctions.—Any person who, to the prejudice of the legitimate owner, commits any infringement of copyright registered in the name of such owner, is liable to a fine of from thirty to one hundred and fifty quotas.

Any person who, for purposes of gain, and without having previously obtained the appropriate authorization or permission from the legitimate owner, reproduces, copies, performs or broadcasts any dramatic, musical, literary or poetic work registered in the name of the author, in accordance with the provisions of the Law of Copyright, is liable to the same penalty.

The owner, manager or director of a theatre, spectacle or broadcasting station who, for purposes of gain and in the knowledge that the requisite authorization has not been obtained, permits the performance, reproduction or broadcasting of the registered and protected work of some other person, is liable to the same penalty.

The proceeds or gains obtained by the persons responsible, shall, after payment of the indemnity due to the injured party, be confiscated and paid into the *Caja de Resarcimiento* (Code of Social Defense, Article 392).

---

[32] Articles 40 to 44.   [33] Article 13.   [34] Article 5.

CZECHOSLOVAKIA

SOURCES

Internal Law.—The main source of the law of copyright in Czechoslovakia is the Law No 35 of March 25, 1965,[1] entitled Law Concerning Literary, Scientific and Artistic Works (Copyright Law). Hereinafter, it is referred to as "the Law," and references to Sections, without further specification, are references to the Sections of this Law.

In addition to matters of copyright law, in the strict sense, the Law also contains provisions on the *domaine public payant*,[2] and on the so-called "neighboring rights," that is, the rights of performing artists,[3] producers of phonograms,[4] and broadcasting and television organizations.[5] As these subjects do not fall within the purview of the Universal Copyright Convention, they are not dealt with in this book.

The Law entered into force on July 1, 1965.[6]

Universal Copyright Convention.—Czechoslovakia became bound by the Universal Copyright Convention and Protocol 2 as from January 6, 1960.[7]

ACQUISITION OF PROTECTION UNDER THE UNIVERSAL COPYRIGHT CONVENTION

The Law does not contain any provision expressly referring to the Universal Copyright Convention. It merely provides that the provisions of the Law apply also to the works of foreign (i.e., non-Czechoslovak) nationals in accordance with international agreements or, in the absence of such agreements, if reciprocity is assured.[8]

---

[1] Published in "Sbírka zákonů," on April 8, 1965. English translation in CLTW, Czechoslovakia, Item 1.

[2] § 35.   [3] §§ 36 to 39.   [4] §§ 45, 47, 48.   [5] §§ 46 to 48.   [6] § 55.

[7] CLTW, Czechoslovakia: Item *4B*. Czechoslovakia is a member of the Berne Copyright Union, having ratified the Berlin Convention of 1908, the Berne Additional Protocol of 1910, and the Rome Convention of 1928 (CLTW, Czechoslovakia: Item 5). A Government Proclamation by Czechoslovakia, dated April 27, 1927, extended the protection of the former Czechoslovak Copyright Law. (Law No. 218 of November 24, 1926, as amended by Law No. 120 of April 24, 1936) to works of United States citizens. This Proclamation does not seem to have been revoked although the Law of 1926 was repealed in 1953. It may be still of significance, particularly for works created or first published prior to the date on which both the United States and Czechoslovakia became party to the Universal Copyright Convention.   [8] § 50(2).

Consequently, the provisions of the Universal Copyright Convention itself, particulary those of Articles II and XVII and Protocol 2, determine which works are protected under the Universal Copyright Convention. Briefly stated, such works, unless they are excluded by virtue of Article XVII of the Universal Copyright Convention and the Appendix Declaration relating to that Article (in which case the applicable Berne Convention governs rather than the Universal Convention) are the following: (i) published works of nationals of a Convention country, irrespective of the place of first publication, (ii) works first published in a Convention country, irrespective of the nationality of the author, (iii) unpublished works of nationals of a Convention country other than Czechoslovakia, (iv) works first published by the United Nations, by any of the Specialized Agencies of the United Nations, or by the Organization of American States, as well as unpublished works of any of those Organizations.

The only case in which it might be necessary to distinguish between works protected under the Universal Copyright Convention and works protected under certain of the Conventions of the Berne Copyright Union is the case of the rule of the shorter term, discussed below.[9]

There are no copyright formalities in Czechoslovakia. Consequently, registration, deposit, or compliance with other formalities, is neither required nor possible in Czechoslovakia, and the absence, in itself, of a Convention notice on the copies of a published work is no bar to the claiming of protection in that country. Furthermore, Czechoslovakia has no renewal system, so that there is nothing in that country which would correspond to the renewal formalities existing in the United States.

PROTECTED WORKS

The Law protects literary, scientific and artistic works resulting from the creative activity of an author. Such works are, in particular: (i) literary works, (ii) theatrical works, (iii) musical works, (iv) works of the fine arts, including works of architecture and works of applied art, (v) cinematographic works, (vi) photographic works, (vii) cartographic works.[10] New, original works resulting from the creative adaptation of works of another person are the subject of copyright.[11] Translations of works into other languages are the subject of copyright.[12] Symposia, periodicals, anthologies, and other compilations

---

[9] Page 284, below. Works having a Berne Union country as country of origin are, roughly stated: (i) unpublished works whose author is a national (*ressortissant*) of a Union country, (ii) published works which were first published in a Union country or which, within 30 days of their first publication in a non-Union country, were also published in a Union country ("simultaneous publication").

[10] § 2(1).   [11] § 3(1).   [12] § 3(2).

are the subject of copyright if their arrangement is the result of creative activity on the part of the compiler.[13]

Works expressed only in oral form are also the subject of copyright.[14]

Copyright in a works applies to both the whole of the work and the parts thereof.[15]

Protection, under the Law, of works of applied art does not exclude protection of such works also as industrial designs, by virtue of the legal provisions concerning industrial designs.[16]   `

The provisions of the Law do not apply to: (i) statutory provisions, (ii) legal decisions, (iii) public documents, (iv) official records, (v) news of the day, (vi) speeches delivered in connection with public matters.[17] Such speeches, however, may be published in a collection or incorporated in a compilation only with the consent of the person who delivered them.[18]

PROTECTED PERSONS

Generally.—Subject to the exceptions stated below, copyright initially vests in the author.[19] The adaptor whose activity has a creative character, and the translator, are treated as authors.[20] Copyright in a compilation as a whole belongs to the compiler, without, however, affecting the rights of the authors of the various works included in the compilation.[21] Copyright in published symposia, cartographic works, and periodicals, is exercised by the publishers of such works.[22] Copyright in a cinematographic work, or in a work produced by a process analogous to cinematography, as a whole, is exercised by the maker of the work; the use, by such maker, of the works which are individual components of a cinematographic (or analogous) work requires the contractual consent of the authors of the component works.[23]

Copyright in a work which, as a simple work, has resulted from the creative activity of several authors belongs to all co-authors jointly and severally.[24]

Anonymous and Pseudonymous Works.—If a work is made public, or is published without an indication of the author's name or under his pseudonym, and as long as the author does not disclose his identity to the public, copyright is exercised by the person who first lawfully published the work or, in the case of an unpublished work, made it public.[25]

[13] § 4(1).   [14] Cf. § 9(1).
[15] § 9(2).   [16] § 52.   [17] § 2(2), first sentence.
[18] § 2(2), second sentence.   [19] Cf. § 2(1).   [20] Cf. §§ 3(1) and (2)
[21] § 4(2).   [22] § 4(3).   [23] § 6.   [24] § 7.   [25] § 8(2), first sentence.

Works of Certain Employees.—The Law contains special provisions in respect of works of employees of socialist organizations[26] but, since the organizations are Czechoslovak organizations and their employees normally Czechoslovak nationals, such works hardly ever come under the provisions of the Universal Copyright Convention in Czechoslovakia.

ASSIGNMENT AND LICENSING

Generally.—The author may transfer only the right to use the work[27] (see "Protected Rights," below). The right to the protection of authorship (see "Moral Rights," below), is not transferable.[28] Transferees of the right to use the work may transfer such rights to a third person only with the consent of the author.[29] The right to use the work publicly in Czechoslovakia may be transferred by the author only to designated Czechoslovak organizations.[30] The right to use the work in foreign countries may be transferred by the author only through the intermediary of designated Czechoslovak organizations.[31]

Contracts for Dissemination of the Work.—Publishing contracts, contracts for the public performance of a work, contracts for the dissemination of copies of a sound recording, and contracts for the radio or television broadcasting of a work, are included among contracts for dissemination (*rozširování*).[32] Contracts for the dissemination of the work must generally be in writing[33] and must provide for the method and extent of dissemination, the time when the dissemination will take place, the amount of the payment to the author, the part to be played by the author in the dissemination, the period for which the contract is made, and the obligation of the organization to disseminate the work at its own expense.[34] Any author bound by a contract for dissemination of a work is obliged to submit the work to the organization in due time and in a form enabling it to be disseminated in the agreed manner.[35] The organization may rescind the contract if the author, without reasonable cause, fails to submit the work in the proper form and in due time.[36] On the other hand, the author may rescind the contract and demand that the work be returned if the work is not disseminated within the term specified in the contract; his right to a fee is not affected thereby.[37]

Publishing Contracts.—By a publishing contract, the author gives his consent to the publisher to publish a literary, dramatico-musical or musical work, or a work of the fine arts, or a photographic

[26] § 17. [27] § 19(1). [28] § 12(2). [29] § 19(2). [30] § 19(3).
[31] § 20. [32] § 22(2). [33] § 22(4). [34] § 22(3). [35] § 23(1).
[36] § 23(2). [37] § 23(3).

work, and the publisher is bound to publish the work at his own expense, to provide for its dissemination, and to pay remuneration to the author.[38] As long as the obligations based on the publishing contract exist, the author is not entitled to grant to any other organization the right to publish the work without the consent of the publisher, except in the case of the publication of the work in a collection of his works or in a periodical.[39] If the work is out of print before the expiration of the term specified in the contract, the author may ask the publisher to republish the work, even though a subsequent edition of the work has not been provided for in the contract. If, thereafter, a publishing contract for a new edition is not made within six months, the author is free to make a contract with another publisher.[40]

Contract for Public Performance of a Work.—By a contract for the public performance of a work the author grants his consent to the organization to perform a theatrical or musical work, and the organization is bound to perform the work at its own expense and to pay the author a remuneration.[41]

Contract for Creation of a Work.—By a contract for the creation of a work, the author assumes the obligation to create for the ordering party, subject to payment, a literary, scientific or artistic work, and grants the right to the ordering party to use the work for the purpose specified by the contract. Under such a contract, the author is obliged to create the work personally and within the stipulated term. Unless otherwise specified, delivery of the work gives rise to the author's right to the agreed remuneration.[42]

Transfer of the Property of the "Corpus Mechanicum".—A person who acquires ownership of the original work or a reproduction thereof does not thereby acquire the right to use the work (see "Protected Rights," below), unless otherwise expressly agreed.[43]

"Droit de Suite."—An author who has transferred the original of his work for valuable consideration may claim a fair share from his transferee or any further transferee if the transferee obtains a socially unjustified profit from transferring the property in the original work. This right—designated as *droit de suite* in French doctrine and law—may not be waived in advance by the author.[44]

Czechoslovak Organizations Representing Authors.—The Law provides that the Czechoslovak Minister of Education and Culture may grant to Czechoslovak socialist organizations representing authors a monopoly—for each organization within its competence—of the right (i) to license the use of works and collect authors' fees, (ii) to act as an intermediary when the rights of Czechoslovak authors

[38] § 24(1).   [39] § 24(2).   [40] § 24(3).
[41] § 26.   [42] § 27(1) and (2).   [43] § 30.   [44] § 31.

are transferred outside Czechoslovakia or when the rights of non-Czechoslovak authors are transferred in Czechoslovakia, (iii) to disseminate works in Czechoslovakia.[45]

PROTECTED RIGHTS

Economic Rights

Generally.—The author has the right to dispose of his work—especially to decide upon making the work public and to give his consent to its use—and he has a right to remuneration.[46] Subject to certain exceptions,[47] a work may be used only with the consent of the author.[48] The consent of the author is given by contract to the competent Czechoslovak socialist organizations.[49] The amount of the remuneration is determined by Government regulations according to the value of the work and its social importance.[50]

Special Cases.—Speeches delivered in connection with public matters may be published in a collection or incorporated in a compilation only with the consent of the person who delivered them.[51] A work may be incorporated in a compilation only with the consent of the author.[52] Works of different authors may be joined together in a composite work only with the consent of their respective authors. The authors of the composite work as such must dispose of such work in common, but the author of each individual work included in the composite work may dispose of his work individually. However, for the performance of a musical work with text, the consent of the composer of the music is sufficient.[53] The use of a work in a cinematographic work, or in a work produced by an analogous process, requires the consent of the author of the work.[54]

Broadcasting.—Czechoslovak broadcasting and television organizations may, without the author's consent, transmit works that have already been made public; they are obliged to indicate, in connection with the transmission, both the author and the work, and to remunerate the author for each transmission.[55]

---

[45] § 44(1).   [46] § 12(1).
[47] If the author is a Czechoslovak national and it is not possible to obtain his consent through reasonable efforts, or he unreasonably refuses to give his consent, and if the work has already been made public, the competent authority may waive the requirement of consent but the right to remuneration remains (see § 18(1)). Other exceptions exist in the case of works created by employees (see "Protected Persons," *supra*). See also "Broadcasting," "Translation," and "Limitations," *infra*.
[48] § 14(1).   [49] § 14(1).   [50] § 13.   [51] § 2(2).   [52] § 4(1).
[53] § 5(1), (2) and (3).   [54] Cf. § 6, first sentence.   [55] § 16.

Translation.—The Law provides that the Czechoslovak Minister of Education and Culture may, within the limits of the applicable international agreements, waive the requirement of the author's consent in the case of the translation of the work of a non-Czechoslovak national into one or more of the languages of the nationalities of the Czechoslovak Socialist Republic.[56] Thus, the Law provides for the possibility of applying Article V of the Universal Copyright Convention concerning the right to translate. However, no cases are known in which this provision of the Law has been made use of.

MORAL RIGHTS

The author has a right to the protection of his authorship, especially the inviolability of his work.[57] This right is not transferable.[58]

If the work is used by a person other than the author, the use must be made in a manner which is not prejudicial to the "value" of the work.[59] It is not permissible to reveal the identity of the author if his work was published without his name or under a pseudonym. Later, of course, the author may give permission for his identity being revealed.[60]

Even a work in the public domain may be used only in a manner which is not prejudicial to the "value" of the work. The name of the author, if known, must be indicated even in works in the public domain. Authors' societies and socialist organizations must see to it that these rules are respected.[61]

LIMITATIONS

The Law permits the free use of a work—that is, use without the consent of the author and without payment of any fee to him—when a person makes any of the following uses: (i) makes for his own personal use a reproduction or copy of a work already made public, provided that, in the case of a work of the fine arts, he identifies it clearly as a reproduction or copy, and provided that, in the case of a work of architecture, he does not construct a building; (ii) quotes excerpts from a published work, provided that he indicates both the author and the title of the work; (iii) includes in a scientific or critical work, to the extent necessary in order to explain the text, or in textbooks or manuals for schools, within reasonable limits, parts of published works or even entire short published works, provided that he indicates both the author and the source; (iv) uses a published work in an individual lecture exclusively for teaching or educational purposes, provided that he indicates both the author and the work; (v)

[56] § 18(2).   [57] § 12(1) (a).   [58] § 12(2).   [59] § 12(1) (a).   [60] § 8(1).
[61] § 35(2).

reprints, in a periodical, articles of current interest on economic or political matters already published in other periodicals, provided that he indicates both the author and the source (however, reprinting is not permitted when it has been expressly forbidden); (vi) adapts to another field of the fine arts a work of the fine arts that has been located in public places (photographs of a work of the fine arts thus located may also be reproduced and disseminated without the consent of its author); (vii) reprints, in the catalog of a public collection or exhibition, a picture of a work of the fine arts included in such a collection or exhibition; (viii) exhibits publicly works of the fine arts or photographic works which have been transferred by the author to a socialist organization (if a work of the fine arts or a photographic work has been transferred to personal ownership, the author's consent shall not be necessary, provided that the work is exhibited free of charge or lent free of charge to a socialist organization to be exhibited); (ix) reproduces for his own personal use or for gratuitous distribution a commissioned photographic portrait of himself, or has it reproduced by a third party.[62]

Free use is also permitted to organizations reporting current events by means of photography, film, radio or television, if reasonable use is made of the work which is performed or exhibited on such occasion.[63]

Copyright is not infringed by a person who uses the ideas contained in the work of another person in order to create a new, original work.[64]

TERM OF PROTECTION

Beginning of Protection.—Copyright in a work originates as soon as the work is expressed orally or in the form of a manuscript, draft, sketch, or in any other perceptible manner.[65]

End of Protection.—Except in the cases stated hereinafter, copyright expires fifty years after the death of the author. In the case of works of joint authorship, the fifty years are calculated from the death of the co-author who is the last to die.[66] If the work is a posthumous work which was first made public during the last ten years of the fifty-year period, copyright expires ten years after the publication of the work.[67]

Copyright in an anonymous or pseudonymous work—where the identity of the author is not known—expires fifty years after the publication of the work.[68]

---

[62] § 15(2).   [63] § 15(3).   [64] § 15(1).   [65] § 9(1).   [66] § 33(1).
[67] § 33(2).   [68] § 33(3).

Copyright in a cinematographic work expires twenty-five years after the date on which the work was made public.[69]

Copyright in a symposium or in a periodical published by an organization expires ten years after publication.[70]

Copyright in a photographic work expires ten years after the death of its author.[71]

As to moral rights, see "Moral Rights," above.

Common Rules.—A work is considered to have been *made public* on the day on which it was first lawfully performed in public, exhibited in public, published, or made accessible to the public in any other way.[72] It is considered to have been *published* on the day on which copies thereof were lawfully put into public circulation.[73]

The number of years indicated under the heading "End of Protection," above, is not counted from the actual date of the relevant event (making public, publication, death) but from the end of the year in which the event occurred.[74]

The term of copyright is governed by the above rules of the Law even if it started to run prior to the entry into force of the Law, but only if the copyright had not already expired prior to the date of such entry into force, i.e., July 1, 1965.[75]

Copyright devolves upon the heirs of the author. The provisions of the Law concerning the author, unless inapplicable by reason of their nature, apply also to the heirs of the author. If a co-author dies without leaving heirs, his share accrues to the shares of the other co-authors.[76]

Rule of the Shorter Term.—The term of copyright in the work of a non-Czechoslovak national may not be longer than in the country of origin of such work.[77] The country of origin of an unpublished work is the country of which the author is a national. The country of origin of a published work is the country in which the work was first lawfully published. A work published within thirty days both in Czechoslovakia and in another country is considered to have Czechoslovakia as its country of origin.[78]

INFRINGEMENTS

Civil Remedies.—Any controversy concerning claims arising out of the Law is within the jurisdiction of the ordinary courts, even if one of the parties is a socialist organization, or both are.[79] An author whose right has been infringed may demand, in particular, that further infringement be prohibited and that the consequences of the infringe-

---

[69] § 33(4).   [70] § 33(5).   [71] § 33(6).   [72] § 10(1).   [73] § 10(2).
[74] § 34.   [75] § 51(1).   [76] § 29.   [77] § 50(4).   [78] § 11.
[79] § 53(2).

ment be remedied. Equitable compensation is among such remedies. In the case of a work of joint authorship, each co-author may sue independently.[80]

Penal Sanctions.—Unauthorized, wilful use of a protected work in any manner which is reserved to the author is a criminal offense, punishable by a fine or imprisonment.[81]

---

[80] § 32.　　[81] Penal Code, § 261.

DENMARK

SOURCES

Internal Law.—The main source of the law of copyright in Denmark is the Copyright Act of May 31, 1961.[1] Hereinafter, it is referred to as "the Act," and references to Sections, without further specification, are references to Sections of this Act.

Photographs are not considered works, rights in them are not considered copyrights, and their protection is not regulated in the Copyright Act, but in a separate law entitled "Act on Rights in Photographic Pictures." The date of this Law is also May 31, 1961.[2] Hereinafter, it will be referred to as the "Act on Photographs."

Universal Copyright Convention.—Denmark became bound by the Universal Copyright Convention and Protocols 1 and 2 as from February 9, 1962.[3] A Royal Decree of October 5, 1961 (hereinafter referred to as "the Royal Decree"),[4] regulates, among other things, the application of the Copyright Act and of the Act on Photographs to works and photographic pictures protected under the Universal Copyright Convention.

ACQUISITION OF PROTECTION UNDER THE UNIVERSAL COPYRIGHT CONVENTION

Subject, where applicable, to the rule of the shorter term,[5] the provisions of the Copyright Act and of the Act on Photographs apply to:

a) works and photographic pictures of nationals of a country party to the Universal Copyright Convention;

b) works and photographic pictures first published in a country party to the Universal Copyright Convention;

c) works and photographic pictures of persons domiciled in a

[1] Published in "Lovtidende A", 1961, page 295; English translation in CLTW, Denmark: Item 1.

[2] Published in "Lovtidende A", 1961, page 292; English translation in CLTW, Denmark: Item 2.

[3] CLTW, Denmark: Item 3B. Denmark is a member of the Berne Copyright Union. It has ratified the Conventions of Berlin, Rome and Brussels (CLTW, Denmark: Item 4).

[4] Published by the Ministry of Cultural Affairs under No. 1690-60-24.

[5] See "Term of Protection," page 293 below.

country party to the Universal Copyright Convention provided that, according to the laws of that country, they have the same rights as nationals of that country insofar as the application of the Universal Copyright Convention is concerned;

d) works and photographic pictures of stateless persons and refugees who have their habitual residence in a country party to Protocol 1 of the Universal Copyright Convention;[6]

e) works and photographic pictures first published by the United Nations, any Specialized Agency of the United Nations, or the Organization of American States, and to any unpublished works these Organizations may in the future publish.[7]

Denmark has no copyright formalities. Consequently, registration, deposit, or compliance with other formalities is not required, and the absence, in itself, of a Convention notice on the copies of a published work is no bar to claiming protection in this country. Furthermore, Denmark has no renewal system, so that there is nothing in this country which would correspond to the renewal formalities existing in the United States.

PROTECTED SUBJECT MATTER

Works.—The Copyright Act protects literary and artistic works. The following are specially mentioned:
—works of *belles lettres* (*skønlitteraer*) or works of a descriptive (nonfictional) nature (*beskrivaende fraemstilling*), whether written or oral,
—musical works,
—dramatic works,
—cinematographic works,
—works of fine arts,
—works of architecture,
—works of applied art,[8]

---

[6] Royal Decree, sections 6 and 10. To works and photographic pictures which meet any of the conditions referred to under (a), (b), (c), and (d), above, but which have, as a country of origin, a country which is a member of the Berne Copyright Union, the provisions of the Copyright Act and of the Act on Photographs apply by virtue of sections 1 and 5 rather than sections 6 and 10 of the Royal Decree (Royal Decree, section 8). However, the distinction is of little practical relevance outside the application of the rule of the shorter term. Works and photographic pictures which have, as country of origin, a State which withdraws from the Berne Copyright Union after January 1, 1951, are not protected in Denmark, even if they meet one or more of the conditions referred to under (a), (b), (c), or (d) above (Royal Decree, sec. 8). No country has withdrawn from the Berne Copyright Union since the said date; consequently, the provision does not yet apply in practice.
[7] Royal Decree, section 9. (Neighboring rights (sec. 45 to 50) do not apply in this case.)
[8] Section 1, first paragraph.

—maps, drawings and other works of a descriptive nature executed in graphic or plastic form,[9]
—translations, adaptations, and other transformations of a work into another literary or artistic form.[10]

Copyright in a work is not lost by the fact that it is registered as a design under provisions other than those of the Copyright Act.[11]

Photographs.—Photographic pictures are protected; a picture produced by a process analogous to photography is considered a photographic picture.[12]

PROTECTED PERSONS

Works.—Copyright belongs to the person who created the work.[13] A person who translates a work or adapts or converts it into a different literary or artistic form, has copyright in the new work thus produced, but may not make dispositions connected therewith contrary to the copyright in the work from which the new work is derived.[14] A person who, by combining works or parts of works, creates a composite work (*samlevaerk*), has copyright in the composite work, but his rights may not restrict the rights in the said works.[15]

If a work has several authors whose respective contributions do not constitute independent works, copyright belongs to them jointly.[16]

In the absence of proof to the contrary, the person whose name, generally-known pseudonym, or signature, is indicated in the usual manner on the copies (*eksemplar*) of the work, or when the work is made available (*tilgaengeligt*) to the public, is deemed to be the author. If a work is published without authorship being indicated in the said manner, the editor, and if he is not named, the publisher, may represent the author until authorship is indicated in a new edition of the work or in a notification filed with the *undervisningsministeriet* (Ministry of Education).[17] The transfer of a copy (*eksemplar*) of the work does not carry with it the transfer of the copyright in the work.[18]

Photographs.—The owner of the rights in a photographic picture is the person who has produced it (*fraemstiller*).[19]

[9] Section 1, second paragraph; these are considered literary works.
[10] *See* Section 4, first paragraph.
[11] Section 10, first paragraph.
[12] Act on Photographs, section 1.
[13] Section 1, first paragraph.
[14] Section 4, first paragraph.
[15] Section 5.   [16] Section 6.   [17] Section 7.
[18] Section 27, first paragraph.
[19] Act on Photographs, section 1, first paragraph. Other provisions refer to him as the photographer (*see*, for example, Act on Photographs, sec. 3).

The person whose name, firm-name (*firma*), or generally known signature is indicated in the usual manner on the copies (*eksemplar*) of the photographic picture, or when the photographic picture is publicly exhibited, is deemed to be the photographer.[20]

In the absence of an express agreement to the contrary, the right in a photographic picture made on commission belongs to the person who commissioned it. However, the photographer may exhibit the picture in the usual manner for advertising purposes, unless the person who commissioned it has prohibited such exhibition. On the other hand, even if the photographer has reserved the right in a photographic picture made on commission, the person who commissioned it may cause it to be published in newspapers, periodicals, or biographical writings, unless the photographer has prohibited such publication. In any case, the moral rights of the photographer are protected.[21]

ASSIGNMENT AND LICENSING

Generally.—Subject to certain limitations concerning moral rights (discussed below), copyright may be transferred entirely or partially.[22]

The transfer of a copy does not include transfer of the copyright.[23] (In the case of a portrait executed on commission, the artist may not exercise his copyright without the permission of the person who commissioned it or, if such person is dead, without the permission of his surviving spouse and heirs.) When a photographer has transferred one or more copies of a photographic picture to another person, or when the picture was published, it may be publicly exhibited without the permission of the photographer.[24]

An agreement transferring copyrights may be wholly or partially repudiated if it is contrary to usage considered as proper in the field of copyright.[25]

In the absence of an agreement to the contrary, the person to whom a copyright has been transferred may not transfer the same to others. If the copyright belongs to a business, it may be transferred, together with the business or part thereof; however, the transferor remains liable for the fulfilment of the original contract.[26]

Public Performance Contracts.—In the absence of an agreement to the contrary, the license to perform a work other than a cinematographic work is considered to be non-exclusive and valid only for three

[20] Act on Photographs, section 3.
[21] Act on Photographs, section 12.
[22] Section 27, first paragraph.
[23] Section 27, first paragraph.
[24] Act on Photographs, section 10, first paragraph.
[25] Section 29.
[26] Section 28, second paragraph.

years. Where a person who has been granted an exclusive right to perform a work (other than a cinematographic work) does not exercise his right for at least three years, the author may—in the absence of an agreement to the contrary—perform, or license third persons to perform, such works.[27]

Publishing Contracts.[28]—In the absence of an agreement to the contrary:

a) a manuscript or other copy from which the reproduction is effected remains the property of the author;[29]

b) the publisher may publish one edition (*oplag*), that is a quantity of copies produced at one and the same time, whose number may not exceed 2,000 for literary works, 1,000 for musical works, and 200 for artistic works;[30]

c) the publisher must publish the work within a reasonable time, and provide for its distribution to the extent permitted by the condition of the market and other relevant circumstances;[31]

d) the author may rescind the contract and retain any remuneration received in either of the following cases:

   i) the work has not been published within two years (in the case of a musical work, within four years) from the date of submission of the manuscript or other copy from which reproduction was to be made,

   ii) the work is out of print, and no new edition is published within one year of the author's demand for a new edition to be published;[32]

e) the publisher must give the author a certification issued by the printer, or whoever was responsible for the reproduction, certifying the number of copies (*eksemplar*) produced;[33]

f) the publisher must render yearly accounts to the author as to the number of copies sold, on rentals, and on the number of copies remaining in stock;[34]

g) the author must be given the opportunity to make changes in the work whenever a year or more has elapsed between the publication of the last edition and the beginning of the production of the new edition;[35]

[27] Section 32.
[28] A publishing contract is a contract by which the author transfers to the publisher the right to multiply (*mangfoldiggøre*), by printing or other similar process, and publish (*udgive*) a literary or artictic work (sec. 33, first paragraph).
[29] Section 33, second paragraph.
[30] Section 34.
[31] Section 35. (If the publisher does not fulfil any of these obligations, the author may rescind the contract, keep any remuneration received, and claim any additional damages.)
[32] Section 36.
[33] Section 37, first paragraph.
[34] Section 37, second paragraph.
[35] Section 38. Such changes must not cause unreasonable costs and must not alter the character of the work.

h) the author may not publish, or authorize third persons to publish, the work in the form or manner stipulated in the contract, as long as the editions allowed the publisher are not out of print.[36]

The rules of interpretation summarized under (a) through (h), above, do not apply to contributions to newspapers or periodicals; and further, those under (c) and (d) do not apply to contributions to other composite works (*samlevaerk*).[37]

Contracts Relating to the Production of Cinematographic Works.—In the absence of agreement to the contrary, the granting of a license to use a literary or artistic work in the production of a film includes a license to make the work (but not a musical work) accessible (*tilgaengeligt*) to the public by means of the film.[38]

The granting of a license to use a literary or musical work in the production of a film intended for public exhibition must produce the film and make it available to the public within a reasonable time.[39]

PROTECTED RIGHTS

ECONOMIC RIGHTS

Works.—Copyright includes the exclusive right to dispose of the work (i) by producing copies (*eksemplar*) thereof; (ii) by making it accessible to the public. It is irrelevant whether these acts are done with the work in its original form or in a modified form. Modified forms include translations, adaptations, expressions in a different literary or artistic genre, and expressions by a different technique.[40]

Production of copies includes fixation on contrivances with the help of which the work may be reproduced.[41]

Making accessible to the public may be effected by public performance, by offering copies for sale, loan or lease, by other diffusion to the public, or by public exhibition.[42]

Once a literary or musical work has been published, any copy being part of the publication may be freely distributed further and publicly exhibited. However, sheet music may not be leased to the public without the author's consent.[43]

[36] Section 39, first paragraph. However, a literary work may be included by the author in an edition of his collected or selected works, when fifteen years have elapsed since the publication of the first edition.
[37] Section 40.   [38] Section 42.   [39] Section 41.
[40] Section 2, first paragraph.   [41] Section 2, second paragraph.
[42] Section 2, third paragraph. Performance before a bigger, although closed, group is considered public performance if it takes place on the premises of an undertaking conducted for profit (*erhvervsvirksomhed*).
[43] Section 23, first paragraph. The provision, however, does not affect the author's right to remuneration for books loaned to the public through libraries (Order No. 128 of April 16, 1959, sec. 7 (2b)).

The author has an exclusive right to publish a compilation of his written or oral statements, even when at the time the statements were made they could be, singly, published without his consent.[44]

Copies produced outside Denmark, which, if produced in Denmark, would have infringed the author's rights, may not be imported into Denmark if the importation serves the purposes of public distribution, exhibition or performance. Unauthorized importations are punishable by fine or imprisonment.[45]

Photographic Pictures.—The right in photographic pictures consists of the exclusive right of (i) making copies of the photographic picture by photography, printing, drawing or other processes; (ii) publicly exhibiting the photographic picture.[46]

Moral Rights

Works.—When copies of a work are produced or when the work is made available to the public, the name of the author must be indicated to the extent and in the manner required by proper usage.[47]

A work may not be changed in a manner, and may not be presented to the public in a form or context, which would be prejudicial to the author's literary or artistic reputation, or which would be inconsistent with his individuality.[48]

However, buildings and useful articles may be altered without the author's consent.[49]

Even if copyright has expired, works may not be altered or made available to the public in violation of the moral rights of the author if cultural interests are thereby adversely affected.[50]

Photographic Pictures.—When copies of a photographic picture are produced, or when the photographic picture is publicly exhibited, the name of the photographer must be indicated, to the extent and in the manner required by proper usage.[51]

Photographic pictures may not be altered in a manner prejudicial to the producer's reputation as a photographer; nor may they be

---

[44] Section 24.
[45] Section 55, second paragraph.
[46] Act on Photographs, section 1, first paragraph.
[47] Section 3, first paragraph. This right may be waived only in respect of utilizations clearly circumscribed as to manner and extent (sec. 3, third para.). *See* also section 26.
[48] Section 3, second paragraph. This right may be waived only in respect of utilizations clearly circumscribed as to manner and extent (sec. 3, third para.).
[49] Section 13. But buildings may be altered only for technical reasons or with a view to their practical utilization.
[50] Section 53. Prosecution is by the public prosecutor pursuant to a finding of the Ministry of Education.
[51] Act on Photographs, section 2, first sentence: *see also* section 12.

exhibited in such a form or context as to prejudice the producer's reputation as a photographer.[52]

LIMITATIONS

The author's (or when applicable, the photographer's) permission is not required *in certain cases* of: copying for private use;[53] photocopying by libraries;[54] quotation, criticism, learned treatise; popular scientific work;[55] reproduction in a newspaper[56] or religious or educational compilations,[57] sound fixation for educational use;[58] uses for the blind;[59] for charitable or some other non-profit-making occasions;[60] performance at divine services, in connection with education, news by broadcast or film;[61] ephemeral fixations for and by broadcasting organizations;[62] etc.[63]

One of the unique features of the Danish Act is that it allows the Danish broadcasting organizations, which have an agreement with an organization representing a large number of Danish authors in the field—under which agreement it may broadcast literary and musical works—also to broadcast published works of authors who are not represented by the organization; such authors are entitled to compensation for the broadcast. This provision does not apply to dramatic works and to works whose broadcasting has been prohibited by the author.[64]

TERM OF PROTECTION

Generally.—Copyright in works subsists until the end of the fiftieth year after the year in which the author, or the last surviving co-author, died.[65]

[52] Act on Photographs, section 2, second sentence.
[53] Section 11. Act on Photographs, section 5.
[54] Section 12. Act on Photographs, section 6.
[55] Section 14; however, in certain cases the author is entitled to compensation. Act on Photographs, section 7; however, in certain cases the photographer is entitled to compensation.
[56] Section 15.
[57] Section 16; however, the author is entitled to compensation.
[58] Section 17.
[59] Section 18.
[60] Section 20; but cinematographic works and dramatic works may not be so performed.
[61] Section 21; Act on Photographs, section 8. "Radio Denmark" may broadcast, in return for compensation, any disseminated photographic picture, unless the photographer has prohibited showing by television (Act on Photographs, sec. 9).
[62] Section 22, first paragraph; Act on Photographs, section 11.
[63] Sections 19, 24, 25; Act on Photographs, sections 7, 10, 13.
[64] Section 22, first paragraph.
[65] Section 43.

Anonymous and Pseudonymous Works.—In the case of a work disseminated[66] without mention of the author's name or generally known pseudonym or signature, copyright subsists until the end of the fiftieth year after the year in which the work was disseminated.[67]

Photographic Pictures.—Rights in photographic pictures subsist until the end of the twenty-fifth year after the year in which the photographic picture has been produced.[68]

Rule of the Shorter Term.—Protection of a given work (or photographic picture)—except protection of the moral rights—ceases in Denmark on the same date as in the country of origin of the work (or photographic picture) if that date precedes the date on which the work (or photographic picture) would, according to the provisions referred to above, cease to be protected in Denmark. The country of origin is the country, party to the Universal Copyright Convention, in which the work (or photographic picture) was first published, or if it was published simultaneously or within thirty days in two or more such countries with different terms of copyright, the country in which such term is the shortest. Works (or photographic pictures) first published in a country not party to the Universal Copyright Convention, and unpublished works (or photographic pictures), are deemed to originate in the country of which their author is a national.[69] A work is considered "published" when copies thereof have been lawfully placed on sale or otherwise distributed to the public.[70,71]

---

[66] "Disseminated" (*offentliggjørt*) means "lawfully made available to the public" (sec. 8, first para.).

[67] Section 44, first para.; if the author's identity is disclosed between the time of dissemination and that of the expiration of the above term, or if it is established that the author died before the work was disseminated, protection ends at the expiration of the fiftieth year after the year in which the author, or the last surviving co-author, died (Section 44, second paragraph).

[68] Act on Photographs, section 15.

[69] Decree, section 7. However, if the work has as country of origin a Berne Union country and that country is not the same as the country of origin under the Universal Copyright Convention, then the term of protection in the *former* country (i.e., country of origin according to the Berne Conventions) serves as a basis of comparison with the term resulting from the Danish laws (Decree, sec. 8). Works having a Union country as country of origin are, roughly stated: (i) unpublished works whose author is a national (*ressortissant*) of a Union country, (ii) published works which were first published in a Union country or which, within 30 days of their first publication of a non-Union country, were also *published* in a Union country ("simultaneous publication").

[70] Section 8, second sentence.

[71] The rule of the shorter term, as laid down in the Decree, is not quite in harmony with the requirements of the Universal Copyright Convention (*see* page 50, above). For example, the Royal Decree calls for a comparison of terms in respect of the individual work rather than the class to which the work belongs.

INFRINGEMENTS

Generally.—Any violation of the economic or moral rights of the author or photographer is an infringement. Importation—with a view to general distribution or public exhibition or performance—into Denmark of copies of the work or photographic picture if the production of such copies outside Denmark took place under circumstances which, if the production had taken place in Denmark, would have made the copies unlawful likewise constitutes infringement.[72]

Infringing copies, and implements serving the infringement, may be seized and destroyed or otherwise disposed of.[73]

Civil Remedies.—Infringers are liable to pay compensation for the damage caused. If it is deemed reasonable, under the circumstances, the injured party may be awarded compensation, even where the infringement was committed in good faith; however, in such cases the compensation may not exceed the profit resulting from the infringement. If the infringer is criminally liable, the court may order him to pay to the injured party compensation for mental suffering.[74]

Penal Sanctions.—If the infringement has been committed wilfully and with gross negligence, the infringer may be punished by fine or imprisonment. If the offence has been committed by a legal entity, the legal entity, as such, may be liable for the fine.[75]

[72] Section 55; Act on Photographs, section 17.
[73] Section 57; Act on Photographs, section 19.
[74] Section 56; Act on Photographs, section 18.
[75] Section 55; Act on Photographs, section 17.

ECUADOR

SOURCES

Internal Law.—The primary source of the law of copyright in Ecuador is the Law on Intellectual Property, dated October 24, 1951—January 22, 1958 (hereinafter referred to as "the Law").[1] References to Articles without further specification, are references to Articles of this Law.

Universal Copyright Convention.—Ecuador became bound by the Universal Copyright Convention and Protocols 1 and 2 as from June 5, 1957.[2]

ACQUISITION OF PROTECTION UNDER THE UNIVERSAL COPYRIGHT CONVENTION

There are no laws in Ecuador which specifically refer to the Universal Copyright Convention. In particular, there are no provisions implementing Article III of the Convention, which provides for the non-applicability or avoidance of domestic formalities for the acquisition of copyright.[3] Consequently, while it is assumed for purposes of the present exposition that conflicts between the Law of Ecuador and the Convention will be resolved in accordance with the provisions of the latter, this assumption cannot, in the absence of relevant authoritative decisions, be regarded as officially confirmed.

The laws of Ecuador do not define the works which are protected in that country by virtue of the Universal Copyright Convention. On the

[1] Published in "Registro Oficial", of February 11, 1958. English translation in CLTW, Ecuador: Item 1. Articles cited in this Chapter without any indication of the statute are Articles of this Law.

[2] CLTW, Ecuador: Item 1A. Ecuador is also party to the Copyright Conventions of Rio de Janeiro of 1906, Buenos Aires of 1910, Caracas of 1911, Havana of 1928, and Washington of 1946 (CLTW, Ecuador: Items 2 through 6). Bilateral treaties concluded with Mexico in 1888, France in 1898, 1905 and 1952, Spain in 1900 and 1953 relate, in whole or in part, to copyright protection, but since all these countries as well as Ecuador are party to the Universal Copyright Convention, the significance of these treaties in the field of copyright relations has become a limited one, except for works created prior to February 11, 1958 (CLTW, Ecuador: Items 7, 8, 9, 11). A Treaty of Friendship concluded with Bolivia stipulates mutual national treatment in respect to copyright (CLTW, Ecuador: Item 10).

[3] Article 25 prescribes registration and deposit.

basis of the provisions of the Convention and the Protocols, it may be assumed that such works are: (i) published works of nationals of a Convention country, irrespective of the place of first publication, (ii) works first published in a Convention country, irrespective of the nationality of the author, (iii) unpublished works of nationals of a Convention country, other than Ecuador, (iv) works of stateless persons and refugees who have their habitual residence in a State party to Protocol 1 (except perhaps Ecuador), either published or unpublished, and, if published, irrespective of the place of first publication, (v) works first published by the United Nations, any of its Specialized Agencies, or the Organization of American States, as well as unpublished works of any of these Organizations.

It may thus be further assumed that works in any of these categories are protected in Ecuador without deposit and registration, provided always that, in the case of published works, the provisions of Article III of the Convention concerning notice have been complied with.

Ecuador has no renewal system, so that there is nothing in this country which would correspond to the renewal formalities existing in the United States.

PROTECTED WORKS

Intellectual productions of any kind are protected, if they are capable of publication and reproduction, whatever is the method of form of expression employed. Their nature may be philosophic, scientific, religious, literary, artistic, or any other. The following are mentioned in the Law as examples: (i) didactic texts, monographs, and other intellectual works; (ii) novels, poems, fables, criticisms, essays and other literary productions; (iii) dramatic and dramatico-musical works, intended for the stage, motion pictures, radio and television broadcasting; (iv) lectures, speeches, sermons and dissertations, in written or recorded form, (v) writings used in judicial proceedings, (vi) choreographic works and pantomimes, the scenic arrangement of which is fixed in writing or otherwise; (vii) musical compositions; (viii) paintings, drawings, illustrations, decorations, sculptures, engravings, lithographs and other plastic works; (ix) photographs, motion pictures, microphotographs and microfilms; (x) astronomical and geographical spheres, maps, plans, sketches, plastic works of geography, topography, architecture or any other science.[4] The following are also considered "works": translations, adaptations, musical arrangements, instrumentations, dramatizations, cinematographic versions and any other transformations of a literary, artistic or scientific work, provided they are authorized by the author or by the person who owns his rights protected by the Law.[5] Finally, compilations of literary or scientific

[4] Article 1.   [5] Article 2, first paragraph.

works, such as encyclopaedias and anthologies, as well as reviews and magazines, are protected if the selection and arrangement of their contents are original and the result of creative effort; rights in such works may not prejudice the rights in the pre-existing works.[6]

PROTECTED PERSONS

"Author" may mean a person or a legal entity. Subject to the exceptions stated below, copyright originally vests in the author,[7] whatever be his race, sex, color, language, religion, national origin, political opinion or social class.[8]

According to the Law, the owner of an unregistered work who publishes it for the first time owns the copyright therein.[9],[10] It is doubtful whether this provision is applicable to such works protectable under the Convention which, pursuant to Article III of the Convention, need not be registered in Ecuador in order to be protected there. Copyright in compilations of popular productions, such as songs, legends, traditions (*tradiciones*), and music, vests in the compiler.[11]

In the case of works produced in collaboration, copyright belongs to the authors in equal parts, unless otherwise provided by contract concluded between them.[12]

An author who is employed to work (*para la redacción*) for a periodical may not, in order to prevent reproduction, reserve to himself the copyright in his works prepared for such periodical (*sus obras periodísticas*). Copyright in such works belongs to the owner of the periodical (*empresario*), but the author may publish his contributions in an independent collection of his articles.[13] Unless otherwise provided by contract, copyright in a work created by a hired author vests in the person or corporation which hired him to work.[14]

In the absence of proof to the contrary, the person whose name or known pseudonym appears on a given work or reproductions thereof, or whose name is announced when the work is used or presented, is presumed to be the author of the work.[15] If, in the case of publication of a work by an anonymous or pseudonymous author, his true name has not been recorded in the Ministry of Education, the publisher is regarded as author of the work.[16]

ASSIGNMENT AND LICENSING

Copyright is capable of transfer, in whole or in part, upon any basis (*a cualquier título*).[17] In order to have legal effect, every contract relating

[6] Article 2, second paragraph.
[7] Article 5.   [8] Article 14.   [9] Article 3, second paragraph.
[10] Article 4(a).   [11] Article 4(c).   [12] Article 10.   [13] Article 8.
[14] Article 9.   [15] Article 3.   [16] Article 15.   [17] Article 23.

to copyright must be recorded in the *Registro General de la Propiedad Intelectual* (General Copyright Register) maintained by the Ministry of Education.[18]

PROTECTED RIGHTS

ECONOMIC RIGHTS

The author of a work has the right to utilize and diffuse his work by any known lawful method. Consequently, he has the right: (i) to publish and reproduce the work by means of printing, photography, engraving (*grabado*), multi-copying or other processes; (ii) to diffuse it by means of radio or television, or by any other system presently known or hereafter invented for the reproduction of signs, sounds or images; (iii) to perform it on the stage, by cinematography or by television; (iv) to adapt, arrange, transpose, dramatize and, in general, transform it for the purposes of diffusion (*publicidad*) or exhibition; (v) to authorize diffusions and adaptations or modifications necessary for theatrical or cinematographic versions, or for any other medium of performance or reproduction; (vi) to authorize translations.[19] No person is entitled to use publicly (*utilizar con fines de publicidad*) scientific, literary, or artistic works that were copied, taken down in shorthand or in the form of notes during a reading, performance or exhibition, or during instruction or oral explanation, except with the express authorization of the author.[20]

Letters are the physical property of the person to whom they were addressed; but the exclusive right of publication belongs to the author, and upon the author's death, to his heirs. However, addressees may reveal the contents of letters received by them when such publication is necessary to defend their personal honor.[21]

MORAL RIGHTS

Even after having alienated his copyright, the author of a work retains the right to claim authorship of the work and to oppose any modification or alteration prejudicial to his reputation. This right is inalienable, and may be exercised by the author and by his successors, until the expiration of 50 years after the date of his death. If the author has no successors the Ministry of Education may exercise his moral rights. After the expiration of 50 years from the death of the author, the moral rights may be exercised by the said Ministry.[22]

[18] Article 28.   [19] Article 5.
[20] Article 13, second paragraph; *see also* article 20.
[21] Article 19.   [22] Article 12.

LIMITATIONS

Short fragments or small selections from works may be freely reproduced in anthologies or chrestomathies, or in books of criticism or
literary history, for scientific or pedagogical purposes, provided the
source is indicated and the borrowed texts are not altered. Subject to
the same conditions and limitations, fragments or selections may be
freely used in recitations, theatrical performances, musical performances, public exhibitions, and broadcasting.[23] Subject to the indication of the source from which they are taken, articles, notices, drawings
photographs and illustrations published in periodicals may be freely
reproduced and diffused by any means, unless such uses are expressly
prohibited.[24]

The State, following a declaration of public utility, issued by the
Ministry of Education, may expropriate any work which its author,
or the successors in title of the author, fail to publish or re-publish.[25]

TERM OF PROTECTION

In the case of works of a natural person, the property rights belong
to the author during his life, to his successors for a period of 50 years
after his death, and thereafter to the State (*dominio del Estado*). In the
case of a work of two or more authors, the rights of their successors
continue for the said period of 50 years in favor of their respective
antecedents.[26]

In the case of works of legal entities, the property rights belong to the
legal entity for a period of 50 years, calculated from the first publication
of the work, and thereafter to the State. In the case of works published
in parts, the term is calculated from the first publication of the last
part.[27]

Since there is no provision in the law of Ecuador for the "rule of the
shorter term" permitted under Article IV (4) of the Universal Copyright
Convention, it would appear that works to which the Universal Copyright Convention applies are protected in Ecuador until the expiration
of the terms indicated above even if in other countries they fall into
the public domain at an earlier date.

INFRINGEMENTS

The following acts are considered as violations of the Law: (i) registration of the work of another person as one's own work, (ii) publication

[23] Article 6.   [24] Article 7.
[25] Article 47.   [26] Article 11, *see also* articles 16 and 17.
[27] Article 11, *see also* articles 16 and 17.

of the work of another person as one's own work, (iii) plagiarism, (iv) the falsification of an edition, (v) the importation or sale of fraudulent (*falsos*) copies, (vi) the dramatic or musical performance of a work, by broadcasting or any other method of diffusion and performance, without the permission of the author, (vii) the unauthorized reproduction of works of art, (viii) the reproduction and sale of infringing editions, (ix) the retention by the printer, publisher, lithographer, etc., of copies in excess of the number of copies agreed with the author, (x) any other infringement of the rights conferred by the Law.[28]

Actions prescribe after two years from the committing of the offence if no proceedings have been initiated, and, if proceedings have been initiated, two years from the initiation of the proceeding.[29]

Civil Remedies.—In case of infringement, the author or his representative may demand (a) discontinuance of the acts violating such rights, (b) confiscation in his favor of infringing copies, and payment of the value of the infringing copies sold, (c) appropriate indemnity for the damage suffered.[30]

In the event of an action for plagiarism, the court must seek the opinion of a literary society, academy or circle for the purpose of establishing the nature of the plagiarism.[31]

When the performance or the exhibition of a work is announced, and the requisite permission has not been obtained for the performance or exhibition, the author or his representative may ask that the performance or exhibition be prohibited or suspended; he may also claim damages.[32]

Penal Sanctions.—Infringers are subject to fine.[33]

---

[28] Article 33.   [29] Article 43.   [30] Article 34.
[31] Article 35.   [32] Article 40.
[33] Article 36; *see also* Articles 37 to 39.

FINLAND

SOURCES

Internal Law.—The main source of the law of copyright in Finland is the Copyright Act of July 8, 1961.[1] Hereinafter, it is referred to as "the Act," and references to Sections, without further specifications, are references to the Sections of this Act.

Photographs are not considered "works"; rights in them are not copyrights, and their protection is not regulated by the Copyright Act but by a separate law entitled "Act on Rights in Photographic Pictures."[2] The date of this Law is equally July 8, 1961. Hereinafter, it is referred to as the "Act on Photographs."

Universal Copyright Convention.—Finland became bound by the Universal Copyright Convention and Protocols 1 and 2 as from April 16, 1963.[3]

ACQUISITION OF PROTECTION UNDER THE UNIVERSAL COPYRIGHT CONVENTION

The Act provides that on condition of reciprocity, the President of the Republic may provide for the application of the Act in relation to other countries and similarly for application to works first published by an international organization and to unpublished works which such organization has a right to publish.[4] The Act on Photographs provides that, on condition of reciprocity, the President of the Republic may provide for the application of the Act on Photographs in relation to other countries and similarly for application to photographic pictures first published by an international organization and to unpublished pictures which such organization has a right to publish.[5] Although the condition of reciprocity is doubtless fulfilled in the case of countries

---

[1] Published in "Suomen Asetuskokoelma," 1961, page 799. English translation in CLTW, Finland: Item 1.

[2] Published in "Suomen Asetuskokoelma," 1961, page 808. English translation in CLTW, Finland: Item 2.

[3] CLTW, Finland: Item 2A. Finland is a member of the Berne Copyright Union, the Brussels Convention of 1948 being the most recent text it has ratified. A Decree of December 8, 1928 (No. 313, published in "Suomen Asetuskokoelma," 1928, page 979; English translation in CLTW, Finland: Item 4) extended protection to works originating in the United States of America.

[4] Section 65.   [5] Act on Photographs, section 25.

party to the Universal Copyright Convention, it would appear that the orders of the President of the Republic concerning such countries have not yet been issued.

Finland being a Member also of the Berne Copyright Union, it would seem that Articles II and XVII, and Protocols 1 and 2, of the Universal Copyright Convention should determine which are the works protected under the said Convention.[6] Briefly stated, such works should be, except if excluded by virtue of Article XVII of the Universal Copyright Convention and the Appendix Declaration relating to the same Article (in which case the applicable Convention of the Berne Copyright Union rather than the Universal Copyright Convention governs): (i) published works of nationals of a Convention country, irrespective of the place of first publication, (ii) works published in a Convention country, irrespective of the nationality of the author, (iii) unpublished works of nationals of a Convention country other than Finland, (iv) works of stateless persons and refugees who have their habitual residence in a State party to Protocol 1, whether published or unpublished, and if published, irrespective of the place of first publication, (v) works first published by the United Nations, by any of the Specialized Agencies of the United Nations, or by the Organization of American States, as well as unpublished works of any of these Organization.[7]

PROTECTED SUBJECT MATTER

Works.—The Copyright Act protects literary and artistic works. The following are specially mentioned:
—works of *belles lettres* (*skönlitterär framställning*) or works of a descriptive (non-fictional) nature (*beskrivande framställning*), whether written or oral,
—musical works,
—dramatic (*sceniskt*) works,
—cinematographic works (*filmverk*),
—works of fine arts (*bildkonst*),
—works of architecture (*byggnadskonst*),
—works of artistic handicraft (*konsthantverk*),
—works of industrial art (*konstindustri*),[8]
—maps and other works of a descriptive nature executed as drawings, engravings, or three-dimensionally,[9]
—translations, adaptations, and other conversions of a work into another literary or artistic form.[10]

[6] See page 50, above.
[7] Cf. Universal Copyright Convention, Articles II, XVII, and Protocols 1 and 2.
[8] Section 1, first paragraph.
[9] Section 1, second paragraph; these are considered literary works.
[10] *See* section 4, first paragraph.

Photographs.—Photographic pictures are protected; a picture produced by a process analogous to photography is considered a photographic picture.[11]

PROTECTED PERSONS

Works.—Copyright belongs to the person who created the work.[12] A person who translates or adapts (*bearbetat*) a work, or converts it into another literary or artistic form, has copyright in the new work thus produced, but may not make dispositions connected therewith (*förfoga däröver*) contrary to the copyright in the work from which the new work is derived.[13] A person who, by combining works or parts of works, creates a composite work (*samlingsverk*), has copyright in the composite work, but his rights may not restrict the rights in the said works.[14]

If a work has several authors whose respective contributions do not constitute independent works, copyright belongs to them jointly.[15]

In the absence of proof to the contrary, the person whose name, generally-known pseudonym, or signature, is indicated in the usual manner on the copies (*exemplar*) of the work, or when the work is made available (*tillgängligt*) to the public, is deemed to be the author. If a work is published without authorship being indicated in the said manner, the editor, and if he is not named, the publisher, will represent the author, until authorship is indicated in a new edition of the work or in a notification filed with the competent Ministry of Justice.[16]

The transfer of a copy (*exemplar*) of the work does not carry with it the transfer of the copyright in the work. However, where a portrait picture was executed on commission, the artist may not exercise his rights without the permission of the person who commissioned it or, if such person is dead, the permission of the surviving spouse and heirs.[17]

Photographs.—The owner of the rights in a photographic picture is the person who has produced (*framställt*) it.[18]

The person whose name, firm name (*firma*), or generally known signature is indicated in the usual manner on the copies (*exemplar*) of the photographic picture, or when the photographic picture is publicly exhibited, is deemed to be the photographer.[19]

In the absence of an express agreement to the contrary, the right in a photographic picture made on commission belongs to the person who

[11] Act on Photograph, section 1.
[12] Section 1, first paragraph.
[13] Section 4.   [14] Section 5.   [15] Section 6.   [16] Section 7.
[17] Section 27, second paragraph.
[18] Act on Photographs, section 1, first paragraph. Other provisions refer to him as the photographer (*see*, for example, Act on Photographs, sec. 3).
[19] Act on Photographs, section 3.

commissioned it. However, the photographer may exhibit the picture in the usual manner for advertising purposes, unless the person who commissioned it has prohibited such exhibition. On the other hand, even if the photographer has reserved the right in a photographic picture made on commission, the person who, commissioned it may cause it to be published in newspapers, periodicals, or biographical writings, unless the photographer has prohibited such publication.[20]

ASSIGNMENT AND LICENSING

Generally.—Subject to certain limitations concerning moral rights (discussed below), copyright may be transferred entirely or partially.[21]

The transfer of a copy does not include transfer of the copyright. In the case of a portrait executed on commission, the artist may not exercise his copyright without the permission of the person who commissioned it or, if such person is dead, without the permission of his surviving spouse and heirs.[22] When a photographer has transferred copies of a photographic picture, they may be publicly exhibited, without the permission of the photographer.[23]

If the application of a condition in a contract concerning transfer of copyright is obviously contrary to usage considered as proper in the field of copyright, or is otherwise obviously unfair, it may be changed or disregarded.[24]

In the absence of an agreement to the contrary, the person to whom a copyright has been transferred may not transfer it to others. If the copyright belongs to a business, it may be transferred, together with the business or part thereof; however, the transferor remains liable for the fulfilment of the original contract.[25]

Public Performance Contracts.—In the absence of an agreement to the contrary, the license to perform a work other than a cinematographic work, is considered to be non-exclusive and valid only for three years. Where a person who has been granted, for a period exceeding three years, the exclusive right to perform a work (other than a cinematographic work) does not exercise his right for at least three years, the author may—in the absence of an agreement to the contrary—perform, or license third persons to perform, such works.[26]

[20] Act on Photographs, section 14.
[21] Section 27, first paragraph.
[22] Section 27, second paragraph.
[23] Act on Photographs, section 10, first paragraph.
[24] Section 29.
[25] Section 28.
[26] Section 30.

Publishing Contracts.[27]—In the absence of an agreement to the contrary:

(a) the manuscript or other copy from which the reproduction is effected remains the property of the author;[28]

(b) the publisher may publish one edition (*upplaga*) (that is, a quantity of copies produced at one and the same time) whose number may not exceed 2,000 in the case of literary works, 1,000 in the case of musical works, and 200 in the case of artistic works;[29]

(c) the publisher must (i) publish the work within a reasonable time, (ii) distribute the copies in the usual manner, (iii) follow up the publishing to the extent determined by the marketing conditions and other circumstances;[30]

(d) the author may rescind the contract and keep the remuneration received, even where there is no negligence on the part of the publisher, in either of the following cases:

(i) the work has not been published within two years (in the case of a musical work, within four years) from the date of submission of the manuscript or other copy from which the multiplication was to be made,

(ii) the work is out of print and no new edition is published within one year of the author's demand for a new edition to be published;[31]

(e) the publisher must give the author a certification issued by the printer, or whoever effectuated the multiplication, concerning the number of copies (*exemplar*) produced;[32]

(f) the publisher must render yearly accounts to the author on the number of copies sold and on the number of copies remaining in stock;[33]

(g) the author must be given a chance to make changes in the work every time a year or more elapses between the publication of the last edition and the beginning of the production of the new edition;[34]

(h) the author may not publish, or authorize third persons to publish, the work in the form or manner stipulated in the contract, as long as the editions allowed the publisher are not out of print.[35]

[27] A publishing contract is a contract by which the author transfers to the publisher the right to multiply (*mangfoldiga*), by printing or other similar process, and publish (*utgiva*) a literary or artistic work (sec. 31, first paragraph).
[28] Section 31, second paragraph.
[29] Section 32.
[30] Section 33. If the publisher negligently does not fulfil any of these obligations, the author may rescind the contract, retain any remuneration received, and, if he has suffered additional damage, he may claim compensation therefore.
[31] Section 34.   [32] Section 35, first paragraph.
[33] Section 35, second paragraph.
[34] Section 36. Such changes must not cause unreasonable costs and must not alter the character of the work.
[35] Section 37, first paragraph. However, a literary work may be included by the author in an edition of his collected or selected works, when fifteen years have elapsed since the publication of the first edition.

The rules of interpretation summarized under (a) through (h), above, do not apply to contributions to newspapers or periodicals; and those under (c) and (d) do not apply to contributions to other composite works (*samlingsverk*) as well.[36]

Contracts Relating to the Production of Cinematographic Works.—In the absence of agreement to the contrary:

(a) the granting of a license to use a literary or artistic work in the production of a film:

(i) includes a license to make the work, other than a musical work, accessible (*tillgängligt*) to the public, by means of a film, in motion picture theatres, on television, or otherwise;

(ii) does not include a license to make the musical work accessible to the public in the said manner;[37]

(b) the grantee of a license to use a literary or musical work in the production of a film intended for public exhibition must produce the film and make it available to the public within a reasonable time.[38]

PROTECTED RIGHTS

ECONOMIC RIGHTS

Works.—Copyright includes the exclusive right to dispose (*förfoga*) of the work (i) by producing copies (*exemplar*) thereof; (ii) by making it accessible to the public. It is irrelevant whether these acts are done with the work in its original form or in a modified form. Modified forms include translations, adaptations (*bearbetning*), expressions in a different literary or artistic form, and expressions by a different technique.[39]

Production of copies includes fixation on contrivances by means of which the work may be reproduced.[40]

Making accessible to the public may be effected by public performance, by offering copies for sale, loan or lease, by other diffusion to the public, or by public exhibition.[41]

[36] Section 38.
[37] Section 39.
[38] Section 40. If through negligence this is not done within a reasonable time, the author may rescind the contract and retain any remuneration received, and if he has suffered additional damage, he may claim compensation therefor. If the film is not produced within five years from the time at which the author carried out his obligations, the author may rescind the contract and retain any remuneration received even if there is no fault on behalf of the grantee.
[39] Section 2, first paragraph.
[40] Section 2, second paragraph.
[41] Section 2, third paragraph. Performance before a larger, although closed, group is considered public performance if it takes place on the premises of an undertaking conducted for profit (*forvärvsverksamhet*).

When a literary or musical work has been published, any copy, being part of the publication, may be freely further distributed and publicly exhibited. However, sheet music may not be leased to the public without the author's consent.[42]

The author has an exclusive right to publish a compilation of his written or oral statements, even when, at the time the statements were made, they could be published singly, without his consent.[43]

Copies produced outside Finland which, if produced in Finland, would have infringed the author's rights, may not be imported into Finland for general distribution. Unauthorized importations are punishable by fine or imprisonment.[44]

Photographs.—The right in photographic pictures consists in the exclusive right of (i) making copies of the photographic picture by photography, printing, drawing or other processes; (ii) publicly exhibiting the photographic picture.[45]

Moral Rights

Works.—When copies of a work are produced or when the work is made available to the public, the name of the author must be indicated, to the extent and in the manner required by proper usage.[46]

A work may not be changed in a manner, and may not be presented to the public in a form or context, which would be prejudicial to the author's literary or artistic reputation, or which would be inconsistent with his individuality.[47] However, buildings and useful articles (*bruks-föremål*) may be altered by the owner without the author's consent.[48]

After the author's death, the courts may restrain, by injunction, performances or reproductions prejudicial to the spiritual interests of culture; the right to ask for injunctions in such cases belongs to certain government-appointed authorities. This provision applies also to works in the public domain.[49]

Photographs.—When copies of a photographic picture are produced, or when the photographic picture is publicly exhibited, the name of the photographer must be indicated to the extent and in the manner required by proper usage.[50]

[42] Section 23.   [43] Section 24.
[44] Section 53, second paragraph.
[45] Act on Photographs, section 1, first paragraph.
[46] Section 3, first paragraph. This right may be waived only in respect of utilizations clearly circumscribed as to manner and extent (sec. 3, third paragraph). *See also* section 26.
[47] Section 3, second paragraph. This right may be waived only in respect of utilizations clearly circumscribed as to manner and extent (sec. 3, third paragraph).
[48] Section 13.
[49] Section 51 and section 60, second paragraph.
[50] Act on Photographs, section 2, first paragraph; *see also* section 13

Photographic pictures may not be altered in a manner prejudicial to the producer's reputation as a photographer; nor may they be publicly exhibited in such a form or context as to prejudice the producer's reputation as a photographer.[51],[52]

LIMITATIONS

The author's (or, when applicable, the photographer's) permission is not required *in certain cases* of: photocopying by libraries;[53] quotation, criticism or learned treatise;[54] reproduction in a newspaper[55] or religious or educational compilations;[56] sound fixation for educational use;[57] uses for the blind;[58] performance at divine services or in connection with education;[59] news by broadcast or film;[60] ephemeral fixations for and by broadcasting organizations;[61] etc.[62]

One of the unique features of the Finnish Act is that it allows any Finnish broadcasting organization which, having obtained a special permission of the Government, has an agreement with an organization representing a large number of Finnish authors in the field— under which agreement it may broadcast literary and musical works— also to broadcast published works of authors who are not represented by the organization; such authors are entitled to compensation for the broadcast. This provision does not apply to dramatic works and to works whose broadcasting has been prohibited by the author. Furthermore, it does not apply in cases where there is a particular reason to assume that the author would oppose the broadcasting.[63]

[51] Act on Photographs, section 2, second sentence.
[52] Section 11; Act on Photographs, section 5.
[53] Section 12; Act on Photographs, section 6; and Royal Decree No. 348 of 1961.
[54] Section 14; however, in certain cases the author is entitled to compensation. Act on Photographs, section 7, first paragraph; however, in certain cases the photographer is entitled to compensation.
[55] Section 15, first paragraph.
[56] Section 16; however, the author is entitled to compensation. Act on Photographs, section 7, second paragraph.
[57] Section 17.   [58] Section 18.
[59] Section 20; but cinematographic works and dramatic works may not be so performed.
[60] Section 21; Act on Photographs, section 8. Swedish television organizations may show, in return for compensation, any disseminated photographic picture, unless the photographer has prohibited such showing or there is a particular reason to assume that he opposes it (Act on Photographs, sec. 9).
[61] Section 22, first paragraph; Act on Photographs, section 11.
[62] Section 15, second paragraph, and secs. 19, 24, 25; Act on Photographs, sections 10, 12.
[63] Section 22, second paragraph.

TERM OF PROTECTION

Works Other than Works of Artistic Handicraft or Industrial Art.—Copyright in works other than works of artistic handicraft or industrial art subsists until the end of the fiftieth year after the year in which the author, or the last surviving co-author, died.[64]

In the case of a work (other than a work of artistic handicraft or industrial art) disseminated[65] without mention of the author's name or generally known pseudonym or signature, copyright subsists until the end of the fiftieth year after the year in which the work was disseminated.[66]

Works of Artistic Handicraft or Industrial Art.—Copyright in a work of artistic handicraft or industrial art subsists until the end of the tenth year after the year in which the work was disseminated, provided it was disseminated before the death of the author. If it was not so disseminated, copyright subsists until the end of the tenth year after the year in which the author died.[67]

Photographs.—One has to distinguish between (i) photographic pictures having an artistic or scientific value and (ii) photographic pictures lacking such value. In the first case, similar rules apply as in the case of works other than works of artistic handicraft or industrial art, discussed above, that is, the duration is generally fifty years *p.m.a.*, etc.[68] In the second case, the right subsists only until the end of the twenty-fifth year after the year in which the photographic picture (having no artistic or scientific value) was produced.[69]

Rule of the Shorter Term.—Protection of a given work (or photographic picture) in Finland ceases on the same date as in the country of origin of the work (or photographic picture) if that date precedes the date on which the work (or phogographic picture) would, according to the provisions referred to above, cease to be protected in Finland. The country of origin is the country, party to the Universal Copyright Convention, in which the work (or photographic picture) was first published, or if it was published simultaneously or within

[64] Section 43, first paragraph.
[65] "Disseminated" (*offentliggjort*) means "lawfully made available to the public" (sec. 8, first paragraph).
[66] Section 44, first paragraph; if the author's identity is disclosed between the time of dissemination and that of the expiration of the above term, or if it is established that the author died before the work was disseminated, protection ends at the expiration of the fiftieth year after the year in which the author, or the last surviving co-author, died (Sec. 44, second paragraph).
[67] Section 43, second paragraph; "disseminated" (*offentliggjort*) means "lawfully made available to the public" (sec. 8, first paragraph).
[68] Act on Photographs, section 15, second and third paragraphs; of course, "photographer" must be substituted for "author."
[69] Act on Photographs, section 15, first paragraph.

thirty days in two or more such countries with different terms of copyright, the country in which such term is the shortest. Works (or photographic pictures) first published in a country not party to the Universal Copyright Convention, and unpublished works (or photographic pictures), are deemed to originate in the country of which their author is a national.[70] A work is considered "published" when copies have been lawfully placed on sale, or otherwise distributed to the public.[71,72]

INFRINGEMENTS

Civil Remedies: Works.—In the case of wilful or negligent infringement constituting exploitation of the work the infringer is liable to pay the author or other copyright proprietor (i) an amount constituting reasonable remuneration for the exploitation, and (ii) damages for loss, mental suffering, or other injury caused by his act.[73]

In the case of infringement which is neither wilful nor negligent, the infringer is liable to pay the author or other copyright proprietor an amount constituting reasonable remuneration for the exploitation.[74]

In the case of wilful or negligent commission of acts subject to penal sanctions (see below), but not constituting an exploitation of the work (e.g., violations of moral rights), the defendant is liable to pay to the author or other copyright proprietor damages for loss, mental suffering, or other injury caused by his act.[75,76]

Civil Remedies: Photographs.—In the case of wilful or negligent infringement constituting exploitation of the work, the infringer is liable to pay to the photographer or other holder of his rights (i) an amount constituting reasonable remuneration for the exploitation, and (ii) damages for loss, mental suffering, or other injury caused by his act.[77]

In the case of infringement which is neither wilful nor negligent, the infringer is liable to pay the photographer or other holder of his rights an amount constituting reasonable remuneration for the exploitation.[78]

In the case of wilful or negligent commission of acts subject to penal

[70] Royal Decree No. 349, article 2, para. (3).
[71] Section 8, second paragraph.
[72] The rule of the shorter term, as laid down in Royal Decree No. 349, is not quite in harmony with the requirements of the Universal Copyright Convention (*see* page 50 above). For example, the Royal Decree calls for a comparison of terms in respect of the individual work rather than the class to which the work belongs.
[73] Section 54, first and second paragraphs.
[74] Section 54, first paragraph.
[75] Section 54, third paragraph.
[76] *See also* sections 55, 56, 58 and 59.
[77] Act on Photographs, section 17, first and second paragraphs.
[78] Act on Photographs, section 17, first paragraph.

sanctions (see below) not constituting exploitation of the work, the defendant is liable to pay to the photographer or other holder of his rights damages for loss, mental suffering, or other injury caused by his act.[79,80]

Penal Sanctions: Works.—Any person who commits any of the following acts wilfully or with gross negligence is punishable by fine or imprisonment: (i) infringes copyright, (ii) makes a work available to the public under such a title, pseudonym, or signature that the work or its author may be easily confused with a previously disseminated work, or the author of such a work, (iii) imports into Finland copies of a work for general distribution, if such copies have been produced outside Finland under such circumstances that a similar production within Finland would have been punishable according to the provisions referred to under (i) and (ii) above.[81,82]

Penal Sanctions: Photographs.—Any person who commits any of the following acts, wilfully or with gross negligence, is punishable by fine or imprisonment: (i) infringes the right in a photographic picture, (ii) offers for sale or otherwise distributes copies of a photographic picture produced in violation of the provisions of the Act on Photographs, (iii) distributes to the public, or imports into Finland for such distribution to the public, copies of a photographic picture if the copies have been produced outside Finland under such circumstances that a similar production within Finland would have been punishable according to the provisions referred to under (i) and (ii), above.[83,84]

---

[79] Act on Photographs, section 17, third paragraph.
[80] *See also* Act on Photographs, sections 18, 19, 20.
[81] Section 53. The author may give directions in his will, having binding effect on his surviving spouse and heirs of the body, as to the exercise of copyright, or authorize another person to give such directions (sec. 41, second paragraph). Persons violating such directions wilfully or with gross negligence are punishable by fine or imprisonment (sec. 53, first paragraph).
[82] *See also* sections 52, 55, 56, 59.
[83] Act on Photographs, section 16.
[84] *See also* Act on Photographs, sections 18, 19, 20, 21.

FRANCE

SOURCES

Internal Law.[1]—The main source of the law of copyright in France is the Law No. 57–296 on Literary and Artistic Property (hereinafter referred to as "the Law"), dated March 11, 1957.[2] Hereinafter, references to Articles, without further specification, are references to Articles of this Law.

The Law also applies, with minor modifications not specified in the present analysis, to the overseas territories of France.[3]

Earlier Laws still in force and of possible major interest in connection with the protection of certain non-French works are: (i) two Laws, from 1919 and 1951, extending the term of copyright by reason of the two World Wars;[4] (ii) the Law of February 9, 1895, punishing fraudu-

[1] A commentary on the pre-1957 law, and also on what then was a draft of the 1957 Law, is Prof. Henri Desbois' "Le Droit d'Auteur (Droit français, Convention de Berne revisée)," published in Paris by the Librairie Dalloz in 1950. Prof. Henri Desbois also analyzed the Law of 1957, in a long article entitled "La loi française du 11 mars 1957," published in the October, November and December 1957 issues of "Le Droit d'Auteur."

Some of the legislative history and analysis of the Law of 1957 may be found in a special issue (No. XIX of April 1958) of the Revue internationale du Droit d'auteur, containing the following articles: Marcel Boutet: "Considérations générales"; Jacques Isorni: "Le vote de la loi"; Jean Vilbois: "Historique"; Alphonse Tournier: "Le bilan de la loi"; Henri Desbois: "Le droit moral"; François Hepp: "Le droit d'auteur propriété incorporelle"; Léon Malaplate: "Le droit représentation et le droit d'exécution"; Jean Matthyssens: "Le droit de la cinématographie"; Roger Fernay: "La cession et le contrat d'édition"; Jacques-Louis Duchemin: "La propriété artistique"; Raoul Castelain: "La durée";***: "La procédure et les sanctions."

Gaston Bonnefoy's "La nouvelle législation sur la propriété littéraire et artistique," published by the Editions Montchrestien, in Paris, in 1959, summarizes the French court decisions under each Article of the 1957 Law.

The bulk of Prof. Robert Plaisant's "Propriété littéraire et artistique" published on loose leaves in the Collection des Juris-Classeurs (Editions Techniques, S.A.) was written in 1953, that is, prior to the promulgation of the 1957 Law, but is still a valuable source of reference.

[2] Published in the Journal Officiel of March 14, 1957, page 2723. A corrigendum was published in the Journal Officiel of April 19, 1957, page 4143. The Law entered into force on March 11, 1958 (Article 79, first paragraph). See English translation in CLTW, France: Item 1.

[3] Decree No. 58-447 of April 19, 1958, published in the Journal Officiel of April 19, 1958. See English translation in CLTW, France: Item 6.

[4] Law of February 3, 1919, and No. 51-1119 of September 21, 1951; published in

lent misrepresentation of authorship in artistic works;[5] (iii) the Law No. 52–300 of March 12, 1952, amended by Law No. 57–296 of March 11, 1957 (i.e., by the basic copyright statute), granting special protection to dresses and other articles of fashion.[6]

Universal Copyright Convention.—France became bound by the Universal Copyright Convention and Protocols 1 and 2 as from January 14, 1956. The Convention is also applicable to Guadeloupe, Martinique, Guiana, and Réunion.[7]

ACQUISITION OF PROTECTION UNDER THE UNIVERSAL COPYRIGHT CONVENTION

The Law does not contain provisions dealing expressly with works protected under the Universal Copyright Convention. The French Law does not differentiate between French and non-French works, and, in France, the protection available to all seems to be the same, whether claimed under the Law, the Universal Copyright Convention, the Berne Conventions[8], or any of the bilateral treaties to which France is a party,[9] except that the extension of the duration of protection under the Law of September 21, 1951, No. 51–1119, seems to apply only to French, Italian, Norwegian and Spanish works.[10]

France has no copyright formalities.[11] Consequently, registration, deposit, or compliance with other formalities is not required nor possible in France, and the absence, in itself, of a Convention notice on the copies of a published work is no bar to claiming protection in France. Furthermore, France has no renewal system, so that there is nothing in this country which would correspond to the renewal formalities existing

the Journal Officiel of February 5, 1919, and September 25, 1951. *See* English translation in CLTW, France: Items 2 and 3.

[5] Journal Officiel of February 12, 1895. *See* English translation in CLTW, France: Item 12.

[6] Journal Officiel of March 13, 1952. *See* English translation in CLTW, France: Item 18.

[7] *See* CLTW, France: Item 19.

[8] France has ratified all the instruments of the Berne Union, including the latest, i.e., the Brussels Convention, by which it became bound on August 1, 1951 (CLTW, France: Item 20).

[9] France has concluded bilateral treaties with the following countries (the number in parentheses is that of the item under CLTW, France): Bolivia (25), Costa Rica (27), Ecuador (28), El Salvador (22), Greece (29), Guatemala (26), Italy (24), Mexico (31), Norway (23A), Spain (23), Turkey (30).

[10] *See* CLTW, France: Items 32 to 35, containing the English translation of the exchange of notes of France with Italy, Norway and Spain.

[11] According to Article 1, first paragraph, the author of a work enjoys protection by the mere fact of the creation of the work, and according to Article 7 a work is considered created, independently of any public divulgation, by the mere fact of the realization—even incomplete realization—of the author's conception.

in the United States. Protection in France will last, without any intervention by the copyright owner or a State authority, until the day on which the work falls into the public domain.

PROTECTED WORKS

Under the General Copyright Law.—The Law protects "intellectual" works (*œuvres d'esprit*).[12] All intellectual works are protected, regardless of their kind, form of expression, merit, or purpose (*destination*).[13] The Law gives the following, non-limitative, enumeration: (i) books, pamphlets, and other literary, artistic and scientific writings; (ii) lectures, addresses, sermons, oral pleadings in court, and other works of the same nature; (iii) dramatic and dramatico-musical works; (iv) choreographic works, and pantomimes, the acting form of which is fixed in writing or otherwise; (v) musical compositions with or without words; (vi) cinematographic works and works made by processes analogous to cinematography; (vii) works of drawing, painting, architecture, sculpture, engraving, litography; (viii) photographic works of an artistic or documentary character and other works of the same character produced by processes analogous to photography; (ix) works of the applied arts; (x) illustrations, geographical maps; (xi) plans, sketches, and plastic works, relative to geography, topography, architecture or the sciences.[14]

Furthermore, the following are protected as works, but without prejudice to the rights of the author of the original work: (i) translations, adaptations, "transformations" (*transformations*), arrangements, (ii) anthologies and collections of various works if, by reason of the selection and arrangement of their contents, they constitute intellectual creations.[15]

The title of a work is protected if it has original characteristics.[16] Even after the work has fallen into the public domain, such title may not be utilized for another work of the same kind under conditions capable of creating confusion.[17]

Under the Special Law Protecting Articles of Fashion.—The Law granting special protection to dresses and other articles of fashion[18] protects artistic creations of the industries which, by reason of the exigencies of fashion, frequently change the form of their products, such as dresses, furs, underwear, embroidery, hats, shoes, gloves, leather goods, fabrics of striking novelty or of special use in connection with *haute couture*, fabrics of upholstery.[19] This protection is additional to that available under the Copyright and Design Laws.[20] The duration

---

[12] Article 1, first paragraph.   [13] Article 2.   [14] Article 3.
[15] Article 4.   [16] Article 5, first paragraph.   [17] Article 5, second paragraph.
[18] *See* citation on page 314, above.
[19] Special Law, Article 2.   [20] Special Law, Article 1.

of the protection is not specified in the special Law; civil and criminal actions may, presumably, be brought under it, until the statute of limitation bars them.

PROTECTED PERSONS

Generally.—Copyright originally vests in the author, that is, the person who created the work,[21] even when he creates a work under a contract for his employer.[22] Copyright in a translation, adaptation, "transformation," arrangement, anthology, or collection vests in the translator, adaptor, etc., but without prejudice to the rights of the author of the original work.[23] The person under whose name the work is disclosed (*divulguer*) is presumed to be the author of the work.[24]

Works of Collaboration, Composite and Collective Works.— A work of collaboration—i.e., a work to the creation of which several physical persons have contributed[25]—is the joint property of the co-authors.[26] They must exercise their rights by common accord.[27] In case of disagreement, the civil courts decide.[28] Different kinds of contributions may be separately exploited by their respective authors if such exploitation does not prejudice the exploitation of the work of collaboration.[29]

A composite work—i.e., a new work into which a pre-existing work is incorporated without the collaboration of the author of the pre-existent work[30]—is the property of the author of the new work, without prejudice to the rights of the author of the pre-existing work.[31]

A collective work is defined as a work created by the initiative of a physical person or a legal entity who edits it, publishes it, and discloses it (*divulguer*) under his direction and name, and in which the contributions of the various authors are indistinguishably merged.[32] Copyright in a collective work originally vests in the said physical person or legal entity.[33]

Cinematographic Works.—In French law, the physical persons intellectually creating the cinematographic work (*qui réalisent la création de l'œuvre cinématographique*) and not the film producer are the authors thereof.[34] The Law presumes—but the presumption may be rebutted by contrary proof[35]—that the following persons are authors of a cinematographic work made in collaboration: (i) the author of the script (*scénario*), the author of the adaptation (*adaptation*), (iii) the author

[21] Article 1, first paragraph.
[22] Article 1, third paragraph.   [23] Article 4.
[24] Article 8.   [25] Article 9, first paragraph.
[26] Article 10, first paragraph.   [27] Article 10, second paragraph.
[28] Article 10, third paragraph.   [29] Article 10, fourth paragraph.
[30] Article 9, second paragraph.   [31] Article 12.
[32] Article 9, third paragraph.   [33] Article 13.
[34] Article 14, first paragraph.   [35] Article 14, second paragraph.

of the dialogue (*texte parlé*), (iv) the author of the musical compositions, with or without words, specially created for the cinematographic work, (v) the director (*réalisateur*). If the cinematographic work is derived from a pre-existing work or script (*scénario*) still under copyright protection, the author of such pre-existing work or script is treated as one of the co-authors of the cinematographic work.[36],[37],[38] As to the producer's special position in connection with the exploitation of the cinematographic work, see page 319, below.

Works Specially Created For Sound or Television Broadcasting.—The psysical persons intellectually creating (*qui assurent la création intellectuelle*) of "radiophonic or radiovisual" works (*œuvres radiophoniques ou radiovisuelles*) are the authors thereof.[39] If such a work is derived from a pre-existent work or script (*scénario*) still under copyright protection, then the authors of such pre-existing work or scenario will be included among the co-authors of the "radiophonic" or "radiovisual" work.[40],[41]

Exercise of Rights in Anonymous and Pseudonymous Works.—Even in anonymous and pseudonymous works, copyright vests in the author. However, until such time as the author declares his identity (*identité civile*) and proves his authorship, he is represented, in the exercise of his rights, by the first publisher (*l'éditeur ou le publicateur originaire*)[42].

Posthumous Works.—The right of exploitation in posthumous works belongs: (i) to the successor of the author, if disclosure is made

[36] Article 14, third paragraph.

[37] The producer will be the author of the cinematographic work if he complies with all these roles; and will be one of the co-authors if he complies with at least one of them (Article 17, second paragraph).

[38] If one of the authors refuses to complete his contribution to a cinematographic work or to a work specially created for broadcasting (see below), as the case may be, or is unable to complete his contribution due to *force majeure*, he may not oppose the use of the part of his contribution already in existence (*déjà réalisé*), for the purpose of completing the work. To the extent of his contribution, he will be deemed co-author. In the absence of an agreement to the contrary, each of the co-authors may freely dispose of his contribution for exploitation in a different field (*genre*) if such exploitation does not prejudice the exploitation of the cinematographic work, or of the work specially created for broadcasting, as the case may be. *See* Articles 10, 15 and 18.

[39] Article 18, first paragraph. This type of work is unknown in the copyright Laws of English speaking countries. The expression is not defined in the French Law. It probably means works specially created for sound and television broadcast, although the dividing line, if any, between a cinematographic work and a fixation of a work specially created for television broadcasting seems to be uncertain.

[40] Article 18, second paragraph.   [41] *See* footnote 38, above.

[42] Article 11, first and second paragraphs. The declaration of identity may be made in a will; in any case, rights previously acquired by third parties remain unaffected (Art. 11, third paragraph). If the pseudonym of the author leaves no doubt as to his identity, he is to be treated as an author whose works appear under his true name (Art. 11, fourth paragraph).

before the expiration of the 50th calendar year following his death, (ii) to the proprietor of the work (i.e., the physical object, such as the manuscript or painting) effecting publication, if disclosure is made after the expiration of the 50th calendar year following the death of the author.[43]

PROTECTED RIGHTS

Generally.—According to the Law, the author of an intellectual work enjoys an "exclusive incorporeal property right in the work, effective against all persons (*opposable à tous*),"[44] and this right includes two kinds of attributes, viz., (i) those of an intellectual and moral nature, and, (ii) those of an economic (*patrimonial*) nature.[45]

Moral Rights

The author enjoys a "perpetual, inalienable and imprescriptible" right, "attached to his person," to respect for (i) his name, (ii) his authorship, (iii) his work.[46] Upon the death of the author, this right devolves upon his heirs or on the persons designated by him in his will.[47]

In the case of a cinematographic work, the author may exercise his moral rights only over the *completed* work.[48]

Notwithstanding the transfer of the exploitation rights (see below), the author, even after the publication of his work, enjoys, in relation to the transferee, the right to correct (*droit de repentir*) and the right to retract (*droit de retrait*). He cannot, however, exercise these rights unless he agrees to indemnify the transferee beforehand for the loss that the correction or retraction may cause him.[49]

The author alone has the right to divulge (*divulguer*) his work.[50]

---

[43] Article 23, second and third paragraphs.   [44] Article 1, first paragraph.
[45] Article 1, second paragraph.   [46] Article 6, first paragraph.
[47] Article 6, fourth and fifth paragraphs. In connection with performance contracts, the Law provides separately that the theatrical producer must ensure the public performance of a work under technical conditions which guarantee respect for the author's intellectual and moral rights (Art. 47).
[48] Article 16, second paragraph, unless Article 1382 of the Civil Code is applicable against a person by whose fault the completion of the film was prevented (Art. 16, second paragraph). According to Article 1382 of the Civil Code, every act whatever of an individual which causes injury to another obliges the person through whose fault the injury occurred to make redress for it. A cinematographic work is considered completed when the first master print (*copie standard*) has been established by common accord between the director (*réalisateur*) or, as the case may be, the co-authors, and the producer (*producteur*) (Art. 16, first paragraph).
[49] Article 32, first paragraph.
[50] Article 19, which, together with Article 20, contains also further details, particularly in respect of cinematographic and posthumous works.

ECONOMIC RIGHTS

Right to Exploit.—The author[51] has the exclusive right to exploit his work in any form whatever and to take an economic profit (*profit pecuniaire*) therefrom.[52] This right includes particularly (i) the right of performance (*représentation*), the right of reproduction (*reproduction*).[53]

Right of Performance.—This right consists of the direct communication of the work to the public, especially by means of (i) recitation, (ii) musical performance, (iii) dramatic performance, (iv) presentation, (v) dissemination (*diffusion*), by any method, of words, sounds or images, (vi) projection, (vii) transmission of a broadcast work by means of loudspeaker, or by means of a television screen, placed in a public place.[54],[55]

Right of Reproduction.—Reproduction consists in the material fixation of the work by all methods that permit of indirect communication to the public.[56] Such reproduction may be effected, in particular, by any of the following means: (i) printing, (ii) drawing, (iii) engraving, (iv) photography, (v) casting (*moulage*) or other processes of the graphic and plastic arts, (vi) fixation (*enregistrement*) by mechanical, cinematographic, or magnetic methods,[57] and, (vii) in the case of architectural works, by repeated execution of a plan or standard model (*projet type*).[58],[59]

Presumption as to the Cinematographic Exploitation of Cinematographic Works.—The authors of a cinematographic work[60]—except the author of the musical compositions (with or without words)[61]—must be bound to the producer by a contract which, in the absence of a clause to the contrary, is deemed to have transferred to the producer the exclusive right of cinematographic exploitation.[62]

EXCEPTIONS AND LIMITATIONS

Once a work is disclosed, the following acts do not require the

[51] Naturally, whenever the author is referred to, his successors in title should be understood if the right is no longer the author's own.
[52] Article 21, first paragraph.   [53] Article 26.
[54] Article 27.
[55] Any complete or partial performance or reproduction made without the consent of the author or his transferees is unlawful; this also applies to translations, adaptations, new versions, arrangements, or reproductions, by any method or process whatsoever (Art. 40).
[56] Article 28, first paragraph.   [57] Article 28, second paragraph.
[58] Article 28, third paragraph.   [59] *See* footnote 12, above.
[60] *See* "Protected Persons: Cinematographic Works," page 316, above.
[61] The public performance right for the film music must, normally, be acquired by the producer from the *Société des auteurs, compositeurs et éditeurs de musique* (SACEM), the French performing right society of authors, composers and their publishers, which has a monopolistic status in France.
[62] Article 17, third paragraph.

author's permission: (i) free, private performances effected exclusively within the family circle, (ii) copying and reproduction reserved strictly for the private use of the copyist and not intended for collective use, (iii) use for analyses or brief quotations justified by the critical, polemical, pedagogical, scientific, or informational character of the work in which the copying is made, (iv) copying in press reviews, (v) in the case of public speeches: use in the press or by broadcast, if it is for the purpose of reporting current events (*à titre d'information d'actualité*), (vi) use in parodies, pastiches, and caricatures, "subject to the laws relating thereto."[63]

ASSIGNMENT AND LICENSING

In General.—Performance rights and reproduction rights may be transferred gratuitously or for compensation.[64] As already stated, copyright vests in the creator, and not in the employer, even when the creator made the work for another person under a contract or in his capacity as employee.[65]

Performance contracts and publishing contracts—defined below—must be in writing.[66] The instrument must: (i) separately mention each transferred right, (ii) specify the limits of the exploitation of the transferred rights in respect to scope, purpose, place, and duration.[67] Gratuitous authorizations of performances must be in writing.[68] In all other cases, the general rules of evidence apply which, roughly, provide for the need of writing if the value of the contract exceeds fifty new francs.[69]

Moral rights are inalienable.[70]

Total transfer of future works is void,[71] but an author may grant a preferential right (*droit de préférence*) to a publisher in respect of (i) the next five of his works of a clearly specified kind, or (ii) all his works of a clearly specified kind to be produced in the next five years.[72]

When the right of exploitation has been transferred and the author suffers a prejudice of more than seven-twelfths on account of a breach (*lésion*) or an insufficient advance estimate of the proceeds of the work,

[63] Article 41. *See also* Article 45 dealing, among other things, with ephemeral recordings by broadcasters.

[64] Article 30, first paragraph.   [65] Article 1, third paragraph.
[66] Article 31, first paragraph.   [67] Article 31, third paragraph.
[68] Article 31, first paragraph.   [69] Civil Code, Articles 1341 to 1348.
[70] *See* "Protected Rights: Moral Right," page 318, above.
[71] Article 33. However, this rule may be put aside in the case of a "general performance contract," i.e., a contract whereby a professional organization of authors confers on an *entrepreneur de spectacles* the power to perform all existing or future works constituting the repertory of the organization, under conditions determined by the author or his successors in title (Art. 43, second and third para.).
[72] Article 34, which also contains further details.

he may demand that the price conditions (*conditions du prix*) of the contract be revised.[73] Such demand may be made only where the transfer was made for a lump sum.[74] The breach is to be evaluated by taking into consideration the totality of the exploitation for which the transferee is responsible in connection with the various works of the author alleging to be prejudiced.[75]

Any clause purporting to grant the right to exploit a work in a manner which, at the date of the conclusion of the contract, was not foreseeable or foreseen, must be express and must stipulate a mutual participation in the profits resulting from the exploitation.[76]

In the case of partial transfer, the transferee is substituted for the author in the exercise of the transferred rights, under the conditions, within the limits, and for the term provided in the contract, and with the obligation to account.[77]

Obligatory Participation of the Author in the Financial Success of his Work.—A unique feature of the French Law is that it requires, as a rule, that transfers, whether total or partial, of the rights of an author must assure him a "proportionate participation in the receipts resulting from the sale or the exploitation."[78] This rule is subject to a number of exceptions; the remuneration of the author may be calculated as a lump sum (*évaluer forfaitairement*) in the following cases:

—where it is impractical to establish a basis for calculating a proportionate participation;[79]

—where the means of controlling the application of proportionate participation are lacking;[80]

—where the expenses of calculating and controlling proportionate participation would be out of proportion to the expected results;[81]

—where the nature or the conditions of the exploitation make the application of proportionate participation impossible, either because the author's contribution does not constitute one of the essential elements of the intellectual creation of the work, or because the use of the work is only of an accessory character in relation to the object exploited;[82]

—in the following cases, if the first edition of a book is involved, and the author has expressly agreed to a lump sum remuneration: scientific and technical works; anthologies and encyclopaedias; prefaces, annotations, introductions, presentations; illustrations for a work; de luxe editions printed in a limited number of copies; prayer books; trans-

---

[73] Article 37, first paragraph. [74] Article 37, second paragraph.
[75] Article 38, third paragraph.
[76] Article 38. [77] Article 39. [78] Article 35, first paragraph.
[79] Article 35, second paragraph, item 1.
[80] Article 35, second paragraph, item 2.
[81] Article 35, second paragraph, item 3.
[82] Article 35, second paragraph, item 4.

lations, provided the translator asks for lump sum remuneration; cheap popular editions; cheap picture books for children;[83]
—where the transferor or the transferee is a person or enterprise established outside France;[84]
—where the author creates a work under contract or as an employee for publication in a newspaper, other kinds of periodicals, or a press service.[85]

General Rules of Interpretation.—Acquisition of the material object incorporating the work (i.e., the manuscript pages, the painting, etc.) does not invest the person acquiring it with any of the rights protected by copyright[86],[87] since "the incorporeal property right defined by Article 1 (i.e., the copyright) is independent of the property of the material object."[88]

The transfer of the right of performance does not imply transfer of the right of reproduction, and *vice versa.*[89] When a contract implies (*comporte*) total transfer of the right of performance, the effect of the transfer is limited to the methods of exploitation specified (*prévus*) in the contract. The same applies in case of the "total" transfer of the right of reproduction.[90]

Where an author creates a work under contract or as an employee for a newspaper or other periodical, and once the work has been published in the newspaper or periodical, the author has the right—unless there is a contrary stipulation—to have the work reproduced or otherwise exploited, in any form whatsoever, provided such acts do not compete with such newspaper or other periodical.[91]

Even where the author has transferred the right of exploitation for a given article or speech, he alone has the right to include it in a collected edition of his articles or speeches.[92]

Performance Contracts.—Performance contracts must be concluded for a limited period or for a specified number of communications to the public.[93] A contract granting an exclusive right to perform a dramatic work may not exceed five years, and the interruption of the

---

[83] Article 36, first paragraph.
[84] Article 36, second paragraph.
[85] Article 36, third paragraph.
[86] Article 29, second paragraph; but *see* "Protected Persons: Posthumous Works," page 317, above.
[87] The copyright remains with the author or his successor. They are, however, not entitled to require the proprietor of the material object to place it at their disposal for the exercise of copyright. If the proprietor of the material object manifestly abuses his right, remedy might be sought from the courts. Article 29, third paragraph.
[88] Article 29, first paragraph.
[89] Article 30, second and third paragraphs.
[90] Article 30, fourth paragraph.
[91] Article 36, third paragraph.
[92] Article 37.   [93] Article 44, first paragraph.

performances for two consecutive years automatically terminates the exclusive right.[94]

Entrepreneurs de spectacles cannot validly transfer their interest in a performance contract without the formal, written assent of the author or his representative.[95]

Authorization to broadcast does not imply authorization to record the broadcast.[96] However, certain recordings may be authorized by the Government for historical reasons.[97]

Entrepreneurs de spectacles must inform the author or his representative of the exact schedule (*programme*) of all public performances organized by them, and must furnish a statement of receipts together with supporting documents.[98]

Publishing Contracts.—A publishing contract (*contrat d'édition*) is a contract whereby the author of an intellectual work or his successors in title transfer, under specified conditions, to a person called the publisher (*éditeur*), the right to manufacture or have manufactured in quantity copies (*exemplaires*) of the work, and the publisher undertakes to publish (*publier*) and disseminate the work.[99]

Publishing contracts not providing for a minimum remuneration must indicate the minimum number of copies constituting the first printing.[100]

Unless the contract provides otherwise, the author may require annual statements on the number of copies manufactured and in stock, and, in the absence of contrary usage or agreement, a royalty statement.[101]

The publisher may only transfer his interest in a publishing contract to a third party—except together with his entire business, unless the prior authorization of the author has been obtained.[102]

When the publisher destroys all copies, or—after the expiration of a suitable period fixed by the author—the publisher fails to publish or, where the printing has been exhausted, fails to reprint, the contract will automatically terminate.[103]

[94] Article 44, third paragraph. However, it may be that this rule does not apply in the case of the so-called general performance contracts (*see* "Assignment and Licensing: In General," footnote 7, page 314, above).
[95] Article 44, fourth paragraph.   [96] Article 45, second paragraph.
[97] Article 45, third paragraph.   [98] Article 46, first paragraph.
[99] Article 48. Contracts for publication at the author's expense or providing the author's participation in the publisher's losses are not publishing contracts within the meaning of the Copyright Law, but are governed by the Civil Code, and the Commercial Code, respectively (Arts. 49 and 50).
[100] Article 51.
[101] Article 59. *See also* Article 60 for further details.
[102] Article 62, first paragraph. If the alienation of the business is of a nature that the material or moral interests of the author will be seriously compromised, the author may even terminate the contract (Art. 62, second paragraph).
[103] Article 63, first and second paragraphs. The printing is considered exhausted if

If the author dies before completion of his work, the contract terminates as far as the unfinished part of the work is concerned.[104]

Contracts Concerning Cinematographic Works.—The authors of a cinematographic work—apart from the author of the musical compositions, with or without words—must be bound to the producer[105] by a contract which, in the absence of a clause to the contrary, constitutes transfer, to the producer, of the exclusive right of cinematographic exploitation.[106] Such transfer is without prejudice to the right of the authors of the cinematographic work to a proportionate participation in the receipts resulting from the exploitation of the cinematographic work unless the circumstances, described above,[107] make it lawful to pay them a lump sum remuneration.[108]

In order to be effective against third parties, most contracts concerning the production, distribution, and exploitation of cinematographic works, and the mortgaging of their proceeds, must be deposited and registered in the *Centre national de cinématographie* in Paris.[109]

TERM OF PROTECTION

Undivulged Works.—As already stated, the author alone has the right to divulge (*divulguer*) his work.[110] After his death, the right to divulge his work posthumously belongs to the executors designated by the author in his will—as long as such executors are alive.[111] If the testamentary executors are dead, or none was designated, and unless the will provides otherwise, the right to divulge the work belongs, in the following order, to: (i) the descendants, (ii) the spouse, provided he or she has not been separated and has not remarried, (iii) other heirs and legatees (if they accept the succession).[112]

There is no timelimit on this right; consequently protection against divulgation appears to be perpetual.[113]

two orders for the delivery of copies addressed to the publisher have not been fulfilled within three months (Art. 63, third paragraph).
[104] Article 63, fourth paragraph.
[105] The producer of a cinematographic work is the physical person or legal entity who takes the initiative of, and is responsible for, the making of the cinematographic work (Art. 17, first paragraph).
[106] Article 17, third paragraph.
[107] *See* "Assignment and Licensing: Obligatory Participation of the Author in the Financial Success of his Work," page 321, above.
[108] Article 17, third paragraph, *in fine*.
[109] Decree No. 56-158, codifying the legislative texts relating to the cinematographic industry, of January 27, 1956 (Journal Officiel of January 31, 1956), Articles 31 to 44. English translation published in CLTW, France: Item 17.
[110] Article 19, first paragraph.   [111] Article 19, second paragraph.
[112] Article 20, second paragraph.
[113] Article 21, third paragraph. However, the court may order appropriate measures

Posthumous Works.—The exclusive right of economic exploitation terminates, in the case of posthumous works, 50 years after the date of the publication.[114] As to who the owner of the right of exploitation is, one must differentiate between (i) works divulged before the expiration of the 50th calendar year after the author's death, and, (ii) works divulged after that date. The successors in title own the right of exploitation in case (i), whereas in case (ii) the right is owned by the proprietor of the work (manuscript, etc.) who publishes the work or causes its publication.[115]

Consequently, it would appear that unpublished works are perpetually protected in France.

Published Works.—"The author shall enjoy, during his lifetime, the exclusive right to exploit his work under any form whatsoever and to take economic profit therefrom. Upon the death of the author, this right shall continue to the benefit of his successors, during the then current calendar year and for 50 years thereafter."[116]

This rule is couched in general terms but, in view of the fact that different rules apply to unpublished and posthumous works (discussed above), as well as to pseudonymous works and collective works (discussed below), the duration of 50 years *post mortem auctoris* seems to apply only to such published works which are not posthumous, pseudonymous, or collective.

Pseudonymous Works.—In the case of pseudonymous works, the exclusive right of economic exploitation terminates at the expiration of the 50th calendar year following the date of publication.[117]

Collective Works.—In the case of collective works, the exclusive right of economic exploitation terminates at the expiration of the 50th calendar year following the date of publication.[118]

Rule of the Shorter Term.—Since there is no provision in the Law for the "rule of the shorter term" permitted under Article IV, paragraph (4) of the Universal Copyright Convention, works protected by virtue of that Convention in France seem to be protected until the expiration of the terms indicated above, even if in other countries they

in any of the following cases: (i) if the right is manifestly abused by persons other than the author, (ii) if such persons disagree among themselves, (ii) if there is no known successor at law, (iii) if there is no heir (*vacance* or *déshérence*) (Article 20).

[114] Article 23, first paragraph.   [115] Article 23, second and third paragraphs.

[116] Article 21, first and second paragraphs. "In the case of works of collaboration, the determinative calendar year shall be the year during which the last surviving collaborator dies" (Art. 21, third paragraph). For possible special rights of the surviving widow, *see* Article 24.

[117] Article 22, first paragraph. If the author of an anonymous or pseudonymous work discloses his identity, the general rules apply (Art. 22, third paragraph).

[118] Article 22, first paragraph. There are special rules for collective works published in instalments (Art. 22, second paragraph).

fall into the public domain at an earlier date. In the absence of court decisions in point, there is, however, no certainty in this matter.

INFRINGEMENTS

The Law contains only a few special rules concerning procedure. Otherwise the general rules of law apply.

In particular, the Law regulates injunction and seizure,[119] and amends most of the provisions of the Criminal Code dealing with the offenses (*délits*) of unlawful reproduction and performance.[120] Apart from the reports drawn up by the agents of the *police judiciaire*, proof of the existence of a performance or diffusion may be determined by statements of agents designated by the professional organizations of authors authorized by the Minister in charge of Arts and Letters.[121]

---

[119] Articles 66 to 69.

[120] Articles 70 to 74; Criminal Code, Articles 425 to 429. A special statute establishes penalties for "fraud in the field of art"; such as the fraudulent application of a usurped name on a work of painting, sculpture, drawing, engraving or music (Law of February 9, 1895; for citation *see* page 313, above).

[121] Article 75. These organizations are: (i) *Société des auteurs, compositeurs et éditeurs de musique (SACEM)*, (ii) *Société pour l'administration du droit de reproduction mécanique des auteurs, compositeurs et éditeurs*, (iii) *Société des auteurs et compositeurs dramatiques*, (iv) *Société des gens de lettres*, (v) *Société de la propriété artistique des dessins et modèles*, (vi) *Association pour la diffusion des arts graphiques et plastiques*, (vii) *Société des orateurs et conférenciers* (Order of April 15, 1958, of the Minister of National Education, Youth and Sport, published in the Journal Officiel of May 4, 1954; *see* English translation in CLTW, France: item 4, footnote 2).

GERMANY (FEDERAL REPUBLIC)

SOURCES

Internal Law.[1]—The main source of the law of copyright in the Federal Republic of Germany (hereinafter referred to as "Germany") is the Law on Copyright and Related Rights (Copyright Law) (*Gesetz über Urheberrecht und verwandte Schutzrechte (Urheberrechtsgesetz)*) of September 9, 1965.[2] Hereinafter, references to Sections, without further specification, are references to Sections of this Law.

A separate law deals with relations between author and publisher. This "Law on Publication" (*Gesetz über das Verlagsrecht*) dates from June 19, 1901. It was amended on May 22, 1910, and September 9, 1965.[3] In the present book, this Law is referred to as "VG," these two letters being the abbreviation of the Law's common name in German (*Verlagsrecht-Gesetz*, i.e., Publication Law Act).[4]

The present book generally does not deal with those parts of the Law which concern related rights since, in international relations, most of these related rights are covered by the Rome Convention of October 26, 1961, on neighboring rights rather than by the Universal Copyright Convention.

Universal Copyright Convention.—Germany became bound by the Universal Copyright Convention and Protocols 1 and 2 as from September 16, 1955. The Convention is also applicable to *Land* Berlin.[5]

---

[1] An excellent introduction to the study of the new German Law is Professor Eugen Ulmer's essay "The new German Copyright Act" published in *Copyright* (Monthly Review of the United International Bureaux for the Protection of Intellectual Property (BIRPI)), 1965, pp. 275 to 286. This essay is hereinafter referred to as "Ulmer."

[2] Published in "Bundesgesetzblatt, I," 1965, No. 51, of September 16, 1965, page 1273. An English translation appears in the CLTW as German Federal Republic: Item 1.

[3] Published in "Reichs-Gesetzblatt," 1901, page 217, and 1910, page 793, and "Bundesgesetzblatt, I," 1965, page 1273. An English translation appears in the CLTW as German Federal Republic: Item 3.

[4] The texts in German of all laws, ordinances, conventions, and treaties concerning the law of copyright in the Federal Republic of Germany are collected in the remarkable "Taschenbuch des Urheberrechts," 2nd Edition, by Dr. Kurt Haertel and Gerhard Schneider, published in 1967 by the Carl Heymanns Verlag in Cologne.

[5] *See* CLTW, German Federal Republic: Item 4.

ACQUISITION OF PROTECTION UNDER THE
UNIVERSAL COPYRIGHT CONVENTION

The protection of works of German nationals, and the works of non-German nationals published (*erschienen*) in the territory of the application (*Geltunsgbereich*) of the Law, is exclusively governed by the Law. Publication outside such territory does not affect this rule, if the said publication preceded by not more than 30 days the publication in the territory of the application of the Law. Publication of a translation has, in this respect, the same effect as the making public of the original.[6]

There is no express reference in the Law to the Universal Copyright Convention. But the Law does provide that "otherwise" (i.e., except, essentially, as to works first published in Germany) non-German nationals enjoy protection according to the provisions of international treaties or conventions.[7] Consequently, for determining which works— from the point of view of their "nationality"—are entitled to protection in Germany under the Universal Copyright Convention, the provisions of that Convention and its Protocols 1 and 2 must be considered as the direct source of the applicable rules. Consequently, and subject to the exceptions stated in the subsequent paragraphs, the following are protected in Germany under the Universal Copyright Convention: (i) published works of nationals of a Convention country, irrespective of the place of first publication, (ii) works first published in a Convention country, irrespective of the nationality of the author, (iii) unpublished works of nationals of a Convention country other than Germany, (iv) works of stateless persons and refugees who have their habitual residence in a State party to Protocol 1 (except perhaps Germany), whether unpublished or published, and, if published, irrespective of the place of first publication, (v) works published for the first time by the United Nations, by any of the Specialized Agencies of the United Nations, or by the Organization of American States, as well as unpublished works of any of these Organizations.

For example, works of U.S. citizens are protected in Germany, whether such works are unpublished or published; and works of a French citizen first published in the United States are protected in Germany.

---

[6] §§ 120 and 121(1). The Law provides that a work has been published if, with the consent of the person having the right thereto (*Berechtigter*), multiplied copies (*Vervielfältigungsstücke*) of the work, after they had been manufactured, have, in sufficient quantity, been offered to the public or put into circulation. An artistic work is also regarded as having been published if, with the consent of the person having the right thereto, the original or a copy thereof has been made permanently accessible to the public (§ 6(2)).

[7] § 121(4), first sentence.

For details *see* the chapter on Article II of the Universal Copyright Convention, above.

If a work coming under any of the definitions (i) to (v) above is a work which has, within the meaning of the applicable Act of the Berne Convention, a Berne Union country as country of origin, its protection in Germany is governed by the applicable Berne Convention rather than by the Universal Copyright Convention.[8] Works falling within this definition are, roughly stated, (i) unpublished works whose author is a national (*ressortissant*) of a Berne Union country, (ii) published works which were first published in a Berne Union country or which, within 30 days of their first publication in a non-Berne Union country, were also published in a Berne Union country ("simultaneous publication").

Examples:

An unpublished work of a French *ressortissant* is protected in Germany by virtue of the Berne Convention, rather than the Universal Copyright Convention.

A work of a French or U.S. citizen first published in Canada is protected in Germany by virtue of the Berne Convention, rather than the Universal Copyright Convention.

A work of a French or U.S. citizen first published in the United States but also published in Canada within 30 days from publication in the United States is protected in Germany by virtue of the Berne Convention, rather than the Universal Copyright Convention.

A work of a French citizen first published in France is protected in Germany by virtue of the Berne Convention, rather than the Universal Copyright Convention.

A work of a USSR citizen first published in France is protected in Germany by virtue of the Berne Convention, rather than the Universal Copyright Convention.

For details and refinements, *see* the chapter on Article XVII of the Universal Copyright Convention, above.

It should be noted that the determination of the question whether a

---

[8] This book does not deal, except for incidental references to the Berne Conventions, with the availability of protection in Germany by virtue of provisions other than those of the Universal Copyright Convention. It might, however, be useful to bear in mind that Germany is a member of the Berne Union (the latest text ratified is that of Brussels, 1948, which came into force in Germany on October 10, 1966), and that Germany has concluded bilateral treaties, wholly or partly dealing with copyright, with Austria (9), Ceylon (17), Egypt (14), Greece (13), Iceland (12A), Iran (10), Mexico (18), Pakistan (12), Peru (15), Thailand (11A), and Turkey (11) (the numbers in parentheses refer to the item number in the CLTW, German Federal Republic, containing the English translation of each of these instruments), and, finally, that Germany promulgated special provisions in respect of works of nationals of the United States (7 and 8). These special provisions, however, may be considered superseded, for all practical purposes, by the Universal Copyright Convention.

given work is protected in Germany by virtue of the Berne Convention rather than the Universal Copyright Convention is of possible relevance only in connection with determining the duration of the protection of the work in Germany, since the "rule of the shorter term" in the Berne Convention may lead to a different expiration date of the protection in Germany than the corresponding, but different, rule in the Universal Copyright Convention. This question is discussed under "Term of Protection: Rule of the Shorter Term," page 349, *infra*. In all other respects, the protection in Germany seems to be the same, whether claimed under the Universal Copyright Convention or the Berne Convention.

Germany has no copyright formalities. Consequently, registration, deposit, or compliance with other formalities, is neither required nor possible in Germany, and the absence, in itself, of the Convention notice on the copies of a published work is no bar to claiming protection in Germany. Furthermore, Germany has no copyright renewal system, so there is nothing in this country which would correspond to the renewal formalities existing, for example, in the United States. Protection in Germany will last, without any intervention by the copyright owner or State authority, until the day on which the work falls into the public domain.

PROTECTED WORKS

The Law protects literary, scientific and artistic works, but does not define these works. It merely gives examples and provides that a "work," within the meaning of the Law, must be a personal individual creation. The examples given are the following: (i) literary works, such as writings and speeches, (ii) musical works, (iii) works of pantomime, including choreographic works, (iv) artistic works, including architectural works and works of applied art and plans and sketches of such works, (v) photographic works, including works produced by processes analogous to photography, (vi) cinematographic works, including works produced by processes analogous to cinematography, (vii) representations of a scientific or technical nature, such as drawings, plans, maps, sketches, tables and plastic representations.[9]

Translations and other adaptations of a work which constitute personal intellectual creations of the adapter are protected in the same manner as independent works, without prejudice to the copyright in the adapted work.[10]

Collections of works or of other contributions which, by virtue of the selection or arrangement thereof, constitute personal intellectual crea-

[9] §§ 1 and 2.   [10] § 3.

tions (*Sammelwerke*) are protected in the same manner as independent works, without prejudice to the copyright in the works thus collected.[11]

Laws, regulations, official decrees and notices, as well as decisions and officially drafted guidelines of decisions, do not enjoy copyright protection. The same applies to other official works published in the official interest for public information; however, such works are protected against certain modifications and require that the indication of their source generally accompany their use.[12]

The protection of cinematographic works and films is governed by special provisions discussed on p. 350, below.

PROTECTED PERSONS

Generally.—As a rule, copyright originally vests in the author of the work, i.e., the person who creates the work.[13]

Adapters, translators, and persons who, by selection and arrangement, create a collection of works (*Sammelwerk*), are protected as authors of the adaptation, translation, or collection.[14]

Co-Authors.—If two or more persons have created a work in common, and their respective contributions cannot be separately exploited (*verwerten*), such persons are considered to be co-authors of the work. The right of publication and of exploitation belongs jointly to the co-authors. Alterations of the work are permissible only with the consent of the co-authors. Nevertheless, a co-author may not in bad faith refuse his consent to the publication, exploitation or alteration of the work. Each co-author is entitled to assert claims arising from infringements of the joint copyright; he must, however, demand payment to all the co-authors.[15]

Combined Works.—If several authors have combined their works for joint exploitation, each of them may require from the other his consent to the publication, exploitation or alteration of the combined works, if such consent can in good faith be demanded.[16]

Presumption of Authorship.—A person who is designated in the customary manner as the author on copies of a work which has been published or on the original of an artistic work is, in the absence of proof to the contrary, regarded as the author of the work. The same applies to a designation which is known as the author's pseudonym or artist's mark. Where the author is not designated in the said manner, it is presumed that the person designated as editor (*Herausgeber*) on the copies of the work is empowered to assert the author's rights. Where no editor is designated, it is presumed that the publisher (*Verleger*) is so empowered.[17]

[11] § 4. [12] § 5. [13] Cf. §§ 1 and 7. [14] Cf. §§ 3 and 4.
[15] § 8(1) and (2). [16] § 9. [17] § 10(1).

Employee-Authors.—Contrary to most copyright laws, the German Law does not vest the copyright in the employer but in the employee. In other words, copyright in works created by an employee belong to the employee and the employer must acquire by contract the right to the utilization of the work.[18] The contract may, however, be a tacit agreement.

ASSIGNMENT AND LICENSING

GENERALLY

When Author Dies.—Copyright passes by inheritance. The author may, by testamentary disposition, entrust the exercise of the copyright to an executor.[19]

Assignment Inter Vivos.—Copyright cannot be assigned *inter vivos*.[20] An author may merely grant (*einräumen*) rights of exploitation (*Nutzungsrechte*), i.e., may license the use or utilization of the work. It is interesting to note in this connection Ulmer's comments on the meaning of the "granting of exploitation rights" (*Einräumung von Nutzungsrechten*):

> "In any case, however, in view of international relationships it must be emphasized that the "*Einräumung von Nutzungsrechten*" mentioned in the Act corresponds logically to the "*cession des droits d'exploitation*" as understood in French law, and to the "assignment (transfer) of copyright" as understood in Anglo-American law. In these systems of law too, it is a familiar concept that, in cases where a time limit is placed on transfer, a reversion of the transferred right to the author occurs. It would therefore be wrong to deny legal validity in Germany to an agreement, concluded in the U.S.A., in which the author transfers the copyright to an assignee, for use both at home and abroad, on the ground that, according to German Law, the copyright might not be conveyed. *Transfer of copyright is to be interpreted in German law rather as the granting of a license.* In Germany itself such an interpretation will be necessary in the undoubtedly numerous cases in which the contracting parties refer also in future to the transfer of rights (*Übertragung*)." (Ulmer, p. 281).

Licensing.—The author may grant a license to another to utilize the work in a particular manner or in any manner.[21] The license may be limited as to place, time or purpose.[22] A license may be exclusive

---

[18] Cf. §§ 11 and 43.   [19] § 28.

[20] Cf. § 29, second sentence. Since this is an innovation in the Law and assignment was possible under the Laws in force before 1966, the Law provides that, if the copyright has been assigned prior to its effective date, the assignee enjoys the corresponding rights of exploitation. In case of doubt, however, the assignment will not be considered as extending to rights established only under the new Law (§ 137(1)). *Inter vivos* assignment under the new Law is possible between co-heirs and by the heirs to the legatees (§ 29). An assignee under such an assignment and an heir (both designated in German by the word *Rechtsnachfolger* = successor in title) has the same rights as the author unless the Law provides otherwise (§ 30).

[21] § 31(1), first sentence.   [22] § 32.

or non-exclusive.[23] A license purporting to grant rights with respect to unknown means of utilization, and the undertaking of any obligations with respect to such means, have no legal effect.[24] If the license does not specify the utilizations it allows, then the scope of the license is governed by the purpose for which it was granted.[25] A non-exclusive license granted by the author to A before he grants an exclusive license to B remains effective vis-à-vis B.[26]

The Law establishes the following norms of interpretation, applicable only in case of doubt, that is, when the contract contains no clear provision to another effect: (i) a license to use the work does not carry with it a license to publish or exploit an adaptation of the work, (ii) a license to reproduce (*vervielfältigen*) does not carry with it a license to make sound recordings or visual recordings, (iii) a license for public communication (*öffentliche Wiedergabe*) does not carry with it a license to make the communication perceptible to the public outside the circle for which the performance is intended, by means of picture screens, loudspeakers, or other similar technical devices,[27] (iv) a license to include a work in a periodical (or other collection of works appearing periodically) carries with it the transfer, to the editor or publisher, of the exclusive right to reproduce (*vervielfältigen*) and distribute (*verbreiten*), but—unless otherwise agreed—the author may, after the lapse of one year from the date of publication, have his work reproduced and distributed in other forms, i.e., in forms other than in a periodical collection. This last rule applies also to contributions to non-periodical collections if the contribution is made gratuitously. If the contribution is to a newspaper, the editor or publisher acquires only a non-exclusive license; if the agreement provides for an exclusive license, the author may, immediately after publication in the newspaper, have his work reproduced and distributed in other forms, i.e., in forms other than in a newspaper. All these rules may, of course, be set aside by clear contractual provisions to the contrary.[28]

Assignment of License.—A license may be assigned (*übertragen*) only with the consent of the author, except when the assignment is effected in connection with the transfer of a part or the whole of the assignor's business. Where consent is needed, the author may refuse such consent only where good faith admits of refusal. All these rules, however, may be set aside by contract between the author and the licensee. Where the contract between the author and the assignor allows the latter to assign his license to a third person (the assignee) without the consent of the author, or where the assignment is effected in connection with the transfer of the assignor's business (and hence without the author's consent), then the assignor and the assignee are jointly and

[23] § 31(1), second sentence.   [24] § 31(4).   [25] § 31(5).   [26] § 33.
[27] § 37.   [28] § 38.

severally responsible towards the author for the discharge of the obligations which the assignor undertook vis-à-vis the author.[29]

Grant of a Non-Exclusive Sub-License.—Any exclusive licensee may grant non-exclusive licenses to third persons, but only with the consent of the author. The author may refuse consent only where good faith admits of refusal. The author may waive his right to consent by contract. The consent of the author is not required when the exclusive licensee has received his license for the sole purpose of safeguarding the interests of the author.[30]

Future Works.—A written contract is required when the author grants licenses in respect of future works which are either not specified or are specified only as to their nature. Either party may terminate such contract, subject to six months' notice, any time after five years from the conclusion of the contract; this right to denounce the contract cannot be waived.[31]

Modifications of the Work.—Unless otherwise agreed between the author and the licensee, the latter may not alter the work, the title of the work, or the designation of the author. However, the author may refuse his consent to alterations in the work and in the title of the work only where good faith admits of such refusal.[32]

Revocation of License.—The Law regulates in detail the conditions under which an author may revoke an exclusive license if the licensee does not utilize, or does not sufficiently utilize, the license.[33] The Law also regulates in detail the conditions under which an author may revoke a license if the work no longer reflects his views and he therefore cannot be expected to agree to the utilization of the work.[34]

Alienation of Corpus Mechanicum.—If the author alienates the original of the work, in case of doubt, he is not deemed, by so doing, to have granted a license for the exploitation of the work by the acquirer. The owner of the original of an artistic or photographic work has the right to exhibit it in public unless the author has expressly excluded this right when he alienated the original.[35]

PUBLICATION CONTRACTS FOR LITERARY AND MUSICAL WORKS

In many countries, including the United States, the law of contracts between author and publisher is the subject of little or no special regulation in the copyright statute, but is largely left to the general law of contracts. This is not the case in Germany where, as indicated above, a separate statute regulates "the law of publication" (*Verlagsrecht*).[36]

[29] § 34.   [30] § 35.   [31] § 40.   [32] § 39.   [33] § 41.   [34] § 42.   [35] § 44.
[36] See page 327.

The VG deals with publication contracts concerning works of literature and music.[37] Its provisions are *ius dispositivum*, i.e., can be put aside by contract[38] and are mainly intended to cover cases not provided for by contract, or serve for the interpretation of contracts.

The rules concerning licensing contracts, discussed above (p. 332), apply also to publishing contracts.

Basic Obligations.—Under a publishing contract, the author[39] is obliged to *deliver* the work to the publisher for the purpose of multiplication and distribution, and the publisher is obliged to *multiply* and *distribute* the work at his (the publisher's) expense.[40]

Extent of Right Where the Work is Protected by Copyright. —During the subsistence of the contractual relationship, and once the manuscript is delivered, not the author but only the publisher has the right to multiply and distribute the work;[41] the author must guarantee this right to the publisher;[42] and the author himself is precluded from publication.[43] These rules are subject to the following qualifications: —The author has the right to multiply and distribute the work in a collected edition (*Gesamtausgabe*) of his works if twenty years have elapsed since the expiration of the calendar year in which the work was published (*erschienen*).[44]

—The publisher is not entitled to exploit (i) a single work as part of a collected edition or collective work, (ii) part of a collected edition or collective work as a separate edition.[45]

—The publisher is authorized to issue one edition only.[46]

—Where the number of copies is not specified, the publisher is authorized to make one thousand copies.[47] This limitation does not apply in the case of contributions to collective works.[48]

[37] VG, § 1.

[38] With the exception of VG, § 36, dealing with the bankruptcy of the publisher.

[39] Any reference in the VG to the author should also be understood as covering the person who is not the author, if such person, and not the author, enters into the publication contract with the publisher (VG, § 48).

[40] VG, § 1. However, where a work is produced according to a plan of the person ordering such work and he prescribes in detail the contents of the work as well as the manner of treatment, he is not, in case of doubt, required to multiply and distribute the work. The same applies in the case of collaboration in encyclopaedic enterprises, auxiliary or supplementary assistance in the work of another person, and collective works. *See* VG, § 47.

[41] VG, §§ 2 and 9.

[42] VG, § 8. Other rights, including the right of translation, remain, in case of doubt, the property of the author.

[43] VG, § 8.   [44] VG, § 2, third paragraph.

[45] VG, § 4. But the publisher may do all this, to the extent that such exploitation is open to any person during the subsistence of copyright (VG, § 4).

[46] VG, § 5, first paragraph. If the publisher has been accorded the right to issue several editions, the conditions applying to the preceding edition apply to each new edition, in case of doubt (VG, § 5, first paragraph).

[47] VG, § 5, second paragraph. If the publisher has fixed a smaller number by a

Extent of Right Where the Work is not Protected by Copyright.—Where the contract relates to a work in which no copyright exists, the author is, of course, not required to secure any publication right to the publisher,[49] but where the author, in bad faith, conceals the fact that the work has already been delivered to a third party for publication (*Verlag*), or has been published (*veröffentlicht*) by a third party, the provisions of civil law governing the warranty of the vendor, or defects in a right, apply by analogy.[50] The author himself must refrain from multiplication and distribution for six months from publication (*Veröffentlichung*).[51] Once the publisher has published the work under the contract, he may multiply it again in like manner as any third party has the right to do, that is, freely, unless the contract provides that the production of new editions or additional copies depends upon a special payment.[52]

Delivery of Manuscript.—The author must deliver the work to the publisher in a condition suitable for multiplication.[53] The author must deliver the work (i) immediately, if the contract relates to a work already completed,[54] (ii) by the date that the purpose to be served by the work requires, if the work is to be completed only after the conclusion of the contract.[55] If the purpose to be served gives no indication as to the length of the term, it will depend on the time which the author requires for completing the work "through an effort corresponding to his circumstances."[56]

Alterations by the Author.—Until the completion of the multiplication, the author, or a third party authorized by him, may make alterations in the work. Before a new edition is issued, the publisher must give the author (or the third party authorized by the author) an opportunity to make alterations. In both cases, alterations are permitted only in so far as they do not prejudice the lawful interest of the publisher.[57] If multiplication has started and the author makes, thereafter, alterations in excess of the customary amount, he must pay the publisher for the cost of such alterations, except when outside circumstances justify the alterations.[58]

---

declaration made to the author prior to the commencement of multiplication, he is entitled only to produce an edition in the number so fixed (VG, § 5, second paragraph). The customary supplementary and free copies are not included in the number of copies permitted, provided the number of the latter does not exceed one-twentieth of the total number of copies permitted (VG, § 6). Copies lost or destroyed from the stock of the publisher may be replaced by him (VG, § 7).

[48] VG, § 43.   [49] VG, § 39, first paragraph.
[50] VG, § 39, second paragraph.   [51] VG, § 39, third paragraph.
[52] VG, § 40.   [53] VG, § 10.   [54] VG, § 11, first paragraph.
[55] VG, § 11, second paragraph. Occupations of the author of which, at the time of concluding the contract, the publisher did not know or could not have been expected to know, may be disregarded (VG, § 12, second paragraph).
[56] VG, § 11.   [57] VG, § 12, first and second paragraphs.
[58] VG, § 12, third paragraph.

Alterations by the Publisher.—The publisher may make alterations to which the author may not, in good faith, refuse his consent.[59] When new copies (*Abzüge*) are made of a collective work, the publisher (*Verleger*), jointly with the editor (*Herausgeber*), may omit certain contributions.[60] Where the contribution to a newspaper or other periodical collective work is to be published without the name of the author, the publisher may make such alterations in the text as are customary in collective works of the same kind.[61]

Format, Make-up, Retail Price.—The format and make-up of the copies are determined by the publisher, with due regard to the usage prevailing in the publishing trade and to the purpose and contents of the work.[62] The publisher determines the retail price for each edition; he may reduce the price, provided that the lawful interests of the author are not prejudiced; and he may increase the price, but only with the consent of the author.[63]

Payments and Accounts.—The publisher must pay on delivery; but where the amount is undetermined or depends on the length of the work, payment becomes due only upon the completion of the multiplication.[64] Where the compensation is fixed in accordance with the number of copies sold, the publisher must render annually to the author an account for the preceding business year, and must permit the inspection of his books, so far as is necessary for the examination of such account.[65]

Free Copies for the Author.—Authors of *literary* works are entitled to a minimum of five and a maximum of fifteen free copies; within these limits, they are entitled to one free copy for each hundred produced.[66] In the case of contributions, separate reprints may replace copies of the entire collective work,[67] but where the contribution is published in a newspaper, the author is not entitled either to free copies or free reprints.[68] Authors of *musical* works are entitled to the "usual number" of free copies.[69]

Transfer of the Rights of the Publisher.—The rights of the publisher may be transferred, provided the transfer has not been precluded by stipulation between the author and publisher. The latter may not, however, transfer his rights respecting a specific work without the consent of the author. Such consent may only be refused for an important reason. Where the publisher has requested the author to give such consent, the consent shall be considered given if the author does not state his refusal to the publisher within two months after receiving the request. The multiplication and distribution incumbent

---

[59] VG, § 14, second paragraph.
[60] VG, § 19.   [61] VG, § 44.   [62] VG, § 14.   [63] VG, § 21.   [64] VG, § 23.
[65] VG, § 24.   [66] VG, § 25, first paragraph.   [67] VG, § 25, third paragraph.
[68] VG, § 46, first paragraph.   [69] VG, § 25, second paragraph.

on the publisher may also be made by his successor. If the successor agrees with the publisher to assume the obligation to multiply and distribute the work, he becomes liable to the author, jointly with the publisher, for the performance of the obligations arising out of the contract of publication. The liability of the successor does not extend to an already existing obligation to pay damages.[70]

Termination of Contract.—Authors may, subject to the conditions and with the consequences regulated in some detail in the VG, terminate the publishing contract in the following cases:
—If the publisher who has the right to publish a new edition chooses not to exercise this right.[71]
—If the publisher fails to multiply or distribute the work in the manner stipulated in the contract.[72]
—Before multiplication has begun, if circumstances arise which could not have been foreseen at the time of making the contract and which would have kept the author from publishing the work if he had known the facts and reasonably evaluated the case.[73]
—Before multiplication has begun, if bankruptcy proceedings start against the publisher.[74]
—If the contribution to a newspaper or other periodical collective work has not been published within a year from the delivery of the work to the publisher.[75]
—If the relations of mutual "trust" (*Vertrauensverhältnis*) are shattered.[76]

Publishers may, subject to the conditions and with the consequences regulated in some detail in the VG, terminate the publishing contract in the following cases:
—If the purpose which the work was to serve ceases to exist.[77]
—If the contract related to a contribution to a collective work, and the multiplication of the collective work does not take place.[78]
—If all or part of the work is not delivered in due time by the author, unless the delay in delivery causes only negligible injury to the publisher.[79]
—If the work is not of the character (*Beschaffenheit*) stipulated in the contract.[80]

Loss of Manuscript.—If the work is accidentally lost or destroyed (*geht unter*) after delivery to the publisher, the author's right to payment remains unaffected. In other respects, both parties stand released from complying with the terms of the contract.[81]

[70] VG, § 28.   [71] VG, § 17.   [72] VG, § 32.   [73] VG, § 35.
[74] VG, § 36.   [75] VG, § 45.
[76] RGZ 79, page 156; RGZ 112, page 188; RGZ 140, page 275.
[77] VG, § 18, first paragraph.   [78] VG, § 18, second paragraph.
[79] VG, § 30.   [80] VG, § 31.
[81] VG, § 33. However, on demand of the publisher, the author must, for an appropriate payment, furnish another substantially identical work, so far as this is

Death of Author.—Where the author dies before completion of the work, and a part of the work has already been delivered to the publisher, the publisher is entitled to maintain the contract with regard to the part delivered, upon notifying the heir of the author. The heir may fix an appropriate term for the publisher to exercise this right. The right terminates if the publisher does not, before the expiration of the term, give the notification to maintain the contract. Similar provisions apply where the completion becomes impossible due to circumstances for which the author is not responsible.[82]

UPWARD REVISION OF AUTHOR'S FEES

The author has a claim to more than he has agreed to in the licensing contract if the stipulated consideration is grossly disproportionate to the income derived by the licensee from the utilization of the work. The new consideration must represent a fair (*angemessene*) participation by the author in the said income. Both the claim and the amount of the claim depend also on the question whether they seem to be justified in the light of the whole of the relationship between the author and the licensee. The claim must be presented within two years from the date on which the author becomes aware of the existence of the circumstances which justify the claim and, in any case, within ten years from the date on which the said circumstances started to exist. This right—which the Law calls "author's participation" (*Beteiligung des Urhebers*)—cannot, of course, be waived in advance.[83]

PROTECTED RIGHTS

Generally.—The Law provides, as an introductory statement to the Section entitled "Content of Copyright" (*Inhalt des Urheberrechts*), that copyright protects the author in his intellectual and personal relations to the work and in the utilization of the work.[84] It distinguishes between personal rights (*Urheberpersönlichkeitsrechte*), rights of exploitation (*Verwertungrechte*), and other rights. The same division is followed in the present Chapter.

---

possible without great labor, on the basis of existing preliminary work or of other existing material. If the author offers to furnish such work without cost within an appropriate term, the publisher is required to multiply and distribute such work in place of the work lost or destroyed. Each party may also claim these rights where the work has been lost or destroyed after delivery, in consequence of a circumstance for which the other party is responsible. Delivery shall be considered as having taken place if the publisher is in default with respect to acceptance. (V.G. § 33).

[82] VG, § 34. [83] § 36. [84] § 11.

PERSONAL RIGHTS

Generally.—Three rights are distinguished: the right to make public (*veröffentlichen*) the work, the right to be recognized as the author of the work, and the right against distortion (*Entstellung*) of the work.[85] The last two fall into the traditional category of moral rights, whereas the first may be regarded either as a moral right—and obviously the German Law is inclined in this direction—or, as other laws would do, as an economic right.

Under the first, the author has the right to determine whether and how his work is to be made public. As long as the work, or its essential content, or a description thereof, has not been made public with the consent of the author, the author alone is entitled to make public, or to describe, the content of his work.[86]

Under the second, the author has the right to recognition of his authorship of the work. He is entitled to determine whether the work should carry an indication as to the identity of its author and, if so, what the indication should consist of.[87]

Under the third, the author has the right to prohibit any distortion of, or any other injury (*Beinträchtigung*) to, his work which may endanger his justifiable intellectual or personal interest in the work.[88]

RIGHTS OF EXPLOITATION

Generally.—The author has the exclusive right to exploit (*verwerten* = to utilize, to derive benefit from, to exploit) his work both in material form (*in körperlicher Form*) and in non-material form (*in unkörperlicher Form*). The Law does not define the concept of exploitation but gives examples of the two kinds it distinguishes.

Under material form of exploitation, the Law mentions the right of reproduction (*Vervielfältigung*), the right of distribution (*Verbreitung*), and the right of exhibition (*Ausstellung*).

Under non-material forms of exploitation, the Law mentions the rights of recitation (or delivery) (*Vortrag*), performance (*Aufführung*) and showing (*Vorführung*), the right of broadcasting (*Senderecht*), the right of communication (*Wiedergabe*) by means of visual or sound recordings (*Bild- oder Tonträger*), and the right of communicating broadcasts (*Wiedergabe von Funksendungen*).

Non-material forms of exploitation, also called rights of communication (*Wiedergabe*), are protected only if the communicating is public. The communication is public (*öffentlich*) when it is intended for several persons (*Mehrzahl* = plurality, a (certain) number, a multiplicity, of persons), unless the circle of those persons is clearly delimited and

[85] §§ 12, 13, 14.   [86] § 12.   [87] § 13.   [88] § 14.

each of them is connected to the others either through mutual relations with each other or through relations with the organizer.[89]

Right of Reproduction.—The right of reproduction is the right to make copies of the work, irrespective of the nature of the process employed or the number of copies produced. The recording (*Übertragung* = transfer, transposition) of the work on devices with the help of which picture or sound sequences may repeatedly be communicated is considered to be reproduction. Such devices are called visual or sound recordings (*Bild- oder Tonträger* = carriers, incorporators of picture or sound). The recording may be that of a live performance (*Aufnahme*) or the recording of a recording (re-recording).[90]

Right of Distribution.—The right of distribution is the right to offer to the public, or to place in circulation, the original of the work or copies thereof. Once the original of the work or copies thereof have been lawfully sold in Germany, and thus brought into circulation, their further distribution does not require the author's consent.[91]

Right of Exhibition.—The right of exhibition is the right to allow the public viewing of the original or copies of the work, provided the work, provided the work is a work of the fine arts (*Werk der bildenden Künste* = of the graphic arts (drawing, painting, etc.), sculpture, etc.) or a photographic work (*Lichtbildwerk*), and provided it has not yet been made public.[92]

Right of Public Recitation.—The recitation must relate to literary works (works which can be expressed by speech (*Sprachwerke*)), must consist of a personal delivery, must be public, and must allow the hearing of the delivery, in order to come under the concept of public recitation.[93]

Right of Public Performance.—If the performance is that of a musical work, it must consist of a personal delivery, must allow the hearing of the delivery, and must be public, to come under the definition of this right. Another kind of performance, also coming under the same definition, is the public production of a work on a stage (*ein Werk öffentlich bühnenmässig darzustellen*).[94]

Common Rules for Public Recitations and Performances.—The rights of public recitation and performance include also the right to allow the viewing or hearing, in public, of the personal delivery, outside the enclosure (room, hall, auditorium, etc.) in which the delivery takes place, with the help of picture screens, loudspeakers, or other similar technical devices.[95]

Right of Public Showing.—The right of public showing relates to works of the fine arts, photographic works, cinematographic works,

[89] § 15.　[90] § 16.　[91] § 17.　[92] § 18.　[93] § 19(1).　[94] § 19(2).
[95] § 19(3).

and representations (*Darstellungen*) of a scientific or technical nature. The right is the right to make such works publicly perceptible (*öffentlich wahrnehmbar*)—i.e., allow their viewing (seeing, beholding) or hearing (listening to)—by means of technical devices. The public communication of broadcasts of such works does not come under the definition of this right but under a *sui generis* right, discussed below.[96]

Right of Broadcasting.—The right of broadcasting is the right to allow access, by the public, to a work by means of wired or wireless radio or television or other similar technical devices. The right is called *Senderecht* in German, and *Sender* is the usual term for designating broadcasting stations, i.e., stations from which broadcasts are originated.[97]

Right of Communication by Means of Visual or Sound Recordings.—This right relates to recitations and performances of works. If they are made publicly perceptible (can be viewed or listened to) by means of visual or sound recordings, they come under the definition of this right. It also covers cases in which the communication, first restricted to the persons gathered in an enclosure (*Raum*), is further communicated, by similar means, to persons outside the said enclosure.[98]

Right of Communicating Broadcasts.—This right relates to broadcasts of works. If the work is broadcast and the received broadcast is made publicly perceptible (can be viewed or listened to) by means of picture screens, loudspeakers, or other similar technical devices, it comes under the definition of this right. It also covers cases in which the communication, first restricted to the persons gathered in an enclosure (*Raum*), is further communicated, by any of the said means, to persons outside of the enclosure.[99]

Rights in Connection With Adaptations and Transformations.—If a work is adapted (*bearbeitet*, including translated) or otherwise transformed (*umgestaltet*), the making public and any exploitation of the new work (i.e., the adaptation, etc.) requires the authorization not only of the adaptor, etc., but also of the author of the work from which the new work is derived. The making itself of an adaptation, etc.—as distinguished from the making public and exploitation thereof —does not require the authorization of the author of the primary work. Not so, however, when the primary work is used in the making of a cinematographic work (*Verfilmung*), or when the primary work consists of plans and drawings for a work of the fine arts and is used for making such work or an adaptation thereof, or when the primary work is a work of architecture and is used as a model for constructing a similar building or an adaptation thereof: in such cases, the authori-

[96] § 19(4).   [97] § 20.   [98] § 21.   [99] § 22.

zation of the author of the primary work is required, irrespective of whether the secondary work will later be made public or will be exploited.[100]

Free Use For Creating New Work.—If a work is independent but has been created by "using freely" (*in freier Benutzung*) the work of another person, the making public or exploitation of such independent work does not require authorization by the author of the "freely used" work. The contrary rule applies, however, when the used work is a musical work, and the use consists of recognizably taking a melody from it and making it a basic feature of the "independent" new work.[101]

OTHER RIGHTS

Right of Access.—The author may demand of the person in whose possession the original work or a copy thereof is that he (the author) be allowed access to the original or copy if such access is necessary for the making of copies or adaptations and if such access is not contrary to the lawful interests of the possessor.[102]

Droit de Suite.—The Law provides for a *droit de suite* but makes this right applicable to non-German nationals only in case of reciprocity the existence of which must be proclaimed by the Federal Minister of Justice.[103] No such proclamation has issued so far (January 1, 1968).

Right of Remuneration for Rental of Copies.—If copies of a work are rented for profit by the renter, the renter must pay an equitable remuneration to the author—except if the work was published for the sole purpose of renting.[104] By "renter" (*Vermieter*) is meant the person who rents out the copies, i.e., lends them for a consideration.

LIMITATIONS

Generally.—The Law contains detailed provisions on the limitations or limits (*Schranken*) of the rights discussed above.[105] These limitations generally mean either that the work may be used freely—for certain purposes and between stated limits—that is, without the author's consent and without an obligation to pay him anything for the use, or that the work may be used without the author's consent but subject to the obligation to pay him for the use (compulsory licenses) or that the author is obliged to grant a license under reasonable conditions.

Compulsory Licenses and Obligation to Contract.—The system of compulsory licenses—no need for authorization but obliga-

[100] § 23.   [101] § 24.   [102] § 25.   [103] §§ 26 and 121(5).   [104] § 27.
[105] §§ 45 to 63.

tion to pay—seems to be provided for in three cases: in connection with recordings of school broadcasts if the recordings are preserved beyond the current school year; in connection with public communication which is not for the profit of the organizer but for the profit of a third party; and in connection with the reproduction, distribution or public communication of certain articles and commentaries concerning political, economic or religious questions of the day. The obligation to grant a license under reasonable conditions is provided in connection with the production of sound recordings (*Herstellung von Tonträgern*).

Free Uses.—Free uses are provided for the purposes of the administration of justice and public safety[106] (not further discussed in this book), and for a variety of other purposes which are discussed below.

Common Rules.—Subject to certain minor exceptions stated in detail in the Law, no protected work which may be used, and is used, without the author's permission, may be modified. Neither may it be used without indicating the source and identifying the author.[107]

Production of Sound Recordings.—Without going into all the details the Law provides for, the rule is that the author of a musical work (as well as the author of the text, if any, connected with the musical work) who has authorized a record manufacturer to make a sound recording of his work for commercial purposes, to reproduce the record and to distribute the copies must—hence the expression "obligation to contract"—grant an authorization for similar purposes to any other domestic record manufacturer. The grant is conditional upon adequate consideration (*angemessene Bedingungen*) on the part of the latter manufacturer. The amount of the compensation is not fixed by law, as it is for example in the United States, nor is it fixed by an administrative authority, as it is for example in the United Kingdom, but will be determined by the courts if the parties cannot agree. Similar provisions have existed in German copyright legislation for more than half a century but no cases are known in which the courts have actually been asked to apply them. In any case, important exceptions are provided: the obligation to contract is not applicable when the rights in question are administered by an authors' society (*Verwertungsgesellschaft*), or when the author has made use of his right to withdraw the original license because the work no longer corresponds to his convictions, or, finally, if the recording is to serve the purposes of the making of a motion picture. The exportation of sound recordings made under a license is allowed only into countries in which the right of recording is not protected.[108]

Incorporation of Work in Collections for Religious, School or Instructional Use.—What is permitted, without the authoriza-

[106] §§ 45   [107] Cf. §§ 62 and 63.   [108] § 61.

tion of the authors, is the reproduction and distribution of a collection of works (*Sammlung*), provided the included works are short literary works (*Sprachwerke*) or short musical works or isolated (*einzelne* = single) works of the fine arts or isolated photographs. The collection must consist of works of a greater number of authors. The works must have been already made public. The nature itself of the work must be such that it is solely destined for religious use (*Kirchengebrauch*), school use, or instructional use. The Law provides for certain minor exceptions and procedural conditions as well.[109]

Recording of School Broadcasts.—Schools may freely make individual (*einzelne*) visual and sound recordings of the broadcasts of works when they are transmitted within the framework of "school broadcasting" (*Schulfunksendung*). Such recordings may be used only for the purposes of instruction. At the end of the school year, they must be erased, unless an adequate remuneration is paid to the author.[110]

Reproduction, Distribution and Public Communication of Public Speeches.—It is freely permitted to reproduce and distribute speeches dealing with questions of current interest (*Reden über Tagesfragen*) in newspapers, periodicals, or other information papers, which mainly cover current events, provided the speeches were made in public meetings or were broadcast. The public communication (broadcast, etc.) of such speeches is also freely permitted. Furthermore, it is freely permitted to reproduce, distribute and publicly communicate speeches which were made in public hearings before State, community or church organs. However, neither kind of speech may be freely reproduced and distributed in the form of a collection when the collection mainly contains the speeches of one and the same author.[111]

Reproduction, Distribution and Public Communication of Newspaper Articles and Broadcast Commentaries.—The said uses of such articles and commentaries are, in the cases and under the conditions regulated in detail in the Law, either free or subject only to the payment of an adequate remuneration to the author.[112]

Reproduction, Distribution and Public Communication of Works in Connection with Reporting on Current Events By Picture or Sound.—The said uses are free whether the medium is broadcasting, film, newspaper, or periodical paper. The reporting—by picture or sound—must relate to current events and the works must have been shown or made audible within the framework of the event to which the reporting relates. The extent of the use is limited by the purpose, i.e., the natural limits of reporting.[113]

Reproduction, Distribution and Public Communication of Quotations.—The said uses are free when, within the limits set by

[109] § 46.   [110] § 47.   [111] § 48.   [112] § 49.   [113] § 50.

their purpose: (i) isolated (*einzelne*) works (already made public) are included in an independent scientific work for the purpose of illustrating or explaining (*Erlauterung*) its content; (ii) passages from a published work are quoted in an independent literary work (*Sprachwerk*); isolated (*einzelne*) passages from a musical work (already made public) are quoted in an independent musical work.[114]

Communication to the Public.—A work which has been made public may be freely communicated (performed, etc.) to the public if the following conditions obtain: (i) the communication serves no profit-making purpose (*Erwerbszweck*) on the part of the organizer of the communication, (ii) the audience (*Teilnehmer*) are admitted free of charge, (iii) in case of recitation or performance, no special remuneration is paid to the artists.

If, however, the event fulfilling the above conditions serves a gainful purpose for a third party, the latter must pay an adequate remuneration to the author. Where the communication to the public is connected with a church service, a religious celebration, or another event organized by a publicly recognized church or religious sect, the authorization of the author is not required and he is entitled to an adequate remuneration only if the above conditions are not fulfilled.

Even if the event fulfills the above conditions, the authorization of the author is required if the communication to the public consists of a stage performance (*bühnenmässige Aufführung*), a broadcast, or a public showing of a cinematographic work.[115]

Reproduction for Personal or Other Internal Use.—The Law provides for two kinds of situations in which isolated (*einzelne*) copies may be freely made: one is called reproduction for personal use (*zum persönlichen Gebrauch*), the other is called reproduction for other internal use (*zum sonstigen eigenen* (= one's own) *Gebrauch*).

Copies for *personal use* may be made by the user himself or by another person for the personal use of the user. The services of another person must, however, be gratuitous when the copying consists of recording on visual or sound records or when the copied work is a work of the fine arts. Copies for *other internal use* may be made by the user himself or by another person for the internal use of the user.

Neither for *personal use* nor for *other internal use* can copies freely be made in the following three cases: (i) a public speech, public performance, or public showing of a work cannot be recorded on picture or sound recordings; (ii) plans and drawings for a work of the fine art cannot be executed (i.e. the work of the fine art made); (iii) an architectural work cannot be copied by building another one like it. In these cases, the recording, execution or building require the author's authorization.

[114] § 51.   [115] § 52.

Otherwise, any kind of work may be copied freely for *personal use*. The cases in which free copying is allowed for *other internal use* are limited in various respects and are specified in the Law. There are four such cases: (i) copying for one's own scientific use, if and to the extent that copying for such use is necessary (*geboten*); (ii) copying for the purposes of inclusion of the work in one's own archives, if and to the extent that copying for this purpose is necessary (*geboten*), and provided that the copying is done from the original or from a copy of the work which is the property of the copier; (iii) copying for one's own information about current questions (*Tagesfragen*) when what is copied is a work transmitted by broadcasting, (iv) for other internal (*eigen* = one's own) uses in two cases: *first*, when what is copied is small parts of a work which has already been published or are isolated items (*einzelne Aufsätze*) which have been published in newspapers or periodicals; *second*, when what is copied is a work out of print (*vergriffenes Werk*) and the owner of the right cannot be traced.

Copies made either for *personal use* or *other internal use* may neither be distributed nor employed in communicating the work to the public.

In one case, the copying for *other internal use* (not for personal use), although permissible without authorization, carries with it the obligation to pay an adequate remuneration, i.e., the free use is replaced by a compulsory license. This is the case where the copying serves the industrial or commercial purposes (*gewerbliche Zwecke*) of the copier.

In connection, with copying for personal use, the Law provides, in a special case, for a source of revenue for the author but places the obligation to pay not on the copier or user but on the person who makes or sells the copying equipment. The case is that of such copying equipment—for example tape recorders—as is apt to be used for the making of visual or sound recordings of broadcasts or of already existing recordings. If it is unlikely that the equipment will be used for such purposes in Germany, the obligation to pay does not exist. The obligation exists in respect of works which, because of their nature, are likely to be copied in the said manner. The individual author cannot, however, enforce the claim. The claim may be enforced only by an authors' society (*Verwertungsgesellschaft*) which then takes care of the distribution of the collected fees to the authors. The fee cannot exceed five percent of the sale price of the equipment.[116]

Copying by Broadcasting Organizations.—Any broadcasting organization licensed to broadcast the work may freely record it by means of its own facilities on visual or sound recordings for the purpose of using these recordings for broadcasting the work, provided that broadcasting is effected over all or any of the organization's transmitters or beam transmitters, but only once over each of them.[117]

---

[116] §§ 53 and 54.   [117] § 55.

Other Cases of Free Uses.—Other cases in which free use is permitted, under the conditions and within the limits specified in detail by the Law, are uses of the work for demonstrating copying or receiving equipment (e.g., television sets) by shops which sell such equipment;[118] use of a work when it is incidentally and unimportantly connected with the reproduction, distribution or communication;[119] use in catalogues;[120] use of works permanently placed in streets and other public places; copying of portraits.[121]

TERM OF PROTECTION

Generally.—Copyright expires seventy years after the author's death.[122] In case of co-authors, the term is calculated from the death of the co-author who dies last.[123]

Certain Posthumous Works.—If a posthumous work is made public (*veröffentlicht*) during the last ten years of the seventy-year period, copyright expires ten years after the work has been made public.[124] A work is made public when, with the consent of the author (or whoever has acquired the right thereto from the author), it is made accessible to the public.[125]

Anonymous and Pseudonymous Works.—Copyright generally expires seventy years after the work has been made public.[126]

Photographic Works.—Copyright in photographic works expires twenty-five years after the work has been published (*erscheinen*) or, if it has not been published within twenty-five years after its making, it expires twenty-five years after it has been made (*herstellen*).[127]

Moral Rights.—The above rules apply to all rights of the author, including moral rights. Thus, moral rights in Germany, unlike those in some other European countries, are not perpetual.[128]

Common Rules.—The periods of seventy or twenty-five years referred to above are calculated from the end of the calendar year in which the relevant event (death, making public, publication) occurred.[129]

Transitional Provisions.—With a few exceptions, the provisions of the Law came into effect on January 1, 1966. Among the exceptions are the provisions on duration, which came into effect on September 16, 1965.[130] The consequence of this distinction is that works which fell into the public domain at the end of 1965 or at the end of any previous

---

[118] § 56.   [119] § 57.   [120] § 58.   [121] § 59.   [122] § 64(1).
[123] § 65.   [124] § 64(2).   [125] § 6(1).
[126] § 66(1); see also §§ 66(2) to (4), 67, and 129(2).   [127] § 68.
[128] See Ulmer, p. 284.   [129] § 69.   [130] § 143.

year[131] remain in the public domain and do not benefit from the extension of the former fifty-year *post mortem auctoris term* to the now prevailing seventy-year *post mortem auctoris term*. On the other hand, works which would have fallen into the public domain at the end of 1965 or later benefit from the new seventy-year rule.

As the former laws provided for a term of protection twenty years less than the new Law, the question arises who should benefit from the extension. The question is answered in the following manner by the new Law:

> If the copyright has been assigned in whole or in part prior to the effective date of the new Law, then, in case of doubt, the assignment applies also to the extension. The same holds good also if, prior to the effective date of the new Law, a license has been granted for the exercise of one of the rights of the author.

In such cases, the assignee or the licensee must pay to the assignor or licensor an adequate remuneration, provided it can be assumed that, had the prolongation of the term been known at the time of the transaction, the assignee or licensee would have undertaken to pay a higher consideration.

The assignee or licensee may avoid the obligation of supplemental remuneration if he waives, or puts at the disposal of the assignor or licensee, his rights for the term which results from the extension.

If, prior to the effective date of the new Law, the assignee or licensee has alienated his rights to a third person, he is required to pay a supplemental remuneration only if, under the circumstances, such payment would not constitute an undue burden for him.[132]

Rule of the Shorter Term.—The Law expressly provides that Article IV, paragraphs 4 to 6, of the Universal Copyright Convention —that is, the provisions concerning the rule of the shorter term—are applicable for the purpose of calculating the term of protection to be accorded under the Convention to foreign nationals with respect to their works.[133] That the—in some respects different—rule of the shorter term under the Berne Convention is applicable to works which are protected under the Berne Convention rather than the Universal Copyright Convention follows from the text of the Berne Convention itself and § 121 (4) of the Law, which provides that the texts of the applicable Conventions govern. In the Berne Convention, the rule of the shorter term is so worded that it is directly applicable,[134] whereas in the Universal Copyright Convention it seems to require implementation by domestic law, which is just what the new German Law does

---

[131] The former laws also provided that the terms expire at the end of the relevant calendar year.

[132] § 137(2) to (4).   [133] § 140.

[134] " ... the term ... shall not exceed the term fixed in the country of origin of the work" (Berne-Brussels Convention, Article 7(2)).

in its § 140. For the consequences of this rule, see p. 50 (Article IV, paragraphs 21 to 24). Since the rules of the shorter term differ from each other in the Berne Convention and the Universal Copyright Convention, it will be necessary in some cases to examine first whether the protection of the work in Germany is governed by the Universal Copyright Convention or by the Berne Convention. As to this question, see p. 328, above (Part entitled "Acquisition of Protection under the Universal Copyright Convention"), of the present Chapter.

Special Provisions concerning Films

Generally.—The Law contains a separate group of provisions on "films" (*Filme*).[135] Films, according to the Law, fall into two categories. They are either cinematographic works (*Filmwerke*, expression which could perhaps be translated, in imitation of the American terminology, as "motion-picture photoplays") or motion pictures (*Laufbilder*, expression which could perhaps be translated, in imitation of the American terminology, as "motion pictures other than photoplays"). However, while in the US Law both are "works," the German Law denies the rank and title of "work" to the latter. The Law does not define either of the two kinds but characterizes the latter kind (i.e., what is here translated as "motion pictures") as sequences of pictures, or sequences of pictures and sound, which are not protected as cinematographic works.[136]

Rights of the Producer of a Cinematographic Work or of a Motion Picture.—The producer of a cinematographic work (*Filmhersteller*) or of a motion picture has four kinds of exclusive rights in connection with the picture recording (*Bildträger* = the carrier of the pictures) or the picture-and-sound recording (*Bild- und Tonträger* = the carrier of the pictures *cum* sound) in which the cinematographic work or the motion picture is incorporated: (i) the right to reproduce (copy) the recording, (ii) the right to distribute the said recording, (iii) the right to use the said recording for the purposes of public showing, (iv) the right to use the said recording for the purposes of broadcasting. Furthermore, the producer has the right to prohibit such distortions or cuts in the said recording as may endanger his lawful interests in such recording.[137] All these rights are assignable (*übertragbar*).[138] The limitations concerning the rights in other works, except the limitation consisting of compulsory licenses for sound recordings, apply also vis-à-vis film producers.[139]

Duration of the Rights of the Producer of a Cinematographic Work or of a Motion Picture.—The said rights expire twenty-five years after the publication of the picture recording or the picture-and-

---

[135] §§ 88 to 95.   [136] § 95.   [137] §§ 94(1) and 95.   [138] §§ 94(2) and 95.
[139] §§ 94(4) and 95.

sound recording. However, if the recording is not made public within twenty-five years from its production (*Herstellung*), the rights expire twenty-five years after production.[140] It would seem that those periods start from the actual dates of making public or publication, and not from the end of the calendar year in which making public or publication took place.

The Right of Cinematographic Adaptation of "Pre-Existing" Works.—If the author of a work authorizes another person to use his work in a cinematographic work or in a motion picture (*sein Werk zu verfilmen*), then, in case of doubt, such authorization implies the grant of an exclusive license for the following uses: (i) to use the work— without modification or with changes and adaptations—in the making of a cinematographic work or motion picture, (ii) to reproduce and distribute the cinematographic work or motion picture, (iii) in case of a cinematographic work or a motion picture intended for public showing, to show it publicly, (iv) in case of a cinematographic work or motion picture intended for broadcasting, to broadcast it, (v) to exploit translations and other cinematographic adaptations (*filmische Bearbeitungen oder Umgestaltungen*) of the cinematographic work or motion picture to the same extent as the cinematographic work or the motion picture itself.[141] In case of doubt, the above authorizations relate only to one such use of the pre-existing work, and, in case of doubt, the exclusive license of the other person lapses ten years after the date of his contract with the author of the pre-existing work.[142]

Rights in the Cinematographic Work.—Any person who undertakes to participate in the production of a cinematographic work and, by so doing, acquires a copyright in such work is deemed, in case of doubt, to have granted the producer the exclusive right to exploit, in every known manner, the cinematographic work, translations thereof and any other cinematographic adaptation (*filmische Bearbeitung oder Umgestaltung*) of the same work. Even if such an author of a cinematographic work had granted in advance to a third party the said exclusive rights, he has the right to grant the same rights to the producer.[143]

Limitations on the Licensing Rights of Authors.—When a person undertakes to participate in the production of a cinematographic work or when the author of a work authorizes the use of his work in a cinematographic work or a motion picture and has authorized or is deemed to have authorized that the producer exploit it by reproduction, distribution, public showing, broadcasting, translation, or cinematographic adaptation, then, the general provisions concerning the need for the author's consent to the assignment of exclusive licenses or the granting of non-exclusive licenses, and the author's

[140] §§ 94(3) and 95.   [141] § 88(1).   [142] § 88(2).   [143] § 89(1) and (2).

right to withdraw the license on account of non-exploitation or change of convictions, are inapplicable.[144]

Limitations on the Moral Rights of Authors.—The right of authors against distortions and other injuries to their works becomes, in the case of cinematographic works, a right only against gross (*gröbliche*) distortions and gross injuries. Beneficiaries of this right are the authors of cinematographic works or of the works used in the making of cinematographic works or motion pictures.[145]

INFRINGEMENTS

Civil Remedies.—The infringer, whether innocent or not, can be ordered to cease and desist by the court. Damages or the infringer's profits may be claimed by the injured party only if the infringement was intentional or negligent. Damages may be claimed also when the prejudice caused is not of an economic nature. The Law provides also for the destruction of unlawful copies or delivery of such copies to the injured party. Limitations, conditions and exceptions are provided for but not detailed here.[146]

Criminal Sanctions.—Intentional infringements are subject to criminal prosecution upon complaint by the injured party and are punished by a fine or imprisonment. Unlawful designations of authorship are subject to similar rules.[147]

---

[144] § 90, first sentence.   [145] § 93, first sentence.   [146] §§ 97 to 105.
[147] §§ 106 to 111.

GHANA

SOURCES

Internal Law.—The main source of the law of copyright in Ghana is the Copyright Act, 1961.[1] Hereinafter it is referred to as "the Act," and references to Sections, without further specification, are references to Sections of the Act. The Act expressly deals with works originating in countries party to the Universal Copyright Convention.

Universal Copyright Convention.—Ghana is bound by the Universal Copyright Convention and Protocols 1 and 2 as from August 22, 1962.[1a]

ACQUISITION OF COPYRIGHT UNDER THE UNIVERSAL COPYRIGHT CONVENTION

Protection is given by Ghana to a work which satisfies any of the following conditions: (i) it is a work of which the author or, in the case of a work of joint authorship,[2] any of the authors is, at the time when the work is made, an individual who is a citizen, domiciliary or resident of a country party to the Universal Copyright Convention, or a body corporate which was incorporated under the laws of such a country,[3] (ii) it is a work which was first published in a country party to the Universal Copyright Convention,[4] (iii) it is a work which was made by or under the direction or control of certain international bodies.[5]

[1] "An Act to make provision for Copyright in literary, musical and artistic works, cinematograph films, gramophone records and broadcasts." Act. No. 85 of the Parliament of the Republic of Ghana, dated November 8, 1961. CLTW, Ghana: Item 1.

[1a] CLTW, Ghana: Item 2.

[2] For the definition of "author" *see* (Protected Persons) page 348 below. "Work of joint authorship" means a work produced by the collaboration of two or more authors in which the contribution of each author is not separable from the contribution of the other author or authors.

[3] Section 2 (1). The Act does not refer generally to countries parties to the Universal Copyright Convention but its schedule names all those which were such parties at the time the Act was promulgated. It is to be expected that the list of countries in the schedule will be kept up to date as changes occur. Section 14.

[4] Section 3 (i).

[5] Section 4 (i). The international bodies are to be named by regulations of the Minister responsible for Information. No such regulations have yet been issued; they will probably name the organizations referred to in Protocol 2.

A work is taken to have been published if, but only if, copies[6] have been issued in sufficient quantities to satisfy the reasonable requirements of the public.[7] Where in the first instance a part only of a work is published, that part is treated as a separate work.[8] Publication in a given country is not treated as being other than first publication by reason only of earlier publication in another country, if the two publications took place within a period of not more than 30 days.[9]

There are no copyright formalities in Ghana. Consequently, registration, deposit, or compliance with other formalities is neither required nor possible in Ghana, and the absence, in itself, of a Convention notice on the copies of a published work is no bar to claiming protection in that country. Furthermore, Ghana has no renewal system, so that there is nothing in this country which would correspond to the renewal formalities existing in the United States.

PROTECTED WORKS

The following works are eligible for copyright: literary works, musical works, artistic works, cinematographic films, gramophone records, and broadcasts, if, and only if, (i) sufficient effort has been expended on making the work to give it an original character, and (ii) the work has been written down, recorded or otherwise reduced to material form, whether with or without consent.[10]

"Literary work" means, irrespective of literary quality, any of the following, or works similar thereto:

(i) novels, stories and poetical works, (ii) plays, stage directions, film scenarios and broadcasting scripts, (iii) textbooks, treatises, histories, biographies, essays and articles, (iv) encyclopaedias, dictionaries, directories and anthologies, (v) letters, reports and memoranda, (vi) lectures, addresses and sermons.[11]

"Musical work" means any musical work, irrespective of musical quality, and includes words composed for musical accompaniment.[12]

"Artistic work" means, irrespective of artistic quality, any of the following, or works similar thereto: (i) paintings, drawings, etchings, lithographs, woodcuts, engravings, and prints, (ii) photographs not

---

[6] "Copy" means a reproduction in written form, in the form of a recording or film, or in any other material form; however, an object is not taken to be a copy of an architectural work unless the object is a building or a model (sec. 15 (1)).

[7] Section 15 (2) (a).

[8] Section 15 (2) (b).

[9] Section 15 (2) (c).

[10] Section 1 (1) and (2). A work is not ineligible for copyright by reason that the making of the work, or the doing of any act in relation to the work, involved an infringement of copyright in some other work (sec. 1 (4)).

[11] Section 15 (1).   [12] Section 15 (1).

comprised in a cinematograph film, (iii) maps, plans and diagrams, (iv) works of sculpture, (v) works of architecture in the form of buildings (including structures) or models, and (vi) works of artistic craftsmanship.[13]

An artistic work is not eligible for copyright if, at the time when the work is made: (i) it constitutes a design of a type capable of registration under the Registered Designs Act, 1949, of the United Kingdom, or any enactment replacing that Act in Ghana, and (ii) it is intended by the author to be used as a model or pattern to be multiplied by any industrial process.[14]

"Cinematograph film" means the material first embodying the recording of a sequence of visual images capable, by the use of that material, of being shown as a moving picture, or of being recorded on other material by the use of which it can be so shown; it includes material first embodying the recording of a sound-track associated with the film.[15]

"Gramophone record" means the material first embodying the recording of a sequence of sounds capable, by the use of that material, of being automatically reproduced aurally, but does not include a sound-track associated with a cinematograph film.[16]

"Broadcast" means a sound or television broadcast of any material not broadcast by the use (whether direct or indirect) of (i) a gramophone record, copies of which have been issued to the public, or (ii) a cinematograph film, copies of which have been issued or exhibited to the public. "Broadcast" includes a broadcast by diffusion over wires.

PROTECTED PERSONS

Generally.—Subject to the exceptions stated below, copyright initially vests in the author.[17] "Author," in the case of a cinematographic film or gramophone record, means the person by whom the arrangements for the making of the film or record were undertaken, or in the case of a broadcast transmitted from within any country, means the person by whom the arrangements for the making of the transmission from within that country were undertaken.[18]

Works Commissioned or Made by Employees.—Where a work (other than a broadcast) is commissioned by a person (who is not the author's employer) or, not having been so commissioned, is made in the course of the author's employment, copyright vests initially in the person who commissioned the work, or the author's employer, as the case may be.[19]

[13] Section 15 (1).   [14] Section 1 (3).   [15] Section 15 (1).   [16] Section 15 (1).
[17] Section 9 (1). Copyright in works made by or under the direction of one of the designated international bodies initially vests in such body (sec. 9 (2)).
[18] Section 15 (1).   [19] Proviso to section 9 (1).

ASSIGNMENT AND LICENSING

Subject to the exceptions stated below, copyright is transmissible by assignment, by testamentary disposition, or by operation of law, as movable property.[20]

An assignment or testamentary disposition may be limited so as to apply to some only of the acts which the owner of the copyright has the exclusive right to control, or to a part only of the period of the copyright.[21]

A purported assignment of copyright is void if it is not in writing signed by or on behalf of the assignor.[22]

Any document purporting to confer an exclusive license to do an act falling within copyright shall be construed as a total or partial assignment of the copyright, as the case may require.[23]

A license to do an act falling within copyright may be written or oral, or may be inferred from conduct, and may be revoked at any time, provided that a license granted by contract cannot be revoked, either by the person who granted the license or his successor in title, except as the contract may provide, or by a further contract.[24]

An assignment or license granted by one copyright owner shall have effect as if granted by his co-owners also, and, subject to any contract between them, fees received by the grantor shall be divided equitably between all the co-owners.[25]

An assignment, license or testamentary disposition may be effectively granted or made in respect of a future work or an existing work in which copyright does not yet subsist; and the prospective copyright in any such work is transmissible by operation of law as movable property.[26]

A testamentary disposition of the material on which a work is first written or otherwise recorded is, in the absence of contrary indication, taken to include the disposition of any copyright or prospective copyright in the work which is vested in the deceased.[27]

PROTECTED RIGHTS

RIGHTS AND CERTAIN LIMITATIONS THEREON

Literary, Musical and Artistic Works.—Copyright in a literary, musical or artistic work is the exclusive right to control the doing in

[20] Section 10 (1).   [21] Section 10 (2).   [22] Section 10 (3).
[23] Section 10 (4).   [24] Section 10 (5).
[25] Section 10 (6).
Persons are deemed to be co-owners (i) if they share a joint interest in the whole or part of a copyright; or (ii) if they have interests in the various copyrights in a composite production, that is a production consisting of two or more works made in collaboration.
[26] Section 10 (7).   [27] Section 10 (8).

Ghana of any of the following acts, namely, the distribution of copies,[28] the public performance[29] for payment, and the broadcasting,[30] of the whole or a substantial part of the work, either in its original form or in any form recognizable derived from the original. However, copyright in any such work does not include the right to control:

a) the doing of any of the aforesaid acts by way of fair dealing for purposes of criticism or review, or the reporting of current events, if any public use of the work is accompanied by an acknowledgement of its title and authorship, except where the work is incidentally included in a broadcast;

b) the doing of any of the aforesaid acts by way of parody, pastiche or caricature;

c) the distribution of copies, or the inclusion in a film or broadcast, of an artistic work situated in a place where it can be viewed by the public;

d) the incidental inclusion of an artistic work in a film or broadcast;

e) the distribution of a collection of literary or musical works which includes not more than two short passages from the work in question, if the collection is designed for use in educational institutions and includes an acknowledgment of the title and authorship of the work;

f) the broadcasting of a work if the broadcast is intended to be used for purposes of instruction in educational institutions;

g) the distribution of sound recordings of a published literary or musical work, if fees are paid to the owner of the copyright in accordance with regulations yet to be issued.[31]

Copyright in a *work of architecture* also includes the exclusive right to control the erection of any building which reproduces the whole or a substantial part of the work, either in its original form or in any form recognizably derived from the original, provided that the copyright in any such work does not include the right to control the reconstruction of a building in the same style as the original.[32]

Cinematograph Films.—Copyright in a film is the exclusive right to control the doing in Ghana of any of the following acts, namely, the distribution of copies,[33] the public exhibition for payment, and the

[28] "Copy" means a reproduction in written form, in the form of a recording or film or in any other material form; however, an object is not taken to be a copy of an architectural work unless the object is a building or model (sec. 15 (1)).
[29] "Performance" includes, in addition to a live performance or delivery, any mode of visual or acoustic presentation (sec. 15 (1)).
[30] "Broadcast" means a sound or television broadcast of any material not broadcast by the use (whether direct or indirect) of (i) a gramophone record, copies of which have been issued to the public, or (ii) a cinematograph film, copies of which have been issued or exhibited to the public. "Broadcast" includes a broadcast by diffusion over wires (sec. 15 (1)).
[31] Section 5 (1).   [32] Section 5 (2).   [33] Section 6.

broadcasting,[34] of the whole or a substantial part of the film, either in its original form or in any form recognizably derived from the original.[35]

Gramophone Records.—Copyright in a gramophone record is the exclusive right to control the distribution in Ghana of copies[1] of the whole or a substantial part of the record, either in its original form or in any form recognizably derived from the original.[36]

Broadcasts.—Copyright in a broadcast is the exclusive right to control the doing in Ghana of any of the following acts, namely, the distribution of copies, the public communication, and the re-broadcasting, of the whole or a substantial part of the broadcast, either in its original form or in any form recognizably derived from the original, provided that copyright in a television broadcast does not include the right to control the distribution or re-broadcasting of still photographs taken from the broadcast, if done by way of fair dealing for purposes of criticism or review, or the reporting of current events.[37]

OTHER POSSIBLE LIMITATIONS

If the Minister responsible for Information is satisfied that a licensing body[38] (i) is unreasonably refusing to grant licenses in respect of copyright, or (ii) is imposing unreasonable terms or conditions on the granting of such licenses, he may, by executive instrument, direct that, as respects the doing of any act specified in the instrument in relation to a work with which the licensing body is concerned, a license shall be deemed to have been granted by the copyright owner, provided the appropriate fees prescribed by the instrument are paid or tendered before the expiration of the prescribed period after the act is done.[39]

TERM OF PROTECTION

WORKS OTHER THAN WORKS OF CERTAIN INTERNATIONAL ORGANIZATIONS

Literary, Musical and Artistic Works.—If the work is *unpublished*, copyright expires 25 years after the end of the year in which the author dies.[40] In the case of a work of joint authorship, the death of the author who dies last is relevant.[41] If the work is *published*, copyright expires

---

[34] Section 7.   [35] Section 8.
[36] "Licensing body" means an organization which has as its main object, or one of its main objects, the negotiation or granting of licenses in respect of works protected by copyright (sec. 12 (2)).
[37] Section 8.
[38] An organization which has as its main object, or one of its main objects, the negotiation or granting of licenses (sec. 12 (2)).
[39] Section 12 (1).   [40] Section 2 (2).   [41] Section 2 (4).

on the later of the following two dates: (i) the end of the year in which the author dies, (ii) 25 years after the end of the year in which the work was first published.[42] Where a work is first published after its copyright as an unpublished work has expired, a new term of copyright begins on first publication and expires 25 years after the end of the year in which such first publication took place.[43]

Cinematograph Films and Gramophone Records.—If the film or record is *unpublished*, copyright expires 25 years after the end of the year in which it was made. If the film or record is *published* (and first publication took place within the said term), copyright expires 20 years after the end of the year in which it was first published.[44]

Broadcasts.—Copyright in broadcasts expires 20 years after the end of the year in which the broadcast was made.[45]

Works of Certain International Organizations

Literary, Musical and Artistic Works.—Copyright in a work which is *not published* during the period ending 50 years from the end of the year in which it was made, expires at the end of that period. If the work is *published* during that period, copyright expires on the date of the expiration of 25 years from the end of the year in which it was first published.[46]

Cinematograph Films, Gramophone Records, and Broadcasts.—The duration of copyright in these works is the same as described above in connection with works other than works of international organizations.[47]

Rule of the Shorter Term

Since there is no provision in the law of Ghana for the "rule of the shorter term" permitted under Article IV (4) of the Universal Copyright Convention, it would appear that works are protected in Ghana until the expiration of the terms indicated above, even if in other countries they fall into the public domain at an earlier date.

INFRINGEMENTS

Copyright is infringed by any person who does, or causes any other person to do, an act falling within the copyright, without the license of the person in whom is vested either the whole of the copyright or,

[42] Section 2 (2).   [43] Section 2 (3).   [44] Section 2 (2).
[45] Section 2 (2).   [46] Section 4 (2).   [47] Section 4 (3).

where there has been a partial assignment or partial testamentary disposition, the relevant portion of the copyright.[48]

The remedies available for infringement of copyright are: (i) damages limited to the loss (if any) incurred by reason of the infringement, together with such additional sum as may be just, having regard to the flagrancy of the infringement, the benefit (if any) gained by the infringer, and such other matters as may be relevant; (ii) an injunction to restrain further infringements or, where no infringement has yet occurred, to restrain any infringement; (iii) an injunction requiring the delivery up to the Court and destruction or other disposal (as the Court may direct) of copies of the work in question, or other articles, which have been, or may otherwise be, used for purposes of infringement.[49]

No injunction is available in proceedings for infringement of copyright which requires a completed or partly-built building to be demolished or prevents the completion of a partly-built building.[50]

---

[48] Section 11 (1).   [49] Section 11 (2).   [50] Section 11 (3).

GREECE

SOURCES

Internal Law.—The main source of the law of copyright in Greece is the Law on Literary Property of June 29, 1920, as amended up to October 7, 1943.[1] Hereinafter it is referred to as "the Law," and references to Articles, without further specification, are references to the Articles of this Law.

Another source is the Law on Copyright of Playwrights (hereinafter referred to as the "Law on Playwrights") of 1909.[2]

Universal Copyright Convention.—Greece became bound by the Universal Copyright Convention and Protocols 1 and 2 as from 1963.[3]

ACQUISITION OF PROTECTION UNDER THE UNIVERSAL COPYRIGHT CONVENTION

The laws of Greece do not contain any special provision in respect of works to which Greece is supposed to grant protection by virtue of the Universal Copyright Convention. The provisions of that Convention, particularly Articles II and XVII, and Protocols 1 and 2, determine which are the works protected under the Universal Copyright

[1] Date of basic Act (Law No. 2387): June 29, 1920; of Amendatory Acts: (Law No. 4301) August 6, 1929; (Legislative Decree No. 619) October 11—November 3, 1941: (Law No. 763) October 7, 1943: (Law No. 1136) January 10—22, 1944: (Law No. 56) November 23—December 7, 1944).

Official Greek text published in "Ephēmeris tēs Kybernēseos" of July 3, 1920, page 1441; August 13, 1929, page 2337; November 3, 1941; October 13, 1943, page 1615; January 25, 1944; December 1, 1944). English translation published in CLTW, Greece: Item 1.

[2] Date of basic Act (Law No. 3483): December 16, 1909; of Amendatory Acts: (Law No. 3637) March 19, 1910; (Law No. 2387) June 29, 1920; (Law No. 4186) July 2, 1929; (Law No. 4301) August 6, 1929; (Law No. 988) November 29, 1943.

Official Greek text published in "Ephēmeris tēs Kybernēseos" of December 16, 1903, page 619; July 3, 1920, page 1441; July 9, 1929, page 2009; August 13, 1929, page 2337; December 1, 1943, page 1958. English translation published in CLTW, Greece: Item 3.

[3] See CLTW, Greece: Item 4A. Greece is a member of the Berne Copyright Union, the Brussels Convention of 1948 being the most recent text of that Union which Greece has ratified (see CLTW, Greece: Item 5). A decree of January 20, 1932 (published in "Ephēmeris tēs Kybernēseos," January 20, 1932, page 155; English translation in CLTW, Greece: Item 6) provides for the protection of "literary works

Convention. Briefly stated, such works are—except if excluded[3a] by virtue of Article XVII of the Universal Copyright Convention and the Appendix Declaration relating to the same Article (in which case the applicable Convention of the Berne Copyright Union rather than the Universal Copyright Convention governs): (i) published works of nationals of a Convention country, irrespective of the place of first publication, (ii) works first published in a Convention country, irrespective of the nationality of the author, (iii) unpublished works of nationals of a Convention country other than Greece, (iv) works of stateless persons and refugees who have their habitual residence in a State party to Protocol 1 (except perhaps Greece), whether published or unpublished, and if published, irrespective of the place of first publication, (v) works first published by the United Nations, by any of the Specialized Agencies of the United Nations, or by the Organization of American States, as well as unpublished works of any of these organizations.

Greece has no copyright formalities. Consequently, registration, deposit, or compliance with other formalities is not required, and the absence, in itself, of a Convention notice on the copies of a published work is no bar to claiming protection in Greece. Furthermore, Greece has no renewal system, so that there is nothing in this country which would correspond to the renewal formalities existing in the United States.

PROTECTED WORKS

The works of writers, composers, painters, authors of drawings, sculptures, turners and engravers are protected, whether they are original works, arrangements or translations.[4] Dramatico-musical works and musical compositions are also protected.[5]

Photographic and other similar works, and motion pictures (whether silent, sound, or talking) are protected "provided that each copy thereof bears the name of the photographer or publisher, his address, and the date of publication."[6] The Law does not provide that this requirement shall be considered as fulfilled if the Convention notice appears on the copies. It is thus uncertain whether it is so considered if

and plays created in the United States of North America." Bilateral agreements were concluded with France in 1912, Italy in 1948, and the German Federal Republic in 1951 (*See* CLTW, Greece: Items 7, 8, 9).

[3a] Such works are: (i) unpublished works whose author is a national (*ressortissant*) of a Berne Union country, (ii) published works which were first published in a Berne Union country or which, within 30 days of their first publication of a non-Union country, were also published in a Union country ("simultaneous publication").

[4] Article 1.   [5] Article 1.   [6] Article 14.

the Convention notice is used as provided in Article III of the Universal Copyright Convention. Original plays, their translations or adaptations are protected.[7]

PROTECTED PERSONS

Copyright originally vests in the author, translator or adaptor, as the case may be.[8]

In the case of anonymous or pseudonymous works, the person who publishes or makes public the work enjoys copyright; however, the rights shall be exercised by the author or artist as soon as he reveals his identity.[9]

In the case of photographs, copyright originally vests in the photographer; and in the case of motion pictures, in the creators of their component artistic parts—whether literary, musical or photographic—that is, in the writers, musical composers, scenographers and actors.[10]

ASSIGNMENT AND LICENSING

Copyright is transferable.[11] The acquisition of a manuscript or of an original work of art does not imply the acquisition of the right of its reproduction.[12]

Any person who receives remuneration for the publication of his work in a newspaper, periodical, year-book, calendar, anthology, etc., is not entitled to republish the said work elsewhere for two years from the completion of such publication, unless otherwise agreed.[13]

In the absence of an express agreement to the contrary, assignment by the author of the right to publish a theatrical work does not imply the assignment of the right to perform the said work; nor does authority to perform imply the right of publication in print, unless accompanied by an explicit statement to that effect.[14]

PROTECTED RIGHTS

Economic rights

Copyright comprises the exclusive right of publication, multiplication by reproduction, copying by any means and in any manner, and public performance.[15,16]

[7] Law on Playwrights, article 1.
[8] Article 1: Law on Playwrights, article 1.
[9] Article 4.   [10] Article 14.   [11] *See* article 1.   [12] Article 8.   [13] Article 11.
[14] Law on Playwrights, article 8.
[15] Article 1; Law on Playwrights, article 1.
[16] *See* also article 9.

As to the right of translation, the Law provides that authors or assignees of the authors' rights have the exclusive right to authorize the translation of such works and, in respect of theatrical works, the public performance of the translation, in all languages for ten years from the 31st of December of the year in which they were published. After ten years, the right of translation falls into the public domain. The possessors of unpublished works of deceased authors have similar rights. In respect of works published in instalments, the ten years are computed from the 31st of December of the year of publication of the last instalment.[17]

It is to be noted that this provision may lead to less protection than that required by Article V of the Universal Copyright Convention. On this point, therefore, Greek law appears to be at variance with the obligations of Greece under the Universal Copyright Convention.

MORAL RIGHTS

Assignees of copyright are not entitled to alter the work in any manner without the author's consent.[18]

LIMITATIONS

Musical compositions may be performed without the permission of the composer by military or other bands for non-profit educational purposes or non-profit entertainment of the public, in public halls without charge for admission, or in schools, or in the open. No compensation is due to the composers or the assignees of their rights in such cases.[19]

The republication, in the original or in translation, of material from periodicals or newspapers by another periodical or newspaper is permissible, unless a prohibition thereof by the author or the publisher appears on the work. However the source from which the republished material was taken, as well as the name of the author or artist, must be indicated.[20]

[17] Article 6. The provisions concerning translations apply also to the republication of texts and to the reproduction of pictures, drawings, etc., in literary collections, anthologies, school textbooks, calendars or yearbooks, souvenir issues, etc. However, those provisions do not apply to the publication of poetic or dramatic works in the original or in translation if set to music, to the dramatic or melodramatic arrangement of novels, to the adaptation of literary or artistic works, to cinematography or mimical representation, to the recording of musical compositions on phonograph records, or to the performance of musical works by mechanical inventions. In these cases the right is exclusive during the normal duration (generally 50 years *post mortem auctoris*) of copyright protection.

[18] Article 15.

[19] Article 9, second paragraph.

[20] Article 13.

The Government may order the printing and publication of a work of a deceased author if the work is of special significance and importance to the letters or the history of Greece or to science, but was either not published or, having been published, is no longer found in the book-trade, the copies being out of print, and if the heirs of the author are dead or cannot be found, or being alive and found are indifferent about the publication or republication of the work, or if they have transferred their rights to a publisher who has not published or republished the work for ten years (the previous publication having been exhausted).[21]

TERM OF PROTECTION

Copyright endures for the life of the author and for 50 years from the end of the calendar year in which he dies.[22] In respect of a work made in collaboration by two or more persons, copyright exists for 50 years, computed from the end of the calendar year in which the last surviving collaborator dies.[23]

INFRINGEMENTS

Perpetrators of certain infringing acts are punishable by imprisonment or fine.[24]

Since there is no provision in Greek law for the "rule of the shorter term" permitted under Article IV(4) of the Universal Copyright Convention, it would appear that works to which the Universal Copyright Convention applies are protected in Greece until the expiration of the terms indicated above even if in other countries they fall into the public domain at an earlier date.

---

[21] Legislative Decree No. 2179/1943 of November 23, 1942, published in "Ephē-meris tēs Kybernēseōs" of March 15, 1943, page 222; *see* English translation in CLTW, Greece: Item 2.
[22] Articles 1 and 2.
[23] Article 3. *See also* article 5.
[24] Article 16. *See also* Law on Playwrights, articles 9 to 15.

GUATEMALA

SOURCES

Internal Law.—The main source of the law of copyright in Guatemala is the Decree-Law No. 1037 of February 8 and 11, 1954, on Copyright (*Ley sobre derecho de autor*).[1] Hereinafter, it is referred to as "the Law," and references to Articles, without further specification, are references to Articles of this Law.

Universal Copyright Convention.—Guatemala became bound by the Universal Copyright Convention and Protocols 1 and 2 as from October 28, 1964.[2]

ACQUISITION OF PROTECTION UNDER THE UNIVERSAL COPYRIGHT CONVENTION

The Law does not contain provisions dealing expressly with works protected under the Universal Copyright Convention. It merely provides that the protection of authors and copyright owners—other than Guatemalan citizens or non-Guatemalan citizens domiciled in Guatemala (who are protected according to the provisions of the Law alone)—are governed by the international treaties and conventions which Guatemala has ratified.[3] Consequently, as far as the Universal Copyright Convention is concerned, the provisions of that Convention and its Protocols determine which works are to be protected in Guatemala by virtue of the said instruments. Briefly stated, then, such works are: (i) published works of nationals of a Convention country, irrespective of the place of first publication; (ii) works first published in a Convention country, irrespective of the nationality of the author; (iii) unpublished works of nationals of a Convention country other than Guatemala; (iv) works of stateless persons and refugees who have their habitual residence in a State party to Protocol 1 (except perhaps

[1] Published in "El Guatemalteco," issue of February 19, 1954. *See* English translation in CLTW, Guatemala: Item 1.

[2] *See* CLTW, Guatemala: Item 1A. Guatemala is also bound by the Rio de Janeiro Copyright Convention, 1906, the Buenos Aires Copyright Convention, 1910, the Havana Copyright Convention, 1928, the Washington Copyright Convention, 1946, and by bilateral treaties with Spain (1893) and France (1895); *See* CLTW, Guatemala: Items 2 to 7.

[3] Article 20.

Guatemala), either published or unpublished, and, if published, irrespective of the place of first publication; (v) works first published by the United Nations, any of its Specialized Agencies, or by the Organization of American States, as well as unpublished works of any of those Organizations.

The acquisition of copyright protection in Guatemala is not subject to any formality.[4] Consequently, registration or deposit is not required, and the absence, in itself, of the Convention notice on the copies of a published work is no bar to the claiming of protection in Guatemala. Furthermore, Guatemala has no renewal system, so there is nothing in that country which would correspond to the renewal formalities existing in the United States. Protection in Guatemala will last, without any intervention by the copyright owner or a Government authority, until the day on which the work falls into the public domain.

PROTECTED WORKS

Generally.—The Law protects authors in so far as concerns their literary, scientific and artistic works, whether published or unpublished.[5] Works, within the meaning of the Law, are the following: literary works, such as novels, poems, short stories or scientific works; lectures, speeches, sermons, lessons and other oral works, provided they have been reduced to writing or have been recorded (*grabadas*); dramatic and dramatico-musical works, theatrical works, cinematographic works; choreographic works and pantomimes, the stage directions of which are fixed in writing or otherwise; musical compositions with or without words; drawings, illustrations, paintings, sculptures, engravings, lithographs; photographs, including those made by cinematography, microphotography or on microfilms; astronomical or geographical globes; maps, plans, sketches, and plastic works relating to geography, geology, topography, architecture, or any other science. All these works, however, are protected only if they constitute an individual creation in the literary, scientific, artistic or musical fields, capable of public utilization by any means of communication known at present or yet to be invented.[6]

Derived Works.—Translations, adaptations, arrangements, instrumentations, transformations, dramatizations, and other versions of or based on (*sobre*) literary, scientific, artistic, musical or cinematographic works, are also "works" within the meaning of the Law, without prejudice to any copyright subsisting in the basic work (*obra primigenia* = the "first-born" work).[7]

---

[4] Article 1, second sentence.　　[5] Article 1, first sentence.　　[6] Article 6.
[7] Article 7.

Works of Applied Art.—Works of art made principally for industrial purposes are "works" within the meaning of the Law, provided they contain an element of individual creativity (*creación individual*).[8]

Compilations, Etc.—Collections of works, periodicals, magazines (*revistas*) and other works of like kind, compilations and anthologies, which, by their selection or arrangement, constitute a work within the meaning of the Law, are protected as such, without prejudice to any copyright subsisting in the various works included in such collections, etc.[9]

Title of the Work.—Copyright extends to the title of the work, provided that, by reason of the title's form or fame, it (i.e., the title) has a distinctive character which invests the work with individuality (*individualizando la obra*).[10]

Exceptions.—The following are not "works" within the meaning of the Law: laws, decrees, regulations, ordinances, treaties, judicial decisions and, in general, all official documents (*actos oficiales*). The same is true in respect of speeches made in public meetings or in the courts. Translations, thereof, however, are protected as works.[11]

PROTECTED PERSONS

Generally.—The Law protects authors.[12] The creator of the work is its author.[13] Copyright in a work created by the collaboration of two or more authors belongs jointly (*en común y pro indiviso*) to the collaborators.[14] Copyright in dramatico-musical works created by several co-authors is deemed to be indivisible unless otherwise provided by contract.[15]

Presumptions.—In the absence of proof to the contrary, the person whose name or known pseudonym is indicated upon the work or its reproductions, or in connection with the public exhibition, performance, recitation, showing, sound or visual broadcasting, of the work, is deemed to be its author.[16]

Works Produced under Certain Types of Central Direction.
—Entrepreneurs (*empresarios*) and firms having legal capacity (*empresas de personería jurídica*) professionally producing works through the intermediary of their employees or contractors, particularly publishers of dictionaries and encyclopedias and producers (*fábricas*) of cinematographic works, enjoy copyright in the said works, without prejudice

---

[8] Article 8.   [9] Article 4.   [10] Article 14.   [11] Article 9.
[12] Article 1, first sentence.   [13] Article 2, first sentence.
[14] Article 5, first paragraph.   [15] Article 5, second paragraph.   [16] Article 2.

to any copyright that the employees or contractors may have in their respective contributions.[17]

ASSIGNMENT AND LICENSING

The author has the exclusive right to utilize his work, to authorize its use by others, to assign his right, and to grant licenses in respect thereof.[18] Any disposal, assignment, or license, must be interpreted strictly.[19] The author's moral right is inalienable, and its exercise cannot be waived in advance.[20]

Copyright, as a whole or in part, cannot be distrained (*es inembargable*). However, the following may be distrained: (i) copies (*ejemplares*) or reproductions of a published work; (ii) any work of the fine arts (*de las artes plásticas*), such as a painting, sculpture or drawing, and any work of art primarily made for industrial exploitation, when finished and put on sale; (iii) any revenue derived from the exploitation of copyright.[21]

PROTECTED RIGHTS

ECONOMIC RIGHTS

The general exclusive right to use the work, according to its nature, by any means at present known or subsequently discovered, includes the following particular exclusive rights:

(i) to reproduce it by means of printing, photography, or fixation upon devices capable of reproducing sounds, or in any other form;

(ii) to diffuse it by means of telephotography, radio or television broadcasting, or any other means at present known or hereafter to be invented capable of reproducing signs, sounds or images;

(iii) to publish it;

(iv) publicly to perform it, show it by means of cinematography, or exhibit it;

(v) to distribute it, commercially or professionally;

(vi) to adapt, transpose, arrange, orchestrate, dramatize and, in general, to transform it in any other manner;

(vii) to authorize the transformations which the foregoing item specifies, especially for the adaptation of the work to cinematography;

(viii) to perform it in public by means of instruments which, mechanically or electrically, serve to reproduce signs, sounds or images;

(ix) to translate it;

---

[17] Article 3. [18] Article 10. [19] Article 12. [20] Article 19. [21] Article 15.

(x) to authorize the utilization of translations, adaptations, transformations, arrangements and other modifications;

(xi) to authorize the performance, diffusion or public presentation of performances and broadcasts, including television, by means of the mechanical or electrical instruments referred to in item (viii) above, including loudspeakers.[22]

"Publication" means the making known or distribution to the public of a work by any means suitable for the purpose, having regard to the nature of the work in question. The first offering of a cinematographic work for sale or hire or distribution for the purposes of public or commercial showing also constitutes publication. Visible performance, recitation, exhibition or showing of a work to a public audience, that is, an audience outside the domestic circle, or by way of broadcasting, television or other mechanical or electrical means also constitutes publication. Only authorized publication is to be considered as publication.[23]

Literary, scientific and artistic works protected by the Law may not be used publicly or with gainful intent (*con fines de lucro*) without the previous authorization of the *Asociación Guatemalteco de Autores y Compositores* (Guatemalan Association of Authors and Composers), which has the right to fix the appropriate royalty rates in the interests of their members and of the persons they represent.[24]

Moral Rights

The author, upon disposing wholly or in part of his economic rights in any manner, retains the moral right to claim the authorship of his work and to oppose any modification or utilization thereof which is prejudicial to his reputation as an author.[25]

Limitations

Articles of Current Interest.—These, if published in a periodical or magazine, may be freely reproduced by the press unless reproduction is prohibited by means of a special or general reservation in the said periodical or magazine. In any case, the source from which such matter is taken must be mentioned, and an indication given in an unmistakable manner of the title of the periodical or magazine, the place of its publication, and the date of the relevant edition. In the absence of such notice, the reproduction is unlawful. The same provisions apply also to the reproduction of drawings and photographs of current events, either in the original or in reduced dimensions.[26]

[22] Article 10.   [23] Article 11.   [24] Article 32.   [25] Article 19.   [26] Article 16.

News Items.—The actual substance of current news items published in the press is not protected by copyright.[27]

Extracts, Etc.—Reproduction of short extracts from literary, scientific and artistic works in publications intended for teaching or for scientific purposes, in anthologies and chrestomathies, or for the purpose of literary criticism or scientific research, is free, provided that an indication is given in an unmistakable manner of the source from which they have been taken and that the extracts in question have not been altered. For the same purposes, and with similar restrictions, extracts and parts of such works may be freely reproduced in translation.[28] Public reproduction, performance, recitation, showing, and radio or television broadcasting, of such extracts or parts are also free.[29]

TERM OF PROTECTION

Economic Rights.—Copyright protection starts upon creation[30] and, subject to the following qualifications and exceptions, expires fifty years after the death of the author.[31]

In the case of works created by two or more authors, the term of fifty years is counted from the death of the author who dies last. If any of the co-authors dies without leaving heirs, his rights accrue in equal parts to the surviving co-authors.[32] The Copyright of legal entities expires fifty years after the publication of the work.[33]

Moral Rights.—The moral rights of the author have the same duration as his economic rights. Upon his death, the moral rights pass to his heirs even if the economic rights were alienated during his lifetime or have been bequeathed to persons other than his heirs. Each heir may exercise the moral rights independently of the other heirs.[34]

Rule of the Shorter Term.—Since there is no provision in the Law for the "rule of the shorter term" permitted under Article IV, paragraph (4), of the Universal Copyright Convention, works protected by virtue of that Convention in Guatemala seem to be protected until the expiration of the terms indicated above, even if in other countries they fall into the public domain at an earlier date.

---

[27] Article 16.   [28] Article 17.   [29] Article 18.   [30] Article 1, second sentence.
[31] Article 13, first sentence.   [32] Article 13, second and third sentences.
[33] Article 13, last sentence.   [34] Article 19, last sentence.

INFRINGEMENTS

CIVIL REMEDIES

Any person whose rights are violated may request from the courts: (i) an order for the cessation of the unlawful acts, (ii) the sequestration or destruction of unlawful copies and implements for making them or, at his option, delivery of such copies and implements to him at cost, (iii) compensation for damages, including moral damages if the violation was wilful or negligent, (iv) the net proceeds of the admittance fees collected in connection with the public performance of dramatic, dramatico-musical or cinematographic works, even when the violation was innocent (*de buena fe*).[35] The violation of moral rights entitles the author or the heir to request the courts to order cessation of the unlawful use and to award damages for moral suffering (*daño moral*).[36] Civil actions prescribe after the expiration of two years from the date when the violation became known.[37]

CRIMINAL SANCTIONS

Fraudulent or grossly negligent violations of copyright are punishable by a fine.[38] So is any publisher or printer who stocks a greater number of copies than contracted for.[39] So is also any person who reproduces the work without mentioning the source when the reproduction is free (see "Protected Rights, Limitations," above).[40] Penal proceedings are instituted at the request of the interested party, but must be instituted *ex officio* in the case of importation into Guatemala of unauthorized copies or reproductions. Such copies must be ordered to be destroyed without regard to who owns them.[41] Failure to announce in advance public performances, showings, broadcasts, etc., to the *Asociación Guatemalteco de Autores y Compositores* (Guatemalan Society of Authors and Composers) is punishable by a fine.[42] Penal actions may be instituted independently of any civil action.[43]

INJUNCTIONS

Any person whose rights are threatened to be violated may request the courts to order adequate preventive measures.[44]

---

[35] Article 21.   [36] Article 19.   [37] Article 25.   [38] Article 26, first sentence.
[39] Article 26, second sentence.   [40] Article 27.   [41] Article 28.
[42] Articles 22 and 23.   [43] Article 29.   [44] Article 24.

HAITI

SOURCES

Internal Law.—The primary source of the law of copyright in Haiti is the Law on Literary and Artistic Property, dated October 8, 1885 (hereinafter referred to as "the Law").[1] The Penal Code provides for criminal sanctions for infringements.[2]

Universal Copyright Convention.—Haiti became bound by the Universal Copyright Convention and Protocols 1 and 2 as from September 16, 1955.[3]

ACQUISITION OF PROTECTION UNDER THE UNIVERSAL COPYRIGHT CONVENTION

There are no laws in Haiti which specifically refer to the Universal Copyright Convention. In particular, there are no provisions implementing Article III of the Convention, which provides for the non-applicability or avoidance of domestic formalities for the acquisition of copyright.[4] Consequently, while it is assumed for purposes of the present exposition that conflicts between the Law of Haiti and the Convention will be resolved in accordance with the provisions of the latter, this assumption cannot, in the absence of relevant authoritative decisions, be regarded as officially confirmed.

The laws of Haiti do not define the works which are protected in that country by virtue of the Universal Copyright Convention. On the basis of the provisions of the Convention and the Protocols, it may be assumed that such works are: (i) published works of nationals of a Convention country, irrespective of the place of first publication; (ii) works first published in a Convention country, irrespective of the nationality of the author; (iii) unpublished works of nationals of a Convention country other than Haiti; (iv) works of stateless persons

---

[1] Published in "Le Moniteur," October 10, 1885. English translation in CLTW, Haiti: Item 1.
[2] Penal Code promulgated on August 11, 1835, as amended up to and including the Law of February 16, 1927. English translation in CLTW, Haiti: Item 2.
[3] CLTW, Haiti: Item 3. Haiti is also a party to the Copyright Conventions of Buenos Aires (1910) and Washington (1946). *See* CLTW, Haiti: Items 4 and 5.
[4] Article 2 prescribes registration and deposit.

and refugees who have their habitual residence in a State party to Protocol 1 (except perhaps Haiti), either published or unpublished, and if published, irrespective of the place of first publication; (v) works first published by the United Nations, any of its Specialized Agencies, or by the Organization of American States, as well as unpublished works of any of these Organizations.

It may thus be further assumed that, with the possible exception of the rule of the shorter term (discussed below), works in any of these categories are protected in Haiti without deposit and registration, provided always that, in the case of published works, the provisions of Article III of the Convention concerning notice have been complied with.

Haiti has no renewal system, so that there is nothing in this country which would correspond to the renewal formalities existing in the United States.

PROTECTED WORKS

Literary and artistic works are protected; they include books, leaflets, writings of all kinds, dramatic works of all kinds, musical compositions with or without words, musical arrangements, drawings, paintings, sculptures, engravings, lithographs, geographical maps, plans, scientific sketches and, in general, any literary, scientific or artistic work capable of publication by any method of printing, or reproduction.[5]

PROTECTED PERSONS

Copyright vests in the author.[6] Proprietors, by inheritance or other title, of posthumous works are assimilated to the authors of such works, provided they print such works separately.[7]

ASSIGNMENT AND LICENSING

Authors have a property right in their works; they may assign their right.[8]

PROTECTED RIGHTS

Authors have the exclusive right to sell, cause the sale of, distribute, perform, translate, or cause the translation of, their works.[9]

[5] Article 1.   [6] Article 2.   [7] Article 4.
[8] Articles 2 and 5.   [9] Article 5.

TERM OF PROTECTION

Copyright belongs to the author during his life.[10] After his death, the right passes to his widow for her life, and to the children for a term of 20 years; if there are no children, the right passes to the heirs or proprietors for a term of 10 years.[11] The term enjoyed by the widow may or may not be longer than the 25 years *post mortem auctoris* minimum prescribed by the Universal Copyright Convention. The terms of 20 and 10 years, referred to above, are necessarily shorter than the Conventional minimum. It may be that in cases where the application of the provisions of the Law would result in a term shorter than the one prescribed by the Convention, Haiti will apply the Conventional minimum. However, no authoritative statement to this effect is known.

INFRINGEMENTS

Any person who, without the written consent of the author, or his successor in title, publishes, reproduces, exhibits, or causes the performance of, a literary or artistic work, is guilty of infringement and is subject to fine, and, upon request of the proprietor, the payment to the proprietor of a sum equivalent to the price of one thousand copies of the original edition.[12] The seller of infringing editions, who is not himself decreed an infringer, may be ordered to pay the proprietor a sum equivalent to the price of two hundred copies of the original edition.[13]

Directors, producers of spectacles (*entrepreneurs de spectacles*) and associations of performers causing dramatic works to be performed in a theatre contrary to the rules and regulations on copyright are punishable by fine and confiscation of the receipts for the benefit of the owner of copyright.[14] Infringing copies are also subject to such confiscation.[15]

---

[10] Article 5.   [11] Articles 5 and 6.   [12] Articles 7 and 9.
[13] Article 10; Penal Code, Articles 347 to 349.
[14] Penal Code, Articles 350 and 351.
[15] Article 8.

HOLY SEE

The Holy See (Vatican City) became bound by the Universal Copyright Convention and Protocols 1 and 2 on October 5, 1955.[1] No special measures for the implementation of the Convention were promulgated by the Holy See.

Law No. XII of January 12, 1960,[2] provides that, in respect of copyright, the legislation of the Italian State shall be observed in the Vatican City, provided such Italian legislation is not contrary to the precepts of divine law, the principles of canon law, or the Treaty and Concordat concluded between the Holy See and the Italian State on February 11, 1929, and provided that, in relation to the factual situation existing in the Vatican City, such legislation is applicable,[3] There are no authoritative interpretations as to the extent, if any, to which the Italian copyright law is inapplicable in the Vatican City on any of the above grounds.

It would appear that most, if not all, that is said, in connection with Italy (*see* pages 400 to 415 below), holds also for the Vatican City.

[1] CLTW, Holy See: Item 2. The Holy See is a member of the Berne Copyright Union, having ratified the Conventions of Rome of 1928, and Brussels of 1948 (CLTW, Holy See: Item 3).

[2] Official Italian text published as "Stato della Città del Vaticano; XII, Legge sul Diritto di Autore"; English translation in CLTW, Holy See: Item 1.

[3] Article 1 of Law No. XII of 1960.

ICELAND

SOURCES

Internal Law.—The main source of the law of copyright is Law
No. 13 of October 20, 1905.[1] This was amended by Laws No. 49 of
April 14, 1943, No. 74 of June 5, 1947, and No. 11 of February 2, 1956.[2]
Hereinafter, it is referred to as "the Law," and references to Sections,
without further specification, are references to Sections of the Law.
The Law has not been amended in connection with the adherence of
Iceland to the Universal Copyright Convention in 1956, and is, in at
least one respect—the right of translation—at variance with the re-
quirements laid down in Article V of that Convention. The question
is further discussed below in connection with the right of translation.[3]

Universal Copyright Convention.—Iceland became bound by
the Universal Copyright Convention as from December 18, 1956.[4]

ACQUISITION OF PROTECTION UNDER THE
UNIVERSAL COPYRIGHT CONVENTION

The laws of Iceland do not contain any special provisions in respect
of works to which Iceland is supposed to grant protection by virtue of
the Universal Copyright Convention. The provisions of that Convention
particularly Articles II and XVII, determine which are the works
protected under the Universal Copyright Convention. Briefly stated,
such works are, unless excluded[5] by virtue of Article XVII of the

---

[1] Published in "Stjornartidindi Fyyrir Island," 1905, page 116. English translation
in CLTW, Iceland: Item 1.

[2] Published in "Stjornartidindi," 1943, page 123, 1947, page 255, and 1956, page
146. English translation in CLTW, Iceland: Item 1.

[3] Page 366, below.

[4] CLTW, Iceland: Item 2. Iceland did not adhere to any of the Protocols attached
to the Universal Copyright Convention. Iceland is party to the Rome Convention,
1928, of the Berne Union, subject to a reservation on the right of translation (CLTW,
Iceland: Item 2).

[5] Such works are: (i) unpublished works whose author is a national (*ressortissant*)
of a Berne Union country, (ii) published works which were first published in a
Berne Union country or which, within 30 days of their first publication of a non-
Union country, were also published in a Union country ("simultaneous publication").

Universal Copyright Convention and the Appendix Declaration relating to the same Article (in which case the Rome Convention of the Berne Union rather than the Universal Convention governs): (i) published works of nationals of a Convention country (i.e., a country party to the Universal Copyright Convention), irrespective of the place of first publication, (ii) works first published in a Convention country, irrespective of the nationality of the author, (iii) unpublished works of nationals of a Convention country, other than Iceland.

It is in connection with the right of translation and the rule of the shorter term, discussed below,[6] that it might be necessary to determine whether a work is protected in Iceland by virtue of the Rome Convention of the Berne Union rather than the Universal Copyright Convention.

There are no copyright formalities in Iceland. Consequently, registration, deposit, or compliance with other formalities is neither required nor possible in Iceland, and the absence, in itself, of a Convention notice on the copies of a published work is no bar to claiming protection in that country. Furthermore, Iceland has no renewal system, so that there is nothing in this country which would correspond to the renewal formalities existing in the United States.

PROTECTED WORKS

All works of an author are protected. These include literary works, whether they are oral addresses and lectures or writings (manuscripts, printed copies, copies reproduced by other methods than printing); musical works; and artistic works (sculptures, engravings, paintings, drawings, all kinds of charts, photographs, works of commercial art, models).[7] An authorized translation of a writing, and a translation of a work not protected by the Law, enjoy the same protection as an original work.[8]

No person may reprint telegrams received and published by another person at the latter's expense, or report their contents in print within five days from their first publication in printed form.[9]

PROTECTED PERSONS

Copyright originally vests in the author.[10]

Publishers of newspapers, periodicals or works that consist of independent contributions by various contributors have the same exclusive

---

[6] *See* pages 366 and 368.

[7] Section 1. *See also* section 8.

[8] Section 5. It is lawful to publish a new, independent translation, without the authorization of the author of the earlier translation.

[9] Section 14.   [10] Section 1.

right of publication as authors with regard to these composite works. The authors of the individual contributions retain copyright therein, in the absence of an agreement to the contrary.[11]

When a work is created by several authors, none of whose contributions constitutes an independent whole, the consent of all authors is required for publication, performance or other use.[12]

In the case of anonymous or pseudonymous works, the editor or publisher whose name appears on the work is presumed to have authority to safeguard the interests of the author, unless there is proof to the contrary.[13]

ASSIGNMENT AND LICENSING

Generally.—The author may transfer the copyright in his work, either wholly or partially. The transfer by the author of his right of publication by a particular means (for example, by printing or by performance) does not authorize the transferee to publish the work by some other means, or to arrange for translations.[14]

Publication Contracts.—When the author (or his successor) transfers the right to publish a writing, the transferee is not entitled, unless otherwise agreed, to publish more than one edition of not more than 1,000 copies. This provision does not apply to publication in newspapers and other periodicals.[15]

Performance Contracts Concerning Dramatic Works.—The person to whom an author has transferred the right of performance of a dramatic work is, in the absence of an agreement to the contrary, entitled to perform the work in any place, and as often as he wishes, but he may not transfer this right to others. Even when an exclusive right of dramatic performance has been transferred, if the transferee has not brought about a public performance during three consecutive years, the author and his heirs, but no other successors, may freely transfer the right of dramatic performance to third persons or themselves arrange for performance.[16]

Performance and Broadcasting of Musical and Non-Dramatic Literary Works.—Owners of literary or musical (non-dramatic) rights, who are neither members of an approved Icelandic organization

[11] Section 3.
[12] Section 6, first and second paragraphs; but this provision may be put aside by contract. For further details see the rest of sections 6 and 1, and, as to music and text, section 7.
[13] Section 25, second paragraph.
[14] Section 9, first and second paragraphs.
[15] Section 9, fourth and fifth paragraphs.
[16] Section 10.

or society of authors or composers, nor have granted to such an organization or society full powers to act on their behalf, enjoy the same protection as members as regards the amount payable for the performances of their works.[17]

PROTECTED RIGHTS

ECONOMIC RIGHTS

Generally.—The author has a property right in his work. Within the limits stated below, he has the exclusive rights: (i) to publish, translate, perform, exhibit by means of cinematography, recite, broadcast, or utilize in any other manner his literary and musical works; (ii) to make copies, photographs, and other reproductions from any of his works, and to reproduce such copies for sale, advertising, or any other profitable purpose; (iii) to exhibit publicly his works, when they have been acquired by another private person, unless the work is exhibited in a private collection only accessible to the public under specified conditions.[18]

Right of Broadcasting.—If no agreement is reached between broadcasting stations and performing right societies on the amount of payments to be made for the broadcasting of literary and musical works, such amount is fixed by arbitration.[19]

Right of Translation.—The right of translation is protected as an exclusive right: (i) as long as the work is under copyright protection (that is, generally, fifty years *post mortem auctoris*) in respect of the language or languages, if any, in which a lawful translation has been published within 25 years from the first publication of the work, (ii) for 25 years from the first publication of the work in respect of all languages in which no lawful translation has been published during these 25 years.[20, 21]

[17] Regulations about Performing Rights of Literary and Musical Works, No. 19 of February 1, 1948, and No. 51 of April 10, 1959. *See* English translations in CLTW, Iceland: Item 1A.
[18] Section 1.
[19] Regulations cited in footnote 17, above.
[20] Section 4, first and second paragraphs. With respect to works published in instalments, the 25 years are calculated from the publication of the last instalment. In the case of works published in several volumes published at intervals, and reports of scientific associations, the individual volumes or reports are considered separate works in regard to the term of ten years. Section 4, third and fourth paragraphs.
[21] In the case of works which originate in a country member of the Berne Union, party to the Rome Convention of 1928, the right of translation is protected as an exclusive right: (i) as long as the work is under copyright protection: (a) in respect of all languages other than the Icelandic language and (b) in respect of the Icelandic language if a lawful translation in the Icelandic language has been published within ten years from the first publication of the work; (ii) for ten years from the

This provision is not in harmony with Article V of the Universal Copyright Convention, under which the right of translation must always be protected until the expiration of the copyright in the work; albeit, under certain circumstances, compulsory licenses may be granted.

MORAL RIGHTS

The transferee of copyright is not entitled to publish the work in an altered form without the consent of the author.[22]

LIMITATIONS

It is permissible to recite and broadcast, without the author's authorization, single poems, short stories, articles, portions of literary works, and to sing or play without the composer's authorization, single melodies and portions of published musical works, if the royalty regulations of the Icelandic authors' associations are observed.[23]

No authorization is needed and no royalties need be paid where single poems, short stories, articles, portions of literary works, single melodies, or portions of published musical works are presented (i) at events organized for charitable purposes, (ii) exclusively for the purpose of popular education, (iii) at any entertainment to which the audience is admitted free of charge, (iv) at meetings of societies or schools if the admittance fee charge is not greater than the amount required to cover the expenses of organizing the meeting.[24]

Furthermore, no authorization is needed and no royalties need be paid for the public performance of: (i) any musical work, if the performance is by choral or other societies and no remuneration is paid to the performers; (ii) dance music, at dances, even though the performers of music are paid at the usual rate, provided such performers do not constitute an organized and permanent orchestra.[25]

Finally, it is permissible: (i) to insert single portions of published works in other works which, taken in their entirety, are independent, (ii) to insert single portions of a work in reading books and school books after two years have elapsed since the first publication of such work, (iii) to reprint published poems as texts of songs in concert programs, (iv) to reprint in the press articles on current economic, political or religious subjects, unless reproduction is expressly prohibited.[26]

first publication of the work in respect of translation into the Icelandic language if no lawful translation into the Icelandic language has been published during these ten years.

[22] Section 9, third paragraph.
[23] Section 2, first paragraph.
[24] Section 2, second paragraph.
[25] Section 2, second and third paragraphs.
[26] Sections 15 and 16.

TERM OF PROTECTION

Generally.—Subject to the exceptions stated below, copyright subsists for the life of the author and for a term of fifty years after his death.[27]

The term of protection is fifty years from the last day of the year in which the work was first published in the case of anonymous works, pseudonymous works, newspapers, periodicals, and works consisting of independent contributions of various contributors.[28]

Rule of the Shorter Term.—Since there is no provision in the Law for the "rule of the shorter term" permitted under Article IV, paragraph (4), of the Universal Copyright Convention, works protected in Iceland by virtue of that Convention appear to be protected until the expiration of the terms indicated above, even if in other countries they fall into the public domain at an earlier date.[29]

INFRINGEMENTS

Wilful or negligent violations of copyright are punishable by fine and give the right to the injured party to claim damages.[30] Violations in good faith render infringers liable to pay to the injured person the estimated profit they gained.[31] The following are considered as violations: (i) publication in violation of the Law, (ii) importation into Iceland of a work published outside Iceland in violation of the Law, (iii) distributing, leasing or selling a work which, to the knowledge of the defendant, was published in or imported into Iceland in violation of the Law, (iv) unlawful public performance of a dramatic work, (v) unlawful public reading of a literary work, (vi) unlawful public performance of musical works, (vii) unlawful use of a text for the text of a musical work.[32]

Under certain circumstances, the confiscation or destruction of infringing copies, and of contrivances used for making them, may be ordered.[33]

[27] Section 22, first paragraph. When a work is created by several authors, none of whose contributions constitutes an independent whole, the death of the last surviving co-author is determinative in computing the term.
[28] Section 23, first paragraph. If the true name of the author is disclosed in the prescribed manner, the *post mortem auctoris* term applies (sec. 23, second para.). *See also* section 24.
[29] However, it is possible that the rule of the shorter term provided in Article 7 of the Rome Convention of the Berne Union applies in the case of works which, within the meaning of the Rome Convention, have as their country of origin a country party to the Rome Convention (or *any* Berne Union country?). *See* page 000, *above*.
[30] Sections 18 and 19.   [31] Section 20.
[32] Sections 18 and 9. Infringement is deemed to have occurred when one copy has been printed or otherwise completed (sec. 18, third para.). *See also* section 21.
[33] Section 17.

All actions prescribe within one year from knowledge by the injured party and, in any case, after two years from commission for criminal actions, and after three years from commission for civil actions. Destruction and confiscation may be claimed at any time while the copyright subsists.[34]

[34] Section 26.

INDIA

SOURCES

Internal Law.—The main source of the law of copyright in India is the Copyright Act, 1957.[1] Hereinafter, it is referred to as "the Act," and references to Sections, without further identification, are references to Sections of the Act.

The Act is supplemented by the Copyright Rules, 1958.[2] Hereinafter, they are referred to as "the Rules."

Universal Copyright Convention.—India became bound by the Universal Copyright Convention and Protocols 1 and 2 as from January 21, 1958.[3] It is also a member of the Berne Copyright Union.[4]

The protection that India grants to works on account of the Universal Copyright Convention and the Conventions of the Berne Copyright Union is regulated in the International Copyright Order, 1958,[5] and its amendments.[6] This Order, as amended, will hereinafter be referred to as "the Order."

ACQUISITION OF PROTECTION UNDER THE UNIVERSAL COPYRIGHT CONVENTION

Hereinafter, a country party to the Universal Copyright Convention is referred to as a "Convention country."

Conditions of Protection.—There is protection in India on

[1] Act No. 14 of June 4, 1957, published in "The Gazette of India, Extraordinary, Part II, Section 1," No. 15, of June 6, 1957. Came into force on January 21, 1958 (S.R.O. 269). The best monograph commenting on the Indian Law is Rustom R. Dadachanji's *Law of Literary and Dramatic Copyright in a Nut-shell*, published at Bombay in 1960.

[2] Date of the Rules: January 21, 1958, published in "The Gazette of India, Extraordinary, Part II, Section 3," No. 34, of January 21, 1958, and No. 54, of April 22, 1958.

[3] CLTW, India: Item 3.

[4] CLTW, India: Item 3.

[5] Date of the Order: January 21, 1958; published in "The Gazette of India, Extraordinary, Part II, Section 3," No. 34, of January 21, 1958. *See* CLTW, India: Item 3.

[6] These merely extend the effect of the basic Order to countries later adhering to the Berne or Universal Conventions. All the amending Orders are cited and covered in CLTW, India: Item 3.

account of the Universal Copyright Convention if the work fulfils any of the following conditions:

(i) If the work was first published in a Convention country (irrespective of the nationality of the author).[7]

(ii) If, at the time the work was first published (or, if the author was dead at that date, then at the time of his death), the author was a national of a Convention country.[8] In the case of a work of joint authorship, all authors must fulfil this condition. If the "author" is a body corporate, such body must be incorporated in a Convention country.[9]

(iii) If the author of the unpublished work (other than an architectural work) was, at the time of making the work.[10] a national of, or domiciled in, a Convention country.[11] In the case of a work of joint authorship, all authors must fulfil this condition.[12] If the "author" is a body corporate, such body must be incorporated in a Convention country.[13]

(iv) If the work is made or first published by or under the direction or control of the United Nations Organization, any of the Specialized Agencies of that Organization, or the Organization of American States.[14]

If the work was first published in a country party to the Berne Copyright Union, *see* page 377, below, as to the right of translation; and if the country of origin of a work is a country member of the Berne Copyright Union, *see* page 381, below, as to the rule of the shorter term.

The definitions of "author" and "work" are discussed below.[15]

Concept of Publication.—"Publication" means:

(a) in the case of a literary, dramatic, musical or artistic work, the issue of copies of the work to the public in sufficient quantities (the issue of records recording a literary, dramatic or musical work does not, in itself, cause the publication of such work; and, the issue of photographs and engravings of a work of sculpture or architecture does not, in itself, cause the publication of such work);

(b) in the case of a cinematograph film, the sale or hire, or offer for sale or hire, of the film or copies thereof to the public;

---

[7] Order, section 3(a).
[8] Order, section 3(b).
[9] Section 13(2), Explanation; section 8; Order section 3(d).
[10] If the making extended over a considerable period, the author must have been a national or domiciliary of a Convention country during a substantial part of that period (sec. 7).
[11] Order, section 3(c).
[12] Section 13(2), Explanation.
[13] Section 8; Order, section 3(d).
[14] *See* section 17(e) and 41, and the Copyright (International Organizations) Orders, 1958, of January 21, 1958; published in "The Gazette of India, Extraordinary, Part II, Section 3," No. 34, of January 21, 1958 (CLTW, India: Item 4).
[15] *See* pages 373 and 374.

(c) in the case of a record, the issue of records to the public, in sufficient quantities.[16]

Except in relation to an infringement of copyright, a work is not deemed to be published if it has been published without the license of the owner of the copyright.[17]

A work first published in a country which is not a Convention country but, within thirty days of publication in such country, has also been published in a Convention country, is considered as published in the latter country (i.e., the Convention country; "simultaneous publication"), provided that the former country (i.e., the non-Convention country) does not grant a shorter term of protection than the latter country.[18]

If any question arises as to the length of term of protection for a given work in a given country, or as to the requirement to issue copies or records in "sufficient" quantity, the Copyright Board decides.[19]

Formalities.—No formalities of any kind need to be complied with in order to acquire or maintain protection in India. There is, however, a Copyright Office in the Ministry of Scientific Research and Cultural Affairs, in New Delhi, to which the author or the publisher of any work, or the owner of or any other person interested in the copyright in a work, may apply to enter particulars of the work in the Register of Copyrights.[20] The Register of Copyrights constitutes *prima facie* evidence of the particulars (names and titles of works; names and addresses of authors, publishers and owners of copyrights; etc.) entered therein.[21]

The absence, in itself, of the Convention notice on the copies of a published work is no bar to claiming protection in India. Furthermore, India has no renewal system, so there is nothing in this country which would correspond to the renewal formalities existing in the United States.

Works Created or Published Prior to the Commencement of the Order.—The Copyright Act, 1957, does "not apply to a work published before the commencement of (the) Order in a Universal Copyright Convention Country, not being a Berne Convention Country, other than any such work published in the United States of America which enjoyed copyright in India immediately before such commencement by virtue of any Order in Council."[22] Consequently, if the work was first, or "simultaneously" with the first publication,

---

[16] Section 3.   [17] Section 4.   [18] Section 5.   [19] Section 6.
[20] Sections 9, 10, 45.
[21] Sections 44, 48. As to the correction of entries, *see* sections 49, 50.
[22] Order, section 4(c). "Commencement" depends on the date of adherence of each country to the Universal Copyright Convention and the implementing Order of India. The date of commencement in respect to the United States is January 21, 1958.

published in a country member of the Berne Union—for example, if the work of a U.S. citizen was first published in 1950 simultaneously in the United States and Canada—it would continue to be protected in India. Protection of works published only in the United States prior to the commencement of the Order appears to be a rather rare and exceptional occurrence, since earlier Orders in Council generally did not provide for such protection. Unpublished works of citizens of a Convention country appear to be protected in India, even if they were created prior to the commencement of the Order in respect to the country of which they are citizens.

PROTECTED WORKS

The following classes of works are protected: (i) original literary, dramatic, musical and artistic works, (ii) cinematograph films, (iii) records.[23]

Literary, Dramatic, Musical and Artistic Works.—Literary works include tables and compilations.[24]

Dramatic works include any piece of recitation, choreographic work or entertainment in dumb show, the scenic arrangement or acting form of which is fixed in writing or otherwise but do not include a cinematograph film.[25]

"Musical work" means any combination of melody or harmony or either of them, printed, reduced to writing or otherwise graphically produced or reproduced.[26]

"Artistic work" means: (i) a painting, a sculpture, a drawing (including a diagram, map, chart or plan), an engraving or a photograph, whether or not any such work possesses artistic quality, (ii) an architectural work of art, (iii) any other work of artistic craftsmanship.[27] A "work of sculpture" includes casts and molds.[28] Engravings include etchings, lithographs, wood-cuts, prints and other similar works, not being photographs.[29] Photographs include photo-lithographs and any work produced by any process analogous to photography, but do not include any part of a cinematograph film.[30]

"Architectural work of art" means any building or structure having an artistic character or design, or any model for such building or structure.[31] In the case of an architectural work of art, copyright subsists only in the artistic character and design and does not extend to processes or methods of construction.[10] Copyright does not subsist in any design: (i) which is registered under the Indian Patents and Designs

[23] Sections 13(1) and 2(y).
[24] Section 2(o).   [25] Section 2(b).   [26] Section 2(p).
[27] Section 2(c).   [28] Section 2(za).   [29] Section 2(i).
[30] Section 2(s).   [31] Section 2(b).

Act, 1911, (ii) which, although capable of registration under that Act, has not been so registered, if any article to which it has been applied has been reproduced more than fifty times by an industrial process by the owner of the copyright or, with his license, by any other person.[32]

Cinematograph Films.—"Cinematograph film" includes the sound track, if any.[33] "Cinematograph" is construed as including any work produced by any process analogous to cinematography.[34] Copyright does not subsist in any cinematograph film if a substantial part of the film is an infringement of the copyright in any other work.[35] Copyright in a cinematograph film does not affect the separate copyright in any work in respect of which, or a substantial part of which, the film is made.[36,37]

Records.—"Record" means any disc, tape, perforated roll or other device in which sounds are embodied so as to be capable of being reproduced therefrom, other than a sound track associated with a cinematograph film.[38] Copyright does not subsist in any record made in respect of a literary, dramatic or musical work if, in making the record, copyright in such work has been infringed.[39] The copyright in a record does not affect the separate copyright in any work in respect of which, or a substantial part of which, the record is made.[40]

PROTECTED PERSONS

Generally.—Subject to certain exceptions, referred to below, the author of a work is the first owner of the copyright in the work.[41] "Author" means in relation to: (i) a literary or dramatic work, the author, (ii) a musical work, the composer, (iii) an artistic work other than a photograph, the artist, (iv) a photograph, the person taking the photograph, (v) a cinematograph film, the owner of the film at the time of its completion, (vi) a record, the owner of the original plate from which the record is made, at the time of the making of the plate.[42] "Plate" includes any matrix or other appliance by which records for the acoustic presentation of the work are or are intended to be made.[43]

The following are exceptions from the general rule:

Works for Newspapers, etc. In the case of a literary, dramatic or artistic work made by the author in the course of his employment by the proprietor of a newspaper, magazine or similar periodical under a contract of service or apprenticeship, for the purpose of publication in a newspaper, magazine or similar periodical, the copyright, in the absence of any agreement to the contrary, is split: (i) the said proprietor

---

[32] Section 13(5).   [33] Section 15.   [34] Section 2(f).   [35] Section 2(f).
[36] Section 13(3) (a).   [37] Section 13(4).   [38] Section 2(w).
[39] Section 13(3) (b).   [40] Section 13 (4).
[41] Section 17.   [42] Section 2(d).   [43] Section 2(t).

is the first owner of the copyright in the work insofar as the copyright relates to the publication of the work in any newspaper, magazine or similar periodical, or to the reproduction of the work for the purpose of its being so published, (ii) in all other respects the author is the first owner of the copyright.[44]

Certain Commissioned Works. Subject to the rule set out in the foregoing paragraph, in the case of a photograph taken, or a painting or portrait drawn, or an engraving or cinematograph film made, for valuable consideration at the instance of any person, such person is, in the absence of any agreement to the contrary, the first owner of the copyright.[45]

Works of Employees. Subject to the rules set out in the two preceding paragraphs, in the case of a work made in the course of the author's employment under a contract of service or apprenticeship, the employer is, in the absence of an agreement to the contrary, the first owner of copyright.[46]

PROTECTED RIGHTS

Economic Rights

Generally.—Copyright means the exclusive right to do, and to authorize the doing of, certain acts.[47]

Literary, Dramatic and Musical Works.—In relation to literary, dramatic and musical works, the following acts require the authorization of the owner of the copyright:

(i) *To reproduce the work in any material form.*[48]
(ii) *To publish the work.*[49]
(iii) *To perform the work in public.*[50] "Performance" includes any mode of visual or acoustic presentation, including any such presentation by the exhibition of a cinematograph film, or by means of radio-diffusion, or by the use of a record, or by any other means and, in relation to a lecture, includes the delivery of such lecture.[51] "Lecture" includes address, speech and sermon.[52] "Radio-diffusion" includes communication to the public by any means of wireless diffusion, whether in the form of sounds, or visual images, or both.[53]

---

[44] Section 17, proviso (a).
[45] Section 17, proviso (b).
[46] Section 17, proviso (c).
[47] Section 14. Works the authors of which are citizens of India may be subject to compulsory licenses if they are withheld from the public (secs. 1(b) and 31).
[48] Section 14(1) (a) (i).   [49] Section 14 (1) (a) (ii).
[50] Section 14(1) (a) (iii).
[51] Section 2(q). "Delivery" in relation to a lecture, includes delivery by means of any mechanical instrument or by radio-diffusion (sec. 2(g)).
[52] Section 2(n).   [53] Section 2(v).

(iv) *To produce, reproduce, perform or publish any translation of the work.*[54] The right of translation may, in certain cases, be subject to compulsory licensing.[55]

(v) *To make any cinematograph film or a record in respect of the work.*[56] The making of records in respect of any literary, dramatic or musical work does not require the authorization, but is merely subject to the payment of a compulsory license fee established by the Copyright Board, if: (a) records recording the work have previously been made by, or with the license or consent of, the owner of the copyright, (b) the person making the records has given the prescribed notice of his intention to make the records.[57]

(vi) *To communicate the work by radio-diffusion. To communicate to the public by a loud speaker or any other similar instrument the radio-diffusion of the work.*[58]

(vii) *To make any adaptation of the work.*[59] "Adaptation" means: (a) in relation to a dramatic work, the conversion of the work into a non-dramatic work, (b) in relation to a literary work, the conversion of the work into a dramatic work by way of performance in public or otherwise, (c) in relation to a literary or dramatic work, any abridgment of the work or any version of the work in which the story or action is conveyed wholly or mainly by means of pictures in a form suitable for reproduction in a book, or in a newspaper, magazine or similar periodical, (d) in relation to a musical work, any arrangement or transcription of the work.[60]

(viii) *To do in relation to a translation or an adaptation of the work any of the acts specified in relation to the work in (i) to (vi), above.*[61]

Artistic Works.—In relation to artistic works, the following acts require the authorization of the owner of the copyright:

(i) *To reproduce the work in any material form.*[62]

(ii) *To publish the work.*[63]

(iii) *To include the work in a cinematograph film.*[64]

(iv) *To make an adaptation of the work.*[65]

(v) *To do, in relation to an adaptation of the work, any of the acts specified in relation to the work in (i) to (iii).*[66]

---

[54] Section 14(1) (a) (iv).   [55] *See* page 377.

[56] Section 14(1) (a) (v). *See* page 374, above, for the definitions of cinematograph film and record.

[57] Section 52(1) (j); Rules, Chapter VII.

[58] Section 14(1) (a) (vi). *See* the definition of radio-diffusion in footnote 7, above.

[59] Section 14(1) (a) (vii).   [60] Section 2(a).

[61] Section 14(1) (a) (viii).   [62] Section 14(1) (b) (i).

[63] Section 14(1) (b) (ii).   [64] Section 14(1) (b) (iii).

[65] Section 14(1) (b) (iv). "'Adaptation' means ... in relation to ... an artistic work, the conversion of the work into a dramatic work by way of performance in public or otherwise" (sec. 2(a) (ii)).

[66] Section 14(1) (b) (v).

Cinematograph Films.—In the case of a cinematograph film, the following acts require the authorization of the owner of the copyright:[67]

(i) *To make a copy of the film.*

(ii) *To cause the film, insofar as it consists of visual images, to be seen in public, and, insofar as it consists of sounds, to be heard in public.*

(iii) *To make any record embodying the recording in any part of the sound track associated with the film by utilizing such sound track.* "Recording" means the aggregate of the sounds embodied in, and capable of being reproduced by means of, a record.[68]

(iv) *To communicate the film by radio-diffusion.*[69]

Records.—In the case of records,[70] the following acts require the authorization of the owner of the copyright.[71]

(i) *To make any other record embodying the same recording.*[72]

(ii) *To cause the recording embodied in the record to be heard in public.*

(iii) *To communicate the recording embodied in the record by radio-diffusion.*

Possible Limitations of the Right of Translation.—The right of translation is protected as an exclusive right of authorization during the entire duration of copyright, i.e., (i) perpetually, if the work is not published, (ii) generally, until the expiration of fifty years from the death of the author if the work is a published work and its first publication took place in a country member of the Berne Copyright Union.[73]

On the other hand, the right of translation may, in certain circumstances, be subject to compulsory licensing in the case of a work: (i) first published in a country party to the Universal Copyright Convention and not a member of the Berne Copyright Union,[74] (ii) of a national of a country party to the Universal Copyright Convention first published in a country other than a country member of the Berne Copyright Union.[75,76]

A compulsory license to produce and publish a translation may be

---

[67] Section 14(1) (c).

[68] Section 2(x). "Record" is defined in section 2(w); *see* page 374, above.

[69] "Radio-diffusion" is defined in section 2(v); *see* footnote 7, above.

[70] "Record" is defined in section 2(w); *see* page 374, above.

[71] Section 14(1) (d). In the case of records, copyright originally vests in the owner of the original plate (sec. 2(t), *see* page 374, above) from which the record is made at the time of the making of the plate (sec. 2(d) (vi)).

[72] "Recording" means the aggregate of the sounds embodied in, and capable of being reproduced by means of, a record (sec. 2(x)).

[73] *See* Order, section 4(a) (i). "Simultaneous" publication is to be considered as first publication (*see* Order, sec. 3(a); Act. secs. 3 and 5).

[74] It would appear that if first publication in such a country is followed, within thirty days, by publication in a country member of the Berne Copyright Union, the right of translation may not be subjected to compulsory licensing.

[75] The statement made in the foregoing footnote equally applies in this case.

[76] Order, section 4(a) (ii).

given only in respect of translation into the following languages: Assamese, Bengali, Gujarati, Hindi, Kannada, Kashmiri, Malayalam, Marathi, Orija, Punjabi, Sanskrit, Tamil, Telegu, Urdin, and only if all the following conditions are met:[77]

(a) a translation in the language to which the application relates: (i) has not been published by, or with the license of, the owner of the copyright, within seven years of the first publication of the work, or, (ii) if a translation has been so published, it has been out of print;

(b) the applicant proves to the satisfaction of the Copyright Board that (i) he had requested and had been denied authorization by the owner of the copyright to produce and publish such translation, or, (ii) he was unable to find the owner of the copyright but had sent a copy of his request for such authorization to the publisher whose name appeared on the work, not less than two months before the application for the license;

(c) the Copyright Board is satisfied that the applicant is competent to produce and publish a correct translation of the work and possesses the means to pay to the owner of the copyright the royalties payable to him for the license;

(d) the author has not withdrawn copies of the work from circulation;

(e) an opportunity of being heard is given, wherever practicable, to the owner of the copyright;

(f) the applicant pays to the owner of the copyright royalties in respect of copies of the translation of the work sold to the public, calculated at the rate established by the Copyright Board.[78]

MORAL RIGHTS

Independently of the author's copyright, and even after the assignment either wholly or partially of the said copyright, the author of a work has the right to claim authorship of the work, as well as the right to restrain or claim damages in respect of: (i) any distortion, mutilation or other modification of the said work, or, (ii) any other action in relation to the said work which would be prejudicial to his honor or reputation.[79]

LIMITATIONS

Fair Dealing.—No fair dealing with a literary, dramatic, musical or artistic work constitutes infringement of copyright for the purposes of: (i) research or private study, (ii) criticism or review, (iii) reporting

---

[77] Order, section 4(a) (ii), and Constitution, Eighth Schedule.
[78] Section 32(4). For the composition of the Copyright Board and procedural details, *see* section 32(1) (2) (3), and Rules, Chapters II and IV.
[79] Section 57(1).

of current events in a newspaper, magazine, similar periodical, radio-diffusion, cinematograph film, or photograph, (iv) judicial proceeding or reporting on such proceeding.[80]

Other Exceptions Concerning Specified Uses of Works are provided in connection with (i) the reading or recitation in public of reasonable extracts from a published literary or dramatic work,[81] (ii) inclusion of works into collections made for educational use, reproduction in examination papers and the like, performance in educational institutions or by certain amateur groups,[82] reporting of current events and the like,[83] (iii) inclusion in a cinematograph work of certain artistic works,[84] (iv) the making or publishing of a painting, drawing, engraving, or photograph of an architectural work of art,[85] or, if situated in a public place, of a sculpture or other work of artistic craftsmanship,[86] (v) the reconstruction of a building,[87] (vi) the playing of a recording in clubs, hotels, etc.[88]

Copies Made for Libraries.—The making of not more than three copies of a book, pamphlet, sheet of music, map, chart or plan, by and for a public library, if such book, etc., is not available for sale in India, does not constitute copyright infringement.[89]

Reproduction of Certain Unpublished Works.—The reproduction, for the purpose of research or private study or with a view to publication, of an unpublished literary, dramatic or musical work kept in a library, museum or other institution to which the public has access, does not constitute copyright infringement, if the identity of the author is not known to the library, etc. If the identity of the author *is* known to the library, etc., reproduction becomes free only after fifty years have elapsed since the date of the death of the author.[90]

Transition from Two-Dimensional Works of Art to Three-Dimensional Objects.—It does not constitute an infringement of copyright to make an object in three dimensions of an artistic work in two dimensions if the object would not appear, to persons who are not expert in relation to such objects, to be a reproduction of the artistic work.[91]

ASSIGNMENT AND LICENSING

Assignments.—Copyright may be assigned in an existing or in a future work. In the latter case, the assignment takes effect only when

[80] Section 52(1) (a) (b) (c).
[81] Section 52(1) (f).   [82] Section 52(1) (g) (h) (i) (1).
[83] Section 52(1) (m) (n).   [84] Section 52(1) (u).
[85] Section 52(1) (s).   [86] Section 52(1) (t).
[87] Section 52(1) (x).   [88] Section 52(1) (r).
[89] Section 52(1) (o).   [90] Section 52(1) (p).   [91] Section 52(1) (w).

the work comes into existence. Copyright may be assigned wholly or partially, generally or subject to limitation, for the whole term of the copyright or only part thereof.[92] Assignments are only valid if they are in writing, signed by the assignor or by his duly authorized agent.[93]

Licenses.—Any interest in the copyright may be granted by license. Licenses must be in writing, signed by the owner of the copyright or by his duly authorized agent. Licenses may be granted in respect of a future work; such licenses take effect only when the work comes into existence.[94]

Bequest of a Manuscript or of an Artistic Work.—Bequest of the manuscript of a literary, dramatic or musical work, or of an artistic work, is deemed to comprise the copyright in the work if the work is unpublished at the time the testator dies. "Manuscript" means the original document embodying the work, whether written by hand or not.[95]

TERM OF COPYRIGHT

Unpublished Works.—Copyright in unpublished works subsists without limitation of time, i.e., perpetually.[96]

Published Literary, Dramatic, Musical and Artistic Works Other than Photographs.—Copyright in literary, dramatic, musical and artistic works (other than photographs) published not anonymously and not pseudonymously within the lifetime of the author subsists until the expiration of the fiftieth calendar year following the year in which the author dies. In the case of a work of joint authorship, the date of the death of the author who dies last is the relevant date.[97]

Copyright in a literary, dramatic or musical work or an engraving which, or an adaptation of which, has not been published before the death of its author, subsists until the expiration of the fiftieth calendar year following the year in which the work (or, if the adaptation was earlier published, the adaptation) was first published.[98] It is important to note that, for the purposes of this rule, "publication" does not mean only the issue of copies of the work to the public in sufficient quantities,[99] but also performance in public of the work and sale (or offer for sale) to the public of records made in respect of the work.[100]

[92] Section 18(1).   [93] Section 19.   [94] Section 30.   [95] Section 20.
[96] For the concept of publication, *see* section 3, discussed on page 371 above. For unpublished manuscripts kept in libraries, etc., *see* section 52(1) (p), discussed on page 379 above.
[97] Section 22. "Work of joint authorship" means a work produced by the collaboration of two or more authors in which the contribution of one author is not distinct from the contribution of the other author or authors (sec. 2(z)).
[98] Section 24(i). Only non-anonymous and non-pseudonymous publication is meant here.
[99] Section 3(a).   [100] Section 24(2).

Copyright in literary, dramatic, musical and artistic works (other than photographs), which are published anonymously or pseudonymously, subsists until the expiration of the fiftieth calendar year following the year in which the first publication of the work took place.[101]

Published Photographs, Cinematograph Films, and Records. —Copyright in published photographs, published cinematograph films, and published records subsists until the expiration of the fiftieth calendar year following the calendar year in which they were first published.[102]

Published Works of Certain International Organizations.— Copyright in the published works of the United Nations Organization, the Specialized Agencies of that Organization, or the Organization of American States subsists until the expiration of the fiftieth calendar year following the calendar year in which they were first published.[103]

Rule of the Shorter Term.—The term of copyright resulting from the above rules of the Act applies only if the term enjoyed by the work in its "country of origin" is not shorter than the term prescribed by the law of India. If the term is shorter in the country of origin, that term, rather than the term of India, applies.[104]

For the purposes of determining which country is the "country of origin" of a given work, the following rules apply: (a) If the work was first published in a Berne Union country (even if also a Universal Convention Country), that country is the country of origin. (b) If the work was first published in a Universal Convention country, that country is the country of origin. (c) If the work was published simultaneously (i.e., within thirty days) in a Berne Union country and a non-Berne Union country, the Berne Union country is the country of origin. (d) If the work was published simultaneously (i.e., within thirty days) in a Universal Convention country and in a non-Berne Union and non-Universal Convention country, the Universal Convention country is the country of origin. (e) If the work was published simultaneously (i.e., within thirty days) in several Berne Union countries, the country whose laws give the shortest term of copyright in the work is the country of origin. (f) If the work was published simultaneously in several

[101] Section 23(i). However, where the identity of the author is disclosed before the expiration of this period, copyright subsists until the expiration of the fiftieth calendar year following the year in which the author dies (sec. 23(1), proviso). For further details, *see* section 23(2) (3).
[102] Sections 25, 26, 27. As to the meaning of "publication," *see* section 3, discussed on page 371 above.
[103] Section 29.
[104] Order, section 4(b). The application of this rule may lead to results at variance with Article IV of the Universal Copyright Convention, since the Convention only allows comparison between categories of works, not between the terms applicable to a given work.

Universal Convention countries, the country whose laws give the shortest term of copyright in the work is the country of origin. (g) If the work is an unpublished work or was first published in a non-Berne Union or a non-Universal Convention country, the country of which the author was a national, or the country in which he was domiciled at the time of making the work or a substantial part thereof or, as the case may be, at the time of first publication thereof, whichever gives the longer term of copyright is the country of origin.[105]

INFRINGEMENTS

Unauthorized Use.—Copyright is infringed by any person who does anything, the exclusive right to do which is conferred upon the owner of the copyright (*see* "Protected Rights," above), (i) without a license granted by the owner of the copyright, or (ii) (in the case of certain compulsory licenses or exceptions) without the license of the Registrar of Copyrights, or (iii) in contravention of the conditions of a license so granted or of any condition imposed by the competent authority.[106]

Permitting Use of Premises When Performance Is Infringing.—Copyright is infringed by any person who permits, for profit, any place to be used for the performance of the work in public where such performance constitutes an infringement, unless he was not aware and had no reasonable grounds to believe that such performance would be an infringement.[107]

Sale, Importation, etc.—Copyright is infringed by any person who: (i) makes for sale or hire, or sells or lets for hire, or by way of trade displays or offers for sale or hire, infringing copies, (ii) distributes infringing copies either for the purpose of trade or to such an extent as to affect prejudicially the owner of the copyright, (iii) by way of trade exhibits in public infringing copies, (iv) imports infringing copies to India, except if the importation is for the private and domestic use of the importer.[108] For the purposes of this rule, the reproduction of a

[105] Order, section 4, Explanations (a) to (f).
[106] Section 51 (a) (i).　　[107] Section 51 (a) (ii).
[108] The following is the form of an application for preventing importation: "The Registrar of Copyrights, Copyright Office, New Delhi—Sir, In accordance with section 53 of the Copyright Act, 1957 (14 of 1957), I hereby state that: (1) I am the owner of the copyright (I am the duly authorised agent of [full name] who is the owner of copyright) in the work specified in the enclosed affidavit and I hereby apply for an order that the copies of the said work as specified in the said affidavit shall not be imported into India. (2) I am also enclosing a copy of the work the copyright in which is being infringed. (3) I produce herewith the following additional evidence in proof of infringement of copyright by the works in respect of which the order is sought: [Give particulars]. (4) The prescribed fee has been paid as per

literary, dramatic, musical or artistic work in the form of cinematograph film is deemed to be an "infringing copy."[109] Furthermore, "infringing copies" are: (a) in relation to a literary, dramatic, musical or artistic work, a reproduction thereof, (b) in relation to a cinematograph film, a copy of the film or a record embodying the recording in any part of the sound track, (c) in relation to a record, any record embodying the same recording.[110]

Civil Remedies.—Depending on the circumstances of the case, the plaintiff may be entitled to damages, an account of profits or injunctions, and may be treated as the owner of the infringing copies (or of the plates used in or intended for making such copies).[111]

details below: [Give particulars]. (5) Communications on this subject may be addressed to: [Give particulars]. Place: .... Date: .... Yours faithfully, [Signature]."

The following is the form of the affidavit which must accompany the application: "I [full name in block letters] of [full address], do hereby on solemn affirmation state that: (1) the particulars in the Statement below are true to the best of my knowledge and belief; (2) the works which are being imported in accordance with the particulars in the said Statement are infringing copies of the work described in the said Statement; and (3) I am interested in the prevention of importation of the said infringing copies for the following reasons: [State reasons]; (4) the infringing copies are not being imported for the private and domestic use of the importer."

The following is the form of the Statement that must be attached to the application: "A. Particulars of the Work and Rights held: (1) Full name, address and nationality of the applicant. (2) Telegraphic address of the applicant. (3) If the applicant is not the owner of the copyright, full name, address and nationality of the owner of the copyright. (4) Description of the Work: (a) Class of the work (Literary, Dramatic, Musical, Artistic, Cinematograph Film, Record). (b) Title of the work. (c) Full name, address and nationality of the author and if the author is deceased, the date of his decease. (d) Language of the work. (e) Name and address of the publisher. [If the work has appeared as a serial or otherwise in a journal or magazine, give the name of the journal or magazine, the volume number of the issue, the date and page reference.] (f) Year of first publication. [If the work has appeared as a serial or otherwise in a journal or magazine, give the name of the journal or magazine, the volume number of the issue, the date and page reference.] (g) Country of first publication. (h) If the copyright in the work is registered under section 45, the Registration Number. B. Details of import of infringing copies: (1) Country of origin of the infringing copies. (2) Name, address and nationality of the importer in India. (3) Name, address and nationality of the maker of the infringing copies. (4) Expected time and place of import of the infringing copies into India. (5) In case a consignment of the infringing copies is detected and detained, will the applicant be prepared to go himself or depute an authorised agent to identify the said copies to the satisfaction of the Registrar of Copyrights. C. Any other relevant information not covered above. Place: .... Date: .... [signature]. Solemnly affirmed before me by [full name of deponent in block letters] who is known to me personally who is identified to me by [name of identifier in block letters] who is known to me personally. Place: .... Date: .... [Signature and seal of the Magistrate]."

The fee accompanying the application is 25 Rupees (Order, First and Third Schedules).

[109] Section 51 (b); Rules, Chapter VIII.
[110] Section 2(m).   [111] Sections 54 through 62.

Criminal Sanctions.—Most infringements, if committed or abetted knowingly, are criminal offenses, punishable with fine, imprisonment, or both.[112] Under certain conditions, the police have the power to seize infringing copies.[113] Any person who knowingly makes, or has in his possession, any plate[114] for the purpose of making infringing copies is punishable with fine, imprisonment, or both.[115,116]

---

[112] Section 63.   [113] Section 64.

[114] "Plate" includes any stereotype or other plate, stone, block, mould, matrix, transfer, negative or other device used or intended to be used for printing or reproducing copies of any work, and any matrix or other appliance by which records for the acoustic presentation of the work are or are intended to be made (sec. 2(t)).

[115] Section 65. The definition of "infringing copy" is the same as given under "Sale, Etc.," above, except that the reproduction of a literary, dramatic, musical or artistic work in the form of a cinematograph film is not considered an infringing copy of such a work (sec. 2(m) (i)).

[116] *See also* sections 66 to 70, as to the question of who is liable where the offense is committed by companies, and other provisions relating to offenses.

IRELAND

SOURCES

Internal Law.—The main source of the law of copyright in Ireland is Part VI, entitled "Copyright," of the Industrial and Commercial Property (Protection) Acts, 1927 to 1958.[1] In the following, it will be referred to as "the Law," and references to Sections, without further specification, are references to Sections of this Law.

Universal Copyright Convention.—Ireland became bound by the Universal Copyright Convention and Protocols 1 and 2 as from January 20, 1959.[2] The application of the Law to works protected under the Universal Copyright Convention is regulated in the Copyright (Foreign Countries) Order 1959, and its amendments.[3] Hereinafter, it is referred to as "the Order."

ACQUISITION OF COPYRIGHT UNDER THE UNIVERSAL COPYRIGHT CONVENTION

Subject to certain exceptions,[4] the Law applies to the following works by virtue of the Universal Copyright Convention or, more exactly, the Order regulating its implementation:[5]

(i) works first published[6] in any of the countries party to the Uni-

---

[1] Date of the Principal Act: May 20, 1927; of the amendatory acts: May 18, 1929; July 13, 1957; July 23, 1958. Official texts published as No. 16 of 1927, No. 13 of 1929, No. 13 of 1957, No. 21 of 1958, of the Public General Acts passed by the Oireachtas. *See also* CLTW, Ireland: Item 1. These Acts still apply to works protected in Ireland under the Universal Copyright Convention although Ireland adopted a new Copyright Law in 1963. However, the effects of the new law have not yet been extended to works protected under the Universal Copyright Convention.

[2] CLTW, Ireland: Item 4.

[3] CLTW, Ireland: Item 4. Ireland is a member of the Berne Copyright Union.

[4] The exceptions concern non-retroactivity (Order, sec. 5), the preservation of acquired rights (Order, sec. 8), and a provision according to which rights in phonograms include the right of public performance only if that right exists in the country (other than Ireland) in which the record was made (Order, sec. 6, *see* page 389 below).

[5] The Order enumerates the countries party to the Universal Copyright Convention. The Order is amended whenever there is a change in membership.

[6] "Publication" means the issue of copies of the work to the public, and does not

versal Copyright Convention (hereinafter referred to as "Convention country"),

(ii) published works the authors of which were, at the time of first publication thereof, subjects or citizens of any Convention country,

(iii) unpublished works the authors of which were, at the time of making of the works,[7] subjects or citizens of any Convention country,

(iv) unpublished works the authors of which were, at the time of making of the works,[8] resident[9] in any Convention country.[10]

There are no copyright formalities in Ireland. Consequently, registration, deposit, or compliance with other formalities is neither required nor possible in Ireland, and the absence, in itself, of a Convention notice on the copies of a published work is no bar to claiming protection in that country. Furthermore, Ireland has no renewal system, so that there is nothing in this country which would correspond to the renewal formalities existing in the United States.

PROTECTED WORKS

The Law provides for the protection of original literary, dramatic, musical, and artistic works. Literary works include maps, charts, tables

include the performance in public of a dramatic or musical work, the delivery in public of a lecture, the exhibition in public of an artistic work, the construction of an architectural work of art, the issue of photographs or engravings of works of sculpture and architectural works of art (sec. 154(3)). A work is not deemed to be published if it is published without the consent or acquiescence of the author, his executors, administrators or assigns (sec. 177(2)). A work is deemed to be first published in a Convention country, notwithstanding that it has been published simultaneously in another country (unless the publication in a Convention country is colourable only and is not intended to satisfy the reasonable requirements of the public), and a work is deemed to be published simultaneously in two countries if the time between publication in one such country and the publication in the other country does not exceed thirty days (sec. 177(3)).

[7] Where the making of the work has extended over a considerable period, the author must have been a subject, citizen or resident of a Convention country for a substantial part of that period (sec. 177(4)).

[8] Residence in a country means being domiciled in that country (sec. 177(5)).

[9] Order, section 4. *See also* Law, section 166(2). Ireland is a member of the Berne Copyright Union. It has ratified the Conventions of Berlin (1908), Rome (1928) and Brussels (1948) (CLTW, Ireland: Item 4). The Order provides for protection of works under the Berne Union Conventions under the same conditions as in the case of the Universal Copyright Convention. Since the nature and extent of the protection is the same in both cases, there is no need to differentiate between works protected under one convention rather than the other.

[10] Artistic works may be registered in the Industrial and Commercial Property Registration Office. The "register of artistic works" constitutes *prima facie* evidence as to the names and addresses of proprietors of the copyright in registered artistic works, and of the registered assignments and transmissions of copyright in such works. *See* section 179.

and compilations.[11] Dramatic works include any piece for recitation, choreographic works, entertainments in dumb show the scenic arrangement or acting form of which is fixed in writing or otherwise, and any cinematographic production. "Cinematograph" includes any work produced by any process analogous to cinematography. Artistic works include works of painting, drawing, sculpture, and artistic craftsmanship; architectural works of art; engravings; photographs. "Work of sculpture" includes casts and moulds. "Architectural work of art" means any building or structure having an artistic character or design, in respect to such character or design, or any model for such building or structure, provided that the protection afforded by the Law is confined to the artistic character and design, and does not extend to processes or methods of construction. "Engravings" include etchings, lithographs, wood-cuts, prints, and other similar works, not being photographs. "Photograph" includes photo-lithograph and any work produced by any process analogous to photography.[12]

Copyright also subsists in records, perforated rolls, and other contrivances by means of which sounds may be mechanically reproduced (hereinafter "phonograms") in like manner as if such contrivances were musical works.[13]

Regarding the protection given to artistic works under the Law, sections 172 (2) provides that the Law shall not apply to works which are capable of being registered under other statutory provisions as industrial designs.

PROTECTED PERSONS

Generally.—Subject to the exceptions stated below, the author of a work is the first owner of copyright in the work.[14]

Certain Works Made on Order.—Where, in the case of an engraving, photograph, or portrait, the plate or other original was ordered by some other person and was made for valuable consideration in pursuance of that order, then, in the absence of an agreement to the contrary, the person by whom such plate or other original was ordered is the first owner of the copyright.[15] "Plate" includes any stereotype or other plate, stone, block, mould, matrix, transfer, or negative used or intended to be used for printing or reproducing copies of any work.[16]

Works of Employees.—Where the author was in the employment of some other person under a contract of service or apprenticeship and the work was made in the course of his employment, the employer is the first owner of copyright, unless there is a different agreement be-

[11] Section 177(1).
[12] Section 177(1).   [13] Section 169(1).
[14] Section 158(1).   [15] Section 158(1).   [16] Section 177(1).

tween the employer and the employee. However, where the work is an article or other contribution to a newspaper, magazine, or similar periodical, it is presumed that the right to restrain the publication of the work, otherwise than as part of a newspaper, magazine, or similar periodical, is reserved to the employee-author.[17]

Phonograms.—Copyright in records, perforated rolls, and other contrivances by means of which sounds may be mechanically reproduced originally vests in the person who was the owner of the original plate from which the contrivance was directly or indirectly derived at the time when such plate was made.[18]

Photographs.—The person who, at the time when the negative from which the photograph was directly or indirectly derived, owns such negative, is deemed to be the author of the work.[19]

ASSIGNMENT AND LICENSING

Generally.—Subject to the limitation set forth below, the owner of the copyright in any work may assign the right either wholly or partially, and either generally or subject to limitation as to place or otherwise, and either for the whole term of the copyright or for any part thereof. Such owner may also grant any interest in his right by license. Assignments and licenses are only valid if they are in writing signed by the owner of the right in respect of which the assignment or grant is made, or by his duly authorized agent.[20]

Reversion of Copyright to the Author's Estate.—Where the author of a work is the first owner of the copyright therein, no assignment of license by him (otherwise than by will) has effect beyond the expiration of 25 years from his death. The reversionary interest in the copyright expectant on the termination of this 25-year period devolves, on the death of the author—and notwithstanding any agreement made by him during his life—, on his legal personal representatives. These provisions do not apply to collective works.[21]

---

[17] Section 158(1). For other presumptions of authorship, *see* section 159(3) (names printed in the copies of works, etc.), and section 167(2) (bequeathed manuscripts).
[18] Section 169(1). Where the owner is a body corporate, it must have established a place of business within a Convention country in order to qualify for protection in Ireland (sec. 169(1), and Order, sec. 4). "Plate" includes any matrix or other appliance by which records, perforated rolls or other contrivances for the acoustic representation of the work are, or are intended to be, made (sec. 177(1)).
[19] Section 171.   [20] Section 158(2).
[21] Section 158(2). "Collective work" means: (i) an encyclopaedia, dictionary, yearbook, or similar work; (ii) a newspaper, review, magazine, or similar periodical; (iii) any work written in distinct parts by different authors, or in which works or parts of works of different authors are incorporated (sec. 177(i)).

PROTECTED RIGHTS

Economic Rights

Generally.—Subject to the exceptions stated below, "copyright" means the sole right: (i) to produce or reproduce the work in any material form whatsoever; (ii) to perform[22] the work in public; (iii) in the case of lectures,[23] to deliver[24] them in public; (iv) to produce, reproduce, perform or publish translations of a work;[25] (v) in the case of a dramatic work, to convert it into a novel or other non-dramatic work; (vi) in the case of a novel or other non-dramatic work, or of an artistic work, to convert it into a dramatic work, by way of performance in public or otherwise; (vii) in the case of a literary, dramatic, or musical work, to make any record, perforated roll, cinematograph film or other contrivance by means of which the work may be mechanically performed or delivered.[26]

Compulsory Licenses for Sound Recording.—Records, perforated rolls and other contrivances by means of which musical works may be mechanically performed (hereinafter "phonograms") may be made in Ireland without the consent of the owner of the copyright in the musical work if phonograms have previously been made by, or with the consent or acquiescence of, such owner. The making of phonograms under "compulsory license" is subject to the payment of a royalty the amount of which is, generally speaking, five per cent of the ordinary retail price of the phonogram.[27]

Performance Rights of Producers of Sound Recordings.—If the owner of the copyright (generally, the producing company) in a sound recording does not have an establishment in Ireland, it enjoys the right of public performance in its records only if the Convention country in which the recording was made grants itself such a right.[28]

Limitations

The Law provides that certain acts, normally subject to the authorization of the owner of the copyright, may be performed without such

[22] "Performance" means any acoustic representation of a work and any visual representation of any dramatic action in a work, including such a representation made by means of any mechanical instrument (sec. 177(1)).
[23] "Lecture" includes address, speech, and sermon (sec. 177(1)).
[24] "Delivery" in relation to a lecture includes delivery by means of any mechanical instrument (sec. 177(1)). However, addresses of a political nature delivered at a public meeting may be freely reported on in newspapers (sec. 170).
[25] Prior to the Amendatory Act of 1958, the author's right of translation into the Irish language was subject to certain limitations; these limitations were removed by this Act with, generally, retrospective effect.
[26] Section 154(2).
[27] Section 169(2); for further details and qualifications *see* sec. 169(2) to (8).
[28] Order, section 6.

authorization. Among such acts are: (i) fair dealing with the work for the purposes of private study, research, criticism, review, or newspaper summary; (ii) publishing of pictures of certain three-dimensional works of art when they are permanently situated in a public place; (iii) certain uses in schools; (iv) certain uses in newspapers of lectures publicly delivered.[29]

TERM OF PROTECTION

Generally.—Subject to the exceptions stated below, copyright subsists for the life of the author and fifty years from the first day of January next after his death.[30] In the case of works of joint authorship, the 50 years start running from the date of the death of the co-author who dies last.[31] In the case of a literary, dramatic, or musical work, or an engraving, in which copyright subsists at the date of the death of the author, but which has not been published (nor, in the case of a dramatic or musical work, been performed in public; nor, in the case of a lecture, been delivered in public) before the date of the author's death, copyright subsists until publication, performance, or delivery, whichever happens first, and for a term of 50 years thereafter.[32]

Sound Recordings.—Copyright in records, perforated rolls, and other contrivances by means of which sounds may be mechanically reproduced subsists for 50 years from the making of the original plate from which the contrivance was directly or indirectly derived.[33]

Photographs.—Copyright in photographs subsists for 50 years from the making of the original negative from which the photograph was directly or indirectly derived.[34]

Rule of the Shorter Term.—Since there is no provision in the Law for the "rule of the shorter term" permitted under Article IV, paragraph (4), of the Universal Copyright Convention, works are protected in Ireland until the expiration of the terms indicated above even if in other countries such works fall into the public domain at an earlier date.

INFRINGEMENTS

Generally.—Subject to the exceptions stated elsewhere,[35] copyright is deemed to be infringed by any person who, without the consent of

[29] Section 155(1) (i) to (vii).
[30] Amendatory Act of 1957, section 9.
[31] Section 166(1). "Work of joint authorship" means a work produced by the collaboration of two or more authors in which the contribution of one author is not distinct from the contribution of the other author or authors (sec. 166(3)).
[32] Section 167(1).   [33] Section 169(1).   [34] Section 171.
[35] Pages 389, above and 391, below.

the owner of the copyright, does anything the sole right to do which is conferred on the owner of the copyright.[36] Furthermore, copyright in a work is deemed to be infringed by any person who does any of the following acts in relation to copies of a work which infringe copyright, or would infringe copyright if they had been made in Ireland: (i) sells or lets for hire, or by way of trade exposes or offers for sale or hire; (ii) distributes either for the purposes of trade or to such an extent as to affect prejudicially the owner of the copyright; (iii) by way of trade exhibits in public; (iv) imports for sale or hire into Ireland.[37] Infringement is also committed by any person who permits a theatre, hall, room, or other place to be used for the public performance for profit of a work without the consent of the owner of the copyright, unless such person was not aware and had no reasonable grounds for suspecting that the performance would be an infringement of copyright.[38]

Civil Remedies.—The injured party is generally entitled to all remedies by way of injunction, damages, accounts, and otherwise, as are conferred by law for the infringement of a right.[39] Infringing copies and plates may be handed over to the injured party.[40] Injunction is the only available remedy where the defendant proves that at the date of the infringement he was not aware and had no reasonable ground for suspecting that copyright subsisted in the work.[41] The limit of time for commencing civil actions is three years from the date of the infringement.[42]

Penal Sanctions.—Most of the infringing acts, if committed knowingly, constitute offences and are punished by fine or imprisonment.[43]

Importation of Infringing Copies.—Copies made outside of Ireland of any work in which copyright subsists which if made in Ireland would infringe copyright, may be prohibited by the Customs authorities on the request of the copyright owner who must indemnify the authorities against possible expense or damages.[44]

Seizure.—Under certain circumstances, seizure of allegedly infringing copies of musical works may be ordered.[45]

---

[36] Section 155(1).   [37] Section 155(2).
[38] Section 155(4). *See also* section 155(3).
[39] Section 159(1).   [40] Section 160.   [41] Section 161.
[42] Section 163.
[43] Sections 155(5) and 164. *See also* sections 184, 185, 186.
[44] Section 165.   [45] Sections 182 and 183.

ISRAEL

SOURCES

Internal Law.—The main source of the law of copyright in Israel is the United Kingdom Copyright Act, 1911,[1] as extended to Palestine in 1924,[2] amended by the Israeli Copyright Ordinance Law of 1953.[3] The 1911 Act and the 1953 Ordinance Law are hereinafter referred to as "the Act" and "the Ordinance," respectively. References to Sections without further specification are references to Sections of the Act. References to Sections of the Ordinance Law are preceded by the word "Ordinance."

Universal Copyright Convention.—Israel is bound by the Universal Copyright Convention and Protocols 1 and 2 as from September 16, 1955. The Copyright (International Convention) Order, 1955, implements certain provisions of the Convention in Israel (hereinafter referred to as "the U.C.C. Order").[4,5,6]

[1] Act of December 16, 1911; 1 & 2 Geo. 5, c. 46. See text in CLTW, Australia: Item 1, The Schedule.
[2] The Copyright Act, 1911 (Extension to Palestine) Order 1924, dated March 21, 1924, published in "Statutory Rules and Orders" of the United Kingdom, 1924, No. 385; and the Copyright Ordinance of the High Commissioner for Palestine, dated June 15, 1924, published in "The Laws of Palestine in force on the 31st December 1933," Revised Edition, 1934, p. 389. See both in CLTW, Israel: Item 1.
[3] The Copyright Ordinance (Amendment) Law, dated February 2, 1953, published in "Sefer Ha-Chukkim," No. 118, February 12, 1953, page 38 (CLTW, Israel: Item 1). See also the Prescription Law, 1958, dated March 27, 1958, published in "Sefer Ha-Chukkim," No. 251, April 6, 1958 (CLTW, Israel: Item 1).
[4] Dated August 21, 1955, published in "Kovetz Ha-Takkanot," No. 542, August 25, 1955, p. 1342 (CLTW, Israel: Item 2).
[5] Israel is a member of the Berne Copyright Union and is bound by the Rome (1928) and Brussels (1948) Conventions. See the Copyright (Berne Convention) Order, 1953, of March 4, 1953, published in "Kovetz Ha-Takkanot," No. 384, March 19, 1953, p. 818 (CLTW, Israel: Item 3); hereinafter referred to as "the Berne Convention Order."
[6] The Copyright (United States) Order, 1953, dated June 3, 1953, published in "Kovetz Ha-Takkanot," No. 365, June 11, 1953, p. 117 (CLTW, Israel: Item 4) provides that "(1) A work first published in the United States of America shall be protected in Israel as though it had been first published in Israel. (2) An unpublished work of an author who at the date of making of the work was a citizen of the United States of America shall be protected as though its author were an Israel national. (3) This Order shall have effect retroactively as from the 5th Iyar, 5708 (14th May, 1958)." This Order contains no provision on the rule of the shorter term. The Universal Copyright Convention Order does. If a work comes under both Orders,

ACQUISITION OF PROTECTION UNDER THE
UNIVERSAL COPYRIGHT CONVENTION

Unless the work is protected by the Berne Conventions, Israel protects the following categories of works under the Universal Copyright Convention: (i) *published* works of an author "who is a citizen or national of one of the member countries" of the Universal Copyright Convention, and works "first published in such a country," and (ii) *unpublished* works of an author "who at the date of making thereof was a citizen or national of one of the member countries" of the Universal Copyright Convention.[7] Although Israel has also ratified Protocols 1 and 2, the U.C.C. Order refers neither to the works of certain refugees and stateless persons, nor to the works of certain international organizations. Because of the incompleteness of the U.C.C. Order on this point, it is uncertain whether works falling into these categories are protected in Israel.

Works protected under the Berne Conventions are: (i) works first published in a country member of the Berne Union, and (ii) unpublished works the author of which was at the time of making the work a subject or national of a country member of the Berne Union.[8]

Whether a given work is protected in Israel under the Berne Conventions rather than the Universal Copyright Convention is a question which requires determination in connection with the application of the rule of the shorter term since this rule is not the same in the Berne and the U.C.C. Orders.[9]

"Publication" means the issue of copies of the work to the public and does not include the performance in public of a dramatic or musical work, the delivery in public of a lecture, the exhibition in public of an artistic work, the construction of an architectural work of art, or the issue of photographs and engravings of works of sculpture and architectural works of art.[10]

There are no copyright formalities in Israel. Consequently, registration, deposit, or compliance with other formalities is neither required nor possible in Israel, and the absence, in itself, of a Convention notice

it is uncertain whether the rule of the shorter term will apply or not. The U.C.C. Order is more recent than this Order, but this Order is a special measure (it deals with only one country, the United States) whereas the U.C.C. Order is a general measure (it deals with all U.C.C. countries). The question is which of the two principles, *lex posterior derogat priori* or *lex specialis derogat generali*, applies.

[7] U.C.C. Order, sections 2 and 3. Where, in the case of an unpublished work, the making of the work has extended over a considerable period, nationality or residence in a Convention country during any substantial part of that period suffices to bring the work under the provision. *See* section 35(4).

[8] Berne Convention Order, sections 2 and 3.

[9] Berne Convention Order, sections 1 and 4(1); U.C.C. Order, sections 4 and 5. The question is discussed on page 397, below.

[10] Section 1(3).

on the copies of a published work is no bar to claiming protection in that country. Furthermore, Israel has no renewal system, so that there is nothing in this country which would correspond to the renewal formalities existing in the United States.

PROTECTED WORKS

The Act does not contain a definition or formal enumeration of protected works but it does refer, *expressis verbis*, to literary, dramatic, musical and artistic works;[11] lectures, novels, other non-dramatic works;[12] records, perforated rolls, and other contrivances by means of which sounds may be mechanically reproduced (hereinafter sometimes referred to as "sound recordings");[13] and photographs.[14]

"Literary work" includes maps, charts, plans, tables, and compilations. "Dramatic work" includes (i) any piece for recitation, choreographic work or entertainment in dumb show, the scenic arrangement or acting form of which is fixed in writing or otherwise, and (ii) any cinematograph production where the arrangement of acting form or the combination of incidents represented give the work an original character. "Artistic work" includes (i) works of painting, drawing, sculpture and artistic craftsmanship, (ii) architectural works of art, (iii) engravings, and (iv) photographs. "Works of sculpture" include casts and moulds. "Architectural work of art" means any building or structure having an artistic character or design, in respect of such character or design, or any model for such building or structure, provided that the protection afforded by copyright is confined to the artistic character and design, and does not extend to processes or methods of construction. "Engravings" include etchings, lithographs, woodcuts, prints, and other similar works, not being photographs. "Photograph" includes photo-lithograph and any work produced by any process analogous to photography. "Cinematograph" includes any work produced by any process analogous to cinematography.[15]

Designs.—The Act does not apply to designs capable of being registered under the Patents and Designs Statutes, except designs which, although capable of being so registered, are not used or intended to be used as models or patterns to be multiplied by any industrial process.[16]

PROTECTED PERSONS

Subject to the exceptions stated below, the first owner of the copyright in a work is the author of the work.[17]

[11] Section 1(2).   [12] Section 1(2).   [13] Section 19(1).   [14] Section 21.
[15] Section 35(1).   [16] Section 22(1).   [17] Section 5(1).

Engravings, Photographs and Portraits Made on Order.—
Where, in the case of an engraving, photograph, or portrait, the plate
or other original was ordered by some other person and was made for
valuable consideration in pursuance of that order, then, in the absence
of any agreement to the contrary, the person by whom such plate or
other original was ordered is the first owner of the copyright.[18] "Plate"
includes any stereotype or other plate, stone, block, mould, matrix,
transfer, or negative used or intended to be used for printing or reproducing copies of any work.[19]

Works of Employees.—Where the author was in the employment
of some other person under a contract of service or apprenticeship and
the work was made in the course of his employment by that person, the
employer is—in the absence of any agreement to the contrary—the
first owner of copyright; but where the work is an article or other
contribution to a newspaper, magazine, or similar periodical, the right
of publication otherwise than as part of a newspaper, etc., is presumed
to belong to the author-employee.[20]

Sound Recordings.—The first owner of copyright in records,
perforated rolls, and other contrivances by means of which sounds may
be mechanically reproduced, is the person who, at the time it is made,
is the owner of the original plate from which such contrivances are
directly or indirectly derived.[21] "Plate" includes any matrix or other
appliance by which records, perforated rolls or other contrivances for
the acoustic representation of the work are or are intended to be made.[22]

Photographs.—The first owner of copyright in a photograph is the
person who, at the time the negative (from which the photograph was
directly or indirectly derived) was made, owned such negative.[23]

ASSIGNMENT AND LICENSING

The owner of the copyright in any work may assign the right (i) either
wholly or partially, (ii) either generally or subject to limitations in
Israel, (iii) either for the whole term of the copyright or any part
thereof. He may grant any interest in the right by license. Assignments
and licenses are valid only if they are in writing, signed by the owner of
the right in respect of which the assignment or grant is made, or by his
duly authorized agent.[24]

Where, under any partial assignment of copyright, the assignee
becomes entitled to a given right, the assignee is treated as the owner of
the copyright as far as the said given right is concerned.[25]

[18] Section 5(1), proviso (a).   [19] Section 35(1).   [20] Section 5(1), proviso (b).
[21] Section 19(1).   [22] Section 35(1).   [23] Section 21.
[24] Section 5(2).   [25] Section 5(3).

PROTECTED RIGHTS

Economic Rights

Generally.—Subject to the exceptions stated below, "copyright" means the sole right: (i) to publish the work if it is an unpublished work; (ii) to produce or reproduce the work in any material form whatsoever; (iii) to perform[27] the work in public; (iv) in the case of lectures,[28] to deliver[29] them in public; (v) to produce, reproduce, perform or publish a translation of a work; (vi) in the case of a novel or other non-dramatic work, or of an artistic work, to convert it into a dramatic work, by way of performance in public or otherwise; (vii) in the case of a dramatic work, to convert it into a novel or other non-dramatic work; (viii) in the case of a literary, dramatic, or musical work, to make any record, perforated roll, cinematograph film or other contrivance by means of which the work may be mechanically performed or delivered.[30]

Compulsory Licenses for Sound Recordings.—Records, perforated rolls and other contrivances by means of which musical works may be mechanically performed (hereinafter referred to as "sound recordings") may be made without the consent of the owner of the copyright in the musical work if sound recordings have previously been made by, or with the consent or acquiescence of, such owner. The making of sound recordings under "compulsory license" is subject to the payment of a royalty, the amount of which, generally speaking, is five per cent of the ordinary retail price of the sound recording.[31]

Limitations

The Act provides that certain acts, normally subject to the authorization of the owner of the copyright, may be performed without such authorization. Among such acts are: (i) fair dealing with the work for purposes of private study, research, criticism, or newspaper summary; (ii) publishing of pictures of certain three-dimensional works of art when they are permanently situated in a public place; (iii) certain uses in schools; (iv) certain uses in newspapers or lectures publicly delivered; (v) public reading or recitation of reasonable extracts from a published work.[32]

---

[27] "Performance" means any acoustic representation of a work and any visual representation of any dramatic action in a work, including such a representation made by means of any mechanical instrument (sec. 35(1)).

[28] "Lecture" includes address, speech, and sermon (sec. 35(1)).

[29] "Delivery" in relation to a lecture, includes delivery by means of any mechanical instrument (sec. 35(1)).

[30] Section 1(2).

[31] Section 19(2); for further details and qualifications, *see* section 19(2) to (8).

[32] Section 2(1) (i) to (vi) and section 20.

TERM OF PROTECTION

Generally.—Subject to the exceptions stated below, copyright subsists until the end of the fiftieth calendar year counted from the first day of January following the date of the death of the author.[33] In the case of a work of joint authorship, the date of the death of the last surviving co-author governs.[34] Copyright in anonymous and pseudonymous works subsists until the expiration of the fiftieth calendar year counted from the first day of January following the publication of the work; if, however, the identity is disclosed during this period, or if the pseudonym leaves no doubt as to the author's identity, copyright subsists until the end of the fiftieth calendar year counted from the first day of January following the date of the author's death.[35]

Sound Recordings.—Copyright in records, perforated rolls, and other contrivances by means of which sounds may be mechanically reproduced subsists for fifty years from the making of the original plate from which the contrivance was directly or indirectly derived.[36]

Photographs.—Copyright in photographs subsists for fifty years from the making of the original negative from which the photograph was directly or indirectly derived.[37]

Rule of the Shorter Term.—In the case of works protected under the Universal Copyright Convention alone (i.e., *not* protected under the Conventions of the Berne Union)[38] the periods of protection which would result from the application of the above rules are limited: (i) in the case of a published work, to the period of protection fixed for a work of the same class in the country of first publication,[39] (ii) in the case of

[33] Section 3; Ordinance, section 5(3).
[34] Ordinance, section 5(2). A "work of joint authorship" means a work produced by the collaboration of two or more authors in which the contribution of one author is not distinct from the contribution of the other author or authors (sec. 16(3)).
[35] Ordinance, section 5(1) and (3).
[36] Section 19(1).   [37] Section 21.
[38] As to the question of which are the works protected under the Universal Copyright Convention, see U.C.C. Order, sections 2, 3, and 6, discussed on page 393, above. Works protected under the Conventions of the Berne Union are (i) works first published in a country of the Berne Union, (ii) unpublished works the author of which was at the time of the making of the work a subject or national of a country of the Berne Union (Berne Convention Order, secs. 2 and 3). In the case of works protected under the Conventions of the Berne Union, there is no provision for the rule of the shorter term in Israel except for cinematographic and photographic works, and works of applied art: the term of protection in the case of such works does not exceed the term fixed for them in their country of origin (Berne Convention Order, sec. 4(1)). "Country of origin" has the meaning assigned to it in Article 4 of the Berne Convention (Berne Convention Order, sec. 1).
[39] For the purpose of determining the country of publication: (i) a work of an author who is a citizen or national of a Convention country, and which was first published in a country not party to the Convention, is deemed to have been first

an unpublished work, to the period of protection granted in the country of which the author is a citizen or national.[40]

INFRINGEMENTS

Generally.—Subject to the exceptions stated elsewhere,[41] copyright is deemed to be infringed by any person who, without the consent of the owner of the copyright, does anything the sole right to do which is conferred on the owner of the copyright.[42] Furthermore, copyright in a work is deemed to be infringed by any person who does any of the following acts in relation to a work which, to his knowledge, infringes copyright, or would infringe copyright if it had been done in Israel: (i) sells or lets for hire, or by way of trade exposes or offers for sale or hire; (ii) distributes either for the purposes of trade or to such an extent as to affect prejudicially the owner of the copyright; (ii) by way of trade exhibits in public; (iv) imports for sale or hire into Israel.[43] Infringement is also committed by any person who, for his private profit, permits a theatre or other place of entertainment to be used for the performance in public of the work without the consent of the owner of the copyright, unless he was not aware, and had no reasonable ground for suspecting, that the performance would be an infringement of copyright.[44]

Civil Remedies.—The injured party is generally entitled to all remedies by way of injunction, interdict, damages, accounts, and otherwise, as are conferred by law for the infringement of a right.[45] Infringing copies and plates may be handed over to the injured party.[46] Injunctions and interdict are the only remedies where the defendant proves that, at the date of the infringement, he was not aware, and had no reasonable ground for suspecting, that copyright subsisted in the work.[47]

Penal Sanctions.—Most of the infringing acts, if committed knowingly, constitute offenses and are punishable by fine or imprisonment.[48]

published in the country of which the author is a citizen or national, (ii) a work published simultaneously in two or more Convention countries is deemed to have been first published in that of the said countries the laws of which grant to that work the shortest period of protection (U.C.C. Order, sec. 5). A work which has been published in several countries within thirty days of its first publication is considered as having been published simultaneously in all such several countries (Ordinance, sec. 7(1)). A work which has been published simultaneously in Israel and in other countries is considered as having been first published in Israel, unless the publication in Israel was colourable only (Ordinance, sec. 7(2)).

[40] U.C.C. Order, section 4.
[41] Page 396, above.
[42] Section 2(1).   [43] Section 2(2).   [44] Section 2(3).
[45] Section 6(1).   [46] Section 7.
[47] Section 8. *See also* section 9.
[48] Sections 11 to 13; Ordinance, section 3.

Importation of Infringing Copies.—Importation into Israel of copies made outside of Israel may be prevented where the copies, if made in Israel, would infringe copyright.[49]

Statute of Limitations.—The period of prescription is seven years.[50]

---

[49] Sections 14 and 35(1); Ordinance, section 2.
[50] Prescription Law, 1958, dated March 25, 1958, published in "Sefer Ha-Chukkim," No. 251, November 6, 1958; section 26 (5).

ITALY

SOURCES

Internal Laws.—The main source is the Law No. 633 of April 22, 1941, on the protection of copyright "and other rights connected with the exercise thereof." This Law was amended by Decree-Law No. 82 of August 23, 1946.[1] Hereinafter, it is referred to as "the Law," and references to Articles, without further specification, are references to the Articles of this Law, as amended.

Regulations implementing certain provisions of the Law were promulgated by Decree No. 1369 of May 18, 1942.[2] Hereinafter, they are referred to as "the Regulations."

Universal Copyright Convention.—Italy became bound by the Universal Copyright Convention and its Protocol 2 as from January 24, 1957.[3] Law No. 923 of July 19, 1956,[4] provides for full and complete enforcement of the Convention and Protocol, and the application of the rule of the shorter term discussed under "Term of Protection," below.[5,6]

[1] "Gazzetta Ufficiale" of July 16, 1944, and September 12, 1946; English translation in CLTW, Italy: Item 1.

[2] "Gazzetta Ufficiale" of December 3, 1942; English translation in CLTW, Italy: Item 2. The best known commentaries are: "Codice del diritto di autore," by Eduardo Piola Caselli, published at Turin by the Unione Tipografico Editrice Torinese in 1943: "Il diritto di autore," by Amadeo Giannini, published by "La Nuova Italia," at Florence in 1942; "Il diritto di autore," by Ettore Valerio and Zara Algardi, published by Giuffré at Milan in 1943. These were written shortly after the promulgation of the 1941 Law. The evolution since that time, including the judicial interpretation of the Law, is fully covered in the excellent "Lettres d'Italie," of Valerio De Sanctis, published in *Le Droit d'auteur*: 1943, p. 97; 1944, p. 62; 1945, p. 122; 1946, p. 65; 1947, pp. 14, 125, 143; 1949, p. 43; 1951, p. 41; 1953, p. 51; 1954, pp. 173, 193; 1955, pp. 104, 124; 1956, pp. 127, 138; 1957, p. 164; 1958, p. 186; 1959, p. 161; 1960, p. 250; 1961, p. 221; 1962, p. 270; 1964, p. 43; 1966, p. 82.

[3] CLTW, Italy: Item 3B.

[4] "Gazzetta Ufficiale" of August 23, 1956; English translation in CLTW, Italy: Item 3B.

[5] Page 413.

[6] Italy is a member of the Berne Copyright Union from its foundation and has ratified all its Conventions, the latest being the Brussels Convention of 1948 (see CLTW, Italy: Item 4). Italy acceded to the Montevideo Copyright Convention of 1889 and established copyright relations under it with Argentina and Paraguay (CLTW, Italy: Item 5); however, since Argentina is also party to the Universal Copyright Convention, the Montevideo Convention is now of little, if any, significance between Italy and Argentina. Italy concluded bilateral treaties with Spain in 1880, France in 1884, and Portugal in 1906 (CLTW, Italy: Items 6, 7, and 11),

ACQUISITION OF PROTECTION UNDER THE
UNIVERSAL COPYRIGHT CONVENTION

The Law provides that the international conventions for the protection of intellectual works govern the field of application of the Law in the case of works of foreign authors.[7] The Law on the ratification of the Universal Copyright Convention provides for the full and complete enforcement of that Convention.[8] Consequently, the Universal Copyright Convention itself determines what works[9] are protected in Italy thereunder. The matter is dealt with in detail in connection with Articles II and XVII of the Universal Copyright Convention and its Protocol 2.[10]

Subject to the possible exception stated in the next paragraph, Italy would thus protect the following works under the Universal Copyright Convention: (i) published works of nationals of a Convention country, irrespective of the place of first publication, (ii) works first published in a Convention country, irrespective of the nationality of the author, (iii) unpublished works of nationals of a Convention country other than Italy, (iv) works first published by the United Nations, by any of the Specialized Agencies of the United Nations, or by the Organization of American States, as well as unpublished works of any of these Organizations.

If a work belongs to any of these four categories but has, within the meaning of the Conventions of the Berne Union, a Union country as country of origin, then such work is protected, in Italy, by virtue of the applicable Convention of the Berne Union, rather than by virtue of the

and there are provisions on copyright in treaties of friendship concluded with Nicaragua in 1906, Greece in 1948, and Lebanon in 1949 (CLTW, Italy: Items 10, 14 and 15); these treaties and treaty provisions, however, do not seem to be of much practical significance since the adherence of the co-contracting countries to the Berne or Universal Copyright Conventions. There is a most-favored-nation provision in respect of literary and artistic property in a treaty concluded with Cuba in 1903 (CLTW, Italy: Item 9). Exchanges of notes with the United States of America effected in 1893 and 1915 (CLTW, Italy: Items 8 and 12) seem to be of limited significance since the two countries are now bound by the Universal Copyright Convention.

[7] Article 186(1); *see* also articles 185(3), 189(1).

[8] Law No. 923 of 1956, article 2.

[9] In the system of the Italian Copyright Law, photographic pictures are not "works." They are called photographs. Their makers are not called "authors," and the rights in them are not copyrights. Since the Universal Copyright Convention uses the expression "photographic works," it is somewhat uncertain whether protection can be claimed in Italy for photographic pictures *under the Universal Copyright Convention*. Subject to this general *caveat*, hereinafter it is assumed that such protection under the Universal Copyright Convention *can* be claimed in Italy, since the object is, at least to a great extent, the same, whether called photograph or photographic work.

[10] Page 50, above.

Universal Copyright Convention. Works having a Union country as country of origin are, roughly stated, (i) unpublished works whose author is a national (*ressortissant*) of a Union country, (ii) published works which were first published in a Union country or which, within 30 days of their first publication in a non-Union country, were also published in a Union country ("simultaneous publication"). It would seem, however, that it is only in connection with the rule of the shorter term that it might be necessary to decide whether a work belonging to any of the four categories set out in the preceding paragraph is a work to which one of the Conventions of the Berne Union applies: in all other respects the protection that Italy grants under the Berne and Universal Conventions appears to be the same.

Copyright is acquired by creation of a work resulting from an intellectual effort, and is not subject to the fulfilment of any formality in Italy.[11] Works may be registered in a register kept in the *Ufficio della proprietà letteraria, artistica e scientifica* (an office of the Presidence of the Council (Cabinet)), but lack of registration does not affect the copyright protection.[12] Assignments and other transactions may be recorded in the same Office.[13] The absence of the Convention notice on the copies of a published work is no bar to claiming protection in Italy.[14] Furthermore, Italy has no copyright renewal system, so there is nothing in this country which would correspond to the renewal formalities existing, for example, in the United States.

PROTECTED SUBJECT MATTER

Works Proper.—The Law protects intellectual works (*opere dell'ingegno*) having a creative character in the fields of literature, music, graphic arts (*arti figurative*), architecture, the theatre and cinematography, whatever their mode or form of expression.[15] The Law mentions the following examples: (i) literary, dramatic, scientific, didactic and religious works, whether written or oral, (ii) musical works and compo-

[11] Article 6. However, articles of current interest of an economic, political or religious character, published in magazines or newspapers, may be freely reproduced in other magazines or newspapers, or in news broadcasts, unless such reproduction is expressly reserved; the source must be acknowledged in such reproduction (art. 62; Regulations, art. 7). Sound recordings sold in commerce must indicate the title of the work, the name of the author, the name of the performers, and the date of manufacture; omission of these indications does not affect the copyright in the recorded work (art. 62). As to photographs, see page 403, below.
[12] Article 103; Regulations, articles 30 to 43. Registration of cinematographic works is effected in the *Società Italiana Autori Editori* (*see* art. 103). In respect of certain photographs, however, *see* p. 403, below.
[13] Article 104; Regulations, articles 30 to 43.
[14] Except, to a certain extent, in the case of photographs; *see* p. 403, below.
[15] Article 1.

sitions, with or without words, dramatico-musical works, and musical variations if, in themselves, they are original works, (iii) choreographic works and pantomimes, the acting form (*la traccia*) of which is fixed in writing or otherwise, (iv) works of sculpture, painting, of the art of drawing, engraving (*incisione*) and similar graphic (*figurativi*) arts, including scenic art (*scenografia*), even when such works are applied to an industrial product if their artistic value is distinguishable (*scindibile*) from the industrial character of the product with which they are associated, (v) architectural plans and works, (vi) works of cinemato-graphic art, whether silent or sound, provided that they are not mere documentaries.[16]

Collective works (*opere collettive*), such as encyclopaedias, dictionaries, anthologies, magazines, and newspapers, are protected as original works, independently of and without prejudice to any copyright sub-sisting in the constituent works or parts of works.[17]

"Elaborations"[18] of a work, if they are of a creative character, are protected as original works but without prejudice to the copyright in the basic work. Examples of elaborations are: translations, conversions (*trasformazioni*) into another literary or artistic form, modifications and additions constituting a substantial recasting of the basic work, adaptations, reductions, abridgments and, unless they are original works in themselves, variations.[19]

Photographs.—Photographs are not considered as "works" by the Law and special provisions apply to them.[20] They will be summarized here. In other parts of the present analysis of the Law of Italy, it should be understood that whatever is said in connection with "works" does not apply to photographs, unless expressly stated.

Photographs (*fotografie*) are pictures of persons, or of aspects, elements or features of the life of nature or society, obtained by photographic or analogous processes. They include reproductions of works of the graphic arts and stills (*fotogrammi*) of cinematographic films. Copies of writings, documents, business papers, material objects, technical drawings and similar products are not "photographs," even if obtained by photo-graphic or analogous processes.[21]

Although acquisition of the rights in photographs is not subject to any formality, providing all copies of the photograph with certain indications is a practical necessity if protection is desired, since un-authorized reproduction is deemed lawful (unless the photographer can prove bad faith on the part of the reproducer) whenever the copies of the photograph do not contain the prescribed indications.[22] These

[16] Article 2.   [17] Article 3.
[18] *Elaborazioni*," i.e., elaborations, developments, transformations, adaptations.
[19] Article 4.
[20] Title II, Chapter V, of the Law.
[21] Article 87.   [22] Article 90, second paragraph.

indications differ somewhat from the elements of the Convention notice. The Law calls for the name of the photographer (or of his employer, or of the person who has commissioned the photograph), the year of production of the photograph, and (if the photograph reproduces a work of art) the name of the author of the work of art which has been photographed.[23] It does not call for the symbol ©, and the date it calls for is not that of the first publication. There is no provision in the Italian Law reconciling these provisions with the requirements of Article III of the Universal Copyright Convention. The Convention notice *should*, it is believed, be considered by Italy as satisfying the requirements of Article 90 of the Law; whether, in fact, Italian courts *would* so hold, is an open question, since the issue has not yet come before them.

The rights in a photograph originally vest in the photographer[24] except (i) if produced in the course of the execution of a contract of employment (*contratto di lavoro*) or work (*contratto di lavoro*), (ii) if produced pursuant to a commission, and the photograph reproduces objects which are in the possession of the person giving the commission. In case (i), the rights belong to the employer (*datore di lavoro*); in case (ii), they belong to the person commissioning the photograph.[25] In the latter case, however, an equitable remuneration must be paid to the photographer whenever the photograph is used commercially.[26]

The rights in a photograph are the exclusive rights of reproduction, distribution (*diffusione*) and circulation (*spaccio*).[27] They are subject to certain limitations in the case of portraits,[28] and the exclusive right of authorization is replaced by a right to equitable remuneration when reproduction is made (i) in anthologies destined for school use, or in other scientific or educational works;[29] (ii) of photographs concerning persons or events "in the news" (*di attualità*) or otherwise of public interest, published in newspapers or other periodicals.[30] Reproductions must indicate the source.[31]

In the absence of agreement to the contrary, the transfer (*cessione*) of the negative (or other similar thing destined for the production of copies) involves the transfer of the rights in the photograph if such rights belong to the transferor.[32]

[23] Article 90, first paragraph.
[24] Article 88, first paragraph. If the photograph is a reproduction of a work of the graphic arts, the rights in the photograph may not prejudice the rights in the work (art. 88, first paragraph).
[25] Article 88, second and third paragraphs.
[26] Article 88, third paragraph.
[27] Article 88, first paragraph.
[28] Discussed below; *see* page 408.
[29] Article 91, first paragraph.
[30] Article 91, third paragraph.
[31] Article 91, second paragraph.
[32] Article 89.

The duration of the protection may vary according to the nature of the photograph. It is forty years for a photograph which (i) reproduces works of the graphic arts or architectural works, or (ii) has a technical or scientific character, or (iii) has a distinctive (*spiccato*) artistic value, provided that (a) the photograph has been deposited in the *Ufficio della proprietà letteraria, artistica e scientifica*, and (b) all copies (*esemplari*) of the photograph bear the indication "*riproduzione riservata per quaranta anni*" (reproduction reserved for forty years).[33] There is no provision in the Italian Law reconciling these requirements of deposit and special notice with the requirements of Article III of the Universal Copyright Convention. The Convention notice *should*, it is believed, be considered by Italy as satisfying not only the general requirement of indicating certain data on any kind of photograph,[34] but also the additional requirements of deposit and special notice on which the forty-year protection of the three kinds of photographs referred to above hinges. Whether, in fact, Italian courts would so hold, is an open question, since the issue has not yet come before them.

Otherwise, the duration of protection of rights in a photograph is twenty years from the making (*produzione*) of the photograph.[35]

The rule of the shorter term, where applicable, qualifies the above results.[36]

Neighboring Rights.—The Copyright Law of Italy also contains provisions concerning the protection of producers of phonograph records and like contrivances,[37] of the licensee (*esercente*) of the broadcasting service (i.e., the *Radiodiffusione Italiana*),[38] and of performing artists.[39] It will be assumed, in the present analysis, that protection of the so-called neighboring rights of these beneficiaries cannot be claimed under the Universal Copyright Convention, whose aim is the protection of the traditional subject matter of copyright.

Sketches of Theatrical Scenes.—Sketches of theatrical scenes (*bozzetti di scene teatrali*) which do *not* constitute a work are dealt with in a special provision of the Law.[40] Their authors have a right to remuneration when their sketches are further used in theatres other than the theatre for which they were created; the right continues for five years from the first performance in which the sketch was used. It is uncertain whether protection for such sketches can be claimed in Italy *under the Universal Copyright Convention*, since the Universal Copyright Convention protects *works* and the provision in question deals with sketches, which are *not* works.

[33] Article 92, second and fourth paragraphs.
[34] Article 90, first paragraph; *see* page 403, above.
[35] Article 92, first paragraph.
[36] *See* page 414, below.
[37] Articles 72 to 78.   [38] Article 79.
[39] Articles 80 to 85.   [40] Article 86.

Engineering Projects.—Another special provision of the Law deals with a right to remuneration of the authors of certain engineering projects (*progetti di lavori dell'ingegneria*) *vis-à-vis* persons realizing the projects.[41] The Law does not treat the right as a copyright. It is believed that, the matter being wholly outside the usual scope of copyright, protection *by virtue of the Universal Copyright Convention* is probably unavailable in Italy, although this is not entirely certain since there are no judicial decisions in point.

Title of Works, etc.—The title, when it uniquely identifies the work, may not be reproduced in connection with any other work without the author's consent. This prohibition does not extend to using the title in a work which is of a kind and character so far removed from the work in which the title was first used as to exclude all possibility of confusion. The reproduction of column headings (*rubriche*) is also prohibited under like conditions, when they are applied to products of the periodic press in such a constant manner that they acquire a connotation of identifying the customary and characteristic contents of the column.[42] The Law contains no timelimit as to the duration of this protection. But as to titles of a newspaper, magazine or other periodical publication, the Law limits the duration of protection against their use in other works of the same character to the time during which they are published and two years after the cessation of their publication.[43] These provisions are not among those characteristic of copyright laws, and it is uncertain whether they may be invoked in Italy merely on the basis of the Universal Copyright Convention.

News.—The reproduction of information and news is lawful, provided it is not effected by way of acts which are contrary to fair practice in journalism, and provided the reproduction contains an indication of the source.[44] It is unlikely that protection of information and news—which are not *works*—may be claimed in Italy *under the Universal Copyright Convention.*

Emblems, etc.—The reproduction or imitation, on another work of the same kind, of headings (*testate*), emblems, ornamentations (*fregi*), arrangements of printing signs or characters, or of any other particularity of form or color in the external appearance of an intellectual work is prohibited as an act of unfair competition if the said reproduction or imitation is capable of creating confusion between works or authors.[45] There is no timelimit provided for in the Law. Whether this kind of

---

[41] Article 99.

[42] Article 100, first, second and third paragraphs.

[43] Article 100, fourth paragraph.

[44] Article 101, first paragraph. Acts which are presumed to be unlawful are defined in article 101, second paragraph.

[45] Article 102.

protection may be invoked by virtue of the Universal Copyright Convention seems to be doubtful.

PROTECTED PERSONS

Generally.—Protection originally vests in the creator of the work.[46] In the case of a collective work, the person who organizes and directs its creation is deemed to be the author.[47] In the case of "elaborations" or adaptations, the "elaborator" or adaptor is deemed to be the author.[48] In the case of pseudonymous or anonymous works, the person performing or publishing it is entitled to assert the rights of the author, until such time as the author reveals his identity.[49]

The Law contains provisions—which, however, may be set aside by contract—as to the respective rights, on the one hand, of the composer of the music, and, on the other hand, of the author of the "literary part" (words, choreography, mimicry) of operas, operettas, melologues, musical compositions with words, dances and ballets.[50]

Collective Works.—In the case of a collective work, the rights of economic utilization belong, in the absence of agreement to the contrary, to the publisher—without prejudice to the rights which the person organizing and directing the creation of the work has, within the limits of his contribution.[51] Unless otherwise agreed by contract, the author of an article (other than a person on the editorial staff) submitting his article to a periodical or newspaper re-acquires his unlimited copyright in the article (i) if he does not receive notice of acceptance within one month from submitting it, or (ii) if reproduction is not effected within six months from the notification of acceptance.[52]

Unless otherwise agreed by contract, the author of an article or other work reproduced in a newspaper, magazine or other collective work, is entitled to reproduce it in a separate form, or in a collection in volume form, or in another newspaper or magazine—provided the original publication is indicated.[53]

Cinematographic Works.—The following persons are considered as co-authors of a cinematographic work: the author of the subject, the

[46] Article 6; for presumption of authorship, *see* article 8; *see also* articles 10 and 11.
[47] Article 7, first paragraph.
[48] Article 7, second paragraph.
[49] Article 9, first paragraph; this does not apply where the pseudonym leaves no doubt as to the identity of the author (art. 9, second paragraph).
[50] Articles 33 to 37.
[51] Articles 38, first paragraph, and article 7.
[52] Article 39, first paragraph: the second paragraph of the same article deals with members of the editorial staff.
[53] Article 42.

author of the scenario (*sceneggiatura*), the composer of the music, and the artistic director[54]—but the exercise of the rights of *cinematographic exploitation* belong to the producer.[55] If the producer fails to complete the cinematographic work within a period of three years from the delivery of the literary or musical parts, or does not exhibit the completed work within three years from its completion, the authors of the said parts are entitled to dispose, unrestrictedly, of their respective contributions.[56]

Authors and Addressees of Letters, etc.—A letter, personal or family memorandum, or any similar writing may not be published, reproduced, or in any other manner brought to the knowledge of the public, without the consent of the author, and, in the case of letters, also of the addressee, irrespective of whether it is or is not protected by copyright.[57] After the death of the author or the addressee, the consent of the surviving spouse and children, and if none exists, the consent of certain other relatives is required;[58] however, the wishes of the deceased person, when expressed in writing, must in all cases be respected.[59]

Persons Portrayed.—Subject to certain exceptions (notoriety, etc.),[60] portraits of a person may not be displayed, reproduced or commercially distributed without the consent of the person portrayed, irrespective of whether they are or are not protected by copyright. After the death of the person portrayed, the consent of the surviving spouse and children, and if none exists, the consent of certain other relatives is required; however, the wishes of the deceased person, when expressed in writing, must in all cases be respected.[61]

ASSIGNMENT AND LICENSING

Generally.—The rights of economic utilization of a work are alienable and transmissible.[62] The transfer of rights of utilization requires documentary evidence (written form).[63]

Unless otherwise agreed by contract, the transfer of one or more copies (*esemplari*) of the work does not imply the transfer of the rights of economic utilization, except when the object of the transfer is a

[54] Article 44.
[55] Articles 45, and 46, first paragraph; for further details and qualifications, *see* "Economic Right," page 409, below.
[56] Article 50.
[57] Article 93, first paragraph, and article 95.
[58] Article 93, second paragraph.
[59] Article 93, fourth paragraph.
[60] Article 97.   [61] Articles 93, 96, 97.
[62] Article 107.   [63] Article 110.

mould, an engraved plate, or any similar contrivance, destined for the making of copies of a work of art.[64]

Publishing Contracts.—The Law contains numerous provisions on publishing contracts.[65] Some of these are rules that can be put aside by contrary contractural arrangements, others are mandatory. The following are included in the latter category:

Future rights which may be granted by future laws and which extend the scope or duration of copyright protection cannot be included in the transfer.[66]

Contracts in respect of future works (i.e., works not yet in existence at the time the contract is concluded) are void if they relate to all the future works, or all the future works of a certain category, of the author.[67] Contracts relating to the alienation of exclusive rights in future works may not extend for a term in excess of ten years.[68]

Publication contracts may not be concluded for a term exceeding twenty years, unless they relate to: encyclopaedias or dictionaries; sketches, drawings, vignettes, illustrations, photographs and similar objects for industrial use; maps; dramatico-musical and symphonic works.[69]

The publisher must publish the work within two years; the author may stipulate a shorter, but not a longer, period than two years.[70]

The remuneration of the author must consist in a "participation" (normally calculated on the basis of a percentage of the retail price of the copies sold), except in the case of certain categories of works for which the remuneration may consist of the payment of a lump sum. These categories are the following: dictionaries, encyclopaedias, anthologies and other works produced in collaboration; translations; newspaper and magazine articles; speeches and lectures; scientific works; maps; musical compositions; dramatico-musical works; works of the plastic (*figurativi*) arts.[71]

PROTECTED RIGHTS

Economic Rights

Generally.—The author has the exclusive right to publish his work and to exploit it ("economic utilization") in any form or manner,

[64] Article 109. The assignment of the right to make phonograph records of a work does not include the right to perform publicly or broadcast the work with the help of such records (article 61, second paragraph).

[65] Articles 118 to 135.

[66] Article 119, third paragraph.

[67] Article 120, first paragraph, item (1).

[68] Article 120, first paragraph, item (2).

[69] Article 122.   [70] Article 127.   [71] Article 130, first paragraph.

whether original or derivative.[72] The various rights expressly referred to in the Law, and discussed below, are mere examples; they do not constitute an exhaustive enumeration. All rights are exclusive rights of authorization, unless otherwise stated.

Rights of Reproduction.—This right has for its object multiplication, in the form of copies (*copie*) of the work, by any means, such as copying by hand, printing, lithography, engraving, photography, phonography, cinematography, etc.[73]

Right to Transcribe.—The right to transcribe (*trascrivere*) has for its object the use of means suitable for transforming an oral work into a written or otherwise reproduced (*see above*) work.[74]

Right of Public Performance and Recitation.—This right has for its object the performance (*esecuzione, rappresentazione*) or recitation— irrespective of the way in which it is effected[75]—of musical, dramatic and cinematographic works, any other works destined to be shown to the public (*opera di pubblico spettacolo*), and of oral works. It is generally irrelevant whether the performance or recitation is effected for or without payment; however, if it is effected within the normal family circle, college (*convitto*), school, or institute of health (*istituto di ricovero*), and if it is not effected for gainful intent, it is not considered to be public.[76]

Right of Diffusion.—This right has for its object the use of any means of diffusion over a distance, such as telegraphy, telephony, radio, television and other similar means.[77] Within certain limits, the *Radiodiffusione Italiana* (the sole radio and broadcasting organization in Italy) may, however, broadcast works from theatres, concert halls or other public places, even without the authorization of the owner of the copyright, except (i) if the work is new, or, (ii) if it is not new, when it is first performed in any given season. A theatrical work is deemed

[72] Article 12, first and second paragraphs.
[73] Article 13. The author has the exclusive right to adapt and record the work on phonograph records, cinematographic films, metal tapes, or any analogous material or mechanical contrivance for reproducing sound and voices; and to reproduce, lease, and put into commercial circulation copies of the work so adapted or recorded (art. 61, first paragraph, items (1) and (2)). *Radiodiffusione Italiana* may, however, record a work without the authorization of the owner of the copyright for the purposes of deferred broadcasting (art. 55).
[74] Article 14.
[75] Including by means of sound fixations (records, films, tapes, etc.) (art. 61, first paragraph, item (3)); as to the performance of film music, *see* "Cinematographic Works," below.
[76] Article 15. The owner of the copyright is entitled to an equitable remuneration for the performance in public establishments of broadcast works by means of sound radio receiving sets; he cannot prohibit such performance (art. 58).
[77] Article 16. Including broadcasting from sound fixations (records, film, tapes) (art. 61, first paragraph, item (3)).

to be new as long as it has not been publicly performed in three different theatres or other public places.[78] The owner of the copyright is entitled to remuneration for such broadcasts, the amount of which is fixed by the courts if the parties are unable to agree.[79] *Radiodiffusione Italiana* may also make special broadcasts of cultural and artistic propaganda intended for countries other than Italy, without the consent of the owner of the copyright, subject to payment of remuneration, the amount of which is fixed by the Government if the parties are unable to agree.[80]

Right of Commercial Distribution.—The exclusive right of commercial distribution (*mettere in commercio*) has for its object the putting into circulation, with gainful intent, a work or copies (*esemplari*) thereof, and includes also the exclusive right of introducing into the territory of Italy, for the purpose of putting into circulation, reproductions which have been made outside Italy.[81]

Right of Translation.—The exclusive right of translation has for its object the translation of the work into another language or dialect.[82]

Right of "Elaboration".—This includes all forms of modification, "elaboration" (adaptation), and transformation.[83]

Right of Publishing in a Collection.—The author has the exclusive right to publish his works in the form of a collection.[84]

Cinematographic Works.—The producer is entitled to exercise the rights of cinematographic exploitation of a cinematographic work. On the other hand, the right of making or exhibiting elaborations, transformations or translations of the cinematographic work belongs to the authors of the work rather than to its producer—unless otherwise agreed by contract. The authors of the music (and words accompanying it) used in a cinematographic work are entitled to collect, directly from the person publicly exhibiting such work, a public performance fee. The amount of the fee is not the subject of separate negotiation for each work, but is established annually by agreements among the SIAE and the trade association of the industry. If they are unable to agree, the amount is fixed by the Government.[85] The authors of the literary or musical elements of a cinematographic work may reproduce them or utilize them separately in any manner, provided no projudice is occasioned thereby to the rights of the producer.[86]

Droit de suite.—The authors of paintings, sculptures, drawings and prints are entitled to between two and ten per cent of the amount

[78] Article 52.   [79] Article 56.   [80] Article 60; Regulation, article 20.
[81] Article 17; article 61, first paragraph, item (2).
[82] Article 18, first paragraph.
[83] Article 18, second paragraph, and article 4.
[84] Article 18, third paragraph.
[85] Article 46.   [86] Article 49.

by which the price of the first public sale of original copies (*esemplari*) of such works exceeds the price of first alienation, provided the excess is higher than certain amounts specified in the Law.[87] It is not entirely clear whether this right—known only in very few countries—may be claimed in Italy under the Universal Copyright Convention.

MORAL RIGHTS

Independently of the rights of economic utilization, and even after the assignment of such rights, the author retains the right to claim authorship (*paternità*) of the work, and to oppose any distortion, mutilation or other modification of the work which may be prejudicial to his honor or reputation.[88] These rights are inalienable; but if the author was aware of and accepted modifications in his work, he is not entitled to intervene to prevent the execution thereof or to demand its suppression.[89] Moral rights are not limited in time; their exercise after the author's death is regulated by the Law.[90] The right of publishing unpublished works belongs to the heirs of the author or to the legatees of the particular works, unless the author has expressly forbidden publication or has entrusted it to other persons.[91]

LIMITATIONS

The reproduction of single works or of portions thereof for the personal use of readers, when made by hand or by a means unsuitable for circulating or diffusing the work in public, is free. The photo-copying of works existing in libraries, when made for personal use or for the services of the library, is free. The use of such copies in competition with the rights of economic utilization belonging to the author is prohibited.[92]

The Law also contains other exceptions under, or limitations of, some of the rights *in certain cases* of: uses of newspaper or magazine articles of current interest; political speeches; judicial proceedings; loans to the public for personal use of copies of a work; criticism, discussion, instruction; use by the armed forces;[93] and uses of photographs by the person who commissioned them.[94]

[87] Article 144 to 155.
[88] Article 20, first paragraph; article 18, fourth paragraph. The right to oppose modifications is qualified in the case of architectural works (art. 20, first paragraph). As to anonymous and pseudonymous works, *see* article 21. For certain qualifications in the case of collective works, including newspapers and magazines, *see* articles 40 and 41; in the case of contributions to cinematographic works, *see* articles 47 and 48; in connection with the broadcasting of works, *see* article 54; in connection with sound fixations, *see* article 63; as to photographs, *see* article 98, second paragraph. The right of withdrawal from commerce is regulated by articles 142 and 143.
[89] Article 22.   [90] Article 23.   [91] Article 24, first paragraph.
[92] Article 68.   [93] Articles 65, 66, 67, 69, 70, 71.   [94] Article 98, first paragraph.

TERM OF PROTECTION

WORKS OTHER THAN CINEMATOGRAPHIC WORKS

Generally.—Subject to the rule of the shorter term, discussed below, the rights of economic utilization of works protected under the Universal Copyright Convention generally continue for the life of the author and until the termination of the fiftieth calendar year after his death.[95]

Collaboration.—In the case of works created by the indistinguishable and inseparable contributions of two or more persons, as well as in the case of dramatico-musical and choreographic works and pantomimes, the death of the last surviving co-author serves as a basis for computing the duration for all the contributions.[96]

Collective Works.—In the case of collective works (encyclopaedias, newspapers, etc.), the duration of the right of each collaborator is determined on the basis of his death, but the duration of the economic rights in the collective work, as such, is fifty years from the date of first publication—subject, where applicable, to the rule of the shorter term (discussed below) and the prolongations referred to above.[97,98]

Anonymous and Pseudonymous Works.—In the case of anonymous and pseudonymous works (unless the pseudonym does not leave any doubt as to the civil identity of the author, or unless the author has revealed his identity), protection of the economic rights ends fifty years after first publication.[99]

Posthumous Works.—In the case of works published for the first

---

[95] Article 25. Italy extended the term of protection: (a) by six years for all works which have been published but have not fallen into the public domain by August 17, 1945 (Legislative Decree No. 440 of July 20, 1945; "Gazzetta Ufficiale," No. 98, of August 16, 1945; CLTW Italy: Item 3), and, (b) until December 31, 1961, for all works which otherwise would have fallen into the public domain between January 1, 1951, and December 31, 1961 (Law No. 1421 of December 19, 1956; "Gazzetta Ufficiale" No. 327 of December 31, 1956; CLTW, Italy: Item 3A). These extensions seem to apply to works protected by virtue of the Universal Copyright Convention (*see* articles 186 and 189 of the Law; article 7 of Legislative Decree No. 440 of 1945; article 3 of Law No. 1421 of 1956) unless the rule of the shorter term (*see above*) does not cut off the protection at some point before or during the extension.

[96] Article 26, first paragraph.

[97] *See* footnote 1, above.

[98] Article 26, second paragraph. Where parts or volumes of a work are published separately in different years and duration is computed from publication rather than death, the term is computed from the year of publication of each part or volume (art. 30, first paragraph). In the case of collective periodical works, such as magazines and newspapers, the term is calculated from the end of the year of publication of the individual parts or number (art. 30, second paragraph).

[99] Articles 27 and 28, subject, where applicable, to the rule of the shorter term (*see below*) and the prolongations (*see* footnote 1).

time after the death of the author, one must differentiate between cases where publication took place (i) within twenty years of the death of the author; (ii) later than the expiration of the twentieth year from the author's death. In case (i), the economic rights continue for fifty years from first publication; in case (ii), the general rules apply (fifty years *p.m.a.*, etc.).[100]

CINEMATOGRAPHIC WORKS

In the case of cinematographic works, one must distinguish between works (i) first exhibited to the public not later than the end of the fifth calendar year following the year in which the work was produced, and (ii) works not exhibited to the public within the stated term. The economic rights in a cinematographic work expire—subject, where applicable, to the rule of the shorter term (see below) and possible prolongations[101] after thirty years; the thirty years are completed in case (i), from the first public exhibition, and, in case (ii), from the end of the year in which the work was produced.[102]

RULE OF THE SHORTER TERM

Works protected in Italy by virtue of the Universal Copyright Convention do not enjoy a longer period of protection in Italy than that fixed, for the class of works to which they belong, by the law of the contracting state (i.e., country party to the Universal Copyright Convention) of which, in the case of an unpublished work, the author is a national and, in the case of published works, a period no longer than that which is fixed by the law of the contracting state (i.e., country party to the Universal Copyright Convention) in which the work has been first published. If the law of a contracting state (i.e., country party to the Universal Copyright Convention) grants two or more successive terms of protection, the works which, for any reason, are not protected for the second or one of the subsequent terms, is not protected in Italy during the same term or terms.[103] Thus, for example, works first published in the United States, if protected in Italy under the Universal Copyright Convention, shall cease to be protected in Italy at the end of twenty-eight years after first publication, if copyright is not renewed in them in the United States for the second term of United States copyright protection.

---

[100] Article 31, subject in both cases, where applicable, to the rule of the shorter term (*see below*) and prolongations (*see* footnote 1).
[101] *See* footnote 1, above.
[102] Article 32.
[103] Law No. 923 of July 19, 1956; "Gazzetta Ufficiale" No. 210 of August 23, 1956; CLTW, Italy: Item 3B.

INFRINGEMENTS

Civil Remedies.—Injunctions are available to prevent threatened infringement.[104] In certain cases, the removal or destruction of the implements or fruits of infringement may be demanded.[105] Any person injured by an infringement may sue for damages.[106] The author of a work under copyright protection may intervene in the action, even if he no longer owns the rights, in order to protect his interests in proceedings instituted by the assignee.[107]

Penal Sanctions.—Most of the violations of the economic or moral rights of the author are punishable by fines or imprisonment. The punishment is less severe when the acts result from negligence.[108]

[104] Articles 156 and 157.
[105] Articles 158 to 164, 169 and 170.
[106] Articles 158 and 167.
[107] Article 165.   [108] Articles 171 to 174.

JAPAN

SOURCES

Internal Law.—The main source of the law of copyright in Japan is the Copyright Act, Law No. 39, of March 4, 1899.[1] This was amended by Laws promulgated in 1910, 1920, 1931, 1934, 1941, 1950, 1951, 1956, 1958 and 1962.[2] Hereinafter, it is referred to as "the Law," and references to Articles, without further specification, are references to Articles of this Law.

Various Ordinances regulate certain details. The most important among these is the one promulgating the Copyright Regulations.[3] Hereinafter, it will be referred to as "the Regulations."

Universal Copyright Convention.—Japan became bound by the Universal Copyright Convention and Protocols 1 and 2 as from April 28, 1956.[4] A Law—hereinafter referred to as Law No. 86—promulgated on the same date,[5] provides for the implementation of certain provisions of the Universal Copyright Convention, particularly those concerning the right of translation and the rule of the shorter term.[6]

ACQUISITION OF PROTECTION UNDER THE UNIVERSAL COPYRIGHT CONVENTION

There are no express provisions in the Japanese laws specifying the works that are protected in Japan by virtue of the Universal Copyright

[1] Published in "Hôrei Zensho," Section of Laws, March, 1899, page 105. English translation in CLTW, Japan: Item 1.

[2] Published in "Hôrei Zensho," Section of Laws: June, 1910, page 233; August, 1920, page 63; May, 1931, page 113; May, 1934, page 41; March, 1941, page 30; May, 1950, page 29; June 1951, page 13; April, 1956, page 99; May, 1958, page 175, and Law No. 74 of April 5, 1962. For English translations, see CLTW, Japan: Item 1.

[3] Ordinance of the Ministry of Home Affairs, No. 18, of July 28, 1931 ("Hôrei Zensho," Section of Ministry Orders, July, 1931, page 17), as amended up to June 18, 1956. See English translation in CLTW, Japan: Item 3. See the other Ordinances in CLTW, Japan: Items, 2, 4, 5, and 6.

[4] CLTW, Japan: Item 7A.

[5] Law No. 86 of April 28, 1956; published in "Hôrei Zensho," Section of Laws, April, 1956, page 97; English translation in CLTW, Japan: Item 7A.

[6] Japan is a member of the Berne Copyright Union. It did not, however, ratify the latest (Brussels, 1948) text, but only the former ones, the original 1886 text being the first and the Rome text of 1928 being the last. See CLTW, Japan: Item 8.

Convention.[7] It is therefore assumed that the provisions of the Convention itself govern in this respect. Accordingly, and subject to the exceptions stated below, the following appear to be protected in Japan under the Universal Copyright Convention: (i) published works of nationals of a Convention country, irrespective of the place of first publication, (ii) works first published in a Convention country, irrespective of the nationality of the author, (iii) unpublished works of nationals of a Convention country other than Japan, (iv) works of stateless persons and refugees who have their habitual residence in a state party to Protocol 1 (except perhaps Japan), whether unpublished or published, and, if published, irrespective of the place of first publication, (v) works first published by the United Nations, by any of the Specialized Agencies of the United Nations, or by the Organization of American States, as well as unpublished works of any of these Organizations. If a work falling within any of the above categories is a work which has, as its country of origin, within the meaning of the Conventions of the Berne Union, a country member of that Union (a "Berne Union work"),[8] protection in Japan is available under the applicable Convention of the Berne Union rather than the Universal Copyright Convention.[9] It appears, however, that there are only two cases in which it may be relevant to determine whether a given work is protected in Japan by virtue of the Berne Conventions or by virtue of the Universal Copyright Convention: (i) in applying the rule of the shorter term, and (ii) in connection with the right of translation.[10] The question is discussed in connection with these two problems.[11]

The acquisition of copyright protection in Japan is not subject to any formality.[12] Consequently, registration or deposit is not required,[13]

---

[7] *See*, however, Art. 28(1), which provides that the provisions of the Law apply to copyright in the works of an alien except in cases where there are other specific provisions in a treaty.

[8] Law No. 86, Article X.

[9] *See* Universal Copyright Convention, Article XVII, and Appendix Declaration relating thereto.

[10] Law No. 86, Article I through X.   [11] Pages 421 and 426.

[12] However, articles on current political events (excluding scientific works) published in a newspaper or periodical may be reproduced in another newspaper or periodical with a clear indication of their sources, unless reproduction is expressly prohibited (Art. 20(1)). Such prohibition, it is assumed, may take the form of the Convention notice.

[13] Certain facts of transactions may be registered in the Copyright Register or the Publication Right Register maintained by the Ministry of Education. Such facts and transactions are: (i) assignments and pledges concerning copyright, (ii) the true name of the author of a pseudonymous or anonymous work, (iii) the date of production of a work, (iv) the date of first publication of a work, (v) contracts concerning publishing. *See* articles 15 and 16, and Regulations, articles 1 to 14. When the date of production or first publication is registered, such date is presumed to be the date of production or first publication, as the case may be (art. 35, fifth and sixth paragraphs).

and the absence, in itself, of the Convention notice on the copies of a published work is no bar to claiming protection in Japan. Furthermore, Japan has no renewal system, so there is nothing in this country which would correspond to the renewal formalities existing in the United States. Protection in Japan will last, without any intervention of the copyright owner or a state authority, until the day on which the work falls into the public domain.

PROTECTED WORKS

Literary, scientific, artistic (including musical) works are protected. Included are works belonging in the domain of writings, speech, drawing, painting, architecture, sculpture, modelling, photography, performance, and singing,[14] works produced by means of cinematography or a process analogous thereto.[15] Works produced by a process analogous to photography enjoy the same protection as works of photography.[16]

PROTECTED PERSONS

Generally.—Copyright originally vests in the author.[17] The publisher or producer of an anonymous or pseudonymous work may exercise the rights of the copyright owner, except where the author has his true name registered in the Copyright Register (and the publisher or producer is not the owner of the copyright).[18] Copyright in a work produced by the collaboration of two or more persons belongs to them jointly.[19]

[14] Article 1, first paragraph. The following are not protected: (i) laws, ordinances and Government documents, (ii) miscellaneous reports and articles on current events, published in a newspaper or periodical, (iii) speeches made in law courts, diets, assemblies, or other political meetings open to the public (art. 11).

[15] Article 22(3).   [16] Article 26.

[17] Article 1, first paragraph, and article 22(3). In civil actions, the person whose name appears on the published work as its author is to be presumed to be its author; in the case of a public performance of an unpublished work of drama, music, or cinematography, the person who is named as the author at such public performance is presumed to be its author; if no author has been named, the person giving the public performance is presumed to be the author of the work (art. 35, first, third and fourth paragraphs).

[18] Article 12. The person whose name appears in the work as that of publisher is presumed to be the publisher (art. 35, second paragraph).

[19] Article 13, first paragraph. If the contributions are not separable and one of the authors refuses to permit publication or public performance, the other authors may acquire his share upon paying an indemnity to him, unless there is agreement to the contrary; in this case the author may demand that his name be omitted (art. 13, second and fourth paragraphs). If the contributions are separable and one of the authors refuses to permit publication or public performance, the other authors may publish or publicly perform their separate contributions as independent works, unless there is an agreement to the contrary (art. 13, third paragraph).

Compilations.—A person who has lawfully compiled various works of other persons is the author of the work so compiled, but the copyright in each part belongs to the author of such part.[20]

Translations.—The translator of a work is considered an author and owns the copyright in the translation, provided, however, that the rights of the author of the original work shall not be prejudiced thereby.[21]

Adaptations of Artistic Works.—A person who has lawfully reproduced an artistic work by a technique different from that of the original author is deemed an author and is protected, as such.[22]

Cinematographic Works.—The author of a work produced by means of cinematography is deemed to be an author and is protected, as such.[23] A person who has reproduced the work of other persons by means of cinematography (including the making of a motion picture which dramatizes the work) is deemed an author and is protected as such, without prejudice, however, to the rights of such other persons in their work.[24]

Phonograms.—A person who has lawfully recorded the work of another person on instruments for the mechanical reproduction of sounds is deemed an author and has copyright in such instruments.[25]

Photographs Serving as Illustrations.—Copyright in a photograph which is inserted in a work of literature or science belongs to the author of such work if the photograph was produced or commissioned specifically for such work.[26]

Commissioned Photographic Portraits.—Copyright in a portrait photograph made pursuant to a commission belongs to the person who commissioned it.[27]

ASSIGNMENTS AND LICENSES

Generally.—Copyright may be assigned in whole or in part.[28] Succession to copyright, its assignment, or its pledge, is effective against third persons only if it is registered in the Copyright Register maintained in the Ministry of Education.[29]

Publishing Contracts.—Publishing contracts may relate to works of writing, drawing or painting.[30]

The following are rules which may be set aside by contract: (i) The publisher has the right to reproduce the work by means of typography or other mechanical or chemical processes, and to sell and circulate

[20] Article 14. [21] Article 21. [22] Article 22(1).
[23] Article 22(3). [24] Article 22(4). [25] Article 22(7).
[26] Article 24. [27] Article 25. [28] Article 2.
[29] Article 15, first paragraph. [30] Article 28(2).

the copies so reproduced; however, when the author is dead and the contract is more than three years old, the copyright owner may publish the work in a collection or compilation, or may publish separately a work of the author that has been included in a collection or compilation.[31] (ii) The right of the publisher to publish subsists for three years from the date of the contract of publication.[32] (iii) The publisher must publish the work within three months from the date of the contract of publication; if he does not do so, the copyright owner may revoke the publisher's right to publish.[33]

Whenever the publisher prepares to publish a new edition, he must notify the author in advance. The author may make alterations in his work within a reasonable time before the publisher has completed reproduction of each edition.[34]

The copyright owner may, at any time, withdraw the right of publication which he has granted to the publisher and have the edition suppressed, provided that he pays indemnity to the publisher.[35] The right of publication may be assigned or pledged only with the consent of the copyright owner.[36]

PROTECTED RIGHTS

ECONOMIC RIGHTS OTHER THAN THE RIGHT OF TRANSLATION

The author has the exclusive right to reproduce his work.[37] Copyright in dramatic works or musical compositions includes the right of public performance.[38] Copyright in a work of literature, science or art (including music) includes the right to reproduce such work by means of cinematography (including the making of a motion picture which dramatizes the work) and the right to exhibit such reproduction.[39] Copyright in a work of literature, science or art (including music) includes the right to adapt the work to instruments for the mechanical reproduction of sounds, and the right publicly to perform the work by means of such instruments.[40] Copyright in a work of literature, science or art (including music) includes the right to authorize the broadcasting of such work.[41] These rights, all exclusive in principle, are subject to limitations in certain cases; they are discussed below.[42]

---

[31] Article 28(3).   [32] Article 28(4).
[33] Article 28(5). *See also* article 28(6).
[34] Article 28(7).   [35] Article 28(8).
[36] Article 28(9). *See also* articles 28(10) and 28(11).
[37] Article 1, first paragraph.   [38] Article 1, second paragraph.
[39] Article 22(2).   [40] Article 22(6).
[41] Article 22(5), first paragraph.   [42] Page 422.

THE RIGHT OF TRANSLATION

Subject to the exceptions stated below, the right of translation is an exclusive right of authorization, the duration of which is equal to the general term of protection (i.e., generally 33 years *post mortem auctoris*).[43]

There are two sets of possible exceptions to this rule, one applying to what will be called in this chapter "Berne works" and other non-Universal Copyright Convention works, the other applying to what will be called in this chapter "U.C.C. works."

It should be borne in mind that not all works which would otherwise seem to qualify for protection under the Universal Copyright Convention belong to the category of "U.C.C. works": if they have as their country of origin, within the meaning of the Conventions of the Berne Union, a country member of that Union, they belong to the category of "Berne works" rather than to the category of "U.C.C. works." The question of what works have a Berne Union country as country of origin is discussed above.[44]

"*Berne Works.*" In the case of "Berne works" (and all other works which are not "U.C.C. works," provided they are protected in Japan), if the copyright owner does not publish (in or outside Japan) a translation of the original work within ten years after the publication, in the original language of the work, his right of translation ceases, in Japan, upon the expiration of that period in respect of all languages (Japanese or other) in which no translation has been published during that period. This means, of course, that if the copyright owner *does* publish, anywhere in the world, and within the stated ten years, a translation, in one or more languages, then his right of translation, in respect of such language or languages, continues in Japan beyond the ten-year period and expires only when all other rights also cease to be protected (i.e., when the work falls into the public domain in Japan).[45]

"*U.C.C. works.*" The following applies to "U.C.C. works" only, that is, it does not apply to "Berne works":

Where, after the expiration of a period of seven years from the year following the year of the first publication of a writing, being a "U.C.C. work," a translation (by the owner of the right of translation or with his authorization) has not been published in the Japanese language, or has been so published but is out of print, a Japanese national may publish a translation in the Japanese language under a compulsory license, that is, without the consent of the owner of the right of translation. The license is given, upon application, by the Minister of Education, in either of the following two cases: (i) where the applicant has requested, and been denied, authorization by the owner of the

---

[43] Article 1, second paragraph, and article 7, second paragraph.
[44] Page 417.   [45] Article 7.

right of translation to translate into Japanese and publish such translation, (ii) where, notwithstanding due diligence exercised by the
applicant, he has failed to find the owner of the right of translation.[46]
Prior to the publication of the Japanese translation under a compulsory
license, a compensation which is just and conforms to international
standards, and which is approved by the Minister of Ecucation of
Japan, must be paid, in whole or in part, to the owner of the right of
translation.[47] The license is not transferable.[48] The original title and
the name of the author of the work must be printed on the copies of the
translation.[49] Copies of the translation may not be exported to a State,
other than the States party to the Universal Copyright Convention, as
designated by Cabinet Order.[50]

MORAL RIGHTS

When a work is published, publicly performed, or broadcast *during
the lifetime of the author*, the name and title of the author may not be
altered or concealed, nor may the work be revised or otherwise altered,
or its title changed, without the consent of the author, whether or not
he actually owns the copyright, and even where the publication, performance or broadcast is free or is effected under a compulsory license.[51]

When a work is published, publicly performed or broadcast *after
the death of the author*, the reputation of the author must not be injured
by revising or otherwise altering his work, nor may its title or the name
and title of the author be altered or concealed, even where the copyright
may have ceased to exist, and even if the publication, performance or
broadcast is free or is effected under a compulsory license.[52]

LIMITATIONS

**Publication or Public Performance under Compulsory
Licenses.**—The right to publish a work is generally an exclusive right

[46] In this case (i.e., when the owner has not been found), the applicant must send
copies of his application to the publisher whose name appears on the work and, if
the nationality of the owner of the right of translation is known, to the diplomatic or
consular representative of the state of which such owner is a national, or to the
organization which may have been designated by the Government of that State,
and he must also send to the Minister of Education of Japan a report that the copies
have been so sent (Law No. 86, article V, paragraph (2)).
[47] Law No. 86, article V, paragraph (1). The Minister of Education must not grant
a license before the expiration of two months from the date of dispatch of the copies
of the application (Law No. 86, art. V, paragraph (3). The Minister of Education
must hear the advice of the Copyright Council.
[48] Law No. 86, article V, paragraph (4).
[49] Law No. 86, article VII.
[50] Law No. 86, article VIII. For further details, see Order No. 259 of July 18, 1964;
English translation published in CLTW, Japan: Item 7B.
[51] Article 18, first and third paragraphs.
[52] Article 18, first and second paragraphs.

of authorization.[53] The same is true in the case of the right publicly to perform.[54] However, without the consent of the owner of the copyright upon the permission of the Minister of Education, when an agreement with the copyright owner is not possible for any of the following reasons: (i) the address of the copyright owner is not known; (ii) the copyright owner is not known and cannot be ascertained from any registration of the work; (iii) the copyright owner does not reside in Japan, and his attorney in Japan is not known.[55] This compulsory license is granted upon application[56] and the depositing by the applicant of a compensation, the amount of which is fixed by the Minister of Education, after consultation with the Copyright Council.[57] Any person who objects to the amount of compensation so fixed may bring action in a civil court.[58]

Cases in Which the Right of Reproduction is not Protected. —Reproduction requires no authorization by, and no payment of any compensation to, the owner of the copyright in the following cases: (i) Reproduction by other than mechanical or chemical processes and without any intention of publishing the reproduction; (ii) Quotation, with appropriate modification, of a reasonable part of the work; (iii) Extracting of reasonable parts and their compilation in a book of ethics or reading material for popular education; (iv) Insertion in a dramatic or musical composition of extracts of a work of literature or science; (v) Insertion, of an artistic work (including musical works) as an illustration in a work of literature or science, or insertion of a work of literature or science as an explanation in an artistic work; (vi) Reproduction of a drawing or painting in the form of a sculpture, or reproduction of a sculpture in the form of a drawing or painting; (vii) Reproduction for the exclusive use of a government agency.[59] In any such free reproduction, the source must be clearly indicated.[60] Articles on current political events (excluding scientific works) published in a newspaper or periodical may be fully reproduced in another newspaper or periodical with a clear indication of their sources, unless reproduction has been expressly prohibited.[61]

Cases in Which the Right of Public Performance is not Protected.—Public performance is free—that is, it requires neither the authorization of the owner of the copyright, nor the payment of

[53] *A contrario* article 27.
[54] Article 1, second paragraph.
[55] Article 27; Regulations, article 20.
[56] Regulation, articles 19 and 21.
[57] Article 27; Regulation, article 23; *see also* Law, article 36(3), and Regulations, articles 24 and 25.
[58] Article 27, third paragraph.
[59] Article 30, first paragraph.
[60] Article 30, second paragraph.   [61] Article 20(1).

any compensation to him—in either of the following two cases: (i) when the performance of a dramatic or musical work is not for profit and the performers do not receive any remuneration, (ii) when the performance is effected by means of lawfully made instruments for the mechanical reproduction of sounds.[62]

Free Publication of Speeches.—Public speeches on topics of current events may be published in a newspaper or periodical with a clear indication of the name of the speaker and the time and place of the speech. A compilation of speeches, however, may be published only with the consent of the speaker.[63]

Broadcasting under Compulsory Licenses.—The right of broadcasting is generally an exclusive right of authorization.[64] In the case of a work which has been published or publicly performed and which a broadcaster intends to broadcast, he must consult the copyright owner, but if they cannot agree on the terms, the broadcaster may obtain a license to broadcast (compulsory license).[65] The license is granted upon request by the Minister of Education,[66] who fixes the amount of a reasonable compensation to the copyright owner,[67] after consulting the Copyright Council.[68] Any person who objects to the amount of the compensation so fixed may bring action in a civil court.[69]

Cases in Which the Right of Broadcasting is not Protected.—Broadcasting is free in either of the following two cases: (i) the public performance that is being broadcast is a performance of a dramatic or musical work and the performance is not for profit and the performers do not receive remuneration; (ii) the broadcasting is effected by means of lawfully made instruments for the mechanical reproduction of sounds.[70]

TERM OF PROTECTION

WORKS OTHER THAN PHOTOGRAPHIC AND CINEMATOGRAPHIC WORKS

Works published or publicly performed during the author's life are protected—subject to the exceptions stated below—during the life of the author and for 33 years after his death.[71] In the case of

[62] Article 30, first paragraph.
[63] Article 20(2).   [64] Article 22(5), first paragraph.
[65] Article 22(5), second paragraph.
[66] Regulations, article 15.
[67] Article 22(5), second paragraph; Regulations, article 16(1).
[68] Regulations, article 16(2); see also Regulations, articles 17 and 18.
[69] Article 22(5), third paragraph.
[70] Article 30, first paragraph, items (vii) and (viii).
[71] Article 3, first paragraph.

works jointly produced, the date of the death of the last surviving author governs.[72]

Works published or publicly performed after the death of the author are protected—subject to the exceptions stated below—for 33 years from the time of the publication or public performance.[73]

Anonymous or pseudonymous works are protected for 33 years from the time of publication or performance; but if the author has his true name registered within this period, protection lasts during the life of the author and for 33 years after his death.[74]

Duration of the Right of Translation.—See above.[75]

Where the author leaves no successors, copyright ceases upon his death.[76]

Unpublished works.—It would appear that unpublished works are protected without limitation in time, since there is no provision in the Law limiting the duration of copyright in them. But the rule according to which copyright ceases upon the death of the author if he leaves no successors, seems to apply also to unpublished works.

Computation of Years.—All periods are calculated from the beginning of the year following the year in which the relevant event (death, publication, performance) occurred.[77]

PHOTOGRAPHED WORKS

Subject to the exceptions stated below, copyright (i) in an *unpublished* photograph lasts ten years from the beginning of the year following the year in which the negative was made, (ii) in a *published* photograph lasts ten years from the beginning of the year following the year in which the photograph was first published.[78]

Copyright in a photograph lawfully reproducing a work of art continues as long as the copyright in the work of art expires.[79] Copyright in a photograph inserted in a work of literature or science continues as long as the copyright in such work expires, provided the photograph was produced or commissioned specifically for such work.[80]

---

[72] Article 3, second paragraph.
[73] Article 4. Presumably the first of these two events counts.
[74] Article 5. Presumably the first of these two events counts.
[75] Page 421.
[76] Article 10.
[77] Article 9. *See also* article 8 for works published in succeeding volumes, issues or instruments.
[78] Article 23, first and second paragraphs.
[79] Article 23, third paragraph.
[80] Article 24.

CINEMATOGRAPHIC WORKS

One must differentiate between cinematographic works with originality, and cinematographic works without originality.

The term of protection for cinematographic works with originality is the same (33 years, etc.), as for works other than photographs.[81]

As to the term of protection for cinematographic works without originality, the same rules apply as to photographs: the term is ten years, subject to the exception relating to the case in which the reproduction of a work of art is involved.[82]

RULE OF THE SHORTER TERM

The rule of the shorter term applies to works protected under Article II and Protocol 1 of the Universal Copyright Convention;[83] *it does not apply to works having as their country of origin, within the meaning of the Conventions of the Berne Union, a country member of that Union.*[84] This should be borne in mind throughout the rest of the present chapter.

For the purposes of the application of the rule of the shorter term, as provided for in Law No. 86 of Japan, one must differentiate between works which, in the relevant country (to be defined hereafter): (i) do not belong to a class of works which, in that country, are protected; (ii) belong to a class of works which, in that country, are protected. If they belong to the latter category, one must examine whether the particular work in which one is interested, enjoys, in the relevant country: (a) a protection as long as, or longer than, it enjoys in Japan under Japanese law, (b) a protection shorter than would, in the absence of the rule of the shorter term, apply in Japan. The rule of the shorter term applies, of course, only in this last case (case (b)).[85]

"Relevant country," in the case of an unpublished work, is the Convention country of which the author is a national.[86] In the case of a published work, the "relevant country" is the Convention country in which the work was first published.[87] A work published in two or more Convention countries within thirty days from first publication is considered as published simultaneously in those countries, and for a work so published the "relevant country" is the country in which the term of protection is the shortest.[88] If the work of a national of a Con-

[81] Article 22(3). *See above*, page 424.   [82] Article 22(3). *See above*, page 425.
[83] *See above*, page 417; and *see* Law No. 86, articles III and IX.
[84] *See above*, page 417; and *see* Law No. 86, article X.
[85] This is contrary to Article IV of the Universal Copyright Convention which allows comparison only between the terms of protection of classes of works, and not between the terms of protection of individual works.
[86] Law No. 86, article III. Or, if he is stateless or a refugee, the country in which he resides if that country is party to Protocol 1 (Law No. 86, art. X).
[87] Law No. 86, article III.
[88] Law No. 86, article IV, paragraph (2).

vention country was first published in a non-Convention country, the former (i.e., the country of which the author is a national) is the "relevant country."[89]

Now, the rule of the shorter term is the following: a particular work ceases to be protected in Japan from the same date as it ceases to be protected in the relevant country, if that date precedes the date at which, under the law of Japan, it would otherwise cease to be protected.[90]

Furthermore, a particular work is not protected at all in Japan if it does not belong, according to the legislation of the relevant country, to a class of works protected according to that legislation.[91] In other words, if the particular work, in the relevant country, is a work belonging to a non-protected class, the duration of its protection in Japan is zero, that is, such work is not protected for any time in Japan.

INFRINGEMENTS

Civil Remedies.—Infringers are liable for damages.[92] But if the act constituting infringement was committed in good faith and without negligence, the infringer is liable only to the extent of his net profits.[93]

The violation of any of the rights protected by the Law constitutes infringement. Furthermore, a person who imports infringing copies for sale in Japan is deemed an infringer.[94]

Penal Sanctions.—Any person who knowingly commits infringement, or knowingly sells or circulates infringing copies, or published a work in which the name of the author is falsified, is punishable by imprisonment or fine or both.[95] Other violations of moral rights, and free uses of works without indication of the source, are punishable by a fine only.[96] False registrations are punishable by fine.[97]

Infringing copies and the implements and tools used solely for the reproduction of such copies are to be confiscated if they are the property of the infringer, the printer, or the person who sells or circulates the infringing copies.[98]

Most offenses are prosecuted only upon the complaint of the injured party.[99]

[89] Law No. 86, article IV, paragraph (1).
[90] Law No. 86, article III, paragraph (1).
[91] Law No. 86, article III, paragraph (2).
[92] Article 29.
[93] Article 33. *See also* article 34. For actions concerning infringements of moral rights, *see* article 36(2).
[94] Article 31. A person who publishes a book of answers to written questions in a textbook is deemed an infringer. (art. 32).
[95] Articles 37 and 40. *See also* article 34.
[96] Articles 37 and 39.
[97] Article 42.   [98] Article 43.   [99] Article 44.

Conservatory Measures.—When a civil or criminal action has been filed, the court may—with or without requiring the posting of a bond—order the suspension of the sale or circulation of the allegedly infringing copies, or may order the suspension of any allegedly infringing public performance of a work.[100]

---

[100] Article 36(1), first paragraph. If the court, in its final judgment, finds that there was no infringement, the applicant for suspension or seizure is liable to indemnify the prevailing party for the damage sustained (art. 36(1), second paragraph).

KENYA

SOURCES

Internal Law.—The main source of the law of copyright in Kenya is the Copyright Act, 1966.[1] Hereinafter, it is referred to as "the Act," and references to Sections, without further specification, are references to Sections of this Act.

Universal Copyright Convention.—Kenya became bound by the Universal Copyright Convention and Protocols 1 and 2 on September 7, 1966.[2]

ACQUISITION OF PROTECTION UNDER THE UNIVERSAL COPYRIGHT CONVENTION

The application of the Act is extended, in respect of literary, musical and artistic works and cinematograph films:

(i) to individuals or bodies corporate who are citizens of, or domiciled or resident in, or incorporated under the laws of, a country bound by the Universal Copyright Convention (hereinafter referred to as a "Convention country"),

(ii) to works, other than sound recordings, first published in a Convention country.[3]

A work is taken to have been published if, but only if, copies have been issued in sufficient quantities to satisfy the reasonable requirements of the public.[4] Where in the first instance a part only of a work is published, that part is treated, for the purposes of the Act, as a separate work.[5] A publication in any country is not treated as being other than the first publication by reason only of an earlier publication elsewhere if the two publications took place within a period of not more than thirty days.[6] The acquisition of copyright protection in Kenya is not subject to

---

[1] Act No. 3 of 1966, entered into force on April 1, 1966 (*see* Legal Notice No. 85 of March 24, 1966, and published in the "Kenya Gazette Supplement No. 25" of March 29, 1966, page 123). Text reprinted in CLTW, Kenya: Item 1.

[2] See CLTW, Kenya: Item 2.

[3] See the Copyright Regulations 1966, Legal Notice No. 322, published in the "Kenya Gazette Supplement No. 97" of November 22, 1966.

[4] Section 2(2) (a).   [5] Section 2(2) (b).   [6] Section 2(2) (c).

any formality. Consequently, registration or deposit is not required, and the absence, in itself, of the Convention notice on the copies of a published work is no bar to the claiming of protection in Kenya. Furthermore, Kenya has no renewal system, so there is nothing in that country which would correspond to the renewal formalities existing in the United States. Protection in Kenya will last, without any intervention on the part of the copyright owner or a State authority, until the day on which the work falls into the public domain.

PROTECTED WORKS

Generally.—The Act distinguishes between six categories of works: literary works, musical works, artistic works, cinematograph films, sound recordings, broadcasts.[7]

The first three—i.e., literary, musical and artistic works—are eligible for copyright only if both of the following conditions are fulfilled: (i) sufficient effort has been expended on making the work to give it an original character, (ii) the work has been written down, recorded, or otherwise reduced to material form.[8]

No work is ineligible for copyright by reason only that the making of the work, or the doing of any act in relation to the work, involved an infringement of copyright in some other work.[9]

"Work" includes translations, adaptations, new versions or arrangements of pre-existing works, and anthologies or collections of works which, by reason of the selection and arrangement of their content, present an original character.[10]

Literary Works.—These include, irrespective of literary quality: (i) novels, stories and poetical works, (ii) plays, stage directions, film scenarios and broadcasting scripts, (iii) textbooks, treatises, histories, biographies, essays and articles, (iv) encyclopaedias and dictionaries, (v) letters, reports and memoranda, (vi) lectures, addresses and sermons.[11]

Musical Works.—These are protected irrespective of musical quality. They include works composed for musical accompaniment.[12]

Artistic Works.—These include, irrespective of artistic quality: (i) paintings, drawings, etchings, lithographs, woodcuts, engravings, prints; (ii) maps, plans, diagrams; (iii) works of sculpture; (iv) photographs not comprised in a cinematograph film; (v) works of architec-

---

[7] Section 3(1). Since the Copyright Regulations 1966 (see footnote 3, above) do not extend protection, under the Universal Copyright Convention, to sound recordings and broadcasts, no further reference is made in this book to these two categories.
[8] Section 3(2). [9] Section 3(3). [10] Section 2(1). [11] Section 2(1).
[12] Section 2(1).

ture in the form of buildings (including any structure) or models, (vi) works of artistic craftsmanship, including pictorial woven tissues and articles of applied handicraft and industrial art.[13]

Cinematograph Films.—A "cinematograph film" means the first fixation on film or on any other medium of a sequence of visual images or electronic impulses capable of being shown as a moving picture and of being the subject of reproduction, and includes the recording of a soundtrack associated with the cinematograph film.[14]

PROTECTED PERSONS

As a general rule, copyright initially vests in the author.[15] In the case of a cinematograph film, "author" means the person by whom the arrangements for the making of the cinematograph film were undertaken.[16]

Where a work has been *commissioned* by a person who is not the author's employer under a contract of service, then, the copyright is deemed to be transferred to the person who commissioned the work, unless it has been agreed otherwise by contract.[17]

Where a work has been made in the course of the author's *employment* (as distinguished from having been made pursuant to a commission referred to above), the copyright is deemed to be transferred to the author's employer, unless it has been agreed otherwise by contract.[18]

Where a work has been made by, or under the direction or control of, the Government of Kenya or an international body or other governmental organization designated in the Regulations issued under the Act, copyright initially vests in the Government, the international body, or the governmental organization.[19]

ASSIGNMENT AND LICENSING

Generally.—Copyright is transmissible by assignment, by testamentary disposition, or by operation of law, as movable property.[20]

An assignment or testamentary disposition of copyright may be limited so as to apply to some only of the acts which the owner of the copyright has the exclusive right to control; or to a part only of the

[13] Section 2(1).　[14] Section 2(1).　[15] Section 11(1).
[16] Section 2(1).　[17] Section 11(1).　[18] Section 11(1).
[19] Sections 6(1), 11(2). According to the Copyright Regulations 1966 (see footnote 3, above), Second Schedule, such international organizations are: (i) the United Nations, (ii) the Specialized Agencies of the United Nations, (iii) the Organization of American States, (iv) the Organization of African Unity.
[20] Section 12(1).

period of the copyright; or to a specified country or other geographical area.[21]

No assignment of copyright and no exclusive license can have effect unless they are in writing signed by or on behalf of the assignor or licensor.[22]

A non-exclusive license to do an act falling within the ambit of copyright may be written or oral, or may be inferred from conduct, and may be revoked at any time, but a license granted by contract may not be revoked, either by the person who granted the license or his successor in title, except as the contract may provide, or by a further contract.[23]

An assignment or license granted by one copyright owner has effect as if granted by his co-owners also, and, subject to any contract between them, fees received by the grantor are to be divided equitably between all the co-owners. Co-ownership exists among persons: (i) if they share a joint interest in the whole or any part of a copyright, or (ii) if they have interests in the various copyrights in a composite production, that is to say, a production consisting of two or more works.[24]

Future Works.—An assignment, license or testamentary disposition may be effectively granted or made in respect of a future work, or an existing work in which copyright does not yet subsist. The prospective copyright in any such work is transmissible by operation of law as movable property.[25]

"Corpus Mechanicum".—A testamentary disposition of the material on which a work is first written or otherwise recorded is, in the absence of contrary indication, to be taken to include the disposition of any copyright or prospective copyright in the work which is vested in the deceased.[26]

Licenses Administered by Licensing Bodies.—"Licensing body" means an organization which has as its main object, or one of its main objects, the negotiation or granting of licenses in respect of works protected by copyright.[27] If a licensing body unreasonably refuses to grant licenses, or is imposing unreasonable terms or conditions on the granting of licenses, the Government authority appointed to that effect may direct that corresponding licenses may be deemed to have been granted by the copyright owner provided that the appropriate fees prescribed by the said Government authority are paid or tendered.[28]

---

[21] Section 12(2).   [22] Section 12(3).   [23] Section 12(4).
[24] Section 12(5).   [25] Section 12(6).   [26] Section 12(7).   [27] Section 14(2).
[28] Section 14(1) and (2).

PROTECTED RIGHTS

Economic Rights

Copyright in a *literary, musical or artistic work*, or in a *cinematograph film*, is the exclusive right to control the doing in Kenya of any of the following acts: (i) reproduction in any material form, (ii) communication to the public, (iii) broadcasting. The right exists in respect of the whole work or a substantial part thereof, both in its original form and in any form recognizably derived from the original.[29]

"Reproduction" means the making of one or more copies of the work or cinematograph film. "Copy" means a reproduction in written form, in the form of a recording or cinematograph film, or in any other material form, so however that an object is not to be taken to be a copy of an architectural work unless the object is a building or a model. "Communication to the public" includes, in addition to any live performance or delivery, any mode of visual or acoustic presentation. "Broadcasting" means the broadcasting of sounds and/or images, and includes diffusion over wires.[30]

Copyright in a *work of architecture* also includes the exclusive right to control the erection of any building which reproduces the whole or any substantial part of the work either in its original form or in any form recognizably derived from the original, provided that this right does not include the right to control the reconstruction of a building in the same style as the original.[31]

Limitations

Free Uses.—The following uses are free, i.e., require neither authorization by nor payment to the copyright owner:

Fair Dealing, i.e., reproduction, communication to the public or broadcasting "by way of fair dealing" for purposes of research, private use, criticism or review, or the reporting of current events. However, if such use is public, it must be accompanied by an acknowledgement of the title of the work and its authorship, except when the work is incidentally included in a broadcast.[32]

Parody, etc.—Reproduction, communication to the public, or broadcasting, is free if it is by way of parody, pastiche or caricature.[33]

Artistic Works Situated in Streets, etc.—The reproduction and distribution of copies, or the inclusion in a film or broadcast, is free if the work is an artistic work which is situated in a place where it can be viewed by the public.[34]

[29] Section 7(1).   [30] Section 2(1).   [31] Section 7(2).
[32] Sections 7(1) (i), 9, and 10.   [33] Section 7(1) (ii).   [34] Section 7(1) (iii).

Incidental Filming or Television of an Artistic Work.—Inclusion of an artistic work in a cinematograph film or in a television broadcast is free if it is incidental.[35]

Collections of Literary or Musical Works.—Inclusion of not more than two short passages from a work in a collection of literary or musical works is free if the collection is designed for use in educational institutions. The included passages must be accompanied by an acknowledgement of the title of the work and its authorship.[36]

Educational Broadcasts.—The broadcasting of a work is free if the broadcast is intended to be used for educational purposes.[37]

School and University Use.—Any use of a work is free in any school registered in accordance with the Kenya Education Act or in any university for the educational purposes of that school or university. Any reproductions made under this exception must be destroyed within twelve months of the making of the reproduction.[38]

Reading, etc. of Extracts.—The reading or recitation in public or in a broadcast of any reasonable extract of a literary work is free, if the work is a published work and if the use is accompanied by a sufficient acknowledgement.[39]

Government-ordered Use in Public Interest.—Use of a work, sound recording, or broadcast by or under the direction or control of the Government, public libraries, non-commercial documentations centers and scientific institutions designated by Regulations, is free if (i) the use is in the public interest, (ii) no revenue is derived from the use, (iii) in cases where the use consists of communication to the public, (iii) no admission fee is charged.[40]

Ephemeral Recording, etc.—The reproduction of a work by or under the direction or control of a broadcasting authority is free if (i) the reproduction or any copies thereof are intended exclusively for lawful broadcast by that broadcasting authority, (ii) the reproduction and any copies thereof are destroyed within six months of reproduction or any longer period agreed under contract. Reproductions of an exceptional documentary character may, however, be preserved but may not be used without the authorization of the copyright owner.[41]

Judicial Proceedings.—Any use made of a work for the purpose of judicial proceedings is free. Any use for the purpose of a report on such proceedings is equally free.[42]

---

[35] Section 7(1) (iv).   [36] Section 7(1) (v).   [37] Section 7(1) (vi).
[38] Section 7(1) (vii).   [39] Section 7(1) ix).   [40] Sections 7(1) (x), 9, and 10.
[41] Sections 7(1) (xi), and 9.   [42] Sections 7(1) (xiii), 9, and 10.

Compulsory Licenses.—In the following three cases, the author-ization of the owner of the relevant copyright is not required but a fair compensation must be paid to him in accordance with Regulations issued under the Act:

(i) *Making, etc., of Sound Recordings,* or, more precisely, when a sound recording of a literary or artistic work is made or imported and the copies thereof are intended for retail sale in Kenya.[43]

(ii) *Broadcasting of Works not in the Repertoire of a Performing Rights Society,* or, more precisely, when a work already lawfully made acces-sible to the public, and with which no licensing body is concerned, is broadcast.[44]

A "licensing body" is an organization which has as its main objects, or one of its main objects, the negotiation and granting of licenses in respect of protected works.[45]

(iii) *Broadcast of Music of a Cinematograph Film,* or, more precisely, when a broadcasting authority broadcasts a cinematograph film in which a musical work is incorporated.[46]

Broadcasting of Works Incorporated in a Cinematograph Film.—Subject to the provision just stated, where the owner of the copyright in any literary, musical or artistic work has authorized a person to incorporate the work in a cinematograph film and a broad-casting authority broadcasts the film, such authority is in the absense of any express agreement to the contrary, deemed to have been author-ized by the owner of the copyright to·effect such broadcast.[47]

TERM OF PROTECTION

Copyright in *literary works, musical works, and artistic works other than photographs,* expires twenty-five years after the end of the year in which the author dies.[48] In the case of a work of joint authorship, the term is counted from the death of the author who dies last.[49] "Work of joint authorship" means a work produced by the collaboration of two or more authors in which the contribution of each author is not sepa-rable from the contribution of the other author or authors.[50] Anony-mous or pseudonymous literary, musical or artistic works are protected until the expiration of twenty-five years from the end of the year in which they were first published, except that, if the identity of the au-thor becomes known in the meantime, the term is calculated according to the general rules, i.e., twenty-five years *post mortem auctoris.*[51] Copy-right in literary, musical or artistic works (other than photographs)

---

[43] Section 7(1) (viii).   [44] Section 7(1) (xii).   [45] Section 14(2).
[46] Section 8(2).   [47] Section 8(1).   [48] Section 4(2).
[49] Sections 4(4), and 5(2).   [50] Section 2(1).   [51] Sections 4(3), and 5(2).

made by or under the direction or control of the Government or any of the designated international bodies or other governmental organizations subsists until the expiration of twenty-five years from the end of the year in which they were first published.[52] "Publication" takes place if, but only if, copies of the work have been issued in sufficient quantities to satisfy the reasonable requirements of the public.[53]

Copyright in *photographs* and *cinematograph films* expires twenty-five years after the end of the year in which they were first made lawfully accessible to the public.[54]

COMPARISON OF TERMS

Since there is no provision in the Act for the "rule of the shorter term" permitted under Article IV (4) of the Universal Copyright Convention, it would appear that works are protected in Kenya until the expiration of the terms indicated above, even if, in other countries, they fall into the public domain at an earlier date.

INFRINGEMENTS

CIVIL REMEDIES

Generally.—Copyright is infringed by any person who does, or causes any other person to do, an act the doing of which is controlled by the copyright without the license of the owner of the copyright.[55]

Infringements are actionable at the suit of the owner of the copyright, and in any action for infringement all such relief—by way of damages, injunction, accounts or otherwise—is available to the plaintiff as is available under the general laws of Kenya in any corresponding proceedings in respect of infringement of other proprietary rights.[56] "Owner of the copyright" means the first owner, the assignee or an exclusive licensee, as the case may be, of the relevant portion of the copyright.[57]

Innocent Infringers.—If, at the time of the infringement, the defendant was not aware, and had no reasonable grounds for suspecting, that copyright subsisted in the work, he is not liable for damages but only for an account of profits.[58]

Flagrant Infringements.—If the infringement is flagrant, if benefit has accrued to the defendant by reason of the infringement, and if the court is satisfied that effective relief would not otherwise be available to the plaintiff, then, the court, in assessing damages for the

---

[52] Section 6(2).   [53] Section 2(2) (a).   [54] Section 4(2), 5(2), and 6(3).
[55] Section 13(1).   [56] Section 13(2).   [57] Section 13(6).   [58] Section 13(3).

infringement, may award such additional damages as it considers appropriate under the circumstances.[59]

CRIMINAL SANCTIONS

The Act does not provide for criminal sanctions.

INJUNCTIONS

See "Civil Remedies," above. It is to be noted, however, that no injunction issues if it would require a completed or partly built building to be demolished or if it would prevent the completion of a partly built building.[60]

---

[59] Section 13(4).   [60] Section 13(5).

LAOS

According to a letter dated September 8, 1951, from the Prime Minister of Laos to UNESCO, matters of copyright law are governed by the texts of France, regularly promulgated in Laos before the coming into force of the National Constitution of Laos, that is, May 11, 1947.[1] However, no information was obtained on the question of which texts were thus promulgated.

Laos became bound by the Universal Copyright Convention and Protocols 1 and 2 as from August 19, 1954.[2]

[1] *See* CLTW, Laos: Item 1.   [2] *See* CLTW, Laos: Item 2.

LEBANON

SOURCES

Internal Law.—The main source of the law of copyright in Lebanon is a decree of January 17, 1924, amended by a decree of September 22, 1926, and a law of January 31, 1946.[1] Hereinafter, it is referred to as "the Law," and references, without further specification, to Articles are references to Articles of the Law.

Universal Copyright Convention.—Lebanon became bound by the Universal Copyright Convention and Protocols 1 and 2 as from October 17, 1959.[2]

ACQUISITION OF PROTECTION UNDER THE UNIVERSAL COPYRIGHT CONVENTION

The Law protects works from the time of their creation, irrespective of the author's nationality and irrespective of the place in which the work was first published.[3]

Acquisition of copyright is not subject to any formality, but there is optional deposit and registration in the *office de protection*, and such deposit is a prerequisite (except for works protected under the Conventions of the Berne Copyright Union) to the institution of lawsuits in the courts.[4] The absence of the Convention notice on the copies of a published work is no bar to claiming protection in Lebanon. Furthermore, Lebanon has no renewal system, so there is nothing in this country which would correspond to the renewal formalities existing, for example, in the United States.

[1] Decree of the French High Commissioner providing regulation of Commercial and Industrial Property Rights in Syria and Lebanon, No. 2385 of January 17, 1924, amended by Decree No. 526 of the French High Commissioner on September 22, 1926 (published in "Bulletin officiel des actes administratifs du Haut Commissariat de la République française en Syrie et au Liban," February 1924, and September 15, 1926, respectively) and further amended by the Law of January 31, 1946 (published in "Journal officiel de la République libanaise," February 6, 1946); *see* the English translations in CLTW, Lebanon: Item 1.

[2] *See* CLTW, Lebanon: Item 2A. Lebanon is a member of the Berne Copyright Union, the Rome Convention of 1928 being the most recent text of that Union extending to Lebanon (*see* CLTW, Lebanon: Item 3).

[3] Article 148.

[4] Articles 137 and 158 to 168. Such deposit may be effected after the event giving raise to a claim has taken place, (article 158, first paragraph).

PROTECTED WORKS

The Law protects all works which are the manifestations of human intelligence, whether written, plastic or oral. They include books, leaflets, periodicals, newspapers and all other writings; dramatic and dramatico-musical works; musical compositions with or without words; choreographic works and pantomimes; drawings, engravings and illustrations: lithographic and calligraphic works, geographical maps, sketches, plans and works in relief; architectural plans, models and sketches, posters and illustrated post cards; paintings, sculptures, photographs, cinematographic films; rolls, discs and perforated cardboard, etc., for talking machines and mechanical musical instruments; works of art of all kinds, whether or not they have an industrial character and whatever their merit, importance, designation, the material composing them, the nationality of their author and the place of their creation.[5] Are also protected: translations, adaptations, arrangements and other reproductions of original works without prejudice to the rights of the author of the original work from which they were derived.[6] Furthermore, the Law protects collections of selected portions of works which, in themselves, are in the public domain, but when grouped together, as a collection, display an original character; reproductions, by writing or by means of talking machines, of speeches, lectures, instruction by professors, or any other oral manifestations of thought; reproductions or publications of ancient texts or manuscripts preserved in public or private archives.[7]

Tales, stories or novels in serial form published in newspapers or periodicals shall be protected without the necessity of specially forbidding their reproduction, adaptation or translation; all other literary, political and scientific articles of which the reproduction, translation or adaptation has not been forbidden may be reproduced, adapted or translated, but in such cases mention of the source and of the author shall be cumpulsory. Only sundry items and news of the day, having merely informative character, may be reproduced or translated without an indication of source or special authorization.[8]

A cinematographic sound film is considered as an original production constituting an independent entity, without the musical, artistic or literary elements therein having any independent existence, but if the cinematographic work is merely the reproduction of a musical, artistic or literary work, such work preserves its individual character. Only the producer of a cinematographic film has the right to authorize its projection, unless there has been express stipulation to the contrary

[5] Article 138.   [6] Article 139.
[7] Article 140. However, such texts or manuscripts may be freely published anew by another person, provided he takes them directly from the originals (art. 140).
[8] Article 148.

and such stipulation has been notified to the person exploiting the film.

The composer of a musical work cannot oppose the exploitation of the work by means of machines designed for its mechanical diffusion or by any other means, if the person exploiting it has paid a consideration to the composer or to his successors in title.[9]

PROTECTED PERSONS

Copyright originally vests in the author.[10]

When the protected work is the product of collaboration, all collaborators have, in the absence of agreement to the contrary, equal rights in respect of the common work.[11]

When the work is the product of collaboration, and in the absence of agreement to the contrary, no collaborators or their successors in title may, without the consent of the other collaborators or their successors in title, cause the common work to be reproduced, performed, translated, etc. In case of dispute, the Courts decide as to the manner in which the work may be exploited.[12]

In the absence of any stipulation to the contrary, the composer of the music and the author of the words of a lyrical work have equal rights in respect of the work, whether an opera or a song: each may separately exploit the complete work, but neither is entitled to combine with a new collaborator for the purpose of transforming the common work.[13]

The publisher of an anonymous work or of a work appearing under the name of a legal entity is entitled to exercise the rights in respect of the work for such time as the author does not make himself known.[14]

ASSIGNMENT AND LICENSING

Copyright is deemed to be movable property, transmissible and assignable (*cessible*) in accordance with the rules of Civil law (*droit civil*).[15]

Assignment of copyright is to be interpreted restrictively.[16]

PROTECTED RIGHTS

Economic Rights

The author of a literary or artistic work has the exclusive right to publish it and to reproduce it in any form. Only the author or his

[9] Law of February 26, 1946, as amended by the Law of December 31, 1951 (published in "Journal officiel de la République libanaise," February 27, 1946; *see* English translation in CLTW, Lebanon: Item 2).
[10] Article 137. [11] Article 144. [12] Article 150.
[13] Article 151. [14] Article 155. [15] Article 157. [16] Article 146.

successors in title may authorize (i) the reproduction, either in whole or in part, of a work, (ii) its translation (iii), its public performance, (iv) its adaptation, (v) its conversion from a literary into a dramatic work, or vice versa, (vi) its utilization by cinematography or its reproduction by some other art, (vii) its illustration, in the case of a book, (viii) its reproduction by talking machines, or, in the case of a musical work, by mechanical musical instrument, and vice versa.[17]

The following acts, among others, are deemed to be unlawful if committed without the express authorization of the author or his successors in title: public performance of a dramatic, dramatico-musical work; public performance of a translated dramatic work; public reading of a literary work; adaptation and arrangement of a musical work or its orchestration; conversion of a work into another work of the same kind or of a different kind, such as the transformation of a story, an account or a novel into a dramatic work, or vice versa; the conversion of a dramatic or literary work into a cinematographic work.[18]

Moral Rights

Authors may oppose any public exhibition of the material object constituting the created work, if modifications have been made in it without their authorization.[19]

The author who has assigned his rights retains the right of opposing any modification made without his consent. He may, at any time, institute judicial proceedings to obtain recognition of his authorship against any person attributing such authorship to himself. The author or his successors in title may require the courts to order the rescission of an assignment by which the publication, execution, translation, performance, illustration, etc., has been authorized by the author or his successors in title, if it is proved that the assignee has distorted, modified or reproduced the work in a manner harmful to the reputation of the author.[20]

No modification may be made of a literary or musical work of a deceased author unless the part which has been modified is reproduced, *in extenso*, in its original form, upon the same page and in equally prominent characters.[21]

Limitations

Extracts from literary, artistic or scientific works for use in the preparation of school works and analyses, and brief quotations in the course of an article or work of criticism may be freely reproduced.

[17] Article 145, first paragraph.
[18] Article 147.   [19] Article 145, second paragraph.
[20] Article 146.   [21] Article 152.

However, the source must always be clearly indicated in the reproductions.[22]

The composer of a musical work cannot oppose the exploitation of the work by means of machines designed for its mechanical diffusion or by any other means, if the person exploiting it has paid to the composer or to his successors in title the fee fixed by the Law itself.[23] In other words, a legal license takes the place of the exclusive right of authorization in these cases.

TERM OF PROTECTION

Copyright is protected throughout the lifetime of the author, and, in favor of his successors in title, for a period of fifty years after his death.[24]

Photographic works or works produced by a process analogous to photography, anonymous and pseudonymous works, works published under the name of a legal entity, and posthumous works are protected for a term of fifty years, calculated from the date of their publication.[25]

An anonymous work of which the author reveals his identity before the expiration of the said term of fifty years is protected until the death of the author and for a period of fifty years thereafter.[26]

A work is deemed to have been published when copies of it have been issued; the exhibition of a work of art, the performance or rendition of a dramatic or musical work, and the construction of an architectural work do not constitute publication.[27]

INFRINGEMENTS

Infringements of copyright are punishable by imprisonment or fines; the infringer is liable to pay damages; and the owner of copyright may ask for various conservatory measures.[28]

---

[22] Article 149.
[23] Article 2 of the Law cited in footnote 9, above.
[24] Article 143.   [25] Articles 153 and 155.   [26] Article 154.
[27] Article 156.   [28] *See* articles 169 to 180.

LIBERIA

SOURCES

Internal Law.—The main source of the law of copyright in Liberia is the Copyright Act of December 22, 1911, as amended by the Act of January 26, 1956.[1] Hereinafter, it is referred to as "the Act." References to Sections, without further specification, are references to Sections of this Act.

Universal Copyright Convention.—Liberia became bound by the Universal Copyright Convention and Protocols 1 and 2 as from January 26, 1956.[2]

AQUISITION OF PROTECTION UNDER THE UNIVERSAL COPYRIGHT CONVENTION

The Act does not differentiate between works according to nationality or place of first publication. Works that are entitled to protection under the Universal Copyright Convention are protected without having to comply with deposit, registration or any other formality.[3]

Furthermore, Liberia has no renewal system, so that there is nothing in this country which would correspond to the renewal formalities existing in the United States.

PROTECTED WORKS

Literary, scientific and artistic works are protected.[4] They comprise "books, pamphlets, other writings, dramatic and dramatico-musical works, chirographic works, pantomimes, musical compositions, cinematographic works, designs, paintings, architectural drawings, plans, sketches, and plastic works relative to geography, topography, architecture of the sciences, translations, adaptation(s), musical arrangements, other reproduction(s) converted into literary or artistic works."[5]

---

[1] Published in "Acts passed by the Legislature of the Republic of Liberia during the Session 1911—1912," page 24, and "Acts passed by the Republic of Liberia during the Session 1955—1956," page 1; reprinted in CLTW, Liberia: Item 1.
[2] CLTW, Liberia: Item 2. [3] Section 10. [4] Section 1.
[5] Section 2.

PROTECTED PERSONS

Copyright vests in the author.[6]

PROTECTED RIGHTS

Authors have the exclusive right to reproduce their works, and to sell or authorize such reproductions.[7] The exclusive right of selling a work comprises the right of forbidding the sale in Liberia of reproductions made outside Liberia without the permission of the author.[8]

TERM OF PROTECTION

Copyright lasts during the life of the author and 25 years after his death.[9]

INFRINGEMENTS

Infringers are punishable by fine, and are liable for damages.[10]

---

[6] Section 1.   [7] Sections 1 and 3.
[8] Section 4.   [9] Section 3.   [10] Section 9.

LIECHTENSTEIN

SOURCES

Internal Law.—The main source of the law of copyright in Liechtenstein is the Law on Copyright in Literary and Artistic Works of October 26, 1928, as amended by the Law of August 8, 1959.[1] Hereinafter it is referred to as "the Law," and references to Articles, without further specification, are references to Articles of this Law, as amended.

Universal Copyright Convention.—Liechtenstein became bound by the Universal Copyright Convention and Protocols 1 and 2 as from January 22, 1959.[2]

ACQUISITION OF PROTECTION UNDER THE UNIVERSAL COPYRIGHT CONVENTION

The Law of Liechtenstein does not contain any special provision in respect of works to which Liechtenstein is supposed to grant protection by virtue of the Universal Copyright Convention. The provisions of that Convention, particularly Articles II and XVII, and Protocols 1 and 2, determine which are the works protected under the Universal Copyright Convention. Briefly stated, such works are—except if excluded by virtue of Article XVII of the Universal Copyright Convention and the Appendix Declaration relating to the same Article (in which case the applicable Convention of the Berne Copyright Union rather than the Universal Copyright Convention governs): (i) published works of nationals of a Convention country, irrespective of the place of first publication, (ii) works first published in a Convention country, irrespective of the nationality of the author, (iii) unpublished works of nationals of a Convention country other than Liechtenstein, (iv) works of stateless persons and refugees who have their habitual residence in a State party to Protocol 1 (except perhaps Liechtenstein), whether published or unpublished, and if published, irrespective of the

---

[1] Published in *Liechtensteinisches Landes-Gesetzblatt*, No. 12 of November 3, 1928, and No. 17 of October 26, 1959. *See* English translation in CLTW, Liechtenstein: Item 1.
[2] *See* CLTW, Liechtenstein: Item 1A. Liechtenstein is a member of the Berne Copyright Union, the Brussels Convention of 1948 being the latest text which it ratified (*see* CLTW, Liechtenstein: Item 2).

place of first publication, (v) works first published by the United Nations, by any of the Specialized Agencies of the United Nations, or by the Organization of American States, as well as unpublished works of any of these organizations.

There seems to be no difference between the protection afforded by Liechtenstein by virtue of its membership in the Berne Union, and the protection granted pursuant to its being party to the Universal Copyright Convention, Consequently, the question of which of the Conventions applies in a concrete situation appears to be largely academic.

Article 65 *bis* of the Law, enacted in 1959, provides in effect that the works of Liechtenstein nationals and works first published (*herausgegeben*) in Liechtenstein, enjoy the more extended (*weitergehende*) protection granted by the Brussels Convention of the Berne Union. The basic principle of the Universal Copyright Convention is national treatment, by virtue of which Liechtenstein would have to grant, in all respects, the same protection to nationals of countries party to the Universal Copyright Convention (and to works first published in such countries) as it grants to its own nationals. Consequently, it could be argued that the "plus" protection guaranteed to Liechtenstein works must also be granted to Convention works. On the other hand, the very specific character of the provision contained in Article 65 *bis*, namely, that it extends certain provisions of the *Brussels* Convention to *Liechtenstein* works, throws some doubt on the correctness of an interpretation according to which Liechtenstein would extend the said "plus" protection to works which are not of Liechtenstein and which may not originate in a country member of the Berne Union. Since, however, the protection granted by the Brussels Convention does not seem to be "more extended" than the protection existing under the Liechtenstein Copyright Law (other than its Article 65 *bis*), it appears to be largely superfluous to try to solve the question. In any case, the following analysis is limited to the Liechtenstein Copyright Law and disregards any additional protection which may or may not be available under the combined application of Article 65 *bis*, the Brussels Convention, and the national treatment provisions of the Universal Copyright Convention.

Acquisition of copyright is not subject to the fulfilment of any formality in Liechtenstein.[3] Consequently, registration, deposit, or compliance with other formalities is neither required nor possible in Liechtenstein, and the absence, in itself, of the Convention notice on the copies of a published work is no bar to claiming protection in Liechtenstein. Furthermore, Liechtenstein has no renewal system, so there is nothing in this country which would correspond to the renewal formalities existing, for example, in the United States.

[3] However, it is lawful to reproduce in the press topical articles relating to economics, politics or religion *if their reproduction is not expressly reserved* or if they are not expressly designated as original contributions or original reports (art. 25(2)).

PROTECTED WORKS

All literary and artistic works are protected.[4] Literary and musical works are protected, even when they are not written or fixed in some other manner unless, by their nature, they can come into existence only through fixation in some form.[5] Photographic works, including works obtained by processes analogous to photography, are protected.[6]

The Law expressly mentions, as examples, the following categories of works as coming under the general expression "literary and artistic works": works of *belles lettres*; scientific works; geographical and topographical maps and other figurative representations of a scientific or technical nature; choreographic works; pantomimes, actions (*Handlungen*) fixed by cinematography or by analogous means and constituting an original creation; musical works; works of art (*Werke der bildenden Künste*), such as works of drawing, painting, sculpture, architecture, engraving, lithography, and of applied art.[7]

Compilations (*Sammlungen*) are protected as works, without prejudice to the copyright subsisting in the individual works included therein.[8]

Translations, and other adaptations (*Wiedergaben*) constituting original literary, artistic or photographic works, are protected, subject to the copyright in the works from which they were derived.[9]

The mere fact that a work has been, either in its finished form or as a project, deposited as an industrial design (*Muster oder Modell*) does not deprive it of protection under the Copyright Law.[10]

PROTECTED PERSONS

Generally.—Copyright originally vests in the author.

Collaboration.—Persons who have jointly created a work in such a manner that their respective contributions cannot be separated possess, as collaborators, a common copyright in the work. They can dispose of it only jointly, but each of them may prosecute infringers by himself.[11]

Presumptions of Authorship.—In the absence of proof to the contrary, the author of the work is deemed to be: (i) the physical person whose true name is indicated upon the copies of the work in the manner in which authors generally are indicated upon such copies,[12] (ii) the physical person who, in connection with the public recitation, performance or exhibition of the work, or in connection with the public

---

[4] Article 1(1).   [5] Article 1(2).   [6] Article 2.   [7] Article 1(2).
[8] Article 3.   [9] Articles 4(1) and (3).   [10] Article 5.   [11] Article 7.
[12] In the case of works of art or photography, the application of a distinctive sign referring to the author is sufficient (art. 8(1) (1)).

exhibition of copies (*Werkexemplare*) of the work, is named as author by his true name.[13]

Anonymous and Pseudonymous Works.—In the case of a published (*herausgegeben*) work, the author of which is not indicated in the manner creating the presumptions referred to above, the person who caused the work to appear (*Herausgeber*), or if such person is not designated, the publisher (*Herausgeber*) is responsible for the safeguarding of copyright, and, in the absence of proof to the contrary, he will be deemed to be the successor in title (*Rechtsnachfolger*) of the author.[14]

Portraits.—In the absence of agreement to the contrary, copies of a commissioned portrait may not be put into circulation or made available for public disclosure without the authorization of the person portrayed.[15]

ASSIGNMENT AND LICENSING

General Rules of Interpretation.—The transfer of one of the rights comprised in copyright does not imply the transfer of other rights comprised in copyright.[16] Transfer of the property in a copy of a work does not imply transfer of the copyright therein, even if what is transferred is the original copy.[17]

PROTECTED RIGHTS

ECONOMIC RIGHTS

Copyright includes the following exclusive rights:

(a) *to reproduce* (*wiedergeben*) the work by any process,[18] in the original form or in a modified form.[19] The latter includes: (i) translation, (ii) transfer (*übertragen*) on contrivances capable of mechanical recitation or performance, (iii) reproduction by means of cinematography or other similar processes,[20] (iv) the realization (carrying out, *Ausführung*) of plans of figurative works of a scientific nature, architectural works, works of applied art, or any other works of art.[21] The transfer of musical works to contrivances capable of mechanical performance, however, is in certain circumstances, subject to compulsory license.[22] Copyright in

[13] Article 8(1).   [14] Article 8(2).
[15] Article 35(1). If he is dead or otherwise not available, the Law prescribes who may exercise the right.
[16] Article 9(2).   [17] Article 9(3).   [18] Article 12(1), item (1).
[19] Article 13(1).   [20] Articles 17 to 20.   [21] Article 14.
[22] Any person having an industrial establishment in Liechtenstein (or in the United States of America; *see* Decree of the Federal Council of September 26, 1924) is

a musical work does not extend to the use of its melody when a new and original work results from such use.[23] Copyright in a photographic work does not exclude the right of any other person to take a new photograph of the same object, even if such new photograph is taken from the same position and, in a general manner, under the same conditions as the first photograph;[24]

(b) *to sell, place on sale* (*feilhalten*), *or put into circulation in any other manner* copies of the work;[25]

(c) *to recite, perform* (*représenter, exécuter*; *aufführen, vorführen*), *or exhibit the work publicly*, or *to transmit publicly over wires* the recitation, performance or exhibition of the work;[26]

(d) *to exhibit* publicly copies (*exemplaires, Werkexemplare*) of the work, or *to disclose* the work to the public in any other manner, as long as the work has not been communicated to the public by or with the permission of the owner of the copyright;[27]

(e) *to broadcast* a work, or otherwise communicate it to the public by any other means capable to diffuse, without wires, signs, sounds or images;[28]

(f) *to communicate the broadcast work publicly*, over wires or otherwise, when such communication is made by an organization other than the originating organization;[29]

entitled to require, against the payment of an equitable remuneration, authorization to adapt a musical work to contrivances capable of performing it mechanically (i) if the author is dead and the work has been published, or, (ii) if, being alive, he has already given a like authorization extending to Liechtenstein or any other country and the instruments to which the work has been adapted have been placed upon the market or the work has been published in some other manner. The authorization has effect only in respect of circulation of the contrivances in Liechtenstein and their export to countries where the work enjoys no protection against an adaptation of this nature. The same principles apply to the text of musical works. *See* articles 17, 18, 19, 20.

[23] Article 15.   [24] Article 16.   [25] Article 12(1), item (2).

[26] Article 12(1), item (3). In the case of the public performance of a musical work with words, the owner of the right of performance in the musical work is, in relation to third parties, deemed to have the right to authorize also the public performance of the words (art. 34(1)). Persons providing a place for unlawful recitation, performance, exhibition or display are civilly responsible only if they were aware of the unlawful character of these acts (art. 60). Any person who utilizes, for public recitation, performance, exhibition (*Vorführung*), or broadcast of a work, copies which have been manufactured or put into circulation in an unlawful manner is an infringer (art. 42(2)), unless he has acquired the copies in good faith at a public auction, in the market, or from a person dealing in objects of like kind, and if, prior to the recitation, performance or exhibition, he was unaware of the unlawful character of the copies so used (art. 61(1)).

[27] Article 12(1), item 4. Any person who publicly exhibits (*Ausstellung*) copies which have been manufactured or put into circulation in an unlawful manner, incurs no responsibility if he has acquired the copies in good faith at a public auction, in the market, or from a person dealing in objects of like kind, and if, prior to the exhibition, he was unaware of the unlawful character of the copies exhibited (art. 61(2)).

[28] Article 12(1), item 5, and (2).   [29] Article 12(1), item 6.

(g) *to communicate publicly by loudspeaker* or by any other like instrument transmitting signs, sounds or images, the broadcast work or the work publicly transmitted over wires.[30]

MORAL RIGHTS

The provisions of the Civil Code and the Code of Obligations protecting the person are expressly reserved by the Law.[31]

Any person who, in such a manner as to deceive others, applies the name of the author, his distinctive sign or his pseudonym to the copies of a reproduction not emanating from the author himself, or to the copies of an original work of another person, is liable both civilly and criminally.[32]

LIMITATIONS

Except for the construction of works of architecture, the reproduction of a work is free if the reproduction is destined exclusively for the personal and private use of the person reproducing it; such reproduction may not be made for profit.[33] The Law also contains limitations or exceptions *in certain cases* of: reproduction or other uses of speeches delivered in public meetings,[34] reproduction of newspaper and magazine articles,[35] reproduction of literary and musical works in scientific works,[36] reproduction of literary works in school textbooks,[37] reproduction of musical or dramatic works in preparation of their public performance,[38] reproduction of works of art or photography in a school book or catalogue or when they are permanently located in a public place,[39] reproduction of commissioned portraits,[40] reproduction of the text of musical works for distribution to the audience,[41] reporting of current events by means of photography, cinematography or broadcasting.[42]

TERM OF PROTECTION

Protection ends at the expiration of the fiftieth calendar year following the death of the author.[43] However, where the work is (i) anonymous, or (ii) pseudonymous and the pseudonym leaves doubt as to the author's identity, protection ends at the expiration of the fiftieth calendar year

---

[30] Article 12(1), item 7.   [31] Article 44.
[32] Article 43.   [33] Article 22. *See also* article 42(2).
[34] Article 24 and 31.   [35] Articles 25 and 31.
[36] Articles 26 and 31.   [37] Articles 27 and 31.   [38] Article 28.
[39] Articles 29 and 31.   [40] Articles 30 and 31.
[41] Article 32.   [42] Article 33 *bis*.
[43] Articles 36, 37, 38, 41. In the case of works of collaboration, the death of the last surviving co-author governs (art. 39).

following the year in which the work was made public (*öffentliche Bekanntgabe*), provided the identity of the author is not revealed before the expiration of this period.[44]

Since there is no provision in Liechtenstein law for the "rule of the shorter term" permitted under Article IV(4) of the Universal Copyright Convention, it would appear that works to which the Universal Copyright Convention applies are protected in Liechtenstein until the expiration of the terms indicated above even if in other countries they fall into the public domain at an earlier date.

INFRINGEMENTS

Generally.—Acts requiring the consent of the owner of copyright, if committed without his consent, constitute infringements.[45] Furthermore, it is a violation of the Law to apply, in such a manner as to deceive others, the name of the author, his distinctive sign or his pseudonym, to the original work or to copies not authorized by the author.[46] Infringing copies (other than buildings), and objects serving exclusively for the manufacture of infringing copies, may be seized[47] and confiscated.[48] If copies of a work (other than sound recordings) lawfully manufactured are put into circulation outside the territory for which the owner of the copyright has authorized their sale, such putting into circulation does not constitute infringement within the meaning of the Copyright Law, but the plaintiff may seek remedy on the grounds of breach of contract.[49]

Civil Remedies.—The general provisions of the Code of Obligations apply, even if the violation is committed outside Liechtenstein but to the detriment of a person domiciled in Liechtenstein.[50]

Penal Sanction.—Penal sanctions apply only where the violation was intentional,[51] and penal proceedings take place only upon complaint of the injured private party.[52] Violations are punishable by fines,[53] and action prescribed within three years.[54]

---

[44] Articles 36, 37, 38, 41. In the case of works consisting of independent separate parts made public at different times, each part is considered a "work" (art. 40(1)). In the case of works appearing in instalments, the date of the making public of the last instalment governs (art. 40(2)).

[45] *See above*, "Economic Rights," page 440.

[46] Article 43, item 1. *See also* items 2 and 3 of the same article.

[47] Articles 51, 52, 54.   [48] Articles 53 and 54.

[49] Article 56.   [50] Article 44.   [51] Article 46.

[52] Article 47.   [53] Article 49.   [54] Article 50(1).

LUXEMBOURG

SOURCES

Internal Law.—The main source of the law of copyright in Luxembourg is the Copyright Law of May 10, 1898.[1] Hereinafter, it is referred to as "the Law," and references to Articles, without further specification, are references to Articles of this Law.

Universal Copyright Convention.—Luxembourg became bound by the Universal Copyright Convention and Protocols 1 and 2 as from October 15, 1955.[2]

ACQUISITION OF PROTECTION UNDER THE UNIVERSAL COPYRIGHT CONVENTION

The Law does not seem to differentiate between works according to the nationality of their authors or the place of their first publication: they are equally protected by the Law whether originating in Luxembourg or outside Luxembourg.[3]

Subject to two exceptions, there are no copyright formalities in Luxembourg. The two exceptions relate to public performance and to posthumous works, discussed below.[4]

Luxembourg has no renewal system, so that there is nothing in this country which would correspond to the renewal formalities existing in the United States.

PROTECTED WORKS

The Law protects "literary and artistic works,"[5] and expressly mentions the following kinds of works as included among those protected: books, pamphlets and all other writings; dramatic or dramatico-

---

[1] Published in the "Mémorial" of May 21, 1898. English translation published in CLTW, Luxembourg: Item 1.

[2] *See* CLTW, Luxembourg: Item 2. Luxembourg is a member of the Berne Copyright Union, the most recent Convention of that Union which it ratified being the Brussels Convention of 1948 (*see* CLTW, Luxembourg: Item 3).

[3] Article 39.

[4] *See* pages 446 and 447, below.

[5] Article 1, first paragraph.

musical works, musical composition with or without words; works of drawing, painting, sculpture, engraving; lithographs, illustrations, geographical maps; plans, sketches and plastic works relative to geography, topography, architecture or to sciences in general; works of architecture; photographic works and works produced by an analogous process; and finally, any production whatsoever in the literary, scientific or artistic domain which is capable of publication in any manner and in any form whatsoever.[6]

Furthermore, oral works, such as lessons, sermons, lectures and speeches, are also protected.[7]

The fact that a work of art is reproduced by an industrial process or applied to an industrial product does not deprive it of protection under the Copyright Law.[8]

PROTECTED PERSONS

Copyright originally vests in the author.[9]

The publisher of an anonymous or pseudonymous work is, in so far as third parties are concerned, regarded as the author of the work. Upon the author's revealing his identity, he resumes the exercise of his right. If the author's real name is revealed, either by the author or by his successors in title authorized to do so, the term of protection is calculated on the basis of the author's life.[10]

ASSIGNMENT AND LICENSING

Copyright is movable property, and is assignable and transmissible in whole or in part, in accordance with the rules of the Civil Code of Luxembourg.[11]

When the copyright is undivided, its exercise is regulated by agreement. In case of agreement, no single co-proprietor may exercise the copyright by himself; failing such agreement, the Courts decide. However, each of the proprietors may, without intervention of the other proprietors, take action in his own name in respect of any infringement of the copyright, and claim damages in respect of his share of the right. The Courts may always subordinate the authorization to publish the work to such conditions as they may consider fit to prescribe. They are

[6] Article 2, second paragraph.
[7] Article 10, first paragraph. However, speeches made in deliberative assemblies, at public court proceedings, or at political gatherings, may be freely published; but only the author shall have the right to print them separately (article 10, second paragraph).
[8] Article 21.   [9] Article 1, first paragraph.
[10] Article 7.   [11] Article 3.

free to decide, upon the request of an opposing co-proprietor, that he can neither share in the costs nor in the profits of publication, or that the name of such collaborator must not appear on the work.[12]

The transfer of a work of art is not deemed to transfer the right of reproduction to the person who acquired the work.[13]

PROTECTED RIGHTS

ECONOMIC RIGHTS

The author of a work has an exclusive right to reproduce it or to authorize its reproduction in any manner or form.[14]

According to the apparently unrepealed provisions of the Law, the exclusive right of translation ceases to exist if the author does not exercise it within 10 years from the first publication of the original work, by publishing or having published a translation in the language for which protection is claimed.[15] This provision, if still in force, is at variance with the minimum provisions of the Universal Copyright Convention (*see* Article V of that Convention).

No work may be publicly performed, either wholly or in part, without the consent of the author. The right of the author or of his successors in title shall apply also to the public performance of unpublished works or of published works in which the author has expressly stated in the title or at the beginning of the work that he prohibits its public performance.[16]

Copyright in musical compositions includes the exclusive right of making arrangements based upon themes from the original work.[17]

In the case of works consisting of words or libretti and music, neither the author nor the composer may independently combine his work with that of another collaborator. Nevertheless, each has the right to exploit the work independently by way of publication, translation or public performance.[18]

[12] Article 6. [13] Article 19. [14] Article 1, first paragraph.
[15] Article 12, first paragraph. In the case of works published in instalments, the term of ten years starts to run from the date of publication of the last instalment of the original work.

In respect of works composed of several volumes published at intervals, as well as in respect of bulletins or pamphlets published by literary or scientific societies or by individuals, each volume, bulletin or pamphlet is considered as a separate work for the purpose of calculating the term of ten years.

The 31st of December of the year in which the work was published is deemed to be the date of publication for the purpose of calculating the term of protection (article 12, second, third and fourth paragraphs).

[16] Articles 15 and 16. It is possible—although no authentic text so states it—that the Convention notice would satisfy this requirement of express reservation of the performance rights in the copies of published works.

[17] Article 17. [18] Article 18.

MORAL RIGHTS

The assignee of copyright or the acquirer of the tangible object incorporating a literary or artistic work may not modify the work in order to sell or exploit it, nor publicly exhibit the modified work, without the consent of the author or his successors in title.[19]

LIMITATIONS

Copyright does not prevent free quotation from a work for the purposes of criticism, polemics or teaching.[20]

Neither the author nor the proprietor of a portrait has the right to reproduce or exhibit it in public without the consent of the person portrayed or that of his successors in title, during 20 years following the date of death of such person. As the result of such consent, the proprietor has the right of reproduction, but the copies must bear no indication of the name of the author.[21]

TERM OF PROTECTION

Copyright endures until the expiration of 50 years from the death of the author.[22]

The proprietors of a posthumous work enjoy copyright for a period of 50 years from the date when the work is published, performed, or exhibited, provided registration is effected in a Government Office within six months of publication, performance or exhibition.[23] There is no indication in the law of Luxembourg that this formality could be avoided by the use of the Convention notice.

When the work is the result of collaboration, copyright subsists for the benefit of all successors in title for 50 years after the death of the last surviving collaborator.[24]

Since there is no provision in the law of Luxembourg for the "rule of the shorter term" permitted under Article IV(4) of the Universal Copyright Convention, it would appear that works to which the Universal Copyright Convention applies are protected in this country until the expiration of the terms indicated above even if in other countries they fall into the public domain at an earlier date.

---

[19] Article 8.   [20] Article 13.   [21] Article 20.   [22] Article 2.
[23] Article 4, first paragraph, and Decree of the Grand Duke of May 10, 1898 (published in "Mémorial" of May 21, 1898).
[24] Article 5.

INFRINGEMENTS

Civil Remedies.—Infringers are liable for damages and various other remedies are available against actual or menacing infringements.[25]

Penal Sanctions.—Certain infringements, if committed wilfully or fraudulently (*böswillige oder betrügerische Verletzung*; (*atteinte méchante ou frauduleuse*) are punishable by fine or imprisonment.[26]

---

[25] *See* Articles 30 to 38.   [26] *See* Articles 22 to 29.

MALAWI

SOURCES

Internal Law.—The main source of the law of copyright in Malawi is the Copyright Act, 1965.[1] Hereinafter, it is referred to as "the Act," and references to Sections, without further specification, are references to Sections of this Act.

Universal Copyright Convention.—Malawi became bound by the Universal Copyright Convention on October 26, 1965.[2] It is not bound by any of the Protocols.

ACQUISITION OF PROTECTION UNDER THE UNIVERSAL COPYRIGHT CONVENTION

The application of the Act is extended in respect of literary, musical and artistic works and cinematograph films:

(i) to individuals or bodies corporate who are citizens of, or domiciled or resident in, or incorporated under the laws of, a country bound by the Universal Copyright Convention (hereinafter referred to as a "Convention country"),

(ii) to works, other than sound recordings, first published in a Convention country.[3]

A work is taken to have been published if, but only if, copies have been issued in sufficient quantities to satisfy the reasonable requirements of the public.[4] Where in the first instance a part only of a work is published, that part is treated, for the purposes of the Act, as a separate work.[5] A publication in any country is not treated as being other than the first publication by reason only of an earlier publication elsewhere if the two publications took place within a period of not more than thirty days.[6]

The acquisition of copyright protection in Malawi is not subject to any formality. Consequently, registration or deposit is not required,

---

[1] Act No. 38 of 1965, published in the "Malawi Government Gazette" of May 14, 1965. Entered into force on May 24, 1965. Reprinted in CLTW, Malawi: Item 1.
[2] See CLTW, Malawi: Item 2.
[3] See the Copyright (Extension) Regulations, 1966, Government Notice No. 248, published in the "Malawi Gazette Supplement" of November 18, 1966, page 432.
[4] Section 2(2) (a).   [5] Section 2(2) (b).   [6] Section 2(2) (c).

and the absence, in itself, of the Convention notice on the copies of a published work is no bar to the claiming of protection in Malawi. Furthermore, Malawi has no renewal system, so there is nothing in that country which would correspond to the renewal formalities existing in the United States. Protection in Malawi will last, without any intervention on the part of the copyright owner or a State authority, until the day on which the work falls into the public domain.

PROTECTED WORKS

Generally.—The Act distinguishes between six categories of works: literary works, musical works, artistic works, cinematograph films, sound recordings, broadcasts.[7]

The first three—i.e., literary, musical and artistic works—are eligible for copyright only if both of the following conditions are fulfilled: (i) sufficient effort has been expended on making the work to give it an original character, (ii) the work has been written down, recorded, or otherwise reduced to material form.[8]

No work is ineligible for copyright by reason only that the making of the work, or the doing of any act in relation to the work, involved an infringement of copyright in some other work.[9]

"Work" includes translations, adaptations, new versions or arrangements of pre-existing works, and anthologies or collections of works which, by reason of the selection and arrangement of their content, present an original character.[10]

Literary Works.—These include, irrespective of literary quality: (i) novels, stories and poetical works, (ii) plays, stage directions, film scenarios and broadcasting scripts, (iii) textbooks, treatises, histories, biographies, essays and articles, (iv) encyclopaedias and dictionaries, (v) letters, reports and memoranda, (vi) lectures, addresses and sermons.[11]

Musical Works.—These are protected irrespective of musical quality. They include works composed for musical accompaniment.[12]

Artistic Works.—These include, irrespective of artistic quality: (i) paintings, drawings, etchings, lithographs, woodcuts, engravings, prints; (ii) maps, plans, diagrams; (iii) works of sculpture; (iv) photographs not comprised in cinematograph film; (v) works of architecture in the form of buildings (including any structures) or models; (vi)

---

[7] Section 3(1). Since the Copyright (Extension) Regulations, 1966 (see footnote 3, above), do not extend protection, under the Universal Copyright Convention, to sound recordings and braodcasts, no further reference is made in this book to these two categories.

[8] Section 3(2).   [9] Section 3(4).   [10] Section 2(1).   [11] Section 2(1).
[12] Section 2(1).

works of artistic craftsmanship, including, subject to the exceptions stated in the following paragraph, pictorial woven tissues and articles of applied handicraft and industrial art.[13]

An artistic work is not eligible for copyright if, at the time the work was made, it was intended by the author to be used as a model or pattern to be multiplied by any industrial process.[14]

Cinematograph Films.—A "cinematograph film" means the first fixation of a sequence of visual images capable of being shown as a moving picture and of being the subject of reproduction and includes the recording of a soundtrack associated with the cinematograph film.[15]

PROTECTED PERSONS

As a general rule, copyright initially vests in the author.[16] In the case of a cinematograph film, "author" means the person by whom the arrangements for the making of the film were undertaken.[17]

Where a work has been *commissioned* by a person who is not the author's employer under a contract of service, then, the copyright is deemed to be transferred to the person who commissioned the work, unless it has been agreed otherwise by contract.[18]

Where a work has been made in the course of the author's *employment* (as distinguished from having been made pursuant to a commission referred to above), the copyright is deemed to be transferred to the author's employer, unless it has been agreed otherwise by contract.[19]

Where a work has been made by, or under the direction or control of, the Government of Malawi, copyright initially vests in the Government.[20]

ASSIGNMENT AND LICENSING

Generally.—Copyright is transmissible by assignment, by testamentary disposition, or by operation of law, as movable property.[21]

An assignment or testamentary disposition of copyright may be limited so as to apply to some only of the acts which the owner of the copyright has the exclusive right to control; or to a part only of the period of the copyright; or to a specified country or other geographical area.[22]

No assignment of copyright and no exclusive license can have effect

---

[13] Section 2(1).   [14] Section 3(3).   [15] Section 2(1).   [16] Section 11(1).
[17] Section 2(1).   [18] Section 11(1).   [19] Section 11(1).   [20] Section 11(2).
[21] Section 12(1).   [22] Section 12(2).

unless they are in writing signed by or on behalf of the assignor or licensor.[23]

A non-exclusive license to do an act falling within the ambit of copyright may be written or oral, or may be inferred from conduct, and may be revoked at any time, but a license granted by contract may not be revoked, either by the person who granted the license or his successor in title, except as the contract may provide, or by a further contract.[24]

An assignment or license granted by one copyright owner has effect as if granted by his co-owners also, and, subject to any contract between them, fees received by the grantor are to be divided equitably between all the co-owners. Co-ownership exists among persons: (i) if they share a joint interest in the whole or any part of a copyright, or (ii) if they have interests in the various copyrights in a composite production, that is to say, a production consisting of two or more works.[25]

Future Works.—An assignment, license or testamentary disposition may be effectively granted or made in respect of a future work, or an existing work in which copyright does not yet subsist. The prospective copyright in any such work is transmissible by operation of law as personal or movable property.[26]

"Corpus Mechanicum".—A testamentary disposition of the material on which a work is first written or otherwise recorded is, in the absence of contrary indication, to be taken to include the disposition of any copyright or prospective copyright in the work which is vested in the deceased.[27]

Licenses Administered by Licensing Bodies.—"Licensing body" means an organization which has as its main object, or one of its main objects, the negotiation or granting of licenses in respect of works protected by copyright.[28] If a licensing body unreasonably refuses to grant licenses, or is imposing unreasonable terms or conditions on the granting of licenses, the Government authority appointed to that effect may direct that corresponding licenses may be deemed to have been granted by the copyright owner provided that the appropriate fees prescribed by the said Government authority are paid or tendered.[29]

---

[23] Section 12(3).   [24] Section 12(4).   [25] Section 12(5).   [26] Section 12(6).
[27] Section 12(7).   [28] Section 14(2).   [29] Section 14(1) and (2).

PROTECTED RIGHTS

Economic Rights

Copyright in a *literary, musical or artistic work*, or in a *cinematograph film*, is the exclusive right to control the doing in Malawi of any of the following acts: (i) reproduction in any material form, (ii) communication to the public, (iii) broadcasting. The right exists in respect of the whole work or a substantial part thereof, both in its original form and in any form recognizably derived from the original.[30]

"Reproduction" means the making of one or more copies of the work or cinematograph film. "Copy" means a reproduction in written form, in the form of a recording or cinematograph film, or in any other material form, so however that an object is not to be taken to be a copy of an architectural work unless the object is a building or a model. "Communication to the public" includes, in addition to any live performance or delivery, any mode of visual or acoustic presentation. "Broadcasting" includes the broadcasting of sounds and/or images, and includes diffusion over wires.[31]

Copyright in a *work of architecture* also includes the exclusive right to control the erection of any building which reproduces the whole or any substantial part of the work either in its original form or in any form recognizably derived from the original, provided that this right does not include the right to control the reconstruction of a building in the same style as the original.[32]

Limitations

Free Uses.—The following uses are free, i.e., require neither authorization by nor payment to the copyright owner:

Fair Dealing.— Reproduction, communication to the public or broadcasting "by way of fair dealing" for purposes of research, private use, criticism or review, or the reporting of current events, is free. However, if such use is public, it must be accompanied by an acknowledgement of the title of the work and its authorship, except when the work is incidentally included in a broadcast.[33]

Parody, etc.—Reproduction, communication to the public, or broadcasting, is free if it is by way of parody, pastiche or caricature.[34]

Artistic Works Situated in Streets, etc.—The reproduction and distribution of copies, or the inclusion in a film or broadcast, is free if the work is an artistic work which is situated in a place where it can be viewed by the public.[35]

---

[30] Section 7(1).   [31] Section 2(1).   [32] Section 7(2).
[33] Sections 7(1) (a), 9 and 10.   [34] Section 7(1) (b).   [35] Section 7(1) (c).

Incidental Filming or Televising of an Artistic Work.—Inclusion of an artistic work in a cinematograph film or in a television broadcast is free if it is incidental.[36]

Collections of Literary or Musical Works.—Inclusion of not more than two short passages from a work in a collection of literary or musical works is free if the collection is designed for use in educational institutions. The included passages must be accompanied by an acknowledgement of the title of the work and its authorship.[37]

Educational Broadcasts.—The broadcasting of a work is free if the broadcast is intended to be used for educational purposes.[38]

School and University Use.—Any use of a work is free in any school or university for the educational purposes of that school or university. Any reproductions made under this exception must be destroyed within twelve months of the making of the reproduction.[39]

Reading, etc. of Extracts.—The reading or recitation in public or in a broadcast of any reasonable extract of a literary work is free if the work is a published work and if the use is accompanied by a sufficient acknowledgement.[40]

Governmen-tordered Use in Public Interest.—Use of a work by or under the direction or control of the Government, public libraries, non-commercial documentation centers and scientific institutions, designated by Regulations, is free if (i) the use is in the public interest, (ii) no revenue is derived from the use, (iii) in cases where the use consists of communication to the public, no admission fee is charged.[41]

Ephemeral Recording, etc.—The reproduction of a work by or under the direction or control of a broadcasting authority is free if (i) the reproduction or any copies thereof are intended exclusively for lawful broadcast by that broadcasting authority, (ii) the reproduction and any copies thereof are destroyed within six months of reproduction or any longer period agreed under contract. Reproductions of an exceptional documentary character may, however, be preserved but may not be used without the authorization of the copyright owner.[42]

Judicial Proceedings.—Any use made of a work for the purpose of judicial proceedings is free. Any use for the purpose of a report on such proceedings is equally free.[43]

Compulsory Licenses.—In the following three cases the authorization of the owner of the relevant copyright is not required but a fair compensation must be paid to him in accordance with Regulations issued under the Act:

[36] Section 7(1) (d).   [37] Section 7(1) (e).   [38] Section 7(1) (f).
[39] Section 7(1) (g).   [40] Section 7(1) (i).   [41] Sections 7(1) (j), 9, and 10.
[42] Sections 7(1) (k) and 9.   [43] Sections 7(1) (m), 9 and 10.

(i) *Making, etc., of Sound Recordings*, or, more precisely, when a sound recording of a literary or artistic work is made or imported and the copies thereof are intended for retail sale in Malawi.[44]

(ii) *Broadcasting of Works not in the Repertoire of a Performing Rights Society*, or, more precisely, when a work already lawfully made accessible to the public, and with which no licensing body is concerned, is broadcast.[45]

A "licensing body" is an organization which has as its main objects, or one of its main objects, the negotiation and granting of licenses in respect of protected works.[46]

(iii) *Broadcast of Music of a Cinematograph Film*, or, more precisely, when a broadcasting authority broadcasts a cinematograph film in which a musical work is incorporated.[47]

Broadcasting of Works Incorporated in a Cinematograph Film.—Subject to the provision just stated, where the owner of the copyright in any literary, musical or artistic work has authorized a person to incorporate the work in a cinematograph film and a broadcasting authority broadcasts the film, such broadcast does not, in the absence of any agreement to the contrary, infringe such copyright.[48]

TERM OF PROTECTION

Copyright in *literary works, musical works, and artistic works other than photographs*, expires twenty-five years after the end of the year in which the author dies.[49] In the case of a work of joint authorship the term is counted from the death of the author who dies last.[50] "Work of joint authorship" means a work produced by the collaboration of two or more authors in which the contribution of each author is not separable from the contribution of the other author or authors.[51] Anonymous or pseudonymous literary, musical or artistic works are protected until the expiration of twenty-five years from the end of the year in which they were first published, except that, if the identity of the author becomes known in the meantime, the term is calculated according to the general rules, i.e., twenty-five years *post mortem auctoris*.[52] Copyright in literary, musical or artistic works (other than photographs) made by or under the direction or control of the Government or any of the designated international bodies or other governmental organizations subsists until the expiration of twenty-five years from the end of the year in which they were first published.[53] "Publication" takes place if, but only if, copies of the work have been issued in sufficient

[44] Section 7(1) (h).   [45] Section 7(1) (l).   [46] Section 14(2).
[47] Section 8(2).   [48] Section 8(1).   [49] Section 4(2).
[50] Sections 4(4) and 5(2).   [51] Section 2(1).   [52] Sections 4(3) and 5(2).
[53] Section 6(2).

quantities to satisfy the reasonable requirements of the public.[54]

Copyright in *photographs* and *cinematograph films* expires twenty-five years after the end of the year in which they were first made lawfully accessible to the public.[55]

COMPARISON OF TERMS

Since there is no provision in the Act for the "rule of the shorter term" permitted under Article IV (4) of the Universal Copyright Convention, it would appear that works are protected in Malawi until the expiration of the terms indicated above, even if, in other countries, they fall into the public domain at an earlier date.

INFRINGEMENTS

CIVIL REMEDIES

Generally.—Copyright is infringed by any person who does, or causes any other person to do, an act the doing of which is controlled by the copyright without the license of the owner of the copyright.[56]

Infringements are actionable at the suit of the owner of the copyright, and in any action for infringement all such relief—by way of damages, injunction, accounts or otherwise—is available to the plaintiff as is available under the general laws of Malawi in any corresponding proceedings in respect of infringement of other proprietary rights.[57] "Owner of the copyright" means the first owner, the assignee or an exclusive licensee, as the case may be, of the relevant portion of the copyright.[58]

Innocent Infringers.—If, at the time of the infringement, the defendant was not aware, and had no reasonable grounds for suspecting, that copyright subsisted in the work, he is not liable for damages but only for an account of profits.[59]

Flagrant Infringements.—If the infringement is flagrant, if benefit has accrued to the defendant by reason of the infringement, and if the court is satisfied that effective relief would not otherwise be available to the plaintiff, then, the court, in assessing damages for the infringement, may award such additional damages as it considers appropriate under the circumstances.[60]

[54] Section 2(2) (a).   [55] Sections 4(2), 5(2) and 6(3).
[56] Section 13(1).   [57] Section 13(2).   [58] Section 13(6).
[58] Section 13(6).   [59] Section 13(3).   [60] Section 13(4).

CRIMINAL SANCTIONS

The Act does not provide for criminal sanctions.

INJUNCTIONS

See "Civil Remedies," above. It is to be noted, however, that no injunction issues if it would require a completed or partly built building to be demolished or if it would prevent the completion of a partly built building.[61]

---

[61] Section 13(5).

MEXICO

SOURCES

Internal Law.—The main source of the law of copyright in Mexico is the Federal Copyright Law of November 4, 1963.[1] Hereinafter, it is referred to as "the Law," and references, without further specification, to Articles are references to Articles of the Law.

Universal Copyright Convention.—Mexico became bound by the Universal Copyright Convention and Protocol 2 as from May 12, 1957.[2]

ACQUISITION OF PROTECTION UNDER THE UNIVERSAL COPYRIGHT CONVENTION

The Law provides that the works of nationals of a State with which Mexico has concluded a treaty or convention in force on copyright enjoy the protection provided by the Law in so far as it is not incompatible with the applicable treaty or convention.[3] It is assumed that the provision means that if the Law is incompatible with the treaty or convention, the treaty or convention applies. Whether this interpretation is correct is uncertain since, as far as is known, the question has not yet been decided by the courts.

The uncertainty stems from the fact that the Law speaks of the works of the *nationals* of certain countries, whereas both the Universal and Berne Conventions provide for the protection of works *first published* in certain countries, irrespective of the nationality of their authors. Perhaps, an argument for the correctness of the assumption stated above could be drawn from that Article of the Law which provides only for a limited and conditional protection for works which were *first published* in a State with which Mexico is *not* bound by a treaty or convention.[4]

[1] Published in "Diario Oficial" of December 21, 1963. *See* English translation in CLTW, Mexico: Item 1.
[2] *See* CLTW, Mexico: Item 1B. Mexico is also a party to the Berne (Brussels, 1948) Convention and the Washington Copyright Convention of 1946, and has concluded bilateral agreements with Ecuador, the Dominican Republic, France, Denmark, the Federal Republic of Germany, and Paraguay (*see* CLTW, Mexico: Items 2 to 8).
[3] Article 30.   [4] Article 28.

Another, minor, source of uncertainty stems from the Article which provides for the protection of works *first published* by any organization of nations of which Mexico is a member but says nothing about the *unpublished* works covered by Protocol 2.[5] Here, too, however, it might be assumed that the provisions of the Universal Copyright Convention will apply notwithstanding the possible difference between the text of the Law and the international instrument.

If both assumptions are correct, then, works protected in Mexico under the Universal Copyright Convention—unless excluded by virtue of Article XVII of that Convention and the Appendix Declaration relating to the said Article (in which case the applicable Convention of the Berne Copyright Union governs rather than the Universal Copyright Convention)—are the following: (i) published works of nationals of a Convention country, irrespective of the place of first publication, (ii) works first published in a Convention country, irrespective of the nationality of the author, (iii) unpublished works of nationals of a Convention country other than Mexico, (iv) works first published by the United Nations, by any of the Specialized Agencies of the United Nations, or by the Organization of American States, as well as unpublished works of any of these Organizations.

The acquisition of copyright is not subject to the fulfilment of any formality.[6] Nevertheless, there does exist a Copyright Register in the *Dirección General del Derecho de Autor* (General Copyright Directorate) in which works and various facts relevant in connection with their copyright protection may be registered.[7] Entries in the Register create a presumption that the facts recorded therein are true.[8] Documents originating outside Mexico and submitted to the *Dirección* as proof that the applicant for registration is the owner of the copyright may, for the purposes of registration, be submitted without legalization of signature.[9]

Mexico has no renewal formalities, so that there is nothing in that country which would correspond to the renewal formalities existing in the United States.

PROTECTED WORKS

Generally.—The Law describes as its objects the protection of the rights which it establishes for the benefit of the author of every *intellectual* or *artistic* work and the safeguarding of the cultural wealth of the Mexican nation.[10]

[5] Article 31, second paragraph.　　[6] Cf. Articles 8 and 27.

[7] Articles 119 to 134. Also, the use of a copyright notice is prescribed for works published in Mexico; the omission of the notice is punishable by a fine imposed upon the publisher (Articles 237 and 143).

[8] Article 122.　　[9] Article 127.　　[10] Article 1.

Copyright subsists in works: (i) if they exist in writing, recording or any other durable fixation (*en forma de objetivación perdurable* = in the form of a durable *thing* or object), (ii) if they are capable—by some medium (irrelevant which)—of reproduction or communication to the public (*susceptible de hacerse del conocimiento público*), and (iii) if they have the characteristics of any of the following categories: (a) literary, (b) scientific, technical, legal, (c) pedagogical or didactical, (d) musical (with or without words), (e) dance, choreographic, pantomime, (f) pictorial (drawings, engravings, lithographs), (g) sculptural and plastic, (h) architectural, (i) photographic, cinematographic, radio and television, (j) any other which, by analogy, may be regarded as being included in the said general categories of intellectual or artistic works.[11] Works meeting these conditions are protected even if they have not been communicated to the public or have not been published (*ineditas*). The purpose for which they are intended is irrelevant.[12]

Intellectual or artistic works published in newspapers and magazines, or transmitted by radio, television or other means of diffusion, are not deprived of legal protection by reason of such publication or transmission.

Secondary Works.—Arrangements, compendiums, amplifications, translations, adaptations, compilations and transformations of any intellectual or artistic work, if they have some original character, are protected, to the extent that they are original. If they are based on a work protected by copyright, they may be published only with the consent of the owner of that copyright.[13] To the extent that they have originality, such versions are protected even when derived from a work in the public domain; but such protection does not include the right to the exclusive use of the basic work, nor does it give rise to any right to prevent the making of other versions thereof.[14]

Compilations, Etc.—Compilations, concordances, interpretations, comparative studies, annotations, commentaries, and other similar works, which entail, on the part of their authors, the creation of an original work, are protected by copyright.[15]

Titles.—The title of a protected intellectual or artistic work or a periodical publication may be used only by the owner of the copyright. This limitation does not apply where the nature of the work or publication excludes any possibility of confusion. Generic titles and proper names do not enjoy protection.[16]

Rights in the title or caption of a newspaper, magazine, newsreel and, in general, of any periodical publication or form of diffusion, whether applicable to the entire publication or only to a part thereof,

---

[11] Article 7. [12] Article 8.
[13] Article 5, second paragraph. [14] Article 9.
[15] Article 21, third paragraph. [16] Article 20.

may be reserved. Such reservation confers upon the person concerned the exclusive right to the use of the title or caption during the whole period of publication or diffusion and for one year thereafter. Publication or diffusion must commence within one year from the date of reservation of the right in the relevant certificate.[17]

Characters.—The right of exclusive use and exploitation of fictitious or symbolic personalities in literary works, story-telling strips (*historietas gráficas*) such as comic strips, or in any periodicals, may be reserved if such personalities have definite originality and are used habitually or periodically. The same applies to characteristic human persons (*personajes humanos de caracterización*) used in artistic performances. Protection of this right is acquired by means of a certificate of reservation. Protection lasts five years from the date of the certificate unless renewed for successive periods of five years each. Renewal is granted after proof of use and exploitation is presented to and accepted by the *Dirección General del Derecho de Autor* (General Copyright Directorate).[18]

Characteristic Graphics and Promotional Matter.—The exclusive right to use original, characteristic graphics (*gráficas originales características*) in intellectual or artistic works, periodicals or magazines, cinematographic films, or similar publications, may be reserved by their publishers or producers, provided they serve to distinguish such works, etc. The same applies in the case of characteristic features of promotional matter (*características de promociones publicitarias*), provided they are definitely original. Protection lasts two years from the date of the certificate unless renewed for successive periods of two years each. Renewal is granted after habitual use has been proved.[19]

PROTECTED PERSONS

Copyright originally vests in the author.[20]

Civil or commercial societies, institutes and academies, and, in general, legal entities, can generally hold copyright only as the successors in title of authors who are physical persons.[21]

However, any legal entity which, or physical person who, produces a work with the special and remunerated participation or collaboration of one or more persons is the original owner of the copyright in such work. When the collaboration is not remunerated, copyright vests in the collaborators.[22]

In the absence of proof to the contrary, the person whose name, or known or registered pseudonym, is indicated as that of the author of a

[17] Article 24.   [18] Article 25.   [19] Article 26.
[20] Cf. Article 1. As to co-authors, see Articles 11 to 15.
[21] Article 31, first sentence.   [22] Article 59.

protected work is presumed to be the author. The competent courts must, in consequence, allow such person to take legal action for infringement of his rights. In the case of anonymous or pseudonymous works whose authors have not disclosed their identity, the action may be brought by the publishers of the works, but this right ceases as soon as the author or the copyright owner becomes a party to the proceedings. In cases where the publisher acts, he is deemed to act as an agent.[23]

ASSIGNMENT AND LICENSING

Generally.—The author may dispose of his rights of use and exploitation. Moral rights cannot be assigned.[24]

Publication Contracts.—The law *defines* a publication contract as a contract by which the owner of the copyright in respect of an intellectual or artistic work undertakes to deliver the work to a publisher who, in turn, undertakes to reproduce it, to distribute and sell the copies on his own account, and to accept liability in respect of the agreed copyright royalties.[25] In any such contract, the owner of the copyright continues to hold the copyright, and the publisher does not have rights in excess of those which, within the limits of the contract, are necessary for its fulfilment during the time required for such purpose.[26]

Stipulations whereby authors commit themselves in respect of their *future productions* are null and void, except insofar as concerns any specific work or works the characteristics of which must be clearly established in the contract.[27]

The publication contract must satisfy the following *conditions*: (i) it must specify the number of copies that constitute the edition (*edición*) contracted for, (ii) the cost of publication (*edición*), distribution, promotion, publicity, advertising, and any other cost, must be borne by the publisher, (iii) each edition (*edición*) must be the subject of an express agreement. The author cannot waive these prescriptions.[28]

On the other hand, the following are *permissive rules* which may be set aside by contractual stipulations: (i) the publisher must place on sale the finished copies of the edition within one year,[29] and, in the case of popular music, within six months,[30] (ii) the edition must be of average quality,[31] (iii) the selling price is fixed by the publisher but must not be prohibitive.[32] The right to publish separately two or more works of the same author does not confer upon the publisher the right to publish them collectively, and vice versa.[33]

---

[23] Article 17, first and second paragraphs.   [24] Article 3.
[25] Article 40, first paragraph.   [26] Article 41.   [27] Article 45 (IV).
[28] Article 45.   [29] Article 46.   [30] Article 47.   [31] Article 48.
[32] Article 49.   [33] Article 52.

The publisher must comply with a certain number of *formalities*: (i) he must register the publishing contract with the *Dirección General del Derecho de Autor* (General Copyright Directorate), (ii) he must number each copy,[34] (iii) he must indicate in each copy his name and address, the year of publication, the number of the edition (whether it is first, second, etc.),[35] (iv) if what is published is a translation, he must indicate, immediately below the title of the translation, the title in the original language,[36] (v) the name or pseudonym of the author and, if what is published is a translation, compilation, adaptation or other version, then also the name or pseudonym of the translator, adaptor, etc. If the work is anonymous, this fact must be indicated.[37] If what is published is an adapted, abridged or modified version of the original, this fact must be indicated.[38] The printer, as distinguished from the publisher, must indicate in each copy his name and address, the total number of copies printed, and the date on which the printing was completed.[39]

Other Contracts Licensing Reproduction.—The rules concerning publication also apply, insofar as the nature of the things permit, in the case of other contracts for the reproduction of intellectual works by means other than printing.[40]

Performance Contracts.—Unless there is agreement to the contrary, dramatic, musical, dramatico-musical and choreographic works, pantomimes and, in general, all works capable of performance, must be performed within six months from the date of the contract.[41]

Contracts Stipulating Royalties.—When a contract stipulates the payment of a royalty (*regalía*) per copy, the producing or importing enterprise must keep books which, at any time, allow the amounts due to be determined.[42]

Rules of Interpretation of Certain Contracts.—The right to publish a work "by any means" does not, of itself, include the right to exploit it by means of performances.[43] Authorization to broadcast does not include authorization to rebroadcast or otherwise exploit publicly.[44] Authorization to record on discs or other phonograms does not include the right to use them for profit.[45]

PROTECTED RIGHTS

Generally.—The Law distinguishes between three kinds of rights of the author: (i) the right to the recognition of his authorship, (ii) the right to oppose unauthorized deformation, mutilation, or modifica-

[34] Article 45.   [35] Article 53.   [36] Article 55.   [37] Article 56.
[38] Article 57.   [39] Article 54.   [40] Article 60.   [41] Article 76.
[42] Article 78.   [43] Article 72.   [44] Article 73.   [45] Article 77.

tion of his work, and any act that is prejudicial to his work or his reputation, (iii) the use and exploitation of the work, for a limited time, for purposes of economic gain (*con propósitos de lucro* = for profit).[46] The first two are discussed hereinafter under "Moral Rights," whereas the last is discussed below under "Economic Rights."

ECONOMIC RIGHTS

Generally.—The rights of use and exploitation for profit include the rights of reproduction, performance (*ejecución*) and adaptation, of the work by any means appropriate to the nature of the work, and particularly by the means referred to in the international treaties by which Mexico is bound.[47] The rights of the author are superior to those of performers, and in case of conflict prevail over the latter.[48]

Right of Public Performance and Exhibition.—It would appear, however, that the rights of performance and exhibition are not necessarily exclusive rights of authorization since the Law provides that, in case of performance or exhibition (*ejecución, representación, projección*) for profit, fees (*derechos*) must be paid and that, in the absence of agreement between the users (*usufructuarios*) and the authors or authors' societies, the fees are governed by the tariff of the *Secretaría de Educación Pública* (Ministry of Public Education). This provision seems to apply not only to live performances but also to the public exhibition of films and the public playing of phonograph discs or other recordings, including playing by jukeboxes.[49]

Right to Translate.—The right to translate is an exclusive right of authorization,[50] lasting the whole term of copyright, except in the following cases, when it is a right subject to compulsory licensing:

The *Secretaría de la Educación Pública* (Ministry of Public Education) may grant to any national or any foreigner domiciled in the Republic of Mexico who so requests a non-exclusive license to translate and publish in Spanish works written in another language if, at the expiration of a period of seven years from the date of first publication of the work, no translation in Spanish has been published by the owner of the right of translation, or with his authorization,[51] or if the Spanish translation is out of print.[52]

In order to obtain the grant of such a license, the applicant is, among other things, required to satisfy the following conditions:

(i) he must make an application;

(ii) he must establish that the work falls within the applicable provisions of the Law;

(iii) he must prove that he has requested authorization from the

---

[46] Article 2.   [47] Article 4.   [48] Article.   [49] Articles 79 and 80.
[50] Cf. Article 36.   [51] Article 33.   [52] Article 37.

owner of the right to make and publish the translation, and that he has been unable to obtain such authorization;

(iv) he must prove, in cases where it has not been possible to obtain the consent of the owner of the right of translation, that he has sent copies of the petition to the publisher whose name appears on the copies of the work and, when the nationality of the owner of the right of translation is known, to the diplomatic and consular representatives of the State of which he is a national (in such cases, no license is granted before the expiration of a period of two months from the date of sending the copy);

(v) he must entrust the translation of the work to a person deemed competent for the purpose by a special committee consisting of a representative of the *Secretaría de la Educación Pública* (Ministry of Public Education), a representative of the *Universidad Nacional Autonoma de Mexico* (Autonomous National University of Mexico) or an institute specializing in languages, and one from the organization representative of the major professional interests of the publishers;

(vi) he must indicate the number of copies to be published and the retail selling price of each copy;

(vii) he must deposit a sum equal to one third of ten per cent of the retail selling price of all unbound copies to be published, and must give a guarantee for the remaining two thirds, which amount must be paid over within a period of two years from the date of the application.[53]

Compulsory licenses are not transferable, and any transfer, in addition to being null and void, gives rise to the ex-officio revocation of the license.[54]

Any compulsory license will be withdrawn if the author has withdrawn from circulation copies of the work which it is sought to translate and publish.[55]

See also "Limitations," below.

.MORAL RIGHTS

Recognition of Authorship.—The author's right to the recognition of his quality as author is provided for both generally[56] and in particular in connection with publication.[57]

Other Moral Rights.—Other moral rights include protection against:

(i) any deformation, mutilation, or modification of the work which he did not authorize,[58]

---

[53] Articles 34 and 35.   [54] Article 38.   [55] Article 39.   [56] Article 2.
[57] Articles 10, 16, 56 and 135.
[58] Articles 2, 5, 43 and 44.

(ii) any act (*acción*) which results in a loss of esteem (*demérito*) for the work,[59]

(iii) any act which reflects on the honor, prestige or reputation of the author,[60]

(iv) disclosure of an unpublished work (*inédita o non publicada*) received in confidence from the copyright owner or a person acting on his behalf.[61]

Common Rules.—Moral rights are perpetual, inalienable, imprescriptible and irrenounceable. They may be exercised only by the author or, after his death, by his heirs or the person designated to that effect by the author in his will,[62] or, in the absence of such persons, the *Secretaría de Educación Pública* (Ministry of Public Education).[63]

LIMITATIONS

Any photographic work may be freely reproduced for educational, scientific or cultural purposes, or in the general interest, but its source and the name of the photographer must be mentioned in the reproduction.[64]

Anonymous works may be freely used as long as their authors do not reveal their identities.[65]

The rights of the author do not extend to the following acts: (i) industrial exploitation of the ideas contained in the work, (ii) reproduction or performance of the work in connection with a current event, unless for profit, (iii) publication of works of art or architecture which are visible from public places, (iv) translation, or reproduction by any means, of brief extracts of the work in scientific or educational publications, in chrestomathies, or in publications devoted to literary criticism or scientific research, (v) copying by hand, typewriter, photography, photostatic procedure, painting, drawing, or microphotography, of any published work, provided that the copy is for the exclusive use of the copier.[66]

Articles on current events published in newspapers, magazines, and other media of communication, may be reproduced unless such reproduction has been prohibited by means of a special or general reservation made at the time of publication. Upon reproduction, however, mention must be made of the source from which they have been taken. The informative contents of the news of the day, as such, may be freely reproduced.[67]

[59] Article 2. [60] Articles 2, 136 and 137. [61] Article 139.
[62] Article 3. [63] Article 144. [64] Article 16, first paragraph.
[65] Article 17, third paragraph. [66] Article 18.
[67] Article 10, second paragraph.

Where, for technical reasons or reasons of timing, broadcasting or television transmitting stations require to record or fix in their studios, for the purpose of a single subsequent emission, sounds or images of musical selections or portions thereof, or of scientific speeches or studies, or of literary, dramatic, choreographic or dramatico-musical works, complete programs and, in general, any work capable of diffusion, they may do so, provided that no simultaneous transmission takes place, and that the recording of fixing is solely for the purpose of one subsequent transmission within the agreed period.[68]

The Government may authorize the publication of works—without the authorization of the owner of the copyright therein or notwithstanding his opposition—if such publication is a matter of public interest, being necessary or helpful to the advancement, diffusion or improvement of science or national culture or education in either of the following two cases:

(i) when, for a period of one year, there have been no copies of the work in Mexico City and in three of the chief cities of Mexico,

(ii) when works are sold at a price which is such as considerably to impede or restrict their general use, to the detriment of culture and teaching.

The owner of the copyright receives, in these cases, a royalty of ten per cent of the retail price of the copies made.[69]

TERM OF PROTECTION

Moral rights are perpetual.[70]

Economic rights continue for the life of the author and for 30 years after his death. When this period has passed, or when the owner of the right dies without heirs, the right of using and exploiting the work passes into the public domain, but any rights previously acquired by third parties must be respected.

The economic rights in posthumous works continue for 30 years from the date of death or first publication.

An anonymous work whose author does not reveal his identity within a period of 30 years from the date of first publication passes into the public domain.

The duration of copyright belonging in common to the collaborators of a work is determined by the death of the last survivor.[71]

Since there is no provision in Mexican law for the "rule of the shorter term" permitted under Article IV (4) of the Universal Copyright Convention, it would appear that works whose protection is governed

[68] Articles 74 and 75, which also provide for further details and qualifications.
[69] Articles 62 to 71, which also provide for further details and qualifications.
[70] Article 3.   [71] Articles 17, third paragraph and 23.

by that Convention are protected in Mexico until the expiration of the terms indicated above, even if in other countries they fall into the public domain at an earlier date.

INFRINGEMENTS

Mediation by the Copyright Directorate.—In the event of any dispute involving only private interests, either party may request the good offices of the *Dirección General del Derecho de Autor* (General Copyright Directorate) of the *Secretaría de Educación Pública* (Ministry of Public Education) to solve the difficulties encountered.[72]

Penal Sanctions.—Infringements are, in many cases, punishable by a fine or imprisonment.[73]

Civil Remedies.—The infringement of the economic or moral rights makes the infringer liable to pay an indemnity. The indemnity for infringing the right of reproduction is at least equivalent to 40 per cent of the retail price of each illegally reproduced copy. If the number of copies cannot be ascertained with precision, the indemnity is fixed by the court after hearing expert evidence.[74]

[72] Article 118.　　[73] Articles 135 to 144.　　[74] Article 156.

MONACO

SOURCES

Internal Law.—The main source of the law of copyright in Monaco is Law No. 491 of November 24, 1948, as amended by Law No. 512 of November 17, 1949.[1] Hereinafter, it is referred to as "the Law," and references to Articles, without further specification, are references to Articles of the Law.

Universal Copyright Convention.—Monaco became bound by the Universal Copyright Convention and Protocols 1 and 2 as from September 16, 1955.[2]

ACQUISITION OF PROTECTION UNDER THE UNIVERSAL COPYRIGHT CONVENTION

The laws of Monaco do not contain any special provisions in respect of works to which Monaco is supposed to grant protection by virtue of the Universal Copyright Convention. The provisions of that Convention, particularly of Articles II and XVII and Protocols 1 and 2, determine which are the works protected under the Universal Copyright Convention. Briefly stated, such works are, except if excluded by virtue of Article XVII of the Universal Copyright Convention and the Appendix Declaration relating to the same Article (in which case the applicable Berne Convention rather than the Universal Convention governs): (i) published works of nationals of a Convention country, irrespective of the place of first publication, (ii) works first published in a Convention country, irrespective of the nationality of the author, (iii) unpublished works of nationals of a Convention country other than Monaco, (iv) works of stateless persons and refugees who have their

---

[1] Published in "Journal de Monaco," 1948, page 742, and 1949, page 597. See English translation in CLTW, under Monaco: Item 1.

[2] CLTW, Monaco: Item 2. Monaco is a member of the Berne Copyright Union and has ratified all its Conventions, the most recent in date being that of Brussels of 1948 (CLTW, Monaco: Item 3). Monaco issued an Ordinance (No. 625) on October 15, 1952 (published in "Journal de Monaco," 1952, page 209; see English translation in CLTW under Monaco: Item 4), extending copyright protection to the works of U.S. citizens. This Ordinance is of limited interest now that both the United States and Monaco are parties to the Universal Copyright Convention.

habitual residence in a State party to Protocol I (except perhaps Monaco), either published or unpublished, and if published, irrespective of the place of first publication, (v) works first published by the United Nations, by any of the Specialized Agencies of the United Nations, or by the Organization of American States, as well as unpublished works of any of these Organizations.

The only case in which it might be necessary to distinguish between works protected under the Universal Copyright Convention and works protected under a Convention of the Berne Copyright Union is the case of the rule of the shorter term, discussed below.

There are no copyright formalities in Monaco.[3] Consequently, registration, deposit, or compliance with other formalities is neither required nor possible in Monaco, and the absence, in itself, of a Convention notice on the copies of a published work is no bar to claiming protection in Monaco. Furthermore, Monaco has no renewal system, so that there is nothing in this country which would correspond to the renewal formalities existing in the United States.

PROTECTED WORKS

The Law protects "literary and artistic" works,[4] and defines them as including every production in the literary, scientific and artistic domain, whatever the mode or form of its expression, such as: books, pamphlets and other writings; lectures, addresses, sermons and other works of the same nature; dramatic or dramatico-musical works, choreographic works and pantomimes, the acting form of which is fixed in writing or otherwise; musical compositions, with or without words; cinematographic works and works produced by a process analogous to cinematography; works of drawing, painting, architecture, sculpture, engraving and lithography, photographic works and works produced by a process analogous to photography; works of applied art; illustrations; geographical charts, plans, sketches and plastic works relative to geography, topography, architecture or science.[5] Translations, arrangements, adaptations and other transformations of literary and artistic works are protected as original works.[6]

PROTECTED PERSONS

Copyright originally vests in the author.[7] Authors of translations, arrangements, adaptations or other transformations of literary or artistic works enjoy the same protection as authors of original works,

[3] Article I.   [4] Article I.   [5] Article 2.   [6] Article 5.
[7] Articles 1, 3, 4.

without prejudice, however, to the rights of the author of the work which they translate, arrange, adapt or otherwise transform.[8]

A work of collaboration is the common property of its authors. However, when such a work does not form an indivisible whole, each of the co-authors may separately exploit his contribution, provided such separate exploitation does not prejudice the exploitation of the work of collaboration. In respect of the latter work, each co-author is entitled to act as an agent (*mandataire*) of the other co-authors vis-à-vis third parties.[9]

As far as an anonymous or pseudonymous work is concerned, its publisher is treated as if he were the author thereof—in the relationships with third parties. However, if the identity of the author is established, the latter, or his successors in title (*ayants cause*), rather than the publisher have the right to exercise the rights inherent in copyright.[10]

ASSIGNMENT AND LICENSING

Copyright, in whole or in part, may be assigned, with or without consideration, and is transmissible by succession, according to the provisions of the Civil Code.[11]

The alienation of a work of art does not, in itself, imply the alienation of the right of reproducing such work. However, in the case of a commissioned portrait or bust, there is a rebuttable presumption that the alienation of the work of art implied the alienation of the right of reproduction.[12]

PROTECTED RIGHTS

Economic Rights

The author has an exclusive right to publish, reproduce or in any other manner disclose (*divulguer*) his work, and to authorize others to publish, reproduce, or in any form disclose the same.[13] He also has the exclusive right to translate or authorize the translation of his work, as well as to arrange, adapt, or make any other transformation thereof.[14]

The author of any work capable of being publicly performed (*exécuter, représenter*), recited or exhibited, has the exclusive right to effect, or authorize other persons to effect, such uses.[15]

---

[8] Article 5.   [9] Article 7.   [10] Article 13.   [11] Article 14.
[12] Article 10. In any case, the owner of the work of art is not required to place it at the disposal of the author or his successor in title in order that reproduction may be made of the work (art. 11).
[13] Article 3.   [14] Article 4.   [15] Article 6.

MORAL RIGHTS

The author has the right to claim authorship (*paternité*) of his work and to object to any distortion, mutilation, or other alteration thereof, or any other harmful act (*atteinte*) against his work which might prejudice his honor or his reputation.[16] This right is inalienable—i.e., it remains with the author—and perpetual. Its exercise is imprescriptible. The author may dispose that, after his death, the right be exercised by his heirs or by persons named to this effect in his will.[17]

LIMITATIONS

Article on current topics (*articles d'actualité*), and those dealing with economic, political or religious subjects may be freely reproduced by the press, unless their reproduction has been expressly reserved. In any case, the source must always be clearly indicated.[18]

Short quotations from articles in newspapers and magazines are permissible in the form of press reviews without the authorization of the copyright owner.[19] It is also permissible, without the authorization of the copyright owner, to publish extracts from literary or artistic works, in publications of a scientific character, or publications made for use in schools, or in chrestomathies, provided an indication is given of the source and of the author of the work.[20]

The authorization of the copyright owner is not required in the case of public performances or exhibitions organized or authorized by the Government, if the proceeds of such performances or exhibitions are destined for a charitable purpose under the direct patronage of the Sovereign, or if they take place on the occasion of civil or religious ceremonies.[21]

TERM OF PROTECTION

Generally.—Copyright is protected during the life of the author and fifty years after his death. In the case of a work of collaboration, the 50 years are counted from the death of the last surviving co-author. In the case of a posthumous work, copyright lasts for 50 years from publication. In all cases, protection lasts until the end of the calendar year in which copyright would otherwise expire.[22]

Rule of the Shorter Term.—Since there is no provision in the Law for the "rule of the shorter term" permitted under Article IV (4) of the Universal Copyright Convention, works protected in Monaco

[16] Article 19.   [17] Article 20.   [18] Article 15, first paragraph.
[19] Article 15, second paragraph.
[20] Article 16.   [21] Article 17.   [22] Article 12.

by virtue of the Convention appear to be protected until the expiration of the terms indicated above, even if in other countries they fall into the public domain at an earlier date.[23]

INFRINGEMENTS

Civil Remedies.—Infringers are liable to pay damages. Various conservatory measures may be ordered.[24]

Penal Sanctions.—Infringements, including plagiarism, if committed in bad faith, are punishable by fine. Confiscation may be ordered.[25]

---

[23] However, it is possible that the rule of the shorter term provided in Article 7 of the Brussels Convention of the Berne Union applies in the case of works which, within the meaning of that Convention, have as their country of origin a country member of the Berne Copyright Union.

[24] Articles 29 to 33.   [25] Articles 21 to 28.

NETHERLANDS

SOURCES

Internal Law.—The main source of the law of copyright in the Netherlands is the Copyright Law (*Auteurswet*) of 1912, amended seven times (in 1914, 1915, 1917, 1931, 1932, 1956, and 1958).[1] Hereinafter, it is referred to as "the Law" and references to Articles, without further specification, are references to Articles of this Law.

Universal Copyright Convention.—The Netherlands became bound by the Universal Copyright Convention and Protocols 1 and 2 as from June 22, 1967.[2]

ACQUISITION OF PROTECTION UNDER THE UNIVERSAL COPYRIGHT CONVENTION

The Law provides that it applies to the unpublished works of nationals of the Netherlands (*Nederlanders*) and other Netherlands subjects (*Nederlandsche onderdanen*), and to published works if they were first published (*uitgegeven*) in the Netherlands.[3] The Law contains no special provisions with respect to works which the Netherlands is supposed to protect by virtue of international treaties. Consequently, the provisions of the Universal Copyright Convention, particularly Articles II and XVII and Protocols 1 and 2, determine which works are protected in the Netherlands under that Convention. Briefly stated, such works, unless they are excluded by virtue of Article XVII of the Universal Copyright Convention and the Appendix Declaration relating to that Article (in which case the applicable Berne Convention

---

[1] The date of the Law is September 23, 1912. It was published in "Staatsblad," 1912, under number 308, whereas the laws amending the basic Law have the following dates and were published in the Staatsblad in the same year as their date under the numbers indicated in parentheses: October 16, 1914 (489), October 29, 1915 (446), December 15, 1917 (702), July 9, 1931 (264), February 11, 1932 (45), June 14, 1956 (343), May 22, 1958 (296). An integrated Dutch text appears in the Law Series published by W. E. J. Tjeenk Willink, Zwolle, Netherlands, under the title "Nederlandse Staatswetten, Editie Schuurman & Jordens" as volume No. 75. English translation in CLTW, Netherlands: Item 1.
[2] See CLTW: Item 2bis. The Netherlands is a member of the Berne Copyright Union, since 1913. The last Act it has acceded to is the Rome Act of 1928.
[3] Article 47, first paragraph.

governs rather than the Universal Copyright Convention) are the following: (i) published works of nationals of a Convention country, irrespective of the place of first publication, (ii) works first published in a Convention country, irrespective of the nationality of the author, (iii) unpublished works of nationals of a Convention country other than the Netherlands, (iv) works of stateless persons and refugees who have their habitual residence in a State party to Protocol 1 (except perhaps the Netherlands), (v) works first published by the United Nations, by any of the Specialized Agencies of the United Nations, or by the Organization of American States, as well as unpublished works of any of those organizations.

The only case in which it might be necessary to distinguish between works protected by virtue of the Universal Copyright Convention and works protected by virtue of a Convention of the Berne Copyright Union is the case of the rule of the shorter term, discussed below.

The Netherlands has no copyright formalities. Consequently, registration, deposit, or compliance with other formalities, is not required, and the absence, in itself, of a Convention notice on the copies of a published work is no bar to the claiming of protection in the Netherlands. Furthermore, the Netherlands has no renewal system, so that there is nothing in that country which would correspond to the renewal formalities existing in the United States.

PROTECTED WORKS

The Law protects literary, scientific and artistic works,[4] that is, any product (*voortbrengsel*) in the field of literature, science or art, whatever the manner or the form in which the product is expressed.[5] The following are expressly mentioned by the Law: (i) books, pamphlets, newspapers, periodicals, and all other writings; (ii) dramatic works and dramatico-musical works; (iii) oral addresses; (iv) choreographic works and pantomimes, the acting form of which is fixed in writing or in some other manner; (v) musical works, with or without words; (vi) drawings, paintings, works of architecture, sculptures, lithographs, engravings and other prints (*plaatwerken*); (vii) geographical maps; (viii) plans, sketches, and plastic works, relating to architecture, geography, topography, or other sciences; (ix) photographic and cinematographic works, and works produced by processes similar to photography or cinematography, (x) works of industrially applied art.[6] Translations, adaptations, musical arrangements, and other reproductions (*verveelvoudigingen* = multiplications) in a changed form of a work of literature, science or art, as well as collections of various

[4] Article 1.   [5] Article 10 (10, in fine).   [6] Article 10(1) to (10).

works, are protected as independent works, without prejudice to the copyright in the pre-existing work (*oorspronkelijk werk* = the original work).[7, 8]

PROTECTED PERSONS

Generally.—The Law protects the author (*maker* = creator).[9] In the absence of proof to the contrary, the following persons are deemed to be the author: (i) if the work carries an indication as to the author, the person so indicated; (ii) if the work is communicated to the public and the person making the communication indicates a person as author, the person so indicated; (iii) if the work is an oral address or a musical work, and such address or work has not been published (*verschenen*) in print and no author is indicated at the time of delivery or performance, the speaker or the performer.[10] If a work appearing in print bears no indication of the name of the author or does not indicate his true name, the publisher (*Uitgever*), and if no publisher is indicated, the printer (*drukker*) indicated may, on behalf of the owner of the copyright, claim the copyright in the work against third parties.[11] However, if a work which does not indicate any natural person as author is published (*openbaar maakt*) by a public institution, association, foundation, or partnership, as a work of its own, it (i.e., the institution, association, foundation, or partnership) is regarded as the author (unless the publication was unlawful).[12]

Employed Author.—If the labor which a person performs in the employment (*dienst* = service) of another person consists of the making of specific works, then, unless there is agreement to the contrary, the person in whose employment the work was produced is regarded as the author.[13]

Composite Works.—If a work is a composite work, i.e., consists of the separate works of two or more persons, then, the person under whose guidance and supervision the composite work (*het gansche werk*) has been produced, or if there is no such person, then, the person who has collected the separate works, is considered to be the author of the composite work. If any of the separate works is protected by copyright

---

[7] Article 10, last paragraph.

[8] There is no copyright in laws, decrees, ordinances issued by the public authorities, judicial decisions, administrative decisions (art. 11, first paragraph). Other publications of public authorities are protected by copyright only either if it is specially so provided by law, decree or ordinance, or if copyright is expressly reserved either by means of a special notice on the work itself or a special statement made at the time when the work is communicated (art. 11 second par.).

[9] Cf. Article 1.   [10] Article 4.   [11] Article 9.   [12] Article 8.

[13] Article 7.

and is used without the consent of its author, the copyright in the composite work in itself will also be deemed to be infringed.[14]

Works Produced With the Help of Others.—If a work is produced according to the plan and under the guidance of any person, such person is deemed to be the author of the work.[15]

ASSIGNMENT AND LICENSING

Copyright is assignable.[16] It is deemed to be movable property.[17] It may be transferred in whole or in part, but any transfer requires an authenticated or private deed (*eene authentieke of onderhandsche akte*).[18]

Any transfer comprises only those rights (*bevoegdheden* = powers) which are specifically mentioned in the deed or which are necessarily implied because of the nature and the purpose of the contract.[19]

Copyright is not subject to seizure.[20]

Copyright is transmissible by inheritance.[21]

PROTECTED RIGHTS

ECONOMIC RIGHTS

Copyright comprises two main rights: the right to communicate the work to the public (*openbaar maken* = to make public) and the right to reproduce it (*verveelvoudigen* = to multiply).[22]

Communication to the public comprises any of the following acts: (i) communication to the public of a reproduction of the work or part thereof, (ii) distribution of the work or part thereof as long as the work has not been published in print, (iii) public recital (*voordracht*) or public performance (*opvoering, uitvoering, voorstelling*) of the work or part thereof or a reproduction thereof.[23]

Recital or performance in a closed circle is considered public recital or public performance if admission is subject to payment. The payment may consist of any kind of contribution. The same rules apply in the case of public showing (*tentoonstelling in het openbaar* = exhibition in the public for the purpose of being seen).[24]

Reproduction comprises translation, musical arrangement, the composing of music for another work, and, in general, any adaptation (*bewerking*) or imitation (*nabootsing*), provided it does not result in a

---

[14] Article 5.   [15] Article 6.   [16] Cf. Article 1.
[17] Article 2, first paragraph.   [18] Article 2, second paragraph.
[19] Article 2, second paragraph.   [20] Article 2, third paragraph.
[21] Article 2, second paragraph.   [22] Article 1.
[23] Article 12, first paragraph.   [24] Article 12, second paragraph.

new, original work.[25] In the case of works which may be aurally perceived, reproduction comprises also the making of cylinders, discs and any other contrivances for rendering all or part of the work audible by mechanical means.[26]

MORAL RIGHTS

No changes may be made in any work, except works of industrially applied art, without the consent of the copyright owner, and without the consent of the author as well—as long as he is alive—even if he no longer owns the copyright.[27]

However, changes such as those to which the author and the copyright owner could not, in good faith, refuse consent may be made without their consent.[28]

No changes may be made in the title of the work or the indication of its author without the consent of the copyright owner, and without the consent of the author as well—as long as he is alive—even if he no longer owns the copyright. If the work remains pseudonymous or anonymous while its author is alive, the true name of the author may be indicated on the work after his death by the owner of the copyright, but only if the author has authorized him to do so.[29]

Even after the transfer of copyright, the author may make such changes in the work as are permissible in good faith according to custom (*naar de regels van het maatschappelijk verkeer* = according to the rules governing relations in society).[30] In the absence of agreement to the contrary, the author of a painting may make further similar paintings, notwithstanding the transfer of the copyright.[31]

LIMITATIONS

The Law provides for limitations on copyright in connection with certain newspaper items,[32] quotations,[33] personal use,[34] works permanently located in public thoroughfares,[35] and portraits.[36]

In the absence of agreement to the contrary, any person who owns a drawing, painting, architectural work, sculpture, or work of industrially applied art, may, without the consent of the copyright owner, display the work publicly and reproduce it in a catalog for the purpose of sale.[37]

---

[25] Article 13.   [26] Article 14.   [27] Article 25, first paragraph.
[28] Article 25, third paragraph.   [29] Article 25, second paragraph.
[30] Article 25, third paragraph.   [31] Article 24.   [32] Article 15.
[33] Article 16.   [34] Article 17.   [35] Article 18.   [36] Articles 19 to 22.
[37] Article 23.

TERM OF PROTECTION

Generally.—Subject to the exceptions stated below, copyright expires fifty years after the death of the author.[38] If the work has two or more authors, the term of copyright is calculated from the death of the last surviving co-author.[39] In the case of pseudonymous or anonymous works, copyright expires at the end of the fiftieth calendar year following the year of the work's first publication (*openbaarmaking*).[40] The same term applies in the case of posthumous works, works of employed authors, and works—not indicating any natural persons as authors—published by a public institution, association, foundation, or partnership.[41]

Photographic Works and Non-Original Motion Pictures.— Copyright in a photographic work, in a work produced by a process analogous to photography, and in a cinematographic work which has no originality (*waaren het Karakter van oorspronkelijkheid ontbreekt*), subsists until the expiration of fifty years from the end of the calendar year in which it was first made public (*eerste openbaarmaking*) by or on behalf of the copyright owner.[42]

Rule of the Shorter Term.—The Law provides that no claim may be made in respect of a work the term of protection of which has expired in its country of origin.[43] This rule is not quite in harmony with the requirements of the Universal Copyright Convention (*see* page 50, above) as the Law (in conformity with the Berne Convention) calls for a comparison of terms in respect of the individual work, whereas the Universal Copyright Convention allows comparison only with the class to which the work belongs.

INFRINGEMENTS

CIVIL REMEDIES

Notwithstanding the transfer of copyright in whole or in part, the author has a right to institute an action against infringers for damages.[44] In certain cases, seizure of infringing copies may be ordered.[45]

CRIMINAL SANCTIONS

Intentional infringements are punishable by a fine,[46] and the courts may order the infringing copies to be destroyed or surrendered to the copyright owner.[47]

---

[38] Article 37, first paragraph.   [39] Article 37, second paragraph.
[40] Article 38, first paragraph.   [41] Article 38, second paragraph.
[42] Article 40.   [43] Article 42.   [44] Article 27.
[45] Articles 28 to 30.   [46] Articles 31 to 35, 44.   [47] Article 36.

NEW ZEALAND

SOURCES

Internal Law.—The main source of the law of copyright in New Zealand is the Copyright Act 1962, dated December 5, 1962 (hereinafter referred to as "the Act").[1] It came into force on April 1, 1963.[2] Hereinafter, references to Sections, without further specification, are references to Sections of this Act. The Act is supplemented by a number of Regulations and Orders.[3]

Universal Copyright Convention.—New Zealand became bound by the Universal Copyright Convention and Protocols 1 and 2 on September 11, 1964.[4]

The protection that New Zealand grants to works on account of the Universal Copyright Convention and the Convention of the Berne Copyright Union is regulated in The Copyright (International Conventions) Order 1964, and its amendments. This Order, as amended, is hereinafter referred to as "the Order."

ACQUISITION OF PROTECTION UNDER THE UNIVERSAL COPYRIGHT CONVENTION

Hereinafter, a country party to the Universal Copyright Convention will be referred to as a "Convention country."[5]

---

[1] No. 33 of 1962, published in Govt. Doc. 6 2942-62 ("Public", No. 33). Reprinted in CLTW, New Zealand: Item 1.

[2] Section 1(2).

[3] The Copyright (Record Royalties) Regulations 1963 (CLTW, New Zealand: Item 3); The Copyright (Customs) Regulations 1963 (CLTW, New Zealand: Item 4); The Copyright (International Conventions) Order 1964 (CLTW, New Zealand: Item 5); The Copyright (International Organizations) Order 1964 (CLTW, New Zealand: Item 6). The last two Orders are based on sections 49, 50, and 51, of the Act.

[4] UNESCO Copyright Bulletin, Volume XVII, page 6. New Zealand is also a member of the Berne Union, the latest text of the Convention of that Union by which it is bound being that of Brussels, 1948.

[5] The Order does not actually speak of Convention countries in general but enumerates them by name and is amended whenever there is a change in membership.

LITERARY, DRAMATIC, AND MUSICAL WORKS
ARTISTIC WORKS

If published.—In any of the following cases, that is:

(i) if the first publication of the work took place in a Convention country,[6]

(ii) if, at the time the work was first published, the author was a citizen, subject, domiciliary, or resident, of a Convention country,[7]

(iii) in cases where copyright originally vests in a body corporate, if, at the time the work was first published, such body corporate was incorporated in a Convention country,[8]

(iv) if the work was first published by or under the direction of the United Nations, any of the Specialized Agencies of the United Nations, or the Organization of American States, (and the publication agreement did not reserve the copyright, if any, to the author),[9]

the work is protected in New Zealand.

If unpublished.—In any of the following cases, that is:

(i) if, at the time the work was made, or if the making of the work extended over a period, then, for a substantial part of that period, the author was a citizen, subject, resident, or domiciliary, of a Convention country,[10]

(ii) in cases where copyright originally vests in a body corporate, if, at the time the work was made, such body corporate was incorporated in a Convention country,[11]

(iii) if the work was made by or under the direction or control of the United Nations, any of the Specialized Agencies of the United Nations, or the Organization of American States,[12] .

the work is protected in New Zealand.

Concept of Publication.—A work is published if reproductions thereof have been issued to the public.[13] The following acts do not constitute publication: (i) performance of a literary, dramatic or musical work, (ii) issue of records of a literary, dramatic or musical work, (iii) exhibition of an artistic work, (iv) issue of photographs or engravings of a work of architecture or of a sculpture, (v) construction of a work of architecture.[14]

---

[6] Order, clause 3(1) (a).   [7] Order, clause 3(1) (b).
[8] Order, clauses 2 (f) (iv) and 3(1) (c).
[9] Section 50; and The Copyright (International Organizations) Order 1964, clause 2.
[10] Order, clauses 2 and 3(1) (b).   [11] Order, clause 3(1) (c).
[12] Section 50; and The Copyright (International Organizations) Order 1964, clause 2.
[13] Section 3(2) (a).   [14] Section 3(2) (d).

Sound Recordings

In any of the following cases, that is:

(i) if, at any time when the recording was made (that is, when the first record embodying the recording is produced), the maker was a citizen, subject, resident, domiciliary of, or a body corporate incorporated in, a Convention country,[15]

(ii) if the first publication of the recording took place in a Convention country,[16]

the recording is protected in New Zealand, but only in the case of reciprocity, that is, if and to the extent to which the country of origin grants protection to New Zealand sound recordings.[17]

"Publication," in relation to a sound recording, means the issue to the public of records embodying the recording or any part thereof.[18] "Sound recording" means the aggregate of the sounds embodied in, and capable of being reproduced by means of, a record of any description, other than a sound track associated with a cinematograph film.[19] "Record" means any disc, tape, perforated roll, or other device, in which sounds are embodied so as to be capable (with or without the aid of some other instrument) of being automatically reproduced therefrom.[20]

Cinematograph Films

In any of the following cases, that is,

(i) if, for the whole or a substantial part of the period during which the film was made, the maker was a citizen, subject, resident, domiciliary of, or a body corporate incorporated in, a Convention country,[21]

(ii) if the first publication of the film took place in a Convention country,[22]

the cinematograph film is protected in New Zealand.

In relation to a cinematograph film, "publication" means the sale, letting on hire, or offer for sale or hire, of copies of the film to the public,[23] and "copy" means any print, negative, tape, or other article on which the film or part of it is recorded.[24]

---

[15] Order, clause 3(1) (b) and (c).   [16] Order, clause 3(1) (a).
[17] Order, clause 3(2) (c).   [18] Section 3(2) (b).   [19] Section 2(1).
[20] Section 2(1).   [21] Order, clause 3(1) (b) and (c).
[22] Order, clause 3(1) (a).   [23] Section 3(2) (c).
[24] Section 2(1). It includes the sound track, whether incorporated in any print or negative or tape or other article, or issued for use in conjunction with any print or negative or tape or other article (section 2(1)).

PUBLISHED EDITIONS

In any of the following cases, that is:

(i) if the first publication of the edition took place in a Convention country,[25]

(ii) if, at the date of the first publication of the edition, the publisher of such edition was a citizen, subject, resident, domiciliary of, or a body corporate incorporated in, a Convention country,[26]

the edition is protected in New Zealand, but only in the case of reciprocity, that is, if and to the extent to which the country of origin grants protection to New Zealand editions.[27]

An edition shall be taken to have been published if, but only if, reproductions of the edition have been issued to the public.[28]

Protection means that no person is allowed, without the consent of the publisher, to make, by any photographic or similar process, a reproduction of the typographical arrangement of the edition.[29] Such protection lasts until the end of the twenty-fifth calendar year following the calendar year in which the edition was first published.[30]

CREATION OR PUBLICATION PRECEDING THE APPLICATION OF THE ORDER TO CONVENTION COUNTRIES

It would seem that *unpublished* works, sound recordings, and cinematograph films, of citizens, etc., of a Convention country *are* protected in New Zealand even if they were created prior to the application of the Order to the Convention country on account of its adherence to the Universal Copyright Convention.[31]

On the other hand, a work, recording, film, or edition, first *published* in a Convention country prior to such date is not protected in New Zealand except if there are grounds other than the Universal Copyright Convention for protecting them. Thus, in particular, if the work was first, or "simultaneously" with the first publication, published in a country member of the Berne Union—for example, if the work of a U.S. citizen was first published in 1950 simultaneously in the United States and Canada—it would continue to be protected in New Zealand.[32]

---

[25] Order, clause 3(1) (a).   [26] Order, clause 3(1) (b) and (c).
[27] Order, clause 3(2) (c).   [28] Section 3(2) (a).   [29] Section 17(3).
[30] Section 17(2).
[31] This argument is based on the fact that the Order, clause 3(2) (a), refers only to publication.
[32] Order, clause 3(2) (a).

General Rules Concerning the Interpretation of the Concept of "Publication"

The following rules of interpretation seem to apply equally to the publication of works, sound recordings, cinematograph films, and editions:

Simultaneous Publication.—A publication in a Convention country is not treated as being other than the first publication by reason only of an earlier publication in a country which is party to neither the Universal Copyright Convention nor the Berne Union if the two publications took place within a period of not more than thirty days.[33]

Colorable Publication.—A publication which is merely colorable and not intended to satisfy the reasonable requirements of the public is not treated as being a publication.[34]

Unauthorized Publication.—A publication effected without the license of the copyright owner (or, if the work is not protected by copyright, without the license of the author or persons lawfully claiming under him) is not treated as being a publication.[35]

Formalities

New Zealand has no copyright formalities. Consequently, registration, deposit, or compliance with other formalities, is neither required nor possible in New Zealand. The absence, in itself, of the Convention notice on the copies of a published work is no bar to the claiming of protection in New Zealand. Furthermore, New Zealand has no renewal system, so there is nothing in that country which would correspond to the renewal formalities existing in the United States. Protection in New Zealand will last, without any intervention on the part of the copyright owner or a State authority, until the day on which the work or other subject matter of copyright falls into the public domain.

PROTECTED WORKS AND OTHER PROTECTED SUBJECT MATTER

Introductory

The Act grants copyright in works and other subject matter. The designation "works" is reserved for literary, dramatic, musical, and artistic works. The other "subject matter" of copyright may be (i) sound recordings, (ii) cinematograph films, (iii) television broadcasts and sound broadcasts, (iv) published editions of works.

[33] Section 3(4).   [34] Section 3(2) (e).   [35] Section 3(5) and (6).

Copyright in television broadcasts and sound broadcasts is not dealt with in this book because it is available only to the New Zealand Broadcasting Corporation[36] and in any case it is not available under the Universal Copyright Convention.

Copyright in published editions of works has been discussed above (page 506), and will be disregarded hereinafter.

WORKS

The following, if original, are protected as works:

(i) **Literary Works.**[37]—These include any written table or compilation.[38]

(ii) **Dramatic Works.**[39]—These include choreographic works, and entertainments in dumb show, if reduced to writing in the form in which the work or entertainment is to be presented. "Dramatic works" include the scenario or script for a cinematograph film but not the cinematograph film itself.[40]

(iii) **Musical Works.**[41]

(iv) **Artistic Works.**[42]—These are:

—paintings, irrespective of artistic quality;

—sculptures (including any cast or model made for purposes of sculpture), irrespective of artistic quality;

—drawings (including diagrams, maps, charts, and plans), irrespective of artistic quality;

—engravings (including etchings, lithographs, woodcuts, prints, and similar works, but not photographs), irrespective of artistic quality;

—photographs (that is, any product of photography or of any process akin to photography, other than a part of a cinematograph film), irrespective of artistic quality;

—works of architecture, being either buildings (structures) or models for buildings, as long as they are artistic.

—works of artistic craftsmanship, not falling within any of the preceding categories, as long as they have artistic quality.[43]

SOUND RECORDINGS

See the definition of sound recordings on page 505, footnote 19, above.

CINEMATOGRAPH FILMS

"Cinematograph film" means any sequence of visual images recorded on material of any description (whether translucent or not)

---

[36] Cf. Section 16.   [37] Section 7.   [38] Section 2(1).   [39] Section 7.
[40] Section 2(1).   [41] Section 7.   [42] Section 7.   [43] Section 2(1).

so as to be capable, by the use of that material: (i) of being shown as a moving picture, (ii) of being recorded on other material (whether translucent or not) by the use of which it can be so shown. A cinematograph film is taken to include the sounds embodied in the sound track associated with the film.[44]

PROTECTED PERSONS

WORKS

Copyright in a literary, dramatic, musical, or artistic work originally vests in its author,[45] subject to the following exceptions or qualifications:

Photographs.—Copyright in a photograph originally vests in the person who, at the time when the photograph is taken, owns the material on which it is taken.[46]

Certain Commissioned Works.—Unless otherwise provided by contract, where a person commissions the taking of a photograph, or the making of a painting, drawing, engraving, or sculpture, and pays or agrees to pay for it in money or money's worth, copyright vests in him rahter than in the author of the work.[47]

Works for Newspapers, etc.—Unless otherwise provided by contract, where a literary, dramatic or artistic (but not musical) work is made by the author in the course of his employment by the proprietor of a newspaper, magazine, or similar periodical, under a contract of service or apprenticeship (and is so made for the purpose of publication in a newspaper, magazine, or similar periodical), the copyright is split between the said proprietor and the author: (i) the said proprietor is entitled to the copyright in so far as it relates to publication in any newspaper, magazine, or similar periodical; (ii) the author is entitled to the copyright in all other respects.[48]

Works of Employees.—Unless otherwise provided by contract, and except where any of the rules referred to in the preceding three paragraphs apply, where a work is made in the course of the author's employment by another person under a contract of service or apprenticeship, copyright vests originally in such other person rather than in the author.[49]

SOUND RECORDINGS

Copyright in a sound recording originally vests in its maker.[50] "Maker" is the person who owns the record embodying the recording

[44] Section 2(1). [45] Section 9(1). [46] Section 2(1). [47] Section 9(3).
[48] Section 9(2). [49] Section 9(4). [50] Section 13(1) and (4).

at the time when the recording is made.[51] In the absence of any agreement to the contrary, where a person commissions the making of a sound recording, and pays or agrees to pay for it in money or money's worth, copyright will vest in him rather than in the maker.[52] As to the meaning of "recording" and "record," see page 505, above.

CINEMATOGRAPH FILMS

Copyright in a cinematograph film originally vests in its maker.[53] "Maker" means the person by whom the arrangements necessary for the making of the film are undertaken.[54] In the absence of any agreement to the contrary, where a person commissions the making of a film, and pays or agrees to pay for it in money or money's worth, copyright will vest in him rather than the maker.[55]

PROTECTED RIGHTS

GENERALLY

Copyright means the exclusive right to do, and to authorize other persons to do, certain acts in relation to protected works in New Zealand.[56]

LITERARY, DRAMATIC, AND MUSICAL

In relation to literary, dramatic, and musical works, the following acts require the authorization of the owner of the copyright:
—*Reproducing the work in any material form.*[57] This includes reproducing the work in the form of a record or of a cinematograph film.[58] The record of a work is any disc, tape, perforated roll, or other device, in which sounds are embodied, and by means of which the work may be performed.[59] In certain cases, the making of records of musical works is subject to a legal license, rather than to consent by the owner of the copyright: Manufacturers are entitled to make, for the purposes of retail sale, records of musical works which have once been recorded with the consent of the copyright owner, provided they pay him the statutory royalty and give him the prescribed notice of their intention to make the record concerned. In such cases, then, the consent of the owner of the copyright is not needed. Generally, the royalty is equal to five per cent of the ordinary retail selling price of the record.[60] In certain cases, reproduction in the form of a record or a cinemato-

[51] Section 13(7).   [52] Section 13(4), proviso.   [53] Section 14(1) and (4).
[54] Section 14(8).   [55] Section 14(4), proviso.   [56] Section 6(1).
[57] Section 7(3) (a).   [58] Section 2(1).
[59] Section 2(1).   [60] Sections 22 and 23.

graph film for broadcasting purposes does not require authorization.[61]
—*Publishing the work*.[62] This seems to include not only first but also
subsequent publications, i.e., the issuance of reproductions to the
public. The performance, or the issue of records, of the work is not
publication.[63]
—*Performing the work in public*.[64] Performance includes any mode of
visual or acoustic presentation, including presentation (i) by the
operation of radio apparatus, (ii) by the exhibition of a cinematograph
film, (iii) by the use of a record.[65] Where performance is done by a
radio or television receiving set or an apparatus playing records, for
example, a coin-operated record player (jukebox), it is the occupier
of the premises where, with his consent, the apparatus is situated who
is considered to be the person giving the performance.[66] Performance
also includes the delivery of lectures, addresses, speeches, or sermons.[67]

The following acts are not considered performance: (i) broadcasting,
(ii) transmission to subscribers to a diffusion service, (iii) transmission
to (*but not* display or emission by) a receiving apparatus.[68]
—*Broadcasting the work*.[69] Broadcasting is broadcasting by radio communication, whether by way of television or of sound broadcasting.[70]
—*Causing the work to be transmitted to subscribers to a diffusion service*.[71]
This means transmission of the work in the course of a service of
distributing (i) broadcast programs, or (ii) other programs, whether,
in both cases, the program was provided by the person operating the
service or by other persons. The distribution must be over wires, or
other paths provided by a material substance, to the premises of the
subscribers to the service.[72] Where the service is only incidental to a
business of keeping or letting premises where persons reside or sleep,
and is operated as part of the amenities provided exclusively or mainly
for residents or inmates, the service is not considered a "diffusion
service."[73] The person operating the diffusion service is not liable for
any infringement if he transmits the program of the New Zealand
Broadcasting Corporation.[74]
—*Making any adaptation of the work*.[75] This includes, in relation to a
musical work, its arrangement or transcription, and, in relation to a
literary or dramatic work, any of the following: (i) translation, (ii)
the making into a dramatic work of a non-dramatic work, and vice
versa, (iii) the making of a version of the work in which the story or
action is conveyed wholly or mainly by means of pictures in a form
suitable for reproduction in a book, or in a newspaper, magazine, or
similar periodical (for example, the "comic-strip treatment").[76]

[61] Section 19(9) and (10).   [62] Section 7(3) (b).   [63] Section 3(2) (d) (i).
[64] Section 7(3) (c).   [65] Section 2(1).   [66] Section 2(6).   [67] Section 2(1).
[68] Section 2(5).   [69] Section 7(3) (d).   [70] Section 2(3).
[71] Section 7(3) (e).   [72] Section 2(4).   [73] Section 2(4), proviso.
[74] Section 60(1).   [75] Section 7(3) (f).   [76] Section 2(1).

—*Doing, in relation to an adaptation of the work, any of the above acts.*[77] For example, performance of a translation of a dramatic work. Unless the owner of the copyright in the original work and in the translation is the same person, exploitation of a translation will thus normally require two authorizations: that of the owner of the copyright in the original work and that of the owner of the copyright in the translation.

ARTISTIC WORKS

In relation to artistic works, the following acts require the authorization of the owner of copyright:
—*Reproducing the work in any material form.*[78] This includes a version produced by converting the two-dimensional work into a three-dimensional form, and vice versa.[79]
—*Publishing the work.*[80] The exhibition of an artistic work, the construction of a work of architecture, and the issue of photographs or engravings of a work of architecture or of a sculpture, do not constitute publication.[81]
—*Including the work in a television broadcast.*[82]
—*Causing a program which includes the work to be transmitted to subscribers to a diffusion service.*[83]

SOUND RECORDINGS

In relation to sound recordings, the following acts require the authorization of the owner of the copyright,[84] whether, in doing them, the record embodying the recording is utilized directly or indirectly:[85]
—*Making a record embodying the recording.*[86]
—*Causing the recording to be heard in public if*: (i) the recording is performed in a place to which a charge is made for admission, (ii) the recording is performed by or upon a coin-operated machine, (iii) the person causing the recording to be heard in public receives any payment in respect of the performance.[87] Causing the recording to be heard in public does not require the authorization of the owner of the copyright therein if it is done as part of the activities of, or for the benefit of, a club, society or other organization which is not established or conducted for profit and whose main objects are charitable or are concerned with the advancement of religion, education, or social welfare,

[77] Section 7(3) (g).   [78] Section 7(4) (a).   [79] Section 2(1).
[80] Section 7(4) (b).   [81] Section 3(2) (d) (ii).   [82] Section 7(4) (c).
[83] Section 7(4) (d). See also the passages connected with footnotes 72, 73, and 74, above.
[84] See passages connected with footnotes 50, 51, and 52, above.
[85] Section 13(5). See, however, the condition of reciprocity referred to in the passage connected with footnote 17, above.
[86] Section 13(5) (a).   [87] Section 13(5) (c).

provided that, if a charge for admission is made, all proceeds go to the organization.[88] Where broadcasting is effected by the New Zealand Broadcasting Corporation and the recording is caused to be heard in public through the operation of a radio or television receiving set, the operator of the receiving set does not require the authorization of the owner of the copyright in the sound recording.[89] Where authorization is needed, the person who needs to secure such authorization is the occupier of the premises on which, with his consent, the receiving set or record-playing apparatus is operated.[90]
—*Broadcasting the recording.*[91]

CINEMATOGRAPH FILMS

In relation to cinematograph films, the following acts require the authorization of the owner of the copyright.[92]
—*Making a copy of the film.*[93] "Copy" means any print, negative, tape or other article on which the film or part of it is recorded.[94]
—*Causing the film, in so far as it consists of visual images, to be seen in public, or in so far as it consists of sounds, to be heard in public.*[95] These acts do not constitute infringement, by the person causing them, even if done without the consent of the maker, if they are effected through the reception of a broadcast by the New Zealand Broadcasting Corporation.[96]
—*Broadcasting the film.*[97]
—*Causing the film to be transmitted to subscribers to a diffusion service,*[98] except if done through the reception of a broadcast by the New Zealand Broadcasting Corporation.[99]

EXCEPTIONS AND LIMITATIONS

Fair Dealing.—No fair dealing with works, sound recordings, or cinematograph films, is an infringement if it is done for the purposes of research or private study,[100] or criticism or review,[101] or, in certain cases, reporting current events.[102]

[88] Section 13(6).   [89] Section 60(1).
[90] Section 2(6).   [91] Section 13(5) (b).
[92] See passages connected with footnotes 53, 54, and 55, above.
[93] Section 14(5) (a).   [94] Section 2(1).   [95] Section 14(5) (b).
[96] Section 60(1).   [97] Section 14(5) (c).   [98] Section 14(5) (d).
[99] Section 60(1).   [100] Sections 19(1) and (5) and 20(1).
[101] Sections 19(2) and (5) and 20(2), provided the criticism or review is accompanied by a sufficient acknowledgement, sufficient acknowledgement meaning an acknowledgement of the work or other subject matter in question by its title or other description and, unless the work is anonymous or the author or the maker has previously agreed that no acknowledgement of his name should be made, also identifying the author or maker (Sec. 2(1)).
[102] In the case of literary, dramatic, or musical works, sound recordings and

Other Exceptions Concerning Specified Uses of Works are provided in connection with certain (i) judicial proceedings,[103] (ii) readings or recitations in public or broadcasting of reasonable extracts,[104] (iii) school and other educational uses,[105] (iv) newspaper reporting on public lectures,[106] (v) fixations for and by the broadcaster,[107] (vi) photographing, etc., of artistic works permanently situated in a public place,[108] (vii) incidental inclusion of an artistic work in photographs, films, or telecasts,[109] (viii) making of objects in three dimensions reproducing a two-dimensional artistic work if the objects would not appear, to non-experts, to be reproductions,[110] (ix) using, by an author, of part of his earlier artistic work in his later artistic works as a secondary feature,[111] (x) reconstructions of buildings,[112] (xi) certain library and instructional uses.[113]

ASSIGNMENT AND LICENSING

Assignments.—Copyright is transmissible by assignment, by testamentary disposition, or by operation of law, as personal and movable property.[114] The assignment of the material object does not necessarily transfer the title to the copyright. For example, the purchaser of a painting can only obtain the right to reproduction of the work he has purchased by insisting upon an assignment of the copyright or, at least, a license.

Assignment may be partial as to time, country and rights.[115] Assignments must be in writing.[116]

Licenses.—A license is binding upon every successor in title to the licensor's interest in the copyright, except a purchaser in good faith for valuable consideration and without actual or constructive notice of the license.[117] It need not be in writing, that is, it may be oral or implied from conduct.

Assignment and Licensing of Future Copyright.—"Future copyright" means copyright which will or may come into existence in respect of any future work or other subject matter, or in any future event.[118] Future copyright may be assigned or licensed in the same way as existing copyright.[119]

cinematograph films, when the reporting is (i) in a newspaper, magazine or similar periodical, or (ii) by means of broadcasting or in a cinematograph film, provided that, when it is in a newspaper, magazine or similar periodical, a sufficient acknowledgement (see footnote 101, above) accompanies the reporting (sec. 19(3) and (5)).
[103] Sections 19(4) and (5) and 20(7).   [104] Section 19(8).
[105] Section 19(6).   [106] Section 19(7).   [107] Section 19(9) and (10).
[108] Section 20(4), (5) and (6).   [109] Section 20(3).   [110] Section 20(8).
[111] Section 20(9).   [112] Section 20(10).   [113] Section 21.
[114] Section 56(1).   [115] Section 56(2).   [116] Section 56(3).
[117] Section 56(4).   [118] Section 2(1).   [119] Section 57.

Bequest of a Manuscript or an Artistic Work.—The bequest of an unpublished manuscript of a literary, dramatic or musical work, or an unpublished artistic work, is deemed to comprise the copyright therein.[120] "Manuscript" means the original document embodying the work, whether written by hand or not.[121]

TERM OF PROTECTION

Works.—Copyright in literary, dramatic, musical and artistic works subsists until the end of a period of fifty years from the end of the calendar year in which the author died, if, during the life of the author, the work has been published, performed in public, or broadcast, or records of the work have been offered for sale to the public.[122]

On the other hand, if a literary, dramatic, musical or artistic work, or an adaptation thereof, in which copyright subsists has not, before the death of the author, been (i) published, (ii) performed in public, (iii) broadcast, and (iv) no records thereof have been offered for sale to the public—then, copyright ends at the end of a period of seventy-five years from the end of the calendar year in which the author died, provided that, if any of those acts has been done after the death of the author, copyright subsists until the end of a period of fifty years from the end of the calendar year in which that act has first been done, or the end of the said seventy-five-year period, whichever period is the shorter.[123]

If copyright in a cinematograph film has expired before the expiration of the copyright in any literary, dramatic, musical or artistic work used in the cinematograph film, copyright in such work is not infringed even if the film is caused to be seen or heard in public without the permission of the owner of the copyright in such work.[124]

Notwithstanding the rules stated above for artistic works, copyright in a photograph subsists until the end of a period of fifty years from the end of the calendar year in which the original photograph was taken.[125]

Works and Cinematograph Films of International Organizations.—Where copyright originally vests in any of the international organizations listed on page 504, above, copyright subsists until the end of a period of fifty years from the end of the calendar year in which the work or the cinematograph film was made or the photograph was taken.[126]

Sound Recordings.—Copyright in sound recordings subsists until

---

[120] Section 59.   [121] Section 2(1).   [122] Section 8(1) (a).
[123] Section 8(1) (b) and proviso.   [124] Section 14(6).   [125] Section 8(2).
[126] Section 50(4).

the end of a period of fifty years from the end of the calendar year in which the recording was made.[127]

Cinematograph Films.—Copyright in cinematograph films subsists until the end of a period of fifty years from the end of the calendar year during which the film was completed.[128]

Rule of the Shorter Term.—The New Zealand term of copyright in a work, sound recording or cinematograph film protected in its country of origin cannot exceed the term enjoyed in that country *without registration, deposit, or compliance with any other formalities,* by a New Zealand work, sound recording or cinematograph film of the class in question, or—if the laws of that country require compliance with any formalities as a condition of protection—*without compliance with any formalities other than those provided for in Article III, paragraph 1, of the Universal Copyright Convention.*[129]

INFRINGEMENTS

Direct and Indirect Infringements.—Where the acts enumerated above under "Protected Rights" require the authorization of the owner of the copyright, the doing of such acts, without the required authorization, constitutes infringement, even when the infringer did not know that he was infringing.[130]

In addition to these "direct" infringements, copyright may be infringed "indirectly," particularly through importation and sale of infringing copies.

Importation.—Copyright in works, sound recordings, or cinematograph films is infringed by any person who, without the license of the owner of the copyright, imports an article (otherwise than for his private and domestic use) into New Zealand, if, to his knowledge, (i) the making of the article constituted an infringement or (ii) would have constituted an infringement if the article had been made in New Zealand.[131]

Sale, etc.—Copyright in works, sound recordings, or cinematograph films, is infringed by any person who, without the license of the owner of the copyright:
—sells,
—lets for hire,
—by way of trade offers for sale or hire,
—by way of trade exposes for sale or hire,
—by way of trade exhibits in public,

[127] Section 13(3).   [128] Section 14(3).
[129] Order, clause 3(2) (b).   [130] Section 24.
[131] Sections 3(10), 10(2), 18(2). Importation of printed copies may be restricted by giving notice to the Minister of Customs (sec. 29).

—distributes for purposes of trade (or other purposes, but to such extent as to cause prejudice to the owner of the copyright),
an article, if, to his knowledge, (i) the making of the article constituted an infringement, or (ii) in the case of an imported article, would have constituted an infringement if it had been made in New Zealand.[132]

Civil Remedies.—Depending on the circumstances, the plaintiff may be entitled to damages, an account of profits, injunctions,[133] and may be treated as the owner of the infringing copies (or of any plates used or intended for making such copies).[134]

Criminal Sanctions.—Most infringements, if committed knowingly, are criminal offenses, punished by a fine, or in case of recidivism, by a fine or imprisonment.[135]

---

[132] Sections 3(10); 10(3), and (4); 18(3) and (4).
[133] Section 24.   [134] Section 25.   [135] Section 28.

NICARAGUA

SOURCES

Internal Law.—The primary source of the law of copyright in Nicaragua is Part IV (*Del trabajo*), Chapter II (*De la propiedad literaria*), of the Civil Code of February 1, 1904 (hereinafter referred to as "the Code").[1] Hereinafter references to Articles, without further specification, are references to Articles of this Code.

Universal Copyright Convention.—Nicaragua became bound by the Universal Copyright Convention and Protocols 1 and 2 as from August 16, 1961.[2]

ACQUISITION OF PROTECTION UNDER THE UNIVERSAL COPYRIGHT CONVENTION

There are no laws in Nicaragua which specifically refer to the Universal Copyright Convention. In particular, there are no provisions implementing Article III of the Convention, which provides for the non-applicability or avoidance of domestic formalities for the acquisition of copyright.[3] Consequently, while it is assumed for purposes of the present exposition that conflicts between the law of Nicaragua and the Convention will be resolved in accordance with the provisions of the latter, this assumption cannot, in the absence of relevant authoritative decisions, be regarded as officially confirmed.

The laws of Nicaragua do not define the works which are protected therein by virtue of the Universal Copyright Convention. On the basis of the provisions of the Convention and the Protocols, it is assumed that such works are: (i) published works of nationals of a Convention

[1] English translation in CLTW, Nicaragua: Item 1.
[2] *See* CLTW, Nicaragua: Item 1A. Nicaragua is also party to the Copyright Conventions of Rio de Janeiro (1906), Buenos Aires (1910), Havana (1928) and Washington (1946); *see* CLTW, Nicaragua: Items 2 through 5. Nicaragua concluded a copyright treaty with Spain in 1934 (CLTW, Nicaragua: Item 7), and there are provisions relating to copyright in a treaty of friendship, commerce and navigation concluded with Italy in 1906 (CLTW, Nicaragua: Item 6). In view of the fact that Italy and Spain, as well as Nicaragua, are party to the Universal Copyright Convention, these bilateral copyright agreements are now of limited practical significance.
[3] As to such domestic formalities, *see* Code, articles 831 to 845.

country, irrespective of the place of first publication, (ii) works first published in a Convention country, irrespective of the nationality of the author, (iii) unpublished works of nationals of a Convention country other than Nicaragua, (iv) works of stateless persons and refugees who have their habitual residence in a State party to Protocol 1 (except perhaps Nicaragua), either published or unpublished, and, if published, irrespective of the place of first publication, (v) works first published by the United Nations, any of its Specialized Agencies, or by the Organization of American States, as well as unpublished works of any of these Organizations.

It may be thus further assumed that works in any of these categories are protected in Nicaragua without deposit and registration, provided always that, in the case of published works, the provisions of Article III of the Convention concerning notice have been complied with.

Nicaragua has no renewal system, so that there is nothing in this country which would correspond to the renewal formalities existing in the United States.

PROTECTED WORKS

Original works are protected.[4] Oral and written instruction (*lecciones*) and speeches are "works."[5] So are manuscripts,[6] sketches of artistic works,[7] and private letters.[8] Dramatic and artistic works and musical compositions are protected.[9]

PROTECTED PERSONS

Copyright vests in the author.[10] Private letters may not be published without the consent of both writer and addressee or their heirs, unless publication is necessary in proof or defense of a right.[11] When an encyclopaedia, dictionary, periodical or any other work is compiled by various individuals whose individual contributions cannot be separated, copyright belongs to all of them;[12] if one of them dies without heirs or transferees, his right accrues to the remaining authors;[13] however, if the identity of authors of separable parts of the work is known or can be proved, each of them has a separate copyright in his contribution, but the complete work may be republished pursuant to a decision of the majority of the authors.[14] If a work compiled by several persons was

---

[4] Article 729.   [5] Article 731.   [6] Article 733.
[7] Article 790.   [8] Article 734.
[9] Articles 765, 789, 791. As to artistic copyright, *see* "Protected Persons," below
[10] Article 726.   [11] Article 734.   [12] Article 745.
[13] Article 746.   [14] Article 747.

organized (*emprendido*) or published by a single person, such person owns the copyright in the work as a whole; each author may republish his own contribution, either singly or assembled in a collection,[15] but the publisher may not separately publish the individual contributions.[16] In the case of a dramatic or musical work written by several persons, each of them may authorize public performance, unless there is agreement to the contrary or unless an allegation of just cause is found to have merit by judicial authority following expert opinion.[17] Translators, in their lawful translations, have the same rights as authors.[18] For legal purposes, the author of the music is considered to be the author of the words associated with the music; but the author of the words may secure rights by means of a written agreement with the composer of the music.[19]

The author of a lawfully published translation has the same rights as the author of an original work, but he may not prohibit further translation of the same work unless the author of the original work granted him an exclusive right.[20] If the translator alleges a new translation to be a reproduction of his own translation, the court must hear the opinion of experts.[21]

The publisher of a work which is already in the public domain has copyright in it for one year; but this right is not effective against editions made outside Nicaragua.[22] Any person who publishes for the first time a *códice* (ancient manuscript), has copyright in it for his life.[23]

If the author transfers the copyright in a work and subsequently makes substantial revisions of such work, the transferee has no right to restrain the author or his heirs from publishing the revised work or from alienating his rights therein.[24]

In respect of posthumous works, heirs and transferees have the same rights as authors; and if there are no heirs or transferees, the publisher owns the copyright in the posthumous work for 30 years.[25,26,27]

According to the Code, the following persons have artistic copyright: (i) authors of geographical, scientific, architectural, etc., maps and plans, and of plans, sketches and drawings of any kind, (ii) architects, (iii) painters, engravers, lithographers, photographers, and photo-engravers, (iv) sculptors in respect of finished works, models, and moulds, (v) musicians (*músicos*; it is not clear whether this means composers or performers, probably only the former), (vi) calligraphers (*calígrafos*).[28] Persons lawfully reproducing works of art have copyright

[15] Article 748.   [16] Article 749.   [17] Articles 781, 782, 783, 791.
[18] Articles 752, 754, 785.   [19] Article 792.   [20] Articles 752, 785, 864.
[21] Article 754. As to annotators, *see* article 755.
[22] Article 759.   [23] Article 762.   [24] Articles 742 and 743.
[25] Articles 739 and 740.
[26] As to anonymous and pseudonymous works, *see* articles 741, 760, 761.
[27] As to several owners, *see* articles 847, 848, 849.
[28] Article 789.

as established by the contract (*sic!*).[29] An artist who produces a work upon commission may not reproduce the work by a similar process (*sic!*).[30]

ASSIGNMENT AND LICENSING

Copyright is transferable,[31] for a limited time or for its entire duration.[32]

If the contract concerning the performance of a dramatic or musical work does not establish a time-limit within which performance must take place, the work may be withdrawn (*sic!*) if no performance takes place within one year from the date of the contract.[33] Even if the contract specifies a time-limit, the work may be withdrawn (*sic!*) if there is no performance during 5 consecutive years.[34] If the contract specifies a time-limit and the work is not performed within such period and under the conditions agreed, the author may withdraw (*sic!*) it.[35] Sums paid in advance to the author need not be returned in any one of these cases.[36]

Authorization to publish a dramatic or musical work does not imply the right to perform it.[37]

Acquisition of a work of art does not imply the acquisition of the right to reproduce it.[38]

PROTECTED RIGHTS

Economic Rights

Authors of literary, dramatic and musical works have the exclusive right to publish and to reproduce, as many times as they desire, by copies or manuscripts (*sic!*), by printing, lithography, or any similar means, the whole or part of their original works.[39]

The author has the right to publish translations of his non-dramatic or dramatic works, but in such cases he must indicate (*declarar*) whether the reservation is limited to any given language, or extends to all languages.[40] The form in which the indication must be made is not specified in the Code. It is not clear whether a copyright notice as provided in Article III of the Universal Copyright Convention would suffice. The Code provides that an author who does not reside in Nicaragua, and who publishes his work outside of Nicaragua, has the right of

[29] Article 795.   [30] Article 797.   [31] Article 736.
[32] Articles 737 and 738. *See also* article 758.
[33] Articles 775 and 791.
[34] Articles 776 and 791; unless there is just cause for the delay.
[35] Articles 774 and 791.   [36] Articles 777 and 791.
[37] Articles 784 and 791.   [38] Article 796.
[39] Articles 729 and 765.   [40] Articles 751 and 787.

translation for 10 years.[41] It is not clear whether this provision would be applied in the case of works protected under the Universal Copyright Convention; it should not be applied to them because, under the principle of national treatment, the right of translation in foreign works protected under the Convention should have the same duration (i.e., for the entire term of copyright) as in the case of domestic works.[42]

Authors of dramatic and musical works also have an exclusive right of performance,[43] and if the performance is in a public theatre in which a charge is made for admission, the permission must result from a writing.[44] The author who enters into a contract for the performance of his dramatic or musical work enjoys (unless otherwise provided in the contract) the right (i) subsequently to make such changes in the work as he may consider necessary (he may not, however, alter any essential part of the work), (ii) to require, if his work is still in manuscript form, that it be not disclosed to persons outside the theatre.[45] Creditors of the theatrical enterprise may not distrain upon the portion of the proceeds due to the dramatic author or musical composer.[46] Copyright in musical compositions includes the right to make arrangements based upon the motifs or themes of the work.[47]

Authors of artistic works have the exclusive right to authorize the reproduction of their works, in whole or in part, by processes similar to or different from the process employed in the making of the original, and either upon the same scale as the original, or on a different scale.[48] In the absence of proof to the contrary, the possession of a model of a work of sculpture is presumed to imply ownership of the right of reproduction.[49]

MORAL RIGHTS

It is unlawful to omit the name of the author or translator; to change the title of a work; to change or suppress any part of the work.[50]

LIMITATIONS

The Code provides that, in respect of certain works and under certain circumstances, quotations, charitable performances, etc., do not require the consent of the owner of the copyright.[51]

[41] Articles 753 and 787.
[42] As to the making of abstracts and abridgments, *see* articles 756, 757, 790; as to annotations and commentaries, *see* articles 755 and 759.
[43] Articles 765 and 791.   [44] Articles 767 and 791.
[45] Articles 769 and 791.
[46] Articles 777 and 791. *See also* articles 772, 773, 774, 778, 779, for further details.
[47] Article 793.   [48] Article 794.   [49] Article 798.
[50] Article 799. *See also* article 768.
[51] Articles 750 and 805.

When the reproduction of a work is desirable and the owner fails to reproduce it, the Government may either order reproduction at the cost of the State or make the right available by public auction.[52]

TERM OF PROTECTION

The author of a literary or artistic work enjoys copyright throughout his lifetime; upon his death, copyright passes to his heirs, but the Code does not state for what period of time.[53]

The author of a dramatic or musical work enjoys the exclusive right of public performance during his lifetime; upon his death, the right passes to his heirs, who enjoy it for a period of 30 years, unless the right has been transferred, in which case it continues for a period of 30 years after the death of the author, to the benefit of the transferee.[54] The Code does not make it clear what the duration of the other rights (reproduction, etc.) is in the case of dramatic and musical works.

The publisher of a posthumous literary work of a known author owns the copyright for a period of 30 years if there is neither an heir nor a transferee of the author;[55] if the work is a dramatic or musical work, the publisher owns the performance right for a period of 20 years only.[56,57]

Since there is no provision in the law of Nicaragua for the "rule of the shorter term" permitted under Article IV (4) of the Universal Copyright Convention, it would appear that works are protected in Nicaragua until the expiration of the terms indicated above, even if they fall into the public domain in other countries at an earlier date.

INFRINGEMENTS

The Code provides that infringement exists when any person, without the consent of the legitimate owner: (i) publishes original literary works, speeches, lessons or articles, (ii) publishes translations of such works, (iii) performs dramatic or musical works, (iv) publishes or reproduces artistic works either by the same or by a different process from that employed in the original work, (v) omits the name of the author or of the translator, (vi) changes the title or suppresses or varies any part of the work, (vii) publishes a greater number of copies than agreed in the publication contract, (viii) reproduces a work of architecture when entry into private houses is necessary for the purpose, (ix) publishes or performs a musical work consisting of extracts from

[52] Article 860. [53] Articles 735 and 790. [54] Articles 766, 769, 770.
[55] Articles 740 and 778. [56] Articles 779 and 791.
[57] *See also* articles 741, 744, 759, 762, 764, 780, 850.

other works, (x) arranges a musical composition for single instruments.[58] Furthermore, the Code provides that trade in infringing works constitutes infringement, whether it takes place in Nicaragua or in any other place.[59]

Infringers are liable to pay damages and may have to give up the infringing copies to the owner of copyright. They may be subject to various injunctions and punishments under the Penal Code.[60]

[58] Article 799; *see also* articles 800, 801, 802, 804.
[59] Article 802.
[60] *See* articles 806 to 830, and 858.

NIGERIA

SOURCES

Although Nigeria has become bound, as from February 14, 1962, by the Universal Copyright Convention[1] and thus it should grant protection to works to be protected under that Convention, it is probable that, in actual fact, protection under the Universal Copyright Convention is not yet available in Nigeria. The legal background of this situation is the following:

Nigeria continues to apply,[2] subject to amendments not relevant here, the provisions of what was the United Kingdom Copyright Act, 1911.[3] That Act provides that it applies to foreign works only when Orders in Council extend it to such works, and only to the extent and in the cases provided in the Orders.[4] As far as works to be protected under the Berne Union Conventions are concerned, the United Kingdom has issued Orders in Council extending the protection of the 1911 Act (we are *not* speaking about the Orders in Countil extending the 1956 Act). These Orders were applicable in Nigeria before its independence and they are continued to be applied by independent Nigeria. But the U.K. Orders in Council dealing with the Universal Copyright Convention (which concern the 1956 Act only and which were never extended to Nigeria) are not applied by Nigeria. Since Nigeria did not, thus far, issue any Orders of its own, it would seem to be logical to conclude that there is no protection in Nigeria under the Universal Copyright Convention. The reason for which no categorical statement is made here on this question is that no Nigerian court decisions or official declarations of the Nigerian Government on the issue are known.

Hereinafter, a brief analysis is given of the copyright law of Nigeria as it applies to domestic, i.e., Nigerian works. This analysis might become of some interest to persons who wish to secure and maintain protection in Nigeria under the Universal Copyright Convention *if and when* Nigeria extends, by Order, the application of its law to works protected under that Convention, and *to the extent to which* the domestic

---

[1] *See* CLTW, Nigeria: Item 2.

[2] *See* the Nigeria Independence Act, 1960, of the United Kingdom (8 & 9 Eliz. 2, Ch. 55), section 1(3).

[3] Dated December 16, 1911; 1 & 2 Geo. 5, c. 46. *See* CLTW, Australia: Item 1, The Schedule.

[4] *See* section 29.

law, at that time, will be the same as it is when these lines are written (early 1963). Of course, even if the domestic law does not change, the future Order may provide for certain modifications when it makes the law applicable to works to be protected by virtue of such Order.

The Copyright Act, 1911, of the United Kingdom, is hereinafter referred to as "the Act"; references, without further specification, to Sections are references to Sections of the Act.

There are no copyright formalities in Nigeria. Consequently, registration, deposit, or compliance with other formalities is neither required nor possible in Nigeria, and the absence, in itself, of a Convention notice on the copies of a published work is no bar to claiming protection in that country. Furthermore, Nigeria has no renewal system, so that there is nothing in Nigeria which would correspond to the renewal formalities existing in the United States.

PROTECTED WORKS

The Act does not contain a definition or formal enumeration of protected works but it does refer, *expressis verbis*, to literary, dramatic, musical and artistic works;[5] lectures, novels, other non-dramatic works;[6] records, perforated rolls, and other contrivances by means of which sounds may be mechanically reproduced (hereinafter sometimes referred to as "sound recordings");[7] and photographs.[8]

"Literary work" includes maps, charts, plans, tables, and compilations. "Dramatic work" includes (i) any piece for recitation, choreographic work or entertainment in dumb show, the scenic arrangement or acting form of which is fixed in writing or otherwise, and (ii) any cinematograph production where the arrangement or acting form or the combination of incidents represented give the work an original character. "Artistic work" includes (i) works of painting, drawing, sculpture and artistic craftsmanship, (ii) architectural works of art, (iii) engravings, and (iv) photographs. "Works of sculpture" include casts and moulds. "Architectural work of art" means any building or structure having an artistic character or design, in respect of such character or design, or any model for such building or structure, provided that the protection afforded by copyright is confined to the artistic character and design, and does not extend to processes or methods of construction. "Engravings" include etchings, lithographs, woodcuts, prints, and other similar works, not being photographs. "Photograph" includes photo-lithograph and any work produced by any process analogous to photography. "Cinematograph" includes any work produced by any process analogous to cinematography.[9]

[5] Section 1(2).   [6] Section 1(2).
[7] Section 19(1).   [8] Section 21.   [9] Section 35(1).

The Act does not apply to designs capable of being registered under the Patents and Designs Statutes, except designs which, although capable of being so registered, are not used or intended to be used as models or patterns to be multiplied by any industrial process.[10]

PROTECTED PERSONS

Subject to the exceptions stated below, the first owner of the copyright in a work is the author of the work.[11]

Engravings, Photographs and Portraits Made on Order.— Where, in the case of an engraving, photograph, or portrait, the plate or other original was ordered by some other person and was made for valuable consideration in pursuance of that order, then, in the absence of any agreement to the contrary, the person by whom such plate or other original was ordered is the first owner of the copyright.[12] "Plate" includes any stereotype or other plate, stone, block, mould, matrix, transfer, or negative used or intended to be used for printing or reproducing copies of any work.[13]

Works of Employees.—Where the author was in the employment of some other person under a contract of service or apprenticeship and the work was made in the course of his employment by that person, the employer is—in the absence of any agreement to the contrary—the first owner of copyright; but where the work is an article or other contribution to a newspaper, magazine, or similar periodical, the right of publication otherwise than as part of a newspaper, etc., is presumed to belong to the author-employee.[14]

Sound Recordings.—The first owner of copyright in records, perforated rolls, and other contrivances by means of which sounds may be mechanically reproduced, is the person who, at the time it is made, is the owner of the original plate from which such contrivances are directly or indirectly derived.[15] "Plate" includes any matrix or other appliance by which records, perforated rolls or other contrivances for the acoustic representation of the work are or are intended to be made.[16]

Photographs.—The first owner of copyright in a photograph is the person who, at the time the negative (from which the photograph was directly or indirectly derived) was made, owned such negative.[17]

---

[10] Section 22(1).   [11] Section 5(1).   [12] Section 5(1), proviso (a).
[13] Section 35(1).   [14] Section 5(1), proviso (b).
[15] Section 19(1).   [16] Section 35(1).   [17] Section 21.

ASSIGNMENT AND LICENSING

Generally.—The owner of the copyright in any work may assign the right (i) either wholly or partially, (ii) either generally or subject to limitations in Nigeria, (iii) either for the whole term of the copyright or any part thereof. He may grant any interest in the right by license. Assignments and licenses are valid only if they are in writing, signed by the owner of the right in respect of which the assignment or grant is made, or by his duly authorized agent.[18] Where, under any partial assignment or copyright, the assignee becomes entitled to a given right, the assignee is treated as the owner of the copyright as far as the said given right is concerned.[19]

Compulsory License After 25 Years Post Mortem Auctoris.—Twenty-five years after the death of the author, any of his works, if published before the expiration of these 25 years, may be reproduced for sale without the authorization of the owner of the copyright therein if the person so reproducing the work proves (i) that he has given the prescribed notice in writing of his intention to reproduce the work, and (ii) that he has paid ten per cent royalty on the publication price of each copy sold.[20]

Compulsory License After the Death of the Author.—If, at any time after the death of the author of a literary, dramatic, or musical work which has been published or performed in public, a complaint is made to the designated Government authority that the owner of the copyright has refused to republish or to allow the republication of the work, or has refused its public performance, and if by reason of such refusal the work is withheld from the public, the owner of the copyright may be ordered to grant a license to reproduce the work or perform the work in public, as the case may be, on such terms and conditions as the said authority may think fit.[21]

Reversion of Copyright to the Author's Estate.—Where the author of a work is the first owner of the copyright therein, no assignment or license by him (otherwise than by will) has effect beyond the expiration of 25 years from his death. The reversionary interest in the copyright on the termination of this 25-year period devolves, on the death of the author—and notwithstanding any agreement made by him during his life—on his legal personal representatives.[22]

[18] Section 5(2).   [19] Section 5(3).   [20] Proviso to section 3.
[21] Section 4.
[22] Proviso to section 5(2). These provisions do not apply to collective works. "Collective work" means: (i) an encyclopaedia, dictionary, year book, or similar work; (ii) a newspaper, review, magazine, or similar periodical; (iii) any work written in distinct parts by different authors, or in which works or parts of works of different authors are incorporated (sec. 35(1)).

PROTECTED RIGHTS

ECONOMIC RIGHTS

Generally.—Subject to the exceptions stated below, "copyright" means the sole right: (i) to publish the work if it is an unpublished work; (ii) to produce or reproduce the work in any material form whatsoever; (iii) to perform[23] the work in public; (iv) in the case of lectures,[24] to deliver[25] them in public; (v) to produce, reproduce, perform or publish a translation of a work; (vi) in the case of a novel or other non-dramatic work, or of an artistic work, to convert it into a dramatic work, by way of performance in public or otherwise; (vii) in the case of a dramatic work, to convert it into a novel or other non-dramatic work; (viii) in the case of a literary, dramatic, or musical work, to make any record, perforated roll, cinematograph film or other contrivance by means of which the work may be mechanically performed or delivered.[26]

Compulsory Licenses for Sound Recordings.—Records, perforated rolls and other contrivances by means of which musical works may be mechanically performed (hereinafter "sound recordings") may be made without the consent of the owner of the copyright in the musical work if sound recordings have previously been made by, or with the consent or acquiescence of, such owner. The making of sound recordings under "compulsory license" is subject to the payment of a royalty, the amount of which, generally speaking, is five per cent of the ordinary retail price of the sound recording.[27]

LIMITATIONS

The Act provides that certain acts, normally subject to the authorization of the owner of the copyright, may be performed without such authorization. Among such acts are: (i) fair dealing with the work for purposes of private study, research, criticism, or newspaper summary; (ii) publishing of pictures of certain three-dimensional works of art when they are permanently situated in a public place; (iii) certain uses in schools; (iv) certain uses in newspapers or lectures publicly delivered; (v) public reading or recitation of reasonable extracts from a published work.[28]

---

[23] "Performance" means any acoustic representation of a work and any visual representation of any dramatic action in a work, including such a representation made by means of any mechanical instrument (sec. 35(1)).
[24] "Lecture" includes address, speech, and sermon (sec. 35(1)).
[25] "Delivery," in relation to a lecture, includes delivery by means of any mechanical instrument (sec. 35(1)).
[26] Section 1(2).
[27] Section 19(2); for further details and qualifications, *see* section 19(2) to (8).
[28] Section 2(1) (i) to (vi); section 20.

TERM OF PROTECTION

Generally.—Subject to the exceptions stated elsewhere,[29] copyright subsists during the life of the author and for a period of 50 years after his death.[30,31]

Sound Recordings.—Copyright in records, perforated rolls, and other contrivances by means of which sounds may be mechanically reproduced subsists for fifty years from the making of the original plate from which the contrivance was directly or indirectly derived.[32]

Photographs.—Copyright in photographs subsists for fifty years from the making of the original negative from which the photograph was directly or indirectly derived.[33]

INFRINGEMENTS

Generally.—Subject to the exceptions stated elsewhere,[34] copyright is deemed to be infringed by any person who, without the consent of the owner of the copyright, does anything the sole right to do which is conferred on the owner of the copyright.[35] Furthermore, copyright in a work is deemed to be infringed by any person who does any of the following acts in relation to a work which, to his knowledge, infringes copyright, or would infringe copyright if it had been done in Nigeria: (i) sells or lets for hire, or by way of trade exposes or offers for sale or hire; (ii) distributes either for the purposes of trade or to such an extent as to affect prejudicially the owner of the copyright; (ii) by way of trade exhibits in public; (iv) imports for sale or hire into Nigeria.[36] Infringement is also committed by any person who, for his private profit, permits a theatre or other place of entertainment to be used for the performance in public of the work without the consent of the owner of the copyright, unless he was not aware, and had no reasonable ground for suspecting, that the performance would be an infringement of copyright.[37]

Civil Remedies.—The injured party is generally entitled to all remedies by way of injunction, interdict, damages, accounts, and otherwise, as are conferred by law for the infringement of a right.[38] Infringing copies and plates may be handed over to the injured party.[39]

[29] *See* page 476, above.
[30] Section 3.
[31] For special provisions concerning works of joint authorship and posthumous works, *see* sections 16 and 17.
[32] Section 19(1).   [33] Section 21.
[34] Page 477, above.
[35] Section 2(1).   [36] Section 2(2).   [37] Section 2(3).
[38] Section 6(1).   [39] Section 7.

Injunctions and interdicts are the only remedies where the defendant proves that, at the date of the infringement, he was not aware and had no reasonable ground for suspecting that copyright subsisted in the work.[40]

Penal Sanctions.—Most of the infringing acts, if committed knowingly, constitute offenses and are punishable by fine or imprisonment.[41]

Importation of Infringing Copies.—Importation into Nigeria of copies made outside Nigeria may be prevented where the copies, if made in Nigeria, would infringe copyright.[42]

---

[40] Section 8. *See also* section 9.
[41] Sections 11 to 13.
[42] Sections 14 and 35(1).

NORWAY

SOURCES

Internal Law.—The main source of the law of copyright in Norway is the Copyright Act of May 12, 1961.[1] Hereinafter, it is referred to as "the Act," and references to Sections without further specification are references to the Sections of this Act.

Photographs are not considered "works"; rights in them are not considered copyrights; and their protection is not regulated by the Copyright Act, but by a separate law entitled "Act on the Property Rights in Photographic Pictures." The date of this law is June 17, 1960.[2] Hereinafter, it is referred to as the "Act on Photographs."

Universal Copyright Convention.—Norway became bound by the Universal Copyright Convention and Protocols 1 and 2 as from January 23, 1963.[3]

ACQUISITION OF PROTECTION UNDER THE UNIVERSAL COPYRIGHT CONVENTION

Unless protected under the Berne Convention rather than the Universal Copyright Convention,[4] the following works and photographs are protected in Norway under the Universal Copyright Convention: (i) works and photographs of nationals of countries other than Norway first published in a Convention country, (ii) works and photographs of nationals of a Convention country, (iii) works and photographs of nationals of a country other than Norway if domiciled in a Conven-

---

[1] Published in "Norsk Lovtidende," 1961, page 377. English translation in CLTW, Norway: Item 1.

[2] Published in "Norsk Lovtidende," 1960, page 453. English translation in CLTW, Norway: Item 2.

[3] CLTW, Norway: Item 3B. Norway is a member of the Berne Union, the latest text ratified by it being that of Brussels of 1948 (CLTW, Norway: Item 4). A Royal Decree of December 11, 1931 ("Norsk Lovtidende," 1931, page 715; CLTW, Norway: Item 5), provided protection for U.S. authors. There are provisions on copyright law in the bilateral treaties of commerce concluded with France in 1881 (CLTW, Norway: Item 5A) and Thailand in 1937 (CLTW, Norway, Item 6).

[4] Royal Decree of April 10, 1964, published in Norsk Lovtidende, 1964 (English translation in CLTW, Norway: Item 4) (hereinafter referred to as "the Decree" (Article 5).

tion country provided that, according to the laws of the latter country, persons domiciled therein have the same rights as nationals as far as the application of the Universal Copyright Convention is concerned,[5] (iv) works and photographs of stateless persons and refugees who have their habitual residence in a Convention country,[6] (v) works first published by the United Nations, by any of the Specialized Agencies of the United Nations, or by the Organization of American States, as well as the unpublished works of these Organizations.[6bis]

There are no copyright formalities in Norway. Consequently, registration, deposit, or compliance with other formalities is neither required nor possible in Norway, and the absence, in itself, of a Convention notice on the copies of a published work is no bar to claiming protection in Norway. Furthermore, Norway has no renewal system, so that there is nothing in Norway which would correspond to the renewal formalities existing in the United States.

PROTECTED SUBJECT MATTER

Works.—The Copyright Act protects literary, scientific and artistic works of any kind, irrespective of the manner or form of expression. The following are expressly mentioned: (i) writings, (ii) oral lectures, (iii) works for state performance, such as dramatic, dramatico-musical, choreographic and pantomimic works, and radio plays (*horespill*), (iv) musical works, with or without words, (v) paintings, drawings, etchings and other pictorial works, (vi) sculpture of all kinds, (vii) architectural works,—the drawings and models as well as the building itself, (viii) pictorial woven tissues (*billedvev*) and objects of handicraft or industrial art—the prototype (*forbildet*) as well as the work itself, (ix) maps, also drawings, and graphic or plastic representations or portrayals of a technical or scientific nature, (x) cinematographic works (*filmverk*), (xi) translations and adaptations of the works referred to above.[7]

Protection under the Design Law does not exclude protection by the Copyright Act.[8]

Photographs.—Photographic pictures are protected. A picture produced by a method similar to photography is regarded as a photographic picture.[9]

---

[5] Decree, Articles 3, 4, and 8.   [6] Decree, Article 6.   [6bis] Decree, Article 7.
[7] Section 1.   [8] Section 10, second paragraph.
[9] Act on Photographs, section 1.

PROTECTED PERSONS

Works.—Copyright belongs to the person who created the work.[10]

A person who translates or adapts (*bearbeider*) a work or transforms it into a different literary or artistic form has copyright in the new work thus produced, but may not make dispositions contrary to the copyright in the original work.[11] A person who, by combining works or parts of works, creates a composite work (*samleverk*), has copyright in the composite work, but his rights may not restrict the rights in the said works.[12] Unless otherwise agreed, the authors of such works are free to publish their works in a manner other than by means of the composite work.[13]

If a work has several authors whose respective contributions cannot be identified as independent works, copyright belongs to the authors jointly.[14] The authorization of all authors is necessary at the initial publication of the work, or when it is published in an altered form. Republication in the initial form, however, may be authorized by any one of the co-authors.[15] Any one of the co-authors is entitled to sue for infringement.[16]

In the absence of proof to the contrary, the person whose name, generally-known pseudonym, or signature, is indicated in the usual manner on the copies (*eksemplar*) of the work, or when the work is made available (*tilgjengelig*) to the public, is deemed to be the author. If a work is published without authorship being indicated in the said manner, the editor, and if he is not named, the publisher, will represent the author until authorship is indicated in a new edition of the work or in a notification filed with the Ministry concerned.[17]

Photographs.—The owner of the rights in a photographic picture is the person who produced it. He is called the photographer (*fotograf*).[18]

The person whose name, firm name (*firma*) or commonly known mark is indicated in the usual manner on the copies (*eksemplar*) of the photographic picture, or when the photographic picture is publicly exhibited, is deemed to be the photographer.[19]

In the absence of express agreement to the contrary, the right in a photographic picture made on commission belongs to the person who has commissioned it. However, the photographer may exhibit the picture in the usual manner for advertising purposes, unless the person who commissioned it has prohibited such exhibition. On the other hand, even if the photographer has reserved the right in a photographic picture made on commission, the person who commissioned

---

[10] Section 1, first paragraph.　　[11] Section 4, second paragraph.
[12] Section 5, first paragraph.　　[13] Section 5, second paragraph.
[14] Section 6, first paragraph.　　[15] Section 6, second paragraph.
[16] Section 6, third paragraph.　　[17] Section 7.
[18] Act on Photographs, section 1.　　[19] Act on Photographs, section 3.

it may cause it to be published in newspapers, periodicals, or biographical writings, unless the photographer has expressly excluded such uses.[20]

ASSIGNMENT AND LICENSING

Generally.—Subject to certain limitations concerning moral rights (discussed below), copyright in a work may be transferred entirely or partially.[21]

If the author transferred to another person his right to make the work available to the public in a certain manner or by certain means, the transferee may not make the work available to the public in another manner or by other means.[22]

If for the transfer of property rights conditions have been laid down which are contrary to proper usage in the copyright field, or if the agreement of transfer leads to manifestly unreasonable results, a claim may be filed to alter the agreement.[23]

In the absence of an agreement to the contrary, the person to whom property rights have been transferred may not transfer them to a third person. If the property rights have been transferred to a commercial establishment, they may be further transferred only together with the business or part thereof; even then, however, the first transferee remains liable for the fulfilment of the contract with the author.[24]

Public Performance Contracts.—In the absence of an agreement to the contrary, the license to perform a work, other than a cinematographic work, is considered to be non-exclusive and valid only for three years. Where a person who has been granted the exclusive right to perform a work (other than a cinematographic work) for a period exceeding three years, does not exercise this right for at least three years, the author may—in the absence of an agreement to the contrary—perform, or license third persons to perform, such works.[25]

Publishing Contracts.[26]—In the absence of an agreement to the contrary:

(a) the manuscript or other copy from which the reproduction is effected remains the property of the author;[27]

(b) the publisher may publish one edition (*opplag*, that is, a quantity of copies produced at one and the same time) whose number may not

---

[20] Act on Photographs, section 10.
[21] Section 25. [22] Section 25. [23] Section 27.
[24] Section 26, second paragraph. [25] Section 30.
[26] A publishing contract is a contract by which the author transfers to the publisher the right to multiply (*mangfoldiggjere*) by printing or other similar process, and publish (*utgi*) a literary or artistic work (sec. 31, first para.).
[27] Section 31, second paragraph.

exceed 2000 in the case of literary works, 1000 in the case of musical works, and 2000 in the case of artistic works;[28]

(c) newspapers and periodicals may reproduce anew blocks of drawings of which they have previously acquired the right to publish;[29]

(d) the author must be given a chance to make changes in the work if a year or more elapses between the publication of the last edition and the beginning of the production of the new edition; the changes must not entail unreasonable expense and must not alter the character of the work.[30]

The publisher must publish the work within a reasonable time and distribute the copies in the usual manner. In the case of serious default on the part of the publisher, the author may rescind the contract, retain the remuneration received, and claim compensation for damages not covered by the remuneration. When the edition is exhausted, the publisher is not obliged to publish a new edition, even if he has the right to do so. But if the author asks him to publish a new edition and the publisher does not do it within a reasonable time, the author may rescind the contract and retain the remuneration received. Contracts considerably deviating from these principles to the detriment of the author are null and void.[31]

The publisher must give an author a certification issued by the printer, or whoever effected the multiplication, concerning the number of copies (*eksemplar*) produced. The publisher must render yearly accounts to the author as to the number of copies sold—or, in the case of the lease of musical scores, as to the results of such rental—and the number of copies remaining in stock. Contracts deviating, to the detriment of the author, from these provisions are null and void.[32]

Unless otherwise agreed, the author may not republish the work in the same form or in the same manner until the editions agreed upon are exhausted. The author does, however, have the right to include a literary or scientific work in an edition of his collected works or of selected works, after the lapse of 15 years from the expiry of the year in which the publisher issued the first edition. The author may not waive this right. The publication of a collective or selected work of this type must, however, first be offered to the publisher or, if the author's

---

[28] Section 32. Inapplicable to contributions to newspapers, periodicals, and other composite works (sec. 38, first and second paras.).

[29] Section 33.

[30] Section 36. Inapplicable to contributions to newspapers and periodicals (sec. 38, first para.).

[31] Section 34. Inapplicable to contributions to newspapers, periodicals and other composite works (sec. 38, first and second paras.). Unless otherwise agreed, also inapplicable to authors of translations (sec. 38, third para.).

[32] Section 35. Inapplicable to contributions to newspapers, periodicals and other composite works (sec. 38, first and second paras.). Unless otherwise agreed, also inapplicable to authors of translations (sec. 38, third para.).

works have been issued by several publishers, to the publisher who can be considered as his main publisher.[33]

Contracts Relating to the Production of Cinematographic Works.—In the absence of an agreement to the contrary:

(a) the granting of a license to use a work for filming also includes the right to make the work available to the public in cinematographic theatres, by television, or otherwise;

(b) if the author has licensed the use of his work for filming, the licensee must, within a reasonable time, make the film and ensure that it is made available to the public. In case of serious default on the part of the licensee, the author may rescind the contract, retain the remuneration received, and claim compensation for damages not covered by such remuneration.[34]

Photographs.—There are no provisions in respect of transfer in the Act on Photographs.

PROTECTED RIGHTS

ECONOMIC RIGHTS

Works.—Copyright includes the exclusive right to dispose of the work (i) by producing copies (*eksemplar*) thereof; (ii) by making it accessible to the public. It is irrelevant whether these acts are done with the work in its original or in a modified form. Modified forms include translations, adaptations (*bearbeidelse*), expressions in a different literary or artistic form, and expressions by a different technique.[35]

Production of copies includes fixation on contrivances by means of which the work may be reproduced.[36]

A work is made accessible to the public when it is presented outside a private circle, or when copies are offered for sale, loan or lease, or otherwise distributed or shown outside private circles.[37]

Once a literary or musical work has been published, any copy, being part of the publication, may freely be further distributed and publicly exhibited. However, sheet music may not be leased to the public without the author's consent.[38]

Once a work of art has been published or the author has transferred copies (*eksemplar*) thereof, such copies may freely be further dissemi-

[33] Section 37. Inapplicable to contributions to newspapers and periodicals (sec. 38, first para.).
[34] Section 39.   [35] Section 2, first paragraph.   [36] Section 2, second paragraph.
[37] Section 3, third paragraph. In cases of commissioned portraits, the author of the work may not make use of his property rights unless both the person portrayed and the person who has ordered the portrait have given their consent (sec. 2, fourth para.).
[38] Section 23, first paragraph.

nated or publicly exhibited. Such copies may also be freely used in films or broadcasts as part of the background or otherwise in a subordinate manner as compared with the main content of the film or broadcast. Works of art which form part of a collection, or which are publicly exhibited or offered for sale, may be freely reproduced in the catalogues of the collection or in announcements of the exhibition or sale. Works of art may also be freely copied when they are permanently situated in a public place, at a public traffic artery, or near such place or artery. But if the work is clearly the main motive and the reproduction is used for profit, the author is entitled to compensation, except when reproduction is effected in a newspaper or periodical or in a broadcast. A building may always be freely reproduced in pictorial form.[39]

Photographic Pictures.—The right in photographic pictures consists in the exclusive right of (i) making copies of the picture by photography, printing, drawing or in any other manner (ii) publicly exhibiting the photographic picture.[40]

Moral Rights

Works.—When copies of the work are produced or when the work is made available to the public, the author may demand that his name be indicated in the manner required by proper usage. If a person other than the author has the right to alter a work or make it available to the public, this must not be done in a manner or in a context prejudicial to the author's literary, scientific or artistic reputation or individuality, or prejudicial to the reputation or individuality of the work.[41]

Even after the work has fallen into the public domain, it may not be made available to the public in a manner or in a context prejudicial to the author's professional reputation or individuality, or to the reputation or individuality of the work itself, or harmful to general cultural interests.[42, 43]

Photographic Pictures.—The photographer may demand that his name be indicated, according to proper usage, in each copy and on each occasion when the photographic picture is publicly shown. He

[39] Section 23, second and third paragraphs.
[40] Act on Photographs, section 1.
[41] Section 3, first and second paragraphs. The author may only waive these rights in cases where the nature and the extent of the use of the work are limited (sec. 3, third para.). These provisions apply even in respect of works in the public domain (sec. 48, third para.).
[42] Section 48, first paragraph. If the author is dead or if the work of a living author is not protected in Norway, uses of this kind may be forbidden by the competent Norwegian Government Department (sec. 48, second para.).
[43] No work may be made available to the public under a title, pseudonym, mark or symbol liable to be confused with a previously disseminated work or its author (sec. 46).

may also demand that the picture be not altered or shown to the public in a manner prejudicial to his reputation as a photographer.[44]

LIMITATIONS

The author's (or, when applicable, the photographer's) permission is not required *in certain cases* of copying for private use,[45] photocopying by libraries,[46] quotation, criticism or learned treatise,[47] reproduction in a newspaper[48] or religious or educational compilations,[49] uses for the blind,[50] performance at religious services in connection with education, and some other non-profit performances,[51] news broadcast or film,[52] ephemeral fixation for and by broadcasting organizations.[53]

One of the unique features of the Norwegian Act is that it allows the Norwegian State Broadcasting Organization, which has an agreement with an organization representing a large number of authors in the field (under which agreement it may broadcast literary and musical works), also to broadcast published works of authors who are not represented by the organization; such authors are entitled to compensation for the broadcast. This provision does not apply to dramatic works and to works whose broadcasting has been prohibited by the author. Furthermore, it does not apply in cases where there is a particular reason to assume that the author would oppose the broadcasting.[54]

TERM OF PROTECTION

Works: Generally.—Property rights in a work subsist during the lifetime of the author and for 50 years after the expiry of the year in which the author died. In the case of works of two or more authors whose individual contributions cannot be separately identified, the period of 50 years is reckoned from the expiry of the year of the death of the last surviving author.[55, 56]

[44] Act on Photographs, section 2.
[45] Section 11; Act on Photographs, section 5.
[46] Section 16; Act on Photographs, section 6.
[47] Section 13; Act on Photographs, section 7.
[48] Section 14; Act on Photographs, section 8.
[49] Section 15; Act on Photographs, section 8.
[50] Section 17; Act on Photographs, section 9.
[51] Section 18.   [52] Section 19.
[53] Section 20, first paragraph. See also Royal Decree of April 2, 1965, published in "Norsk Lovtidende", 1965, No. 14; English translation published in CLTW, Norway: Item 1A.
[54] Section 20, second paragraph.   [55] Section 40.
[56] Where the owner of the copyright in a work has died before the end of 1955 and the term of protection has not expired before December 2, 1955, the term of protection is generally extended by six years (Law of December 2, 1955, published in

Anonymous and Pseudonymous Works.—If a work has been disseminated without indicating the author's name or generally-known pseudonym, mark or symbol, the property rights subsist for 50 years after the expiry of the year in which the work was first made available to the public.[57]

Photographic Pictures.—The exclusive rights in a photographic picture terminate 15 years after the death of the first owner, and if the exclusive rights initially vested in several persons, after the death of the last surviving among them.[58]

Rule of the Shorter Term.—The term of protection for works or photographs protected in Norway under the Universal Copyright Convention cannot exceed the term of protection provided for by the legislation of the country of origin. The following country is considered as country of origin: (i) the Convention country in which the work or photograph was first published; (ii) the Convention country providing for the shortest term of protection in cases of works or photographs published simultaneously, or within a period of 30 days, in two or more Convention countries providing for terms of unequal lengths; (iii) the country of which the author is a national, if the work or the photograph is unpublished or has been published only in a country not party to the Universal Copyright Convention.[59]

INFRINGEMENTS

Civil Remedies: Works.—Damage caused by infringement of copyright must be compensated by the infringer. If the infringement was committed intentionally or by gross negligence, the court may adjudge an additional sum of money as redress for damages of a non-economic nature. Even if the infringer acted in good faith, the infringed party may ask for the net profit resulting from the infringement, irrespective of the amount of the actual damage suffered.[60]

Civil Remedies: Photographic Pictures.—Damage caused by violation of the rights protected must be compensated by the offender.

"Norsk Lovtidende," 1955, page 1140; English translation in CLTW, Norway: Item 1A). This exceptional measure applies to works of Norwegian nationals and works first published in Norway (cited Law, sec. 3). It also applies to works of nationals of Austria, Brazil, France, Italy and Spain (*see* CLTW, Norway: Item 1A).
[57] Section 41. For certain exceptions, *see* the same section.
[58] Act on Photographs, section 13. If the rights originally vest in a legal entity, they terminate 25 years after the end of the year in which the picture was published (Act on Photographs, sec. 13).
[59] Decree, Article 4. However, if the work or the photograph has a country member of the Berne Union as a country of origin, different provisions apply (Decree, Article 5).
[60] Section 55.

Even if the offender acted in good faith, the injured party may ask for the net profit resulting from the unlawful act, irrespective of the amount of the actual damage suffered.[61]

Penal Sanctions: Works.—Persons intentionally or negligently violating the provisions for the protection of the property rights or moral rights protected by the Copyright Act are punishable by fine or imprisonment. The same applies to persons who, with the intention of making them available to the public, import into Norway copies of works, if such copies may not lawfully be produced in Norway.[62]

Penal Sanctions: Photographic Pictures.—Any person shall be punishable by fine who intentionally or negligently violates the provisions of the Act on Photographs by (i) reproducing copies of a photographic picture or making it available to the public, or (ii) importing a photographic picture into Norway, to which another person holds exclusive right in Norway, with a view to making the picture available to the public.[63]

Seizure, Confiscation, etc.—Both the Copyright Act and the Act on Photographs provides for the possibility of seizure, confiscation, destruction or transfer, in favor of the injured party, of infringing copies made in, or intended to be imported into, Norway.[64]

---

[61] Act on Photographs, section 17.
[62] Section 54, first paragraph.   [63] Act on Photographs, section 16.
[64] Section 56; Act on Photographs, section 18.

PAKISTAN

SOURCES

Internal Law.—The main source of the law of copyright in Pakistan is the Copyright Ordinance, 1962.[1] Hereinafter, it is referred to as "the Ordinance," and references to Sections, without further identifications, are references to this Ordinance.

Universal Copyright Convention.—Pakistan became bound by the Universal Copyright Convention and Protocols 1 and 2 as from September 16, 1958.[2] It is also a member of the Berne Copyright Union.[3]

The Ordinance provides[4] that protection of non-Pakistani works requires the extension of the application of the Ordinance by orders of the Central Government.

No information is available whether such an Ordinance has been issued in respect of works which, because of its being party to the Universal Copyright Convention, Pakistan is supposed to protect.

Consequently, uncertainty exists as to whether the Ordinance is applicable to the said works.

Hereinafter, a brief analysis is given of the copyright law as it applies to domestic, i.e., Pakistani works. This analysis will be of interest to persons who wish to secure and maintain protection in Pakistan under the Universal Copyright Convention if and when Pakistan extends, by order, the application of the Ordinance to works protected under that Convention, and to the extent to which the domestic law, at that time, will be the same as it is when these lines are written (January 1968). Of course, even if the domestic law does not change in the meantime, the future order may provide for certain modifications when it makes the Ordinance applicable to works to be protected by virtue of such order.

---

[1] No XXXIV of June 2, 1962, published in "The Gazette of Pakistan, Extraordinary," of June 2, 1962. Came into force on February 27, 1967 (see S.R.O. 26 (R) 67. The text of the Ordinance is reprinted in 1967 Copyright (BIRPI) 91, 112.
[2] CLTW, Pakistan: Item 2.
[3] CLTW, Pakistan: Item 3. The most recent Act Pakistan is bound by is that of Rome (1928).
[4] Sections 53, 54, 55.

PROTECTED WORKS

The following classes of works are protected: (i) original literary, dramatic, musical and artistic works, (ii) cinematographic works, (iii) records.[5]

Literary, Dramatic, Musical and Artistic Works.—Literary works include works on humanity, religion, social and physical sciences, tables and compilations.[6]

Dramatic works include any piece for recitation, choreographic works and entertainments in dumb show, the scenic arrangement or acting form of which is fixed in writing or otherwise but do not include a cinematographic work.[7]

"Musical work" means any combination of melody or harmony or either of them, printed, reduced to writing or otherwise graphically produced or reproduced.[8]

"Artistic work" means: (i) a painting, a sculpture, a drawing (including a diagram, map, chart or plan), an engraving or a photograph, whether or not any such work possesses artistic quality, (ii) an architectural work of art, (iii) any other work of artistic craftsmanship.[9] A "work of sculpture" includes casts and molds.[10] Engravings include etchings, lithographs, wood-cuts, prints and other similar works, not being photographs.[11] Photographs include photo-lithographs and any work produced by any process analogous to photography, but do not include any part of a cinematographic work.[12]

"Architectural work of art" means any building or structure having an artistic character or design, or any model for such building or structure.[13] In the case of an architectural work of art, copyright subsists only in the artistic character and design and does not extend to processes or methods of construction.[14] Copyright does not subsist in any design: (i) which is registered under the Indian Patents and Designs Act, 1911, (ii) which, although capable of registration under that Act, has not been so registered, if any article to which it has been applied has been reproduced more than fifty times by an industrial process by the owner of the copyright or, with his license, by any other person.[15]

Cinematographic Works.—"Cinematographic work" means any sequence of visual images recorded on material of any description (whether translucent or not), whether silent or accompanied by sound, which, if shown (played back, exhibited) conveys the sensations of motion.[16] Copyright does not subsist in any cinematographic work if a substantial part of the work is an infringement of the copyright in

[5] Sections 10(1), 2(zf).   [6] Section 2(p).   [7] Section 2(j).
[8] Section 2(r).   [9] Section 2(c).   [10] Section 2(zh).   [11] Section 2(k).
[12] Section 2(w).   [13] Section 2(b).   [14] Section 10(5).   [15] Section 12.
[16] Section 2(h).

any other work.[17] Copyright or the lack of copyright in a cinematographic work does not affect the separate copyright in any work in respect of which, or a substantial part of which the cinematographic work is made.[18]

Records.—"Record" means any disc, tape wire, perforated roll or other device in which sounds are embodied so as to be capable of being reproduced therefrom, other than a sound track associated with a cinematographic work.[19] Copyright does not subsist in any record made in respect of a literary, dramatic or musical work if, in making the record, copyright in such work has been infringed.[20] The copyright or lack of copyright in a record does not affect the separate copyright in any work in respect of which, or a substantial part of which, the record is made.[21]

PROTECTED PERSONS

Generally.—Subject to certain exceptions, referred to below, the author of a work is the first owner of the copyright in the work.[22] "Author" means in relation to: (i) a literary or dramatic work, the author, (ii) a musical work, the composer, (iii) an artistic work other than a photograph, the artist, (iv) a photograph, the person taking the photograph, (v) a cinematograph work, the owner of the work at the time of its completion, (vi) a record, the owner of the original plate from which the record is made, at the time of the making of the plate.[23] "Plate" includes any matrix or other appliance by which records for the acoustic presentation of the work are or are intended to be made.[24] The following are exceptions from the general rule:

Works for Newspapers, etc.—In the case of a literary, dramatic or artistic work made by the author in the course of his employment by the proprietor of a newspaper, magazine or similar periodical under a contract of service or apprenticeship, for the purpose of publication in a newspaper, magazine or similar periodical, the copyright, in the absence of any agreement to the contrary, is split: (i) the said proprietor is the first owner of the copyright in the work insofar as the copyright related to the publication of the work in any newspaper, magazine or similar periodical, or to the reproduction of the work for the purpose of its being so published, (ii) in all other respects the author is the first owner of the copyright.[25]

Certain Commissioned Works.—Subject to the rule set out in the foregoing paragraph, in the case of a photograph taken, or a

[17] Section 10(3)(a).   [18] Section 10(4).   [19] Section 2(zb).
[20] Section 10(3)(b).   [21] Section 10(4).   [22] Section 13.
[23] Section 2(d).   [24] Section 2(x).   [25] Section 13(a).

painting or portrait drawn, or an engraving or cinematographic work made, for valuable consideration at the instance of any person, such person is, in the absence of any agreement to the contrary, the first owner of the copyright.[26]

Works of Employees.—Subject to the rules set out in the two preceding paragraphs, in the case of a work made in the course of the author's employment under a contract of service or apprenticeship, the employer is, in the absence of an agreement to the contrary, the first owner of the copyright.[27]

Government Works.—In the case of a Government work, the Government is, in the absence of any agreement to the countrary, the first owner of the copyright.[28, 29]

Works of International Organizations.—In the case of a work which is made or first published by or under the direction of an international organization designated for this purpose by the central government of Pakistan, the international organization concerned is the first owner of copyright.[30]

PROTECTED RIGHTS

ECONOMIC RIGHTS

Generally.—Copyright means the ·exclusive right to do, and to authorize the doing of, certain acts in relation to a work, or in relation to a part of the work.[31]

Literary, Dramatic and Musical Works.—In relation to literary, dramatic and musical works, the following acts require the authorization of the owner of the copyright:
(i) *To reproduce the work in any material form.*[32]
(ii) *To publish the work.*[33]
(iii) *To perform the work in public.*[34] "Performance" includes any mode of visual or acoustic presentation, including any such presentation by the exhibition of a cinematographic work, or by means of radio-diffusion, or by the use of a record, or by any other means and, in relation to a lecture, includes the delivery of such lecture.[35] "Lecture" includes address, speech and sermon.[36] "Radio-diffusion" includes communication to the public by any means of wireless diffusion, whether in the form of sounds, or visual images, or both.[37] "Delivery"

---

[26] Section 13(b).   [27] Section 13(c).   [28] Section 13(d).
[29] Section 2(m).   [30] Sections 13(e), 53(2)(a).   [31] Cf. Section 3(1), (2).
[32] Section 3(1)(a)(i).   [33] Section 3(1)(a)(ii).   [34] Section 3(1)(a)(iii).
[35] Section 2(u).   [36] Section 2(o).   . [37] Section 2(za).

in relation to a lecture, includes delivery by means of any mechanical instrument or by radio-diffusion.[38]

(iv) *To produce, reproduce, perform or publish any translation of the work.*[39] The right of translation may, in certain cases, be subject to compulsory licensing.[40]

(v) *To use the work in a cinematographic work or make a record in respect of the work.*[41] The making of records in respect of any literary, dramatic or musical work or in respect of any translation or adaptation thereof, does not require authorization, but is merely subject to the payment, to the owner of the copyright, of a compulsory license fee established by the Copyright Board, if: (a) records recording the work have previously been made by, or with the license or consent of, the owner of the copyright, (b) the person making the records has given the prescribed notice of his intention to make the records.[42]

(vi) *To communicate the work by radio-diffusion. To communicate to the public by a loudspeaker or any other similar instrument the radio-diffusion of the work.*[43] "Radio-diffusion" includes communications to the public by any means of wireless diffusion whether in the form of sounds or visual images or both.[44]

(vii) *To make any adaptation of the work.*[45] "Adaptation" means: (a) in relation to a dramatic work, the conversion of the work into a non-dramatic work, (b) in relation to a literary work, the conversion of the work into a dramatic work by way of performance in public or otherwise, (c) in relation to a literary or dramatic work, any abridgment of the work or any version of the work in which the story or action is conveyed wholly or mainly by means of pictures in a form suitable for reproduction in a book, or in a newspaper, magazine or similar periodical, (d) in relation to a musical work, any arrangement or transcription of the work.[46]

(viii) *To do in relation to a translation or an adaptation of the work any of the acts specified in relation to the work in (i) to (vi), above.*[47]

Artistic Works.—In relation to artistic works, the following acts require the authorization of the owner of the copyright:

(i) *To reproduce the work in any material form.*[48]

(ii) *To publish the work.*[49]

(iii) *To use the work in a cinematographic work.*[50]

(iv) *To show the work in television.*[51]

(v) *To make any adaptation of the work.*[52] "Adaptation means...in relation to...an artistic work, the conversion of the work into a dra-

---

[38] Section 2(i).   [39] Section 3(1)(a)(iv).   [40] See page 547.
[41] Section 3(1)(a)(v).   [42] Section 57(1)(j) and (2).   [43] Section 3(1)(a)(vi).
[44] Section 2(za).   [45] Section 3(1)(a)(vii).   [46] Section 2(a).
[47] Section 3(1)(a)(viii).   [48] Section 3(1)(b)(i).   [49] Section 3(1)(b)(ii).
[50] Section 3(1)(b)(iii).   [51] Section 3(1)(b)(iv).   [52] Section 3(1)(b)(v).

matic work by way of performance in public or otherwise".[53]

(vi) *To do, in relation to an adaptation of the work, any of the acts specified in relation to the work in (i) to (v), above.*[54]

Cinematographic Works.—In the case of a cinematographic work, the following acts require the authorization of the owner of the copyright:

(i) *To make a copy of the work.*[55]

(ii) *To cause the work, insofar as it consists of visual images, to be seen in public, and, insofar as it consists of sounds, to be heard in public.*[56]

(iii) *To make any record embodying the recording in any part of the sound track associated with the film by utilizing such sound track.*[57] "Recording" means the aggregate of the sounds embodied in, and capable of being reproduced by means of, a record.[58]

(iv) *To communicate the film by radio-diffusion.*[59]

Records.—In the case of records, the following acts require the authorization of the owner of the copyright:

(i) *To make any other record embodying the same recording.*[60]

(ii) *To use the record in the sound track of a cinematographic work.*[61]

(iii) *To cause the recording embodied in the record to be heard in public.*[62]

(iv) *To communicate the recording embodied in the record by radio-diffusion.*[63]

Possible Limitations of the Right of Translation.—The right of translation is protected as an exclusive right of authorization during the entire duration of copyright, i.e., generally, until the expiration of fifty years from the death of the author. However, any citizen of Pakistan or any person domiciled in Pakistan may apply to the Copyright Board for a license to produce and publish—without the authorization of the owner of the copyright, i.e., under a compulsory license —a translation of a literary or dramatic work in any Pakistani language or a language ordinarily used in Pakistan (this, presumably, means English).[64] The application must state the proposed retail price of a copy of the translation[65] and must be accompanied by the prescribed fee.[66] The Copyright Board may, after an inquiry, grant to the applicant a non-exclusive license to produce and publish a translation in the language applied for on conditions that the applicant shall pay to the owner of the copyright in the work royalties in respect of copies of the translation of the work sold to the public calculated at such rate as the Board, in the circumstances of each case, determines.[67] The following conditions must be met too:

(a) a translation in the language to which the application relates (i) has not been published by, or with the license of, the owner of the

[53] Section 2(a)(ii).   [54] Section 3(1)(b)(vi).   [55] Section 3(1)(c)(i).
[56] Section 3(1)(c)(ii).   [57] Section 3(1)(c)(iii).   [58] Section 2(zc).
[59] Section 3(1)(c)(iv).   [60] Section 3(1)(d)(i).   [61] Section 3(1)(d)(ii).
[62] Section 2(d)(iii).   [63] Section 3(1)(d)(iv).   [64] Section 37(1).
[65] Section 37(2).   [66] Section 37(3).   [67] Section 37(4).

copyright, within seven years of the first publication of the work, or, (ii) if a translation has been so published, it has been out of print;

(b) the applicant proves to the satisfaction of the Copyright Board that (i) he had requested and had been denied authorization by the owner of the copyright to produce and publish such translation, or, (ii) he was unable to find the owner of the copyright but had sent a copy of his request for such authorization to the publisher whose name appeared on the work, not less than two months before the application for the license;

(c) the Copyright Board is satisfied that the applicant is competent to produce and publish a correct translation of the work and possesses the means to pay to the owner of the copyright the royalties payable to him for the license;

(d) the author has not withdrawn from circulation copies of the work;

(e) an opportunity of being heard is given, wherever practicable, to the owner of the copyright;

(f) the Copyright Board is satisfied that the grant of the compulsory license will be in the public interest.[68]

Moral Rights

Even if the author has assigned or relinquished the copyright in his work, he has the right to claim authorship of the work, as well as the right to restain, or claim damages in respect of, (i) any distortion, mutilation or other modification of the said work, or, (ii) any other action in relation to the said work which would be prejudicial to his honor or reputation.[69] These rights, called by the Ordinance "author's special rights," may be exercised also by the legal representatives of the author.[70]

Limitations

Fair Dealing.—No fair dealing with a literary, dramatic, musical or artistic work constitutes infringement of copyright for the purposes of (i) research or private study, (ii) criticism or review, (iii) reporting of current events in a newspaper, magazine, similar periodical, radio-diffusion, cinematographic work, or photograph.[71] In relation to a literary or dramatic work *in prose*, a single abstract up to 400 words, or a series of extracts (with comments interposed) up to a total of 800 words with no extract exceeding 300 words, may be deemed to be fair dealing. In relations to a literary or dramatic work *in poetry*, an extract or extracts up to a total of 40 lines and in no case exceeding

---

[68] Section 37(4) proviso.   [69] Section 62(1).   [70] Section 62(2).
[71] Section 57(1)(a) and (b).

one quarter of the whole of any poem may be deemed to be fair dealing. Reasonably longer extracts may be deemed to be fair dealing in the review of a newly published work.[72]

Other Exceptions Concerning Specified Uses of Works are provided, among others, in connection with (i) the reading or recitation in public of reasonable extracts from a published literary or dramatic work,[73] (ii) inclusion of works into collections made for educational use, reproduction in examination papers and the like, performance in educational institutions or by certain amateur groups,[74] (iii) reporting of current events and the like,[75] (iv) inclusion in a cinematograph work of certain artistic works,[75bis] (v) the making or publishing of a painting, drawing, engraving, or photograph of an architectural work of art,[76] or, if situated in a public place, of a sculpture or other work of artistic craftsmanship,[77] (vi) the reconstruction of a building, (vii) the playing of a recording in clubs, hotels, etc.[78] (viii) judicial proceedings and reporting on such proceedings,[79] reporting on public political speeches,[80] (ix) reconstructions of buildings,[81] the exhibition of a no longer protected cinematographic work when it contains still protected literary, dramatic or musical works.[82]

Copies Made for Libraries.—The making of not more than three copies of a book, pamphlet, sheet of music, map, chart or plan, by and for a public library, if such book, etc., is not available for sale in Pakistan, does not constitute copyright infringement.[83]

Reproduction of Certain Unpublished Works.—The reproduction, for the purpose of research or private study or with a view to publication, of an unpublished literary, dramatic or musical work kept in a library, museum or other institution to which the public has access, does not constitute copyright infringement if the identity of the author is not known to the library, etc. If the identity of the author is known to the library, etc., reproduction becomes free only after fifty years have elapsed since the date of the death of the author.[84]

Transition from Two-Dimensional Works of Art to Three-Dimensional Objects.—It does not constitute an infringement of copyright to make an object in three dimensions of an artistic work in two dimensions if the object would not appear, to persons who are not expert in relation to such objects, to be a reproduction of the artistic work.[85]

Other Limitations.—As to the cases of compulsory licenses in

---

[72] Section 57(1), *in fine*.   [73] Section 57(1)(f).
[74] Section 57(1)(g), (h), (i), (l).   [75] Section 57(1)(m).   [75bis] Section 57(1)(t).
[76] Section 57(1)(r).   [77] Section 57(1)(s).   [78] Section 57(1)(k).
[79] Section 57(1)(c).   [80] Section 57(1)(d).   [81] Section 57(1)(w).
[82] Section 57(1)(x).   [83] Section 57(1)(o).   [84] Section 57(1)(p).
[85] Section 57(1)(v).

connection with the making of records or translations, see pages 546 and 547, above.

ASSIGNMENT AND LICENSING

Assignments.—Copyright may be assigned in an existing or in a future work. In the latter case, the assignment takes effect only when the work comes into existence. Copyright may be assigned wholly or partially, generally or subject to limitation, for the whole term of the copyright or only part thereof.[86] Assignments are only valid if they are in writing, signed by the assignor or by his duly authorized agent.[87] *No author may assign his right for more than ten years.* If he purported to assign it for a longer period, the copyright will revent to him or, if he is dead, to his representatives of interest, upon the expiration of the ten year period.[88]

Licenses.—Any interest in the copyright may be granted by license. Licenses must be in writing, signed by the owner of the copyright or by his duly authorized agent. Licenses may be granted in respect of a future work; such licenses take effect only when the work comes into existence.[89]

Bequest of a Manuscript or of an Artistic Work.—Bequest of the manuscript of a literary, dramatic or musical work or of an artistic work, is deemed to comprise the copyright in the work if the work is unpublished at the time the testator dies.[90] "Manuscript" means the original document embodying the work, whether written by hand or not.[91]

TERM OF COPYRIGHT

Published Literary, Dramatic, Musical and Artistic Works Other than Photographs.—Copyright in literary, dramatic, musical and artistic works (other than photographs) published not anonymously and not pseudonymously within the lifetime of the author subsists until the expiration of the fiftieth calendar year following the year in which the author dies.[92] A work is published if copies thereof have been issued to the public in sufficient quantities.[93] In the case of a work of joint authorship, the date of the death of the author who dies last is the relevant date.[94] "Work of joint authorship" means a work produced by the collaboration of two or more authors in which

---

[86] Section 14(1).   [87] Section 15.   [88] Section 14(1), proviso.
[89] Section 35.   [90] Section 16.   [91] Section 2(q).   [92] Section 18.
[93] Section 4(1)(a).   [94] Section 18.

the contribution of one author is not distinct from the contribution of the other author or authors.[95]

Copyright in a literary, dramatic or musical work or an engraving which, or an adaptation of which, has not been published before the death of its author, (posthumous works), subsists until the expiration of the fiftieth calendar year following the year in which the work (or, if the adaptation was earlier published, the adaptation) was first published.[96] It is important to note that, for the purposes of this rule, "publication" does not mean only the issue of copies of the work to the public in sufficient quantities, but—if the work is literary, dramatic or musical work—also performance in public of the work and sale (or offer for sale) to the public of records made in respect of the work.[97]

Copyright in literary, dramatic, musical and artistic works (other than photographs), which are published anonymously or pseudonymously, subsists until the expiration of the fiftieth calendar year following the year in which the first publication of the work took place. However, where the identity of the author is disclosee before the expiration of this period, copyright subsists until the expiration of the fiftieth calendar year following the year in which the author dies.[98]

Published Photographs, Cinematographic Works, and Records.—Copyright in published photographs, published cinematographic works, and published records, subsists until the expiration of the fiftieth calendar year following the calendar year in which they were first published.[99]

Published Works of Certain International Organizations.—Copyright in Government works and published Government work and works of the designated international organizations, subsists until the expiration of the fiftieth calendar year following the calendar year in which they were first published.[100]

Unpublished Works.—Works not published either during the lifetime of the author or within fifty years after his death fall into the public domain after fifty years from the beginning of the calendar year next following the year in which the author dies. This rule applies to any work whose author's identity is known.[101] If such identity is *not* known, and if the work is not published within fifty years from the work's creation, the work falls into the public domain after fifty years from the beginning of the calendar year next following the year in which the work was created.[102]

Relinquishment of Copyright.—The owner of the copyright may relinquish all or some of his rights by giving notice to the Registrar of

[95] Section 2(zgu). [96] Section 19(1). [97] Section 19(2).
[98] Section 21(1), proviso. For further details, see section 21(2), (3).
[99] Section 20. [100] Section 22. [101] Section 23(1).
[102] Section 23(2).

Copyrights of Pakistan.[103] Relinquishment does not affect any subsisting rights of persons other than the owner.[104]

INFRINGEMENTS

Unauthorized Use.—Copyright is infringed by any person who does anything, the exclusive right to do which is conferred upon the owner of the copyright (see "Protected Rights," above), (i) without the consent of or a license granted by the owner of the copyright, or (ii) (in the case of certain compulsory licenses or exceptions) without the license of the Registrar of Copyrights, or (iii) in contravention of the conditions of a license so granted or of any condition imposed by the competent authority.[105]

Permitting Use of Premises When Performance Is Infringing.—Copyright is infringed by any person who permits, for profit, any place to be used for the performance of the work in public where such performance constitutes an infringement, unless he was not aware and had no reasonable grounds to believe that such performance would be an infringement.[106]

Sale, Importation, etc.—Copyright is infringed by any person who (i) makes for sale or hire, or sells or lets for hire, or by way of trade displays or offers for sale or hire, infringing copies, (ii) distributes infringing copies either for the purpose of trade or to such an extent as to affect prejudicially the owner of the copyright, (iii) by way of trade exhibits in public infringing copies, (iv) imports infringing copies into Pakistan.[107] For the purposes of this rule, the reproduction of a literary, dramatic, musical or artistic work in the form of cinematographic work is deemed to be an "infringing copy."[108] Furthermore, "infringing copies" are (a) in relation to a literary, dramatic musical or artistic work, a reproduction thereof otherwise than in the form of a cinematographic work, (b) in relation to a cinematographic work, a copy of the work or a record embodying the record embodying the same recording.[109] "Reproduction" includes recording and records.[110]

Civil Remedies.—Depending on the circumstances of the case, the plaintiff may be entitled to damages, an account of profits, or injunctions, and may be treated as the owner of the infringing copies (or of the plates used in or intended for making such copies).[111]

[103] Section 17(1).   [104] Section 17(3).   [105] Section 56(a).
[106] Section 56(b).
[107] The owner of the copyright in a work, or his duly authorized agent, may ask the Registrar of Copyrights (Pakistan Copyright Office) that he prevent the importation into Pakistan of copies made out of Pakistan which, if made in Pakistan, would infringe copyright (sec. 58).
[108] Section 56(b).   [109] Section 2(n).   [110] Section 2(zd).
[111] Sections 60, 61, 62, 63, 64.

The parties may stipulate the exclusive jurisdiction of the Copyright Board.[112] This Board is a quasi judicial authority established by the Central Government of Pakistan.[113]

Criminal Sanctions.—Most infringements, if committed or abetted knowingly, are criminal offenses, punishable with fine, imprisonment, or both.[114] Under certain conditions, the police have the power to seize infringing copies.[115] Any person who knowingly makes, or has in his possession, any plate for the purpose of making infringing copies is punishable with fine, imprisonment, or both. "Plate" includes any stereotype or other plate, stone, block, mould, matrix, transfer, negative tape, wire, optical film, or other device used or intended to be used for printing or reproducing copies of any work, and any matrix or other appliance by which records for the acoustic presentation of the work are or are intended to be made.[116]

The following acts, infringing moral rights, are also among those punishable with a fine, imprisonment, or both: (i) inserting or affixing the name of any person in or on a work of which that person is not the author, or in or on a reproduction of such a work, in such a way as to imply that such a person is the author of the work (*"false attribution of authorship"*), (ii) publishing, or selling or letting for hire, or by way of trade offering, exposing for sale or hire, or by way of trade exhibiting in public, or distributing such a work or reproductions thereof. False attribution of publishership is similarly punished.[117]

The Ordinance defines which individuals are punishable if the offence has been committed by a company, i.e., a body corporate, including a firm or an association of persons.[118]

[112] Section 65. [113] Sections 45, 46. [114] Sections 66, 67.
[115] Section 74. [116] Section 2(x). [117] Section 70.
[118] Section 71.

PANAMA

SOURCES

Domestic Law.—The primary source of the law of copyright in Panama is Book IV, Title V (*Propiedad literaria y artística*) of the Administrative Code (*Código administrativo*) of August 22, 1916.[1] Hereinafter, it is referred to as "the Code" and references to Articles, without further specification, are references to Articles of this Code.

Universal Copyright Convention.—Panama became bound by the Universal Copyright Convention and Protocols 1 and 2 as from January 23, 1963.[2]

ACQUISITION OF PROTECTION UNDER THE UNIVERSAL COPYRIGHT CONVENTION

There are no laws in Panama which specifically refer to the Universal Copyright Convention. In particular, there are no provisions implementing Article III of the Convention, which provides for the non-applicability or avoidance of domestic formalities for the acquisition of copyright.[3] Consequently, while it is assumed for purposes of the present exposition that conflicts between the law of Panama and the Convention will be resolved in accordance with the provisions of the latter, this assumption cannot, in the absence of relevant authoritative decisions, be regarded as officially confirmed.

The laws of Panama do not define the works that are protected therein by virtue of the Universal Copyright Convention. On the basis of the provisions of the Convention and the Protocols, it may be assumed that such works are: (i) published works of nationals of a Convention country irrespective of the place of first publication, (ii) works first published in a Convention country, irrespective of the nationality of the author,

---

[1] Law No. 1 of 1916; English translation in CLTW, Panama: Item 1.

[2] *See* CLTW, Panama: Itam 1A. Panama is also party to the Copyright Conventions of Rio de Janeiro (1906), Buenos Aires (1910), and Havana (1928); *see* CLTW, Panama: Items 2, 3, 4. Panama concluded a copyright treaty with Spain in 1912 (CLTW, Panama: Item 5). In view of the fact that Spain as well as Panama are party to the Universal Copyright Convention, this treaty is now of limited practical significance.

[3] As to such domestic formalities, *see* Code, articles 1906 through 1918, and 1959 through 1966.

(iii) unpublished works of nationals of a Convention country other than Panama, (iv) works of stateless persons and refugees who have their habitual residence in a State party to Protocol 1 (except perhaps Panama), either published or unpublished, and if published, irrespective of the place of first publication, (v) works first published by the United Nations, any of its Specialized Agencies, or by the Organization of American States, as well as unpublished works of any of these Organizations.

It may thus be further assumed that works in any of these categories are protected in Panama without deposit and registration, provided always that, in the case of published works, the provisions of Article III of the Convention concerning notice have been complied with.

Panama has no renewal system, so that there is nothing in this country which would correspond to the renewal formalities existing in the United States.

PROTECTED WORKS

Every work (*obra*) which is the result of personal work (*trabajo*) or effort of intelligence, imagination or art is eligible for copyright protection. Even if a work is not completely original, it is eligible for protection if it is a production whose elements—although taken from other authors—have been selected with discernment, invested with a new form, and applied with intelligence to some more or less general use.[4]

Compilations of works and information which are in the public domain are eligible for copyright protection if they involve a new effort of arrangement or co-ordination.[5]

A collection of folk songs or stories is the subject of copyright if it is the result of direct research on the part of the collector or his agents and if it assumes a special literary form.[6]

PROTECTED PERSONS

The term "author" means any person who produces an original work or who—with permission, if such is required—recasts, compiles,

[4] Article 1894. Scientific ideas and inventions are not susceptible of copyright protection (art. 1895 and 1896). *See also* article 1897. Letters are protected (art. 1919), *See also* article 1897. Letters are protected (art. 1919), and so are the lectures of teachers (art. 1921). As to parliamentary speeches *see* article 1922.
[5] Article 1930.
[6] Article 1931. As to manuscripts in public archives and libraries, *see* article 1932; as to titles of works, particularly of newspapers or reviews, *see* article 1940.

extracts from or abridges other works.[7] "Author" also means a person who first publishes an unpublished work which has no owner, if he utilizes a manuscript that is his own property.[8] Legal entities are entitled to copyright.[9]

Copyright in a commissioned work belongs to the person who commissioned it.[10] Letters are the property of the addressee, but the right to publish them belongs to their writer or, if he is deceased, to members of his family for a period of 80 years *post mortem auctoris*.[11]

Translators and arrangers of works are considered as authors of their translations or adaptations.[12]

In the case of anonymous or pseudonymous works, the publisher is regarded as the owner of copyright, as long as the author does not reveal his identity.[13]

Copyright in compilations originally vests in the person who is the author or director thereof, and not in the collaborators, unless otherwise agreed by contract.[14]

In the absence of agreement to the contrary, articles written for a newspaper may be published by that newspaper only once; for all other purposes, the copyright in the article belongs to its writer.[15]

ASSIGNMENT AND LICENSING

Copyright is transmissible in the same way as any movable property.[16] Where copyright has been transmitted *inter vivos*, it remains the property of the transferee until the expiration of 80 years from the author's death, provided the author leaves neither parents nor children as heirs. If, however, he does leave parents or children as heirs, the rights acquired by the transferee expire 25 years after the author's death, and for the remaining 55 years they belong to the said heirs.[17]

Transfers of copyright must be executed in a public document (*documento público*), and such document must be recorded in the appropriate register by the *Secretario de Instrucción Pública* (Minister of Public Education). Otherwise the transferee will be given no assistance by the courts to enforce his rights.[18]

---

[7] Article 1890.   [8] Article 1892.   [9] Article 1893.   [10] Article 1905.
[11] Articles 1919 and 1920.
[12] Articles 1927, 1928, 1929, 1945, 1946.
[13] Article 1933. For posthumous works, *see* articles 1934 and 1935.
[14] Articles 1936 and 1937.   [15] Article 1938.   [16] Article 1902.
[17] Article 1903.   [18] Article 1917.

PROTECTED RIGHTS

Economic Rights

No person may reproduce a work, either wholly or in part, without the permission of the author.[19]

As to translation, the Code provides that a work may not be translated without the permission of the author. However, it also provides that works of non-Panamanian authors, printed in non-Spanish speaking countries, may be freely translated. Furthermore, the Code provides that this freedom of translation may not be given up by international conventions concluded by the Executive.[20] These provisions are in conflict with the Universal Copyright Convention, under which Panama is obligated to protect the right of translation. If international treaties prevail over domestic laws in Panama—as they probably do—Panama protects the right of translation in works to which the Universal Copyright Convention applies in the same manner as it protects this right in the case of works of Panamanian authors, that is, as an exclusive right of authorization until the expiration of the years *post mortem auctoris*. Whether this is actually the case seems, however, to be subject to some uncertainty.

The author of a dramatic or musical work has an exclusive right of authorization in respect of performance in a theatre or other public place. The Code seems to deny this right to most non-Panamanian works.[21] As in the case of the right of translation—and for similar reasons—it may be that this denial of the performance right does not apply to works protected under the Universal Copyright Convention.

In respect of artistic works, the Code provides as follows: The question whether the painter or sculptor, after having alienated his work, retains the exclusive right to reproduce it by engraving or other analogous means shall, in general, be resolved negatively, and in individual cases shall be decided in the light of the provisions contained in the contract of alienation.[22]

Moral Rights

Works in the public domain, if reprinted, must bear the author's name, and they may not be altered without clearly indicating all alterations or additions.[23]

Assignees may not alter or modify a work without the permission of the author or, if he is dead, without the permission of his family.[24]

[19] Articles 1889, 1900, 1909.
[20] Articles 1925, 1926, 1929.
[21] Articles 1942 and 1943.
[22] Article 1947. [23] Article 1901. [24] Article 1904.

LIMITATIONS

It is permissible to quote an author by copying the necessary passages without his permission, provided that such passages are not so numerous and so consecutive that they might be considered by experts as a disguised or substantial reproduction that might harm the work from which they are taken.[25]

Selected passages, in prose or verse, may also be reproduced without the consent of the author in anthologies for use in schools or serving some definite literary end, provided the number of passages from the same author is not so high as to prejudice his interests and that they are not contrary to his express wishes.[26]

Items published in newspapers may be freely reprinted in other newspapers, unless such reproduction is expressly prohibited.[27]

TERM OF PROTECTION

Copyright is protected during the life of the author and 80 years thereafter.[28]

Since there is no provision in the law of Panama for the "rule of the shorter term" permitted under Article IV (4) of the Universal Copyright Convention, it would appear that works are protected in Panama until the expiration of the terms indicated above, even if they fall into the public domain in other countries at an earlier date.

INFRINGEMENTS

Any person who registers or sells as his own work a work which is in the private domain, or causes such a work to be published as if it were in the public domain, or who, in any other respect, infringes copyright, is punishable by fine.[29]

---

[25] Article 1923.   [26] Article 1924.
[27] Article 1939; the source must be indicated.
[28] Article 1898.   [29] Articles 1948 to 1958.

PARAGUAY

SOURCES

Domestic Law.—The primary source of the law of copyright in Paraguay is the Copyright Law of 1951.[1] Hereinafter it is referred to as "the Law." References to Articles, without further specification, are references to Articles of this Law.

Universal Copyright Convention.—Paraguay became bound by the Universal Copyright Convention and Protocols 1 and 2 as from March 11, 1962.[2]

ACQUISITION OF PROTECTION UNDER THE UNIVERSAL COPYRIGHT CONVENTION

There are no laws in Paraguay which specifically refer to the Universal Copyright Convention. In particular, there are no provisions implementing Article III of the Convention, which provides for the non-applicability or avoidance of domestic formalities for the acquisition of copyright.[3] Consequently, while it is assumed for purposes of the present exposition that conflicts between the law of Paraguay and the Convention will be resolved in accordance with the provisions of the latter, this assumption cannot, in the absence of relevant authoritative decisions, be regarded as officially confirmed.

The laws of Paraguay do not define the works which are protected in that country by virtue of the Universal Copyright Convention. On the basis of the provisions of the Convention and the Protocols, it is assumed that such works are: (i) published works of nationals of a Convention country, irrespective of the place of first publication,

---

[1] Law No. 94 of July 5/10, 1951, approving Decree Law No. 3649 of March 31, 1951. English translation in CLTW, Paraguay: Item 1.

[2] See CLTW, Paraguay: Item 2A. Paraguay is also party to the Copyright Conventions of Montevideo (1889), Buenos Aires (1910), and Washington (1946); see CLTW, Paraguay: Items 3, 4, 5. Paraguay concluded a copyright treaty with Spain in 1925 (CLTW, Paraguay: Item 6), and there are provisions on copyright in a general treaty that Paraguay concluded with Mexico in 1958 (CLTW, Paraguay: Item 7). In view of the fact that Spain and Mexico, as well as Paraguay, are party to the Universal Copyright Convention, these bilateral copyright agreements are now of limited practical significance.

[3] As to such domestic formalities, see Law, articles 16, 47, 49 to 60, 65, 66.

(ii) works first published in a Convention country, irrespective of the nationality of the author, (iii) unpublished works of nationals of a Convention country other than Paraguay, (iv) works of stateless persons and refugees who have their habitual residence in a State party to Protocol 1 (except perhaps Paraguay), either published or unpublished, and if published, irrespective of the place of first publication, (v) works first published by the United Nations, any of its Specialized Agencies, or by the Organization of American States, as well as unpublished works of any of these Organizations.

It may be thus further assumed that works in any of these categories are protected in Paraguay without deposit and registration, provided always that, in the case of published works, the provisions of Article III of the Convention concerning notice have been complied with.

Paraguay has no renewal system, so that there is nothing in this country which would correspond to the renewal formalities existing in the United States.

PROTECTED WORKS

Literary, scientific and artistic works are protected if they are capable of being published or reproduced. They include books, writings and leaflets of all kinds, irrespective of their length; dramatic and dramatico-musical works, choreographic works or pantomimes, the arrangement of which is fixed in writing or otherwise; the written or recorded versions of lectures, speeches, lessons, sermons and other works of the same kind; musical compositions with or without words; drawings, illustrations, paintings, sculptures, engravings, lithographs, photographic and cinematographic works; maps, plans, sketches, plastic works relating to geography, geology, topography, architecture, or to any other science; and astronomical or geographical spheres.[4]

Unpublished works, including manuscripts, are protected by copyright. The right to publish a work which has been noted or copied on the occasion of its public or private reading, performance, or exhibition belongs to the author.[5]

Translations, adaptations, compilations, arrangements, dramatizations and other new versions of a work are protected as original works, without prejudice to the copyright in the work from which they were derived.[6]

PROTECTED PERSONS

Copyright originally vests in the author.[7]

Any person who, with the authorization of the author, adapts,

---

[4] Articles 1 and 4.   [5] Article 5. *See also* article 17.   [6] Article 7.   [7] Article 2.

translates, modifies or parodies a work has, in the absence of any stipulation to the contrary, the rights of a co-author in respect of the adaptation, transposition, modification or parody. If the said actions are carried out in respect of works in the public domain, the resultant works are protected as original works.[8]

Unsigned articles, anonymous contributions, feature stories, engravings, or news in general, having an original character and published exclusively by a daily newspaper, a review or an information agency, are the property of such newspaper, review or agency.[9] Unless otherwise agreed by contract, the authors of signed contributions to newspapers, magazines, or other periodical publications, retain the copyright in their contributions, and may publish them in selected or complete collections.[10]

The producer of a cinematographic film has the right to show the film without the authorization of the author of the plot or of the composer of the music, but without prejudice to the rights which may flow from their collaboration with him.[11]

The translator of a work has, in respect of his translation, the rights resulting from any agreement he has concluded with the author, provided the translation contract has been registered with the Ministry of Education. The translator of a work in the public domain has copyright in his translation.[12,13]

ASSIGNMENT AND LICENSING

Copyright includes the right to use and authorize the use of the work; to dispose of this right, either wholly or in part, upon any basis, and to transmit the right *mortis causa*.[14]

The author or his successor may sell, exchange, rent, assign, or donate his work, wholly or in part.[15] The transferee acquires the right of commercial exploitation—not any right to alter the work.[16]

The rights of the transferee are protected only if the transfer is registered with the Ministry of Education.[17]

In the absence of agreement to the contrary, the alienation of a work of art or the transfer of rights in respect of a work of painting, photography, sculpture or analogous art, does not imply the right of reproduction, which remains vested in the author.[18,19]

[8] Article 8. [9] Article 13. [10] Article 15.
[11] Article 26, second paragraph. For other questions of collaboration, *see* the rest of article 26 and articles 23, 24, 25, 27.
[12] Article 28.
[13] For portraits, photographs, caricatures, and letters, *see* articles 29 to 31.
[14] Article 2. [15] Article 43. [16] Article 45, first paragraph.
[17] Article 45, second paragraph. [18] Article 46.
[19] Articles 33 to 36 contain some interpretative provisions concerning publication and performance contracts.

PROTECTED RIGHTS

ECONOMIC RIGHTS

Copyright includes the exclusive right of the author to use and to authorize the use of the work.[20] Utilization of a work may take place, according to its nature, by any of the following means, or by any others which may become known in the future: (i) publication by means of printing or in any other form, (ii) public performance, recitation, or exhibition, (iii) reproduction, adaptation, or performance, by means of cinematography, (iv) adaptation to instruments for mechanical or electrical reproduction, (v) public performance by instruments referred to in (iv) above, (vi) diffusion by means of photography, telephotography, television, broadcasting, or other means diffusing signs, sounds or images, (vii) translation, transposition, arrangement, instrumentation, dramatization, adaptation or transformation by any other means, (viii) reproduction, total or partial, in any form whatsoever.[21]

When passages from works of other persons constitute the major portion of a new work, the courts may fix the proportionate amount due to those persons who have the rights in the works from which the passages were taken.[22]

MORAL RIGHTS

Works may be performed, reproduced, published or otherwise utilized only with the title and in the form given to them by their authors.[23]

LIMITATIONS

It is permitted to copy, translate and publish, without the permission of the copyright owner, in commentaries, criticisms or notes, up to 1000 words from scientific and literary works, and up to 8 bars from musical compositions, if such acts are necessary for educational or scientific purposes. The source must always be indicated.[24]

News items of general interest may be freely transmitted or retransmitted by any means whatsoever. Articles of current interest contained in periodicals may be reproduced by the press or may be publicly read or broadcast, unless reproduction has been expressly prohibited. Signature of the author is equivalent to such a reservation.[25]

TERM OF PROTECTION

Generally.—Copyright continues for the life of the author and 50 years after his death or, if there are several authors, after the death of

[20] Articles 2 and 9.   [21] Article 3.   [22] Article 11.
[23] Article 9, first paragraph.   [24] Article 10.   [25] Article 12.

the last surviving co-author.[26] The term of copyright is 15 years from first publication in the case of portraits, photographs, caricatures and letters; the publication of portraits, photographs and caricatures generally requires the authorization of the person portrayed (and the publication of letters generally requires the authorization of the writer) and, for 20 years after his death, the authorization of certain relatives.[27]

Rule of the Shorter Term.—Protection in Paraguay of works published outside Paraguay does not continue for a longer period than that recognized by the laws of the country in which the work has been "published and registered."[28]

INFRINGEMENTS

Civil Remedies.—The author has a right to damages for the violation of his economic or moral rights.[29]

Preventive measures may be ordered.[30]

Penal Sanctions.—Copyright infringements are punishable by fine or imprisonment.[31]

---

[26] Articles 19 and 22. There might be exceptions in the case of posthumous works (articles 20 and 21).

[27] Article 32.

[28] Article 48. This provision is not entirely in harmony with Article IV of the Universal Copyright Convention.

[29] Article 9, second paragraph.

[30] Article 69.   [31] Articles 61, 62, 63.

PERU

SOURCES

Internal Law.—The main source of the law of copyright in Peru is the Law No. 13714 of October 31, 1961, entitled *Ley de Derechos de Autor* (Copyright Law).[1] Hereinafter, it is referred to as "the Law," and references to Articles, without further specification, are references to Articles of this Law.

Universal Copyright Convention.—Peru became bound by the Universal Copyright Convention as from October 16, 1963.[2]

ACQUISITION OF PROTECTION UNDER THE UNIVERSAL COPYRIGHT CONVENTION

The Law provides that authors who are not nationals of or are not domiciled in Peru are protected in accordance with the international conventions which Peru has subscribed to and ratified.[3] On the basis of the provisions of the Universal Copyright Convention, it may be therefor assumed that the following are protected in Peru by virtue of that Convention: (i) published works of nationals of a Convention country, irrespective of the place of first publication, (ii) works first published in a Convention country irrespective of the nationality of the author, (iii) unpublished works of nationals of a Convention country other than Peru.[4]

The acquisition and the exercise of copyright are not conditional upon the fulfilment of any formality.[5,6]

[1] Published in "El Peruano," November 3, 1961, page 2. English translation in CLTW, Peru: Item 1. See also the Regulations (entitled *Reglamento de La Ley No 13714 de Derechos de Autor*) of October 18, 1962.

[2] *See* CLTW, Peru: Item 2A. Peru is also party to the Copyright Conventions of Montevideo (1889), Buenos Aires (1910), and Caracas (1912), and has concluded a copyright Treaty with Spain in 1924. See CLTW, Peru: Items 8, 9, 10, and 11, respectively.

[3] Article 6, second paragraph.

[4] The Law itself provides that if the non-Peruvian author is a stateless person, or is of disputed nationality, he is considered to be a national of the country in which he has established his habitual residence (art. 6(3)).

[5] *See* Articles 9, second paragraph, and 79.

[6] Manufacturers of phonograms must register in the *Registro Nacional de Derecho de Autor* (National Copyright Registry), certain particulars concerning the phonograms

Peru has no renewal system, so that there is nothing in that country which would correspond to the renewal formalities existing in the United States.

PROTECTED WORKS

Generally.—The Law protects all works or productions of the human intellect, provided they have a creative character and fall within the field of literature, science or art, whatever may be the mode or form of expression.[7] As far as scientific productions are concerned, the Law protects their literary or artistic form but not the ideas they contain, their technological content, or the industrial exploitation thereof.[8]

Specially.—The following categories are among the works protected: (i) books, articles, writings, pamphlets, whatever their form or character; encyclopedias, guides, dictionaries, anthologies and compilations of any kind; (ii) lectures, speeches, outlines (*planos*), lessons, sermons, discourses (*memorias*) and works of a like kind, either in oral form or in written or recorded versions; (iii) complete or partial collections certified or authorized by their authors; (iv) dramatic, dramatico-musical, and theatrical works in general; choreographic works and pantomimes, provided their acting form is fixed in writing or otherwise; (v) musical compositions, with or without words; (vi) radio or television adaptations of any literary production; works originally produced for radio or television as well as the corresponding libretti and scripts (*guiónes*); (vii) written versions of folklore, but not their subject matter; (viii) newspapers, magazines and other publications of a similar kind; (ix) titles and slogans provided they are registered in the *Registro Nacional de Derecho de Autor* (National Copyright Registry), (x) reports and writings issued in the exercise of a profession; (xi) photographs, engravings, and lithographs; (xii) cinematographic works; (xiii) architectural plans, sketches, and models, outlines for maps (*sistemas de eleboración de mapas*) and other similar works; (xiii) geographical or celestial globes, and plastic works relating to geography, geology, topography, sculpture, and any other science or

they make and the works such phonograms incorporate (art. 55(1)). Photographic works must bear a notice to be protected (art. 58); however, if the notice fulfils the conditions laid down in Article III of the Universal Copyright Convention, the special provisions of the Law will be inapplicable. Titles of works and slogans (*lemas, frases*) are protected only if registered in the said *Registro* (Articles 60 and 61), and it is uncertain whether a notice satisfying the requirements of Article III of the Universal Copyright Convention would replace such registration or, rather, the need for it. Voluntary registration in the *Registro* establishes certain presumptions (*see* art. 80). As to the procedure of registration, see Articles 78, 81, 82, and 83.

[7] Article 1, first paragraph.   [8] Article 1, second paragraph.

art; (xiv) paintings, sculptures, drawings, illustrations, caricatures, sketches, and the like; sketches for theatrical décor and the décor itself, when the author of the décor and the sketches is the same person; (xv) authorized translations, adaptations, and other transformations of works;[9] (xvi) photographic works[10] other than photographs of a documentary character.[11]

Works Not Protected.—Works, including songs, legends and other expressions of folklore, whose authors are unknown, are not protected by copyright.[12]

Legal texts, decrees, regulations, resolutions, judgements, and other writings emanating from a public authority are not protected by copyright except that the Law provides that any person who reproduces them must faithfully render the original.[13]

The informative content of news items published by the press or broadcast by radio or television is not protected by copyright. When the reproduction is textual, the source must be indicated.[14]

PROTECTED PERSONS

Generally.—Copyright vests in the author.[15]

In the absence of proof to the contrary, the person whose name or known pseudonym, initials, monogram or any other usual sign appears on the work or on reproductions of the work or who is announced as the author in connection with the work's public performance or public communication (*representación, ejecución o difusión pública*), is presumed to be the author.[16]

In Relation to Certain Categories of Works.—In the case of a work of divisible collaboration (*colaboración-divisible*), each collaborator is the owner of the rights in that part of the work of which he is the author. In the case of a work of indivisible collaboration (*colaboración-indivisible*), the rights belong jointly and indivisibly to the co-authors. These rules may be set aside by contract.[17, 18]

In the case of a collective work, the person who has organized, coordinated, directed or published the work under his name, whether such person be a natural person or a legal entity, is regarded as the owner of the copyright, without prejudice to the rights of the authors

[9] Article 7.   [10] Article 56.   [11] Article 57(c).   [12] Article 62(a).
[13] Article 64.   [14] Article 65.   [15] *See* Article 9, first paragraph, *in fine*.
[16] Article 9, first paragraph.   [17] Article 10.
[18] A work produced in collaboration (*obra en colaboración*) is defined as a work in the making of which two or more persons have participated. The Law distinguishes between two kinds: works of divisible collaboration and works of indivisible collaboration, according to whether the individual contributions of each co-author can or cannot be clearly identified within the joint work (*obra común*) (art. 8(1) (b)).

of the parts or productions which are included in the collective work.[19]

In the case of an anonymous work (that is, a work which bears no indication as to the name of the author),[20] and in the case of a work published under a pseudonym[21] and where the author has not revealed his identity, the publisher (*editor*) is regarded as the owner of the copyright until the author reveals himself and proves that he is the author.[22]

In the case of a posthumous work, the successors in title (*causahabientes*) of the author are the owners of copyright.[23]

Any person who transforms, arranges or translates a work, "with the authorization of the Law and with due regard (*respectando*) to the participation of the author of the original work," is considered to be the owner of the new, derivative work.[24] A derivative work is defined as a work which results from the authorized transformation of an original work in such a manner that the new (derivative) work constitutes an independent creation (*creación autónoma*) as a consequence of adding to, translating, arranging, adapting, or otherwise modifying, the original work.[25]

"Editio Princeps."—There are special rules for works owned by public authorities,[26] for *editio princeps*,[27] and regarding the influence of the matrimonial régime (*sociedad conjugal*),[28] age,[29] and civil incompetence[30] on the exercise of the rights protected by copyright.

ASSIGNMENT AND LICENSING

Generally.—The author may transmit his proprietary rights (*disponer de su derecho patrimonial*) in any manner (*a cualquier título*) and may transmit them *mortis causa*.[31] He may alienate or transfer (*ceder*) his work.[32]

Theatrical and Musical Works.—Authorization for the public performance of theatrical, choreographic, musical and pantomimic works, and the payment of royalties for such performance, are regulated, in the absence of other agreements, by the rules of the lawfully registered professional associations of authors of such works.[33]

Certain Collective Works.—The Law contains special provisions on the respective rights of the organizer of a collective work and the authors of the productions included in such a work. For this purpose,

[19] Articles 11 and 8, first paragraph, (c).
[20] Article 18, first paragraph, (d).
[21] A work is considered *pseudonymous* when the author is indicated by a name, sign or phrase which is other than his real name (art. 18(1) (e)).
[22] Article 12.   [23] Articles 8, first paragraph, (f), and 13.   [24] Article 14.
[25] Article 8, second paragraph, *in fine*; an original work is defined as a work consisting of the "primigenial" creation of an author (*ibid.*).
[26] Article 15.   [27] Article 16.   [28] Article 17.   [29] Article 18.
[30] Article 19.   [31] Article 35.   [32] Article 90.   [33] Article 43.

the Law differentiates between: (i) anthologies, chrestomathies, and other similar compilations, (ii) encyclopedias, dictionaries, and other similar compilations, produced on order, (iii) newspapers, magazines, and other similar publications. As to the last category, productions of the editorial staff (*personal de redacción*) are distinguished from productions of persons not belonging to such staff. Generally, and subject to contractual arrangements to the contrary, the exercise of the proprietary rights is reserved to the organizer of the collective work, at least for a limited period or for certain purposes.[34]

Phonograms.—Transfer of the right to make phonograms of a work or of the right to distribute phonograms does not, in the absence of agreement to the contrary, include the right publicly to perform the work by means of such phonograms. In the absence of agreement to the contrary, a license to make phonograms is considered to be non-exclusive.[35] Even an exclusive license may be rescinded if it is not exploited within the stipulated period or, if no such period has been stipulated, within six months from the date of the authorization.[36] Manufacturers of phonograms must, at not less than six-monthly intervals, pay the author the moneys due to him, and the author or his representative has the inalienable right to examine the books in which the manufacturer is obliged to keep the necessary accounts.[37]

Photographic Works.—In the absence of proof to the contrary, the transfer of the negative carries with it the transfer of the copyright in the photographic work.[38]

"Corpus Mechanicum."—Copyright is independent of the ownership of the material object containing (*el que conste*) the creation. The acquisition of the material object does not confer upon the acquiror any rights not transferred to him.[39] However, as to photographs, see the preceding paragraph. As to paintings, sculptures, drawings and other works of art (*de las artes visuales* = of art appealing to sight), the acquirer of the *corpus* obtains, nevertheless, the following rights (unless otherwise agreed by contract): (i) the right to enjoyment in private (*disfrute in privado*), (ii) the right of public exhibition, but not for profit, (iii) the right of publication in newspapers and magazines, but not for profit, (iv) the right to reproduce for purely personal or family use, provided the work is a portrait and the process employed in the reproduction is different from the process employed in the making of the work, (iv) the right to transfer the property of the *corpus* to third parties.[40] The acquisition of an architectural plan or design implies the right to execute the architectural work.[41]

[34] Article 44.   [35] Article 51.   [36] Article 52. See also Article 53.
[37] Article 55, second paragraph.   [38] Article 59.   [39] Article 5.
[40] Article 91, first paragraph. As to the rights retained by the author, see Article 91, last paragraph.
[41] Article 94. For further details concerning architectural works, see also Article 95.

Publication Contracts.—The Law contains detailed rules on publication contracts.[42] Any transfer of rights must be narrowly interpreted: in the absence of other contractual provisions, the publisher acquires the right to publish only one edition, and does not acquire the right to translate, perform, record, or adapt to cinematography or television.[43] Subject to punishment by a fine, the publisher must indicate in each copy the name of the author, a copyright notice (*mención de reserva*), his own and the printer's name and address, and the number of each copy.[44] He must have the publication registered in the *Registro de Derechos de Autor* (Copyright Registry).[45]

Contracts Concerning the Publication and Diffusion of Musical Works.—Contracts concerning the publication and diffusion (*edición-difusión*) of musical works are governed by different rules.[46] Such contracts imply not only the right to publish in print but also the rights to record, to adapt in cinematographic and television works, and to translate,[47] but do not include the right publicly to perform.[48]

Performance Contracts.—It would appear that the rules concerning public performance (*representación*) apply to live performances on the stage, which would thus include dramatic, dramatico-musical, choreographic and pantomimic works.[49] License to perform is not, unless otherwise agreed, transferable.[50] Public recitation and public reading are governed by similar rules.[51]

Future Works.—Alienation of the entire future production of an author, or an agreement not to produce, even for a limited period, is invalid.[52]

PROTECTED RIGHTS

Copyright (*derecho de autor*) consists of intellectual, moral and proprietary (*patrimonial*) attributes.[53]

ECONOMIC RIGHTS

Generally.—The proprietary attributes (economic rights) allow the exploitation of the work or of the production within a limited period of time and in the ways (*forma*) defined in the Law.[54] The three main ways of exploiting the work, according to the terminology of the Law, are "publication," "reproduction," and "transformation."[55] However, each of these terms has a special meaning, as described below.

[42] Articles 96 to 109.   [43] Article 97.   [44] Article 98.   [45] Article 99.
[46] Articles 110 to 115.   [47] Article 110(1).   [48] Article 110(2).
[49] Articles 116 to 121.   [50] Article 116(2).   [51] Article 122.
[52] Article 3.   [53] Article 2(1).   [54] Article 2(2).   [55] Articles 36 and 37.

"Publication."—Publication "may be by means of typographic publication (*edición*), sale, distribution, radio broadcasting, television broadcasting, performance (*representación, ejecución*), reading, recitation, exhibition, and, in general, by communication to the public or diffusion by any means whatsoever."[56] Performance, reading, recitation, and exhibition, require authorization when they are public, that is, are (i) effected in a place which is not a private home, or (ii) even if in a private home, when the performance, reading, recitation, or exhibition taking place elsewhere reaches the private home through the use of radio broadcasting, television broadcasting, loudspeakers, phonograms, cinematography, or other adequate means.[57] The said authorization must emanate from the owner of the copyright or the association or other entity which represents him.[58]

"Reproduction."—"Reproduction" means reproduction or transmission (*emisión*) of sounds or images by any appropriate means, in particular by means of discs, tapes, motion pictures, photography, telephotography, and microphotography.[59]

"Transformation."—This includes translation into another language or dialect, adaptation to a different art form (*género*), or any other transformation which results in a new version or application of the original work.[60]

Cinematographic Works.—In the case of a cinematographic work, the producer is the person entitled to exploit it and thus owns the right to show it in public (*proyectarla in público*), broadcast it by means of television, reproduce copies thereof, rent it out, alienate it, and dispose of it in any form whatsoever; all this, however, without prejudice to any rights of the authors of the works used in the cinematographic work, and to any rights of other collaborators.[61] In the absence of agreement to the contrary, the authors of the script (*argumento*), of the music, of the words of the songs, and of any other work which has been the subject of cinematographic adaptation, retain the right to utilize their respective contributions as long as it is not for the purposes of another cinematographic or television production.[62]

Phonographic Reproduction.—Authors of musical, literary or scientific works have the exclusive right to do or authorize the doing of the following acts: (i) to reproduce the work by means of adaptation, recording on phonographic disc, cinematographic film, magnetic tape, or any other similar material or mechanical device capable of reproducing sound or voice; (ii) to sell and distribute the copies (*ejemplares*) incorporating the work so performed (*representada*) and recorded, (iii) publicly, to perform the work (*ejecución*), or to broad-

---

[56] Articles 36, first paragraph, (a), 38, and 42.   [57] Articles 39.
[58] Article 40.   [59] Article 36, first paragraph (b).
[60] Article 36, first paragraph, (c).   [61] Article 45.   [62] Article 48.

cast it by radio or television, by means of discs or any other of the materials or mechanical devices referred to above.[63]

Photographic Works.—The photographer has the exclusive right to reproduce, exhibit, publish, and sell, the photograph.[64]

"Droit de Suite."—The author of a painting, sculpture, sketch, or drawing, is entitled to a percentage of the increase in value, if any, which its owner may realize when he sells the original work at a public sale. The percentage is to be agreed upon between the parties. The right devolves upon the heirs and legatees of the author for 30 years after the author's death.[65]

MORAL RIGHTS

Generally.—The author, even after the alienation of his proprietary rights, has the right to claim authorship of the work, to oppose any deformation, mutilation or modification of it, and to require that this name or known pseudonym be mentioned whenever the work is used.[66]

Cinematographic Works.—In the absence of agreement to the contrary, the producer of a cinematographic work is entitled to modify, to the extent required by the adaptation, the works used in his cinematographic production.[67] The producer must indicate on the film his own name or trade name (*razón social*), as well as the names of the artistic director, the authors of the plot (*argumento*), of the dialogue, of the music, and of the words of the songs, and of the names of the principal performers.[68]

Phonograms.—Whenever possible, the disc or other device capable of reproducing sound or voice must indicate the title of the work, the names of the performing artists (or the name of the orchestra or choir and the name of the conductor). If such indication cannot be given on the disc or other device, it must be given on its container.[69]

LIMITATIONS

Expropriation.—The State may, in certain cases, expropriate copyright in the public interest, but not until five years after the author's death.[70]

Free Uses.—Subject to certain conditions and within certain limits, the Law provides for free use in connection with: commentaries on current events,[71] speeches delivered at public meetings,[72] lessons of

[63] Article 50. [64] Article 56. [65] Articles 22, 92, 93.
[66] Article 32. For further details, including the exercise of the moral right after the author's death, see Articles 33, 34, 65, 66, 69, 71, 73, second paragraph.
[67] Article 46. [68] Article 47. [69] Article 54. [70] Article 63.
[71] Article 66. [72] Article 67.

professors or teachers;[73] reproduction of brief portions of longer works or of entire brief works for purely cultural purposes,[74] reproduction for exclusively personal use,[75] reproduction by photography, cinematography or television of architectural works,[76] reproduction for the purposes of courts or public administration,[77] reproduction of artistic works located in public museums,[78] reproduction of monuments and artistic works located in public thoroughfares,[79] the demonstration of phonograms, radios, television sets and the like,[80] the setting to music of poems or other literary works,[81] and use in centers of learning for teaching purposes.[82]

TERM OF PROTECTION

Generally.—Subject to the exceptions stated below, copyright subsists during the life of the author and for fifty years thereafter. The fifty-year period is counted from the first day of the year following the author's death.[83] When the copyright has been assigned, it expires twenty years earlier, that is, thirty years after the author's death.[84] If the author dies without leaving heirs and without having assigned the copyright, the work falls into the public domain upon the author's death,[85] except that the author may prohibit by will (testament) or other written document that his work be published for a certain period, not exceeding one hundred years from his death.[86] In case of collaboration, the period of fifty years is counted from the death of the co-author who dies last.[87]

Cinematographic Works.—The rights of the producer subsist for a period of twenty-five years from the end of the year in which the work was first shown in public (*se proyectó en público la obra por primera vez*).[88]

Photographs.—Copyright in photographs subsists for twenty years from the end of the year indicated upon the copies (*ejemplares*).[89] Photographs are protected only if they bear a notice indicating the name of the photographer or the owner of the copyright and the year in which the negative was exposed (i.e., the picture taken).[90] The notice, according to the Law, is "*prohibida la reproducción*" (reproduction prohibited) but, according to the Universal Copyright Convention, this may be replaced by the symbol ©. As far as the year date is concerned, the Universal Copyright Convention prescribes the indication

[73] Article 68.   [74] Article 69.   [75] Article 70.   [76] Article 72.
[77] Article 71.   [78] Article 73.   [79] Article 74.   [80] Article 75.
[81] Article 76.   [82] Article 77.   [83] Article 21.   [84] Article 22.
[85] Articles 23, 62(c), 21, second paragraph, and 84 to 89.
[86] Article 34 (c).   [87] Article 25.   [88] Article 26.
[89] Article 27, first paragraph.   [90] Article 58.

of the year in which first publication occurred. If the year of first publication is different from the year of the making of the work and the year of the making is indicated, the notice might still be valid since making necessarily precedes publication and an antedated notice does not curtail the rights of third persons. However, this argument is subject to doubt.[91]

If the photograph forms an integral part of a literary or scientific work, and if the copyright in the photograph is the property of the owner of such work, copyright in the photograph will subsist as long as copyright subsists in the said work.[92]

Posthumous Works.—Copyright in a posthumous work subsists for at least thirty years from the date of first publication, provided such date is indicated in the work.[93]

Anonymous and Pseudonymous Works.—The rights of the publisher expire fifteen years after first publication, but if, during this period, the identity of the author is revealed, the general rules apply. The general rules apply also when the pseudonym is well known or has been recorded in the *Registro de Derecho de Autor* (Copyright Registry).[94]

Slogans.—Slogans are protected from the date of their registration in the *Registro Nacional de los Derechos de Autor* (National Copyright Registry). Their protection lasts as long as the objects or things to which they refer continue to exist.[95]

Works Consisting of Several Volumes.—If a work consists of several volumes and the volumes are not published at the same time, any period to be calculated from first publication is to be calculated from the first publication of the last volume.[96]

Renunciation.—Any work falls into the public domain and may be freely used (subject to respect for the moral rights) if the owner of the copyright in the work decides to place the work in the public domain by renouncing his copyright.[97]

Moral Rights.—Moral rights are protected without limitation in time. They can be neither assigned nor renounced.[98]

Rule of the Shorter Term.—Since there is no provision in the Law for the "rule of the shorter term" permitted under Article IV (4) of the Universal Copyright Convention, it would appear that works which are protected in Peru by virtue of the Universal Copyright Convention are protected there until the expiration of the terms indicated above even if in other countries they fall into the public domain at an earlier date.

[91] See page 29, *supra.*   [92] Article 27, second paragraph.   [93] Article 28.
[94] Article 30.   [95] Article 31.   [96] Article 29.   [97] Article 62 (d).
[98] Articles 2(2), 62, and 90.

INFRINGEMENTS

Generally.—The following acts constitute infringement (*infracción*): (i) the publication (*edición*), reproduction, distribution or sale of a work under the name of the infringer, under the name of a third person, or under a pseudonym, or without a name (in anonymous form), by usurping the authorship of the work or by attributing authorship to a person when such person is not the author; (ii) the publication (*edición*), reproduction, distribution or sale of the work with its text deformed, changed or mutilated, or its title altered; (iii) the publication (*edición*), reproduction, distribution, sale, or any other use, of a previously published work without the authorization of the author or his successors in title (*causahabientes*); (iv) the publication (*edición*) of a previously published work by falsely applying the name of the authorized publisher; (v) the publication (*edición*) or reproduction of a work in a greater number of copies than the authorized number; (vi) the public performance of theatrical, literary, or musical works without the authorization of the owners of the right; (vii) the obtaining of the suspension of a public performance which was to take place by a person falsely alleging that he is the author, his successor in title, or his agent; (viii) the usurpation of the name, pseudonym, *nom de plume*, or monogram, of the author; (ix) unfair competition consisting in the usurpation of the title of the work; (x) the public performance of a dramatic or musical work under a changed title, or omitting, altering, or adding to, its various passages, without the author's consent; (xi) the omission of the name of the author or of any other element whose indication is required by the Law;[99] (xii) the commission of the offense (*delito*) of plagiarism, that is, to disseminate (*difundir*) the work of another person as one's own, in whole or in part, either without changes in the text or with certain alterations in it designed to disguise the appropriation.[100]

CIVIL REMEDIES

The injured party has a right to compensation for the pecuniary and moral prejudice suffered by him[101] and to the payment by the infringer to him of any royalties which he (the infringer) has earned.[102] Furthermore, he is entitled to eighty per cent of the "civil fine" which must be imposed on every infringer by the public authority. Infringing copies or implements may be seized and either destroyed or their property transferred to the injured party or a public institution. The infringer may be ordered to correct any omissions or adulterations effected by him in the work.[103]

[99] Article 123.   [100] Article 124, first paragraph
[101] Article 134, first paragraph. *See* also Articles 130 to 132, ad 141 to 143.
[102] Article 131.   [103] Article 129.

CRIMINAL SANCTIONS

Criminal sanctions[104] include the penalty of imprisonment.[105]

INJUNCTIONS

The competent authority may prohibit unauthorized public performances,[106] and the court may order preventive distraint (*embargo preventivo*) upon paintings, sculptures, discs, tapes, films, books, and in general any copies (*ejemplares materiales*) of a work, as well as any pecuniary proceeds (*rendimientos pecuniarios*) derived from the work.[107]

---

[104] Article 133 to 140. *See* also Article 144.   [105] Article 133.
[106] Articles 125 to 127.   [107] Article 128.

PHILIPPINES

The Philippines deposited its instrument of accession to the Universal Copyright Convention and the Protocols with the Director General of UNESCO on August 19, 1955. However, on November 14, 1955, the Philippines addressed the following communication to the Director General of UNESCO: "His Excellency the President of the Republic of the Philippines has directed the withdrawal of the instrument of accession of the Republic of the Philippines to the Universal Copyright Convention prior to the date of November 19, 1955, at which the Convention would become effective in respect of the Philippines." This communication was received by UNESCO on November 16, 1955.[1]

Although the Convention does not provide for withdrawal of instruments of accession, there is good reason to believe that legally the Philippines has not become bound by the Convention and its Protocols, since the above communication was made prior to the date on which the accession of the Philippines would have become effective. As a practical matter, the Philippines never gave any indication of considering itself bound by the Convention or its Protocols.

Consequently, and for the purposes of the present book, it is assumed that no copyright protection is available in the Philippines by virtue of the Universal Copyright Convention or its Protocols.

---

[1] CLTW, Philippines, Item 3.

PORTUGAL

SOURCES

Internal Law.—The main source of the law of copyright in Portugal is the Copyright Code (*Código do Direito de Autor*) promulgated by Decree-Law No. 46980 of April 27, 1966, and entered into force on May 2, 1966.[1] Hereinafter, it is referred to as "the Code," and references to Articles without further specification are references to Articles of this Code.

Universal Copyright Convention.—Portugal became bound by the Universal Copyright Convention and Protocols 1 and 2 as from December 25, 1956.[2]

ACQUISITION OF COPYRIGHT UNDER THE UNIVERSAL COPYRIGHT CONVENTION

The Code does not differentiate between nationals and foreigners. It expressly states that copyright is recognized even if the work is not protected in its country of origin.[3] It does, however, contain the rule of the shorter term, so that works whose country of origin is a country other than Portugal may, in fact, fall into the public domain earlier than works whose country of origin is Portugal.[4]

There are no copyright formalities in Portugal. Consequently, registration, deposit, or compliance with other formalities, is not required in Portugal, and the absence, in itself, of a Convention notice on the copies of a published work is no bar to the claiming of protection in Portugal. Furthermore, Portugal has no renewal system, so that there is nothing in that country which would correspond to the renewal formalities existing in the United States.

---

[1] Published in "Diário do Govêrno," No. 99 of April 27, 1966. English translation in CLTW, Portugal: Item 1.
[2] CLTW, Portugal: Item 2A. Portugal is a member of the Berne Copyright Union, having ratified the Conventions of Berlin, 1908, Rome, 1928, and Brussels, 1948 (CLTW, Portugal: Item 3).
[3] Article 4(3).   [4] Article 26.

PROTECTED WORKS

Generally.—The Code protects "intellectual works" (*obras intelectuais*), which are defined as creations of the human intellect, whatever may be the mode or form of expression.[5] The following are included among intellectual works: (i) literary, artistic and scientific writings, (ii) lectures, lessons, addresses, sermons and other works of the same nature, (iii) dramatic or dramatico-musical works, (iv) choreographic works and entertainments in dumb show, the acting form of which is fixed in writing or otherwise, (v) musical compositions with or without words, (vi) cinematographic works and works produced by a process analogous to cinematography, (vii) works of drawing, painting, architecture, sculpture, engraving and lithography, (viii) photographic works and works produced by a process analogous to photography, (ix) works of applied art, (x) illustrations and maps, (xi) plans, sketches and three-dimensional works relative to geography, topography, architecture or science.[6]

Derivative Works.—Without prejudice to the rights in the works from which they are derived, the following derivative works are protected as if they were original works: (i) translations, adaptations, transpositions, arrangements, instrumentations, dramatizations, and other alterations, (ii) collections of works—such as collections of selected passages, compendia, and anthologies—which, by reason of the selection or the arrangement, constitute intellectual creations, (iii) systematic or annotated compilations of legal texts.[7]

Titles.—Protection of the work extends to its title, provided the title is original and cannot be confused with the title of another work of the same kind by another author which has previously been disclosed.[8] The title of a *newspaper* or *periodical*, regularly and continuously published, is protected until the expiration of one year (in the case of annual periodicals, two years) from the appearance of the last issue.[9] The title of a work *not yet published* may, under certain conditions, be protected through registration.[10]

PROTECTED PERSONS

Generally.—Copyright belongs to the intellectual creator of the work.[11] An entity which subsidizes the publication, reproduction or completion (*conclusão*) of a work does not thereby acquire any rights in the work.[12] But it may be expressly agreed, or it may be deduced from the terms or circumstances of the agreement, between the author

---

[5] Article 1(1).   [6] Article 2.   [7] Article 3(1).   [8] Article 6(1).
[9] Article 6(3).   [10] Article 6(4).   [11] Article 8(1).   [12] Article 8(2).

and the entity financing the creation or the publication of the work, that copyright belongs to such entity. In that case, the author may not ask for more than was agreed upon, i.e., the remuneration, if any, or the mere fact of publication, if applicable.[13]

Commissioned Works and Works of Employees.—Subject to the exceptions stated below, copyright vests in the author even when he has created the work pursuant to a commission or in the course of the performance of his duties as an employee.[14] In those cases or where the author agrees with another person that the latter may publish the work at his expense,[15] the author may not use the work in any way prejudicial to the objective for which the work was produced, or for objectives analogous to the objective for which the work was produced (provided the body for which the work was produced is a non-profit body), or for a purpose prejudicial to the edition which he has authorized.[16]

Works of Joint Authorship (obras de colaboração).—An intellectual work created by several persons is a work of joint authorship, whether or not it is possible to determine the personal contribution of each, if the work is disclosed or published in the name of one, some or all of the collaborators.[17] Copyright is owned jointly by all of them, and exercised generally by majority decisions.[18] However, any of the authors may exercise individually his rights in regard to his personal contribution to the extent that such exercise is not prejudicial to the use of the work of joint authorship.[19]

Collective Works (obras colectivas).—A collective work is a work which was created on the initiative of, whose creation was directed by, and which was disclosed or published under the name of, an individual or a legal entity.[20] Newspapers and similar periodicals are examples of collective works.[21] Cinematographic works are not collective works.[22] Copyright in a collective work belongs to the individual or body referred to above,[23] but, if the individual contribution of any collaborator may be identified, the rules concerning works of joint authorship are applicable to such contribution.[24]

Radiophonic and Televisual Works (obras radiofonicas ou radiovisuais).—These are: (i) works created with a view to the special conditions of their use for sound or television broadcasting, and (ii) adaptations of works originally created for another form of use, when the adaptation has been made with a view to the special conditions of use for sound or television broadcasting.[25] The authors

---

[13] Article 9(1). *See also* Article 9(2).   [14] Article 8(3).   [15] Article 8(4).
[16] Article 8(5). *See also* Article 8(6).   [17] Article 10, first sentence.
[18] Article 11.   [19] Article 12.   [20] Articles 10, second sentence, and 13(1).
[21] Article 13(3).   [22] Article 13(4).   [23] Article 13(1).
[24] Article 13(2).   [25] Article 15(3).

of the words, the music, or the artistic composition (*composição artística*) transmitted are deemed to be the authors.[26] Performers and technical personnel engaged in the broadcasting of such works are not included among the authors of such work.[27]

Phonographic Works.—The authors of the words or of the music fixed on the record are deemed to be the authors of a phonographic work.[28] Performers, the technical personnel, and the producer of the phonogram, are not authors.[29]

Cinematographic Works.—A cinematographic work is a work of joint authorship and the following are deemed to be the authors: (i) the author of the scenario or of the literary, musical, or literary-musical script, (ii) the director (*o realizador*), (iii) the author of the adaptation, when the cinematographic work is an adaptation of a work not expressly composed for the cinema.[30] No other persons engaged in the making of the cinematographic work are deemed to be authors of such work.[31]

Presumptions.—The natural person or the legal entity whose name is indicated on the work as being that of the author, in accordance with general practice, or whose name is announced as being that of the author in connection with the performance, recitation or other use of the work, is presumed to be the author.[32] An abbreviated form of the name, initials, pseudonyms, a conventional symbol—if generally associated with the particular person—all have the same effect as his full name.[33]

Anonymous and Certain Pseudonymous Works.—Where the work is presented under a pseudonym or any other designation that does *not*, in fact, reveal the author's identity, or where the work is published anonymously, the publisher has the right and obligation to defend the copyright vis-à-vis third persons, as long as the author does not reveal his identity.[34]

ASSIGNMENT AND LICENSING

Generally.—Copyright may be *assigned* in whole or in part.[35] Rights of a purely personal nature, however, cannot be transferred.[36] Partial transfer is a transfer which relates only to certain specified modes or forms of use.[37] A *simple authorization* (license) to exploit the work in a certain way is not a transfer.[38] Both assignments and licenses must be *in writing*.[39] Total assignment requires a document also signed

[26] Article 15(1).   [27] Article 15(2).   [28] Article 16.   [29] Article16.
[30] Article 17.   [31] Article 18. *See also* Article 19.   [32] Article 20.
[33] Article 21(1). *See also* Articles 21(2), 22 and 23.   [34] Article 24.
[35] Article 38.   [36] Article 39.   [37] Article 39.   [38] Article 40(1).
[39] Articles 39, 40(2).

by witnesses.[40] Modes of exploitation which, at the time of the conclusion of the contract, were unknown are covered by the contract only if the contract expressly states such fact.[41]

Future Works.—Assignment of copyright with respect to future works may relate to works to be produced over a period of ten years at the most.[42] Contracts providing for a longer specified term are valid only for ten years, and contracts providing for all future works are null and void.[43]

Works Out of Print.—If a work is out of print and the holder of the copyright refuses to republish it, the author or other interested party may apply to the courts for an authorization to republish.[44]

Other Questions.—Copyright may not be acquired by prescription.[45] There are special rules with respect to the rights of spouses,[46] usufruct,[47] pledge,[48] and attachment.[49] Furthermore, there are special provisions concerning the exercise of rights by heirs,[50] authors' societies,[51] minors,[52] bankrupt persons,[53] and married women.[54]

"Droit de Suite."—Any author who has transferred an original work of art, an original manuscript or the copyright in any (other) intellectual work has the right to benefit from any increase in value (*maisvalia*) which occurs at any subsequent alienation where the seller makes a considerable profit. This right cannot be waived or alienated.[55] The author's participation amounts to ten percent of the increase if the sales price is 10,000 escudos or less, and twenty percent if the sales price is above 10,000 escudos.[56] If the difference is due to the devaluation of the currency (*desvalorização da moeda*), these provisions do not apply.[57]

The author of a work of art has the exclusive right to authorize the making of reproductions of his work and to authorize the sale of copies of his work. Authorization must be in writing.[58] Each reproduction must bear an indication of the author's identity unless the author waives this requirement.[59] Copies offered for sale require the approval of the author.[60]

Unexpected High Profits.—If the author who has sold his right of exploitation in a particular work suffers—because of miscalculation of the probable profits of the exploitation—"enormous" injury (*lesão enorme*) on account of the fact that his own remuneration (*proventos*) is greatly out of proportion to the profits of the acquirer of such right, he (the author) may claim additional compensation from the ac-

[40] Articles 44(1). See also Article 44(2).   [41] Article 45(1).
[42] Article 46(1), first sentence.   [43] Article 46(1), second sentence, and (2).
[44] Article 52(1). For further details, *see* Article 52(2), (3), (4), and Article 53.
[45] Article 54.   [46] Article 43.   [47] Article 47.   [48] Article 48.
[49] Articles 49 to 51.   [50] Article 65.   [51] Article 67.   [52] Article 68.
[53] Article 69.   [54] Article 70.   [55] Article 59(1).   [56] Article 59(2).
[57] Article 59(3).   [58] Article 172(1).   [59] Article 173.   [60] Article 174.

quirer. The amount is to be determined by the courts.[61] These provisions apply only when the alienation was for a fixed amount, paid in one sum or in instalments, or when the remuneration of the author consists in a participation in the profits but the participation stipulated is not in conformity with current practice (*usos correntes*) in transactions of the kind involved.[62]

PROTECTED RIGHTS

ECONOMIC RIGHTS

Generally.—The exclusive right to enjoy (*fruir*) and use an intellectual work includes the right to disclose (*divulgar*) the work and to use it commercially (*explorar econòmicamente*).[63] Use relates to all means currently known or which may be invented in the future. The following uses are expressly mentioned by the Code: (i) publication (*publicação*), by printing or any other method of graphic reproduction, (ii) performance, recitation, exhibition, in public (*representação, recitação, execução, exhibição ou exposição em público*), (iii) cinematographic reproduction, adaptation, showing, distribution, (iv) recording on or adaptation to any contrivance destined for mechanical, electric or chemical reproduction, as well as public performance, communication or retransmission by such contrivance, (v) diffusion by photography, telephotography, television, sound broadcasting, or any other means of reproducing signs, sounds or images, public communication by loudspeaker or similar instruments and, in general, any communication to the public, by wire or by wireless means, of the diffused work when such communication is effected by an organization other than the original one, (vi) indirect appropriation in any form, (vii) translation and adaptation into a language other than that in which the work was created, (viii) adaptation, alteration, arrangement, instrumentation, elaboration (*ampliação*), direct utilization in another work, (ix) total or partial reproduction by any means.[64]

The Code regulates with an unusual wealth of detail (in altogether 106 articles) the various contracts concerning the exploitation of works. Only some of the more important provisions are mentioned here.

Publishing.[65]—Authorization to publish does not imply authorization to translate.[66] The publishing contract must be in writing and must specify the number of copies to be produced.[67] The author may audit the accounts of the publisher to verify the number of copies

---

[61] Article 60(1).   [62] Article 60(2).   [63] Article 61(1).   [64] Article 62(1).
[65] Articles 71 to 101.   [66] Article 74.   [67] Article 77(1).

actually produced[68] and, where his remuneration depends on the number of copies sold, to verify the sales.[69]

Stage Performance.[70]—The author's consent for stage performance is necessary whether the performance is public or private, whether an entrance fee is or is not charged, and whether the performance is or is not for profit. The contract must be in writing.[71] The broadcasting, whether by radio or television, of a stage performance requires the special, written authorization of the impresario and the author.[72] The above rules apply to the stage performance not only of dramatic works but also of dramatico-musical works, choreographic works, pantomimes, and similar works.[73]

Musical Performance and Recitation.[74]—The organizer of the performance or recitation must display a written program on the premises before the performance or recitation starts. The program must indicate the titles of the works and the names of the authors.[75]

Cinematographic Works.[76]—Whether a work has been expressly created for use in a cinematographic work or is a work which was created without such intent, its use for the making of a cinematographic work requires the written authorization of its author.[77] The contract must specify the conditions of production, public exhibition and distribution.[78] Where the authors have authorized the public exhibition of the cinematographic work, the rights of economic use in the work will be exercised by the maker, i.e., the person or legal entity who undertakes and organizes the making of the film and is responsible for both the technical and the financial aspects of such undertaking.[79]

Recording.[80]—Authorization for recording must be in writing.[81] It must be strictly interpreted: unless expressly stipulated otherwise, the authorization to record does not include authorization to broadcast or perform in public the work recorded.[82]

Photographs.[83]—Photographs come under the provisions of the Code only if they are personal artistic creations on account of the choice of the subject or because of the conditions in which they were created.[84] The author of a photographic work has the exclusive right to reproduce it, disclose it, and to offer it for sale, with restrictions regarding exhibition, reproduction and sale of portraits.[85] Where the photograph is made pursuant to an employment contract (*contrato de trabalho*), copyright in the photograph belongs to the employer (*entitade patronal*).[86] Alienation of the negative implies the presumption that the copyright

[68] Article 77(4). [69] Article 80. [70] Articles 102 to 118.
[71] Articles 103 and 104. [72] Article 115. [73] Article 102.
[74] Articles 119 to 121. [75] Article 120. [76] Articles 122 to 136.
[77] Article 122. [78] Article 123. [79] Article 125.
[80] Articles 137 to 146. [81] Article 137. [82] Article 137.
[83] Articles 147 to 154. [84] Article 147(1). [85] Article 148.
[86] Article 148(2).

was also transferred.[87] The copies of the photograph must indicate (i) the name of the owner of the copyright, (ii) the year in which it was made, (iii) in the case of a photograph of a work of art, the name of the author of such work.[88] If these indications are missing, action will lie only against infringers whose bad faith can be proven.[89] Subject to the payment of equitable remuneration to the owner of the copyright therein, the reproduction of photographs in scientific or educational works does not require the authorization of the copyright owner.[90]

Broadcasting.[91]—Unless expressly stipulated otherwise, authorization to broadcast does not include authorization to record broadcast works.[92] Nevertheless, broadcasting organizations may, without the authorization of the copyright owner, record works to be broadcast, but solely for use by their transmitting stations in cases where the broadcast is deferred because of time program scheduling considerations or technical requirements.[93]

If the parties cannot agree on the remuneration for broadcasting, such remuneration will be fixed by the courts.[94] The same applies where the broadcast work is publicly communicated by a receiving set.[95]

Subject to authorization by the competent Government authorities, the official broadcasting services may make special broadcasts in the national interest without the authorization of the copyright owner. In such a case, the latter has a right to equitable remuneration.[96]

Translation.[97]—Subject to the exception stated below, the right to translate is an exclusive right of authorization.[98] If, after the expiration of seven years from the publication of a work written in a language other than Portuguese, the owner of the right of translation, or any person authorized by him, has not published the work in Portuguese, any other person may apply to the courts for a non-exclusive license to translate and publish the work.[99] Such license may be granted only where the applicant proves that he has sought permission, from the owner of the right of translation, to translate and publish the translation and that, after due diligence on his part, he has not been able to find the owner of the right of translation or to obtain permission from him.[100]

In these same conditions license may also be granted where previous editions of a translation already published in Portuguese are out of print.[101]

Where the applicant has been unable to find the holder of the right

---

[87] Article 149.   [88] Article 150(1).   [89] Article 150(2).
[90] Article 151(1).   [91] Articles 155 to 162.   [92] Article 157(1).
[93] Article 157(2).   [94] Article 160(1).   [95] Article 160(2).
[96] Article 161.   [97] Articles 163 to 168.   [98] Article 163.
[99] Article 164(1).   [100] Article 164(2).   [101] Article 164(3).

of translation, he must send copies of his application to the publisher whose name appears on the work and to the diplomatic or consular representative of the State of which the owner of the right of translation is a national—in the event that the nationality of the holder of the right of translation is known—or to any organization designated for such purpose by the Government of that State. License may not be granted until two months after the date on which the copies of the application were despatched.[102]

The title and the name of the author of the original work must be printed on all copies of the published translation.[103]

Licenses obtained in a country other than Portugal are not deemed valid; however, copies of translations obtained in this manner may be imported and sold.[104]

Translation licenses obtained from a court are not transferable.[105]

Where the author has withdrawn the copies of the work from circulation, license may not be granted by the court.[106]

Works of Art.[107]—Only the author may publicly exhibit or authorize the public exhibition of his work of art.[108] Transfer of ownership of the work of art is deemed to imply assignment of the right to exhibit in public.[109]

MORAL RIGHTS

The Code provides that copyright (*o direito de autor*) consists of rights of an economic nature (*direitos de carácter patrimonial*) and rights of a personal nature (*direitos de carácter pessoal*) and that the latter are called moral rights.[110] Whereas economic rights may be transferred by any means recognized in law (*direito*), moral rights may be transferred only according to the provisions of the Code.[111]

The moral right of the author consists in being entitled, during his lifetime, to claim authorship of the work and to ensure that the work's integrity be maintained. He is protected against any distortion, mutilation or other modification of the work, and against any other act in relation to his work which is prejudicial to his honor or reputation. These rights are independent of the economic rights and may be claimed even after the transfer of the economic rights.[112] After the death of the author and until the work falls into the public domain, moral rights are exercised by his heirs or representatives.[113] After the work falls into the public domain, the State is responsible for watching

[102] Article 164(4).   [103] Article 164(5).   [104] Article 164(6).
[105] Article 164(7).   [106] Article 164(8).   [107] Articles 169 to 177.
[108] Article 169(1).   [109] Article 169(2).   [110] Article 5(1).
[111] Article 5(2).
[112] Article 55. There are special rules for architectural works (Article 56).
[113] Article 57(1).

over the integrity and authenticity (*genuinidade*) of the work.[114]
Moral rights are inalienable and imprescriptible.[115]

LIMITATIONS

Newspapers, etc.—Although copyright in serials (*romances-folhetins*), short stories (*novelas*) and other works—even if unsigned—published in newspapers or other periodicals belongs to their authors, the proprietor or publisher of the newspaper or other periodical may reproduce copies of the newspaper or other periodical containing the said serials, etc.[116] The right of *separate* reproduction belongs to the author.[117] If the work is an article on current economic, political or religious topics, and reproduction is not expressly reserved, it may be freely reproduced by third persons in the press (*imprensa*). However, the name of the author and the source must be clearly indicated in such reproductions.[118]

In the case of newspaper or periodical items produced pursuant to an employment contract, a distinction is made between signed and unsigned items. Signed articles may be published separately by their authors, but not until three months after the issue of the newspaper or periodical containing them is put into circulation.[119] No right of separate publication by the author exists in the case of unsigned items.[120]

News of the day may be freely reproduced.[121]

Other Free Uses.—The Code contains special rules in connection with certain public speeches,[122] performances for school purposes,[123] literary criticism,[124] commentaries and annotations,[125] and letters missive.[126]

Other Limitations.—As to limitations in connection with broadcasting, recording, and translation, see pages 583 and 584, above.

TERM OF PROTECTION

Generally.—Subject to the exceptions and qualifications stated below, copyright expires fifty years after the death of the author.[127]

In the case of a work of *joint authorship*, the term is computed from the death of the last surviving author.[128] In the case of a *collective work*, other than a periodical, copyright expires fifty years after first publication or disclosure (*divulgaçao*),[129] unless the collective work is the prop-

---

[114] Article 57(2).   [115] Article 57(1).   [116] Article 178(2).
[117] Article 178(1).   [118] Article 178(3).   [119] Article 179(1).
[120] Article 179(2).   [121] Article 180.   [122] Articles 181 to 183.
[123] Article 184.   [124] Article 185.   [125] Article 186.
[126] Article 188.   [127] Article 25.   [128] Article 30.   [129] Article 31(1).

erty of a single individual (*empresario*), in which case copyright expires fifty years after his death.[130]

In the case of a *posthumous* work, copyright expires fifty years after the death of the author.[131]

In the case of *anonymous, cryptonymous* or *pseudonymous works*, copyright expires fifty years after publication or disclosure, as long as the identity of the author remains unknown.[132]

Works in Several Instalments.—In the case of a work published in various parts or volumes at different times, and in the case of a collective work published periodically (newspapers and the like), the term is computed separately for each part, volume, or issue, whenever computation is based on publication.[133]

Rule of the Shorter Term.—If the country of origin of the work is a country other than Portugal and the law of that country grants a term of protection less than life plus fifty years, the term of protection in Portugal will be the same as in the country of origin.[134] In the case of published works, the country of origin is the country of first publication, without prejudice to the provisions of Article IV (5) of the Universal Copyright Convention.[135] (Those provisions state that the work of a national of a Contracting State (e.g., the United States), first published in a non-Contracting State (e.g., the Soviet Union), is to be treated as if it had been first published in the Contracting State of which the author is a national (i.e., in the example given, the United States).[136] Otherwise the concept of publication is governed by Article 4 (4) of the Berne Convention (which, presumably, means the Brussels Act since, at the time the Code was promulgated, Portugal was bound by the Brussels Act).[137] In the case of unpublished works, the country to which the author belongs (*pertence*) is considered the country of origin, unless the work is a work of architecture or a work of the graphic or plastic arts forming part of a building, in which case the country in which the building is situated is the country of origin.[138]

Computation of Years.—The terms are computed from the first day of the year following the year in which the relevant event (death, publication, disclosure) occurred.[139]

Transitional Provision.—The law which was in effect in Portugal before the entry into force of the Code provided for perpetual protection. Works which, at the date of the entry into force of the Code, were under this perpetuity rule, continue to be protected at least until May 2, 1991 (i.e., 25 years from the entry into force of the Code), at which time new provisions will regulate their subsequent fate.[140]

---

[130] Article 31(2).   [131] Article 33.   [132] Article 34.   [133] Article 36.
[134] Article 26.   [135] Article 27(1).   [136] Article 27(1).
[137] Article 27(2). Article 28 (simultaneous publication).
[138] Article 29.   [139] Article 35.   [140] Article 37

INFRINGEMENTS

Civil Remedies

Infringers of copyright are liable for damages.[141] The sale, offering for sale, or other placing on the market of infringing copies is also deemed to be infringement, whether the infringing copies were produced in Portugal or outside Portugal.[142]

Penal Sanctions

Certain acts of infringement are punishable by imprisonment or a fine.[143]

Injunctions

To prevent repetition of infringement or the commission of threatened infringement,[144] the courts may issue injunctions, seizure of copies or apparatus,[145] or the suspension of performances or exhibitions.[146]

---

[141] Article 190.　[142] Article 200.　[143] Article 197.
[144] Article 202.　[145] Article 203.　[146] Article 207.

SPAIN

SOURCES

Internal Law.—The main source of the law of copyright in Spain is the Copyright Law of January 10, 1879.[1] Hereinafter, it is referred to as "the Law," and references to Articles, without further specification, are references to Articles of the Law.[2]

Protection of phonographic works is provided by a Decree dated July 10, 1942.[3] Hereinafter it is referred to as "the Decree."

Universal Copyright Convention.—Spain became bound by the Universal Copyright Convention and Protocol 2 as from September 16, 1955.[4]

[1] Published in "Gaceta de Madrid" of January 12, 1879, No. 12, page 107. English translation in CLTW, Spain: Item 1.

[2] Other sources are: The Copyright Regulations of September 3, 1880, as amended in 1888, 1894, 1913 and 1919 (English translation in CLTW, Spain: Item 2), hereafter referred to as "the Regulations"; a Royal Decree of July 26, 1929, amended on December 26, 1947, on the registration of cinematographic films, published in the "Gaceta de Madrid" of May 7, 1930, and the "Boletín Oficial" of January 24, 1948 (English translation in CLTW, Spain: Item 3), the Law on Intellectual Property Rights in Cinematographic Works (Law No. 17/1966) of May 31, 1966, published in "Boletín Oficial del Estado" No. 131 of June 2, 1966 (English translation in CLTW, Spain: Item 2A), hereinafter referred to as "the Cinematographic Copyright Law," the Decree of February 10, 1967, concerning the percentages and remunerations to be paid to the authors of cinematographic works, published in "Boletín Oficial del Estado," No. 49 of February 27, 1967 (English translation published in CLTW, Spain: Item 2B).

[3] Published in the "Boletín Oficial" of July 18, 1942, English translation in CLTW, Spain: Item 4.

[4] CLTW, Spain: Item 5. Spain is a member of the Berne Copyright Union and has ratified all its instruments, including the latest (Brussels) revision of 1948 (CLTW, Spain: Item 6). Spain is also a party to the Montevideo Copyright Convention of 1899 and is bound, under the Convention, with Argentina and Paraguay (CLTW, Spain: Item 7), but since both these countries are now also parties to the Universal Copyright Convention, the significance of the ties under the Montevideo Convention is now small, if any. Spain has concluded bilateral treaties with France (1880), Italy (1880), and Portugal (1880), but the ties under the Berne Conventions have, to a large extent, superseded these treaties (CLTW, Costa Rica: Item 8; Ecuador: Item 9; Spain: Item 26; Peru: Item 11; Paraguay: Item 6; Nicaragua: Item 7). Diplomatic notes deal with the protection of Bolivian (1936), and U.S. (1895) works, and special decrees deal with the protection of Austrian (1912) and Cuban (1928) works (CLTW, Spain: Items 24, 15, 17 and 21), but except for Bolivia, the ties under the Berne Union or theUniversal CopyrightConvention have reduced the significance of these notes and decrees. Bilateral treaties were concluded with El Salvador (1880),

ACQUISITION OF PROTECTION UNDER THE
UNIVERSAL COPYRIGHT CONVENTION

The laws of Spain do not contain any special provisions in respect to works to which Spain is supposed to grant protection by virtue of the Universal Copyright Convention. The provisions of that Convention, particularly of Articles II and XVII and Protocol 2, determine which are the works protected under the Universal Copyright Convention. Briefly stated, such works are, except if excluded by virtue of Article XVII of the Universal Copyright Convention and the Appendix Declaration relating to the same Article (in which case the applicable Berne Convention rather than the Universal Convention governs): (i) published works of nationals of a Convention country, irrespective of the place of first publication, (ii) works first published in a Convention country, irrespective of the nationality of the author, (iii) unpublished works of nationals of a Convention country other than Spain, (iv) works first published by the United Nations, by any of the Specialized Agencies of the United Nations, or by the Organization of American States, as well as unpublished works of any of these organizations.

The Law requires, as a condition of copyright protection, deposit and registration in the Copyright Register (Ministry of *Fomento*) in the case of all works other than works of the fine arts;[5, 5 bis] this requirement, however, is inapplicable in the case of works enjoying protection by virtue of the Conventions of the Berne Copyright Union or the Universal Copyright Convention.[6] It would seem that Spain grants protection to such works even if the Convention notice is missing from the copies of published works, since protection of such works is exempt from *any* formality.

Spain has no renewal system; thus there is nothing in Spain corresponding to the renewal formalities existing in the United States.

PROTECTED WORKS

Scientific, literary and artistic works are protected, whatever the manner of their expression (*que puedan darse a luz por cualquier medio*).[7]

Colombia (1885), Guatemala (1893), and the Dominican Republic (1930), and since none of these countries is party to any multilateral convention to which Spain is party, these treaties still have practical significance (CLTW, El Salvador: Item 6; Colombia: Item 6; Guatemala: Item 6; Dominican Republic: Item 6). Exchanges of notes concerning the term of protection concerning Austria, France, Italy and Norway are discussed under "Term of Protection," page 518, below.

[5] Articles 29, 33 to 39.

[5 bis] The Cinematographic Copyright Law expressly provides (art. 8) that all cinematographic works and the rights of the authors thereof must be recorded in the Copyright Register.

[6] *Cf.* article 51.   [7] Article 1.

The Law expressly mentions maps, plans, scientific drawings, musical compositions, reproductions of works of art,[8] dramatic works,[9] translations.[10] Indirect reference is made to authorized recasts, extracts and abridgments.[11] The Decree extends copyright protection to authorized phonographic adaptations, transformations and reproductions, and calls them "phonographic works."[12]

According to the Regulations, all works produced or capable of publication by means of writing, drawing, printing, painting, engraving, lithography, stamping, autography, photography, or by any other means of printing or reproduction, are deemed to be works for the purposes of the Law.[13]

PROTECTED PERSONS

Copyright belongs to: (i) the author in his own work, (ii) the translator in his translation, which must be an authorized one if the original work is protected, (iii) any person who recasts, copies, extracts from, abridges or reproduces original works, insofar as the product of his effort is concerned (but the permission of the author of the original work, if protected by copyright, is required), (iv) to the publishers (*editores*) of hitherto unpublished works whose author is not known, and to the publishers of hitherto unpublished works of known authorship, which have passed into the public domain, (v) the authors of maps, plans and scientific drawings, (vi) the composers of music, (vii) the authors of works of art, in respect of any kind of reproductions of such works, (viii) the successors in title (*derechohabientes*), whether by inheritance, or by any other title conveying ownership, of the abovementioned persons.[14]

Copyright in phonographic works belongs jointly to the author of the recorded work and the phonograph record company: in the absence of any prior agreement between them, each of them is entitled to oppose the use of the record, or any analogous object derived from the original phonographic recording, for the reproduction or transmission of sounds for purposes of profit.[15] If the recorded work is in the public domain, the copyright in the phonographic work belongs to the record company alone.[16]

As far as cinematographic works are concerned, one must distinguish between the producer and the authors of the cinematographic work. The physical person or the legal entity who takes the initiative

---

[8] Articles 3 and 19. [9] Article 19. [10] Article 14.
[11] Article 2. [12] Decree, article 1. [13] Regulations, article 1.
[14] Articles 2, 3, 14, 26. The person who conceives and gives form to the scientific or literary work, or who creates and executes the artistic work is deemed to be the author of the work (Regulations, article 2).
[15] Decree, article 2. [16] Decree, article 5.

and assumes the responsibility for the realization of a cinematographic work is considered to be the producer thereof. The person or legal entity who or which has been authorized to "shoot" the film is presumed to have taken the said responsibility.[16 bis] The following are considered to be the authors of a cinematographic work: (i) the authors of the plot, of the adaptation, of the scenario, of the dialogue, and of the commentary, (ii) the authors of the musical works and of the texts of such works, (iii) the director of the film. Other persons may also be authors of a cinematographic work if, on account of their intellectual-creative activity, they actually participate in the creation of the cinematographic work.[16 ter]

ASSIGNMENT AND LICENSING

Copyright devolves upon the author's heirs or legatees. It is also transferable by act *inter vivos*. In the latter case, it belongs to the assignee during the life of the author and for 80 years thereafter if the author leaves no "compulsory heirs" (*herederos forzosos*), i.e., heirs whose rights cannot be put aside by will unless there is a legitimate cause for disinheriting them. If the author does leave compulsory heirs, the rights of the assignee end 25 years after the death of the author, and for the remaining 55 years they pass to the compulsory heirs.[17]

In the absence of agreement to the contrary, alienation of a work of art does not imply alienation of the right of reproduction, nor the right of public exhibition.[18]

Transfers of copyright must be incorporated in a public deed and registered in the Copyright Registry: otherwise the transferee is not entitled to the benefits of the Law.[19]

PROTECTED RIGHTS

ECONOMIC RIGHTS

No person has the right to *publish*, without the permission of the author, a scientific, literary or artistic work, including lectures, taken down by means of shorthand, or noted or copied during its reading, performance, or public or private exhibition.[20]

No person may, even for the purpose of annotating, adding to or improving the edition of a work, *reproduce* the work of another person

[16bis] Cinematographic Copyright Law, Article 1.
[16ter] Cinematographic Copyright Law, Article 3.
[17] Article 6. [18] Article 9. [19] Regulations, article 9. [20] Article 8.

without the permission of the owner thereof.[21] In the case of musical works, the prohibition equally extends to the total or partial publication of the melody, with or without accompaniment, transposed or arranged for other instruments or with different words or in any other form than in which the work was published by the author.[22] Authors of works of art have an exclusive right of *public exhibition* as well as reproduction.[23]

No dramatic or musical work may be *performed,* wholly or in part, in any theatre or public place without the previous permission of the owner.[24] In the case of a dramatic or musical work which has been performed in public but has not been printed, no person may make, sell or rent copies thereof without the permission of the owner.[25] In the absence of agreement to the contrary, one half of the performance royalties of all dramatico-musical works belongs to the owner of the copyright in the libretto and the other half to the owner of the copyright in the music.[26]

The author or translator of writings included in periodical publications, or the successors in title of such persons, may publish such writings in the form of a collection, complete or selected, unless otherwise agreed with the owner of the periodical.[27]

Copyright in phonographic works consists of the same rights as those granted in the case of musical works. These include the right to oppose the use of records, or of analogous objects derived from the original phonographic recording, for the reproduction or transmission of sounds for purposes of profit by broadcasting, cinematography, television or sound-reproducing devices or amplifiers used in theatres, bars, cafés, dance-halls and places of amusement in general, as well as by means of any analogous processes which may be invented in the future for the same or similar purposes.[28]

The right to exploit a cinematographic work belongs exclusively to the producer or his successors in title. This right includes the right to reproduce the film in as many copies as may be necessary for its exploitation and the right of public showing of the cinematographic work.[28 bis] The authors of a cinematographic work have the right to collect, for persons who show in public the work, a percentage, as well as the right to dispose of their contributions, for uses outside the film, provided such uses do not prejudice the normal exploitation of the cinematographic work.[28 ter]

---

[21] Article 7, first paragraph.   [22] Article 7, second paragraph.
[23] Articles 9 and 10.   [24] Articles 19 and 20. *See also* Regulations, article 62.
[25] Article 21.   [26] Article 22.   [27] Article 30.
[28] Decree, article 2.
[28bis] Cinematographic Copyright Law, Article 1.
[28ter] Cinematographic Copyright Law, Article 4.

Moral Rights

Authors are protected against changes in the title or text of their works.[29]

Enterprises, societies or private persons who, when proceeding to the public performance of a dramatic or musical work, announce it with a change in title, or suppress, add to or alter certain passages thereof, without the permission of the author, are deemed infringers of copyright.[30]

Producers of phonographic plates or records may refuse to grant permission for reproduction or public performance if such acts would prejudice their artistic reputation or financial interests.[31]

The authors of a cinematographic work have the right to be appropriately mentioned in the "credit titles" as well as the right to their contributions being respected both in the making and the exploitation of the cinematographic work.[31 bis]

Limitations

Any person may publish, as his own property, commentaries, criticisms or notes referring to the work of another person but including therewith only those parts of the work as are necessary for the purpose.[32]

Writings and telegrams included in periodical publications may be reproduced in any other publication of a like kind, provided that in the original publications no indication is given immediately following the title, or at the end of the article, to the effect that reproduction is prohibited: in all cases, the source from which the reproduction is made must be indicated.[33]

The performance of phonograph records is free in *centros*, lectures or meetings of the official education system of the State, or for propaganda purposes of the State.[34]

TERM OF PROTECTION

Generally.—Subject to the exceptions referred to below, copyright is protected during the life of the author and 80 years thereafter.[35] As to the reversionary interest of heirs, *see* "Assignment and Licensing," above.[36]

Works which are not republished by their owner over a period of

---

[29] Articles 47 and 48.   [30] Article 24.   [31] Decree, article 3.
[31bis] Cinematographic Copyright Law, Article 4.
[32] Article 7, first paragraph. *See also* article 23.   [33] Article 31. *See also* article 32.
[34] Decree, article 6.   [35] Article 6. *See also* article 10.
[36] Page 516 above.

20 years may, in certain circumstances, fall into the public domain.[37] It is uncertain whether this provision is also applicable when its effects would lead to a protection shorter than the minimum terms provided in the Universal Copyright Convention or the Berne Conventions.

The rights of phonograph record companies in phonographic works continue for a period of 40 years, calculated from the date of accomplishment of certain formalities.[38] It is not clear how this provision may be applied in the case of such non-Spanish phonographic works which, seemingly, should be protected without the accomplishment of any formalities.

Rule of the Shorter Term.—It would appear that a given work does not enjoy copyright protection in Spain beyond the date on which it falls into the public domain in the country "of its proprietor," and copyright in the translation of a work is not protected in Spain beyond the date on which the original work falls into the public domain in the country of the proprietor of the copyright in the original work.[39]

INFRINGEMENTS

Civil Remedies.—The law provides that copyright is governed by the general rules of law.[40] These undoubtedly include the general rules concerning compensation for damage caused by infringing acts.

Criminal Sanctions.—Infringers are punished criminally and suffer the forfeiture of the illegally published copies.[41] Such copies are delivered up to the owner of the copyright whose rights have been infringed.[42] The proceeds of admission to the unauthorized public performance of a dramatic or musical work are forfeited in favor of the owner of the performance right.[43]

Importation of infringing copies of a protected work is deemed infringement.[44]

---

[37] Articles 40 to 44.   [38] Decree, article 5.
[39] Article 13. The prolongations made on account of one or both of the World Wars in Australia, France, Italy and Norway were expressly recognized by Spain for purposes of computing the term of protection in Spain of works originating in these countries. *See* CLTW, Spain: Item 27, 28, 29, 30.
[40] Article 5.
[41] Articles 45 and 46; Decree, article 7. *See also* Law, articles 48 and 49 and the Penal Code (Text of 1963), Article 534.
[42] Article 46.   [43] Article 25.   [44] Article 47.

SWEDEN

SOURCES

Internal Law.—The main source of the law of copyright in Sweden is the Copyright Act of December 30, 1960.[1] Hereinafter, it is referred to as "the Act," and references to Sections, without further specification, are references to the Sections of this Act.

Photographs are not considered "works"; rights in them are not considered copyrights; and their protection is not regulated by the Copyright Act, but by a separate law entitled "Act on Rights in Photographic Pictures." The date of this law is also December 30, 1960.[2] Hereinafter, it is referred to as the "Act on Photographs."

Universal Copyright Convention.—Sweden became bound by the Universal Copyright Convention and Protocols 1 and 2 as from July 1, 1961.[3] The Royal Decree No. 349 of June 2, 1961 (hereinafter referred to as "the Royal Decree"),[4] regulates, among other things, the application of the Copyright Act and the Act on Photographs to works and photographic pictures protected under the Universal Copyright Convention.

ACQUISITION OF PROTECTION UNDER THE UNIVERSAL COPYRIGHT CONVENTION

Subject, where applicable, to the rule of the shorter term,[5] the provisions of the Copyright Act and of the Act on Photographs apply to:

(a) works and photographic pictures "of foreign nationals in a foreign country party to the Universal Copyright Convention" (*av utländsk medborgare i främmande land, anslutet till Världskonventionen om upphovsrätt*);[6]

---

[1] Published in "Svensk Författningssamling," 1960, page 1949; English translation in CLTW, Sweden: Item 1. An excellent commentary is Torwald Hesser's "La nouvelle législation suédoise sur le droit d'auteur," published in "Le Droit d'auteur," 1961, page 191.

[2] Published in "Svensk Författningssamling," 1960, page 1960; English translation in CLTW, Sweden: Item 2.

[3] CLTW, Sweden: Item 3A. Sweden is a member of the Berne Copyright Union. It has ratified the Conventions of Berlin, Rome and Brussels (1948). CLTW, Sweden: Item 4.

[4] Published in "Svensk Författningssamling," 1961, page 830.

[5] *See* "Term of Protection," page 528, below.

[6] Probably should be understood as meaning nationals of a country, other than

(b) works and photographic pictures of foreign nationals first published in a country party to the Universal Copyright Convention;

(c) works and photographic pictures of foreign nationals domiciled (*med hemvist*) in a country party to the Universal Copyright Convention, provided that the laws of that country treat them in the same manner as its own nationals, as far as the application of the Universal Copyright Convention is concerned;

(d) works and photographic pictures of stateless persons and refugees who have their habitual residence in a country party to Protocol 1 of the Universal Copyright Convention;[7]

(e) works and photographic pictures first published by the United Nations, any specialized agency of the United Nations, or the Organization of American States, and to unpublished works these Organizations may in the future publish.[8]

Sweden has no copyright formalities. Consequently, registration, deposit, or compliance with other formalities is not required, and the absence, in itself, of a Convention notice on the copies of a published work is no bar to claiming protection in Sweden. Furthermore, Sweden has no renewal system, so that there is nothing in this country which would correspond to the renewal formalities existing in the United States.

PROTECTED SUBJECT MATTER

Works.—The Copyright Act protects literary and artistic works. The following are specially mentioned:

—works of *belles lettres* (*skönlitterär framställning*) or works of a descriptive (non-fictional) nature (*beskrivande framställning*), whether written or oral,

—musical works,

—dramatic (*sceniskt*) works,

Sweden, if they are domiciled outside Sweden. If they are domiciled in Sweden, their works and photographic pictures are protected by virtue of section 60 of the Copyright Act, and section 22 of the Act on Photographs.

[7] Royal Decree, section 2, paragraph (1), and section 5. To works and photographic pictures which meet any of the conditions referred to under (a), (b), (c), and (d), above, but which have, as country of origin, a country which is a member of the Berne Copyright Union, the provisions of the Copyright Act and of the Act on Photographs apply by virtue of section 1, rather than section 2, of the Royal Decree (Royal Decree, sec. 2, para. (4)). However, the distinction is of no practical relevance since the effects of the two Sections are the same. Works and photographic pictures which have, as country of origin, a State which withdraws from the Berne Copyright Union after July 1, 1961, will not be protected in Sweden even if they meet one or more of the conditions referred to under (a), (b), (c), or (d) above (Royal Decree, sec. 2, para. (4)). Since no country has withdrawn from the Berne Copyright Union since the said date, the provision does not apply, in practice, at the time these lines are written (March, 1963).

[8] Royal Decree, section 3.

—cinematographic works (*filmverk*),
—works of fine arts (*bildkonst*),
—works of architecture (*byggnadskonst*),
—works of artistic handicraft (*konsthantverk*),
—works of industrial art (*konstindustri*),[9]
—maps and other works of a descriptive nature executed as drawings, engraving, or three-dimensionally,[10]
—translations, adaptations, and other conversions of a work into another literary or artistic form.[11]

Copyright in a work is not lost by the fact that the work is registered as a design under provisions other than those of the Copyright Act.[12]

Photographs.—Photographic pictures are protected; a picture produced by a process analogous to photography is considered a photographic picture.[13]

PROTECTED PERSONS

Works.—Copyright belongs to the person who created the work.[14] A person who translates or adapts (*bearbetat*) a work, or converts it into another literary or artistic form, has copyright in the new work thus produced, but may not make dispositions connected therewith (*förfoga däröver*) contrary to the copyright in the work from which the new work is derived.[15] A person who, by combining works or parts of works, creates a composite work (*samlingsverk*), has copyright in the composite work, but his rights may not restrict the rights in the said works.[16]

If a work has several authors whose respective contributions do not constitute independent works, copyright belongs to them jointly.[17]

In the absence of proof to the contrary, the person whose name, generally known pseudonym, or signature, is indicated in the usual manner on the copies (*exemplar*) of the work, or when the work is made available (*tillgängligt*) to the public, is deemed to be the author. If a work is published without authorship being indicated in the said manner, the editor, and if he is not named, the publisher, will represent the author until authorship is indicated in a new edition of the work or in a notification filed with the *justitiedepartementet* (Ministry of Justice).[18]

The transfer of a copy (*exemplar*) of the work does not carry with it the transfer of the copyright in the work. However, where a portrait picture was executed on commission, the artist may not exercise his

[9] Section 1, first paragraph.
[10] Section 1, second paragraph; these are considered literary works.
[11] *See* section 4, first paragraph.
[12] Section 10, first paragraph.
[13] Act on Photographs, section 1.
[14] Section 1, first paragraph.
[15] Section 4.   [16] Section 5.   [17] Section 6.   [18] Section 7.

rights without the permission of the person who commissioned it or, if such person is dead, the permission of the surviving spouse and heirs.[19]

Photographs.—The owner of the rights in a photographic picture is the person who has produced (*framställt*) it.[20]

The person whose name, firm name (*firma*), or generally known signature is indicated in the usual manner on the copies (*exemplar*) of the photographic picture, or when the photographic picture is publicly exhibited, is deemed to be the photographer.[21]

In the absence of an express agreement to the contrary, the right in a photographic picture made on commission belongs to the person who commissioned it. However, the photographer may exhibit the picture in the usual manner for advertising purposes unless the person who commissioned it has prohibited such exhibition. On the other hand, even if the photographer has reserved the right in a photographic picture made on commission, the person who commissioned it may cause it to be published in newspapers, periodicals, or biographical writings, unless the photographer has prohibited such publication.[22]

ASSIGNMENT AND LICENSING

Generally.—Subject to certain limitations concerning moral rights (discussed below), copyright may be transferred entirely or partially.[23]

The transfer of a copy does not include transfer of the copyright. In the case of a portrait executed on commission, the artist may not exercise his copyright without the permission of the person who commissioned it or, if such person is dead, without the permission of his surviving spouse and heirs.[24] When a photographer has transferred copies of a photographic picture, they may be publicly exhibited without the permission of the photographer.[25]

If the application of a condition in a contract concerning transfer of copyright is obviously contrary to usage considered as proper in the field of copyright, or is otherwise obviously unfair, it may be changed or disregarded.[26]

In the absence of an agreement to the contrary, the person to whom a copyright has been transferred may not transfer it to others. If the copyright belongs to a business, it may be transferred together with the

[19] Section 27, second paragraph.
[20] Act on Photographs, section 1, first paragraph. Other provisions refer to him as the photographer (*see* for example, Act on Photographs, sec. 3).
[21] Act on Photographs, section 3.
[22] Act on Photographs, section 14.
[23] Section 27, first paragraph.
[24] Section 27, second paragraph.
[25] Act on Photographs, section 10, first paragraph.
[26] Section 29.

business or part thereof; however, the transferor remains liable for the fulfilment of the original contract.[27]

Public Performance Contracts.—In the absence of an agreement to the contrary, the license to perform a work, other than a cinematographic work, is considered to be non-exclusive and valid only for three years. Where a person who has been granted, for a period exceeding three years, the exclusive right to perform a work (other than a cinematographic work) does not exercise his right for at least three years, the author may—in the absence of an agreement to the contrary—perform, or license third persons to perform, such works.[28]

Publishing Contracts.[29]—In the absence of an agreement to the contrary:

(a) the manuscript or other copy from which the reproduction is effected remains the property of the author;[30]

(b) the publisher may publish one edition (*upplaga*) (that is, a quantity of copies produced at one and the same time) whose number may not exceed 2,000 in the case of literary works, 1,000 in the case of musical works, and 200 in the case of artistic works;[31]

(c) the publisher must (i) publish the work within a reasonable time, (ii) distribute the copies in the usual manner, (iii) follow up the publishing to the extent determined by the marketing conditions and other circumstances;[32]

(d) the author may rescind the contract and keep the remuneration received, even where there is no negligence on the part of the publisher, in either of the following cases:

(i) the work has not been published within two years (in the case of a musical work, within four years) from the date of submission of the manuscript or other copy from which the multiplication was to be made,

(ii) the work is out of print and no new edition is published within one year of the author's demand for a new edition to be published;[33]

(e) the publisher must give the author a certification issued by the printer, or whoever effected the multiplication, concerning the number of copies (*exemplar*) produced;[34]

(f) the publisher must render yearly accounts to the author on the number of copies sold and on the number of copies remaining in stock;[35]

---

[27] Section 28.   [28] Section 30.

[29] A publishing contract is a contract by which the author transfers to the publisher the right to multiply (*mångfaldiga*), by printing or other similar process, and publish (*utgiva*) a literary or artistic work (sec. 31, first paragraph).

[30] Section 31, second paragraph.

[31] Section 32.

[32] Section 33. If the publisher negligently does not fulfil any of these obligations, the author may rescind the contract, retain any remuneration received, and, if he has suffered additional damage, he may claim compensation therefore.

[33] Section 34.   [34] Section 35, first paragraph.   [35] Section 35, second paragraph.

(g) the author must be given a chance to make changes in the work every time a year or more elapses between the publication of the last edition and the beginning of the production of the new edition;[36]

(h) the author may not publish, or authorize third persons to publish, the work in the form or manner stipulated in the contract, as long as the editions allowed the publisher are not out of print.[37]

The rules of interpretation summarized under (a) through (h), above, do not apply to contributions to newspapers or periodicals; and those under (c) and (d) do not apply to contributions to other composite works (*samlingsverk*) as well.

Contracts Relating to the Production of Cinematographic Works.—In the absence of agreement to the contrary:

(a) the granting of a license to use a literary or artistic work in the production of a film:

(i) includes a license to make the work, other than a musical work, accessible (*tillgängligt*) to the public, by means of a film, in motion picture theatres, on television, or otherwise;

(ii) does not include a license to make the musical work accessible to the public in the said manner;[38]

(b) the grantee of a license to use a literary or musical work in the production of a film intended for public exhibition must produce the film and make it available to the public within a reasonable time.[39]

PROTECTED RIGHTS

Economic Rights

Works.—Copyright includes the exclusive right to dispose (*förfoga*) of the work (i) by producing copies (*exemplar*) thereof; (ii) by making it accessible to the public. It is irrelevant whether these acts are done with the work in its original form or in a modified form. Modified forms include translations, adaptations (*bearbetning*), expressions in a different literary or artistic form, and expressions by a different technique.[40]

[36] Section 36. Such changes must not cause unreasonable costs and must not alter the character of the work.

[37] Section 37, first paragraph. However, a literary work may be included by the author in an edition of his collected or selected works, when fifteen years have elapsed since the publication of the first edition.

[38] Section 39.

[39] Section 40. If, through negligence, this is not done within a reasonable time, the author may rescind the contract and retain any remuneration received, and, if he has suffered additional damage, he may claim compensation therefor. If the film is not produced within five years from the time at which the author carried out his obligations, the author may rescind the contract and retain any remuneration received, even if there is no fault on behalf of the grantee.

[40] Section 2, first paragraph.

Production of copies includes fixation on contrivances by means of which the work may be reproduced.[41]

Making accessible to the public may be effected by public performance, by offering copies for sale, loan or lease, by other diffusion to the public, or by public exhibition.[42]

When a literary or musical work has been published, any copy, being part of the publication, may be freely further distributed and publicly exhibited. However, sheet music may not be leased to the public without the author's consent.[43]

The author has an exclusive right to publish a compilation of his written or oral statements, even when, at the time the statements were made, they could be published singly without his consent.[44]

Copies produced outside Sweden which, if produced in Sweden, would have infringed the author's rights, may not be imported into Sweden for general distribution. Unauthorized importations are punishable by fine or imprisonment.[45]

Photographs.—The right in photographic pictures consists in the exclusive right of (i) making copies of the photographic picture by photography, printing, drawing or other processes; (ii) publicly exhibiting the photographic picture.[46]

Moral Rights

Works.—When copies of a work are produced or when the work is made available to the public, the name of the author must be indicated to the extent and in the manner required by proper usage.[47]

A work may not be changed in a manner, and may not be presented to the public in a form or context, which would be prejudicial to the author's literary or artistic reputation, or which would be inconsistent with his individuality.[48] However, buildings and useful articles (*bruksföremål*) may be altered by the owner without the author's consent.[49]

After the author's death, the courts may restrain, by injunction, performances or reproductions prejudicial to the spiritual interests of culture; the right to ask for injunctions in such cases belongs to certain

---

[41] Section 2, second paragraph.
[42] Section 2, third paragraph. Performance before a larger, although closed, group is considered public performance if it takes place on the premises of an undertaking conducted for profit (*förvärvsverksamhet*).
[43] Section 23.   [44] Section 24.
[45] Section 53, second paragraph.
[46] Act on Photographs, Section 1, first paragraph.
[47] Section 3, first paragraph. This right may be waived only in respect of utilizations clearly circumscribed as to manner and extent (sec. 3, third para.). See also Section 26.
[48] Section 3, second paragraph. This right may be waived only in respect of utilizations clearly circumscribed as to manner and extent (sec. 3, third paragraph).
[49] Section 13.

government-appointed authorities. This provision applies also to works in the public domain.[50]

Photographs.—When copies of a photographic picture are produced, or when the photographic picture is publicly exhibited, the name of the photographer must be indicated to the extent and in the manner required by proper usage.[51]

Photographic pictures may not be altered in a manner prejudicial to the producer's reputation as a photographer; nor may they be publicly exhibited in such a form or context as to prejudice the producer's reputation as a photographer.[52,53]

LIMITATIONS

The author's (or, when applicable, the photographer's) permission is not required *in certain cases* of: photocopying by libraries;[54] quotation, criticism or learned treatise;[55] reproduction in a newspaper[56] or religious or educational compilations;[57] sound fixation for educational use;[58] uses for the blind;[59] performance at divine services or in connection with education;[60] news by broadcast or film;[61] ephemeral fixations for and by broadcasting organizations;[62] etc.[63]

One of the unique features of the Swedish Act is that it allows any Swedish broadcasting organization which, having obtained a special permission by the King in Council, has an agreement with an organization representing a large number of Swedish authors in the field— under which agreement it may broadcast literary and musical works— also to broadcast published works of authors who are not represented by the organization; such authors are entitled to compensation for the broadcast. This provision does not apply to dramatic works and to

---

[50] Section 51 and section 60, second paragraph.
[51] Act on Photographs, section 2, first paragraph; *see also* section 13.
[52] Act on Photographs, section 2, second sentence.
[53] Section 11; Act on Photographs, section 5.
[54] Section 12; Act on Photographs, section 6; and Royal Decree No. 348 of 1961.
[55] Section 14; however, in certain cases the author is entitled to compensation. Act on Photographs, section 7, first paragraph.
[56] Section 15, first paragraph.
[57] Section 16; however, the author is entitled to compensation. Act on Photographs, section 7, second paragraph.
[58] Section 17.   [59] Section 18.
[60] Section 20; but cinematographic works and dramatic works may not be so performed.
[61] Section 21; Act on Photographs, section 8. Swedish television organizations may show, in return for compensation, any disseminated photographic picture, unless the photographer has prohibited such showing or there is a particular reason to assume that he opposes it (Act on Photographs, section 9).
[62] Section 22, first paragraph; Act on Photographs, section 11.
[63] Sections 15, second paragraph, 19, 24, 25; Act on Photographs, sections 10, 12.

works whose broadcasting has been prohibited by the author. Furthermore, it does not apply in cases where there is a particular reason to assume that the author would oppose the broadcasting.[64]

TERM OF PROTECTION

Works Other than Works of Artistic Handicraft or Industrial Art.—Copyright in works other than works of artistic handicraft or industrial art subsists until the end of the fiftieth year after the year in which the author, or the last surviving co-author, died.[65]

Anonymous and Pseudonymous Works.—In the case of a work (other than a work of artistic handicraft or industrial art) disseminated[66] without mention of the author's name or generally known pseudonym or signature, copyright subsists until the end of the fiftieth year after the year in which the work was disseminated.[67]

Works of Artistic Handicraft or Industrial Art.—Copyrigt in a work of artistic handicraft or industrial art susbsists until the end of the tenth year after the year in which the work was disseminated, provided it was disseminated before the death of the author. If it was not so disseminated, copyright subsists until the end of the tenth year after the year in which the author died.[68]

Photographs.—One has to distinguish between (i) photographic pictures having an artistic or scientific value and (ii) photographic pictures lacking such value. In the first case similar rules apply as in the case of works other than works of artistic handicraft or industrial art, discussed above, that is, the duration is generally fifty years *p.m.a.*, etc.[69] In the second case, the right subsists only until the end of the twenty-fifth year after the year in which the photographic picture (having no artistic or scientific value) was produced.[70]

Rule of the Shorter Term.—Protection of a given work (or photographic picture) in Sweden ceases on the same date as in the country of

---

[64] Section 22, second paragraph.
[65] Section 43, first paragraph.
[66] "Disseminated" (*offentliggjort*) means "lawfully made available to the public" (sec. 8, first paragraph).
[67] Section 44, first paragraph; if the author's identity is disclosed between the time of dissemination and that of the expiration of the above term, or if it is established that the author died before the work was disseminated, protection ends at the expiration of the fiftieth year after the year in which the author, or the last surviving co-author, died (sec. 44, second paragraph).
[68] Section 43, second paragraph; "disseminated" (*offentliggjort*) means "lawfully made available to the public" (sec. 8, first paragraph).
[69] Act on Photographs, section 15, second and third paragraphs; of course, "photographer" must be substituted for "author."
[70] Act on Photographs, section 15, first paragraph.

origin of the work (or photographic picture) if that date precedes the date on which the work (or photographic picture) would, according to the provisions referred to above, cease to be protected in Sweden. The country of origin is the country, party to the Universal Copyright Convention, in which the work (or photographic picture) was first published, or if it was published simultaneously or within thirty days in two or more such countries with different terms of copyright, the country in which such term is the shortest. Works (or photographic pictures) first published in a country not party to the Universal Copyright Convention, and unpublished works (or photographic pictures), are deemed to originate in the country of which their author is a national.[71] A work is considered "published" when copies have been lawfully placed on sale, or otherwise distributed to the public.[72,73]

INFRINGEMENTS

Civil Remedies: Works.—In the case of wilful or negligent infringement constituting exploitation of the work, the infringer is liable to pay the author or other copyright proprietor (i) an amount constituting reasonable remuneration for the exploitation, and (ii) damages for loss, mental suffering, or other injury caused by his act.[74]

In the case of infringement which is neither wilful nor negligent, the infringer is liable to pay the author or other copyright proprietor an amount constituting reasonable remuneration for the exploitation.[75]

In the case of wilful or negligent commission of acts subject to penal sanctions (see below), but not constituting an exploitation of the work (e.g., violations of moral rights), the defendant is liable to pay the author or other copyright proprietor damages for loss, mental suffering, or other injury caused by his act.[76,77]

Civil Remedies: Photographs.—In the case of wilful or negligent infringement constituting exploitation of the work, the infringer is liable to pay the photographer or other holder of his rights (i) an amount constituting reasonable remuneration for the exploitation, and (ii) damages for loss, mental suffering, or other injury caused by his act.[78]

[71] Royal Decree No. 349, article 2, paragraph (3).
[72] Section 8, second paragraph.
[73] The rule of the shorter term, as laid down in Royal Decree No. 349, is not quite in harmony with the requirements of the Universal Copyright Convention (*see* page 50, above). For example, the Royal Decree calls for a comparison of terms in respect to the individual work rather than the class to which the work belongs.
[74] Section 54, first and second paragraphs.
[75] Section 54, first paragraph.   [76] Section 54, third paragraph.
[77] *See also* sections 55, 56, 58, 59.
[78] Act on Photographs, section 17, first and second paragraphs.

In the case of infringement which is neither wilful nor negligent, the infringer is liable to pay the photographer or other holder of his rights an amount constituting reasonable remuneration for the exploitation.[79]

In the case of wilful or negligent commission of acts subject to penal sanctions (see below) not constituting exploitation of the work, the defendant is liable to pay to the photographer or other holder of his rights damages for loss, mental suffering, or other injury caused by his act.[80],[81]

Penal Sanctions: Works.—Any person who commits any of the following acts, wilfully or with gross negligence, is punishable by fine or imprisonment: (i) infringes copyright, (ii) makes a work available to the public under such a title, pseudonym, or signature that the work or its author may be easily confused with a previously disseminated work or the author of such a work, (iii) imports into Sweden copies of a work for general distribution, if such copies have been produced outside Sweden under such circumstances that a similar production within Sweden would have been punishable according to the provisions referred to under (i) and (ii) above.[82],[83]

Penal Sanctions: Photographs.—Any person who commits any of the following acts, wilfully or with gross negligence, is punishable by fine or imprisonment: (i) infringes the right in a photographic picture, (ii) offers for sale or otherwise distributes copies of a photographic picture produced in violation of the provisions of the Act on Photographs, (iii) distributes to the public, or imports into Sweden for such distribution to the public, copies of a photographic picture if the copies have been produced outside Sweden under such circumstances that a similar production within Sweden would have been punishable according to the provisions referred to under (i) and (ii), above.[84],[85]

---

[79] Act on Photographs, section 17, first paragraph.
[80] Act on Photographs, section 17, third paragraph.
[81] *See also* Act on Photographs, sections 18, 19, 20.
[82] Section 53. The author may give directions in his will, having binding effect on his surviving spouse and heirs of the body, as to the exercise of copyright, or authorize another person to give such directions (sec. 41, second paragraph). Persons violating such directions wilfully or with gross negligence are punishable by fine or imprisonment (sec. 53, first paragraph).
[83] *See also* sections 52, 55, 56, 59.
[84] Act on Photographs, section 16.
[85] *See also* Act on Photographs, sections 18, 19, 20, 21.

SWITZERLAND

SOURCES

Internal Law.—The main source of the law of copyright in Switzerland is the Federal Law on Copyright in Literary and Artistic Works of December 7, 1922, as amended by the Law of June 24, 1955.[1] Hereinafter it is referred to as "the Law," and references to Articles, without further specification, are references to Articles of this Law, as amended.

The Code of Obligations contains fourteen Articles dealing with certain questions concerning publishing contracts.[2]

Universal Copyright Convention.—Switzerland became bound by the Universal Copyright Convention and Protocols 1 and 2 as from March 30, 1955.[3]

ACQUISITION OF PROTECTION UNDER THE UNIVERSAL COPYRIGHT CONVENTION

There is no express reference to the Universal Copyright Convention in the Swiss Copyright Law which, however, provides for the supremacy

---

[1] All laws have French, German and Italian texts, equivalent as regards legal effect. The German text of the 1922 Law is published in "Bereinigte Sammlung der Bundesgesetze und Verordnungen," 1848–1947, Vol. 2, page 817; the French text of the 1955 amendatory Law is published in "Recueil des lois fédérales," 1955, page 877. The English translation of both appears in CLTW, Switzerland: Item 1.

German language commentaries are those of E. Röthlisberger and Bénigne Mentha, entitled "Schweizerisches Urheber- und Verlagsrecht an Werken der Literatur und Kunst," Second Edition, published at Zurich in 1932; and that of Adolf Streuli, entitled "Urheberrecht in der Schweiz," published at Geneva, by Schweizerische Juristische Karthotek in 1943. In French, there is Charles Dürr's "Droit d'auteur suisse," published at Berne, by Éditions Aréthousa, in 1953.

[2] Code of Obligations, Articles 380 to 393; English translation in CLTW, Switzerland: Item 2.

[3] CLTW, Switzerland: Item 5. Switzerland is a member of the Berne Copyright Union from its inception and ratified all its Conventions, including the Brussels Convention of 1948. There are provisions on copyright in the Treaty of Friendship and Commerce that Switzerland concluded with Columbia in 1908 (CLTW, Switzerland: Item 7). A decree of the Swiss Federal Council of September 26, 1924, deals with the protection of works first published in the United States of America (Recueil des lois fédérales, 1924, page 492; CLTW, Switzerland: Item 8) but is of limited practical significance since the adherence of both countries to the Universal Copyright Convention.

of international treaties.[4] Consequently, the Universal Copyright Convention itself determines what works are protected by Switzerland under that Convention. The matter is dealt with in detail in connection with Articles II and XVII of the Universal Copyright Convention.[5]

Subject to the possible exception stated in the next paragraph, Switzerland would thus protect the following under the Universal Copyright Convention: (i) published works of nationals of a Convention country, irrespective of the place of first publication, (ii) works first published in a Convention country, irrespective of the nationality of the author, (iii) unpublished works of nationals of a Convention country other than Switzerland, (iv) works of stateless persons and refugees who have their habitual residence in a State party to Protocol 1 (except perhaps Switzerland), whether unpublished or published, and, if published, irrespective of the place of first publication, (v) works first published by the United Nations, by any of the Specialized Agencies of the United Nations, or by the Organization of American States, as well as unpublished works of any of these organizations.

If a work belongs to any of these five categories but has, within the meaning of the Conventions of the Berne Union, a Union country as country of origin, then such work is protected, in Switzerland, by virtue of the applicable Convention of the Berne Union, rather than by virtue of the Universal Copyright Convention. Works having a Union country as country of origin are, roughly stated, (i) unpublished works whose author is a national (*ressortissant*) of a Union country, (ii) published works which were first published in a Union country or which, within 30 days of their first publication in a non-Berne Union country, were also published in a Union country ("simultaneous publication"). Since, however, there seems to be no difference between the protection afforded by Switzerland by virtue of its membership in the Berne Union and the protection granted pursuant to its being party to the Universal Copyright Convention, the question of which of the Conventions applies in a concrete situation appears to be largely academic.

Article 68*bis* of the Law, enacted in 1955, provides in effect that the works of Swiss nationals, and works first published (*éditées, herausgegeben*) in Switzerland, enjoy the more extended (*plus étendue, weitergehende*) protection granted by the Brussels Convention of the Berne Union. The basic principle of the Universal Copyright Convention is national treatment by virtue of which Switzerland would have to grant, in all respects, the same protection to nationals of countries party to the Universal Copyright Convention (and to works first published in such countries) as it grants to its own nationals. Consequently, it could be argued that the "plus" protection guaranteed to Swiss works must also be granted to Convention works. On the other hand, the very specific

[4] Article 6 (2), last sentence.
[5] Pages 11 and 110, above.

character of the provision contained in Article 68*bis*, namely, that it extends certain provisions of the *Brussels* Convention to *Swiss* works, throws some doubt on the correctness of an interpretation according to which Switzerland would extend the said "plus" protection to works which are not Swiss and which may not originate in a country member of the Berne Union. Since, however, the protection granted by the Brussels Convention does not seem to be "more extended" than the protection existing under the Swiss Copyright Act (other than its Article 68*bis*), it appears to be largely superfluous to try to solve the question. In any case, the following analysis is limited to the Swiss Copyright Law and disregards any additional protection which may or may not be available under the combined application of Article 68*bis*, the Brussels Convention, and the national treatment provisions of the Universal Copyright Convention.

Acquisition of copyright is not subject to the fulfilment of any formality in Switzerland.[6] Consequently, registration, deposit, or compliance with other formalities is neither required nor possible in Switzerland, and the absence, in itself, of the Convention notice on the copies of a published work is no bar to claiming protection in Switzerland. Furthermore, Switzerland has no renewal system, so there is nothing in this country which would correspond to the renewal formalities existing, for example, in the United States.

PROTECTED WORKS

All literary and artistic works are protected.[7] Literary and musical works are protected even when they are not written or fixed in some other manner unless, by their nature, they can come into existence only through fixation in some form.[8] Photographic works, including works obtained by processes analogous to photography, are protected.[9]

The Law expressly mentions, as examples, the following categories of works, as coming under the general expression "literary and artistic works": works of *belles lettres*; scientific works; geographical and topographical maps and other figurative representations of a scientific or technical nature; choreographic works; pantomimes; actions (*arrangements scéniques, Handlungen*) fixed by cinematography or by analogous means of art (*œuvres des arts figuratifs, Werke der bildenden Künste*), such as works of drawing, painting, sculpture, architecture, engraving, lithography, and of applied art.[10]

Compilations (*recueils, Sammlungen*) are protected as works, without

---

[6] However, it is lawful to reproduce in the press topical articles relating to economics, politics or religion *if their reproduction is not expressly reserved* or if they are not expressly designated as original contributions or original reports (art. 25 (2)).

[7] Article 1 (1).　　[8] Article 1 (2).　　[9] Article 2.　　[10] Article 1 (2).

prejudice to the copyright subsisting in the individual works included therein.[11]

Translations, and other adaptations (*reproductions, Wiedergaben*) constituting original literary, artistic or photographic works, are protected, subject to the copyright in the works from which they were derived.[12,13]

The mere fact that a work has been, either in its finished form or as a project, deposited as an industrial design (*dessin ou modèle, Muster oder Modell*) does not deprive it of protection under the Copyright Law.[14]

PROTECTED PERSONS

Generally.—Only physical persons may be authors, so that copyright always vests originally in the creator (*in der Person des geistig Schöpfenden*). This holds also in the case of cinematographic works.[15]

Collaboration.—Persons who have jointly created a work in such a manner that their respective contributions cannot be separated possess, as collaborators, a common copyright in the work. They can dispose of it only jointly, but each of them may prosecute infringers by himself.[16]

Presumptions of Authorship.—In the absence of proof to the contrary, the author of the work is deemed to be: (i) the physical person whose true name is indicated upon the copies of the work in the manner in which authors generally are indicated upon such copies,[17] (ii) the physical person who, in connection with the public recitation, performance or exhibition of the work, or in connection with the public exhibition of copies (*exemplaires, Werkexemplare*) of the work, is named as author by his true name.[18]

Anonymous and Pseudonymous Works.—In the case of a published (*édité, herausgegeben*) work, the author of which is not indicated

---

[11] Article 3.   [12] Article 4 (1) and (3).
[13] Although sound recordings are specifically mentioned among adaptations, the highest Swiss court held that performing artists did not enjoy any copyright in them; and that the maker of the recording merely enjoyed protection against unauthorized copying and not also against boradcasting, public performance or other exploitation (Judgment of Dec. 8, 1959, No. 6251/ES, published in Entscheidungen des Schweizerischen Bundesgerichtes, 86, II, 1).
[14] Article 5.
[15] Swiss Federal Tribunal (the highest court in Switzerland) in Suisa *vs.* Koch, Entscheidungen des Schweizerischen Bundesgerichtes, 1958, Vol. 74, Part II, page 106.
[16] Article 7.
[17] In the case of works of art or photography, the application of a distinctive sign referring to the author is sufficient (art. 8 (1)).
[18] Article 8 (1).

in the manner creating the presumptions referred to above, the person who caused the work to appear (*celui qui l'a fait paraître, Herausgeber*), or if such person is not designated, the publisher (*l'éditeur, Herausgeber*) is responsible for the safeguarding of copyright, and, in the absence of proof to the contrary, he will be deemed to be the successor in title (*ayant cause, Rechtsnachfolger*) of the author.[19]

Portraits.—In the absence of agreement to the contrary, copies of a commissioned portrait may' not be put into circulation or made available for public disclosure without the authorization of the person portrayed.[20]

ASSIGNMENT AND LICENSING

General Rules of Interpretation.—The transfer of one of the rights comprised in copyright does not imply the transfer of other rights comprised in copyright.[21] Transfer of the property in a copy of a work does not imply transfer of the copyright therein, even if what is transferred is the original copy.[22]

Publishing Contracts.—The Code of Obligations contains a definition of publishing contracts,[23] makes the transferor of the right of publication responsible for the undisturbed enjoyment of the right by the publisher,[24] regulates the author's residual rights in certain articles and contributions to collective works,[25] his right to make alterations in later editions,[26] the publisher's obligation to render accounts and give free copies to the transferor of the right,[27] and the consequences of the loss of the manuscript[28] or of the edition.[29] If the publishing contract authorizes the publication of several or all editions of a work, and if the publisher fails to prepare a new edition after the exhaustion of the previous one, the court may be asked to fix a deadline for the publication of the new edition; if the publisher fails to comply, his right lapses.[30] The publisher is responsible for reproduction in a suitable form, without abbreviations, additions or other modifications.[31] The right to re-

---

[19] Article 8 (2).
[20] Article 35 (1). If he is dead or otherwise not available, the Law prescribes who may exercise the right.
[21] Article 9 (2).   [22] Article 9 (3).
[23] Code of Obligations, article 380.
[24] Code of Obligations, article 381.
[25] Code of Obligations, article 382.
[26] Code of Obligations, article 385.
[27] Code of Obligations, article 389.
[28] Code of Obligations, article 390.
[29] Code of Obligations, article 391.
[30] Code of Obligations, article 383.
[31] Code of Obligations, article 384.

muneration by the publisher is presumed, unless the circumstances indicate a contrary intention.[32] The right to publish separately different works of the same author is not presumed to include the right to publish them in the form of a collection,[33] and the right to publish the complete works of an author, or a category of his works, is not presumed to include the right to publish the works separately.[34] Transfer of the right of publication is not presumed to include transfer of the right of translation.[35] The contract of publication is terminated by operation of law if, before completion of the work, the author dies, becomes incapable, or, through no fault of his own, is unable to finish the work.[36] When one or more authors undertake to prepare a work according to a plan furnished by the publisher, they may only claim such payment as has been agreed upon; the copyright in this case belongs to the publisher.[37]

PROTECTED RIGHTS

ECONOMIC RIGHTS

Copyright includes the following exclusive rights:

(a) *to reproduce* (*reproduire, wiedergeben*) the work by any process,[38] in the original form or in a modified form.[39] The latter includes (i) translation, (ii) transfer (*adapter, übertragen*) on contrivances capable of mechanical recitation or performance, (iii) reproduction by means of cinematography or other similar processes,[40] (iv) the realization (carrying out, *exécution, Ausführung*) of plans of figurative works of a scientific nature, architectural works, works of applied art, or any other works of art.[41] The transfer of musical works on contrivances capable of mechanical performance, however, is, in certain circumstances, subject to compulsory license.[42] Copyright in a musical work

[32] Code of Obligations, article 388 (1).
[33] Code of Obligations, article 386 (1).
[34] Code of Obligations, article 386 (2).
[35] Code of Obligations, article 387.
[36] Code of Obligations, article 392 (1).
[37] Code of Obligations, article 393.
[38] Article 12 (1), item (1).   [39] Article 13 (1).
[40] Articles 17 to 20.   [41] Article 14.
[42] Any person having an industrial establishment in Switzerland (or in the United States of America; *see* Decree of the Federal Council of September 26, 1924) is entitled to require, against the payment of an equitable remuneration, authorization to adapt a musical work to contrivances capable of performing it mechanically (i) if the author is dead and the work has been published, or, (ii) if, being alive, he has already given a like authorization extending to Switzerland or any other country and the instruments to which the work has been adapted have been placed upon the market or the work has been published in some other manner. The authorization has effect only in respect of circulation of the contrivances in Switzerland and their export to countries where the work enjoys no protection against an adaptation of this nature. The same principles apply to the text of musical works. *See* articles 17, 18, 19, 20.

does not extend to the use of its melody when a new and original work results from such use.[43] Copyright in a photographic work does not exclude the right of any other person to take a new photograph of the same object, even if such new photograph is taken from the same position and, in a general manner, under the same conditions as the first photograph;[44]

(b) *to sell, place on sale (mettre en vente, feilhalten),* or *put into circulation in any other manner* copies of the work;[45]

(c) *to recite, perform (représenter, exécuter; aufführen, vorführen),* or *exhibit* the work publicly, or *to transmit publicly over wires* the recitation, performance or exhibition of the work;[46]

(d) *to exhibit publicly* copies *(exemplaires, Werkexemplare)* of the work, or *to disclose* the work to the public in any other manner, as long as the work has not been communicated to the public by or with the permission of the owner of the copyright;[47]

(e) *to broadcast* a work or otherwise communicate it to the public by any other means capable to diffuse, without wires, signs, sounds or images;[48]

(f) *to communicate the broadcast work publicly,* over wires or otherwise, when such communication is made by an organization other than the originating organization;[49]

(g) *to communicate publicly by loudspeaker* or by any other like instrument transmitting signs, sounds or images, the broadcast work or the work publicly transmitted over wires.[50]

---

[43] Article 15.   [44] Article 16.   [45] Article 12 (1), item (2).

[46] Article 12 (1), item (3). In the case of the public performance of a musical work with words, the owner of the right of performance in the musical work is, in relation to third parties, deemed to have the right to authorize also the public performance of the words (art. 34 (1)). Persons providing a place for unlawful recitation, performance, exhibition or display are civilly responsible only if they were aware of the unlawful character of these acts (art. 60). Any person who utilizes, for public recitation, performance, exhibition *(exhibition, Vorführung),* or broadcast, of a work, copies which have been manufactured or put into circulation in an unlawful manner is an infringer (art. 42 (2)), unless he has acquired the copies in good faith at a public auction, in the market, or from a person dealing in objects of like kind, and if, prior to the recitation, performance or exhibition, he was unaware of the unlawful character of the copies so used (art. 61 (1)).

[47] Article 12 (1), item 4. Any person who publicly exhibits *(exposition, Ausstellung)* copies which have been manufactured or put into circulation in an unlawful manner, incurs no responsibility if he has acquired the copies in good faith at a public auction, in the market, or from a person dealing in objects of like kind, and if, prior to the exhibition, he was unaware of the unlawful character of the copies exhibited (art. 61 (2)).

[48] Article 12 (1), item 5, and (2).   [49] Article 12 (1), item 6.

[50] Article 12 (1), item 7.

Moral Rights

The provisions of the Civil Code and the Code of Obligations protecting the person (*personnalité, Persönlichkeit*) are expressly reserved by the Law.[51] The highest court in Switzerland held that it follows from those provisions that (i) the author has the right to his name's appearing, without alteration, on his work, and that no other name appear on such work, (ii) the author has the right to oppose any deformation, mutilation, or other alteration of his work in a way which would prejudice his honour or reputation.[52] Remedies for violation of moral rights must be claimed within a short time after the plaintiff acquires knowledge of the violation.[53] Any person who, in such a manner as to deceive others, applies the name of the author, his distinctive sign or his pseudonym to the copies of a reproduction not emanating from the author himself, or to the copies of an original work of another person, is liable both civilly and criminally.[54]

Limitations

Except for the construction of works of architecture,[55] the reproduction of a work is free if the reproduction is destined exclusively for the personal and private use of the person reproducing it; such reproduction may not be made for profit.[56] The Law also contains limitations or exceptions *in certain cases* of: reproduction or other uses of speeches delivered in public meetings,[57] reproduction of newspaper and magazine articles,[58] reproduction of literary and musical works in scientific works,[59] reproduction of literary works in school textbooks,[60] reproduction of musical or dramatic works in preparation of their public performance,[61] reproduction of works of art or photography in a school book or catalogue or when they are permanently located in a public place,[62] reproduction of commissioned portraits,[63] reproduction of the text of musical works for distribution to the audience,[64] reporting of current events by means of photography, cinematography or broadcasting.[65]

[51] Article 44; Civil Code, arts. 27 to 29; Code of Obligations, article 49.
[52] Collombet *vs.* Union des Banques Suisses, Strittmatter & Kurz, Entscheidungen des Schweizerischen Bundesgerichtes, 1932, Volume 58, Part II, page 290.
[53] The highest court of Switzerland held that the actual author preserves his so-called "*Individual-Idealrecht*" (personal intangible right) even where he has alienated his copyrights. Entscheidungen des Schweizerischen Bundesgerichtes, 1931, Volume 57, Part II, page 72.
[54] So held by the highest court of Switzerland in Stöcklin *vs.* Kanton Aargau, Entscheidungen des Schweizerischen Bundesgerichtes, 1943, Volume 69, Part II, page 53.
[55] Article 43.
[56] Article 22. *See also* article 42 (2).
[57] Articles 24 and 31.   [58] Articles 25 and 31.   [59] Articles 26 and 31.
[60] Articles 27 and 31.   [61] Article 28.   [62] Articles 29 and 31.
[63] Articles 30 and 31.   [64] Article 32.   [65] Article 33 bis.

TERM OF PROTECTION

Protection ends at the expiration of the fiftieth calendar year following the death of the author.[66] However, where the work is (i) anonymous, or (ii) pseudonymous and the pseudonym leaves doubt as to the author's identity, protection ends at the expiration of the fiftieth calendar year following the year in which the work was made public (*rendre publique, öffentliche Bekanntgabe*), provided the identity of the author is not revealed before the expiration of this period.[67]

Since there is no provision in Swiss law for the "rule of the shorter term" permitted under Article IV (4) of the Universal Copyright Conventions, it would appear that works are protected in Switzerland until the expiration of the terms indicated above even if in other countries they fall into the public domain at an earlier date.

INFRINGEMENTS

Generally.—Acts requiring the consent of the owner of copyright, if committed without his consent, constitute infringements.[68] Furthermore, it is a violation of the law to apply, in such a manner as to deceive others, the name of the author, his distinctive sign or his pseudonym, to the original work or to copies not authorized by the author.[69] Infringing copies (other than buildings) and objects serving exclusively for the manufacture of infringing copies may be seized[70] and confiscated.[71] If copies of a work (other than sound recordings) lawfully manufactured are put into circulation outside the territory for which the owner of the copyright has authorized their sale, such putting into circulation does not constitute infringement within the meaning of the Copyright Law, but the plaintiff may seek remedy on the grounds of breach of contract.[72]

Civil Remedies.—The general provisions of the Code of Obligations apply even if the violation is committed outside Switzerland but to the detriment of a person domiciled in Switzerland.[73]

Penal Sanctions.—Penal sanctions apply only where the violation was intentional,[74] and penal proceeding takes place only upon complaint of the injured private party.[75] Violations are punished by fines,[76] and action prescribed within three years.[77]

[66] Articles 36, 37, 38, 41. In the case of works of collaboration, the death of the last surviving co-author governs (art. 39).
[67] Articles 36, 37, 38, 41. In the case of works consisting of independent separate parts made public at different times, each part is considered a "work" (art. 40 (1)). In the case of works appearing in instalments, the date of the making public of the last instalment governs (art. 40 (2)).
[68] *See above*, "Economic Rights," page 536.
[69] Article 43, item 1. *See also* items 2 and 3 of the same article.
[70] Articles 52, 53, 55.   [71] Articles 54 and 55.   [72] Article 58.   [73] Article 44.
[74] Article 46.   [75] Article 47.   [76] Article 50.   [77] Article 51 (1).

UNITED KINGDOM
OF GREAT BRITAIN AND NORTHERN IRELAND

SOURCES

Internal Law.—The main source is the Copyright Act, 1956, 4 & 5 Eliz. 2 Ch. 74, dated November 5, 1956 (hereinafter referred to as the "Act"). It came into force on June 1, 1957. This Act is supplemented by a number of Orders, Regulations and Rules.[1] Hereinafter, references to Sections, without further specification, are references to Sections of this Act.

Universal Copyright Convention.—The United Kingdom became bound by the Universal Copyright Convention and Protocols 1 and 2 on September 27, 1957.[2]

The protection that the United Kingdom grants to works on account of the Universal Copyright Convention and the Conventions of the Berne Copyright Union is regulated in The Copyright (International Conventions) Order, 1957,[3] and its amendments.[4] This Order, as amended, is hereinafter referred to as the "Order."

[1] The Copyright (Notice of Publication) Regulations, 1957 (Statutory Instruments, 1957, No. 865); The Copyright (Libraries) Regulations, 1957 (Statutory Instruments, 1957, No. 868); The Copyright Royalty System (Records) Regulations, 1957 (Statutory Instruments, 1957, No. 866); The Copyright (Industrial Designs) Rules, 1957 (Statutory Instruments, 1957, No. 867); Copyright (Customs) Regulations, 1957 (Statutory Instruments, 1957, No. 875); The Performing Right Tribunal Rules, 1957 (Statutory Instruments, 1957, No. 924; 1959, No. 1170; 1960, No. 2428). These texts are reprinted in the CLTW, United Kingdom, as Items 1 through 7.

The copyright statute dates from 1956. Consequently, there are not many court decisions interpreting its various provisions. A good source for the rationale of the statute can be found in "Report on the Committee on the Law of Copyright, 1952, Cd. 8662."

"Copinger and Skone James on the Law of Copyright," Ninth Edition, by F. E. Skone James and E. P. Skone James, published at London by Sweet & Maxwell, Limited, in 1958, is the best known manual on British copyright law. It analyzes and comments upon both the 1956 Act and its predecessor, the 1911 Act.

Another commentary on the 1956 Act is "The Law of Copyright" by J. P. Eddy, published by Butterworth & Co. (Publishers) Ltd., at London in 1957.

[2] CLTW, United Kingdom: Item 8.

[3] Dated August 23, 1957, and published in Statutory Instruments, 1957, under No. 1523. See CLTW, United Kingdom: Item 8. The United Kingdom is a member of the Berne Union since the creation of that Union. It has ratified all the Conventions of the Union, including that of Brussels, 1948.

[4] Among these The Copyright (International Conventions) (Amendment) Order,

ACQUISITION OF PROTECTION UNDER THE UNIVERSAL COPYRIGHT CONVENTION

In the following, a country party to the Universal Copyright Convention will be referred to as a "Convention country."

LITERARY, DRAMATIC, MUSICAL AND ARTISTIC WORKS

If published.—In any of the following cases, that is:

(i) if the first publication of the work took place in a Convention country,[5]

(ii) if, at the time the work was first published, the author was a citizen, subject, domiciliary, or resident, of a Convention country,

(iii) in cases where copyright originally vests in a body corporate, if, at the time the work was first published, such body corporate was incorporated in a Convention country,

(iv) in the case of works first published after the death of the author, if the author was a citizen, subject, domiciliary, or resident, of a Convention country at the time of his death,

(v) if the work was first published by or under the direction of the United Nations, any of the Specialized Agencies of the United Nations, the Organization of American States, the Council of Europe, the Organization for European Economic Cooperation, the Baghdad Pact Organization, or the Western European Union (and the publication agreement did not reserve the copyright, if any, to the author),

the work is protected in the United Kingdom.[6]

If unpublished.—In any of the following cases, that is:

(i) if, at the time the work was made,[7] the author was a citizen, subject, resident or domiciliary, of a Convention country,

(ii) in cases where copyright originally vests in a body corporate,

1958 (Statutory Instruments, 1958, No. 1254) made changes concerning the law; the other Orders merely extended the effect of the Orders to countries later adhering to the Berne or Universal Conventions. All the amending Orders are covered in CLTW, United Kingdom; Item 8.

[5] The Order does not actually speak of Convention countries in general but enumerates them by name and is amended whenever there is a change in membership.

[6] Order, section 1; The Copyright (International Organizations) Order, 1957, of August 23, 1957, and The Copyright (International Organizations) (Amendment) Order, 1958, of June 25, 1958 (published in Statutory Instruments 1957, No. 1524, and 1958, No. 1052; in CLTW, United Kingdom: Item 9); Act, sections 2 (2), 3 (3), 33 (3). If, in the case of a work of joint authorship (i.e., a work produced by the collaboration of two or more authors in which the contribution of each author is not separate from the contribution of the other author or authors; Act, sec. 11 (3)), eligibility for protection turns on citizenship, etc., the work will be protected even if only one of the authors fulfils the said conditions (Act, Third Schedule, sec. 1).

[7] Or, if the making of the work extended over a period, then, for a substantial part of that period (Order, sec. 4 (4)).

if, at the time the work was made, such body corporate was incorporated in a Convention country,

(iii) if the work was made by or under the direction or control of the United Nations, any of its Specialized Agencies, the Organization of American States, the Council of Europe, the Organization for European Economic Cooperation, the Baghdad Pact Organization, or the Western European Union,
the work is protected in the United Kingdom.[8]

Concept of Publication.—A work is published if reproductions thereof have been issued to the public.[9] The following acts do not constitute publication: (i) performance of a literary, dramatic or musical work, (ii) issue of records of a literary, dramatic or musical work, (iii) exhibition of an artistic work, (iv) issue of photographs or engravings of a work of architecture or of a sculpture.[10]

SOUND RECORDINGS

In any of the following cases, that is:

(i) if, at the time when the recording was made (that is, when the first record embodying the recording is produced), the maker was a citizen, subject, resident, domiciliary of, or a body corporate incorporated in, a Convention country,[11]

(ii) if the first publication of the recording took place in a Convention country,[12]
the recording is protected[13] in the United Kingdom.[14]

"Publication," in relation to a sound recording, means the issue to the public of records embodying the recording or any part thereof.[15] "Sound recording" means the aggregate of the sounds embodied in, and capable of being reproduced by means of, a record of any description, other than a sound track associated with a cinematograph film.[16] "Record" means any disc, tape, perforated roll or other device in which sounds are embodied so as to be capable (with or without the aid of some other instrument) of being automatically reproduced therefrom.[17]

[8] Order, section 1; The Copyright (International Organizations) Order, 1957, and The Copyright (International Organizations) (Amendment) Order, 1958, cited in footnote 2, above; in CLTW, United Kingdom: Item 9; Act, sections 2 (1), 3 (2), 33 (2). In case of works of joint authorship the rule referred to under footnote 6, above, applies.
[9] Section 49 (2) (c).   [10] Section 49 (2) (a).
[11] Irrespective of whether the recording is later published, and if it is, irrespective of the place of its first publication (see sec. 12 (1), (2) and (8)).
[12] Irrespective of the citizenship, etc., of the maker of the recording (Act, sec. 12 (2)).
[13] The extent of protection is not the same for all Convention countries. *See* page 550, *infra*.
[14] Order, section 1; Act, section 12 (1) and (2).
[15] Section 12 (9).   [16] Section 12 (9).   [17] Section 48 (1).

CINEMATOGRAPH FILMS

In any of the following cases, that is,

(i) if, for the whole or substantial part of the period during which the film was made, the maker was a citizen, subject, resident, domiciliary of, or a body corporate incorporated in, a Convention country,[18]

(ii) if the first publication of the film took place in a Convention country,[19]

the cinematograph film is protected in the United Kingdom.[20]

In relation to a cinematograph film, "publication" means the sale, letting on hire, or offer for sale or hire, of copies of the film to the public; and "copy" means any print, negative, tape or other article on which the film or part of it is recorded.[21]

PUBLISHED EDITIONS

In any of the following cases, that is:

(i) if the first publication of the edition took place in a Convention country,

(ii) if, at the date of the first publication of the edition, the publisher of such edition was a citizen, subject, resident, domiciliary of, or a body corporate incorporated in, a Convention country,

the edition is protected in the United Kingdom.[22]

An edition shall be taken to have been published if, but only if, reproductions of the edition have been issued to the public.[23]

The protection means that no person is allowed, without the consent of the publisher, to make, by any photographic or similar process, a reproduction of the typographical arrangement of the edition.[24] The protection lasts until the end of the twenty-fifth calendar year following the calendar year in which the edition was first published.[25]

CREATION OR PUBLICATION PRECEDING THE APPLICATION OF THE ORDER TO CONVENTION COUNTRIES

It would seem that *unpublished* works, sound recordings, and cinematograph films, of citizens, etc., of a Convention country *are* protected in

[18] Irrespective of whether the film is later published, and if it is, irrespective of the place of its first publication (*see* Act, sec. 13 (1) and (2)).

[19] Irrespective of the citizenship, etc., of the maker (*see* Act, sec. 13 (2)).

[20] Order, section 1; Act, section 13 (1) and (2).

[21] Section 13 (10).

[22] Order, section 1; Act, section 15 (1).

[23] Section 49 (2) (c).

[24] Act, section 15 (3); however, certain libraries, under specified conditions, may make reproductions without the publisher's consent (sec. 15 (4), and The Copyright (Libraries) Regulations, 1957, of May 17, 1957 (Statutory Instruments, 1957, No. 868; CLTW, United Kingdom: Item 3).

[25] Act, section 15 (2).

the United Kingdom even if they were created prior to the application of the Order to the Convention country on account of its adherence to the Universal Copyright Convention.[26]

On the other hand, it would seem that a work, recording, film, or edition, first *published* in a Convention country prior to such date is not protected in the United Kingdom except if there are other grounds than the Universal Copyright Convention to protect them. Thus, in particular, if the work was first, or "simultaneously" with the first publication, published in a country member of the Berne Union—for example, if the work of a U.S. citizen was first published in 1950 simultaneously in the United States and Canada—it would continue to be protected in the United Kingdom.[27]

General Rules Concerning the Interpretation of the Concept of "Publication"

The following rules of interpretation seem to apply equally to the publication of works, sound recordings, cinematograph films, and editions:

Simultaneous Publication.—A publication in a Convention country is not treated as being other than the first publication by reason only of an earlier publication in a country which is party to neither the Universal Copyright Convention nor the Berne Union if the two publications took place within a period of not more than thirty days.[28]

Colorable Publication.—A publication which is merely colorable and not intended to satisfy the reasonable requirements of the public is not treated as being a publication.[29]

Unauthorized Publication.—A publication effected without the license of the copyright owner (or, if the work is not protected by copyright, without the license of the author or persons lawfully claiming under him) is not treated as being a publication.[30]

Formalities

Subject to one exception relating to sound recordings, discussed below, the United Kingdom has no copyright formalities. Consequently, registration, deposit, or compliance with other formalities is neither

[26] This argument is based on the fact that the Order, section 1, proviso (i), refers only to publication. Acquired rights of other persons are safeguarded (Order, sec. 2).
[27] *See* Act, Seventh Schedule, section 1, and Order, section 1, proviso (i). Acquired rights are safeguarded (Order, sec. 2).
[28] Section 49 (2) (d).
[29] Section 49 (2) (b)—except in so far as it may constitute an infringement of the copyright.
[30] Section 49 (3).

required nor possible in the United Kingdom. The absence, in itself, of the Convention notice on the copies of a published work is no bar to claiming protection in the United Kingdom. Furthermore, the United Kingdom has no renewal system, so there is nothing in this country which would correspond to the renewal formalities existing in the United States. Protection in the United Kingdom will last, without any intervention by the copyright owner or a State authority, until the day on which the work or other subject matter of copyright falls into the public domain.

The exception referred to above is the following: Copyright in a sound recording is not protected if any of the records issued to the public in the United Kingdom, or the containers in which they were so issued, failed to bear a label or other mark indicating the year in which the recording was first published.[31] This rule does not apply (i) if it is shown that the records were not issued by or with the license of the owner of the copyright in the recording, or, (ii) if it is shown that such owner had taken all reasonable steps for securing that records embodying the recording would not be issued to the public in the United Kingdom without the said label or mark.[32]

PROTECTED WORKS AND OTHER PROTECTED SUBJECT MATTER

INTRODUCTORY

The Act grants copyright in works and other subject matter. The designation "works" is reserved for literary, dramatic, musical, and artistic works. The other "subject matter" of copyright may be (i) sound recordings, (ii) cinematograph films, (iii) television and sound broadcasts, (iv) published editions of works.

Copyright in television and sound broadcasts is not dealt with in this book because it is available only to the British Broadcasting Corporation and the Independent Television Authority, and to television broadcasts made from countries named in the Copyright (Foreign Television Broadcasts) Order 1961, and the Copyright (Foreign Television Broadcasts) (Amendment) Order 1962, that is, France, Sweden and Denmark. It is not available under the Universal Copyright Convention.

Copyright in published editions of works has been discussed above (page 543), and will be disregarded in the following.

---

[31] Section 12 (6).   [32] Section 12 (6), proviso.

WORKS

The following, if original, are protected as works:

(i) **Literary Works.**[33]—These include any written table or compilation.[34] Literary works are protected only if they are reduced to writing or some other material form.[35]

(ii) **Dramatic Works.**[36]—They are protected only if they are reduced to writing or some other material form.[37] The category of dramatic works include choreographic works, and entertainments in dumb show, if reduced to writing in the form in which the work or entertainment is to be presented.[38] "Dramatic works" include the scenario or script for a cinematograph film but not the cinematograph film itself.[39]

(iii) **Musical Works.**[40]—They are protected only if they are reduced to writing or some other material form.[41]

(iv) **Artistic Works.**—They are:
—paintings, irrespective of artistic quality;
—sculptures (including any cast or model made for purposes of sculpture), irrespective of artistic quality;
—drawings (including diagrams, maps, charts and plans), irrespective of artistic quality;
—engravings (including etchings, lithographs, woodcuts, prints, and similar works, but not photographs), irrespective of artistic quality;
—photographs (that is, any product of photography or of any process akin to photography, other than a part of a cinematograph film), irrespective of artistic quality;
—works of architecture, being either buildings (structures) or models for buildings, as long as they are artistic;
—works of artistic craftsmanship, not falling within any of the preceding categories, as long as they have artistic quality.[42]

SOUND RECORDINGS

See the definition of sound recordings on page 542, footnote 16, above.

CINEMATOGRAPH FILMS

"Cinematograph film" means any sequence of visual images recorded on material of any description (whether translucent or not) so as to

---

[33] Section 2.   [34] Section 48 (1).   [35] *See* Section 49 (4).   [36] Section 2.
[37] *See* section 49 (4).   [38] Section 48 (1).   [39] Section 48 (1).
[40] Section 2.   [41] *See* section 49 (4).
[42] Sections 3 (1) and 48 (1). As to the effect of (i) reprinting a design under the Registered Designs Act corresponding to the artistic work, or (ii) selling articles to which unregistered designs corresponding to the artistic work have been applied, *see* section 10.

be capable, by the use of that material: (i) of being shown as a moving picture, (ii) of being recorded on other material (whether translucent or not) by the use of which it can be so shown.[43]

A cinematograph film is taken to include the sounds embodied in the sound track associated with the film.[44]

"Sound track associated with the film" means any record of sounds (i) which is incorporated in any print, negative, tape or other article on which the film or part of it, insofar as it consists of visual images, is recorded, or (ii) which is issued by the maker of the film for use in conjunction with such an article.[45]

PROTECTED PERSONS

Works

Copyright in a literary, dramatic, musical, or artistic work originally vests in its author,[46] subject to the following exceptions or qualifications:

Photographs.—Copyright in a photograph originally vests in the person who, at the time when the photograph is taken, owns the material on which it is taken.[47] Unless otherwise provided by contract, where a person commissions the taking of a photograph and pays or agrees to pay for it in money or money's worth, copyright vests in him rather than in the owner of the material on which the photograph was taken.[48]

Commissioned Portrait Paintings or Drawings, Commissioned Engravings.—Unless otherwise provided by contract, where a person commissions the painting or drawing of a portrait, or the making of any kind of engraving, and pays or agrees to pay for it in money or money's worth, copyright vests in him rather than in the artist.[49]

Works for Newspapers, etc.—Unless otherwise provided by contract, where a literary, dramatic or artistic (but not musical) work is made by the author in the course of his employment by the proprietor of a newspaper, magazine or similar periodical under a contract of service or apprenticeship (and is so made for the purpose of publication in a newspaper, magazine, or similar periodical), the copyright is split between the said proprietor and the author: (i) the said proprietor is entitled to the copyright insofar as it relates to publication in any newspaper, magazine or similar periodical; (ii) the author is entitled to the copyright in all other respects.[50]

Works of Employees.—Unless otherwise provided by contract,

[43] Section 13 (10).   [44] Section 13 (9).   [45] Section 13 (10).
[46] Section 4 (1).   [47] Section 48 (1).   [48] Section 4 (3) and (4).
[49] Section 4 (3) and (4).   [50] Section 4 (2).

and except where any of the rules referred to in the preceding three paragraphs apply, where a work is made in the course of the author's employment by another person under a contract of service or apprenticeship, copyright vests originally in such other person rather than in the author.[51]

Sound Recordings

Copyright in a sound recording originally vests in its maker.[52] "Maker" is the person who owns the record embodying the recording at the time when the recording is made.[53] In the absence of any agreement to the contrary, where a person commissions the making of a sound recording, and pays or agrees to pay for it in money or money's worth, copyright will vest in him rather than in the maker.[54] As to the meaning of "recording" and "record," *see* page 542, *above*.

Cinematograph Films

Copyright in a cinematograph film originally vests in its maker.[55] "Maker" means the person by whom the arrangements necessary for the making of the film are undertaken.[56]

PROTECTED RIGHTS

GENERALLY

Copyright means the exclusive right to do, and to authorize other persons to do, certain acts.[57]

Literary, Dramatic, and Musical Works

In relation to literary, dramatic, and musical works, the following acts require the authorization of the owner of copyright:[58]
—*Reproducing the Work in Any Material Form*.[59] This includes reproducing the work in the form of a record or of a cinematograph film.[60] The record of a work is any disc, tape, perforated roll, or other device, in which sounds are embodied, and by means of which the work may be performed.[61] In certain cases, the making of records of musical works is subject to a legal license, rather than to consent by the owner of the

---

[51] Section 4 (4) and (5).   [52] Section 12 (4).   [53] Section 12 (8).
[54] Section 12 (4), proviso.   [55] Section 13 (4).   [56] Section 13 (10).
[57] Section 1 (1). Exceptions and qualifications are mentioned in the appropriate places, *below*.
[58] *See* section 49 (5).   [59] Section 2 (5) (a).   [60] Section 48 (1).
[61] Section 48 (1).

copyright.[62] In certain cases, reproduction in the form of record or cinematograph film for broadcasting purposes does not require authorization.[63]

—*Publishing the Work*.[64] This seems to include not only first but also subsequent publications, i.e., the issuance of reproductions to the public. The issuing of photographs or engravings of a work of architecture or of a sculpture is not publication.[65]

—*Performing the Work in Public*.[66] Performance includes any mode of visual or acoustic presentation, including presentation (i) by the operation of wireless telegraphy apparatus (for example by a radio or television receiving set), (ii) by the exhibition of a cinematograph film, (iii) by the use of a record. Where performance is done by a radio or television receiving set or an apparatus playing records, for example, a coin-operated record player (jukebox), it is the occupier of the premises where the apparatus is, with his consent, situated, who is considered to be the person giving the performance.[67] Performance also includes the delivery of lectures, addresses, speeches or sermons.[68]

The following acts are not considered performance: (i) broadcasting, (ii) transmission to subscribers to a diffusion service, (iii) transmission to (*but not* display or emission by) a receiving apparatus.[69]

—*Broadcasting the Work*.[70] Broadcasting is broadcasting by wireless telegraphy, whether by way of sound broadcasting or of television.[71]

—*Causing the Work to be Transmitted to Subscribers to a Diffusion Service*.[72] This means transmission of the work in the course of a service of distributing (i) broadcast programs, or (ii) other programs, whether, in both cases, the program was provided by the person operating the service or by other persons. The distribution must be over wires, or other paths provided by a material substance, to the premises of the subscribers to the service. Where the service is only incidental to a business of keeping or letting premises where persons reside or sleep, and is operated as part of the amenities provided exclusively or mainly for

---

[62] Section 8. Manufacturers are entitled to make, for the purposes of retail sale, records of musical works which have once been recorded with the consent of the copyright owner, provided they pay him the statutory royalty and give him the prescribed notice of their intention to make the record concerned. In such cases, then, the consent of the owner of the copyright is not needed. Generally, the royalty is equal to 6.25 per cent of the ordinary retail selling price of the record.
[63] Section 6 (7), discussed on page 552, below.
[64] Section 2 (5) (b).   [65] Copinger, p. 176; section 49 (2) (a).
[66] Section 2 (5) (c). The Performing Right Tribunal may, in certain cases, force the granting of licenses or prescribe the conditions thereof (secs. 23 to 30).
[67] Section 48 (6).   [68] Section 48 (1).   [69] Section 48 (5).
[70] Section 2 (5) (d). The Performing Right Tribunal may, in certain cases, force the granting of licenses or prescribe the conditions thereof (secs. 28 to 30).
[71] Section 48 (2).
[72] Section 2 (5) (e). The Performing Right Tribunal may, in certain cases, force the granting of licenses or prescribe the conditions thereof (secs. 23 to 30).

residents or inmates, the service is not considered a "diffusion service."[73] The person operating the diffusion service is not liable for any infringement if he transmitted the program of the British Broadcasting Corporation or the Independent Television Authority.[74] Where the diffusion service uses programs of other (non-United Kingdom) broadcasting organizations, the Performance Right Tribunal may, in certain cases, make the use of the works free or may prescribe the amount of the license fee.[75]

—*Making any Adaptation of the Work*.[76] This includes, in relation to a musical work, its arrangement or transcription,[77] and in relation to a literary or dramatic work any of the following: (i) translation, (ii) the making of a dramatic work of a non-dramatic work, and vice versa, (iii) the making of a version of the work in which the story or action is conveyed wholly or mainly by means of pictures in a form suitable for reproduction in a book, or in a newspaper, magazine or similar periodical (for example, the "comic-strip treatment").[78]

—*Doing, in Relation to an Adaptation of the Work, Any of the Above Acts*.[79] For example, performance of a translation of a dramatic work. Unless the owner of the copyright in the original work and in the translation is the same person, exploitation of a translation will thus normally require two authorizations: that of the owner of the copyright in the original work and that of the owner of the copyright in the translation.[80]

ARTISTIC WORKS

In relation to artistic works, the following acts require the authorization of the owner of copyright:[81]

—*Reproducing the work in any material form*.[82] This includes a version produced by converting the two-dimensional work into a three-dimensional form, and vice versa.[83]

—*Publishing the work*.[84]

—*Including the work in a television broadcast*.[85]

—*Causing a television program which includes the work to be transmitted to subscribers to a diffusion service*.[86]

SOUND RECORDINGS

In relation to sound recordings, the following acts require the authorization of the owner of the copyright[87] (that is, generally, of the

[73] Section 48 (3).   [74] Section 40 (3).   [75] Section 28.
[76] Section 2 (5) (f).   [77] Section 2 (6) (b).   [78] Section 2 (6) (a).
[79] Section 2 (5) (g).   [80] *See* Copinger, p. 158.   [81] *See* section 49 (5).
[82] Section 3 (5) (a).   [83] Section 48 (1).   [84] Section 3 (5) (b).
[85] Section 3 (5) (c).
[86] Section 3 (5) (d). The provisions referred to under footnotes 17 and 18, above, also apply here (sec. 48 (3)).
[87] *See* section 49 (5).

maker of the sound recording), whether, in doing them, the record embodying the recording is utilized directly or indirectly:

—*Making a record embodying the recording.*[88]

—*Causing the recording to be heard in public,*[89] but only if the recording was first published in, or the maker of the first record was a citizen, subject, resident, domiciliary, or corporation of Australia, Canada, Ceylon, Denmark, the Federal Republic of Germany, India, Ireland, Israel, Italy, New Zealand, Nigeria, Norway, Pakistan, South Africa, Spain, Switzerland,[90] or the United Kingdom.[91] Causing the recording to be heard in public does not require the authorization of the maker in the following cases: (i) if it is done at any premises where persons reside or sleep, as part of the amenities provided exclusively or mainly for residents or inmates, provided no special charge is made for admission to such premises;[92] (ii) if it is done as part of the activities of, or for the benefit of a club, society or other organization which is not conducted for profit and whose main objects are charitable or are otherwise concerned with the advancement of religion, education or social welfare, provided that, if a charge of admission is made, all proceeds go to the organization.[93] Where the recording is caused to be heard in public through the operation of a radio or television receiving set, the operator of the receiving set does not require the maker's authorization.[94] Causing the recording to be heard in public by a coin-operated record player (jukebox) requires the authorization of the maker.[95] The person who needs to secure the authorization is the occupier of the premises on which, with his consent, the receiving set or record playing apparatus is operated.[96]

—*Broadcasting the recording,*[97] but only if the recording was first published in, or the maker of the first record was a citizen, subject, resident, domiciliary, or corporation of Australia, Canada, Denmark, Ceylon, the Federal Republic of Germany, India, Ireland, Israel, Italy, New Zealand, Nigeria, Norway, Pakistan, South Africa, Spain, Switzerland,[98] or the United Kingdom.[99]

---

[88] Section 12 (5) (e).

[89] Section 12 (5) (b). The Performing Right Tribunal may, in certain cases, force the granting of licenses or prescribe certain conditions thereof (secs. 23 to 30).

[90] Order, section 1, proviso (iii).

[91] Section 12 (1) and (2).

[92] Section 12 (7).

[93] Section 12 (7). The Performing Right Tribunal may reduce or exempt the license fee even in cases where the exemption otherwise would not apply (sec. 29 (5)).

[94] Section 40 (1). *See also* section 28 (4).

[95] Section 48 (6).   [96] Section 48 (6).

[97] Section 12 (5) (c). The Performing Right Tribunal may, in certain cases, force the granting of licenses or prescribe certain conditions thereof (secs. 28 to 30).

[98] Order, section 1, proviso (iii).

[99] Section 12 (1) and (2).

CINEMATOGRAPH FILMS

In relation to cinematograph films, the following acts require the authorization of the owner of the copyright[100] (that is, generally, of the maker of the film):

—*Making a copy of the film.*[101] "Copy" means any print, negative, tape or other article on which the film or part of it is recorded.[102]

—*Causing the film, insofar as it consists of visual images, to be seen in public, or insofar as it consists of sound, to be heard in public.*[103] These acts do not constitute infringement, by the person causing them,[104] even if done without the consent of the maker, if they are effected through the reception of a broadcast of the British Broadcasting Corporation or the Independent Television Authority using the film.[105]

—*Broadcasting the film.*[106]

—*Causing the film to be transmitted to subscribers to a diffusion service.*[107]

EXCEPTIONS AND LIMITATIONS RELATING TO WORKS

Fair Dealing.—No fair dealing with works is an infringement if it done for the purpose of:

—research or private study;[108]

—criticism or review;[109]

—reporting current events (i) in a newspaper, magazine or similar periodical, or (ii) by means of broadcasting, or in a cinematograph film.[110]

Other Exceptions Concerning Specified Uses of Works are provided in connection with certain (i) judicial proceedings,[111] (ii) readings or recitations of reasonable extracts,[112] (iii) school and other educational uses,[113] (iv) fixations for and by the broadcaster,[114] (vi)

[100] *See* section 49 (5). Where the sounds embodied in the sound track of a film are also embodied in a record (other than a record directly or indirectly derived from the sound track), the copyright in the film is not infringed by any use made of the record (sec. 13 (9)).

[101] Section 13 (5) (a), but not if copying is made for the purposes of a judicial proceeding (sec. 13 (6)).

[102] Section 13 (10).

[103] Section 13 (5) (b), but not if this is done for the purposes of a judicial proceeding (sec. 13 (6)).

[104] But they may influence the liability of the BBC or the ITA if the broadcast was not authorized by the owner of the copyright in the film (secs. 40 (4) and (5)).

[105] Section 40 (2).   [106] Section 13 (5) (c).

[107] Section 13 (5) (d). The Principles expressed in connection with footnotes 48 and 49, above, apply here too.

[108] Sections 6 (1) and 9 (1).

[109] Sections 6 (2) and 9 (2), provided it is accompanied by sufficient acknowledgment (sec. 6 (9)).

[110] Section 6 (3). This provision does not apply to artistic works.

[111] Sections 6 (4) and 9 (7).

[112] Section 6 (5).   [113] Sections 6 (6) and 41.   [114] Section 6 (7).

copying and publication of some, more than a century old, manuscripts kept in libraries, museums or similar institutions,[115,116] (vii) photographing, etc., of artistic works permanently situated in a public place,[117] (viii) inclusions of an artistic work in films or telecasts,[118] (ix) making of objects in three dimensions reproducing a two-dimensional artistic work if the objects would not appear, to non-experts, to be reproductions,[119] (x) using, by an author, part of his earlier artistic work in his later artistic works as a secondary feature,[120] (xi) reconstructions of buildings.[121]

ASSIGNMENT AND LICENSING

Assignments.—Copyright is transmissible by assignment, by testamentary disposition, or by operation of law, as personal and movable property.[122] The assignment of the material object does not necessarily transfer the title to the copyright. For example, the purchaser of a painting can only obtain the right to reproduction of the work he has purchased by insisting upon an assignment of the copyright or, at least, a license.

Assignment may be partial as to time, country and rights.[123] Assignments (and exclusive licenses, see below) must be in writing.[124]

Licenses.—A *"simple"* (i.e., non-exclusive) license is binding upon every successor in title to the licensor's interest in the copyright, except a purchaser in good faith for valuable consideration and without actual or constructive notice of the license.[125] It need not be in writing, that is, it may be oral or implied from conduct.

An *"exclusive"* license authorizes the licensee to exercise a certain right or rights to the exclusion of any other person, including the grantor of the license.[126] It must be in writing.[127] The standing in court proceedings of an exclusive licensee is rather similar to that of an assignee.[128]

Assignment of Future Copyright.—"Future copyright" means copyright which will or may come into existence in respect to a work or other subject matter not yet in existence at the time the contract of assignment is concluded ("future work").[129]

[115] Section 7 (1), (2), (3), (4), (5), (9), and (10).
[116] Section 7 (6) to (10).
[117] Section 9 (3), (4) and (6).
[118] Section 9 (5) and (6).
[119] Section 9 (8).   [120] Section 9 (9).   [121] Section 9 (10).
[122] Section 36 (1).   [123] Section 36 (2).
[124] Section 36 (3). Writing is also essential by reason of the Statute of Frauds where the agreement cannot be performed within a year.
[125] Section 36 (4).   [126] Section 19 (9).   [127] Section 19 (9).
[128] Section 19 (1) to (9).   [129] *See* section 37 (5).

Where by an agreement made in relation to any future copyright the prospective owner purports to assign the future copyright to another person, then, on the coming into existence of the copyright, the copyright vests in the assignee or his successor in title.[130] The agreement must be in writing.[131]

Bequest of a Manuscript or an Artistic Work.—Bequest of an unpublished manuscript of a literary, dramatic or musical work, or an unpublished artistic work, is deemed to comprise the copyright therein.[132] Manuscript means the original document embodying the work whether written by hand or not.[133]

TERM OF PROTECTION

Literary, Dramatic and Musical Works.—Copyright in literary, dramatic and musical works subsists until the end of a period of fifty years from the end of the calendar year in which the author dies, if, during the life of the author, the work has been published, performed in public, or broadcast, or records of the work have been offered for sale to the public.[134]

On the other hand, if a literary, dramatic or musical work, or an adaptation thereof, in which copyright subsists has not, before the death of the author, been (i) published, (ii) performed in public, (iii) broadcast, and (iv) no records thereof have been offered for sale to the public —then copyright ends at the end of a period of fifty years from the end of the calendar year which includes the earliest occasion on which one of these acts was done.[135]

If none of these acts is ever done, copyright is perpetual.

If copyright in a cinematograph film has expired[136] before the expiration of the copyright in any literary, dramatic or musical work used in the cinematograph film, copyright in such work is not infringed even if the film is caused to be shown or heard in public without the permission of the owner of the performance right in the work.[137]

Artistic Work Other than Photographs.—Copyright in artistic works subsists until the end of a period of fifty years from the end of the calendar year in which the author dies.[138]

---

[130] Section 37 (1).   [131] Section 37 (1).   [132] Section 38.   [133] Section 48 (1).
[134] Section 2 (3). In case of joint authorship, the death of the last surviving author is generally taken into account (Third Schedule, sec. 2). There are special rules where the publication was anonymous or pseudonymous (Second Schedule).
[135] Section 2 (3), (4), and (6).
[136] *See* page 555, below.
[137] Section 13 (7).
[138] Section 3 (4). In case of joint authorship, the death of the last surviving author is generally taken into account (Third Schedule, sec. 2). There are special rules where the publication was anonymous or pseudonymous (Second Schedule).

However, in the case of an engraving not published before the death of the author, copyright subsists until the end of a period of fifty years from the end of the calendar year in which it is first published.[139] It would seem that the copyright in unpublished engravings is perpetual.

Photographs.—Copyright in a photograph subsists until the end of a period of fifty years from the calendar year in which the photograph has been first published.[140]

Copyright in unpublished photographs is perpetual.

Works of International Organizations.—Where copyright originally vests in any of the international organizations listed on page 541, above, copyright subsists until the end of a period of fifty years from the end of the calendar year in which the work was first published.[141]

Copyright in unpublished works of this kind is perpetual.

Sound Recordings.—Copyright in sound recordings subsists until the end of a period of fifty years from the end of the calendar year in which the recording was first published.[142]

It would seem that copyright in unpublished sound recordings is perpetual.

Cinematograph Films.—One must differentiate between films registrable under the Films Act, 1960,[143] and films not so registrable.

Films registrable under the Films Act, 1960, are "standard" films (i.e., films on 35 mm), except advertising films and certain news reels.[144] Copyright in such films subsists until the film is registered under the Films Act, 1960, and thereafter until the end of a period of 50 years from the end of the calendar year in which it was so registered.[145] It would seem that copyright in registrable but actually unregistered films is perpetual.

In the case of a film which is not registrable under the Films Act, 1960, a further distinction must be made between (i) films protected on account of the nationality, residence, domicile, or place of incorporation, of the maker of the film, and (ii) films protected only on account of the place of first publication of the film. Copyright in films belonging to category (i) subsists until the film is published, and thereafter until the end of the period of 50 years from the end of the calendar year which includes the date of its first publication;[146] it would seem that copyright in such films, if not published, is perpetual. Copyright in films belonging to category (ii) lasts from the date of first publication until the end of the period of 50 years from the end of the calendar year which includes that date;[147] unpublished films of this

---

[139] Section 3 (4), proviso (a).   [140] Section 3 (4), proviso (b).
[141] Section 33 (3).   [142] Section 12 (3).   [143] 8 & 9 Eliz. 2, ch. 57.
[144] Films Act, 1960, sec. 38.   [145] Section 13 (3) (a).
[146] Section 13 (3) (b).   [147] Section 13 (3) (c).

category are, of course, not protected (since it is the act of publication which brings them under copyright protection).

Rule of the Shorter Term.—Since there is no provision in United Kingdom law for the "rule of the shorter term" permitted under Article IV (4) of the Universal Copyright Convention, works are protected in the United Kingdom until the expiration of the terms indicated above even if in other countries they fall into the public domain at an earlier date.

INFRINGEMENTS

Direct and Indirect Infringements.—Where the acts enumerated above under "Protected Rights" require the authorization of the owner of the copyright, the doing of such acts, without the required authorization, constitutes infringement, even when the infringer did not know that he was infringing.[148]

In addition to these "direct" infringements, copyright may be infringed "indirectly" by certain cases of importation, distribution, or permitting the use of premises when the performance was infringing.

Importation.—Copyright in works, sound recordings, or cinematograph films is infringed by any person who, without the license of the owner of the copyright, imports an article (otherwise than for his private and domestic use) into the United Kingdom if to his knowledge (i) the making of the article constituted an infringement or (ii) would have constituted an infringement if the article had been made in the United Kingdom.[149] This provision allows publishers owning the publishing rights for the United Kingdom to prevent the flooding of the United Kingdom market by cheap reprints made outside the United Kingdom even if the reprint, where made, was made with the authorization of the author.

Sale, etc.—Copyright in works, sound recordings, or cinematograph films, is infringed by any person who, without the license of the owner of the copyright:
—sells,
—lets for hire,
—by way of trade offers for sale or hire,
—by way of trade exposes for sale or hire,
—by way of trade exhibits in public,

---

[148] *See* Sections 1 (2) and 17.
[149] Sections 5 (2), 16 (2), 49 (6). Importation of printed copies may be restricted by giving notice to the Commissioners of Customs (sec. 22). The definition of "infringing copy" does not include reproductions of a work in the form of a cinematograph film (sec. 18 (3)).

—distributes for purposes of sale (or other purposes but to such extent as to cause prejudice to the owner of the copyright),
an article, if, to his knowledge (i) the making of the article constituted an infringement, or (ii) in the case of an imported article, would have constituted an infringement if it had been made in the United Kingdom.[150]

Permitting Use of Premises When Performance is Infringing.
—Copyright in literary, dramatic, or musical works—but not in artistic works, sound recordings, or cinematograph films—is infringed by any person who permits a place of public entertainment to be used for public performance where the performance constitutes an infringement. Such person, however, will not be liable if: (i) he was not aware, and had no reasonable ground for suspecting, that the performance would be an infringement, or (ii) gave the permission gratuitously or for a fee not exceeding his own expenses.[151]

Civil Remedies.—Depending on the circumstances, the plaintiff may be entitled to damages, an account of profits, injunctions,[152] and may be treated as the owner of the infringing copies (or of any plates used or intended for making such copies).[153]

Criminal Sanctions.—Most infringements, if committed knowingly, are criminal offenses, punished by fine, or in case of recidivism, by fine or imprisonment.[154]

[150] Section 5 (3), (4), 16 (3), (4); 49 (6).
[151] Sections 5 (5), (6); 49 (6).
[152] Section 17.
[153] Section 18. According to the Limitation Act, 1939, actions in conversion are barred after six years.
[154] Section 21.

UNITED STATES OF AMERICA

SOURCES

Domestic Law.—There are two main sources of protection for works in the United States of America: the federal law and the state law.

The main source of the federal law is Title 17 of the United States Code.[1] The "Code" is a systematic assemblage of all the general legislative enactments of the United States (federal) Congress. Title 17 is entitled and entirely devoted to "Copyrights." Most of the present contents of Title 17 are identical with the Copyright Act of March 4, 1909. But there have been several amendatory acts since then, among which the Act of August 31, 1954 (effective as from September 16, 1955),[2] which was passed in order to conform with certain requirements of the Universal Copyright Convention. Title 17 is hereinafter referred to as "the statute" or "the federal statute," and copyright protection under it as "copyright" or "statutory copyright."

Regulations of the Copyright Office supplement the federal statute. Hereinafter, they will be referred to as the "Regulations."[3]

The sources of the law of each of the fifty states are the enactments of its legislature ("state statutes")[4] and the "common law," the latter mainly resulting from court decisions. Less than half of the states have enacted measures concerning the protection of authors' rights; these enactments usually deal only with isolated aspects of such rights; most enactments simply confirm some of the generally accepted common law principles prevalent in this field, and since there is very little difference in essentials between the state laws of the various states, they will not be separately analyzed. In the following, the law of each state is considered as identical and is referred to as "common law protection.",

Generally stated, the federal statute or statutory copyright applies to (a) published works, and (b) unpublished works if the claim to copyright in them (i.e., in the unpublished work) has been registered in the U.S. Copyright Office in Washington, D.C., a federal instrumentality. In the following, the latter kind of works will be referred to as "unpublished registered works."

---

[1] Text reprinted in CLTW, USA: Item 2.
[2] Public Law No. 743, published in U.S. Statutes at Large, Volume 68, page 1030.
[3] Code of Federal Regulations, Title 37, Chapter II. Reprinted in CLTW, USA: Item 3.
[4] The state statutes are reprinted in CLTW, USA: Items 49 through 66.

As long as a work is unpublished and unregistered, it is protected by the common law. Thus, every work, upon creation, is first protected by common law. Some kinds of unpublished works are eligible for registration in the U.S. Copyright Office, others (for example, most non-dramatic literary works) are not. If an unpublished work is of a kind which is eligible for registration and is registered, its protection ceases to be governed by the common law and is governed by the federal statute. If an unpublished work (i) is of a kind which is not eligible for registration, or (ii) is of a kind which is eligible for registration but is not registered, then its protection is governed by the common law. There is no obligation to apply for registration of unpublished works. Thus, whether an unpublished work is registered or not depends on the will of the owner of the common law rights therein. It is a matter of individual judgment whether it is preferable to register an unpublished work (when eligible for registration) or not. Each course of action has advantages: common law protection has the advantage that it is unlimited in time; statutory protection has the advantages that it offers easier proof of ownership and better defined remedies against infringers. Both have other advantages too.

Once a work is published, it ceases to be protected by common law. If publication was made with the prescribed "notice" (i.e., the symbol © with the name of the copyright proprietor and the year date of publication),[5] the work acquires statutory copyright protection. If the publication is effected without the prescribed notice, the work falls into the public domain because it ceases to be protected by common law and fails to acquire statutory protection.

There is one notable exception as to the notice requirement. A book or periodical in the English language, even though published without a notice, may secure *ad interim* copyright, if it was first published outside the United States and if registration in the U.S. Copyright Office is made within six months after publication. *Ad interim* copyright endures for only five years; however, it may be extended to the full term by publication and registration of an edition of the work manufactured in the United States provided this occurs within the five-year period. Also, only 1,500 copies of such a work may be imported into the United States, and all copies imported must bear the notice.[6]

A work which acquired statutory protection will lose such protection if, generally stated, copies are later put into circulation without the required notice. If protection is lost in this manner, the work falls into the public domain. Common law protection cannot be acquired anew because a published work is ineligible for common law protection.

Universal Copyright Convention.—The United States became

[5] For a more complete statement of the notice requirement, see page 26, above.
[6] §§ 16, 22, 23.

bound by the Universal Copyright Convention and Protocols 1 and 2 as from September 16, 1955.[7]

ACQUISITION OF COPYRIGHT UNDER THE UNIVERSAL COPYRIGHT CONVENTION

Caveat: It should be noted that this chapter and all other chapters deal only with works which the United States is obligated to protect on account of the Universal Copyright Convention. Protection in the United States is or may be available on other grounds for the same and other works, but such cases are not covered by the present analysis.

UNDER THE FEDERAL STATUTE

Unpublished Works.—It is stated below[8] which kinds of unpublished works are eligible for statutory protection. If the work is of such kind, and if statutory protection is preferred to common law protection, statutory protection may be acquired if the author of the unpublished work is a citizen or subject of a state or nation party to the Universal Copyright Convention[9] by registering the claim to protection in the U.S. Copyright Office.

Common law protection is available for any kind of unpublished

[7] CLTW, USA: Item 6. The Convention is also applied in Guam, the Panama Canal Zone, Puerto Rico, and the Virgin Islands (CLTW: Universal Copyright Convention: Item 2). The United States is also a party to the Copyright Conventions of Mexico City (1902) and Buenos Aires (1910); see CLTW, USA: Items 7 and 8. It concluded a bilateral copyright treaty with Hungary in 1912 (CLTW, USA: Item 9) and there are provisions concerning copyright protection in more general treaties concluded with Thailand (1937, then Siam) and China (1947); see CLTW, USA: Items 10 and 11. Presidential proclamations extending some or all the benefits of the copyright statute to nationals of Argentina, Australia, Austria, Belgium, Brazil, Canada, Chile, Costa Rica, Cuba, Czechoslovakia, Denmark, Finland, France, Germany, Greece, India, Ireland, Italy, Luxembourg, Mexico, Monaco, the Netherlands, New Zealand, Norway, Philippines, Poland, Portugal, Rumania, South Africa, Spain, Sweden, Switzerland, Tunisia and the United Kingdom, were promulgated (CLTW, USA: Items 12 through 48).

[8] Page 563.

[9] § 9 (c). Under Protocol 1, the United States is obliged to protect the works of stateless persons and refugees who have their habitual residence in a state party to that Protocol. The works of stateless authors seem to be eligible for statutory protection whether such works are published or unpublished, and irrespective of the place of habitual residence of the author (Houghton Mifflin Co. v. Stackpole Sons, Inc., 104 F. 2d 306 (2d Cir.), *cert. denied*, 308 U.S. 597 (1939)). On the other hand, there is no provision or court decision which would provide for statutory protection of the unpublished work of a refugee merely on the basis of his domicile in a Convention country. (Such work is, however, eligible for statutory protection if the author's nationality qualified it for protection.) The same is true in respect to unpublished works of the international organizations named in Protocol 2. But in any case, these, like all other unpublished works, are protected by common law.

work without registration or any other formality. But if *statutory* protection is desired for an *unpublished* work, the same formalities must be complied with in the case of works of authors who are nationals of Convention countries as in the case of authors who are U.S. nationals.

Generally stated, these requirements are the following:

An application for registration must be filled out on a form furnished by the U.S. Copyright Office,[10] and this application must be filed with the same Office. The application must be accompanied by a fee of $ 4.00[11] and the deposit of: (i) *one copy*, if the work is a lecture, sermon or speech; a dramatic, musical or dramatico-musical composition; (ii) *a title, a description, and one print taken from each scene or act*, if the work is a motion-picture photoplay; (iii) *one photographic print*, if the work is a photograph; (iv) *a title, a description, and at least two prints taken from different sections of the complete motion picture*, if the work is a motion picture other than a photoplay; (v) *one photograph or other identifying reproduction*, if the work is a work of art or a plastic work or drawing.[12]

Published Works.—Published works enjoy statutory protection in the United States: (i) if their author is a citizen or subject of a state or nation that is party to the Universal Copyright Convention, irrespective of the place of first publication, or, (ii) if the work was first published in a state or nation party to the Universal Copyright Convention, irrespective of the nationality of the author, *provided*, in both cases, that "from the time of first publication all the copies of the work published with the authority of the author or other copyright proprietor shall bear the symbol © accompanied by the name of the copyright proprietor and the year of first publication placed in such a manner and location as to give reasonable notice of claim of protection," *and provided* that the author is not a citizen or domiciliary of the United States and that the work was not first published in the United States.[13,14]

---

[10] Communications should be addressed to the Register of Copyrights, Library of Congress, Washington 25, D.C. Forms and information relative to the operations of the Copyright Office are furnished free of charge.

[11] § 215.   [12] § 12.

[13] § 9 (c). Works meeting these conditions are exempt from the requirement of manufacture in the United States (§ 16) to which most publications in English and some other kinds of works are otherwise generally subjected.

[14] As to the works of stateless persons, *see* footnote 2, above. It would seem that a published work of a refugee (who is not stateless) is not eligible for statutory protection merely on the basis of the fact that its author is domiciled in a Convention country. (Such a work is, however, eligible for statutory protection if the author's nationality or the place of the work's first publication qualifies it for protection, or if the author is domiciled in the United States; § 9). Furthermore, it would seem that a work first published by an international organization named in Protocol 2 is not eligible for statutory protection merely on the basis of the fact that it was first published by such organization. (Such a work is, however, eligible for statutory protection if the author's nationality, his statelessness, or the place of the work's first publication qualified it for protection, or if the author is domiciled in the United States; § 9).

The form and location of the notice,[15] the concept of publication,[16] the notion of "author" when his nationality is of relevance,[17] the question who is meant by "copyright proprietor" in connection with the notice,[18] and other questions which are of relevance in connection with the application of the provisions concerning the eligibility of published works for statutory protection are discussed in Part I of this book.

Copies of such published works *may* be deposited in the U.S. Copyright Office and the copyright claim in them *may* be there registered, but such deposit and registration are *not necessary* for the acquisition of statutory protection. Deposit and registration, however, *are* necessary before a lawsuit can be initiated before a U.S. court, since the statute provides that "No action or proceeding shall be maintained for infringement of copyright in any work until the provisions of this title with respect to the deposit of copies and registration of such work shall have been complied with."[19]

Even if not necessary, deposit and registration in the U.S. Copyright Office may have certain advantages, such as: (i) the certificate of registration constitutes *prima facie* evidence of the facts stated therein, (ii) the catalogs published by the Copyright Office constitute a certain publicity, (iii) renewal of copyright might be more easily available if copyright for the first term has been registered.[20]

UNDER COMMON LAW

Unpublished Works.—Unpublished works are protected by

---

[15] Page 24, above.   [16] Page 67, above.   [17] Page 161, above.
[18] Page 261, above.
[19] § 13. Application forms and information as to the objects to be deposited, the possible fees, and all other questions concerning deposit and registration are furnished free of charge by the U.S. Copyright Office. Roughly stated, the procedure is the following: An application has to be filled out and sent to the Register of Copyrights, Library of Congress, Washington 25, D.C. The application must be accompanied by
   either (a) the registration fee ($ 6.oo for prints or labels used for articles of merchandise; $ 4.oo for all other kinds of works) and one copy of the best edition of the work (in certain cases a photograph or other identifying reproduction of the work may take the place of such copy),
   or (b) if application is made within six months of the first application, a catalog card (form supplied by the U.S. Copyright Office) and two copies (or, where applicable, photographs or other identifying reproductions) of the work.
[20] At the present time, the Copyright Office effects renewal registrations only in respect to works the claim of copyright in which for the first term has been registered. It will not be before 1983 that works protected under the Universal Copyright Convention will ordinarily be eligible for renewal. By that time the present statutory provisions may be different. Even if they remain as they are today, it is not possible to state today what the practice of the U.S. Copyright Office will be: will it require registration of the "first" copyright before registering renewals, or will it register renewal without such "first" registration?

common law irrespective of the nationality or domicile of the author, and without any formality (notice, deposit, registration, or other).

Published Works.—No published work is eligible for protection by common law. As to the notion of publication, *see* page 561, above.

PROTECTED WORKS

Under the Federal Statute

"All the writings of an author" are susceptible of statutory copyright protection.[21] The word "writing" has a much broader meaning than it has in its everyday use. It is not limited to works expressed in the form of written words, as will be seen below. "Author," too, has a broad meaning: essentially, one who creates a work without copying is an author.

For the purposes of registration, the statute distinguishes thirteen classes of works but provides that these "specifications shall not be held to limit the subject matter of copyright."[22]

The following classes of works are eligible for statutory protection (a) if published with a proper notice, or (b) as long as unpublished ("not reproduced for sale"), only if they are registered in the U.S. Copyright Office:

(i) "Dramatic or dramatico-musical compositions."[23] This class includes "works dramatic in character such as the acting version of plays for the stage, motion pictures, radio, television and the like, operas, operettas, musical comedies and similar productions and pantomimes[;] choreographic works of a dramatic character, whether the story or theme be expressed by music and action combined or by action alone..."[24]

(ii) "Musical compositions."[25] This class includes "musical compositions in the form of visible notation (other than dramatico-musical compositions), with or without words, as well as new versions of musical compositions, such as adaptations or arrangements, and editing when such editing is the writing of an author."[26]

(iii) "Works of art; models and designs for works of art."[27] This class includes "works of artistic craftsmanship, in so far as their form but not their mechanical or utilitarian aspects are concerned, such as artistic jewelry, enamels, glassware, and tapestries, as well as works

---

[21] § 4.   [22] § 5.   [23] § 5 (d).
[24] Regulations, § 202.7.   [25] § 5 (e).
[26] Regulations, § 202.8 (a). A phonograph record or sound recording is not considered a "copy" of the work recorded on it, and it is not accepted for registration purposes (Regulations, § 202.8 (b)).
[27] § 5 (g).

belonging to the fine arts, such as paintings, drawings and sculpture."[28] Statuettes of a human dancing figure used as a lamp base,[29] certain textile fabrics,[30] and artificial flowers[31] may be registered too.

(iv) "Drawings or plastic works of a scientific or technical character."[32] This class includes "two-dimensional drawings or three-dimensional plastic works which have been designed for a scientific or technical use and which contain copyrightable graphic, pictorial, or sculpture material, [such as] diagrams or models illustrating scientific or technical works or formulating scientific or technical information in linear or plastic form, such as, for example: a mechanical drawing, an astronomical chart, an architect's blueprint, an anatomical model, or an engineering diagram."[33]

(v) "Photographs."[34] This class includes photographic prints and filmstrips, slide films and individual slides."[35]

(vi) "Motion-picture photoplays."[36] This class includes "motion pictures that are dramatic in character and tell a connected story, such as feature films, filmed television plays, short subjects and animated cartoons having a plot."[37]

(vii) "Motion pictures other than photoplays."[38] This class includes "non-dramatic films such as newsreels, travelogs, training or promotional films, nature studies, and filmed television programs having no plot."[39]

The following classes of works are eligible for statutory protection only if published with a proper notice (i.e., as long as unpublished, they are not eligible for statutory protection):[40]

(i) "Books, including composite and cyclopaedic works, directories, gazetteers, and other compilations."[41] The Regulations provide that this class "includes such published works as fiction or non-fiction, poems, compilations, composite works, directories, catalogs, annual publications, information in tabular form, and similar text matter, with or without illustrations, as books, either bound or in loose-leaf form, pamphlets, leaflets, cards, single pages or the like."[42]

(ii) "Periodicals, including newspapers."[43] According to the Regulations, "this class includes such works as newspapers, magazines,

[28] Regulations, § 202.10.
[29] Mazer v. Stein, 347 U.S. 201 (1954).
[30] Peter Pan Fabrics, Inc. v. Brenda Fabrics, Inc., 169 F. Supp. 142, (S.D.N.Y. 1959).
[31] Prestige Floral S.A. v. California Artificial Flower Co., 201 F. Supp. 287 (S.D.N.Y. 1962).
[32] § 5 (i).   [33] Regulations, § 202.12 (a).
[34] § 5 (j).   [35] Regulations, § 202.13.   [36] § 5 (l).
[37] Regulations, § 202.15 (a). It is indifferent whether they are incorporated in films or in video tapes.
[38] § 5 (m).
[39] Regulations, § 202.15 (b). It is indifferent whether they are incorporated in films or video tapes.
[40] See § 10.   [41] § 5 (a).   [42] Regulations, § 202.4 (a).   [43] § 5 (b).

reviews, bulletins, and serial publications, published at intervals of less than a year."[44]

(iii) "Maps."[45] This class includes "cartographic representation of area, such as terrestrial maps and atlases, marine charts, celestial maps and such three-dimensional works as globes and relief models."[46]

(iv) "Reproductions of a work of art."[47] This class includes "reproductions of existing works of art in the same or different medium, such as a lithograph, photoengraving, etching or drawing of a painting, sculpture or other work or art."[48]

(v) "Prints and pictorial illustrations including prints or labels used for articles of merchandise."[49] This class includes "prints or pictorial illustrations, greeting cards, picture postcards and similar prints, produced by means of lithography, photoengraving or other methods of reproduction...[50] A print or label, not a trademark, containing copyrightable pictorial matter, text, or both, published in connection with the sale or advertisement of an article or articles of merchandise."[51]

A special class is constituted by "lectures, sermons, addresses (prepared for oral delivery)."[52] This class includes "the scripts of unpublished works prepared in the first instance for oral delivery, such as lectures, sermons, addresses, monologs, panel discussions, and variety programs prepared for radio and television. The script ... should consist of the actual text of the works to be presented orally."[53] Consequently, such scripts are eligible for statutory protection only through registration in the U.S. Copyright Office.

UNDER COMMON LAW

There is common law protection for any "unpublished work,"[54] as long as it is not registered in the U.S. Copyright Office. It would seem that all the kinds of works which are eligible for statutory protection are also eligible (as long as not published and not registered) for common law protection. Oral works are probably also protected by common law.

PROTECTED PERSONS

UNDER THE FEDERAL STATUTE

Copyright originally—i.e., at the beginning of the first term of twenty-eight years—vests in the person who secures it by registration in

[44] Regulations, § 202.5.   [45] § 5 (f).   [46] Regulations, § 202.9.
[47] § 5 (h).   [48] Regulations, § 202.11.
[49] § 5 (k).   [50] Regulations, § 202.14 (a).
[51] Regulations, § 202.14 (b).
[52] § 5 (c).   [53] Regulations, § 202.6   [54] § 2.

the U.S. Copyright Office if the work is unpublished, and by publication with the proper notice if the work is published without having been registered prior to publication. Such person is the author or, if he has not yet secured copyright, the person to whom he assigned the right to secure copyright. If the author (or the person, if any, to whom he has assigned the right to secure copyright) dies before copyright has been secured, then the right to secure copyright will, depending on the circumstances, belong to the administrator or executor of the author or such assignee, or to the heir or legatee of the author or such assignee.[55]

"Author" has a technical meaning as it does not necessarily mean the person or persons who created the work: in the case of works created for hire, it means the employer.[56] The employer may be either a person or a legal entity.

As to the question of who may secure copyright for the second term (equally twenty-eight years in length), *see* "Duration: Renewal," below.

UNDER COMMON LAW

Common law property in works vests in the author upon creation. But if the author has assigned his property rights before the work has been created, common law property will vest in such assignee upon creation.

ASSIGNMENT AND LICENSING

UNDER THE FEDERAL STATUTE

Assignment.—Copyright may be "assigned, granted, or mortgaged by an instrument in writing signed by the proprietor of copyright, or may be bequeathed by will."[57]

Assignments may be recorded in the U.S. Copyright Office.[58] This is effected by sending to the Copyright Office the original,[59] signed instrument with a fee. The fee is $ 3.00 if the instrument relates to one work and does not exceed six pages. Each additional page and each additional title comprised in the same instrument requires the payment of fifty cents in addition to the basic fee of $ 3.00.[60] After recordation, the Copyright Office returns the original instrument with a certificate of recordation.[61]

If the assignment was executed (i.e., the papers were signed) outside

---

[55] § 9.   [56] § 26.   [57] § 28.   [58] § 30.
[59] Where the original instrument is not available, a certified or other copy may be submitted, but it must be accompanied by a statement that the original is not available (Regulation, § 201.4).
[60] § 215.   [61] § 31.

the United States, it should be acknowledged by the assignor before an officer of a U.S. embassy, legation or consulate.[62] But the U.S. Copyright Office records assignments even if such acknowledgment is missing. Lack of acknowledgment may deprive the recordation of its *prima facie* evidenciary quality—even this is doubtful, however—but in no case does it make the assignment ineffective between assignor and assignee.

Failure to record does not invalidate the assignment. But if recordation of the assignment effected outside the United States is not applied for in the U.S. Copyright Office within six months, the assignment will have no effect "against any subsequent purchaser or mortgagee for a valuable consideration, without notice, whose assignment has been duly recorded" in the U.S. Copyright Office.[63] Thus unrecorded assignments are effective even in respect to third parties for six months in any case, and even beyond the six months if the second assignee knew about the first assignment or if the second assignment is not recorded in the U.S. Copyright Office.

Licenses.—Every transfer of right or rights that amounts to less than the transfer of the entire copyright is a license rather than an assignment. Licenses may be granted orally, though, in practice, they are normally granted in written contracts.

Licenses need not be recorded and the lack of their recordation does not produce effects similar to the effects of failure to record assignments. Still, licenses to use a work *may* be recorded. So may be other papers relative to copyright. Examples of such papers are powers of attorney, agreements between authors and publishers covering a particular work or works and the rights thereto, certificates of change of corporate titles, wills and decrees of distribution.[64] The procedure for obtaining a certificate of recordation from the U.S. Copyright Office is the same as in the case of recordation of assignments (see above).

Mortgaging.—As already stated, mortgaging of copyright is only valid if it is done in a written instrument signed by the owner of the copyright.[65]

Mortgages may be recorded in the U.S. Copyright Office in a similar way and with similar effects as licenses.

UNDER COMMON LAW

The author's rights in a work which has not secured statutory copyright and which thus is protected by the common law may be assigned or licensed in writing or orally. Assignments, licenses and other docu-

---

[62] § 29. "To acknowledge" generally means that the assignor declares, under oa before the counselor or other like U.S. officer that the document was signed by him. The officer attests this declaration on the document and signs and seals the attestation.
[63] § 30.   [64] Regulations, § 201.4.   [65] § 28.

ments relating to works under common law protection may be recorded in the U.S. Copyright Office.

The right to secure statutory copyright may be granted in writing or orally.

If copyright is secured by registration prior to publication and the applicant is not the author, the U.S. Copyright Office does not ask for proof that the applicant has acquired the right so to secure copyright. If the application to register relates to a published work and the applicant is not the author, the U.S. Copyright Office does not ask for proof either that the publication has been effected by a person who had the right to secure copyright by publication, or that the applicant is the copyright owner. But, as a general rule, the person named in the copyright notice and the claimant of copyright in the application must be the same person.

PROTECTED RIGHTS

ECONOMIC RIGHTS UNDER THE FEDERAL STATUTE

Copyright includes a number of exclusive rights of authorization and one right to remuneration ("legal license").

The exclusive rights of authorization, as provided in the somewhat clumsy language of the statute, are the following:

(i) "To print, reprint, publish, copy and vend the copyrighted work," i.e., work of any class or description which is capable of copyright protection and in which copyright has been secured.[66] To print or reprint is necessarily included in "to copy." Copying does not only mean literal repetition or exact duplication but also the various modes in which the work may be substantially reproduced by imitation, paraphrasing or colorable alteration.[67] Copying exists even if only part of the original work is copied or if the copy is not reproducing exactly the original. Producing the substance of a copyrighted work in the same medium, or generally even in a different medium, is "copying." For example, it was held that the making of toys in the semblance of cartoons constitutes copying of the artist's conception as expressed in pictorial form.[68] The right "to vend" is generally considered as limited to and exhausted by the first sale.[69]

(ii) "To translate the copyright work into other languages or dialects ... if it be a literary work."[70]

[66] § 1 (a).
[67] Nutt *v.* National Institute, 31 F. 2d 236 (2d Cir. 1929).
[68] King Features Syndicate *v.* Fleischer, 299 Fed. 533 (2d Cir. 1924).
[69] Fawcett Publications, Inc. *v.* Elliot Publishing Co., 46 F. Supp. 717 (S.D.N.Y. 1942).
[70] § 1 (b).

(iii) "To ... make any other version [other than a translation] thereof, if it be a literary work."[71]

(iv) "To dramatize it if it be a non-dramatic work."[72]

(v) "To convert it into a novel or other non-dramatic work if it be a drama."[73]

(vi) "To arrange or adapt it if it be a musical work."[74]

(vii) "To complete, execute or finish it if it be a model or design for a work of art."[75]

(viii) "To deliver, authorize the delivery of, read, or present the copyrighted work in public for profit if it be a lecture, sermon, address or similar production, or other non-dramatic literary work."[76] This includes the right to broadcast.[77]

(ix) "To make or procure the making of any transcription or record thereof [i.e., of any non-dramatic literary work] by or from which [transcription or record], in whole or in part, it [i.e., such work] may in any manner or by any method be exhibited, delivered, presented, produced, or reproduced."[78]

(x) "To play or perform it [i.e., any non-dramatic literary work] in public for profit, and to exhibit, represent, produce, or reproduce it [the non-dramatic literary work] in any manner or by any method whatsoever."[79]

(xi) "To perform or represent the copyrighted work publicly if it be a drama."[80] Thus, in case of dramatic works, the public performance right is also recognized when the performance is not for profit; in the case of non-dramatic literary works and musical works, it is recognized only when the performance is for profit. Dramatico-musical works are treated in this respect as dramatic works, not as musical works.[81] The public exhibition of motion picture photoplays falls under this provision.[82]

(xii) "To vend any manuscript or any record whatsoever ... if it be a dramatic work ... not reproduced in copies for sale."[83]

(xiii) "To make or procure the making of any transcription or record thereof [i.e., of a dramatic work] by or from which, in whole or in part, it may in any manner or by any method be exhibited, performed, represented, produced, or reproduced."[84] This seems to apply also to dramatico-musical works.

(xiv) "To exhibit, perform, represent, produce, or reproduce it in

[71] § 1 (b).   [72] § 1 (b).   [73] § 1 (b).   [74] § 1 (b).   [75] § 1 (b).
[76] § 1 (c).   [77] *Cf.* last sentence of § 1 (c).
[78] § 1 (c).   [79] § 1 (c).   [80] § 1 (d).
[81] Herbert *v.* Shanley Co., 220 Fed. 340 (2d Cir. 1916).
[82] Universal Pictures Co., Inc., *v.* Harold Lloyd Corp., 162 F. 2d 354 (9th Cir. 1947). The public exhibition of motion pictures other than photoplays was held to constitute copying falling under § 1 (a) (Patterson *v.* Century Productions, Inc., 93 F. 2d 489 (2d Cir. 1937)), *cert. denied* 303 U.S. 655 (1938).
[83] § 1 (d).   [84] § 1 (d).

any manner or by any method whatsoever."[85] It is not entirely clear whether "it" refers to "dramatic work" (in which case the provision partly overlaps that discussed under (xi) above) or to the transcription or record of a dramatic work (this interpretation would be based on the repetition of the five acts referred to in (xiii), above), or both. In any case, the result seems to be the same. It is clear that what are involved are dramatic works which also seem to include dramatico-musical works and motion picture photoplays. Protection is available even if the acts are not for profit. It would, however, seem to be logical to consider that they must be "public."

(xv) "To perform the copyrighted work publicly for profit if it be a musical composition,"[86] but "the reproduction or rendition of a musical composition by or upon coin-operated machines ["juke boxes"] shall not be deemed public performance for profit unless a fee is charged for admission to the place where such reproduction or rendition occurs."[87] Roughly stated, musical compositions are protected against unauthorized public performance for profit, except if the performance is by juke box (unless an admission fee is charged). Public performance includes performance in concert halls, theatres, cabarets, dance halls, and other public places. The charging of admission fees is not a criterion of "for profit."[88] Broadcasting is generally considered public performance for profit,[89] and so is the making available of the received broadcast to guests in the public rooms[90] of the hotel or in the individual bedrooms of the guests.[91] Performance of the music incorporated in the sound track of a motion picture in connection with the exhibition in a theatre of the sound motion picture is public performance for profit, but usually does not give rise to a separate collection by the owner of the musical performance right since U.S. courts have, for anti-trust reasons, forced the two largest American performance rights societies to include the right of such performance in the sale of the right to use the music in the motion picture.[92]

(xvi) "To make any arrangement or setting of it [i.e., of the musical composition] or of the melody of it in any system of notation ... in which the thought of the author may be recorded and from which it may be read for the purpose of public performance for profit, and for the purposes set forth in subsection (a) hereof [i.e., for the purposes of printing, reprinting, publishing, copying or vending]."[93]

[85] § 1 (d).   [86] § 1 (c).   [87] § 1 (e), last paragraph.
[88] § Herbert *v.* Shanley Co., 242 U.S. 591 (1917).
[89] Associated Music Publishers, Inc. *v.* Debs Memorial Radio Fund, Inc., 141 F. 2d 852 (2d Cir.), *cert. denied*, 323 U.S. 766 (1944).
[90] Associated Music Publishers, Inc., *v.* Debs Memorial Radio Fund, Inc., 141 F. 2d 852 (2d Cir. 1944).
[91] Society of European Stage Authors and Composers, Inc., *v.* New York Hotel Statler Co., 19 F. Supp 1 (S.D.N.Y. 1937).
[92] Alden-Rochelle, Inc., v. A.S.C.A.P., 80 F. Supp. 888 (S.D.N.Y. 1948).   [93] § 1 (e).

(xvii) "To make any arrangement or setting of it [i.e., of a musical composition] or of the melody of it in ... any form of record ... from which it may be ... reproduced for the purpose of public performance for profit, and for the purposes set forth in subsection (a) hereof [i.e., for the purposes of printing, reprinting, publishing, copying or vending]."[94] However, once the owner of a musical copyright has used or permitted or knowingly acquiesced in the making of sound recordings, he loses the exclusive right of authorization and "any other person may make similar use of the copyrighted work upon the payment to the copyright proprietor of a royalty of two cents [of a U.S. dollar]" on each record manufactured, "to be paid by the manufacturer thereof."[95] In other words, the right of sound recording becomes subject to a legal license.[96]

Economic Rights under Common Law

Paradoxically, the best expression of the rights of an author in a work not under statutory copyright is to be found in the federal copyright statute which provides that "nothing in this Act [i.e., the federal copyright statute] shall be construed to annul or limit the right of the author or proprietor of an unpublished [and unregistered] work, at common law or in equity, to prevent the copying, publication or use of such unpublished work without his consent."[97]

Thus, at common law, there is an exclusive right of authorization against (i) publication, (ii) copying, and (iii) any other use, of the work. These rights seem to be absolute. They are not limited by the exceptions or qualifications which certain rights suffer under the federal statute. Thus, for example, it would appear that unpublished and unregistered works are protected even against private performance, that such dramatic works are protected even against performances which are not for profit, and that the right of recording of musical works is never subject to the legal license.

Moral Rights under the Federal Statute and under Common Law

There are no provisions in the statute recognizing moral rights. The courts have, however, in a number of lawsuits granted relief in cases which, in the sense most European laws use the term, would be infringements of moral rights. Relief, however, is not based on provisions of the copyright statute but on the law of contracts (particularly on the interpretation of the express or implied intent of the contracting parties) or other legal principles.

[94] § 1 (e). [95] § 1 (e).
[96] Further details are provided in other parts of § 1 (e).
[97] § 2.

LIMITATIONS UNDER THE FEDERAL STATUTE

The federal statute does not provide for limitations beyond the qualifications already referred to in the discussion of the rights.[98] Nevertheless, the courts have established what is usually called the "fair use doctrine" according to which certain uses, within certain limits, are lawful even if done without the authorization of the copyright owner and without the payment of any remuneration to him. It is well-nigh impossible to give a definition of "fair use" or to enumerate the cases in which free uses are considered as lawful. The circumstances of each case determine when this "rule of reason" becomes applicable.

The factors which are usually taken into consideration are: (i) the quantity and value of the portion of the work which is used without authorization, (ii) the extent to which such use is likely to interfere with the sale or other exploitation of the work (so-called harmful competitive effect), (iii) the purpose of the use, (iv) the nature of the work.

LIMITATIONS UNDER COMMON LAW

The doctrine of fair use does not seem to apply to unpublished, unregistered works.[99]

TERM OF PROTECTION

UNDER THE FEDERAL STATUTE

The statute provides for two successive copyright terms totaling fifty-six years. Each term is twenty-eight years.[100]

The first term of twenty-eight years begins to run: (i) for works registered prior to publication, from the date of registration,[101] (ii) for works which are published without having been previously registered as unpublished works, from the date of publication.[102] It follows from the above that if a work is published after it has been registered as an unpublished work, the term does not start to run anew but is still reckoned from the date of registration.

The second term of twenty-eight years is computed from the expiration of the first term. But only those works enjoy copyright for the second term for which "renewal" has been effected through an application deposited in the U.S. Copyright Office. The application must be

[98] *See* page 571, above.
[99] *See* Golding *v.* R.K.O. Radio Pictures, Inc., 193 P. 2d 153 (Cal. Dist. Ct. App. 1948), *aff'd*, 35 Cal. 2d 690 (1956).
[100] However, the second term of copyright is longer for works copyright in which was renewed between September 19, 1934, and December 31, 1940. Copyright in such works expires on December 31, 1968 (Act of November 16, 1967, 81 Stat. 464).
[101] Regulations, § 202.17 (a).
[102] § 24.

received by the Copyright Office during the last (twenty-eight) year of the first term: neither before, nor after. The application is written on a form furnished free of charge by the Copyright Office.[103] It must be accompanied by a fee of $ 2.00.[104] If the renewal is not so applied for within the stated year, the work enters into the public domain.[105] The time limits of renewal cannot be extended by the Copyright Office.[106]

The formalities required for renewal are applicable to works protectible under the Universal Copyright Convention.

Subject to the exceptions stated below, renewal may be secured only (i) by the author (not his assignee!), (ii) if the author is not living, by his widow or children, (iii) if the author is not living and there is no widow and there are no children, by the executors of his will, or, if he left no will, by his next of kin.[107] (The *ratio legis* of the renewal system is to give the author or his family a second chance to negotiate the sale of rights which may fetch a higher price during the second term than they were capable of fetching when they were sold during the first term of copyright.) The author (or the widow, widower, children, etc.) cannot bequeath his contingent right to renew, or bind the surviving beneficiaries to renew it on behalf of someone designated by him in a prior contract. But a contract in which the author promises to renew on behalf of someone is enforceable if the author is alive when the renewal is effected.[108]

The exceptions, simply stated, are the following: if the work is a posthumous work, or if it is a composite work, or if it is a work made for hire, the person entitled to secure renewal is the owner of the copyright (for example, an assignee) at the time of renewal.[109]

Since there is no provision in the federal statute for the "rule of the shorter term" permitted under Article IV (4) of the Universal Copyright Convention, works are protected in the United States until the expiration of the terms indicated above even if in other countries they fall into the public domain at an earlier date.

UNDER COMMON LAW

Protection of a work not published anywhere in the world and not registered in the U.S. Copyright Office is not limited in time—that is,

---

[103] § 24.   [104] § 215.   [105] § 24.

[106] But such terms have been extended, on account of the World Wars, in the case of the works of nationals of certain countries, by proclamations of the President of the United States. None of these extensions is, however, any longer in force.

[107] § 24.

[108] *Cf.* Fred Fisher Music Co., Inc. *v.* M. Witmark Sons, 318 U.S. 643 (1943)—a decision by the Supreme Court. Licenses granted by the owner of the copyright during the first term do not bind the owner of the copyright of the second term. *Cf.* G. Ricordi & Co. *v.* Paramount Pictures, Inc., 189 F. 2d 469 (2d Cir. 1951).

[109] § 24.

such a work is protected under common law as long as it remains both unpublished and unregistered. The fact that such a work may not be protected, or has fallen into the public domain after a certain time—for example, fifty years after the author's death—in a country other than the United States does not make it fall into the public domain in the United States.

INFRINGEMENTS

Under the Federal Statute

Injunction and Impounding.—The court in its discretion may enjoin the infringement.[110] The court may order the impounding, during the pendency of the action, of all articles alleged to be infringing, and may order the destruction of all infringing copies and devices for making them.[111] Piratical copies and copies bearing false copyright notices may be seized when their importation is attempted.[112]

Civil Remedies.—The infringer is liable for actual damages suffered by the copyright owner, as well as the infringer's profits. Or, in lieu of a smaller sum of actual damages or profits, the court is to award "statutory damages" (i.e., damages within the limits fixed in the federal statute) it deems just; this amount, with certain exceptions, is to be not less than $ 250 and not more than $ 5,000.[113] Civil actions cannot be maintained unless commenced within three years after the claim accrued.[114]

Penal Sanctions.—Wilful infringements for profit are punishable by imprisonment or fine. The unlawful use, removal with fraudulent intent, or altering of the copyright notice is punishable with fine. So is the sale or importation of articles if the seller or importer knows that they bear a copyright notice although they are in the public domain.[115] Criminal actions can be maintained only if commenced within three years of the commission of the criminal act.[116]

Under Common Law

At common law, the remedies are the same as for any other property.[117] Both injunctions and actual damages are available.

---

[110] § 101 (a).   [111] § 101 (c) and (d).   [112] §§ 108 and 109.
[113] § 101 (b).   [114] § 115 (b).   [115] §§ 104 and 105.   [116] § 115 (a).
[117] *Cf.* Palmer *v.* DeWitt, 47 N.Y. 532 (1872).

VENEZUELA

SOURCES

Domestic Law.—The primary source of the law of copyright in Venezuela is the Copyright Law (*Ley sobre el derecho de autor*) of 1962.[1] Hereinafter it is referred to as "the Law". References to Articles, without further specification, are references to Articles of this Law.

Universal Copyright Convention.—Venezuela became bound by the Universal Copyright Convention and Protocols 1 and 2 as from September 30, 1966.[2]

ACQUISITION OF PROTECTION UNDER THE UNIVERSAL COPYRIGHT CONVENTION

The Law provides that works whose author is a national of a country other than Venezuela are protected in accordance with the international conventions by which Venezuela is bound,[3] and that stateless persons and refugees are assimilated to the nationals of the country in which they are domiciled.[4] On the basis of the Universal Copyright Convention and the Protocols, it would appear therefore that the following are protected in Venezuela by virtue of that Convention: (i) published works of nationals of a Convention country, irrespective of the place of first publication, (ii) works first published in a Convention country, irrespective of the nationality of the author, (iii) unpublished works of nationals of a Convention country other than Venezuela; (iv) works of stateless persons and refugees who have their habitual residence in a State party to Protocol 1 (except perhaps Venezuela), either published or unpublished, and, if published, irrespective of the place of first publication, (v) works first published by the United Nations, by any of the Specialized Agencies of the United Nations, or by the Organization of American States, as well as unpublished works of any of those Organizations.

---

[1] The date of the Law is November 29—December 12, 1962. It was published in the January 3, 1963, issue of the "Gaceta Oficial de la República de Venezuela." English translation in CLTW, Venezuela: Item 1.
[2] See CLTW, Venezuela: Item 1A. Venezuela is also party to the Caracas (1911) Copyright Agreement (see CLTW, Venezuela: Item 2).
[3] Articles 109 and 111.   [4] Articles 110 and 111.

The acquisition and maintenance of copyright protection are not dependent on compliance with any formalities in Venezuela.[5] The absence of a Convention notice on the copies of a published work is no bar to claiming protection in Venezuela. Furthermore, Venezuela has no renewal system, so that there is nothing in that country which would correspond to the renewal formalities existing in the United States.

PROTECTED WORKS

Generally.—The Law protects the rights of authors in respect of all intellectual works (*obras del ingenio* = works of the mind) of a creative character, whether literary, scientific or artistic and whatever their kind (*genero*), form of expression, merit or destination.[6] They include, in particular: books, pamphlets, and other literary, artistic or scientific writings; lectures, speeches, sermons and other works of a similar kind; dramatic and dramatico-musical works; choreographic works and pantomimes, provided the movements to be produced on the stage (*movimiento escenico*) have been fixed in writing or in some other form; musical compositions with or without words; cinematographic works and works obtained by any process analogous to cinematography; works of drawing, painting, architecture, engraving and lithography; works of applied art, other than mere industrial designs (*modelos o dibujos industriales*); geographical illustrations and maps; plans, plastic works and sketches relating to geography, topography, architecture or the sciences;[7] photographs, reproductions or prints obtained by any process analogous to photography, including the individual pictures in a film strip (provided they do not constitute a cinematographic work).[8]

Secondary Works.—The following are protected as works, independently of the pre-existing works on which they are based or which they include: translations; adaptations; transformations; arrangements; anthologies and compilations which, by reason of the selection or the arrangement (*disposición*) of the various works which they include, constitute personal creations.[9] The fact that the pre-existing work may not be protected does not influence the secondary work's eligibility for copyright protection. The creation of a secondary

---

[5] Cf. Article 5, first paragraph, which provides that the rights in a work come into existence by the sole fact of its creation. Articles 90 to 94 provide for deposit and registration in the *Registro Público* (Public Register) but failure to register does not result in no, or less, protection (cf. Article 94). Transfers of copyright may be recorded in the *Registro Público* (Article 92).

[6] Article 1.   [7] Article 2.   [8] Article 38.

[9] Article 3. See also Articles 4 and 115.

work does not establish any right in the pre-existing work as far as the author of the secondary work is concerned.[10]

"Corpus Mechanicum."—Copyright in a work is independent of the ownership of the material object in which the work is incorporated.[11]

Titles of Works.—The title of a work which effectively individualizes the work may not, without the consent of the author of the work, be used to identify another work of the same kind when there is a risk that such use could cause confusion between the two works.[12]

Scientific Editions.—Editions of another person's works or of texts are protected as intellectual works when the edition is the result of scientific effort.[13]

"Editio Princeps."—The publisher (*divulgador* = the person who divulges) of an intellectual work which has not been made accessible to the public before the end of the fiftieth year from the death of its author is protected as an author.[14]

PROTECTED PERSONS

Generally.—Rights in respect of a work originally vest, as a rule, in the author of the work.[15] In the absence of proof to the contrary, it is presumed that the author of a work is the person whose name is indicated, in the customary manner, in or on the work, as the name of the author, or whose name is announced as that of the author in connection with the performance of the work.[16] The indication or announcement of a pseudonym or sign which leaves no doubt as to the author's identity gives rise to the same presumption.[17]

Works Not Revealing the Author's Identity.—As long as the author does not reveal his identity and does not prove his authorship, the original publisher of the work is entitled to exercise the copyright in his own name.[18]

Co-Authors.—Copyright in works created through the collaboration of several authors belongs to the co-authors in common. The co-

[10] Article 5, second paragraph.
[11] Article 5, third paragraph. The alienation of the material object in which a work of art is incorporated does not imply, in favor of the person acquiring it, the transfer of the author's rights of exploitation. However, in the absence of agreement to the contrary, the alienation of the material object confers upon the person acquiring it the right of publicly exhibiting the work, or having it photographed, or having it used in a documentary motion picture (Article 54).
[12] Article 24.   [13] Article 36, first paragraph.
[14] Article 37, first paragraph.   [15] Article 5, first paragraph.
[16] Article 7, first paragraph.   [17] Article 7, second paragraph.
[18] Article 8.

authors must exercise their rights by common agreement. In the absence of proof to the contrary, it is presumed that each co-author is an agent of the other co-authors in any dealings with third parties. If the co-authors disagree, any of them may turn for relief to the courts. Any co-author whose contribution belongs to a category different from the category to which any other contribution belongs may, in the absence of agreement to the contrary, exploit separately his contribution provided that such exploitation is not prejudicial to the exploitation of the common work.[19]

Composite Works.—A composite work is a new work in which a pre-existing work has been incorporated without the collaboration of the author of the pre-existing work.[20] Copyright in the composite work vests in its author. The rights of the author of the pre-existing work are not affected.[21]

Cinematographic Works.—Authorship of a cinematographic work is recognized as belonging to the physical person or persons who have brought it about as an intellectual creation (*que realizan su creación intelectual*). In the absence of proof to the contrary, the following persons are presumed to be co-authors: (i) the author of the scenario (*escenificación*), (ii) the author of the adaptation, (iii) the author of the script (*guión*), (iv) the composer of the music specially composed for the cinematographic work, (v) the director (*realizador o director*). If the cinematographic work is derived from a pre-existing work or scenario protected by copyright, the authors of such pre-existing works are also presumed to be co-authors of the cinematographic work.[22]

The producer of a cinematographic work is regarded as a co-author only if he is a physical person and fulfils any of the above conditions. The producer may be a physical person or a legal entity. What makes the person or legal entity a producer is the fact that he or it takes the initiative in and is responsible for the making of the cinematographic work. In the absence of proof to the contrary, the physical person or legal entity whose name is indicated in the cinematographic work as the name of the producer is presumed to be the producer.[23]

A cinematographic work is considered to be terminated when the first standard copy has been established by common agreement between, on the one hand, the director and any other co-author, and, on the other hand, the producer.[24]

In the absence of agreement to the contrary, the contract concluded between the authors of the cinematographic work and its producer implies the assignment (*cesión*) to the producer of all rights of exploitation and the right of deciding the manner (*modo*) of making the cinematographic work accessible to the public.[25]

[19] Articles 9, first paragraph, and 10.
[20] Article 9, second paragraph.   [21] Article 11.   [22] Article 12.
[23] Article 15.   [24] Article 14.   [25] Article 16, first paragraph.

If a co-author refuses to complete his contribution to the cinematographic work, or is prevented from completing his contribution by *vis major*, he may not oppose the continued use of his part-contribution already furnished.[26]

In the absence of agreement to the contrary, each of the co-authors may freely dispose of his contribution for the purpose of exploiting it in a different field (*en un género diferente*), provided such exploitation does not prejudice the exploitation of the cinematographic work itself.[27]

Broadcast Works.—The physical person who or the legal entity which is responsible for the intellectual creation (*que realizan la creación intelectual*) of a broadcast work, radio work, or television work (*obra radiodifundida, radiofónica o radiovisual (televisión)*), is treated as the author of that work. The legal situation of the authors of any pre-existing work or any co-author is similar to that which prevails in the case of cinematographic works.[28]

ASSIGNMENT AND LICENSING

Generally.—The right of performance and the right of reproduction may be assigned (*pueden ser cedidos*).[29] Assignment (*cesión*) of one of these rights does not imply assignment of the other. Contracts must be interpreted strictly as to the scope of the rights assigned.[30] Performance and publication contracts (see below) must be in writing.[31]

As a rule, no rights may be assigned for a lump sum. The contract must provide for a participation by the transferor in the revenues of the assignee derived from the exploitation of the work. The participation must be proportionate to such revenues.[32]

As exceptions to this rule, the compensation of the author may be stipulated in a lump sum (*cantidad fija*) in the following cases: (i) if it is not practicable to determine a basis for calculating a proportional participation, (ii) if the means of controlling the application of a proportional participation are lacking, (iii) if the cost of calculating and controlling the application of a proportional participation would be excessive when compared with the expected amount of the compensation to be paid to the author, (iv) if the nature or the circumstances of the exploitation are such that the author's contribution does not constitute one of the essential elements of the intellectual creation to be exploited, or that the utilization of the work is only of an incidental character in relation to the object exploited, (v) if the author or the assignee is domiciled outside Venezuela,[33] (vi) if the contract con-

[26] Article 13, first paragraph.   [27] Article 13, second paragraph.
[28] Article 17.   [29] Article 50.   [30] Article 51.   [31] Article 53.
[32] Article 55, first paragraph.   [33] Article 55, second and third paragraphs.

cerns the publication of a book and the work is a translation or is of a purely scientific character, or consists of a preface, annotation, introduction, presentation or illustration, or if the book is an anthology, encyclopedia, a limited *de luxe* edition, an album for children, a popular edition, or a prayer book.[34]

The author has the right—which he cannot waive by contract—to revoke the assignment, provided he indemnifies the assignee for the prejudice caused to him by such revocation.[35]

Publication Contracts.—The Law regulates in detail the matter of publication contracts.[36] The following is a summary of the most important provisions.

"Publication contract" (*contrato de edición*) is defined as a contract by which the author of an intellectual work or his successors in title assign (*ceden*), subject to specified conditions, the right to produce or cause to be produced a certain number of copies of the work, to a person called the publisher (*editor*), who undertakes to publish and distribute the work. In the absence of express stipulation to the contrary, the publisher is presumed to have acquired an exclusive right to publish.[37]

The contract must indicate the minimum number of copies of the first edition unless it provides for the payment of a sum of a fixed amount as minimum remuneration (*provento*).[38] In the absence of agreement to the contrary, the contract confers upon the publisher the right to publish only one edition.[39]

The work must be delivered to the publisher in a form which allows reproduction by the usual means.[40] The assignor has both the right and the obligation to correct the proofs.[41] The assignor may make changes in the manuscript already delivered provided such changes do not alter the nature and the purpose of the work and provided the assignor pays for the expenses caused by the changes.[42] The publisher has no right to make changes in the work.[43]

Unless otherwise agreed, each copy of the work must indicate the name, pseudonym or distinctive sign of the author and, if what is published is a translation, also the name of the translator and the title of the work in its original language.[44]

In the case of articles for periodicals or magazines, it is presumed that they may be published only once in the periodical or magazine.[45] If signed, they cannot be changed by the publisher. If not signed, they may be changed by the publisher.[46]

Performance Contracts.—"Performance contract" (*contrato de representación*) is defined as a contract by which the author of an intellectual work or his successor in title assign (*ceden*), subject to specified

---

[34] Article 56.   [35] Article 58.   [36] Articles 71 to 85.   [37] Article 71.
[38] Article 72.   [39] Article 73.   [40] Article 74.   [41] Article 76.
[42] Article 77.   [43] Article 78.   [44] Article 80.   [45] Article 86.
[46] Article 87.

conditions, to a physical person or legal entity the right to perform the work. The contract may be concluded for a certain period of time or a certain number of public performances.[47] In the absence of express stipulation to the contrary, the assignee-impresario is not presumed to have acquired an exclusive right to perform.[48]

If, in the case of a dramatic work, an exclusive right has been granted, the grant will be valid only for five years and if no public performance has been given for two consecutive years, the grant will automatically become invalid.[49]

If the contract provides for royalties, the impresario must send to the assignor or his representatives the exact program of the public performances of the work and a true report on the receipts.[50]

Permission to broadcast does not imply permission to record, except that the broadcasting organization may, by its own means, make a recording intended for a single use, within twelve months, over any of its transmitters reaching the same audience.[51]

Permission to broadcast does not imply permission publicly to communicate the broadcast by loudspeaker or any other similar instrument transmitting sounds or images.[52]

Future Works.—An author may assign the rights of exploitation in respect of his future works only if the contract describes the works either specifically or by type. The contract will be valid only for five years.[53, 54]

PROTECTED RIGHTS

Copyright includes economic rights (*derechos de orden patrimonial*) and moral rights (*derechos de orden moral*).[55]

The author has the exclusive right to decide the total or partial disclosure (*divulgación*) of his work and the manner of the disclosure.[56] No person other than the author may, without the consent of the author, cause to be made known (*dar a conocer*) the essential contents or the description of the work before the author himself has done so or before he has disclosed the work.[57] The grant of usufruct of copyright, whether *inter vivos* or *mortis causa*, implies authorization to disclose the work and to decide the manner of disclosure.[58]

[47] Article 65.   [48] Article 66, first paragraph.   [49] Article 66(2).
[50] Article 68.   [51] Article 67, first paragraph.
[52] Article 67, second paragraph.   [53] Article 52.
[54] The Law contains special provisions on the transmission of copyright *causa mortis* (Articles 29 and 30), the legal capacity of authors who are minors (Articles 31 to 33), and the effects of the matrimonial régime on copyright (Articles 34 and 35).
[55] Article 5(1).   [56] Article 18(1).   [57] Article 18(2).   [58] Article 19(1).

ECONOMIC RIGHTS

Generally.—The author has the exclusive right to exploit his work in whatever manner pleases him and to derive benefit from his work.[59]

The right of exploitation includes the right of performance and the right of reproduction.[60]

Right of Performance.—Performance consists in the direct communication of the work to the public, particularly by means of: (i) public recitation, (ii) musical performance, (iii) dramatic performance, (iv) public presentation or exhibition, (v) broadcasting (*difusión*), by any method, of words, sounds and images, (vi) public showing (*proyección*), (vii) transmission of a broadcast work by means of a loudspeaker and possibly also by means of a television screen located in a public place (*lugar público*).[61]

Right of Reproduction.—Reproduction consists in the material fixation of the work by any method that permits the work to be made known to the public in an indirect manner. Reproduction may be effected, in particular, by means of: (i) printing, (ii) drawing, (iii) engraving, (iv) photography, (v) modeling or any other process of the fine arts, (vi) mechanical recording, (vii) cinematographic recording.[62]

Unauthorized Acts.—The total or partial performance or reproduction of a work is unlawful if it is done without the consent of the author or his successors in title (*derecho-habientes o causa-habientes*). This rule applies also to the translation, adaptation, transformation, arrangement, or copy by any art or process, of the work. However, the free use of a work in the making of a new original work is lawful.[63]

MORAL RIGHTS

Paternity.—If a work is published or disclosed by a person other than its author, the author has the right: (i) to be recognized as such, (ii) to decide whether the work should indicate the identity of the author, and (iii) to determine the manner in which such indication, if any, must be given.[64]

Modifications.—The author has the right to prohibit any modification of the work which may prejudice his dignity or reputation. The author may exercise this right also in respect of a person who is the owner of the material object embodying the work. However, the author of a work of architecture may not oppose changes which become necessary during or after construction. Nevertheless, if the architectural work has special artistic merit, the author has priority for planning and carrying out such changes.[65]

[59] Article 23, first paragraph.   [60] Article 39.   [61] Article 40.
[62] Article 41.   [63] Article 42.   [64] Article 20.   [65] Article 21.

Access.—The author may require the proprietor of the material object embodying the work to grant him access to the same whenever such access is necessary for the exercise of his rights of exploitation or the protection of his interests in general.[66]

Cinematographic Works.—Moral rights in a cinematographic work may be exercised by the producer in his own name, as long as there is no contractual agreement to the contrary and as long as such exercise does not prejudice the rights of the authors of the cinematographic work.[67]

LIMITATIONS

Expropriation.—It would appear that the rights of an author may be expropriated in the public interest and that in such cases the general rules of law concerning expropriation apply.[68]

Certain Non-Profit Performances.—The performance of a work is free (i.e., requires neither authorization nor payment): (i) if it is effected in a closed circle of persons and no admission fee is charged and, (ii) if it is in the public interest (*con fines de utilidad general*) the participants derive no profit (*obtengan ningún provecho*).[69]

Certain Non-Profit Reproductions.—The reproduction of a *work of art* is free if it is effected for the sole purpose of study.

The reproduction of a *portrait* is free if it is effected by or on behalf of a competent authority for the purposes of justice or public security.

The reproduction of a *work of art* is free if it is permanently exhibited in a street, square or other public place, and if the reproduction is effected in an art form other than that in which the original exists.

The reproduction of any *work which can be read* is free if it is effected for the personal use of the reader, and if it is effected by the reader or a third person, but in the latter case only if the reproduction is made for the exclusive use of the said reader. However, reproduction by photographic means is free only if (i) reproduction is limited to small portions of a protected work, or (ii) the work is out of print, or (iii) acquisition of a copy of the work would be extremely difficult.[70]

Other Free Uses.—The Law also provides for free uses in connection with words accompanying music,[71] inclusion of works in scientific works to clarify their contents,[72] quotations,[73] reporting of current events in the press, by broadcasting, or in motion pictures.[74]

[66] Article 22. [67] Article 16, second paragraph. [68] Article 1, *in fine*.
[69] Article 43. [70] Article 44. [71] Article 45.
[72] Article 46, first paragraph. [73] Article 46, first paragraph.
[74] Articles 47, 48, 49.

TERM OF PROTECTION

Generally.—Copyright subsists during the life of the author and until the expiration of fifty years from the beginning of the year immediately following the year in which the author died.[75] In the case of works by several co-authors, the fifty-year period is calculated from the beginning of the year immediately following the year in which the last surviving co-author died.[76]

Cinematographic Works.—The right of exploitation of a cinematographic work subsists until the expiration of fifty years from the beginning of the year immediately following that of the work's first publication or, if the work remains unpublished, of its completion.[77]

Anonymous and Pseudonymous Works.—Copyright in anonymous or pseudonymous works subsists until the expiration of fifty years from the beginning of the year immediately following that of the work's first publication.[78]

Titles.—Even after the expiration of copyright, the title of a work may not be used for another work of the same kind if there is a risk that such use would cause confusion with the earlier work and would cause prejudice to the persons who have disseminated the earlier work.[79]

Scientific Editions.—Scientific editions (see "Protected Works," page 000, above) are protected for fifteen years from first publication or, if the scientific edition remains unpublished, for fifteen years from the preparation of the edition. The term begins to run from the beginning of the year immediately following the year of first publication or preparation.[80]

"Editio princeps."—The rights of the publisher of an *editio princeps* (see "Protected Works", page 652, above) subsist until the expiration of ten years from the beginning of the year immediately following the year in which the work was divulged.[81]

Photographs.—Rights in photographs subsist until the expiration of fifteen years from the beginning of the year immediately following the year in which the photograph was divulged or, if it remained undivulged, in which it was made.[82]

Definition of "Divulgation" and "Publication."—A work is deemed to be disclosed or divulged (*divulgada*) when it has been made accessible to the public.

A written work (*la escrita*) is deemed to be published (*publicada*)

---

[75] Article 25.   [76] Article 26, first paragraph.
[77] Article 26, second paragraph.
[78] Article 27, which also provides further details.
[79] Article 28.   [80] Article 36, second paragraph.
[81] Article 37, second paragraph.   [82] Article 38, first paragraph.

when it has been reproduced in a material form and made available to the public in a number of copies sufficient to enable it to be read, or to take visual cognizance of it.[83]

Rule of the Shorter Term.—Since there is no provision in the Law of Venezuela for the "rule of the shorter term" permitted under Article IV (4) of the Universal Copyright Convention, it would appear that works are protected in Venezuela until the expiration of the terms indicated above, even if they fall into the public domain in other countries at an earlier date.

INFRINGEMENTS

CIVIL REMEDIES

The Law provides for injunctions, damages, destruction of unlawfully produced copies, and the publication of the court's decision.[84]

PENAL SANCTIONS

Intentional violations of the rights protected by the Law are punishable by a fine and, in certain cases, by imprisonment.[85] The court may order the publication of its decision.[86] The injured party, in bringing a civil action, may also request the application of penal sanctions.[87]

---

[83] Article 6. [84] Articles 95 to 104. [85] Article 105.
[86] Article 106. [87] Article 107.

YUGOSLAVIA

SOURCES

Internal Law.—The main source of the law of copyright in Yugoslavia is the Law Concerning Copyright of July 10, 1957,[1] as amended by the Law of March 8, 1965.[2] Hereinafter it is referred to as "the Law," and references to Articles, without further specification, are references to Articles of this Law, as amended.

Universal Copyright Convention.—Yugoslavia became bound by the Universal Copyright Convention and Protocols 1 and 2 as from May 11, 1966.[3]

ACQUISITION OF COPYRIGHT UNDER THE UNIVERSAL COPYRIGHT CONVENTION

There is no express reference to the Universal Copyright Convention in the Yugoslav Copyright Law, which, however, provides that the works of foreign nationals (other than those first published in Yugoslavia) enjoy, in accordance with the Law, protection within the limits of the obligations that Yugoslavia has assumed by international treaties.[4] It is not entirely clear which provision is applicable when there is a conflict—as there is at least in the case of the right of translation (see below)—between the Law and the Universal Copyright Convention.

Since there are no express provisions in the Law specifying the works that are protected in Yugoslavia by virtue of the Universal Copyright Convention, it is assumed that the provisions of the Convention itself govern in this respect. Accordingly, and subject to the exceptions stated below, the following appear to be protected in

---

[1] Published in "Sluzbeni List," August 28, 1957, page 681. English translation in CLTW, Yugoslavia: Item 1.

[2] Published in "Sluzbeni List," on March 17, 1965, under No. 11/1965. English translation in Copyright (BIRPI), 1967, page 122.

[3] CLTW, Yugoslavia: Item 1A. Yugoslavia is a member of the Berne Copyright Union. It ratified the Brussels Convention of 1948 but maintained its reservation as to the right of translation. In this respect it is still bound by Article 5 of the original (Berne) Convention of 1886, in the version of the Additional Act of 1896, with regard to translations into the languages of Yugoslavia.

[4] Article 2, third paragraph.

Yugoslavia under the Universal Copyright Convention: (i) published works of nationals of a Convention country, irrespective of the place of first publication (except if first publication took place in Yugoslavia),[5] (ii) works first published in a Convention country, irrespective of the nationality of the author (except if the author is a Yugoslav national),[6] (iii) unpublished works of nationals of a Convention country other than Yugoslavia, (iv) works of stateless persons and refugees who have their habitual residence in a State party to Protocol 1 (except Yugoslavia), whether unpublished or published, and, if published, irrespective of the place of first publication, (v) works first published by the United Nations, by any of the Specialized Agencies of the United Nations, or by the Organization of American States, as well as unpublished works of any of those Organizations. If a work falling within any of the above categories is a work which has, as its country of origin, within the meaning of the Conventions of the Berne Union, a country member of that Union, protection in Yugoslavia is available under the applicable Convention of the Berne Union rather than the Universal Copyright Convention.

The acquisition of copyright protection in Yugoslavia is not subject to any formality. Consequently, registration or deposit is not required, and the absence, in itself, of the Convention notice on the copies of a published work is no bar to the claiming of protection in Yugoslavia. Furthermore, Yugoslavia has no renewal system, so there is nothing in that country which would correspond to the renewal formalities existing in the United States. Protection in Yugoslavia will last, without any intervention by the copyright owner or a State authority, until the day on which the work falls into the public domain.

PROTECTED WORKS

The Law protects intellectual works. Every intellectual creation, whatever its kind and method or form of expression, is an intellectual work. Intellectual works include, in particular, productions in the literary, scientific and artistic domain, such as: (i) books, pamphlets, articles and other writings; addresses, discussions, speeches, and other works of a like nature; (ii) dramatic and dramatico-musical works; (iii) choreographic works and pantomimes, the acting form of which is fixed in writing or otherwise; (iv) musical works, with or without words; (v) cinematographic works and works produced by a process analogous to cinematography; (vi) works of drawing, painting, sculp-

[5] Cf. Article 2, second paragraph, which might mean that works first published in Yugoslavia are protected only by the Law and not (also) by the Convention.

[6] Cf. Article 2, first paragraph, which might mean that works of Yugoslav nationals are protected only by the Law and not (also) by the Convention.

ture and architecture; works of engraving upon metal, wood and other substances; other works of figurative art; (vii) works of all branches of applied art, graphic art, and lithography; (viii) works of artistic or documentary photography and such works obtained by a process analogous to photography; (ix) illustrations and geographical maps; (x) plans, sketches and plastic works relating to geography, topography, architecture or other sciences.[7]

Compendia of intellectual works, such as encyclopedias, directories, anthologies, as well as musical, photographic and like collections which, by reason of selection or arrangement of matter, constitute independent intellectual creations are protected, but without prejudice to the rights of the authors of the individual works which constitute them.[8]

Collections of popular literary and artistic creations, of documents, of judicial decisions, and of other like matter, which do not, of themselves, constitute protected intellectual works, are protected if such collections, by reason of selection, arrangement and method of presentation of matter, constitute independent intellectual creations.[9]

Translations, adaptations, musical arrangements and other transformations of intellectual works are protected as original works, without prejudice to the rights of the author of the original work.[10]

The title of a work is protected in the same way as the work itself of which it is the title.[11] It is unlawful to give a work a title which has already been utilized for an intellectual work of a like kind, if confusion could thereby be caused.[12]

A cinematographic work created by the adaptation or reproduction of a literary, musical, scientific or artistic work is protected as an original work, but without prejudice to the rights of the author of the work adapted or reproduced.[13]

PROTECTED PERSONS

Generally.—Copyright originally vests in the author, that is, the person who has created the work. In the absence of proof to the contrary, the person whose name appears on the work shall be deemed to be the author thereof.[14]

Collections.—The author of a collection of intellectual works which have been translated, adapted, musically arranged, or transformed in any other manner, is the person who has translated, adapted, musically arranged, or otherwise transformed the said works.[15]

---

[7] Article 3.   [8] Article 4, first paragraph.   [9] Article 4, second paragraph.
[10] Article 5.   [11] Article 7, first paragraph.
[12] Article 7, second paragraph.   [13] Article 37, second paragraph.
[14] Article 8.   [15] Article 9, first paragraph.

Works Based on Popular Creations.—Any person who has created a literary, artistic or scientific work based on popular literary and artistic creations is deemed to be the author of the work so created.[16]

Collaboration.—When a work created in collaboration by two or more persons constitutes an indivisible entity, the collaborators have an indivisible copyright therein.[17]

When a work created in collaboration by two or more persons does not constitute an indivisible entity, each collaborator retains copyright in respect of his contribution.[18]

Anonymous and Pseudonymous Works.—In the case of anonymous works, and in the case of works published under a pseudonym and of which the author is unknown, copyright is exercised by the publisher.[19]

Copyright in respect of unpublished works of which the author is unknown is exercised by the competent association of authors.[20]

Cinematographic Works.—The following persons are deemed to be the authors of a completed cinematographic work: the author of the scenario, the composer, the director, and the principal cameraman. The relationship of the producer with the authors of a cinematographic work, and also the relationship between the authors of a cinematographic work, are governed by contract, whereas, in relation to third parties, the copyright governing the utilization of a cinematographic work considered in its entirety is exercisable by the producer.[21]

Memoirs and Personal Notes; Portraits.—Memoirs, personal notes and other like writings of a personal character not destined for the public may not be published without the consent of their author. If important interests are capable of being damaged by the publication of private letters, the consent of the person to whom they were addressed is also necessary. After the death of the said person, such writings may be published if the surviving spouse and the children approve. In their absence, publication may take place if the ascendants of the deceased person have given their consent. These provisions do not apply to memoirs, letters and other like writings which are kept in official archives, museums, libraries and like institutions.[22]

Portraits, works of figurative art or photographs of a person may not be put into circulation or publicly displayed without the consent of such person. After the death of the said person, and for ten years thereafter, the consent of the spouse and the children of the deceased are necessary for the said acts. Should no such person exist, publication may be authorized by his ascendants.[23]

---

[16] Article 9, second paragraph.   [17] Article 10, first paragraph.
[18] Article 10, third paragraph.   [19] Article 11, first paragraph.
[20] Article 11, third paragraph.   [21] Article 12.   [22] Article 76.
[23] Article 77.

The above restrictions do not apply in the case of (i) portraits, works of figurative art or photographs of contemporary historical persons; (ii) pictures representing persons who figure therein only in a capacity incidental to the principal subject; (iii) pictures illustrating assemblies, parades and similar events in which the persons concerned have taken part; (iv) uncommissioned portraits, works of figurative art or photographs, if their public display, presentation or putting into circulation is justified by some superior artistic interest.[24]

ASSIGNMENT AND LICENSING

Generally.—Economic rights may be assigned, wholly or in part.[25] Transfer of specific economic rights is also possible. Such transfer may be limited in time, to a given territory, and to publication or performance in a given language. The contract must be in writing. Otherwise it has no legal effect.[26]

Interpretation of Contracts.—Permission granted for the public performance, for public transmission of the performance, for public diffusion by radio or by any other communication to the public, does not imply permission to record the work by means of instruments recording sounds or images.[27]

Transfer of "Corpus Mechanicum."—The authors of works of figurative art, in relation to such works, and writers and composers, in so far as concerns their original manuscripts, have the right to be informed by the owners of such works or manuscripts of any transfer of the property of the work or of the manuscript, and of the identity of the new owner thereof.[28]

PROTECTED RIGHTS

Generally.—The Law distinguishes between economic and moral rights.[29]

Economic Rights

Generally.—Economic rights consist of rights of utilization, particularly by means of publication, reproduction, multiplication, transformation (arrangement, adaptation), performance, public recitation and reading, public communication, and translation.[30] Communication to the public includes broadcasting, further communication of

[24] Article 78.   [25] Article 13, first paragraph.   [26] Article 44.
[27] Article 33, first paragraph.   [28] Article 24.   [29] Article 24.
[30] Articles 25, 28, 30, 35, 36.

the broadcast by re-broadcasting, by loudspeaker, or any other device transmitting signs, sounds or images.[31] Reproduction includes recording, and performance includes performance by means of recordings.[32] Authors have the exclusive right to authorize (i) the cinematographic adaptation and reproduction of their works, (ii) the distribution and the public performance (showing) of their works thus adapted or reproduced.[33] The same holds good for reproduction or production by means analogous to cinematography.[34] The adaptation of cinematographic works to other artistic forms requires the consent of the authors of the cinematographic work and of the authors of the works used in the cinematographic work.[35] The same holds good in the case of works produced by processes analogous to cinematography.[36] As to the right of exhibition, the Law provides that the author of a painting, sculpture, photography and the like may, on occasions individually specified, forbid the exhibition of "certain" of his works, but he may not prohibit the exhibition of works belonging to museums, galleries and similar institutions.[37]

Right of Translation.—The author has an exclusive right of translation,[38] but when no translation is published in one of the languages of Yugoslavia within ten years from the publication of the original work, translation into and publication in that language do not require the consent of the copyright owner but do require the payment of a fee to him. Further use of the translated work is fully protected.[39] It is to be noted that the safeguards written into Article V of the Universal Copyright Convention are not written into the Law, although the basic feature of that Article (not required from Yugoslavia, as a country making reservations under the Berne Convention) —indemnity to the author—*is* provided for by the Law.

Exercise of the Rights of Authors.—When foreign authors do not exercise their rights in Yugoslavia directly, they can exercise them only through the intermediary of Yugoslav authors' societies officially recognized and supervised by the Yugoslav Government.[40]

Moral Rights

Generally.—Moral rights include: (i) the right of the author to be recognized and indicated as the author of his work,[41] (ii) the right to oppose any deformation, mutilation or modification of the work,

---

[31] Article 31.   [32] Article 32.   [33] Article 37(1) and (2).
[34] Article 37, fourth paragraph.   [35] Article 37, third paragraph.
[36] Article 37, fourth paragraph.   [37] Article 39.   [38] Article 29.
[39] Article 52.   [40] Articles 68 to 75.
[41] Any person who publishes, adapts, performs, translates, records, or publicly utilizes the work of an author is required to indicate the name of the author in connection with each and every utilization (Article 27).

(iii) the right to oppose any unworthy use of the work which would be prejudicial to the honor or reputation of the author.[42]

After the Author's Death.—After the author's death, his moral rights may be exercised by the owner of the copyright or by the competent Yugoslav authors' society.[43]

LIMITATIONS

Right of Translation.—See "Economic Rights," above.

Free Uses.—The following acts are among the acts permissible without the author's consent and without any payment to him: school performances; reproduction for private study; reproduction of paintings in the form of sculpture and vice versa; reproduction of architectural works by painting or sculpture;[44] ephemeral recording by broadcasting organizations;[45] broadcasting and publication in the press of public speeches.[46]

Compulsory Licenses.—The following acts are among the acts permissible without the author's consent but subject to the payment of an equitable indemnity to him: broadcasting of phonograph records and like devices;[47] publication and reproduction for educational purposes of extracts from a literary or scientific work; reproduction in newspapers and periodicals of photographs of current events, illustrations, technical and like sketches published in newspapers or other periodicals; reproduction of works of applied art;[48] re-use of ephemeral recordings by broadcasting organizations.[49]

TERM OF PROTECTION

Generally.—Subject to the exceptions stated below, *economic rights* expire 50 years after the death of the author,[50] whereas *moral rights* continue without limitation in time.[51]

In the case of co-authors, the death of the last surviving co-author is taken as the starting point of the 50-year period.[52]

The economic rights in anonymous and pseudonymous works expire 50 years after first publication. However, when a pseudonym leaves no doubt as to the identity of the author, or if the author reveals his

---

[42] Article 26.   [43] Article 47.   [44] Article 41.
[45] Article 33, second paragraph.   [46] Article 42(1).   [47] Article 34.
[48] Article 40(1) to (7) and third paragraph; the name of the author and the source must be indicated (Article 40, second paragraph).
[49] Article 33, second paragraph, *in fine*.   [50] Article 48.
[51] Article 49. The provisions of the general law of succession govern the matter of inheritance of the economic and moral rights of the author (article 45).
[52] Article 53.

identity, the said rights expire 50 years after the death of the author, or, in the case of co-authors, 50 years after the death of the last surviving co-author.[53]

All periods are calculated from January 1 of the year following the year in which the relevant event (death or first publication) occurred.[54]

Photographic Works and Certain Cinematographic Works.—The economic rights in photographic works and such cinematographic works as have the character of photographic works expire five years after first publication.[55]

Works of Applied Art.—The economic rights in works of applied art expire ten years after first publication.[56]

Rule of the Shorter Term.—Since there is no provision in the Law of Yugoslavia for the "rule of the shorter term" permitted under Article IV (4) of the Universal Copyright Convention, it would appear that works are protected in Yugoslavia until the expiration of the terms indicated above, even if they fall into the public domain in other countries at an earlier date.

INFRINGEMENTS

Civil Remedies

Damages.—Any person whose copyright has been infringed is entitled to damages in accordance with the provisions of the general rules of law relating to damages.[57] If the infringement consists in using the work without indicating the name of the author, the author may also require that in subsequent uses his name be mentioned.[58]

Other Possible Remedies.—According to the circumstances of the case, the courts may also order: seizure; prohibition of the continuation of acts which may constitute in the future or may have caused in the past infringement of copyright; destruction of infringing objects or their transfer (subject to compensation) to the plaintiff.[59]

Distraint.—Unfinished works, unpublished manuscripts, and copyright, cannot be distrained.[60]

Criminal Sanctions

Certain infringements under certain circumstances are punishable by a fine or imprisonment.[61]

[53] Article 51.   [54] Article 54.
[55] Article 50, first paragraph.   [56] Article 50, second paragraph.
[57] Article 55.   [58] Article 60.   [59] Articles 56 to 59.
[60] Article 61.   [61] Articles 62 to 67.

ZAMBIA

SOURCES

Internal Law.—The main source of the Law of copyright in Zambia is the Copyright Act, 1965.[1] Hereinafter, it is referred to as "the Act," and references to Sections, without further specification, are references to Sections of this Act.

Universal Copyright Convention.—Zambia became bound by the Universal Copyright Convention on June 1, 1965.[2] It is not bound by any of the Protocols.

ACQUISITION OF PROTECTION UNDER THE UNIVERSAL COPYRIGHT CONVENTION

The application of the Act is extended in respect of literary, musical and artistic works and cinematograph films:

(i) to individuals or bodies corporate who are citizens of, or domiciled or resident in, or incorporated under the laws of, a country bound by the Universal Copyright Convention (hereinafter referred to as a "Convention country"),

(ii) to works, other than sound recordings, first published in a Convention country.[3]

A work is taken to have been published if, but only if, copies have been issued in sufficient quantities to satisfy the reasonable requirements of the public.[4] Where in the first instance a part only of a work is published, that part is treated, for the purposes of the Act, as a separate work.[5] A publication in any country is not treated as being other than the first publication by reason only of an earlier publication elsewhere if the two publications took place within a period of not more than thirty days.[6]

The acquisition of copyright protection in Zambia is not subject

[1] Act No. 14 of 1965; published in the "Republic of Zambia Government Gazette" of February 12, 1965; entered into force on March 1, 1965; reprinted in CLTW, Zambia: Item 1.

[2] See CLTW, Zambia: Item 2.

[3] See the Copyright Regulations, 1965, published in the "Supplement to the Republic of Zambia Government Gazette" of June 18, 1965, page 1081, as Statutory Instrument No. 216 of 1965.

[4] Section 2(2) (a).　　[5] Section 2(2) (b).　　[6] Section 2(2) (c).

to any formality. Consequently, registration or deposit is not required, and the absence, in itself, of the Convention notice on the copies of a published work is no bar to the claiming of protection in Zambia. Furthermore, Zambia has no renewal system, so there is nothing in that country which would correspond to the renewal formalities existing in the United States. Protection in Zambia will last, without any intervention on the part of the copyright owner or a State authority, until the day on which the work falls into the public domain.

PROTECTED WORKS

Generally.—The Act distinguishes between six categories of works: literary works, musical works, artistic works, cinematograph films, sound recordings, broadcasts.[7]

The first three—i.e., literary, musical and artistic works—are eligible for copyright only if both of the following conditions are fulfilled: (i) sufficient effort has been expended on making the work to give it an original character, (ii) the work has been written down, recorded, or otherwise reduced to material form.[8]

No work is ineligible for copyright by reason only that the making of the work, or the doing of any act in relation to the work, involved an infringement of copyright in some other work.[9]

"Work" includes translations, adaptations, new versions or arrangements of pre-existing works, and anthologies or collections of works which, by reason of the selection and arrangement of their content, present an original character.[10]

Literary Works.—These include, irrespective of literary quality: (i) novels, stories and poetical works, (ii) plays, stage directions, film scenarios and broadcasting scripts, (iii) textbooks, treatises, histories, biographies, essays and articles, (iv) encyclopaedias and dictionaries, (v) letters, reports and memoranda, (vi) lectures, addresses and sermons.[11]

Musical Works.—These are protected irrespective of musical quality. They include works composed for musical accompaniment.[12]

Artistic Works.—These include, irrespective of artistic quality: (i) paintings, drawings, etchings, lithographs, woodcuts, engravings, prints; (ii) maps, plans, diagrams; (iii) works of sculpture; (iv) photographs not comprised in a cinematograph film; (v) works of architec-

[7] Section 3(1). Since the Copyright Regulations, 1965 (see footnote 3, above), do not extend protection, under the Universal Copyright Convention, to sound recordings and broadcasts, no further reference is made in this book to these two categories.

[8] Section 3(2).   [9] Section 3(4).   [10] Section 2(1).   [11] Section 2(1).
[12] Section 2(1).

ture in the form of buildings (including any structure) or models; (vi) works of artistic craftsmanship.[13]

An artistic work is not eligible for copyright if, at the time the work was made, it was intended by the author to be used as a model or pattern to be multiplied by any industrial process.[14]

Cinematograph Films.—A "cinematograph film" means the first fixation of a sequence of visual images capable of being shown as a moving picture and of being the subject of reproduction and includes the recording of a soundtrack associated with the cinematograph film.[15]

PROTECTED PERSONS

As a general rule, copyright initially vests in the author.[16] In the case of a cinematograph film, "author" means the person by whom the arrangements for the making of the film were undertaken.[17]

Where a work has been *commissioned* by a person who is not the author's employer under a contract of service, then, the copyright is deemed to be transferred to the person who commissioned the work, unless it has been agreed otherwise by contract.[18]

Where a work has been made in the course of the author's *employment* (as distinguished from having been made pursuant to a commission referred to above), the copyright is deemed to be transferred to the author's employer, unless it has been agreed otherwise by contract.[19]

Where a work has been made by, or under the direction or control of, the Government of Zambia, or an international body or other governmental organization designated in the Regulations issued under the Act, copyright initially vests in the Government, the international body or the governmental organization.[20]

ASSIGNMENT AND LICENSING

Generally.—Copyright is transmissible by assignment, by testamentary disposition, or by operation of law, as movable property.[21]

An assignment or testamentary disposition of copyright may be limited so as to apply to some only of the acts which the owner of the copyright has the exclusive right to control; or to a part only of the period of the copyright; or to a specified country or other geographical area.[22]

[13] Section 2(1).   [14] Section 3(3).   [15] Section 2(1).
[16] Section 11(1).   [17] Section 2(1).   [18] Section 11(1).
[19] Section 11(1).   [20] Section 11(2).   [21] Section 12(1).   [22] Section 12(2).

A purported assignment of copyright is void if it is not in writing signed by or on behalf of the assignor.[23]

Any document purporting to confer an exclusive license to do an act falling within the ambit of copyright is to be construed as a total or partial assignment of the copyright, as the case may require.[24]

A license to do an act falling within the ambit of copyright may be written or oral, or may be inferred from conduct, and may be revoked at any time, but a license granted by contract may not be revoked, either by the person who granted the license or his successor in title, except as the contract may provide, or by a further contract.[25]

An assignment or license granted by one copyright owner has effect as if granted by his co-owners also, and, subject to any contract between them, fees received by the grantor are to be divided equitably between all the co-owners. Co-ownership exists among persons: (i) if they share a joint interest in the whole or any part of a copyright, or (ii) if they have interests in the various copyrights in a composite production, that is to say, a production consisting of two or more works.[26]

Future Works.—An assignment, license or testamentary disposition may be effectively granted or made in respect of a future work, or an existing work in which copyright does not yet subsist. The prospective copyright in any such work is transmissible by operation of law as movable property.[27]

"Corpus Mechanicum."—A testamentary disposition of the material on which a work is first written or otherwise recorded is, in the absence of contrary indication, to be taken to include the disposition of any copyright or prospective copyright in the work which is vested in the deceased.[28]

Licenses Administered by Licensing Bodies.—"Licensing body" means an organization which has as its main object, or one of its main objects, the negotiation or granting of licenses in respect of works protected by copyright.[29] If a licensing body unreasonably refuses to grant licenses, or is imposing unreasonable terms or conditions on the granting of licenses, the Government authority appointed to that effect may direct that corresponding licenses may be deemed to have been granted by the copyright owner provided that the appropriate fees prescribed by the said Government authority are paid or tendered.[30]

---

[23] Section 12(3). [24] Section 12(4). [25] Section 12(5).
[26] Section 12(6). [27] Section 12(7). [28] Section 12(8).
[29] Section 14(3). [30] Section 14(1) and (2).

PROTECTED RIGHTS

Economic Rights

Copyright in a *literary, musical or artistic work*, or in *a cinematograph film*, is the exclusive right to control the doing in Zambia of any of the following acts: (i) reproduction in any material form, (ii) communication to the public, (iii) broadcasting. The right exists in respect of the whole work or a substantial part thereof, both in its original form and in any form recognizably derived from the original.[31]

"Reproduction" means the making of one or more copies of the work or cinematograph film. "Copy" means a reproduction in written form, in the form of a recording or cinematograph film, or in any other material form, so however that an object is not to be taken to be a copy of an architectural work unless the object is a building or a model. "Communication to the public" includes, in addition to any live performance or delivery, any mode of visual or acoustic presentation. "Broadcasting" means the broadcasting of sounds and/or images, and includes diffusion over wires.[32]

Copyright in a *work of architecture* also includes the exclusive right to control the erection of any building which reproduces the whole or any substantial part of the work either in its original form or in any form recognizably derived from the original, provided that this right does not include the right to control the reconstruction of a building in the same style as the original.[33]

Limitations

Free Uses.—The following uses are free, i.e., require neither authorization by nor payment to the copyright owner:

Fair Dealing.—Reproduction, communication to the public or broadcasting "by way of fair dealing" for purposes of research, private use, criticism or review, or the reporting of current events, is free. However, if such use is public, it must be accompanied by an acknowledgement of the title of the work and its authorship, except when the work is incidentally included in a broadcast.[34]

Parody, etc.—Reproduction, communication to the public, or broadcasting, is free if it is by way of parody, pastiche or caricature.[35]

Artistic Works Situated in Streets, etc.—The reproduction and distribution of copies, or the inclusion in a film or broadcast, is free if the work is an artistic work which is situated in a place where it can be viewed by the public.[36]

[31] Section 7(1).   [32] Section 2(1).   [33] Section 7(2).
[34] Sections 7(1) (a), 9, and 10.   [35] Section 7(1) (b).   [36] Section 7(1) (c).

Incidental Filming or Televising of an Artistic Work.—Inclusion of an artistic work in a cinematograph film or in a television broadcast is free if it is incidental.[37]

Collections of Literary or Musical Works.—Inclusion of not more than two short passages from a work in a collection of literary or musical works is free if the collection is designed for use in educational institutions. The included passages must be accompanied by an acknowledgement of the title of the work and its authorship.[38]

Educational Broadcasts.—The broadcasting of a work is free if the broadcast is intended to be used for educational purposes.[39]

Reading, etc., of Extracts.—The reading or recitation in public or in a broadcast of any reasonable extract of a literary work is free, if the work is a published work and if the use is accompanied by a sufficient acknowledgement.[40]

Government-ordered Use in Public Interest.—Use of a work, for purposes of communication to the public by or under the direction or control of the Government is free if (i) the use is in the public interest, (ii) no revenue is derived from the use, (iii) in cases where the use consists of communication to the public, no admission fee is charged.[41]

Library, etc., Uses.—Reproduction is free—for the purposes of their activities—of such number of copies of such works by such public or institutional libraries, non-commercial documentation centers or scientific institutions as are specified in the Regulations issued under the Act.[42]

Ephemeral Recording, etc.—The reproduction of a work by or under the direction or control of a broadcasting authority is free if (i) the reproduction or any copies thereof are intended exclusively for lawful broadcast by that broadcasting authority, (ii) the reproduction and any copies thereof are destroyed within six months of reproduction or any longer period agreed under contract. Reproductions of an exceptional documentary character may, however, be preserved but may not be used without the authorization of the copyright owner.[43]

Judicial Proceedings.—Any use made of a work for the purpose of judicial proceedings is free. Any use for the purpose of a report on such proceeding is equally free.[44]

Compulsory Licenses.—In the following three cases the authorization of the owner of the relevant copyright is not required but a fair compensation must be paid to him in accordance with Regulations issued under the Act:

[37] Section 7(1) (d).   [38] Section 7(1) (e).   [39] Section 7(1) (f).
[40] Section 7(1) (h).   [41] Sections 7(1) (i), 9, and 10.   [42] Section 7(1) (j).
[43] Sections 7(1) (k), 9.   [44] Sections 7(1) (m), 9, and 10.

(i) *Making, etc., of Sound Recordings*, or, more precisely, when a sound recording of a literary or artistic work is made or imported and the copies thereof are intended for retail sale in Zambia.[45]

(ii) *Broadcasting of Works not in the Repertoire of a Performing Rights Society*, or, more precisely, when a work already lawfully made accessible to the public, and with which no licensing body is concerned, is broadcast.[46]

A "licensing body" is an organization which has as its main object, or one of its main objects, the negotiation and granting of licenses in respect of protected works.[47]

(iii) *Broadcast of Music of a Cinematograph Film*, or, more precisely, when a broadcasting authority broadcasts a cinematograph film in which a musical work is incorporated.[48]

Broadcasting of Works Incorporated in a Cinematograph Film.—Subject to the provision just stated, where the owner of the copyright in any literary, musical or artistic work authorized a person to incorporate the work in a cinematograph film and a broadcasting authority broadcasts the film, such broadcast does not, in the absence of any agreement to the contrary, infringe such copyright.[49]

TERM OF PROTECTION

Copyright in *literary works, musical works, and artistic works other than photographs*, expires twenty-five years after the end of the year in which the author dies.[50] In the case of a work of joint authorship the term is counted from the death of the author who dies last.[51]

"Work of joint authorship" means a work produced by the collaboration of two or more authors in which the contribution of each author is not separable from the contribution of the other author or authors.[52] Anonymous or pseudonymous literary, musical or artistic works are protected until the expiration of twenty-five years from the end of the year in which they were first published, except that, if the identity of the author becomes known in the meantime, the term is calculated according to the general rules, i.e., twenty-five years *post mortem auctoris*.[53] Copyright in literary, musical or artistic works (other than photographs) made by or under the direction or control of the Government or any of the designated international bodies or other governmental organizations subsists until the expiration of twenty-five years from the end of the year in which they were first published.[54] "Publication" takes place if, but only if, copies of the work have been issued in

[45] Section 7(1) (g).   [46] Section 7(1) (b).   [47] Section 14(3).
[48] Section 8(2).   [49] Section 8(1).   [50] Section 4(2).
[51] Sections 4(4), and 5(2).   [52] Section 2(1).   [53] Sections 4(3), and 5(2).
[54] Section 6(2).

sufficient quantities to satisfy the reasonable requirements of the public.[55]

Copyright in *photographs* and *cinematograph films* expires twenty-five years after the end of the year in which they were first made lawfully accessible to the public.[56]

COMPARISON OF TERMS

Since there is no provision in the Act for the "rule of the shorter term" permitted under Article IV (4) of the Universal Copyright Convention, it would appear that works are protected in Zambia until the expiration of the terms indicated above, even if, in other countries, they fall into the public domain at an earlier date.

INFRINGEMENTS

CIVIL REMEDIES

Generally.—Copyright is infringed by any person who does, or causes any other person to do, an act falling within the ambit of copyright without the license of the person in whom is vested either the whole of the copyright or, where there has been a partial assignment or partial testamentary disposition, the relevant portion of the copyright.[57]

Infringements are actionable at the suit of the owner of the copyright, and in any action for infringement all such relief—by way of damages, injunction, accounts or otherwise—is available to the plaintiff as is available under the general laws of Zambia in any corresponding proceedings in respect of infringement of other proprietary rights.[58]

Innocent Infringers.—If, at the time of the infringement, the defendant was not aware, and had no reasonable grounds for suspecting, that copyright subsisted in the work or other subject-matter to which the action relates, he is not liable for damages but only for an account of profits.[59]

Flagrant Infringements.—If the infringement is flagrant, if benefit has accrued to the defendant by reason of the infringement, and if the court is satisfied that effective relief would not otherwise be available to the plaintiff, then, the court, in assessing damages for the infringement, may award such additional damages as it considers appropriate under the circumstances.[60]

[55] Section 2(2) (a).   [56] Sections 4(2), 5(2), and 6(3).   [57] Section 13(1).
[58] Section 13(2).   [59] Section 13(3).   [60] Section 13(4).

CRIMINAL SANCTIONS

The Act does not provide for criminal sanctions.

INJUNCTIONS

See "Civil Remedies," above. It is to be noted, however, that no injunction issues if it would require a completed or partly built building to be demolished or if it would prevent the completion of a partly built building.[61]

---

[61] Section 13(5).

INDEX TO THE ARTICLES
OF THE UNIVERSAL COPYRIGHT CONVENTION

(Heavy type denotes the place of principal discussion)

INDEX TO SUBJECTS

Roman numerals (I to XXII), P1, P2 and P3 designate the twenty-one Articles and the three Protocols, respectively, of the Universal Copyright Convention. Arabic numerals designate pages.

MOTION PICTURES. *See* Cinematographic works

MULTILATERAL CONVENTIONS. *See* Berne Conventions; Inter-American Conventions; Montevideo Convention

MULTIPLICATION, RIGHT OF. *See* Right of reproduction

MUSICAL WORKS. Whether protected, I, 7, 8

N

NATIONAL LANGUAGES. Translation into –, V, 61

NATIONAL TREATMENT
Subject matter of Article II, 11, 22, 23
In case of published works, II, 23
In case of unpublished works, II, 23
In respect to duration (term) of protection, IV, 43, 44

Source of domestic protection, II, 23

NATIONALITY OF AUTHOR
As condition of protection, II, 11 to 13
Controverted –, II, 18
In case of anonymous or pseudonymous works, II, 18
In case of several authors, II, 18
In case of works of employees, II, 19
In case of works of legal entities, II, 19

NATIONALITY OF WORKS
As condition of protection, II, 11 to 22
Published works, II, 11 to 19
Works of nationals of the contracting country in which protection is sought, first published in another contracting country, II, 12, 13
Works first published in the contracting country in which protection is sought, and authored by a national of another contracting country, II, 12, 13
Works of nationals of a contracting country first published in a contracting country, seeking protection in another contracting country, II, 14
Works of nationals of a non-contracting country, first published in the contracting country where protection is sought, II, 14
Works of a national of a contracting country first published in a non-contracting country, II, 15
Unpublished works, II, 16
Definition of publication, VI, 79
See also Nationality of author

"NATIONALS." Meaning of the word –, II, 16

NETHERLANDS. Exposition of the law o the –, 497

"NEW MATTER." Effect of – on Convention notice, III, 28

NEWSPAPERS. Whether protected, I, 8

NEWSREELS. *See* Cinematographic Works

NEW ZEALAND. Exposition of the law of –, 503

NICARAGUA. Exposition of the law of –, 518

NIGERIA. Exposition of the law of –, 525

NON-SELF-GOVERNING TERRITORIES, APPLICATION OF CONVENTION TO –,
Subject matter of Article XIII, 104

NORWAY. Exposition of the law of –, 532

NOTARIAL CERTIFICATES. *See* Notice